# THE ECONOMIC ANALYSIS
## OF
## THE JAPANESE FIRM

# CONTRIBUTIONS
# TO
# ECONOMIC ANALYSIS

151

*Honorary Editor:*

J. TINBERGEN

*Editors:*

D. W. JORGENSON
J. WAELBROECK

NORTH-HOLLAND
AMSTERDAM • NEW YORK • OXFORD

# THE ECONOMIC ANALYSIS
# OF
# THE JAPANESE FIRM

*Edited by*

**MASAHIKO AOKI**
*Kyoto Institute of Economic Research*
*Kyoto University*
*Kyoto*
*Japan*

1984
NORTH-HOLLAND
AMSTERDAM • NEW YORK • OXFORD

ISBN: 0  444  86822  4

*Publishers:*

ELSEVIER SCIENCE PUBLISHERS B.V.
P.O. Box 1991
1000 BZ  Amsterdam
The Netherlands

*Sole distributors for the U.S.A. and Canada:*

ELSEVIER SCIENCE PUBLISHING COMPANY, INC.
52 Vanderbilt Avenue
New York, N.Y. 10017
U.S.A.

**Library of Congress Cataloging in Publication Data**

Main entry under title:

The Economic analysis of the Japanese firm.

(Contributions to economic analysis ;151)
Bibliography: p.
Includes index.
    1. Industrial organization--Japan--Addresses, essays,
lectures.  2. Industrial management--Japan--Addresses,
essays, lectures.  3. Business enterprises--Japan--
Addresses, essays, lectures.  4. Corporations--Japan--
Addresses, essays, lectures.  I. Aoki, Masahiko,
1938-    .  II. Series. *86-1843*
HD70.J3E26  1984      338.7'4'0952      83-20718
ISBN 0-444-86822-4

# PREFACE

This book is an outgrowth of a collective project conducted over
the period 1981-83. The idea of forming the project occurred to
the present editor while he was visiting Harvard University during
the academic year 1979-80 to lecture on the Japanese Economy. That
was the time when an unprecedented interest in the Japanese Economy
had been aroused in the Western world due to public concern over
the slowdown of productivity growth therein and the widespread
recognition of the relatively better performance of Japan in that
respect. However, the books on the Japanese Economy that were
available then were becoming rapidly out-of-date as many new
environmental factors, such as supply shocks, increasing international competition, the aging of population, the new wave of
technological innovation and so on, had begun to considerably alter
the economy from the way it had been during the era of stable high
growth and as new interpretations of the workings of economic
institutions theretofore regarded only as culturally unique and
traditional had emerged during the 1970s. Popular writings
mushrooming then on this subject did not seem to offer a better
alternative either. Most of them were still emphasizing only the
cultural uniqueness of Japan or else ardently advocating the
transplantation of the Japanese way into the Western soil to cure
the latter's so-called "industrial disease." To me it seemed that
the fault of the first approach was to ignore the economic rationality
operating behind apparently unique institutional set-ups. Throwing
everything incomprehensible and/or objectionable into the black box
of "culture" sometimes leads to unscientific and irrational conclusions. For instance, at that time, one U.S. congressman went so
far as to say that "the Japanese language is a non-trariff barrier."
On the other hand, the fault of the second approach may be thought
of as being the neglect of the social and historical context in which
the economic motives of human behavior function. Certainly, one
cannot slice out a piece of Japanese practice, such as the industrial
policy of the Ministry of International Trade and Industry, from
the social contextual whole and transplant it successfully elsewhere.
If such an attempt is earnestly proposed, however, it may be partly
due to an inadequate understanding of the economic aspects of the
practice under consideration.

Ideally, we need to strike a delicate balance between an economic
approach and a social as well as cultural approach in order to
understand any economic institution. However, as an economist, my
feeling was that in spite of the apparent uniqueness of Japanese
economic institutions (and, to repeat, one cannot possibly deny that
there is at least a certain degree of uniqueness in them), certain
aspects of their workings could be and should be explained in terms
of economic reasoning comprehensible to Western and other foreign
readers. I felt that if one could succeed in delving deeply enough

into the economic aspects of an institution, one would thereby contribute to a better understanding of the institution as a whole.

After my return to Kyoto University in the summer of 1980, I spoke to several persons who eventually became contributors to this volume, and we agreed to embark on a joint project to produce a book on the "economic analysis" of a Japanese economic institution. We chose the "firm" as a focal point. The project came to be financed partly by a grant from the Ministry of Education received during the academic years 1981-83 (Grant-in-aid No. 56330003) and by grants from the Suntory Foundation received during the period 1981-83. The participation of Professor Harvey Leibenstein was made possible through a grant for a Distinguised Visiting Professorship to Kyoto University from the Ministry of Education. After a couple of preliminary sessions in which ideas and critical remarks were exchanged among the eventual contributors to this volume, we held a symposium in July 1983 in Rokko to discuss the semifinal versions of the papers. To this symposium we were able to invite four foreign scholars who acted as discussants and whose comments are included in this volume. Also, Professor Susumu Koizumi of Osaka University and Dr. Eisuke Sakakibara of the Ministry of Finace kindly participated as discussants in the symposium. Professor Masao Baba of Kyoto University joined us for discussions at the preliminary sessions. We are very grateful to all of these discussants and acknowledge that their comments were helpful to us in improving upon our papers although some points of disagreement naturally remained. Two caveats: First, although this volume is an outcome of our collective project, no effort whatsoever was made to unify our views, and each author alone is responsible for the content of his paper. Secondly, most of the papers were revised after the symposium and some commentators wrote their comments without seeing the final versions of the papers. Therefore, there are a few points on which the discussants' comments are no longer relevent. However, in the editor's judgement, these are very minor points. The final typescripts were handed over to the publisher in the middle of September 1983.

Throughout this project, we greatly benefited from secretarial assistance from Ms. Tomoko Kashima, who skillfully and cheerfully managed the conferences and facilitated communication between the contributors and the editor in addition to editing and preparing the final typescript. To her we owe a particular debt of thanks. We also acknowledge with appreciation various editorial assistance received from Mr. Charles Horioka and Mr. Kei-ichi Shimazaki.

September 1983
Kyoto

The Editor

# CONTRIBUTORS

MASAHIKO AOKI, Kyoto University, Japan

TUVIA BLUMENTHAL, Ben-Gurion University, Israel

RICHARD B. FREEMAN, Harvard University and National Bureau
    of Economic Research, U.S.A.

ELEANOR M. Hadley, The George Washington University, U.S.A.

TSUNEO ISHIKAWA, University of Tokyo, Japan

MERVYN KING, The University of Birmingham, U.K.

KAZUO KOIKE, Kyoto Univeristy, Japan

HARVEY LEIBENSTEIN, Harvard University, U.S.A. and Kyoto
    University, Japan

KURAMITSU MURAMATSU, Nanzan University, Japan

IWAO NAKAKATANI, Osaka University, Japan

MASAHIRO OKUNO, Yokohama National University, Japan

TOSHIAKI TACHIBANAKI, Kyoto University, Japan

KAZUO UEDA, Osaka University, Japan

TAIZO YAKUSHIJI, Saitama University, Japan

# CONTENTS

Preface                                                                                    v

Contributors                                                                              vii

INTRODUCTION

Chapter I                    Aspects of the Japanese Firm
                             *Masahiko Aoki*                                                 3

PART ONE: THE INTERNAL ORGANIZATION AND INDUSTRIAL RELATIONS

Chapter II                   Skill Formation Systems in the U.S. and Japan:
                             A Comparative Study
                             *Kazuo Koike*                                                  47

Chapter III                  Labor Mobility and Job Tenure
                             *Toshiaki Tachibanaki*                                         77

Chapter IV                   The Effect of Trade Unions on Productivity in
                             Japanese Manufacturing Industries
                             *Kuramitsu Muramatsu*                                         103

Comments on II, III & IV     De-Mystifying the Japanese Labor Markets
                             *Richard B. Freeman*                                         125

PART TWO: PERSONAL SAVING AND CORPORATE FINANCE

Chapter V                    The Bonus Payment System and Japanese
                             Personal Savings
                             *Tsuneo Ishikawa and Kazuo Ueda*                              133

Chapter VI                   Shareholders' Non-Unanimity on Investment
                             Financing: Banks vs. Individual Investors
                             *Masahiko Aoki*                                               193

PART THREE: EXTERNAL RELATIONS

Chapter VII                  The Economic Role of Financial Corporate
                             Grouping
                             *Iwao Nakatani*                                               227

Mathematical Appendix        Risk Sharing in the Corporate Group
                             *Masahiko Aoki*                                               259

Chapter VIII                The Government in a Spiral Dilemma: Dynamic
                            Policy Interventions Vis-à-Vis Auto Firms.
                            C.1900-C.1960
                            *Taizo Yakushiji*                                    265

Comments on V, VI & VII     The Ownership and Financing of Corporations
                            *Mervyn King*                                        311

Comments on VII & VIII      Counterpoint on Business Groupings and
                            Government-Industry Relations in Automobiles
                            *Eleanor Hadley*                                     319


PART FOUR: MANAGERIAL EFFICIENCY AND THE MOTIVATION SYSTEM

Chapter IX                  The Japanese Management System:
                            An X-Efficiency-Game Theory Analysis
                            *Harvey Leibenstein*                                 331

Chapter X                   Reshuffling Firms for Technology?: An Aggregate
                            Time Series Analysis of B. Klein's "Dynamic
                            Efficiency"
                            *Taizo Yakushiji*                                    359

Chapter  XI                 Corporate Loyalty and Bonus Payments:
                            An Analysis of Work Incentives in Japan
                            *Masahiro Okuno*                                     387

Comments on IX & XI         Some Reflections on the Japanese Motivation
                            System
                            *Tuvia Blumenthal*                                   413

Author Index                                                                    417

Subject Index                                                                   421

# INTRODUCTION

THE ECONOMIC ANALYSIS OF THE JAPANESE FIRM
M. Aoki (editor)
© Elsevier Science Publishers B.V. (North-Holland), 1984

II

# ASPECTS OF THE JAPANESE FIRM

MASAHIKO AOKI

## Are the Neoclassical Paradigm and the Culturalist Parable only Alternatives?

The neoclassical paradigm, which has thrived in its Anglo-American homeland and propagated to other industrial nations including Japan, reflects a rather simplistic and mechanistic view of the firm.  According to the textbook treatment of the subject, the firm is nothing but a technological black box, as summarized by the production function, which transforms combinations of marketed inputs into marketable outputs.  It is claimed that economists need not explore the contents of this black box but may be exclusively concerned with how a creature dubbed "entrepreneur" operates it.  Two functions are normally attributed to the entrepreneur: control and risk-taking.  First, he is assumed to control the combination and amounts of marketed inputs and to set them so as to maximize the revenue from outputs net of payments to input-holders given terms of trade of those goods that are determined exogenously in the market.  In so doing, entrepreneur contributes to the overall efficiency of the economy.  Secondly, when future demands for outputs are uncertain, the entrepreneur solely assumes the risk of uncertain future revenues by guaranteeing contractual payments to input-holders and thereby relieves risk-averse input-holders of the risk of uncertain results of production. In so doing, he contributes to efficient risk-shifting in the economy.  A great number of the post-World War II generation of Japanese economists have been trained in this frame of thinking. Some students of the Japanese economy might have felt ambivalence toward this paradigm, however.

On one hand, the aggressive, competitive philosophy of neoclassicism appeared to provide a powerful impetus for the removal of supposed impediments to rapid industrial development in the 1950s and 60s. For instance, characteristics of the Japanese employment structure, such as enterprise unionism, seniority wages and dualistic wage structure, were at first thought of as remnants of "old" society which would fade away with the gradual modernization of the economy.  In this respect, neoclassical and Marxian economists were curiously consensual.  "Equal wage for equal labor" backed up by industrial unionism was an agreed upon beau ideal.  In the sphere of government-business relations, the industrial policy of Japan tends to be glorified nowadays as an omnipotent magic cane that fostered high growth in the 1950s and early '60s.  In retrospect, however, the Ministry of International Trade and Industry (MITI) was actually apt to indulge in pessimistic assessments of the prospects for industrial growth and the competitive  power of industries.  This tendency manifested

itself, for example, ill-conceived plan to create a "people's
car," discussed by T. Yakushiji in this volume, and its unsuccessful effort to limit the construction of new blast furnaces in
the steel industry in the early '60s.[1] Competitive policy prescrip-
tions by neoclassical economists furnished a countervailing standpoint to the conservative and/or meddlesome tendency of bureaucrats
backing up established companies. Moreover, as the population,
released from traditional bonds, apparently began to pursue more
overtly materialistic welfare through individualistic efforts
and as obstacles to the competitive operation of markets were
gradually removed domestically as well as at the national border,
it began to appear that the neoclassical theory provided a better
explanation of the performance of the economy.

On the other hand, in spite of the success of rapid industrialization,
the neoclassical _beau_ ideal turned out to be a never-never land.
Employees seem to be attached to their employing companies as
much as ever. Whereas in England the word "company" is associated
with the shareholdings institution emerging out of the partnership
tradition, in Japan it is more often the employees who talk about
"my company." As a result of the _zaibatsu_ dissolution, the mighty
owners of dominant holding companies disappeared form the main
stage, and shareholdings became dispersed among banks, business
partners, employees, and many small investors. Where can one
find the neoclassical entrepreneur? Is the impact of the employees'
voice on corporate affairs appropriately treatable by the "black
box" paradigm?

Furthermore, the unexpected praise and envy of Japan's economic
success have given rise since the late 1970s to the "Japanism"
myth. Seniority wages, lifetime employment, and enterprise unionism,
once regarded as historical residues, have now been elevated to
the position of "the three sacred tools"[2] which allegedly harmonize
industrial relations and elicit employee cooperation. The "Japanese
management system," based on consensual decision-making, is said
to elicit greater contributions from, as well as to yield fairer
shares to, all corporate constituents concerned. These are ecohoes
of the "culturalist" argument of the type presented in an influential
book by James Abegglen [1], who wrote that the Japanese employment
and management systems are culturally unique and hence are not
transplantable elsewhere.[3] However, the resurrected version of
the myth sounds more proud and suggests that other nations can
learn some lessons from the Japanese about how to cure the industrial
disease.

But if there is an economic rationale for the firm-specific
employment structure and the accompanying constituent management
techniques, why do not similar structures exist elsewhere? As
documented by some Japanese labor economists (e.g., Hazama [20]
and Hyodo [22]), and as introduced to English readers by Cole
[11], Dore [13], and Taira [40], the allegedly traditional practices
of lifetime employment, seniority wages and so on are, in fact,
fairly modern inventions consciously designed by rationality-
minded entrepreneurs after the Russo-Japanese War (1904-5), to
cope with the shortage and resulting excessive quits of skilled
workers. Even at the prestigious Nagasaki Shipbuilding Yard,
the turnover rate of workers is said to have been almost always
at 100% annually before the introduction of the formal dualistic
employment structure, __ i.e., the differentiation of privileged
"lifetime" employees from temporary workers, in 1910.[4]

Actually, the neoclassical homeland as well, some labor economists
have started to emphasize the importance of the internal labor
market, in which allocation and pricing are subject to administrative
rule. Other labor economists have advanced the argument that
unions might also contribute to the productivity of the firm by
providing an effective outlet for employees' voices and complaints,
thereby reducing costly quits.[5] The management of large corporations
everywhere have begun to seek an appropriate channel for reflecting
employees' voice on corporate policy-making. In continental Europe,
employee participation in the corporate organ have become legally
institutionalized. In Anglo-American unionized firms, the scope
of collective bargaining is being broadened beyond the traditional
realm of wage negotiation. Even in England where the industrial
union has been the norm, the focus of bargaining has tended to
shift to the enterprise and plant level. Thus, the institutionaliza-
tion of firm-specific employment structures and the search for
ways to reflect employee voice into managerial decision-making
appear to be universal tendencies in spite of national differences
in their institutional forms due to historical inertia.[6]

These observations are indicative of the general perspective of
this book. First, although we attempt to devote adequate attention
to unique features of the institutional and cultural framework
of the Japanese firm we want to emphasize that at least certain
facets of the Japanese firm should be, and can be, explained by
economic reasoning, based on the rationality principle or otherwise.
We would like to detect universal elements of the modern corporate
firm behind the unique strucutre of the Japanese firm. In spite
of this emphasis on universality, however. we would like to go
beyond the simple neoclassical view of the firm. Although we
will not try to present a unified grand theory of the firm in
this book, all of the contributors seem to agree, implicitly or
explicitly, that the modern corporate firm needs to be regarded
as a coalitional association of diverse constituents, such as
managers, employees, banks, investors, business partners and so
on rather than as a mere technological black box. Or, to put
it in somewhat more neoclassical terms, the modern corporate firm
is a legal fiction which serves as a nexus for the bundle of long-
term contractual relationships with the owners of human and financial
resources as well as business partners. It may be only differences
in the mode and extent of these associations, or contructual
coalitions, among firm-specific resource holders that give rise
to national and individual differences in the character of firms.

## The Firm-Specific Employment Structure and the Union

A popular version of the neoclassical theory regards entrepreneurship
in the modern corporate firm as residing in the body of shareholders.
They place their assets in risky investments and at the same time
exercise ultimate control over corporate affairs through controlling
the selection of managers who direct the activities of the firm.
However, the association of individual shareholders with portfolio
corporations may, in some cases, not be enduring. On the other
hand, although the relationship between the firm and its employees
is taken to be merely contractual and the employees are never
considered as members of the firm in this theory, this view is
unreal in that it ignores the undisputed fact that the employees
form an integral part of the firm for which they work to a far
greater extent than is the case for most of the shareholders whom
the neoclassical theory persists in identifying with the firm.

This general issue underlies Part I, which consists of three papers dealing with labor aspects of the Japanese firm. They address the following questions: To what extent are Japanese workers associated with employing firms permanently? In other words, to what extent does the mythology of lifetime employment reflect reality? What is the economic rationale for the firm-specific employment structure, if any? What implications would it have on the work organization on the shop-floor as well as to the function of the union?

In the United States, studies in human capital theory seem to have placed relatively greater emphasis on the role of general training, as compared to specific training on the job, in the formation of workers' skills. In Japan, by contrast, relatively greater emphasis has been placed on skill formation on the job in theory as well as in practice. (Business schools for teaching general managerial skills have never been developed seriously in Japan.) Skill formation on the job may be more or less of a collective nature. Skills acquired over a period of time in cooperation with fellow workers may lose some of their economic value when the worker is dissociated from the team. Also, customs and uncodified rules of work may contribute to the formation and transmission of firm-specific skills. Workers quits may be also costly to employers in terms of recruiting and re-training new workers.

Kazuo Koike has been engaged in the investigation of the skill formation process on the job in Japan through extensive field work, and he summarizes some of his main findings in his contribution to this volume (Chapter II). He argues persuasively that there are mutual benefits both on the side of management and on the side of workers to making a commitment to long-run employment if the workers skills involved are of a nature fostered efficiently only through the career development of employees in the context of group-interaction within the firm. Thus, one would expect the extent of life-time employment to be very much related to the nature of the skills involved.

The paper by Tachibanaki (Chapter III) examines the extent of lifetime employment (long-run employment) in Japan through careful statistical studies of panel data as well as aggregate data. His findings conform to a recent excellent socioeconomic study by Robert Cole [11] in that the difference in the prevalence of long-run employment between Japan and the United States is found to be smaller than popularly believed. In Japan, lifetime employment is assured for more educated male employees having better jobs at larger firms. For the majority of workers, lifetime employment is often a wishful ideal rather than an established convention. But, as Leibenstein argues in his contribution to this volume, from a motivational point of view the widespread belief that lifetime employment is desirable and subjectively likely may be just as important as the fact.

It is commonly believed that Japanese unionism is characterised by enterprise unions, but there is no legal provision for enterprise unionism. In fact, article 28 of the Constitution guarantees the fundamental right of workers association, and the Labor Union Act guarantees that any association of workers will be recognized as a bargaining partner if its rule book satisfies requirements of independence as stipulated by the Act. Under this legal

framework, it is often the case that union rivalry emerges in
a single firm, which then finds itself mired in serious labor
disputes. One enterprise-one unionism is rather an evolutionary
outcome. The management may be interested in running its own
industiral relations to elicit employees cooperativeness, and
the employees may wish to have a say in wage determination as
well as on the way in which work is organized, the way in which
managerial choices are made which would affect their lives, etc.
It should be recalled that many American labor specialists also
hold that, in spite of apparent industrial unionism a conspicuous
feature of American unionism, in contrast to that of Europe, is
the fact that important bargaining takes place primarily on the
level of the enterprise and/or plant.[7] It may be further added
that, even in Europe, the tendency is toward enterprise and plant-
level bargaining.[8] In this sense, the Japanese unionism may have
a modicum of universality. It may be only that, as widespread
unionism re-emerged in Japan only after World War II after the
monopolistic positions of large corporate firms had been firmly
established, there was neither historical inertia nor politico-
economic imperatives for industrial unionism and that the historical
tendency toward enterprise-level bargaining in mature monopolistically
competitive economies manifested itself in a "purer" form in Japan
for this reason.[9] Of course, the cultural tradition of familyism
in Japan might have played some role.

As Freeman's comment reports, Muramatsu's finding in chapter IV
within the framework developed by Brown, Medoff and Freeman, conforms
to an American finding that unions' contribution to productivity
was significantly larger in the late '70s than in the early '70s.[10]
Muramatsu interpretes this finding as suggesting that, when labor
market conditions become unfavorable toward workers, employees
tend to try to channel their complaints and opinions through union
institutions rather than to quit their jobs and search for another
job, and that this tendency contributes to the improvement of
productivity because quits and retraining are costly to the firm.

## Corporate Finance and Shareholdings

The two papers in Part II deal with aspects of corporate finance
of the Japanese firms, and the two papers in Part III deal with
their external relationships with business partners and the
government. From one point of view, one paper each from the both
Parts (Chapters VI and VII) may be thought of as being concerned
with a similar subject, i.e., the functioning of shareholdings
in the Japanese firm by institutional shareholders.

The paper by Ishikawa and Ueda (Chapter V) on the bonus payment
system bridges Parts I and II nicely. On one hand, the bonus
payment system is commonly counted as one of the unique characteristics
of the Japanese employment structure. The paper by Okuno (Chapter
XI) is concerned with this aspect. On the other hand, bonus payments
are also frequently thought of as an important source of saving
that is channeled into the corporate sector as investible funds.
Japan has experienced a remarkably high personal saving propensity
amounting to 20.0% on average during 1958-78. Many hypotheses
have been offered to explain the phenomenon, but the statistical
tests have been inconclusive.[11] Ishikawa and Ueda challenge the
permanent income-life cycle saving hypothesis and argue that households differentiate bonus earnings from the rest of their income
and regard them as a sort of buffer income, capable of being

dispensed discretionarily. Moreover, they conclude that in normal
years of stable growth, households seem to follow a conventional
rule of thumb that dictates that they save about half of their
bonus income; a theory they label the "habit-buffer income hypothesis". According to their statistical tests, the bonus payment
system has a statistically significant impact on the rate of
personal saving, but its magnitude is not large enough to fully
account for the differential between Japan and other industrialized
countries in the saving rate.

Personal savings out of bonuses and otherwise are channeled into
the corporate sector through the stock market, financial intermediaries, as well as private and public pension funds. The next
questions to be addressed in a treatise on the Japanese firm would
inclde: What are the relative importance of the stock market
and financial intermediaries, particularly city banks, as conduits
of investment funds? What debt-equity structure has been chosen
by the Japanese firm and why? What are the characteristics of
the ownership structure of Japanese firms and what role do different
types of shareholders play? As a way of introducing the next
two analytical papers (Chapters VI and VII) which deal with aspects
of corporate finance and the ownership structure of the Japanese
firm, I present below, in some detail, certain stylized facts
regarding the share ownership patterns and the equity structures
of the large non-financial corporations as listed on the Tokyo
Securities Exchange.

Table I-1 compares the general structure of share ownership in
Japan and the United States. Two caveats regarding differences
between the two sets of data in statistical coverage, definitions,
and underlying legal regulations must be noted before any meaningful
comparisons can be made. First of all, the composition of share
holdings by type of investor is calculated, in the case of Japan,
only for the corporations listed on the Tokyo and other Securities
Exchanges whereas the corresponding figures for the United States
show the pattern of share holdings not only for all listed stocks
of the New York, American and other Stock Exchanges, but also
all Over-the-Counter (OTC) stocks and all closely-held stocks.
(The relative proportions of OTC stocks and closedly-held stocks
in total corporate stocks in 1978 were 19.8% and 14.8% respectively.)
Therefore, the proportion of U.S. individual share holdings may
be somewhat upward biased since a relatively large proportion
of closely-held stock is allegedly held by owner-managers.

Secondly, the proportional figures of share ownership are calculated
in terms of the market value of stock in the case of the U.S.
but in terms of the number of shares held, most of which normally
has a face value of ¥50, in the case of Japan. In order to make
the comparison more tenable, an estimate of the relative composition
of shares held by investors of different types in Japan in terms
of market value at the end of March 1981 is recorded in the last
column of Table I-1. It turns out that there is no substantial
difference between figures calculated in terms of face value and
those in terms of market value except for the fact that the market
value of foreigners' holdings is relatively higher.

(a) Institutional Shareholdings
The institutional holdings in the United States are scattered
among private noninsured pension funds (11.2% of total domestic
stock excluding intercorporate holdings in 1980), investment

Table I-1  Shareholder Composition

(unit: %)

| Japan (End of March) | 1975 | 1976 | 1977 | 1978 | 1979 | 1980 | 1981 | 1981 (market value) |
|---|---|---|---|---|---|---|---|---|
| Government | 0.2 | 0.2 | 0.2 | 0.2 | 0.2 | 0.2 | 0.2 | 0.4 |
| Financial Institutions | 36.1 | 36.5 | 37.9 | 38.8 | 38.8 | 38.8 | 38.6 | 38.2 |
| Intercorporate Holdings | 26.3 | 26.5 | 26.2 | 26.3 | 26.1 | 26.0 | 26.3 | 26.2 |
| Securities Brokers | 1.4 | 1.4 | 1.5 | 1.8 | 2.0 | 1.7 | 1.7 | 1.5 |
| Foreign Investors | 2.6 | 2.6 | 2.3 | 2.1 | 2.5 | 4.0 | 4.6 | 5.8 |
| Individuals | 33.5 | 32.9 | 32.0 | 30.8 | 30.4 | 29.2 | 28.4 | 27.9 |
| (directorate holdings) | (2.7 | 2.4 | 2.3 | 2.3 | 2.1 | 1.9 | 1.8 | 2.4) |

| United States (End of Year) | 1974 | 1975 | 1976 | 1977 | 1978 | 1979 | 1980 |
|---|---|---|---|---|---|---|---|
| Institutional Investors | 32.9 | 32.9 | 31.4 | 31.2 | 30.8 | 29.7 | 28.3 |
| Intercorporate Holdings | 10.7 | 10.7 | 15.3 | 15.3 | 15.2 | 15.2 | 15.4 |
| Foreign Investors | 4.0 | 5.5 | 5.4 | 5.4 | 5.8 | 5.7 | 6.2 |
| Other Domestic Investors (primarily Individuals) | 51.5 | 50.8 | 48.0 | 48.1 | 48.1 | 49.3 | 51.1 |

Source: Japan.  The National Conference of Securities Exchanges, Survey of Stockholding Distribution [32].  The estimates of directorate holdings were computed from the NEEDS corporate financial data.

U.S.  Computed from A-530 and A-540, SEC Monthly Statistical Review.

companies (2.7%), insurance companies (3.8%), personal trust funds
(8.4%), state and local retirement funds (2.9%), foundations and
other educational endowments (2.7%).  In Japan, banks and insurance
companies dominate other financial institutions in terms of shareholdings.  According to the survey done by the National Conference
Board of Securities Exchanges, nearly 47% of all listed stocks
held by financial institutions were held by commercial and trust
banks, 30.1% by life insurance companies, and 13.2% by casualty
insurance companies in 1980.  While in the United States the
commercial departments of banks are not allowed to hold stocks
of other companies on their own account, city banks in Japan are
allowed to do so subject to anti-monopoly regulation.  At present,
the maximum fraction of shares of a single corporation that may
be held by a bank is 10%, but Article 11 of the Revised Anti-
Monopoly Act of 1977 stipulates that the upper ceiling should
be reduced to 5%, and commercial and trust banks will be required
to comply with this requirement by 1987.  Since banks' holdings
of the stocks of certain portfolio corporations still exceeded
that limit in 1981, the proportion of banks holdings may decrease
in the near future unless banks diversify their shareholdings
among many more corporations and/or portfolio corporations issue
new shares without banks' subscriptions.  At present, however,
banks and insurance companies remain among the largest stock
voters in large Japanese corporations, and their power to
influence the managerial policy of portfolio corporations,
although latent in the normal course of affairs, often manifests
itself in cases in which portfolio corporations are caught in
financial difficulties or internally insurmountable management
strife.  Particularly noteworthy in this connection is the provision
of the Japanese corporate statute (Commercial Code, Article 278)
that directors of corporations are removable at any time without
cause by an ordinary resolution of  a shareholders general meeting.
This provision endows major shareholders with a powerful threat
at critical moments.

The potential power of banks to influence other companies may
not be limited to Japan, however, notwithstanding the fact that
direct share holdings by banks are prohibited in the United States.
As we have seen, holdings of pension funds and trust funds are
substantial in the United States, and most of these funds are
not self-administered.  They are usually managed by the trust
departments of banks and insurance companies, and voting rights
are usually exercised by those trustees.  Therefore, in order
to assess the potential power of banks vested in the form of
voting rights, data on share ownership are not enough.  An
interesting study was done by the Subcommittee on Reports,
Accounting and Management of the Senate Committee of Government
Affairs headed by  the late Senator Lee Metcalf [44] regarding
the concentration of voting rights of 122 large corporations which
include some of the giant financial institutions.  (The enormous
size of the 122 corporations is indicated by one statistic:  The
market value of their common stock amounted to 41% of the market
value of all outstanding common stock at the end of 1976).  The
study found that 25.2% of the stock voting authority in the 122
corporations is vested in banks and trust companies and 4.3% in
insurance companies.

If the exercise of influence by banks is made possible by the
concentration of trust assets, there may arise the problem of
a potential conflict of interest between a bank's position as

a trustee and as a lender.  For instance, if a bank's trust
department owns a large block of stock of a corporation, which
also happens to be a good customer of its commercial department,
it may not sell the stock even if that is the proper decision
to make, when this action would jeopardize the bank's business
relationship with that corporation.  In order to prevent this
type of conflict of interest problem from arising, the trust
manager legally owes fiduciary duty to beneficial owners of
trust, and an internal code, commonly called the "China Wall",
is voluntarily imposed by banks to regulate information exchanges
between commercial departments and trust departments.  Some cast
doubts on the effectiveness of such regulation, but whether or
not commercial banks actually use their potential power of
influencing portfolio corporations through voting to their own
advantage is not readily ascertainable.

Since city banks do not normally engage in trust management in
Japan pursuant to administrative guidance by the Ministry of
Finance,[12] and trade stock accordingly on their own account,
the conflict of interest problem of the American type will not
arise.  But there may arise another type of conflict of interest
problem, as clarified by the following series of questions: What
is the motive for the holding of stocks by city banks?  Do they
hold stocks of non-financial corporations simply because they
will yield higher returns?  Or do they hold stocks only in order
to maintain good customer relationships with portfolio corporations
as well as to reserve the right to influence, if necessary, policy
decisions of portfolio corporations to their own advantage?  Are
there then any conflicts of interest, or the absence of unanimity,
between ordinary shareholders and bank-cum-shareholders with
respect to the policy making of portfolio corporations?  The
paper by Aoki (Chapter VI) considers these issues.

(b) Inter-Corporate Shareholdings and Corporate Groupings
The role of banks as shareholders in Japan should be understood
in the broader perspective of intercorporate shareholdings.  Even
a casual glance at Table I-1 would not fail to detect that intercorporate share holdings are substantial in Japan.  Article 9
of the Anti-Monopoly Law illegalizes the establishment of a
holding company whose "principle business is to control...the
business activities of another company."  However, non-financial
large corporations may hold stocks of other corporations, where
the effect is not "substantially to restrain competition," and
only to the extent that the acquisition value of those stocks
does not exceed the value of their own net assets.  Even this
limitation may be lifted in some cases, e.g., when a joint venture
is set up with a foreigner or foreign corporation, when a corporation
spins off a part of its business as a subsidiary and acquires
100% of its shares, etc.[13]

Inter-corporate shareholdings permissible under such a statutory
framework have given rise to two types of corporate groupings:
one is the so-called ex-Zaibatsu corporate groups (kigyo shudan),
or financial keiretsu, in which major corporations are grouped
toghether through mutual shareholdings primarily along the old
Zaibatsu lines and/or with banks as nuclei; and the other type
is subsidiary groupings, or capital keiretsu, in which dominant
parent corporations are connected with many satellite corporations
(subsidiaries) through share holdings and vertial relations.
The ex-Zaibatsu groups or financial keiretsu have corresponding

Presidents' Clubs which meet regularly. There are six such major
groups as Table I-2.

Member corporations of each financial group are connected only
partially, and non-exclusively, with other member corporations
through vertical relations, but each group includes, as a rule,
(at least) one city bank and one trust bank as members.   The
extent of intra-group bank financing and the extent of intra-
group mutual shareholdings indicate the coherence of the group.
In this respect, the Mitsubishi Group and the Sumitomo Group
are superior to the others.   The Presidents' Club is said to
discuss matters relevant to the whole group informally and does
not have any statutory standing nor even formal decision-making
power, but one cannot dismiss its important role, for instance,
in organizing joint projects, such as those involving resource
development abroad, nuclear energy, ocean development, electronic
transactions systems, etc., which require substantial investments,
diverse technologies, the collective use of information channels
and the like.

The present day ex-Zaibatsu groups (represented by Mitsui,
Mitsubishi and Sumitomo) are quite different in their organizational
form from the pre-war Zaibatsu. The latter were controlled by
more or less closely-held holding companies.  This organizational
form, becuase of its closed nature, was already becoming increasingly
obsolete even in the prewar period as the need for financing
the development of capital-intensive heavy industries arose.
The military government initiated policies to direct (forced)
saving toward heavy industries and the war effort through financial
intermediaries, and the role of holding companies went into eclipse
after the 1930s.   The Zaibatsu dissolution by the Supreme Commander
for Allied Powers (SCAP) was thus not a traumatic event in the
development of the Japanese industiral structure but rather had
the not-entirely-precaluculated effect of accelerating the
evolutionary process which had already begun.   There was no open
criticism against the outlawing of holding companies.   No voice
was raised favoring their revival.   Instead, "headless" groupings
(to use Eleanor Hadley's term [17]) were reorganized dexterously
through mutual shareholdings somewhat along the old Zaibatsu
lines.

The 1947 Anti-monopoly Law originally outlawed inter-corporate
shareholdings by nonfinancial corporations except with the
permission of the Fair Trade Commission, which might grant
approval in situations of single tier subsidiaries technologically
related to the parent corpoation.   However this stiff provision
was quickly reversed in 1949. Particularly important to the rise
of inter-corporate shareholdings was the following incident.
When the share market plunged in 1965 causing the near bankruptcy
of one of the four largest securities houses (Yamaichi Securities
Co.), the Japan Joint Securities Corporation and Securities
Holding Union were created under the direction of the Ministry
of Finance to buy and freeze a certain amount of stock to stabilize
the market.   After stabilization was achieved, these stocks were
sold.   At around this time, foreign investments were being
liberalized and many major firms were fearful of a possible
take-over by foreign corporations.   Major corporations built
up mutual shareholdings in order to insulate themselves from
take-overs using old Zaibatsu connections or with financial

Table I-2  Six Major Corporate Groups (1980)

|  | Mitsui | Mitsubishi | Sumitomo | Sanwa | Fuyo | Ikkan | Total |
|---|---|---|---|---|---|---|---|
| Number of Corporations in Presidents' Club | 24 | 28 | 21 | 40 | 29 | 45 | 182 |
| Intra-group shareholdings (%) | 17.4 | 29.3 | 26.8 | 16.8 | 16.2 | 14.7 | |
| Intra-group bank finance (%) | 19.1 | 24.9 | 27.8 | 27.0 | 18.8 | 13.2 | |
| Intra-group directorate holdings (%) | 3.8 | 13.1 | 13.4 | 5.8 | 4.2 | 8.2 | |
| Weight of Groups in the entire non-financial sector in terms of assets (%) | 2.47 | 2.89 | 1.52 | 3.01 | 2.79 | 4.03 | 15.34 |
| in terms of profits (%) | 2.54 | 1.84 | 1.28 | 2.22 | 1.52 | 3.05 | 12.84 |
| in terms of employees (%) | 0.75 | 0.75 | 0.43 | 1.24 | 1.03 | 1.57 | 4.91 |

Source: The Oriental Economist, *Kigyo Keiretsu Soran*, 1982. Since there are several corporations which belong to two groups, the numbers of six presidents' clubs do not add up to the total number of corporations which belong to at least one of the six groups.

institutions acting as intermediaries.  The relative importance
and coherence of these financial groups may have eroded somewhat
recently but they remain a conspicuous phenomenon.

Leaving aside their function as an insulator against take-over,
what is the function of these financial groupings?  Among the
many possible motives for such groupings, the one emphasized by
Nakatani (Chapter VII) is uncertainty and the consequent need
for reduction in collective risk costs on which I would like to
comment in more detail later.

The other type of corporate grouping, the subsidiary grouping
or capital keiretsu, is one in which one dominant parent corporation
is connected with many other subsidiary or keiretsu firms through
shareholdings.  The parent corporation and keiretsu corporations
are normally connectied vertically.  For example, keiretsu firms
can be firms set up as subsidiaries by the parent firm which spins
off part of its activities; they can be subcontractors of parts
production; they can be suppliers of materials to the parent firm;
they can be engaged in marketing the products of the parent corporation; etc.  It had often been the case that keiretsu firms also
own shares of the parent corporation.  The possible motives for
this reciprocal shareholding are many, but to quote a few: to
save on the cost of new share issues of the parent corporations
by assigning a certain number of shares to keiretsu firms (a
practice which would be regulated in the U.S. by the Security
Exchange Rule 240.10b), to insulate the parent corporations from
take-overs by outsiders, and to give keiretsu firms an incentive
for group efficiency.  However, this practice is banned in principle
under the newly effective Commercial Code (October 1982), and
subsidiaries of which more than 50% of shares are owned by parent
corporations are being required to make plans for divesting their
holdings of parent corporate stock in due time.  A plan being
considered within the Matsushita (Panasonic) Group is to transfer
all subsidiary holdings to the employees' stock ownership plan.

Such practices as subcontracting and creating spin-off firms are
widespread in Japan, and subsidiary groupings or capital-keiretsu
are accordingly very extensive.  Kigyo Keiretsu Soran 1982 [35]
by the Oriental Economist defines group members of a subsidiary
group as those corporations of which more than 10% of the stock
is owned by the parent corporation as the first or second largest
stock voter or of which more than 20% of the stock is owned by
other keiretsu firms as the first largest stock voter.  The study
identifies the number of member firms of subsidiary groupings
headed by such major corporations as Shin Nihon Steel, Toyota,
Nissan, Hitachi, and Matsushita as 151, 64, 231, 190, and 611,
respectively.  Those parent corporations invested between 81.5%
(Matsushita) and 36.6% (Shin Nihon Steel) of their total financial
investments in their keiretsu firms in 1981.  It is estimated
that the ten largest subsidiary groupings headed by major
manufacturing corporations owned 5.92% of the total assets,
employed 3.10% of the total employees, and generated 10.68% of
the total profits of the non-fianncial corporate sector in 1977.
Thus, major subsidiary groupings appear to have surpassed the
financial groupings in their cohesiveness.

The prima facie reason for such extensive deployment of subsidiary
relations has been thought to lie in its shock-absorbing funciton,

Table I-3.   The Ratio of Investments in Subsidiaries to
             the Paid-in Capital of Non-Financial Listed
             Corporations

(unit: %)

|      | All Industries | Manufacturng Industries | Non-Manufacturing Industries |
|------|------|------|------|
| 1966 | 10.8 | 11.0 | 10.5 |
| 1967 | 12.0 | 12.4 | 11.3 |
| 1968 | 12.8 | 13.0 | 12.4 |
| 1969 | 14.1 | 13.9 | 14.4 |
| 1970 | 15.3 | 15.1 | 15.6 |
| 1971 | 16.5 | 16.4 | 16.5 |
| 1972 | 17.4 | 17.6 | 17.1 |
| 1973 | 19.8 | 20.1 | 19.3 |
| 1974 | 22.3 | 23.1 | 21.1 |
| 1975 | 24.3 | 25.4 | 22.7 |
| 1976 | 24.4 | 25.8 | 22.2 |
| 1977 | 25.3 | 27.1 | 22.8 |
| 1978 | 26.5 | 28.1 | 24.2 |
| 1979 | 27.7 | 30.3 | 24.1 |
| 1980 | 29.2 | 32.3 | 24.9 |
| 1981 | 30.9 | 34.9 | 25.6 |

i.e., the brunt of recessions is borne by weaker subsidiaries
and subcontractors through lay-offs and losses, while lifetime
employment is guaranteed for employees of the parent corporation.
Subsidiary groupings with such unegalitarian connotations have
been regarded as remnants of semi-feudalistic relations which
would, and should, fade away as the economy develops.   Contrary
to the prediction of this semi-feudalistic paradigm, however,
the subsidiary grouping does not seem to be declinig.   As indicated
in Table I-3, major corporations' investment in their subsidiaries
as a proportion of the value of their total shareholders' paid-
in capitals (shihonkin) has increased remarkably in the 1970s.
At present, more than one-third of the total paid-in capitals
of the manufacturing industry is re-invested in subsidiaries.
Does this mean that the Japanese are still tolerating semi-
feudalistic relations?   Or is there another economic rationale
for the extensive deployment of subsidiary relations?   We shall
discuss possible economic motives for groupings, financial as
well as subsidiary, afterwards.

(c) How Significant is Individual Shareholding?
The final, but not the least important, characteristic of the
Japanese structure of share ownership is the apparent insignificance
and declining proportion of individual shareholdings.   Examining
individuals' assets, shareholdings appear to comprise only 2.0%
of totoal financial assets of individual in 1980 in terms of book
value.   By far the most important item in individual portfolios
is bank deposits and similar assets (61.9% of individual financial
assets in 1980).[14]   However, if the relative proportion of
shareholdings is recomputed using an estimated market value (an

estimate in the <u>Annual</u> <u>Social</u> <u>Account</u> [15] of the Economic Planning
Agency), it would rise to as high as 8.2%, which cannot be considered
insignificant (The ratio is 26.0% in the United States and 4.4%
in Germany).

Despite the relatively small percentage of shareholdings in
individual financial asset portfolios, the importance of the
securities exchange to individual investors should not be
neglected.   The Tokyo Securities Exchange is now the second
largest exchange in the world, second only to the New York
Exchange in terms of market value of stock trades.   (The market
value of total stock transactions on the Tokyo Securities Exchange
in 1980 was $179.8 billion, whereas those on the New York, London,
and Paris Exchanges were $382.4 billion, $36.7 billion and $12.6
billion, respectively.)   Its turnover, as measured by the ratio
of annual sales to the total market value of listed stocks, exceeds
that of the New York Exchange (50.2% for the Tokyo Securities
Exchange and 35.6% for the New York Exchange).   Also, 42.2% of
total share transactions on the Tokyo Securities Exchange in 1981
was on behalf of individuals in terms of market value, and
individuals play a significant role in share price formation.
On the other hand, share transactions by banks, insurance companies,
and non-financial corporations comprised only 2.9%, 0.8% and 6.9%
of total share transactions respectively, indicating that
institutional shareholdings are relatively locked in. (27.7% of
share transactions is self-dealings by securities houses and 10.0%
is transactions by foreigners.)

As indicated in Table I-1, holdings by directors of corporations
are also not negligible, when we take account of the fact that
most of them are salaried managers who have worked their way
through the internal organization and that the stock-option plan
is not practiced in Japan.   The management may not be as conscious
as its American counterpart of short-run movements in the price
or the price-earnings ratio of its own stock because the Board
of Directors functions only as a <u>de facto</u> substructure of top
management, and top managers are rarely disciplined solely in
terms of stock market performance.   But if we were to say that
management is completely indifferent to the movement of the
value of its own stock, we would be incorrect.   As salaried
managers, their retirement incomes will be intimately related
to the future performance of their company's stock.   Also, in
a cultural environment in which even a small difference with one's
neighbors can be a source of great concern, management cannot
be entirely indifferent to the "relative" performance of its own
stock as compared with that of other comparable stocks.   Thus,
while share price is not the criterion used to evaluate managers,
it does impose a certain degree of discipline on them.   One of
the tasks of Chapter VII by Aoki is to analyze how the objective
of value-maximization is reconciled with, or sacrificed in favor
of, other motives in the Japanese firm.

<u>Is Debt-Equity Ratio Really High?</u>

Table I-4 is based on Japanese and U.S. official balance-sheet
statistics in the manufacturing industry.   After comparing such
statistics casually, it is often concluded that Japanese firms
incur relatively higher debt-equity ratio and that there is a
need for them to strengthen their financial positions.   For
instance, the <u>Economic</u> <u>White</u> <u>Paper</u> for 1976 of the Economic

Planning Agency devoted an entire section to the problem of improving
the ability of Japanese firms to withstand fluctuations in the
business cycle and cited the elimination of excessive reliance
on debt financing as an important aspect of this problem.  However,
in order to gain a realistic view of the financial position of
the Japanese firm and the degree of its reliance on debt financing
of investments, we need to pay some attention to the unique economic
institutions and practices in Japan which generate such apparently
high debt-equity ratios.

First of all, we notice that one of the causes of high debt-equity
ratios is the high proportion of accounts payable.  The figure
for Japanese firms has been approximately twice that of their
American counterparts.  Parallel to this phenomenon, the proportion
of accounts receivable on the asset side is also relatively high
for Japanese firms, but the difference is not as  marked as it
is in the case of accounts payable.  One of the important reasons
for the higher proportions of accounts payable and accounts
receivable is one feature of Japan's unique industrial sturcture
to which we have already referred, i.e., the extensive interaction
with subsidiaries and subcontractors.  As we will discuss presently,
there are many motives in the Japanese firm for quasi-disintegration,
and the average size of major firms tends to be kept slim.  Major
firms spin off substantial parts of their activities to their
susidiaries or other keiretsu firms, and extensive use is made
of inter-firm trade credits between them.  A large proportion
of accounts receivable and accounts payable is the result of
transactions between quasi-independent firms within subsidiary
groupings which would have taken the form of intra-firm transactions
in major American integrated firms.  The relatively high proportion
of inventories in total assets in the United States indicates,
on the other hand, the greater prevalence of intra-firm transactions.
Within Japanese subsidiary groupings, major firms tend to sell
on longer term notes, while paying their own bills on a short
term basis, thus playing a financing role. The large amount of accounts payable indicates that major firms are able to pay in cash,
but smaller subcontractors often prefer to sell on short-term credit
because bills issued by major firms are brought to banks for
discount and may serve as signals of the credit worthiness of
the subcontractors.

The second major factor which accounts for the apparently high
debt-equity ratios of Japanese firms is the absence of inflation
accounting.  Plant, equipment, land, and financial securities
are recorded at their acquisition value adjusted only for
depreciation.  In the case of land and equity shares particularly,
this implies a non-negligible distortion of the value of assets
which results in a substantial amount of fukumi-shisan ("hidden"
or off-balance-sheet assets).  This can be inferred from just
one statistic: the price index of land for industrial uses was
3,287 at the end of March 1981, whereas it was 707 at the end
of March 1965 (100 at the end of March 1955).  The price of land
has more than quadrupled in the past sixteen years.  Since banks
normally require firms to offer collateral, particularly in the
form of real estate, against long-term loans, the distortion
should be corrected in order to gain insight into the real
financial position of firms.

An attempt is made to correct the distortion in the debt-equity
ratio by reassessing the value of land owned by firms.  Column 1

Table I-4   Balance Sheet Composition

Total Liabilities and Capital

(unit: %)

| Year | Sharehilders's Equity | Stock | Total Liabilities | Long-term Debts | Current Debts | Short-Term Borrowings | Current Payables |
|---|---|---|---|---|---|---|---|
| **Japan** | | | | | | | |
| 1969 | 23.3 | 12.3 | 76.8 | 24.7 | 49.9 | 13.5 | 19.8 |
| 1970 | 22.3 | 11.1 | 77.8 | 24.5 | 50.7 | 12.7 | 21.2 |
| 1971 | 21.5 | 10.3 | 78.6 | 25.7 | 50.3 | 12.3 | 21.1 |
| 1972 | 20.8 | 9.8 | 79.3 | 28.2 | 48.5 | 12.6 | 18.1 |
| 1973 | 21.1 | 9.2 | 79.0 | 26.7 | 49.5 | 12.2 | 18.3 |
| 1974 | 19.6 | 7.8 | 80.5 | 23.7 | 53.9 | 11.6 | 23.0 |
| 1975 | 19.0 | 7.3 | 81.1 | 25.0 | 53.6 | 13.5 | 21.2 |
| 1976 | 18.4 | 7.3 | 81.7 | 27.8 | 53.6 | 13.4 | 20.0 |
| 1977 | 18.7 | 7.1 | 81.4 | 27.9 | 51.9 | 12.3 | 20.6 |
| 1978 | 20.0 | 7.2 | 80.1 | 27.2 | 51.6 | 12.4 | 19.6 |
| 1979 | 21.5 | 7.2 | 78.6 | 25.2 | 52.2 | 12.4 | 19.6 |
| 1980 | 22.0 | 6.7 | 78.1 | 22.3 | 54.9 | 12.5 | 22.8 |
| 1981 | 23.7 | 6.5 | 76.4 | 21.3 | 54.3 | 12.4 | 22.6 |
| **U.S.** | | | | | | | |
| 1968 | 56.2 | 19.2 | 43.8 | 19.8 | 23.9 | 3.8 | 9.8 |
| 1969 | 54.6 | 18.7 | 45.4 | 20.5 | 24.9 | 4.5 | 10.1 |
| 1970 | 53.8 | 18.4 | 46.2 | 21.6 | 24.6 | 4.7 | 9.6 |
| 1971 | 53.5 | 18.2 | 46.5 | 24.1 | 22.1 | 4.1 | 8.8 |
| 1972 | 53.2 | 17.8 | 46.8 | 22.2 | 24.6 | 3.6 | 9.4 |
| 1973 | 52.1 | 16.2 | 47.9 | 21.5 | 26.4 | 4.2 | 10.2 |
| 1974 | 53.2 | 16.9 | 46.9 | 21.8 | 25.1 | 4.7 | 8.9 |
| 1975 | 53.7 | 16.7 | 46.3 | 23.1 | 23.2 | 3.3 | 8.6 |
| 1976 | 53.8 | 16.0 | 46.2 | 22.7 | 23.5 | 2.9 | 8.4 |
| 1977 | 53.1 | 15.3 | 46.9 | 22.9 | 24.0 | 3.1 | 8.8 |
| 1978 | 51.8 | 14.2 | 48.3 | 22.8 | 25.5 | 3.2 | 8.8 |
| 1979 | 50.2 | 13.0 | 49.8 | 22.8 | 27.0 | 3.8 | 9.5 |
| 1980 | 49.6 | 12.7 | 50.4 | 23.6 | 26.7 | 3.8 | 9.8 |

Assets

(unit: %)

| | Year | Liquid Assets | Current Assets | Current Receivables | Inventories | Fixed Assets | Tangibles | Others Fixed Assets |
|---|---|---|---|---|---|---|---|---|
| Japan | 1969 | 57.9 | 39.2 | 26.1 | 15.9 | 42.0 | 31.3 | 10.7 |
| | 1970 | 58.8 | 40.1 | 27.1 | 16.0 | 41.1 | 30.8 | 10.4 |
| | 1971 | 58.5 | 39.1 | 25.9 | 16.6 | 41.4 | 30.8 | 10.7 |
| | 1972 | 57.3 | 38.9 | 23.6 | 15.6 | 42.7 | 31.2 | 11.5 |
| | 1973 | 56.9 | 39.7 | 23.4 | 14.6 | 43.1 | 30.4 | 12.8 |
| | 1974 | 60.2 | 40.4 | 26.0 | 17.0 | 39.8 | 27.6 | 12.3 |
| | 1975 | 59.9 | 35.9 | 22.6 | 20.9 | 40.1 | 27.8 | 12.3 |
| | 1976 | 60.4 | 37.7 | 22.3 | 19.5 | 39.6 | 27.1 | 12.5 |
| | 1977 | 60.9 | 38.9 | 23.4 | 18.6 | 39.1 | 26.4 | 12.8 |
| | 1978 | 60.3 | 39.1 | 23.1 | 17.7 | 39.7 | 26.6 | 13.1 |
| | 1979 | 60.2 | 40.1 | 23.3 | 16.5 | 39.8 | 26.6 | 13.3 |
| | 1980 | 62.7 | 41.6 | 25.2 | 17.4 | 37.4 | 24.8 | 12.7 |
| | 1981 | 62.9 | 40.0 | 24.0 | 19.3 | 37.1 | 24.4 | 12.7 |
| U.S. | 1968 | 51.2 | 24.4 | 17.5 | 23.3 | 48.8 | 39.6 | 9.1 |
| | 1969 | 50.2 | 23.4 | 17.8 | 23.2 | 49.8 | 39.6 | 10.2 |
| | 1970 | 48.7 | 22.3 | 17.3 | 23.0 | 51.3 | 40.3 | 11.0 |
| | 1971 | 48.9 | 23.0 | 17.1 | 22.1 | 51.1 | 39.9 | 11.2 |
| | 1972 | 50.1 | 24.0 | 18.2 | 22.0 | 49.9 | 38.8 | 11.1 |
| | 1973 | 52.0 | 24.8 | 18.8 | 23.0 | 48.0 | 37.5 | 10.5 |
| | 1974 | 48.8 | 22.9 | 16.8 | 23.4 | 51.2 | 34.1 | 17.1 |
| | 1975 | 47.0 | 23.1 | 15.8 | 21.5 | 53.0 | 35.0 | 18.0 |
| | 1976 | 47.2 | 23.6 | 15.7 | 21.2 | 52.8 | 34.8 | 18.0 |
| | 1977 | 47.0 | 23.4 | 16.3 | 20.8 | 53.0 | 35.3 | 17.7 |
| | 1978 | 46.8 | 23.6 | 17.1 | 20.5 | 53.2 | 35.3 | 17.9 |
| | 1979 | 46.2 | 23.0 | 17.3 | 20.6 | 53.8 | 35.5 | 18.3 |
| | 1980 | 44.5 | 23.9 | 16.3 | 18.6 | 55.5 | 36.6 | 18.9 |

Source: JAPAN. computed from the NEEDS Corporate Financial Date. Figure are for manufacturing corporations listed on the Tokyo Exchange. Current Debts and Long-term Debts do not add up to Total Liabilities which include specific reserves (tokutei hikiatekin). End of March.
U.S.. Federal Trade Commission, Quarterly Financial Report for Manufacturing, Mining and Trade Corporation. The number of corporations surveyed is about 10.000. End of Year.

Table I-5   Debt-Equity Ratio Adjusted for Inflation and Reserves

(end of March)

| F.Y | (1) | (2) | (3) | (4) | (5) | (6) | (7) | (8) | (9) |
|------|------|-------|------|------|---------|------|------|------|------|
| 1970 | 81.1 | 1,911 | 4.2 | 23.7 | 15,055 | 64.7 | 2.5 | 2.7 | 61.3 |
| 1971 | 81.8 | 2,215 | 4.1 | 23.9 | 18,180 | 65.1 | 2.7 | 2.7 | 61.6 |
| 1972 | 82.5 | 2,593 | 4.2 | 24.8 | 21,610 | 65.0 | 2.7 | 2.8 | 61.4 |
| 1973 | 82.5 | 3,021 | 4.3 | 26.7 | 27,485 | 63.4 | 2.8 | 2.8 | 59.9 |
| 1974 | 84.3 | 3,563 | 4.0 | 26.2 | 33,523 | 65.0 | 2.7 | 2.8 | 61.5 |
| 1975 | 84.7 | 3,987 | 4.1 | 23.3 | 31 787 | 67.9 | 2.6 | 3.2 | 64.1 |
| 1976 | 84.9 | 4,354 | 4.1 | 23.3 | 34,476 | 68.1 | 2.1 | 3.3 | 64.6 |
| 1977 | 84.8 | 4,665 | 4.1 | 21.5 | 33,447 | 69.5 | 1.9 | 3.4 | 66.0 |
| 1978 | 83.7 | 5,001 | 4.2 | 21.5 | 34,226 | 68.8 | 1.8 | 3.6 | 65.2 |
| 1979 | 82.8 | 5,279 | 4.3 | 22.2 | 37.427 | 67.4 | 1.6 | 3.7 | 64.0 |
| 1980 | 83.0 | 5,690 | 4.1 | 23.2 | 44,454 | 66.6 | 1.4 | 3.5 | 63.5 |
| 1981 | 81.8 | 6,124 | 4.1 | 24.5 | 51 536 | 64.6 | 1.3 | 3.5 | 61.6 |

of Table I-5 records balance sheets data on debt-equity ratio of
all non-financial corporations listed on the Tokyo Securities
Exchanges. Column 2 indicates the book value of land (billion ¥)
recorded on the balance sheets and column 3 shows its ratio to
total assets.  Column 4 of that table shows the ratio of the value
of land owned by the non-financial corporate sector as a whole
to its total asset value, estimated by the Economic Planning Agency
and reported in the National Accounts [15].  The latter presumably
reflects the real value of land holdings by non-financial corporations more acculately.  There is a wide discrepancy between the
two ratios, e.g., 4.1% and 24.5% in 1981.  Now we shall make the
bold assumption that listed corporations hold exactly the same
proportion of their assets in the form of land as the non-financial
corporate sector as a whole.  This assumption allows us to estimate
the "real value" (billion ¥) of land owned by listed corporations
(shown in column 5).  By adding the difference between the real
value of land and the book value (column 2), i.e., the estimated
capital gain from land-holding, to the value of equity capital,
we can compute data on the debt-equity ratio that have been adjusted
for appreciation in land value.  The results are recorded in column
6.  The same adjustment should be tried regarding the value of
equity shares owned by listed corporations although I have not
tried this.

The third factor that accounts for the apparently high debt-equity
ratio of Japanese firms is the widespread practice of so-called
buzumi-ryodate deposits (compensating balances).  When bank credits
are extended to non-financial corporations, the latter are normally
required to retain a portion of the borrowed amount and to hold
it with the same bank as compensating balances, the use of which
is constrained.  The rate of retention is considered to be determined
by bilateral negotiations between the bank and the borrower and
to reflect the relative bargaining power of the two parties as
well as the state of the financial market.  As long as the retention
rate is positive, firms are forced to incerase their nominal
borrowings in excess of their actual investment requirements.
According to an unofficial estimate by Mr. Y. Wakita of the Bank

of Japan [42], the rate of retention between 1962 and 1981 fluctuated
between 40% and 55%.

The fourth factor we must take into account before making any
meaningful comparison between U.S. and Japanese debt-equity ratios
is the provision whereby Japanese firms have been allowed to
accumulate various non-taxable reserves and to include them under
long-term debt when in fact they are usable at the discretion of
the management.  There are two types of such reserves: one is the
so-called tokutei-hikiate-kin (specific reserves) and the other
is reserves for employees' retirement compensation.  Specific
reserves include, for instance, Reserves for Doubtful Receivables,
Reserves for Price Fluctuations, Reserves for Overseas Market
Development, and Reserves for Losses Incurred due to Exchange Rate
Fluctuations.  Their effect has been to reduce reported corporate
income before tax according to a prescribed formula, reduce the
effective tax rate and increase the amount of internal funds available for use at managerial discretion.  However, pursuant to the
revised Commercial Code which became effective in October 1982,
these reserves will henceforth be included under equity capital.

Column 7 of Table I-5 indicates the magnitude of these reserves
as a percent of the total book value of assets.  The ratio reached
its peak in 1973 and has declined since then.  Even at their highest,
the inclusion of specific reserves in equity capital increases the
debt-equity ratio by only a little bit more than 2%, but their
impact has not been negligible in certain years.  For instance,
in 1974, the net increase in depreciable assets of all listed
corporations in the manufacturing sector was ¥825,454 million,
while the net increase in specific reserves was ¥301,952 million.
Thus, tax-exempt internal funds financed about one-third of all
net investments in equipment, plant, buildings, and the like in
that year.

Employees' de facto Capital Participation

The Reserve for Employees' Retirement Compensation is unique to
the Japanese firm and its economic implications are worthy of
comment.  The Japanese firm offers two types of retirement
benefits, normally combined, to its employees.  One is the lump-
sum payment of retirement compensation (taishoku-kin) at the time
of the employee's retirement, and the other is a pension scheme
administered jointly with the government's welfare pension (Kosei-
nenkin) program.  On the average, according to a survey done by
the Institute for Research in Labor Administration [23] and covering
all listed corporations in Japan, about 30% of total retirement
benefits in terms of present value are in the form of pensions.
Company pensions are financed by contributions from employers as
well as employees and are funded, with pension funds being managed
by insurance companies or trust banks, as is the case in the United
States.  However, reserves for employees' retirement compensation
may be accumulated within the firm and are usable at the discretion
of the management subject to possible consultation with unions.
Firms can set aside as tax-free reserves a fixed percentage (50%
up to 1979 and 40% thereafter, with some transitory adjustments)
of the total estimated amount which they would have to pay under
the assumption that all employees will retire at the end of the
current accounting period.  The firm can accumulate more than that
 roportion, if it opts to do so, but the additional amount would

be subject to corporate taxes.   For instance, financial institutions
are required, pursuant to administrative guidance from the Ministry
of Finance, to accumulate an amount equal to their full retirement
compensation obligations calculated under the same assumption.   The
reserves were entered on the firm's balance sheet as long-term
liabilities.   However, they are of a significantly different nature
than other liabilities.   The whole retirement compensation liabilities are payable prior to any of the firm's other liabilities in
the event of reorganization and employees are protected from firm
risks to that extent.   The accumulation of reserves within the firm
may be thought of as having the effect of employee participation in
the capital formation of the firm.   Employees of major firms can be
regarded as purchasing a membership in the corporation when they are
employed, as starting salaries at major firms are normally set lower
than earnings available for more mobile jobs.   Since their potential
claims for retirement compensation will increase with their salaries
and the duration of their service to the firm, their participation
in capital formation will deepen year by year.   At the time of
retirement, they, in a sense, sell their membership in the corporation by receiving retirement compensation.

As retirement compensation benefits are not portable, this system
discourages the mobility of employees.   When a firm has growth
potential, the immobility of employees contributes to the accumulation of human capital as well as financial capital (in the form of
accumulated claims for retirement compensation).   However, when the
firm enters a stagnant stage, worker immobility may have reverse,
inefficient implications.   As employees are reluctant to "exit" from
the firm in spite of its decline, allocative efficiency will be
violated.   Further, since the absence of any credible threat of exit
also hampers the effectiveness of the employees' "voice" to re-
cuperate the firm from internal inefficiency, intra-firm efficiency
or X-efficiency will be affected unfavorably as well.   Also, as
the firm grows older and a higher proportion of its employees
reaches retirement age, the firm will have to decumulate its
retirement compensation reserves faster, and internal funds for
recuperation will be squeezed.   However, one may say that, on
balance, reserves have had positive effects on the capital accumulation of firms in the past.   Column 8 of Table I-5 indicates that
reserves have amounted to between 2.7% and 3.7% of total assets in
the past.   A more meaningful ratio, however, may be the ratio of
reserves to stockholders' equity (net worth).   This ratio increased
from 8.4% in 1966 to 18.5% in 1979 and then declined to 15.9% in
1981 in all listed non-financial corporations.   At present, one may
say that there is about a one-sixth de facto participation in
capital by employees at major corporations.   Since corporations'
retirement compensation obligations must be met prior to any other
liabilities in the event of reorganization, one may even say that
employees' claims for retirement compensation are fully funded
latently within the corporation partly under the guise of net assets
on the official balance sheet or as an off-balance sheet asset.
Thus, the degree of de facto employees' participation in capital may
be said to be even higher.

In summary, in order to gain a realistic picture of the financial
position of Japanese firms, some adjustments must be made in the
figures reported on the balance sheets, taking into consideration
various institutional characteristics and their economic functions.
We have seen that such adjustments reduce the effective debt-equity

ratio of Japanese firms considerably. The column 9 of Table I-5
summarizes the adjustments made so far regarding the debt-equity
ratio of the listed non-financial corporations for land price
appreciation and reserves. As indicated in the paper by Aoki
(Chapter VI), the dependence of Japanese firms on the debt financing
of investments declined significantly in flow terms as well toward
the end of the 1970s. Why did this occur? Is it because the growth
rate of the corporate sector declined so that there was not as much
need for external funds in the late 1970s as there had been previously? Or is it because the corporate sector had borrowed "too
much" from the capital cost point of view before and remedial
measures were taken as the influence of the banking sector eroded?
These are among the problems analysed in the paper by Aoki.

## "Visible Handshaking"

Japanese firms are usually connected with many other firms through
reciprocal relationships supported by the extensive use of inter-
firm trade credits as well as shareholdings. One may wonder
whether the terms of trade in these customer relations approximate
competitive conditions. The dramatic events of the first oil shock
revealed that such a suspicion is not entirely groundless. The
suppliers of oil and related products gave priority of delivery to
those customers who had not been too demanding in their bad days,
relative to those who had been relentless bidders in the past.
Mutual favortism manifested itself. In the bank-debtor relationship, the terms of credit are adjusted bilaterally between the two
parties through the practice of compensating balances, but the
extent of adjustment seems to have been too limited to be rightfully
called competitive. When credit conditions are tightened, customer-
debtors are treated relatively favorably by banks with respect to
compensating balance requirements, and when credit conditions are
loosened, they are not asked to pay off all debts even if they are
financially capable of doing so.[15] Even in collective bargaining,
as is the case in the steel industry, the smoothing out of contractual conditions over a period of years has been observed in recent
years. For example, the unions restrained their wage demands when
the hardship of the second oil shock hit the industry, but in
return, a moderately generous wage concession was made by the
management in 1982. Thus, long-run kashi-kari kankei (mutual
favoritism) or, to twist Okun's wording,[16] "visible handshaking,"
seems to be a widespread practice in Japan.

Among the many possible motives for such "mutual favoritism," the
one emphasized here is uncertainty and the consequent need for some
kind of reduction in collective risk costs. The Appendix pursuant
to Chapter VII constructs and analyzes a simple model of corporate
groups in which member firms are connected through vertical trade
relations and in which the supply price of the primary input to the
group as well as the demand price of the final output of the group
are uncertain. Grouping itself cannot, of course, eliminate the
uncertainty regarding the generation of aggregate income of member
firms. It can be shown, however, that a group of firms, if at least
one of them is risk-averse, can reduce aggregate risk costs in the
long-run by deviating from the competitive norm and by agreeing on a
specific set of terms of trade among themselves contingent upon
states of external markets surrounding the group. However, such a
specification of contingent intra-group prices will be extremely
cumbersome, and normally, a group-efficient risk reallocation will

be possible and realistic only in the form of a mutual understanding
or implicit agreement.  It is possible that the expectation of
higher utility in the long-run under the agreement and concern with
one's reputation as a good business partner may lead to voluntary
compliance.  However, there may still be an incentive for some firms
to default on the long-run agreement for short-run advantage.[17]
Mutual shareholdings among member firms, that is, reciprocal control
over corporate machinery, may act as an effective mechanism for
enforcing the implicit group agreement.

The paper by Nakatani in this volume asserts that financial groupings are able to arrange and enforce a long-run implicit agreement
for risk-sharing among member firms and member financial institutions with the latter pooling risks and hence assuming a relatively larger role in risk taking.  Various explanations have been
offered to explain the economic raison d'être of ex-<u>Zaibatsu</u> or
financial groupings based upon hypotheses relating to joint profit
maximization by member firms.  For instance, Richard Caves and Masu
Uekusa [10] examined the hypothesis of "profit maximizing reciprocity."  According to this hypothesis, member firms of a group are
assumed to agree to effectuate efficient internal prices among
themselves in the midst of an oligopolistic market environment
where efficient prices are distorted.  Akira Goto [16] advanced the
hypothesis that groups can save on various transactions costs of
using markets relating to information collection, repeated bargaining, and the like.  He also claims that semi-autonomy of member
firms can prevent diseconomies of scale or X-inefficiency associated
with excessive centralization.  However, as econometric studies by
Caves and Uekusa have found, and as a similar study by Nakatani in
this volume reaffirms, there is no evidence that ex-Zaibatsu and
other financial groups perform better in terms of profitability.  If
grouping can always increase profitability either by using efficient
intra-group prices or by saving on transaction costs, why do there
exist more profitable and efficient outsiders which do not belong
to any group?  From the various evidence, we seem compelled to
accept the view that there are two types of firms in the Japanese
economy.  One may hypothesize that one factor responsible for this
dichotomization is the risk attitude of firms.  By this I mean
properly weighted aggregates of the risk attitudes of the various
constituents of firms.[18]

There are several important reasons why member firms of major
ex-<u>Zaibatsu</u> groups might tend to be relatively more risk-averse, in
this sense, than independent outsiders.  On the shareholders' side,
significant portions of the stock of member firms are owned by banks
and other financial institutions (insurance companies, trust banks,
etc.), which are required to behave prudently.  Further, member
firms are mostly mature firms which are managed by directors who
have been promoted through highly bureaucratic internal organizations.  They are motivated personally to maintain and enhance the
prestigeous status associated with their positions and therefore
tend to "play it safe."  On the employees' side, the "life-time"
employment scheme is more firmly instituted in member firms, and the
employees are more interested in secure long-run benefits.  For
these and possibly other reasons, it seems not entirely unreasonable
to hypothesize that member firms of <u>Zaibatsu</u> groups tend to behave
in relatively risk-averse ways.  In fact, Nakatani shows that the
variances of member firms' profits within ex-<u>Zaibatsu</u> groups are, on
the average, smaller than the variances of outsiders' profits, while
the levels of profits are relatively low and the amounts of interest

payments are relatively large for member firms.  These findings may
be explained by the hypothesis that the ex-Zaibatsu group functions
as a social contrivance for reducing aggregate risk costs for
relatively risk-averse member firms, with financial institutions
acting as insurers.

It should be noted that allegedly aggressive Japanese business
practices are not inconsistent with this hypothesis for the following reasons:  (1) most member firms in ex-Zaibatsu groups have,
until recently, remained largely technological followers of foreign
(and sometimes domestic) forerunners rather than innovators so that
the risks involved have been of a more or less calculable nature
(i.e., risk proper in the sense of Frank Knight rather than uncertainty); and (2) even risk-averse individuals may be willing to
engage in enterprising activities if the incidence of risk on
themselves can be mitigated by collective risk sharing.

The Cultural Root of Sharing

It is worth noting that a similar trade-off between the average
level of performance and the amount of variability therein also
appears to exist in the case of labor mobility, as suggested by
Tachibanaki (Chapter IV).  He reports that, in comparison to one-
time job changers, employees enjoying lifetime employment receive,
somewhat surprisingly, less income on the average in exchange for
stability of employment as well as lower variability of income.
Thus, one might conjecture that the supposedly "traditional"
customs and institutions, such as life-time employment and corporate
groupings, are actually associated with a more risk-averse segment
of the population.

One can only speculate about whether the average Japanese is less
willing to take risk "individually" than other nationalities.  The
current judgement of the present writer (which may not be shared by
some of the other contributors to this volume) is that the risk-
bearing function has come to be performed in Japan not so much as
the contractual role of a specific social class as through the use
of implicit agreements of sharing, although, as the findings by
Tachibanaki and Nakatani (as well as Aoki in Chapter VI) indicate,
the reality is not as monolithic as some culturalists tend to claim,
and individual risk taking also has nonnegligible, and possibly
increasing, importance.

Nonetheless, the sharing of decision-making (the so-called consensual
decision-making) as well as its uncertain consequences may be partly
rooted in Japanese culture.  One may trace one of its origins to
certain conventions developed over the centuries in and among village
communities.  Needless to say, economic development during the pre-
industrial period was crucially dependent upon increases in the
scale and productivity of rice production, but most Japanese land
was not suited to rice paddy cultivation in its original form.
Particularly important was the control of water.  As more than two-
thirds of Japan's land is mountainous and as the natural water
supply is concentrated in the "tsuyu (plum season rain)" and the
typhoon seasons, considerable effort had to be expended in the areas
of agriculture and civil engineering in order to develop water
control systems which could preserve water supplies, irrigate and
drain paddies as needed, control floods, and so on.  The rise and
fall of feudal lords during the Warrior Period (15th-16th centuries)
and the enormous increase in rice production during the early Edo

Period (17th century) were very much affected by the large-scale
extension of, and innovation in, irrigation-flood control systems.[19]

The management of a large-scale irrigation system, however, required
intricate intra-and inter-village adjustments of diverse interests.
The names of many agrarian leaders in the Edo Period, such as
Sontoku Ninomiya and Chiyozaburo Mutsugawa, are associated with the
development of inter-village irrigation systems and the consequent
personification of codes for upstream-downstream interest adjustment
and the like.  Without such social codes, ad hoc resolution of conflicts often resulted in bloody clashes among villages known as
"mizuarasoi (water struggle)."  In traditional agricultural areas
such as Kinai, the older practice of so-called "ageta (paddy-
drainage)" had been known for hundreds of years before the Edo
period.  According to this practice, in years in which there was a
shortage of water stocks in reservoirs, irrigable acreage was cut
equiproportionately across villages and families, and the remaining
drained paddies were transformed into other uses such as cotton
production.  Simple and egalitarian conventions of a similar nature
developed in many other areas as well to economize on conflict-
resolution costs.  Such conventions of sharing had become so deeply
rooted during the pre-industrial period that it does not seem
unreasonable to infer that the convention was carried over to the
organization of modern industry.  Many writers have suggested that
the driving force behind Japan's industrial development was the
traditional moral code of "loyalty" to one's group or quasi-family
association,[20] but I am inclined to feel that a more fundamental
force for the "groupism" of the Japanese is rooted in the egalitarian conventions of traditional agricultural production and that
the emphasis of the code of loyalty to modern industrial organization is rather a derivative of this fundamental force, which made
compliance with sharing schemes more easily enforceable.

Spinning off Shocks?

Another type of corporate grouping besides the ex-Zaibatsu or
financial grouping is, as mentioned already, one in which a relatively strong parent firm is surrounded, like Saturn, by many
satellite firms, to which production of parts, sales of products,
and so on, are contracted out or spun off.

Subcontracting systems are not themselves a peculiarly Japanese
institution.  However, because of the strong monopolistic and/or
monopsonistic positions normally enjoyed by parent corporations, the
subcontracting system in Japan has been widely considered a remnant
of semi-feudalism which should (and would) fade away as modernization progressed.  Notwithstanding this expectation, the subcontracting system has not declined in significance during the
1970s, but on the contrary, there are signs that its relative
significance might even have increased from a certain viewpoint.
According to a survey done by the Agency for Medium-and Small-
Sized Enterprises [29], the relative proportion of medium-and
small-sized firm in the manufacturing sector remained stable at
99.5% between 1966 and 1981.  Among these medium and small firms,
however, the relative proportion of subcontractors increased from
53.2% in 1966 to 58.1% in 1971 to 60.7% in 1976 to 65.5% in 1981.
It still has to be empirically ascertained whether the monopolistic
position, or the relative bargaining power, of parent firms increased
throughout the 1970s, but I am not aware of any strong a priori
reason to support this statement.  As noted already, the tendency of

major corporations to spin off subsidiaries has also been accelerating in recent years.

To quote a self-evident example, while General Motors Corporation
turned out 4.62 million four-wheel cars in 1981 with 758,000
employees (126,000 were laid off), the Toyota Motor Corporation
turned out 3.22 millions four-wheel cars with only 48,000 employees.
This difference arised primarily because the Toyota Motor Corporation makes extensive use of subcontracting as well as the spinning
off of many peripheral activities to its subsidiaries.  The Toyota
Motor Corporation merged with the Toyota Auto Sales Corporation in
1982, but the merger increased the number of employees by no more
than 5,000.

The question arises of why the arrangement is in the form of
groupings of quasi-autonomous firms rather than of integrated firms.
That is, cannot the same resource allocation and risk-redistribution
obtained through subsidiary groupings be realized by integrating
member firms into a single giant firm and directing resource allocation and distribution through administrative direction, i.e., by
the guidance of, to use Chandler's expression, "the visible hand"?
Possible reasons for the preference for quasi-independence are many,
intricate, and diverse, and vary from case to case.  Because of the
lack of a paper in this volume specifically devoted to this subject
in spite of its importance, I dare here to take the risk of enumer-
ating in an unsystematic way some possible motives for subsidiary
groupings which I have gathered primarily through interviews with
managers and union leaders of Japanese firms.  The factors are
stated below in terms of positive motives for spin-offs or subcontracting but may indicate disincentives for integration as well.

It is generally agreed that the deepening of the internal employment
structure, a characteristic of the Japanese firm (as discussed by
Kazuo Koike in this volume), provides a managerial motive for
keeping the hontai (main body) as slim as possible.  In the deepened
internal employment structure, the expectations of employees are
long-ranged, extending even to retirement benefits, and it is
difficult for the management to adjust the number of employees with
flexibility over the business cycle without spoiling the expectations of some employees.  This is generally considered to be a
primary motive for the extensive use of subcontracting in Japan.
Certainly, by reacting to the business cycle primarily through the
adjustment of volume and the conditions of subcontracting, while
keeping the "amount" of employment (if not its conditions) intact at
the hontai, the difficult problem of personnel administration and
industrial relations may be spun off and localized.  However, three
cautions must be raised against this conventional explanation:
first, if the managerial motive is merely to keep the lifetime
employed work force as slim as possible, the management could also
achieve this objective by creating different statuses of employment
within the firm.  In fact, the management actually used such a differentiated employment structure extensively and more conspicuously
in the 1950s and early 1960s.  However, the differentiation of employment status within a single firm is not easy to administer from
the industrial relations point of view.  Also, under the institution
of enterprise-based unions organized on the union-shop principle, it
may become difficult for the union to represent the divergent
interests of different groups of employees fairly.  Both the
management and the union may prefer a more undifferentiated employment structure or a more finely graded employment structure in

which differentiation has been made more obscure.[21]  This tendency
toward blurring differences in employment status within a given firm
seems to have been reinforced in the period of rapid economic
growth in the late 1960s when the recruitment of new workers of
relatively inferior employment status became increasingly difficult
due to the shortage of labor.   There is no strong evidence that this
tendency has continued during the 1970s, but it is often observed
that firms spin off or subcontract those activities which require
qualitatively different working conditions (in terms of working
hours, possibility of advancement, etc.) from those faced by the
main work force.   Thus, the managerial preference for a relatively
homogeneous labor force should be reckoned as one of the most
fundamental forces affecting the determination of the size of the
firm.

A second caution against the conventional explanation is that it
should not be taken as implying that the internalization of the
employment structure and its deepining are exclusively limited to
the parent firm.   As discussed in the paper by Kazuo Koike in this
volume, the internalization of the employment structure is also
observable, albeit to a lesser degree, even in small-and medium-
sized firms.   These two cautions combined lead to the third point.
The conventional explanation for the extensive use of subcontracting
emphasizes its shock-absorbing function, but one must be specific
here in regards to what is protected from shocks.   I would argue
that what is protected at the hontai is the employment status of the
main work force but not necessarily its working conditions (wages,
working hours, etc).   Shocks are at least partially absorbed by
the parent firm as well through fluctuating actual earnings of
employees and fluctuating profits.   As the experience of the
mid-1970s shows, if the hardship is extraordinary, then the adjustment may extend even to the sacrifice of seniority rights by older
"permanent" employees.   On the other hand, if small-and medium-
sized firms acquire and accumulate specific internal and technological resources, then their long-run viability may assume vital
importance for the efficiency of the total group.   Human capital
and technological knowledge accumulated at small-and medium-sized
firms can not be scrapped and built in the short-run at the parent
firms' will.   According to a recently released survey [30] on
subcontracting by the MITI, parent companies attach ever higher
importance to resources of subcontractors such as specific technical
expertises, positive attitudes for developments, and managerial
skills.[22]

The conventional view emphasizes the relative weakness of the
bargaining power of satellite firms (with which I do not disagree),
but it tends to identify enforced shock absorption by satellite
firms as the only consequence.   In actuality, the monopolistic
and/or monopsonistic power of parent firms may be located in their
ability to extract monopolistic and/or monopsonistic gains on the
average over the business cycle, while absorbing by themselves a
portion of any shocks via variations in earnings.   The mode of risk-
sharing between parent firms and their satellite firms will vary
from case to case, but we cannot entirely preclude the possibility
that parent firms will absorb more risk and perform an insurance
function in exchange for premiums payable in the form of monopolistic (and/or monopsonic) gains.   According to the just-mentioned
survey by MITI, those of subcontractors and subcontractees who
reckon the shock absorbing by subcontractors among important reasons
for the wide-spread practice of subcontracting are now very

minorities (7.7% and 12.2% respectively). Instead, the "long-run reliable relation" is cited as an important reasons more by sub-contractors (74.5%) than by parent companies (46.5%).[23] In an interview with an executive of a fast growing electronics firm, I was told that a policy of the firm is to require its subcontractors to reduce their shipments to the firm to no more than 20% of their total sales. Although subcontractors desire to increase their shipments to this successful firm above the current 50% level for more "secure" incomes, the firm does not want subcontractors to become "too dependent" on it. According to a survey done by Shoko-Chukin Bank [38], the average number of parent firms of the 1,592 small and medium sized subcontractors surveyed was 6.5. However, the degree of dependence on first parent firms is as high as 82.3% in terms of sales. Still, 38.9% of the surveyed subcontractors wanted to increase their dependencies on first parent firms and 35.3% of them are satisfied to maintain the current levels of dependency. Those subcontractors, particularly relatively smaller ones, tended to regard that strengthening and maintaining close relationships with single parent firms would contribute to "the security of stable contracts". (p.107). The traditional paradigm ascribing shock-absorbing functions exclusively to subcontractors does not seem to capture all of the subtleties involved in the subcontracting system.

In sum, it should be recognized that the deepened employment structure of the Japanese firm is certainly one cause of the extensive use of subcontracting and frequent spin-offs, but the causality should be understood in more general terms than the mere spinning off of shocks. The more fundamental, underlying motive of management seems to be its preference for the maintenance of a relatively undifferentiated employment structure.

Another possible motive for disintegration is also related to the tendency toward deepening (or increased independence from the market) of the internal organization of the firm, but bears upon managers rather than workers. That motive is to create more execu-tive positions. In times of rapid growth of the corporate sector, more executive and senior managerial positions can be created through expansion of the internal organization of the firm, but when the firm and the economy in which the firm is embedded enter a period of slow growth, the long-cherished expectations of many middle managers to be promoted will tend to be disappointed unless some counter-measure is taken. Also, in order to provide relatively young promising managers with opportunities for promotion within the slow-growing internal organization of the hontai, there must be some face-saving outlets for senior managers. For these reasons, some firms spin off various peripheral and related activities as subsidiaries and create positions as executives and directors in these subsidiaries for middle and senior managers who cannot expect any further career advancement in the internal organization of the hontai. Also, it may be added that consensus-oriented decision-making will become increasingly more costly in terms of time, effort, etc., as the number of people to be consulted becomes larger. The saving of decision-making costs may also account for the disintegration of certain nonessential activities.

## Other Motives for Quasi-Disintegration

The two motives for quasi-disintegration mentioned above may be, to some extent, peculiar to the Japanese culture, in which open class

distinctions are generally abhorred, but obscure gradations of
status are more easily acceptable.  However, the following two
motives are more explicitly efficiency-oriented and may be univer-
sally applicable, if to a lesser degree elsewhere.  One is related
to the efficient design of organizations, and the other to the
efficient use of internal resources.  If specialized lines of
production and services are placed in quasi-independent organizational units and those organizational units are made responsible
for the quality of products, timing of delivery, servicing of
products, etc., the efficiency of the whole group comprising such
quasi-independent units may be higher than under the rigid guidance
of the visible hand (hierarchical control).  The quality of products
made by subcontractors is carefully inspected by parent corporations, and any defects in the products or delays in delivery lead to
the deduction of penalties from contractual fees or even the
termination of subcontracting relations.  The sense of responsi-
bility of subunits and the incentive compatibility of fulfilling
hierarchical orders may be enhanced by elevating subunits to quasi-
independent units through subcontracting or spin-off.

The multi-divisional form is also used in major Japanese firms,
particularly in the electronics industry and trading companies.  But
one can risk broad generalization by saying that the main body of
subsidiary groups tends to be specialized more in strategic corporate planning, research and development, integration of group
activities (including assembly of parts into final products), and
other major activities.  The choice of whether to integrate other
specialized or peripheral activities into the hontai as divisions
thereof or to spin them off is a matter for management to decide on
a case-by-case basis, and shafū (the individual character of the
company), molded by the history of the company as well as by the
philosophy of top management, may affect those decisions.  But,
generally speaking, one may say that the degree of integration is
less in Japan than in the United States, as can be seen by comparing
the number of employees of major firms in both countries comparable
in other respects such as sales.

Another efficiency consideration affecting the disintegration
decision, particularly decisions concerning the setting up of
subsidiaries, is related to need for efficient utilization of
internal resources whose services are also of value to other firms.
For instance, a textile firm may have accumulated engineering
skills as a result of maintaining its machinery, or the research
division of a chemical firm may have become equipped with a set of
expensive analytical equipment.  Suppose that the intra-firm demand
for the services of those resources falls far short of requiring
full utilization.  In a cultural atmosphere where the distinction
between uchi (inside) and yoso (outside) are clearly drawn, it may
be rather difficult to elicit outside demand for those services.  In
such cases, firms may decide to set up subsidiaries specializing in
mechanical engineering or analytical engineering in order to realize
the efficient use of those resources by attracting outside demand.

Subsidiaries are also used, in some cases, to raise outside funds
for financing costly equipment.  For instance, it may happen that an
electronics firm has developed a technology for the mass production
of integrated-circuit products, but investment in equipment which
will become quickly obsolete requires a substantial amount of funds.
In such cases, the firm may wish to set up a subsidiary specializing
in parts production in order to attract outside funds.  For instance,

there are subsidiaries of electronics firms on Kyushu Island (the
so-called "Silicon Island") whose co-owners are local financiers and
businessmen. The parent firm saves on initial capital costs, while
the partner can reap substantial capital gains afterwards. The
local owners are also instrumental in recruiting teams of diligent
workers locally. Thus, the formation of subsidiaries in such cases
creates additional benefits unavailable through normal new equity
issues.

Finally, I would like to introduce one more possible motive for the
spinning-off tendency of Japanese firms which is related to uncertainty — fundamental uncertainty in product opportunity rather than
mere business-cyclic risk associated with the "semi feudalisitic"
shock-absorbing paradigm. Suppose that a firm wants to introduce a
new product whose prospects are very uncertain. In order to localize
the risk involved in such an enterprise, the firm may wish to set
up a subsidiary so that possible failure will not seriously affect
the financial position and reputation of the hontai. In this case,
a risk-bearing function is assigned to the subsidiary. If the new
product turns out to be successful and the subsidiary becomes very
profitable, it is often reabsorbed into the hontai through formal
acquisition or merger or is itself elevated to the position of a
parent firm.[24] Otherwise, the subsidiary may be left to quietly fade
away into an obscure position.

## The Government vis-a-vis Firms

Chapter VIII by T. Yakushiji looks at an important external relation
of Japanese firms—namely, their relationship with the government—
from the viewpoint of a political scientist. Yakushiji deals with
government intervention vis-a-vis auto firms, mainly during the
period 1900-60. In spite of the fact, or rather because of the
fact, that the period covered is the preliminary stage during which
the Japanese auto industry successfully established its position as
a world-class competitor, the analysis reveals some essential
problems associated with government interventions. The War Economy
of the 1930s and the first half of the 1940s is apt to be treated as
an aberration from the normal development of the market economy, but
in my judgement, it is during this period that the prototypes of
many of the economic factors which played such an important role
during the high growth period of the 1950s and 1960s had first
emerged. For instance, at that time, equity financing through
Zaibatsu holding companies was beginning to yield to debt financing
through private and public financial intermediaries as the main
method of industrial financing. Enterprise unionism would not have
spread like wildfire after the Second World War, had employees,
blue-collar as well as white-collar, not experienced full-force-
based quasi-labor organizations (the Industrial Patriotic Society)
amidst the scarcity of the War Economy. The development of industrial policies to foster particular industries selected by the
government is another notable example of a phenomenon that has its
roots in the War Economy.

Nowadays, the industrial policy of the Ministry of Industry and
International Trade (MITI) is glorified as a key to the Japanese
success in penetrating world markets. As Yakushiji puts it, however,
"it is a typical trait for policy makers to preserve the past record
which are worth recording", i.e., instances of successful policy
implementation. However, relations between the government and the
auto firms were not always as monolithic and congenial as some

casual observers believe.  Yakushiji reveals by descriptive as well
as numerical policy analysis the following dilemma of policy intervention:  when government intervention to help attain a stable
productive structure in the auto industry succeeded, the industry
inevitably started to drift away from intervention.  At this stage,
the government inevitably became coercive, and unless a new relationship was created, the intervention was no longer lasting or
effective.  Based on this analysis, Yakushiji draws some important
lessons for industrial policy in developing countries.

National Planning and Firms' Long-Run Expectations

One important aspect of government-business interaction which is not
dealt with in this volume is national economic planning.  The
mechanism of national economic planning in Japan is described
succinctly in "Planning in Japan" by R. Komiya [28].  The formal
process of plan-making starts with a request by the Prime Minister
to the Economic Council to prepare a national plan, after which the
Council prepares its report and presents it to the Prime Minister.
The report becomes a guideline for economic management by the
government when it has been adopted by a ministerial meeting.  The
Economic Council is an advisory committee reporting to the Prime
Minister and consisted in 1982 of about thirty members.  A majority
are presidents and chairmen of big corporations and ex-government
officials who remain active in public life.  It also includes some
academics and labor union and consumer representatives.  The actual
preparation of plans and deliberations thereon were done at meetings
of a large number of subcommittees, the total number of members of
which amounted to more than one hundred and sixty in the case of the
latest plan (the New Economic-Social Seven Year Plan-1979).  These
subcommittees are again dominated by businessmen and ex-government
officials.  The secretariat for the Council is the Economic Planning
Agency (EPA), which collects the necessary materials, coordinates
the various ministries concerned, prepares documents, and drafts
plans.  Formal and informal exchanges of information and opinions
between the government and business as part of the consensual plan-
making process are substantial.  What is the essential function of
this interaction?[25]

As Schonfield [31] puts it, there are three approaches to national
economic planning in decentralized capitalist economies:  (i)
forecasting approach, (ii) policy approach, and (iii) corporative
approach.  This classification should be understood not as suggesting that a plan must adopt one of these approaches but as
saying that planning has more or less of all these aspects.  As
regards national planning in Japan, I will, however, refer below
only to (i), particularly the role of macro growth rate forecasting.

One of the important tasks of national planning in Japan is to
forecast important macro variables including the growth rate, the
rate of price increase, and the balance of payments.  As can be
easily detected from the following tabulation, the forecast values of
the rate of growth were consistently lower than the realized values
in the 1960s, and the opposite was the case in the 1970s.  In light
of this poor performance of forecasts, some economists propose that
national plans should present not a single growth rate forecast, but
multiple forecasts of the growth rate contingent upon various
probable scenarios or a range of growth rates.  Mr. M. Sakisaka and
Mr. J. Shimokobe, who were once in charge of plan-making at the

Table I-6   Planned and Actual Real Rates of Macro Growth

| Plan | planning period | planned growth rate | actual growth rate |
|------|-----------------|---------------------|--------------------|
| Five Year Plan for Economic Independence | 1956-60 | 5.0 % | 8.7 % |
| New Long-Range Economic Plan | 1958-62 | 6.5 | 9.9 |
| National Income Doubling Plan | 1961-70 | 7.2 | 10.7 |
| Medium-Term Economic Plan | 1964-68 | 8.1 | 10.6 |
| Economic and Social Development Plan | 1967-71 | 8.2 | 10.9 |
| New Economic and Social Development Plan | 1970-75 | 10.6 | 5.9 |
| Basic Economic and Social Plan | 1973-77 | 9.4 | 4.2 |
| First Half of the Showa 50's Economic Plan | 1976-80 | 6.0 | 3.9 |
| New Economic and Social Seven Year Plan | 1979-85 | 5.5 | ? |

Note:  Planning periods of plans are overlapped because all the plans were replaced by succeeding ones before completion.

EPA, respond to such proposals as follows:

> Sakisaka: "The reality is that industrialists want a reliable figure. They say that in making their own long-range plans a double standard of 5.7% and 7.7%, is disturbing. The foremost needs is a single figure and we don't care about the economic mechanism."

> Shimokobe: "People would not be sympathetic with a proposal of a range. Therefore, planners should always have strong conviction. Whether or not that conviction would turn out to be false is not that important."[26]

I would like to clarify the logical substance behind these impressionistic statements by well-known planners in the light of theoretical economics.

As a starting point, I would like to point out one interesting, albeit not so well known, property of the high growth process of the 1960s. That is, the Japanese economy grew macroscopically at a much faster speed than planned rates, but its growth path approximated sectoral-wise the so-called "turn-pike trajectory." The Fifth Report by the Econometric Committee of the Economic Council [14] comments on this as follows: "... If, based on a long-run sectoral model, we compute the optimal growth path (the path which approximates the turnpike trajectory) by employing actually observed capital and employment coefficients, it is found that the optimal path was very close to the average trend of the actual growth path

involving business cycles.  One may say that it is a natural
consequence of the presumption that the actually observed technologies were the results of (rational) choices.  But, as even under
the same technological coefficients it was possible to follow a path
other than the optimal path, this fact may be interpreted as showing
that the past Japanese economy kept growing in the neighborhood of
the efficient path."(p.349)  This Report only points to the fact and
does not give any explanation at all as to why it happened.  Roughly
speaking, the turnpike trajectory is a special balanced growth path
of industries having the following property:  Regardless of national
planning target in remote future concerning the composition of
industrial capacities, the fastest method to achieve the target is
to approximate that special path in the most of interim period.  The
analogy with the efficient use of a turnpike to arrive at a remote
geographical target in the shortest time is obvious.  Such a
turnpike growth path is usually determined uniquely by technological
conditions as represented by the capital and labor coefficients of
each industry and by the consumption pattern of the household sector
as represented by consumption coefficients.  Since it is not possible
for each individual industry, and furthermore each firm, to know the
properties of the technological matrix necessary for the computation
of the turnpike trajectory beforehand and since national planning
did not direct industries to the turnpike trajectory based upon a
well-prepared blueprint, it remains a mystery why the Japanese
economy was able to approximate the turnpike trajectory in the
1960s.  It was not a driver who consulted a road map that sped on
the turnpike.  The actual sectoral growth path was only the aggregative result of decentralized investment decisions by many firms.

Neoclassical economics, specifically Walrasian general equilibrium
theory, cannot solve this mystery.  Neoclassical economics presumes
as its fundamental axiom that prices of all goods including labor
are determined by market equilibrium.  If we imagine the ultra-
neoclassical world with many capital goods in which (1) the market
for each good including labor is equilibrated at each point on the
growth path, and (2) the demands for capital goods are determined so
as to equalize the rates of return of investments inclusive of the
rationally expected rate of capital gains, then its theoretical
implication is as follows:  unless the initial relative composition
of capital goods happens to be on the turnpike trajectory, the
economy will diverge from it as time passes.[27]  Thus, neoclassical
economics can explain the mystery only as a pure accident.

Therefore, we have to abandon the neoclassical viewpoint in order to
explain the fact that the relative composition of industries did
approximate the turnpike ex post without clear guidance from planners.  But let us restrict the meaning of the abandonment of
neoclassical viewpoint in the sense that the economy may not
necessarily realize general equilibrium, i.e. that excess capacities
may exist in some industries whereas bottlenecks may exist in
others, but let us agree with the Hayekian Weltanschauung characterized by the following two traits:

    (1) informational decentralization in the sense that the
    technological knowledge of firms and taste structures of
    consumers are fully known only to the agents concerned, and

    (2) the impossibility of ideal industrial planning which is
    able to centralize economic knowledge concerning technologies
    and preferences, to compute the turnpike trajectory, and to

direct industries to it.

If the approximation to the turnpike is possible through the aggregation of decentralized and autonomous choices by individual agents in such an economy, what mechanism makes it possible? I considered this problem rigorously elsewhere [2] and summarize only the main results here. Suppose that the rate of utilization of the existing capital stock is determined by demand conditions and that the prices of produced goods are set by firms according to the mark-up principle, with the mark-up depending on the degree of market monopoly enjoyed by firms. (Recall that we have dropped the assumption of equality of demand and supply.) If, in these non-neoclassical decentralized markets, expectations concerning macro growth rates used by firms as a frame of reference for their own investment planning are uniform, then the relative composition of capital equipments will approximate the turnpike trajectory as time passes. In order to relate this sufficient condition to the function of economic planning, I would like to add two explanations.

Firstly, it is the expectations concerning the rate of macro growth but not the actual rates of growth of capital equipment of individual firms that must be made uniform in order to realize the approximation of the turnpike. If a producer owns relatively excessive capital stocks, then the rate of investment of this firm will be at a lower level even if it shares the same expectation concerning the macro growth rate as other firms and conversely. What the above theory states is that if all firms adjust their own investment by employing a particular rate of macro growth as a common reference point, then as time passes, the turnpike trajectory will be approximated, and the convergence of actual growth rates will emerge as a result. Of course, the actual economy is subject to incessant technological and taste changes so that the economy will not conceivably approximate the turnpike trajectory smoothly and remain on it forever. However, it is inferred from the above analysis that the sharing of long-run expectations plays a very important role--namely, that of insuring that the structure of the economy will not be destabilized despite continuous environmental changes.

Secondly, what is deduced from the assumption of uniform long-run expectations is stability in a relative sense but not the stability of an absolute growth level. The approximation of the turnpike trajectory in its relative composition means that a common rate of operation of equipment over industries will emerge, but there is no guarantee that it will be the optimal rate of operation realizing full employment. Even if the economy is running along the turnpike, it might be running with its side brake on or with an overheated engine. Hence, one may say that there is an independent <u>raison d'être</u> for macroeconomic management--namely, to approximate the natural rate of growth--in addition to the necessity of forecasting to stabilize the economy in a relative sense.

I have argued as though long-run expectation formation were exclusively fostered by economic planning, but this is of course an oversimplification. Forecasts of the macro growth rate are competitively made by the private sector as well, and forecasts by the EPA are not always accepted as suitable and reasonable by all firms. However, formal and informal exchanges of information between the government and the private sector in the course of plan-making, as well as announcements of final planning targets, constitute an

important communication process within the economy which helps to
form the general state of expectations.  From the above viewpoint,
one cannot support the proposal of some economists that economic
planners should make multiple contingent forecasts or a range
forecast.  Roughly speaking, what is crucial is not whether or not
the forecast is realized, but that a single pursuasive macro forecast
be proposed which can serve as a frame of reference for investment
planning by individual firms.  It is important that "when all
things began, the macro forecast already was."

In order that future forecasts will be accepted with confidence, it
is desirable that the EPA makes a fairly precise forecast now, but
this is not an absolute prerequisite for relative stability.  For
instance, as already noted, during the 1960s the EPA consistently
underestimated the potential macro growth rate.  It is said that
firms added a few percentage points to the macro planned rates in
the course of their investment planning in order to expand their own
market shares.[28]  As a result, the planned rates were not realized,
but they played the role of a common reference point nonetheless.
Thus, national economic planning in Japan during the 1960s may be
considered a "failure" from the viewpoint of its implementation, but
its significance lay rather in its role as an information exchange
process as well as in its role of providing a solid foundation for
long-run expectations that was used by individual firms in their
decentralized investment decision-making.  The government acted as
an effective coordinator of this informational exchange process.  In
my judgement, this role as a coordinator is also an important aspect
of other government interventions such as industrial policy and the
so-called practice of "window guidance" by the Bank of Japan.

Internal Efficiency

As the concept of the firm is broadened from the neoclassical notion
of a single maximizer, i.e., the enterpreneur, operating well-
defined production functions to the managerialist notion of a
coalitional association of diverse constituents including the body of
employees,[29] the concept of efficiency needs to be broadened accordingly.  What matters is not only the firm's contribution to market
efficiency (or allocative efficiency), but also internal efficiency
among the constituents of the firm.  In some cases, there may not be
a well-defined production function which is independent of the modes
of interaction among these constituents.  However, notions of
internal efficiency may not be limited to one kind.

In recent articles that appeared elsewhere [3] [5], I developed one
notion of internal efficiency in the sense of Pareto involving the
value-maximizing shareholders and the utility-maximizing employees.
If the employees are embedded in the firm-specific employment structure, they may derive utility not only from the current level of
wages but also from employment security as well as enhanced opportunities for promotion within the firm.  In other words, policies relating to employment and investment that are adopted by the management may be highly relevant to the welfare of employees.  Under these
circumstances, if only the wage schedule is agreed upon first through
collective bargaining or otherwise, and then the manager unilaterally
chooses those managerial policies which maximize share price
subject to the predetermined wages, internal efficiency cannot be
achieved.  Such two-stage decision-making results in an outcome off
the so-called Edgeworth contract curve now traced in the multi-

dimensional space spanned by wage vectors as well as vectors
representing policy choices highly relevant to the welfare of
employees. Within the context of the firm-specific employment
structure, bargaining between the management and the employees
becomes, implicitly or explicitly, the multiple issue type. There
may be mutually advantageous trade-offs between gains in one area
(for instance, less risk of lay offs from the employees' viewpoint)
and losses in other areas (e.g., restraints on wage increases).

This is exactly what Raiffa [36] calls "integrative bargaining"
under which the bargaining skills of both partners and better
communication between them may help lead to a Pareto–improving
situation--i.e., to the enlargement of the pie that they will
eventually have to divide. An important aspect of the above argument is, in my opinion, the inefficiency of value maximization
posterior to wage determination. Therefore, the achievement of
internal efficiency in the present sense seems to hinge upon the
frequency of wage adjustments and the importance of value maximization as a disciplining force on management. The longer the
duration of wage contracts and the more pressure for incessant
value maximization to which the management is exposed, the more
likely it is for internal efficiency to be spoiled. In Japan,
wage adjustments are more frequent and value-maximizing pressure
seems to be less stringent relative to the U.S.[30]

## X-Efficiency vs. Dynamic Efficiency?

The last two papers in Part III deal with issues relating to the
internal efficiency of the Japanese firm from different perspectives.
Harvey Leibenstein, a pioneer in the development of a now popular
notion of internal efficiency called "X-efficiency", has been
recently deepening his thoughts by employing a game-theoretic
approach. He now views X-efficiency as a game-theoretic problem
involving the management and employees and applied this idea to a
comparison of American and Japanese management systems in his
contribution (Chapter IX). He based this comparative study on
field work in Japanese factories and interviews with Japanese
managers which he conducted during his visit to Japan. In comparison
to the Japanese contributors, he seems to be relatively more inclined to emphasize cultural elements, such as what he calls
"effort conventions," in the performance of different management
systems, but readers, Western as well as Japanese, will find it
interesting to see how the implications of cultural differences
can be analytically treated using a game-theoretic approach.

Chapter X by T. Yakushiji examines the relative importance of the
original notion of static X-efficiency (of producing more output
with a given level of inputs) and B. Klein's notion of dynamic
efficiency in Japanese firms using a sophisticated technique of
time series analysis. Dynamic efficiency refers to the efficiency
of feedback from market uncertainty to managerial policies such as
undertaking research and development which eventually leads to the
introduction of new goods. The results of the empirical tests
differ depending upon the industry, but generally speaking, Japanese
manufacturing firms have responded to market uncertainty by R&D as
well as operative efficiency. In that sense, they are both dynamically efficient and X-efficient. But as far as auto firms are
concerned, it was found that Klein's dynamic efficiency was hardly
detectable and that X-efficiency was dominant. Steel firms, on the
other hand, responded to market uncertainty by increasing equipment

investments at the expense of decreased X-efficiency. Since the
problems of what factors affect input decisions on research and
development and of how inventions and innovations are generated are
still controversial and unsettled issues in economics, Yakushiji's
exploration would undoubtedly stimulate further inquiries into
these intricate topics.

## Two Layer Games within the Firm

The last, but of course not the least, important paper by Okuno
(Chapter XI) discusses internal efficiency from another perspective.
This analysis has a direct bearing on the bonus payment system, as
already noted.  If the individual performance of employees can be
accurately observed by the management, an output-related wage system
can be used to elicit efficient effort expenditure from employees.
Otherwise, there may be an incentive for individual employees to
shirk to egoistic advantage.  However, such strategic behavior will
damage the collective efficiency of the employees and ultimately
individuals' welfare.  This is a typical game situation.  One may
thus perceive that there are multiple layers of games within the
firm:  a game between the management and the body of employees at
the upper level and a game within the body of employees at the
lower level.  Okuno shows that if "ostracization" of deviants is
instituted as a rule of the non-cooperative game within the body of
employees, then an efficient cooperative game solution is achievable
as an equilibrium outcome.  His analysis thus sheds light on the
role of the "conformist" behavioral pattern of employees in the
Japanese firm.

## The Proof of the Pudding is in the Eating

This introduction has tried to offer a possible synthetic view of
the diverse contributions to this volume on various aspects of the
Japanese firm.  But the author himself is most aware that such an
effort is bound to be somewhat misleading.  As readers would eventually detect, these contributions are neither so monolithic nor
unified in their views as this introduction might have suggested.
They are more rich and diverse in their contents and discourses.
Furthermore, comments by world-leading authorities in the field of
labor (Richard Freeman), corporate finance (Mervyn King), and the
Japanese economy (Eleanor Hadley and Tuvia Blumenthal) are more than
appendices.  Their comments, while providing useful comments and
criticisms on the main contributions, also offer their own thoughts
on the Japanese firm in comparative perspectives.  It is now left to
the reader to examine, and strike his own balance among, those
diverse points of view concerning how the Japanese.firm operates
internally and externally.

NOTES

[1]The details of the two cases are accessible to English readers through Kaplan [26].

[2]In the Japanese mythology, three sacred tresures: magatama (a kind of accessory), tsurugi (sword), and kagami (mirror) symbolize the Emperor and are said to be inherited through generations by the Imperial family. It is the president of the Federation of Employers' Association who drew first the analogy between the three sacred treasures and the three elements of the labor practice. The analogy has now become very popular.

[3]This foremost authority on Japanese management has considerably modified his views in the 1970s. See the expanded and updated edition of the book, entitled Management and Worker: The Japanese Solution, 1973, Tokyo: Sophia University Press. A good neoclassical criticism of Abegglen, as well as a concise description of the emergence of the "Japanese" employment structure in the early 20th century can be found in Taira [40].

[4]See Hazama [20], pp. 453-7.

[5]See Chapter IV of this volume.

[6]This tendency is documented and its implications are discussed in my forthcoming book [7].

[7]See for instance Bok [9].

[8]Aoki [7] discusses this issue in detail.

[9]This may be considered as one instance of the "late development effect." The hypothesis that late-developing societies generally find it easier to build a modern educational system as well as a modern manufacturing industry was advanced by Dore [13].

[10]See references in Chapter IV.

[11]See Chapter V of this volume. A good reference on this subject for English readers is Komiya [27].

[12]The only one exception is the Daiwa Bank.

[13]Strictly speaking, this provision of the Anti-Monopoly Law is applicable only to large corporations where paid-in capitals exceed ¥10 billion or whose net assets exceed ¥30 billion.

[14]A reason often cited for individuals' relative preference for bank deposits and other related forms of assets is the preferential tax treatment of interest income. By the Small Saving Tax Exempt System introduced in 1963, interest income from bank deposits not exceeding ¥3 million per individual and from postal saving deposits not exceeding ¥3 million per individual are currently tax-exempt. Interest income from deposits exceeding this upper limit can be taxed at 35% separately from other types of income if the depositor opts to do so. However, there are substantial preferential tax measures for individual income from share holdings as well. First of all, capital gains are in principle not taxable. Dividend income not exceeding ¥0.5 million can be taxed separately from other types of income at lower rates (20% for dividend income of less than ¥0.1 million per stock, and 35% for dividend income between ¥0.1 and ¥0.5 million per stock).

[15]See Wakita [42].

[16]Okun [34] used the cute expression "invisible handshaking" for long-run implicit employment contracts.

[17]The efficiency of a contingent agreement in an ex ante sense does not insure that the execution of implicitly agreed terms of transaction corresponding to the evolving state of the external market will also be efficient in an ex post sense. In general, it will not. For instance, the marginal product of an upstream firm in a vertically related group in terms of intra-group price may become lower in a particular state than the externally-determined supply price of primary input. Then, the firm's net income falls short of the maximized level ex post. Suppose that there is a firm outside the group which is willing to offer a higher price for the product of the upstream firm, because the outsider is risk-neutral, and that the competitive price for the intermediate product is higher in that particular state than the price implicitly agreed upon by the group. If the upstream firm leaves the group arrangement and starts to transact with the outsider in that state, it can increase its spot net income ex post. Likewise, suppose that the marginal cost of a downstream firm in terms of implicitly agreed intra-group price becomes higher in a particular state than the externally determined demand price of final output. If there is a competitive outsider who offers to sell the intermediate goods for a lower price, then the downstream member firm would be better off defaulting on the group arrangement ex post in that particular state. Even though defaulting on an implicit group agreement may increase its spot net income ex post, however, this will damage the collective efficiency of the group in the long-run. In order to regulate such deviant behavior of member firms, there must be some mechanism to enforce the implicit group arrangement.

[18]For an analytical treatment of the aggregation of preferences of firm's constituents, see Aoki [3] [7].

[19]For more on the importance of water control and its implications for Japanese society, see Hatade and Tamaki [19], particularly Chapter I, and Tamaki [41]. English readers may wish to refer to Smith [39].

[20]An example of such claims is the emphasis placed on the samurai spirit of early Meiji entrepreneurs by, for instance, Hirschmeier and Yui [21]. But this theory is, in my judgement, rightfully refuted by Yamamura [45] who did a careful study of the family origins of famous business leaders during the industrialization period. For instance, the founders of the Mitsubishi and Yasuda Zaibatsu were not authentic samurai but rather farmer-marchants who had succeeded in purchasing the lower title of samurai (Goshi).

[21]Dore [13] argues that while the British employment structure has a clear demarcation between managers and workers, the Japanese employment structure is characterized by a system of finely divisible strata resulting in blurring of class distinction. See particularly pp. 251-9.

[22]See [30] p. 180.

[23]ibid. p.181.

[24]For instance, the Toyota Motor Corporation was originally set up as a subsidiary of the Toyota Automatic Loom Company.

[25]The following is drawn from a part of my report [4] presented before the Research Committee on Economic Planning, EPA, chaired by Professor Y. Murakami, 1980-1.

[26]These statements are drawn from the NIRA Report on Fundamental Problems of Economic Policy [33].

[27]See, for instance, Hahn [18].

[28]See Komiya [28].

[29]Nowadays "managerialism" is identified with the theory which assumes the utility maximization of managers of corporate firms. But after the influential book which pioneered managerialism was first published by Adolph Berle and Gardner Means [8] in 1932, their theory that the manager should act as a trustee for shareholders came to be criticized by Emerick Dodd [12] who argued that the management should, if it had not, act as a trustee for all constituents of the firm including employees and the public in general. Later, Berle accepted this view. See Aoki [6] for more on this development.

[30]See Aoki [3] [5] and [7].

REFERENCES

[1] Abegglen, James C, The Japanese Factory, Glencoe, Illinois: Free Press, 1958.

[2] Aoki, Masahiko, "Dual Stability in a Cambridge-type Model," Review of Economic Studies, 44, 1977, 143-51.

[3] _____, "A Model of the Firm as a Stockholder-Employee Cooperative Game," American Economic Review, 1980, 70: 600-10.

[4] _____, "The Functions of Economic Planning Reconsidered," (in Japanese) in [31] Keizaigaku no Atarashii Nagare, Tokyo: Toyo Keizai Shinpo-sha, 1981, 163-91.

[5] _____, "Equilibrium Growth of the Hierarchical Firm: Shareholder-Employee Cooperative Game Approach," American Economic Review, 1982, 72: 1097-110.

[6] _____, "Managerialism Revisited in the Light of Bargaining-Game Theory," International Journal of Industrial Organization, 1983, 1: 1-21.

[7] _____, The Cooperative Game Theory of the Firm, Oxford: Oxford University Press, 1984, forthcoming.

[8] Berle, Adolf Jr. and Gardiner Means, The Modern Corporation and Private Property, New York: Macmillan, 1932. Revised edition, New York: Harcourt, Brace & World, 1967.

[9] Bok, Derek, "Reflections on the Distinctive Character of American Labor Laws," Harvard Law Review, 1971, 84: 1394-463.

[10] Caves, Richard and Masu Uekusa, Industrial Organization in Japan, Washington D.C.: Brookings Institution, 1976.

[11] Cole, Robert E, Work, Mobility, and Participation: A Comparative Study of American and Japanese Industry, Berkeley and Los Angels: University of California Press, 1979.

[12] Dodd, E. Merrick, "For Whom are Corporate Managers Trustees?" Harvard Law Review, 1932, 45: 1145-63.

[13] Dore, Ronald, British Factory-Japanese Factory, Berkeley and Los Angels:

University of California Press, 1973.

[14] Economic Council (Japan), Econometric Committee, Multi-Sector Model for Economic Planning: the Fifth Report of the Econometric Committee, Tokyo, 1977.

[15] Economic Planning Agency (Japan), National Accounts, 1981, Tokyo, 1982.

[16] Goto, Akira, "Business Groups in a Market Economy," European Economic Review, 1982, 19: 53-70.

[17] Hadley, Eleanor, Antitrust in Japan, Princeton:   Princeton University Press, 1970.

[18] Hahn, Frank H, "Equilibrium Dynamics with Heterogeneous Capital Goods," Quarterly Journal of Economics, 80, 1966, 633-46.

[19] Hatade, Isao and Akira Tamaki, Fûdo: Taichi to Ningen no Rekishi (Landscape: The History of Land and Human-beings), Tokyo:  Heibon-sha, 1974.

[20] Hazama, Hiroshi, Nihon Rômu Kanri-shi Kenkyu (A Study of the History of Japanese Personnel Administration), Tokyo:  Daiamond-sha, 1964.

[21] Hirschmeier, Johannes and Tsunehiko Yui, The Development of Japanese Business, 1600-1973, Cambridge, Mass.:  Harvard University Press, 1975.

[22] Hyodo, Tsutomu, Nihon ni okeru Rôshi Kankei no Tenkai (The Development of Industrial Relations in Japan), Tokyo:  Tokyo University Press, 1971.

[23] Institute for Research in Labor Administration (Rômu Gyôsei Kenkyu-sho), Taishokukin Nenkin Jijyo (Facts about Retirement Compensations and Pensions), Tokyo, 1979.

[24] Johnson, Chalmers, "MITI and Japanese International Economic Policy" in Robert A. Scalapino, The Foreign Policy of Modern Japan, Berkeley and Los Angels: University of California Press.

[25] _____, MITI and the Japanese Miracle: the Growth of Industrial Policy 1925-1975, Stanford:  Stanford University Press, 1982.

[26] Kaplan, Eugene, Japan: the Government-Business Relationship, Washington D.C.: Government Printing Office, 1972.

[27] Komiya, Ryutaro, "Supply of Personal Savings" in Ryutaro Komiya(ed.), Postwar Economic Growth in Japan, Berkeley and Los Angels:  University of California Press, 1969.

[28] _____, "Planning in Japan" in Morris Bornstein(ed.), Economic Planning: East and West, Cambridge, Mass.:  Ballinger, 1975.

[29] Ministry of International Trade and Industry (Japan), Kogyo Jittai Chosa (A Survey of Industrial Situations), Tokyo, 1983.

[30] _____, Chusho Kigyo Hakusho (White Paper on Small and Medium Sized Enterprises), Tokyo, 1983.

[31] Murakami, Taisuke and Hamada Koichi(eds.), Keizaigaku no Atarashii Nagare (New Currents in Economics), Tokyo:  Toyo Keizai Shinpo-sha, 1981.

[32] National Conference Board for Securities Exchanges (Zenkoku Shoken

Torihikijyo Kyogikai), <u>Kabushiki</u> <u>Bunpu</u> <u>Jyokyo</u> <u>Chosa</u> (<u>A</u> <u>Survey</u> <u>of</u> <u>Shareholdings</u>), Tokyo, 1982.

[33] National Institute for Research Advancement (Sôgo Kenkyu Kaihatsu Kiko), <u>Keizaiseisaku</u> <u>Kihonmondai</u> <u>Kondankai</u> <u>Hokokusho</u> (<u>Report</u> <u>of</u> <u>Economic</u> <u>Policy</u> <u>Forum</u>), Tokyo, 1978.

[34] Okun Arthur, <u>Prices</u> <u>and</u> <u>Quantities</u>: <u>a</u> <u>Macroeconomic</u> <u>Analysis</u>, Oxford: Basil Blackwell, 1981.

[35] Oriental Economist (Toyo Keizai Shinposha), <u>Kigyo</u> <u>Keiretsu</u> <u>Soran</u> (<u>Survey</u> <u>of</u> <u>Enterprises</u> <u>Keiretsu</u>), Tokyo, 1982

[36] Raiffa, Howard, <u>The</u> <u>Art</u> <u>and</u> <u>Science</u> <u>of</u> <u>Negotiation</u>, Cambridge, Mass.: Harvard University Press, 1982.

[37] Shonfield, Andrew, <u>Modern</u> <u>Capitalism</u>, Oxford: Oxford University Press, 1965.

[38] Shyôko Chukin Bank, <u>Shitauke</u> <u>Chûsho</u> <u>Kigyo</u> <u>no</u> <u>Shintenkai</u> (<u>New</u> <u>Development</u> <u>of</u> <u>Subcontracting</u> <u>Small</u> <u>and</u> <u>Medium</u> <u>Sized</u> <u>Enterprises</u>), Tokyo, 1983.

[39] Smith, Thomas, <u>The</u> <u>Agrarian</u> <u>Origins</u> <u>of</u> <u>Modern</u> Japan, Stanford: Stanford University Press, 1959.

[40] Taira, Koji, <u>Economic</u> <u>Development</u> <u>and</u> <u>the</u> <u>Labor</u> <u>Market</u> <u>in</u> <u>Japan</u>, New York: Columbia University Press, 1970.

[41] Tamaki, Akira, <u>Mizu</u> <u>Shakai</u> <u>no</u> <u>Kôzô</u> (<u>The</u> <u>Structure</u> <u>of</u> <u>the</u> <u>Water</u> <u>Society</u>), Tokyo: Ronsosha, 1983.

[42] Wakita, Yasuhiro, "Wagakuni no Kashidashi Shijyo to Keiyaku Torihiki (The Loan Market and Contractual Transactions in Japan)," <u>Kinyu</u> <u>Kenkyu</u>, 1983, 2: 47-76.

[43] U.S. Securities and Exchange Commission, <u>SEC</u> <u>Monthly</u> <u>Statistical</u> <u>Review</u>.

[44] U.S. Senate, Subcommittee on Reports, Accounting and Management of the Committee on Governmental Affiars, <u>Voting</u> <u>Rights</u> <u>in</u> <u>Major</u> <u>Corporations</u>, Washington D.C.: Government Printing Office, 1978.

[45] Yamamura, Kozo, <u>A</u> <u>Study</u> <u>of</u> <u>Samurai</u> <u>Income</u> <u>and</u> <u>Entreprenurship</u>, Cambridge, Mass.: Harvard University Press, 1974.

Part One

# THE INTERNAL ORGANIZATION
# AND INDUSTRIAL RELATIONS

THE ECONOMIC ANALYSIS OF THE JAPANESE FIRM
M. Aoki (editor)
© Elsevier Science Publishers B.V. (North-Holland), 1984

# II

# SKILL FORMATION SYSTEMS IN THE U.S. AND JAPAN: A COMPARATIVE STUDY

KAZUO KOIKE

## A. Focus on Workers Skills

This paper aims, firstly and mainly, to compare skill formation systems on the shop floor in the U.S. and Japan. Secondly, it tries to observe industrial democracy, or workers voice on the shop floor in two countries. With these two investigations, it will present an alternative explanation of Japanese industrial relations systems, completely different from the culturalists' view.

Let me begin with the reasons why we concentrate on skill formation systems. Workers' skill is one of the most crucial variables in promoting the standard of living of a country in the long run. Except for a few countries which are fortunately endowed with a multitude of resources, most countries have to export their products in order to import their necessities through international trades. In order to maintain their living, it is of prime importance to be competitive in international markets. Among those economic variables which contribute to competitiveness such as machines, natural resources and money, workers' skills are of a different nature. Machines as well as natural resources can be purchased with money, whereas, except for a handful of engineers and specialists, workers on the shop floor cannot largely be transferred from other countries. The skills to effectively operate machines must be formed in their own country. Therefore, workers skills on the shop floor are vital in the performance of an economy.

Because workers skills are of prime importance in an economy, an insight into them leads to a crucial explanation of Japanese industrial society. This explanation is extremely different from prevailing opinions which stress the uniqueness of Japanese culture and consequently promote the mysteries of Japanese economy. For example, it has been widely said that Japanese workers work hard, due to her traditional culture. If we pay attention to so-called QC circle activities (quality control circles), apart from quantity of work, it is difficult to deny that Japanese workers are more industrious than the Western counterparts, though to a lesser extent than what has been described. Even the blue collar workers in large firms in contemporary Japan are eager to devise better ways how to conduct jobs and production. According to the culturalists' view, this is due to the group-oriented way of thinking and behavior of Japanese workers. One of the most important "groups" to them is undoubtedly their company. It is natural for them to make strong efforts in finding better ways of work, so that their company will avoid being defeated by rivals. By the same token, it has long been insisted that Japanese workers are uniquely loyal to their firm, and that

industrial relations are harmonious as well as cooperative. Once we
observe the character and skills of Japanese workers in large firms,
however, it turns out that they are the natural outcomes of rational
behaviors.   The Japanese blue collar workers in large firms can
develop their careers within the firms far better than outside the
firms.   Although quite the contrary in classical textbooks, it is to
their benefit upon securing their employment to devise more efficient
ways of production.

Even though workers have the skills to devise better means of production, it is difficult to utilize the skills without their discretion.
If they were required to have a supervisor's sanction every time
they experiment their ideas, then few would want to practice their
ideas. It is necessary, therefore, to allocate power to workers to
some extent. This is an industrial democracy on the shop floor.  The
crucial issues on the shop floor are the character skills, how to
develop skills and how to utilize them, because skills ultimately
determine wages and employment.  The way how to develop skills appropriately depends on deployment and promotion, while the way how
to utilizing them appear in the one how to conduct a job.  Accordingly it is necessary to compare workers voice in deciding the ways of
promotion and of conducting a job in two countries.

B. Indicators

Workers skills are not easy to investigate.  A common way of approaching them employs years of schooling and experience as indicators in
econometric models.   This is significant as a first step, though it
rarely portrays the content of experience.  Now that the core of
skill formation is on-the-job-training in any industrialized country,
the content of experience is of crucial importance.  Another approach
must be developed.

Let us consider the nature of OJT.  OJT is not costless.  Although
training always takes place while working, there is a cost in terms
of inefficiency until the workers has acquired necessary skills.
This cost is greatly reduced as he gradually proceeds on to the next
job which is closely related to the former one.  Through such a progression, OJT diminishes the cost of training for the next job,
because the job contents, and accordingly the skill needed in both
jobs largely overlap.  In order to lessen the cost of OJT, therefore,
a series of jobs which are technologically related tend to form a
career through which a worker progresses.  Once workers' careers are
developed, the grade of skill can be identified; the broader and/or
more profound the career, the higher the skills achieved.

From this the operational indicators can be derived; (A) the breadth
of a career, (B) the depth of a career, and (C) whether a career
develops internally or not. (A) By breadth of a career, we mean how
many jobs in a workshop or in a cluster of workshops workers tend to
experience through their careers.  Whether workers of long service
have commonly conducted almost all jobs within the workshop and
whether or not they are reluctant to move even to neighbouring workshops which are closely related to their own, such as transfers to
the assembly shop of large units from that of small units, are the
major indicators.  (B) A career has not only a horizontal span but
also a vertical one.  The supervisory positions which a career includes are a measure of the vertical extent.  (C) If a career spreads
widely in both the vertical and horizontal directions, it tends to

develop within a firm, rather than covering various firms.  In order
to lessen the cost of OJT, the career needs to consist of a series
of jobs which overlap largely in terms of job content.  These
sequences of jobs can be favourably utilized in one plant.  It would
be possible, contrarily, for a career to develop beyond one firm.
This implies that workers can move from one firm to another without
the loss in remuneration.  Presuming OJT systems, it is necessary to
distinctly classify the grade of skill for securing mobility without
the loss.  This in turn increases the cost of OJT, because of the
decreased overlapping in job content.  Thus, we can hypothesize that
the higher the skills, the more apt a career is to expand internally.

No statistical evidence is available to measure the span of workers
careers.  Most of the careers are, when they develop well, inclined
to be enterprise specific, though to a slight extent.  It is hard to
formulate statistics on what entails enterprise specific.  A feasible
way is to conduct case studies collecting more detailed information.
Case studies cannot, however, prevent the danger of selecting biased
cases.  We need to reinforce them with other materials.  There are
statistical materials which are relevant, though indirectly.  When
they are integrated with the findings of case studies, we can have
firmer-foundations.  In short, we employ the method of so-called
triangulation, integrating various data of different character.


1. STEEL WORKERS IN THE U.S.


A. BLS Survey; An Overview

Collective agreements in the U.S. are far more detailed than those
in the U.K., Germany and Japan.  This makes it possible to conduct
an intensive survey to classify the languages in agreements.  The
most extensive one is Bureau of Labor Statistics, MAJOR COLLECTIVE
AGREEMENTS, for the years, 1967-8.  This deals with almost all
agreements applicable to 1,000 and more workers, which stands for
nearly a half of those who are covered by all collective agreements.

In the U.S. systems of industrial relations, the mobility within a
plant takes the form of promotion or transfer.  Layoff is also relevant, because it implies an interception or even a destruction in
the development of careers.  As for promotion, this survey employs
the following items to classify agreements.

   (A) Whether or not an agreement has detailed provisions on promotion.

   (B) Whether or not seniority is one of the criteria in promotion.

   (C) To what extent seniority is stressed as one of the criteria
   in promotion.

   (D) What procedure is adopted in deciding promotion.

Here, we employ Item (A) and (B) in measuring the span of careers.
If careers are well developed, then promotions are such important
events to both workers and management, that detailed provisions
become indispensable.  As careers develop well internally, experi-

ence in one firm is of prime importance, which is precisely seniority. Provisions of seniority must be significant.

Figure II-1 describes these two times by industry.  The two coincide
remarkably, and we can identify following three groups in industries.

> (A) High score group consisting of most heavy industries.  In
> particular, primary metals and process industries such as chemi-
> cals, petro-refinery, pulp and papers have the highest figures,
> more than 95%.  The only exception in process industries is curi-
> ously rubber.  Although no space is available to deal with
> rubber in this paper, it is certain that the rubber industry
> have well developed careers.  This suggests a constraint to
> statistical materials and a necessity to observe practices on
> the shop floor.  Another exception in heavy industries is
> metals, where there are more smaller firms with less developed
> careers.

> (B) Medium group composed on non-heavy manufacturing industries
> and most of non-manufacturing group, as retail and wholesales,
> and transportation.

> (C) An exceptionally small one is construction whose score is
> nearly nil in both terms.

These findings distinctly tell that workers careers are likely to
develop within a plant in heavy industries.  Little is disclosed,
however, on how largely careers extent both in the vertical and
horizontal span.  To observe it, we need a case study.  An integrated iron and steel plant is selected as a field of study, which is,
as the figure suggests, a common case in heavy industries in the
U.S.

B. The Nature of the Data

It is because the data obtained is of such high quality that we pick
a steel plant.  These are written judgements of Federal courts concerning Civil Rights Act, 1964, whose Title VII strongly prohibits
discrimination in employment[2]  The core of discrimination in employment occurs in promotion.  To examine whether or not there is discrimination in promotion by color, it is crucial to identify the
practice of promotion among the white employees as a criterion.  The
practice of promotion naturally reveals workers careers.  Only but a
few cases in law books refer to career.  Among them, the court decision, U.S. vs. U.S. Steel, dealing with the case of Fairfields
Works, affords the most detailed information; 42 career patterns are
described in the decision.  Fairfield Works, with about 12,000
workers, was one of the major integrated steel establishments in the
U.S. Steel Corporation at that date.  I myself have never been in
the plant, but have visited another integrated steel plant.  Information through interviews with union officials and personnel managers
as well as published documents are also utilized.  These are the
sources on which the following analysis is based.

C. "Labor Pool"

Workers careers in the steel industry begin with entry into a plant.
In a giant steel plant, the ports of entry are confined to "labor
pools", which comprise the lowest three or four grades of jobs.  The

Figure II-1.  Detailed Provisions on Promotion and Provisions on Seniority: U.S. Collective Agreements, 1967-68

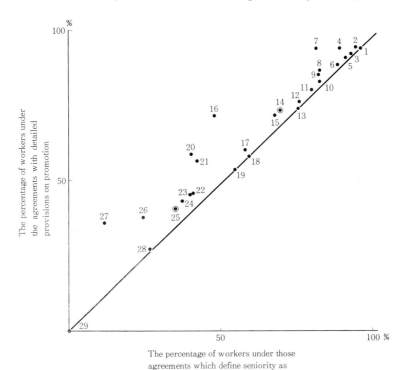

The percentage of workers under those
agreements which define seniority as
one of the criteria in promotion

| | |
|---|---|
| 1.  Petroleum refining | 16.  Leather |
| 2.  Chemicals | 17.  Wood |
| 3.  Primary metals | 18.  Facricated metals |
| 4.  Tobacco | 19.  Textile |
| 5.  Pulp and paper | 20.  Apparel |
| 6.  Electric and gas service | 21.  Retail trade |
| 7.  Munitions | 22.  Wholesale trade |
| 8.  Transportation equipment | 23.  Transportation |
| 9.  Instruments | 24.  Services |
| 10.  Mining | 25.  Non-manufacturing total |
| 11.  Stone and clay | 26.  Printing and publishing |
| 12.  Food | 27.  Hotels and restaurants |
| 13.  Communication | 28.  Rubber |
| 14.  Manufacturing total | 29.  Construction |
| 15.  Machinery | |

Source: U.S. BLS [1969] No. 1425-11.

U.S. Steel Corporation is well known for its early adoption of the
jobs classification plan in the 1940s.  All hourly paid jobs are
classified into 33 ranks.  Thus, the story has to start with the
workings of "labor pools".  Interestingly, a close observation reveals that a functional equivalent exists also in large Japanese
steel plants.  It is of prime importance, therefore, to identify and
compare the functions of labor pools to their Japanese counterparts.

(A) Work in the labor pools is based on unskilled jobs: the
loading and unloading of materials, and transportation and
miscellaneous jobs, which are mostly shared with Japanese
"pools".  These two resemble one another in being paid lower
than other jobs.

(B) The main differences lie firstly, in the fact that workers
in the U.S. pools are employed by the U.S. Steel Corporation,
while their Japanese counterparts are not the employees of a
giant firm, but of smaller contracting firms in charge of transportation or miscellaneous tasks.  Because they are "out" of
any employment contract with the large firm, they are called
"Shagai-kō", which literally means "outside workers", though
they work daily within the campus of the giant plant conducting
work for the giant firm.  Secondly, Japanese pools cover a
wider span of work than U.S. pools.  From these two differences,
much diversity follows.

(C) The U.S. pools are practically the only ports of entry.
Even a worker who has long experience in a similar occupation
with other steel firms cannot be recruited directly to upper
grade jobs.  He has to start again as a member of the labor
pools.  The Japanese labor pool counterparts are not ports of
entry, because they are not employed by the giant firm.

(D) The U.S. pools suffer a burden in being laid off when the
labor market becomes slack.  On one labor pool, there are commonly a dozen workshops.  In any workshop where a surplus of labor
is produced,  the workers are not laid off but downgraded to the
pool, from which the least senior are instead laid off.  Pools
work as a shock absorber.  The Japanese counterparts play a
similar role but to a far lesser extent.  The redundant employees of the large firm cannot easily move into the pools work,
because those who work in pools are not employees of the large
firm.  When we combine Feature D with Feature B, it follows that
Japanese adjustment capability is less, or not larger at least,
than that of the U.S.  Generally, the larger the pool, the greater the adjustment capability becomes, on one hand, and on the
other, the more rigid the demarcation, the smaller the adjustment.  Japan has larger pools, yet with rigid demarcation.
Therefore, although Japanese systems have long been said to have
larger adjustment capability through exploiting a dual structure,
it is hardly the actual case.

(E) The workers in the U.S. pools are also the members of the
local union, while the Japanese counterparts do not affiliate
to the same local which organizes the employees of the large
corporation, and even remain unorganized.

With these differences, it is common in the two countries that the lowest paid workers groups play the role of shock absorber, on which
industrial relations systems are based.

D. Lines of Progression

Upon a labor pool, there may exist one or two dozen workshops.  Each
workshop consists of one or two dozen jobs, which make for one or a
few "progression lines".  A progression line is a sequence of jobs
through which workers are promoted.  There is a great diversity in
the formation of a progression line: long or short, and wide or
narrow ones.  It is extremely difficult to identify, what types of
lines are established.  Firstly, because it is at the plant level
that the content of lines are decided, and it is not easy to gather
statistics on those issues which are specific to each enterprise.
Secondly, because even in the detailed local agreements only the
titles of lines are mentioned; they are so  familiar to the related
workers that no necessity exists to describe them in details.  These
reasons, consequently, indicate the tremendous preciousness of
Fairfield court decisions which describe 42 progression lines.

42 lines are not the total in Fairfield Works, but stand for roughly
one-fifth.  There might be biases in the ways of extracting these 42
lines.  They are confined to those which are sentenced to be modified.
The sentence states that the longer lines were once occupied by
whites while the shorter ones by blacks.  The Federal judge ordered
to combine two lines into a single large one.  Even though the 42
lines are modified to be longer, the original one was shorter.  It
is likely, therefore, that the 42 lines tend to be shorter ones
among the total in the works. Supporting evidence to this presumption
is that a few key lines as open hearth chargers or rollers are not
included.  These are the limitations to Table II-1 and -2.

Table II-1 shows the number of jobs within one progression line.  A
large variation can be perceived: there are shorter lines with only
a couple of jobs, while longer lines have more than ten jobs.  Table
II-2 provides more information on progression lines; the extent of
wage increase and the content of work.  Four groups can be identified:

(A) The shortest lines, arriving at the eighth or lower grades
with 15% increase in terms of wage ratio of the highest jobs to
lowest jobs.  Their work is mostly transportation, such as a
crane operator not in charge of hot materials.  In Japanese
plants this work is done by "outside workers".

(B) Shorter lines stretching to the 14th grade with 25-30%
increase in wage profiles.  Scaling, shearing and sawing are the
main examples of this work.  These are also conducted by "outside
workers" in Japanese plants.

(C) Longer lines with around 40% increase of wages.  They exist
in submain lines in major departments such as furnace operators
in rolling mill departments, or main positions in sub-main
departments, but not in the main positions within major departments.  In these fields, we can recognize regular workers in
Japanese giant plants.

(D) The longest lines with more than 50% increase in wages.
They are found in the main positions in major departments such
as rollers in rolling mill departments.  According to the BLS
survey on job classification, however, the longest lines in the
table are likely to be slightly shorter than the typical cases
in main positions within major departments.

### Table II-1. Number of Rungs in Job-Ladder in Each Progression Line :U.S.

| Number of rungs in a progression line | Number of progression lines | Number of rungs in a progression line | Number of progression lines |
|---|---|---|---|
| 1 | – | 10 | 2 |
| 2 | 6 | 11 | 1 |
| 3 | 4 | 12 | 1 |
| 4 | 8 | 13 | 1 |
| 5 | 7 | 14 | |
| 6 | 3 | 15 | |
| 7 | 5 | 16 | |
| 8 | 3 | 17 | |
| 9 | – | 18 | 1 |

Source: Fair Employment Practice Cases, op. cit., vol. 5, pp. 1272-1296.

### Table II-2. Progression Lines :U.S.

| The highest job-grade in the progression line | The percentage increase of the highest wages in the progression line to the wages for job grade 1-2 | Number of progression lines | Job content of the progression line |
|---|---|---|---|
| 6 | 9.3 | 2 | Weighing raw materials; raw material crane operators |
| 7 | 11.6 | – | |
| 8 | 13.9 | 7 | Crane operators |
| 9 | 16.3 | 3 | Crane operators; truck drivers |
| 10 | 18.6 | 2 | Rear processors, billet rolling mill |
| 11 | 20.9 | 3 | Crane operator of hot metal; boilerman, engine room |
| 12 | 23.2 | 8 | Rear processors, strip mill, rail rolling mill: Maintenance furnaces |
| 13 | 25.6 | 3 | Transportation arround open hearth; powers in moulding shops, maintenance of open hearth furnace |
| 14 | 27.9 | 5 | Stove operators; blast furnace tranportation; reheat furnace |
| 15 | 30.2 | – | Operators, billet mill |
| 16 | 32.5 | 3 | Tin plate mill operators |
| 17 | 34.8 | – | – |
| 18 | 37.2 | – | – |
| 19 | 39.5 | 1 | Reheating furnace operators, slab mill |
| 20 | 41.8 | 1 | Operators, engine room |
| 24 | 51.1 | 2 | Assistant charges, open hearth; rollers billet mill |
| 27 | 58.1 | 2 | Rollers, blooming mill; rollers rail mill |

Source: Fair Employment Practice Cases, vol. 5, pp. 1274-1296.

We cannot accurately infer the relative weight of each group from
the tables.  A rough presumption is that Group D would gain largely
and Group C might also increase slightly.  In comparison with
Japanese giant plants, it is crucial that a large diversity exist in
progression lines.  Japanese "progression lines" among regular
workers are more egalitarian with less differentials by lines in
terms of wage profiles.

E. Seniority in Agreements and in Practice

Progression lines indicate job-ladders, but never reveal the process
and order through which workers are promoted.  How do the detailed
agreements describe these procedures?  National Agreement, U.S.
Steel Corp. and United Steel Workers, says "...in all cases of
promotion, the following factors as listed below shall be considered;
however, only where factors "a" and "b" are relatively equal, shall
length of continuous service be the determining factors: a. Ability to
perform the work, b. Physical fitness, c. Continuous service" (Art.
13-3).  If this is literally interpreted, the primary factors determ-
ing who would be promoted are ability and fitness.  These two factors
are particularly complicated in context.  A question arises: what
are the actual indicators for these two factors, merit rating by
supervisors or some other assessment?  National agreement leaves
room to local agreements.  Although we could not collect the local
agreement of Fairfield Works, another local agreement uses similar
language to that of the National Agreement, except for one point, a
more detailed provision of length of service.  This says that,
ability to perform work and physical fitness being relatively equal,
the most senior person shall be promoted among those who occupy the
position just below the vacant one.  Again the primary factors are
ability and fitness, and still the same question remains: what are
the practical procedures which clarify ability and fitness?

Few documents investigate the practice of promotion.  One of the
exception is this sentence of Fairfield Works, which states: "When a
vacancy arises in a job in a LOP (line of progression), those
persons on the immediately preceding rung of the ladder are entitled
to first consideration.  If one of these persons is selected, this
may create a vacancy on that step of the ladder, which in turn is
filled by promotion of a person on the next preceding rung, etc...

"The selection of which of several employees on the same step of the
LOP is to be promoted is essentially a question of which is the
'oldest' employee..Under some local plant rules the oldest employee
is the one who has been on the preceding job longest (occupational
seniority), while in others it is the employee with longest service
in the LOP (LOP seniority) or in the plant (plant seniority)."[3]

Here is a footnote, which says: "Under the contract 'age' is the
determining factor only where ability to perform the work and relative
fitness of the competing employees are relatively equal.  In practice
most vacancies are filled in accordance with the age factor."[4]

Although there is little written evidence, it becomes very apparent
that the practice of promotion depends heavily on strict seniority,
when we interview relevant individuals.  Not only local and district
union officials but also personnel staff in other steel plants,
clearly admited that this is commonly the case.  A few exceptions
are, according to union officials, those rare cases in which manage-

ment can prove the lack of ability or fitness of a candidate.
Strict seniority powerfully governs the practice of promotion.

Ability and fitness are, however, not decorative but have practical
implications.  The two set constraints that confine candidates to
those on the preceding jobs in the same line.  It is natural to
presume that those workers on the preceding jobs have both ability
and fitness, because they have operated the same machines and conducted closely related jobs. This is important in assessing industrial democracy or allocation of power between management and
labor.  Strict seniority practically implies that no discretion is
left to management in deploying workers and that industrial democracy on the shop floor is greatly promoted.

This strict seniority policy incidentally produces a crucial feature
in careers; transfers between progression lines markedly decrease
and the breadth of careers becomes narrow.  Even among those lines
which are closely related, workers can rarely move.  This is the
most noteworthy difference in skill formation systems between the
U.S. and Japan, which will be discussed later.

Strict seniority in promotion, when combined with diversity in
length of lines, causes serious problems.  Workers in shorter lines
naturally want to move to longer lines, which becomes very difficult
through strict seniority.  This diversity in lines was once applied
to discrimination.  Now the opportunities to move from one line to
another are open only to entry jobs in the line.  When there is a
vacancy in the bottom rung of the line, it is posted and bid by any
worker in department as well as in the pool.  Again, strict seniority
in the department is applied to the person who shall be transferred.

## F. Foremen Are Off Workers Careers

How does this strict seniority in promotion affect the vertical span
of workers career?  It is not straight forward.  Needless to say, it
is evident that workers tend to stay within one plant, and that
careers are inclined to be long.  On the other hand, strict seniority
unintentionally shortens the careers.  The rigid rule of strict
seniority hardly allows room for management discretion.  In selecting
foremen, management does need to have discretion.  Consequently,
foremen as well as other supervisory positions are excluded from
union demarcation, and no union voice is applied to the selection of
foremen.  It had long been common that most foremen were promoted
from the rank and file on the shop floor that foremen had maintained
workers careers, both in the U.S. and Japan.  Now that strict seniority governs blue collar workers, and that foremen are out of union
membership, a part of the candidates have recently been reluctant to
be promoted to foremen in the U.S.  It is because, people say, union
members are protected by unions, while foremen cannot have any
shelter from management discretion.  This means that the vertical
span of workers careers on the shop floor does not extend to the
position of foremen.  In contrast to that, foremen in Japanese
plants still maintain workers careers, firstly because they are
union members as in German unions, and secondly because the economy
growth is rapid resulting in that more workers can be promoted to
foremen.  Several differences in career span between the U.S. and
Japan have so far been suggested.  Now we need to examine this
suggestion through observing Japanese practice on the shop floors.

## 2. THE WIDE RANGE OF CAREERS

### A. Length of Service and Experience

A first step in the study of the U.S. situation is to examine the
BLS's survey on collective agreements.  A similar method cannot be
applied in Japan, though we also have surveys on collective agreements.  It is mainly because the word "promotion" has not been
clarified.  In U.S. cases, it is clear to imply mobility to higher
paid jobs.  In Japanese large firms, there is no job rate.  Job
careers coincide with wage profiles in a long run, though no wage
rate is set by job.  Consequently no one can definitely say whether
mobility is promotion or not, except for promotion to supervisory
positions.  No mobility in a workershop is recorded, because it is
not directly accompanied by a wage increment. It is quite natural,
therefore, that little provisions on promotion among non-supervisory
position exist in collective agreements.  It is of no use examining
the Ministry of Labour's survey on collective agreements. Other
statistical materials have to be searched for.  The most detailed
statistics on the background characteristics of workers are in the
Ministry of Labour, BASIC SURVEY OF WAGE STRUCTURE, yearly statistics
since 1954.  This series provides, for a part of the period, two
figures: average length of service and of experience by occupation,
by industry and by size of firm.  How can we utilize these data?

First, we presume the following two: that if workers careers in a
particular occupation are long and internalised or, of late and high
ceiling in terms of wage profiles, (A) these two figures are big,
say longer than five or ten years, and (B) that both figures do not
differ much.  As discussed above, long careers tend to develop in
one workshop in a plant; it is most efficient to form a career
through a sequence of jobs closely related, and a sequence of jobs
closely related naturally concentrates in a workshop.  The definition
of occupation in these statistics roughly stands for one workshop.
Thus, when workers careers are long, both experience and service are
apt to coincide and be long.  The next step is to operationalize
these two presumptions.  Presumption A is turned into an indicator
that both average service and experience are longer than five years.
Presumption B is measured by two indicators.  Strict indicator is
that length of service is the same as, or more than, average length
of experience; if there are transfers to other occupations in a
plant, then service exceeds experience.  Relaxed indicator is that
average service may be shorter than experience but by less than one
year.

The Basic Survey of Wage Structure has yearly statistics since 1954.
But it does not always provide the figures fit to the examination
described above.  Two series of figures are available; (A) average
length of service and of experience by occupation, by industry and
by size of firm, for the period, 1955-61, and (B) average length of
service by class of experience in an occupation, by industry and by
size of firm for 1964-69.  Variety also exists in the coverage and
size of survey by year.  The most detailed is the one for the year
1961.  Thus, we first examine where long and internalized careers
exists, for the year 1961, and then we observe changes over time
for two periods.  Observation is confined to male workers in the
manufacturing industries.

B. Long Careers Exist Generally in Large Firms?

Figure II-2 shows the ratios of occupations with long careers to all
occupations by incustry for the year 1961.  The oblique lines indicate the figures by strict measure, while the white sections by relaxed measure.  The figure tells that:

    (A) In any industry group, the larger the firms, the more long
    careers exist.

    (B) Differences by industry are obvious.  Chemicals as well as
    primary metals have the highest figures.  In the largest firms,
    those with 1,000 employees and over, the ratio amounts to more
    than 80% even by strict measure, while the machinery group shows
    the lowest figures, and the non-heavy manufacturing group is lo-
    cates in between.

    (C) Even in machineries, the largest firms score more than 50% by
    relaxed measure.  Transportation machinery is, though exceptional
    at a glance, not a deviator, if we observe in greater detail.
    Many occupations in this category are involved with shipbuilding,
    not the automobile industry.  Shipbuilding has a long history in
    modern Japan, to such an extent that service tends to be longer
    and accordingly the difference between service and experience
    becomes longer than one year though experience is also lengthy.
    If we employed a modified indicator for occupations with long
    experiences, say the difference being less than 2 or 3 years,
    then most occupations in shipbuilding would turn out to be
    with late and high ceilings.

    (D) Even in the non-heavy manufacturing sector, the largest
    firms have higher scores than those in machineries.  This is
    extremely noteworthy in comparing with the U.S.  Figure II-1
    shows that U.S. non-heavy manufacturing scored lower.  Although
    the U.S. figures are not confined to large firms, they are
    particularly inclined to large firms because they are the data
    from cases which are covered by labor unions.  Here lies the
    crucial difference between the two countries; internal careers
    with late and high ceilings extend commonly in large firms in
    any industry in Japan, while they are confined to heavy indus-
    tries in the U.S.

C. Long Careers Has Increased in Large Firms

Figure II-3 describes changes over time by industry group.  There is
variance  in the size of survey; the smallest is the one for 1955,
covering only 55 occupations, while 246 are covered by the largest
one, 1961. This makes observation by a two-digit industry difficult.
A wider classification is employed.  As stated above, the character
of the data varies with two period: (A) 1955-61 and (B) 1964-69.  In
the former period figures for average length of service and experience are available.  In the latter period, average length of service
by class of experience is given.  Experience is classified as (a)
less than one year, (b) 1-4 years, (c) 5-9 years, and (d) over 9
years.

The largest class (d) being open ended, the class of 5-9 years has
to be used.  As a result, those occupations with 5-9 years of experience whose average length of service is 7 years and more are identifi-

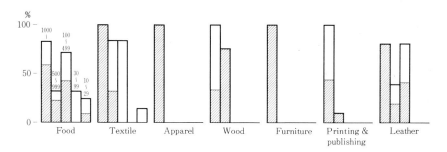

Light industries

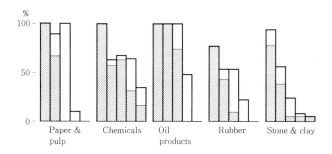

Chemicals

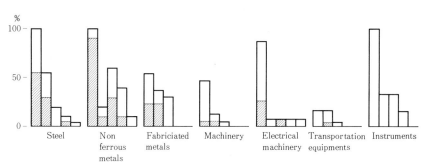

Metals

Source: Rōdōshō <u>Chingin Kōzō Kihon Tōkei Chōsa</u> (Basic Survey of Wage Structure) [1961].

Figure II-2. The Weight of Internal Promotion Type: Percentage of Occupations of Internal Promotion Type to the Whole Occupations, by Industry and by Size of Firm, Manufacturing Industry, Male 1961

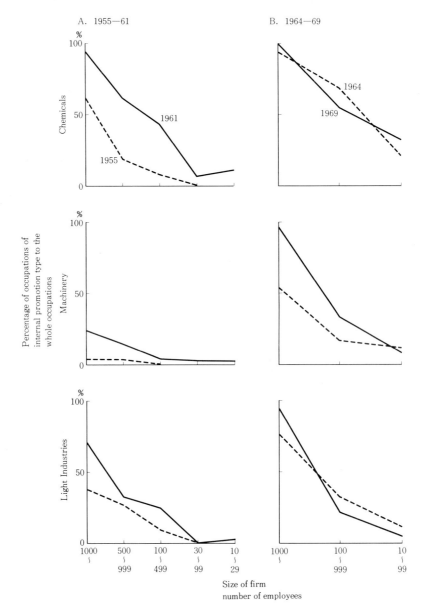

Source: Rōdōshō Chingin Kōzō Kihon Tōkei Chōsa (Basic Survey of Wage Structure).

Figure II-3.    Changes in the Weight of Internal Promotion Type:
Chemicals, Machinery and Light Industries, Male
1955, 61, 64 and 69

ed as long careers. This measure seems looser than that of the
former period, and we cannot compare the two periods directly.  The
figure states that:

    (A) For the former period, 1955-61, the amount of long career
    occupations grew in all industry groups and in all firm-sizes.

    (B) In the latter period, 1964-69, the ratio of long careers for
    the largest firms increased in all industry groups.  The growth
    rate is the largest in the machineries sector, then in the non-
    heavy manufacturing group, and smallest in chemicals.  This
    never implies that long careers have declined in chemicals;
    they were so high (nearly 100%) in 1964 that there was little
    room to grow.  In contrast, in the smallest firms, the figures
    have decreased, though slightly.

    (C) Through combining the results of two periods, it is clear
    that internal careers with late and high ceilings have, in
    general, increased in large firms.  It is our regret that no
    statistical evidence is obtainable after 1970.  We need to
    examine in greater detail long careers which widely extend in
    Japanese large firms.  A case study of a steel plant might
    prove informative.

## D. Egalitarian Rotation

It has long been believed that Japanese workshops are full of seniority. Senior workers, people say, would definitely occupy better
positions in a workshop.  Observation into cases reveals the reverse
practice: seniority affects the situation little.  Let us observe a
blast furnace workshop in a large steel plant.  Two marked features
in deployment come out: (A) egalitarian rotation systems and (B) a
wide range of mobility.  This workshop consists of ten workers
operating five positions under a sub-foreman.  The way to allocate
ten workers to five positions is clear in practice; every a half
day, they rotate all positions egalitarianly.  The subforeman,
taking after administration, works sometimes in place of the absentee.  This egalitarian way is not the outcome of negotiation between
the unions and management at any level.  The local union in the
plant has little regulation of mobility within a workshop; no a-
greement exists on it.  It can hardly be said that this is due to
management policy.  Firstly, because such management policy has
never been announced.  Secondly and more importantly, because the
practice of rotation or deployment in a workshop differs from one
shop to another even within the same plant: some rotate regularly,
some irregularly, the others rotate only partially and some others
do not rotate.  Then, who decides the rotation systems?  Answers
given by local union officials are that it is the foreman as well as
the subforeman.  It is true that the foreman decides, but it is also
true that the foreman largely depends on the practice of the work
group. With such an egalitarian system, there is small room left for
the foreman's discretion in deployment.  Here are two marked aspects
of industrial democracy.  One is that deployment in a workshop
practically depends on the work group including the foreman.  The
other is that there is little room for the foreman's discretion in
deployment.

The second feature is the wide range of mobility between similar
workshops.  There are three blast furnaces in this case.  Each

varies slightly in its way of operation; one is very mechanized,
while another is less and the other is the least mechanized, because
of the different dates of construction.  In addition to egalitarian
rotation within a workshop, one or two workers move to another blast
furnace every year. This mobility firstly utilizes workers experience from the former furnace.  Secondly, this provides a good opportunity for workers to acquire the knowledge to operate furnaces of
slightly different types, which makes workers experience more complete.  Moreover, workers also move to a maintenance workshop in
charge of all blast furnaces, where they gain the knowledge of the
mechanics of the furnaces.  Never foreget that this mobility is
confined to those workshops which are technologically related, to
the extent that workers experience acquired so far is not only fully
utilized but also enlarged.  Mobility to remote workshops is quite a
different matter, which is called "transfer".

Two questions might be raised in relation to such egalitarian
systems.  First, is it technologically possible or efficient to
rotate workers including the unexperienced so egalitarianly?  Secondly, if it is possible, is it because of exceptionally favourable
environments?

Let us examine the first question.  A possible solution is to train
unexperienced workers well before deploying them into rotation.  The
practice in this workshop is almost reverse.  Only two months formal
training is provided before deploying to the workshop.  New recruits
have little experience in the same occupations in other firms.  Two
months training is usually too short to conduct most jobs.  Moreover,
the content of formal training is of general character, say the
nature of steel and the history of the firm.  In spite of that,
usually workers are deployed directly into the rotation immediately
after two months training.  What are the keys to adjust green boys
into rotation systems?  The veteran workers always occupy the positions next to the beginners, looking after him and teaching him.
The task of the veteran is, thus, not only to operate his own position but to teach the beginner.  The ratio between these two parts
varies with each case and with time; the greater the beginners
apptitude, and the more skill he has acquired, the more the weight
of his role of teaching diminishes.  In short, egalitarian systems
in appearance are backed up with practical divisions of labor in
accordance with skill grades.

E. 79 Workshops

The second question is whether these egalitarian systems are exceptional or not.  Little statistical evidence is available on this
point. Fortunately, however, a survey on the rotation systems in 79
workshops of Nippon Steel, the largest corporation, has been published.  As is well known, Nippon Steel was formed by merger in 1971.
At this merger, two former corporations, Yahata and Fuji, as well as
labor unions at the enterprise level tried to coordinate and integrate their wage systems into one.  Wages in Japanese large steel
firms are generally composed of two major parts: (A) basic rates and
(B) job rates.  (A) Basic rates occupy nearly  60% of wage earnings,
having yearly increments with merit-rating, and consequently roughly
in accordance to the length of service and occupation.  This is not
particular to steel, but a common feature of basic rates shared with
most large firms irrespective of industry.  The steel industries
feature is that basic rates occupy not all but 60%; in other words,

large steel firms are exceptional in having job rates amounting to
40% of wages.  (B) Job rates are set under job classification plans
with smaller differentials within a workshop than those in basic
rates.  In trying to integrate wage systems, union officials were
aware that, if regular rotation systems with short intervals as
described above prevail, no job rate can be applicable; workers have
to be paid with different rates every day or every half day.  Union
officials felt the necessities to investigate the practice of rotation.  The results are published in a union bulletin, from which
Table II-3 is derived.

This investigation deals with 79 workshops in eight main establishments of Nippon Steel.  The 79 workshops do not cover all, but we
can say they cover many of the major shops.  This investigation
classifies 79 workshops into five categories with short comments to
each shop: (1) regular rotation to all positions in the workshop,
(2) rotation to all jobs, but not regularly, (3) partial rotation,
(4) no rotation used (5) no reference to rotation (that is, unlikely
to have any rotation).  The table tells us that:

(A) It becomes clear that this blast furnace case is not exceptional, though not commonplace.  Among seven blast furnace
workshops, three rotate regularly all jobs and other two do irregularly.  Of 79 workshops mentioned, 16 rotate all positions
regularly, 15 all jobs irregularly, and another 26 rotate
partially.

(B) A variety can be recognized in the manner and extent of rotation by the establishment and by the workshop even in the same
establishment.  It is partly due to the former firm.  Fuji plants
have more rotations than Yahata plants; the ratio of workshops
with rotation in any style, to all workshops amounts to 78% in
Fuji plants, while 59% in the Yahata group.  Within the Fuji
group, however, diversity is large; Nagoya Works, a new plant
in the Fuji group, shows the highest figures, while Hirohata,
an old plant, has by far lower scores.  Even in the same plant,
variance is not small.  Moreover, plants with the highest scores
do not always adopt egalitarian systems for all workshops;
Nagoya which has the highest percentage in the table uses
partial rotation systems in five workshops out of twelve and
similar workshops in other plants use total rotation systems.
To sum up, the practice within a workshop is one of the vital
factors in adopting rotation systems.

F. Since the Fifties

Since when have these rotation systems existed?  No statistical evidence is avilable.  The only avilable evidence is that of four case
studies of various large steel plants in the late fifties.  Two
studies, the Tsuda and Totsuka/Takahashi Surveys, examine the Yahata
establishment, which is the oldest plant, and find it to be the
least extensive in the adoption of rotation systems in the table.
The Tsuda Survey points out that partial rotation systems were
recognized in a new workshop with most advanced technology and
facilities, while not in older workshops.  Totsuka and Takahashi
observe five workshops in rolling departments and state that now
rotation systems have been introduced, though not before.  But no
description of rotation systems is given.  According to Table II-3
above, the rolling mill workshop in Yahata was still in partial
rotation in 1971.  Accordingly, we can reasonably presume that the

*K. Koike*

Table II-3.  Mobility in a Workshop

| | Yahata | Hikari | Hiro-hata | Sakai | Nago-ya | Kimitsu | Kama-ishi | Muroran |
|---|---|---|---|---|---|---|---|---|
| Blast furnace charging | − | | * | − | ⊙ | * | ⊙ | ⊙ |
| Stove operation | + | | * | − | □ | * | ⊙ | ⊙ |
| Coke oven operation | + | | □ | | ⊙ | | □ | ⊙ |
| Steel converter operation | □ | * | − | □ | ⊙ | − | * | □ |
| Steel pouring | □ | | ⊙ | □ | ⊙ | − | + | * |
| Reheating furnace operation, hot strip mill | □ | | □ | □ | □ | □ | | * |
| Hot strip finishing mill operation | □ | | * | □ | □ | * | | ⊙ |
| Plate finishing mill operation | | | * | | ⊙ | | | |
| Crane operation | | | − | ⊙ | | − | ⊙ | − |
| Cold strip mill operation | + | | + | | □ | □ | | |
| Pipe mill operation | | □ | | | | | | |
| Gilding | + | | □ | | □ | | | |
| Boilers engine room | □ | □ | * | □ | ⊙ | − | − | − |
| Analysis | | □ | | − | | □ | − | − |
| DL driving | * | | * | | ⊙ | | * | − |

Source: Shin-Nittetsu Rōdō Kumiai, (Nippon Steel Workers Union), <u>Chōsa Jihō</u>
(Bulletin) Aug. 1971.

Note: ⊙ Regular rotation to all positions in the workshop
      * Rotation to all positions, not regularly
      □ Partial rotation
      + No rotation
      − No reference to rotation.

rotation referred to in the Totsuka and Takahashi Survey was partial. Two other studies, the Koshiro and Takanashi Surveys, investigating large integrated steel plants in Keihin area, indicate that the grade of rotation is slightly higher than that of Yahata cases; the Koshiro Survey reveals both partial and total rotation systems in two rolling mill workshops, and the Takanashi Survey recognizes partial rotation in a rolling mill shop. To sum up, in the latter half of the fifties, partial rotation systems were not exceptional, and even total rotation could been perceived. Since then, rotation systems have proceeded with slow space, as a practice on the shop floor.

Compared with the U.S. counterparts, it is safe to say that these egalitarian rotations tend to produce wider worker careers. What the incidents of this difference are  will be discussed later.

G. Transfer

In any industrial society, it is inevitable for the economy to fluctuate. "Labor pools" play a major role in adjustment to changes in demand in the U.S.; if a particular workshop needs more labor, it calls back workers from the pool, and conversely when a surplus of labor exists, it returns the surplus back to the pool, from which some are laid off. In large Japanese steel plants, it has long been believed that "outside workers" would play a similar role; when the demand for labor contracts, mostly they are laid off, and regular workers take over their work instead. As the outside workers are more numerous than in the U.S. pool, Japanese steel plants would have larger adjustment capacity, and accordingly regular workers could enjoy larger security of employment. This is known as the dual structure of the Japanese economy, or the foundation on which harmonious industrial relations in regular workers ground.

The facts revealed in the case study differ from this conventional view. This steel plant has a figure which describes deployment of regular workers to each job. Formally it is not a part of collective agreements, and management formally reserves the right to change it without unions approval. In practice, however, it has been rare for management to alter it without union negotiation. Although this figure refers to regular workers only, this is enough to make demarcation distinct. We are not implying that this demarcation has rarely been changed. It has been changed in the long run, but it has taken a considerable time to change, for negotiation with unions is necessary. Consequently, when demand for labor contracts, it is not easy to move immediately regular workers into the field of outside workers. In practice, regular workers and outside workers are non-competing groups in the short run.

With less adjustment capability of "pools", how do Japanese steel plants deal with changes in demand for labor? Along with shorter hours and no new recruting, one of the major ways to adjust is the transfer of workers from declining workshops to others within the same firm, usually in the same plant. These transfers are differ vastly from mobility in a workshop or within a cluster of similar shops. Mobility within a workshop never does damage to workers skill acquired so far, but rather affords better opportunities to enrich it. In contrast to that, transfers to remote workshops cannot fully utilize skills acquired hitherto, and compel workers to learn other skills. The former is favorable for workers, while the latter

is unfavorable, so that unions have negotiated over the latter.  The
local union in this case has been successful in regulating conditions of transfer in detail; how many workers, from where to where,
for how long, temporary or permanent, and how long former wages are
guaranteed in a new shop, are negotiated effectively by the union.
One exception is the issue of who is to be transferred.  The local
union officers definetely have the right and opportunity to verify
whether the candidate is willing to accept.  And, if the candidate
says no, union officials will not approve that transfer.  But, as to
how the candidate is selected is out of union regulation.  There is
neither the rule of seniority, nor custom of seniority.  According
to information obtained through interviews, few workers naturally
prefer to be transferred.  Many tend to stay in their work groups.
How the candidate is selected has not yet been made clear.  Consideration on performance through merit rating would be one factor.
Without strict seniority the foreman's discretion may work.

Again no seniority can be found in layoff.  Fortunately this case
has not experienced any layoff for these two decades.  Generally
speaking, however, layoff occurs once demand for labor drastically
decreases.  And this practice is reversed in regard to seniority;
workers older than age fifty are the most vulnerable.  One of the
most crucial problems in the contemporary Japanese industrial society
is the increasing number of old workers, though no space is available
to deal with them.


3. WHITE-COLLARIZATION


A. Similarity and Dissimilarity between the U.S. and Japan

Observation so far reveals similarity as well as dissimilarity in
the steel plants of the two countries.  Both share a common feature
that workers tend to stay longer in a plant in order to develop
skill through OJT, though they are mobile while they are young in
both countries.  Here additional comments may be necessary, bacause
Japanese workers have long been believed to be immobile for all
their occupational lifes.  Japan has most detailed statistics on
separation by size of firm, by industry and by age group[5].  According
to this data, even in the largest firms of 1,000 employees and over,
the separation rate per year exceeds 20% for male blue collar workers
in the first half of their twenties.  This sharply drops after the
mid-twenties.  Again in the U.S., Job Tenure Survey of BLS says
that, while there is a vast troop of short serviced workers, those
of long service are numerous as in Japan[6].

Two dissimilarities are noteworthy; one is the wide range of experience, and the other is the practice on the shop floor of deploying
workers in a workshop.  These two feature are not peculiar to large
steel plants but common in  most larger firms irrespective of industry in Japan.  Take for example the automobile industry as a case of
mass production industry.  There is no difference in the division of
labor along assemble lines in both countries.  The main difference
lies in allocation and mobility of workers in a workshop.  Suppose
one workshop consists of 20 positions under one subforeman.  In
Japanese assembly lines, regular workers tend to move from one
position to another, regularly or irregularly, ultimately to experi-

ence almost all positions in the workshop.  The opposite holding in
the U.S. line, most jobs are paid nearly equally, so that workers
naturally do not want to move to unaccustomed jobs.  Under Japanese
systems, workers of long experience can do most jobs in the workshop.
If changes in deployment are required, workers of long experience can
contribute much, because they can substitute any position in the
group.  And changes in employment occur in an assembly line far more
frequently than imagined.  Even when an assembly line deals with the
same car model, minor changes follow; variety in attatchments, two
door types or four door types and so on.  All these minor changes
easily require exchange of deployment of workers; a position which
has been held by an inexperienced worker needs an experienced one
when the products change even slightly, say from two door to four door
types.  A skill of wide range can lessen adjustment costs to changes.

Non-mass production workshops are not exceptions.  Take for example
an assembly department of various switch boards in an electrical
machinery plant.  This department consists of three workshops, in
charge of assembling large units, medium, all small ones respectively.  Each workshop is composed of 35-40 workers.  They are divided
into several small sub-groups of which each erects a particular type
of a certain size.  Every year sub-groups are reshuffled, so that
workers can experience all types of switch boards in the workshop.
Moreover, many of the workers, if not all, move to other two workshops in the department.  Consequently, many workers have acquired
the skill and experience to deal with almost all types and sizes of
switch boards which this plant produces.

Through three types of workshops, it is also common that these
systems of mobility within a workshop and a cluster of familiar
workshops largely depend  on the practice on the shop floor.  In
short, as far as large firms in heavy industries in both the U.S.
and Japan are concerned, two Japanese features become evident; skill
of wide range and workers voice in mobility within a workshop.
What is the incidence of these features?

B. QC Circle Activities

These two features can explain many characteristics of Japanese
workers.  Explanations employed so far stress "traditional culture".
One of the most remarkable features of contemporary Japanese workers
seems, they say, to be high morale; little absenteeism and wide
spread QC circle activities in particular.  "QC" means literally
quality control.  In practice, QC circle activities are small groups
consisting of a dozen workers who are eager to devise better ways of
work and production.  It is true that these activities have widely
prevailed among blue collar workers in large firms since 1960s.
That even the blue collar workers find and practice more efficient
ways to work is really noteworthy, because ordinarily it is not a
job for the blue collar workers but for the engineers to devise more
efficient ways of production.  According to the culturalists' view,
this is due to the group-oriented behavior of Japanese people.  The
company to which workers belong is the most important group to them
in contemporary Japanese society.  For the prosperity of their
company, they naturally make the effort to conduct vigorous QC
circle activities.  Another explanation given by some of the western
scholars emphasizes another cultural aspect of Japanese society.
Japanese people are obedient to authority.  Qc circle activities
are, when closely observed, initiated by management and workers

loyally follow management policy.  At a glance, these two explanations appear completely in reverse to each other.  However, they are
similar in the point that both clearly emphasize the attitude of
workers: loyalty to the company and obedience to authority.  No one
can deny the role of workers attitude.  But attitude alone cannot
yield QC circles.  A close observation reveals that many ideas of QC
circle activities are more or less technological.  Can technological
devices be born without technological knowledge and skill?

The explanation presented here highlights the skill of wide range
described above to be the very foundation of QC circle activities.
The skill of wide range affords workers better opportunities to
understand the production mechanism through their wide range of experience.  Recollect the case of a Japanese steel plant.  Workers in
a blast furnace workshop move not only to other blast furnace shops,
but also to the one in charge of maintenance of three furnaces.
This mobility gives them ample opportunity to understand the mechanics of blast furnaces.  To understand the mechanics of production
is the basis of technology, on which various devices to efficient
ways of production flourish.  The skill of wide range is the first
and most important factor of QC circles.

Secondly, though workers possess this skill, they do not necessarily
utilize it, if they do not feel the need to do so.  The similarity
between the U.S. and Japanese steel plants, that is, internalized
careers, causes a strong need to do so.  Once careers are internalized, it is of immense damage to the workers if their company
declines; promotions come late and less frequently, and in worse
cases, layoff is inevitable, which destroys the careers formed so
far, because internalized careers tend to make skill enterprise-
specific, and to make it unfavorable to quit  and move to other
firms.  Workers with internalized careers naturally work to prevent
their company from being defeated by its rivals, not because of
loyalty to their company, but simply in order to secure their
employment.  In other words, QC circles activities are not peculiar
to Japanese workers, and rather the outcome of internalized careers.
U.S. workers in steel firms also have the motivation to conduct QC
circle activities, at least to a certain extent.

Thirdly, workers power to exercise their ideas is necessary.  With
both skill and needs, if they are required to get sanctions from
supervisors every time they think of new ideas, it certainly would
discourage them to conduct QC circle activities.  As shown above,
Japanese work groups on the shop floor practically hold the power to
regulate mobility in a workshop and the way of conducting jobs.
This is an industrial democracy on the shop floor.  In short, without
any bit of groupism and of loyalty to their company, QC circles can
be explained.  And supporting evidence shows that QC circles prevail
mostly in large firms where skill of wide range spreads.

C. Adjustments to Changes on the Shop Floor

This skill of wide range may lessen the adjustment costs to changes
on the shop floor.  Changes on the shop floor occur frequently.  The
largest change is the introduction of new machines.  As indicated in
the productivity index, Japan has the  most frequent and rapid
introduction of new machines.  It is vital whether workers can
operate new machines without much difficulty.  The skill of wide
range, as shown above, affords workers better understanding of

mechanics.  Once they acquire the mechanics, no difficulty remains
in operating the new machines, because fundamental principles are
commonly shared among the old and new machines.

Minor changes take place daily on the shop floor: variation in
products and in composition of the work force.  The example of the
former case is given above for car assembly lines.  Here the latter
example is described.  Even if the number of workers in a workshop
is constant, modification in labor mix occurs; when more "green
boys" come in the labor mix is diluted, while it is more dense when
veteran occupy most positions.  In accordance with variation in the
labor mix, changes in deployment is needed in order to maintain a
smooth flow of production, just like the cases of variations in
products.  This can be easily done, if there are more workers of
wide range of skill.  Less adjustment costs to changes as well as QC
circles are the significant sources of Japanese economic achievements.

D. Seniority Wages

The so-called three pillars of Japanese industrial relations can
also be easily explained without any bit of cultural traits.  Seniority wages, the number one among the three pillars, implies two
features; (A) age-wage profiles are markedly positive, and (B) wage
rates are not set by each job.  It has long been insisted that these
two are due to the cultural tradition of groupism; loyalty to the
group, that is, to the company.  As far as workers are loyal to
their firm, the firm gurantees workers a living with paying wages
which cover living costs. As living costs roughly coincide with age,
age-wage profiles become positive.  On the same token, firms pay
wages not for the job, but prefer regular wage increments, because
they roughly correspond to living costs.  This is only one example
among many explanations based on culture.

The skill of wide range can present an important alternative.  Under
this system, the longer the service, the wider the workers skill
becomes to produce QC circles as well as less adjustment costs to
changes.  Moreover, the veteran workers not only conduct their own
job but also play a role of instructors to the unexperienced.  All
these merits of long service clearly deserve higher wages.  Or,
without paying more to senior workers than to the junior, how can we
expect these merits? This is the reasoning behind Feature A.

Feature B is also necessary in the formation of skill of wide
range. To acquire this type of skill, workers exchange their positions frequently, and move to other familiar shops; in the most
extreme cases, workers rotate positions in an egalitarian way, as
described in a blast furnace workshop.  In this extreme case, if job
rates systems are adopted, wage for each worker would have to vary
every half day.  In this steel case, though job rates are partially
adopted in formal plans, practically no job rates are exercised;
instead, job rates are pooled and redistributed not according to the
job.  And, precisely because wages are not directly connected to
jobs, frequent rotation systems, and accordingly skill formation of
wide range become feasible.

Supporting evidence to the above reasoning is that where seniority
wages exist there exists also skills of wide range.  Even those who
conduct the jobs of large firms are not necessarily paid with se-

niority wages.  Look at "outside workers" in large steel plants in
Japan.  It is a fact that they do the work of the large firms daily
within the very campus of the firm.  It is very clear, however, that
they are hardly paid with seniority wages.  In other words, Japanese
large firms employ regular workers only for the work which requires
skill of wide range, and pay seniority wages only to the workers
who have acquired this type of skill.  This is a very rational
choice.

E. Life-time Commitment and Enterprise Unionism

Almost the same story can be applied to other two pillars; the so-
called life-time commitment and enterprise unionism.  With internalized careers, it is favorable for workers to stay in one plant
from the view points of both management and workers.  For workers,
the longer the service, the higher the skill and wages become.  And
enterprise specific skill makes quitting unfavorable.  For management, the longer the service, the greater the contribution of workers
to productivity, and the cost of training the substitutes becomes
higher if they quit.  As a result, workers of this type of skill
tend to stay within a firm, in which allocation of labor is maintained.  Since allocation as well as pricing is provided within a firm,
this is called an internal labor market.

Once internal labor markets are established, the most important
issues for workers are promotion, transfer, layoff and wage rate for
each job or each worker, because these determine workers skill, work,
and accordingly earnings.  All these take place within one firm and
differ from one to another.  It is, therefore, at the work-place
that workers negotiate and regulate these issues effectively.  Work-
place unionism is required, and enterprise unionism is its subtype.
This reasoning is not particular to Japan, but commonly applicable
to any countries where internal labor markets exist.  If we take
into account workers organizations in general, not confined to
formal union organization, we will find work-place unionism widespread.  U.S. local unions are practically plant-wide or enterprise-
wide in most manufacturing industries.  Workers organizations in the
management participation systems in Germany are also plant- and
enterprise-wide.

F. Common in the White Collar

Skill of wide range, which has really played the key role, is not
particular to Japan, in two senses.  First, this can presumably be
commonly found in the male white collar in the U.S. and EC countries,
and second, this is confined only to a minority of Japanese workers.

Let us examine the first point.  Investigation on skill formation
systems or on careers of white collar workers is not sufficient.  It
is safe to say, however, from present studies that the careers of
the male white collar in the U.S. and Western Europe are mostly
internalized with late and high ceilings.  Supporting evidence is
age-wage profiles.  The EC made a large scale wage structure survey
for the year, 1972, which provided for the first time to most EC
countries, wages by age. The sample size is large and its reliability is high.  Japan has even a more detailed survey.  A comparison
between the two reveals that :

    (A) Japanese male blue collar workers in large firms have almost

similar age-wage profiles to those of EC white collar workers.
The differences occur after the mid fifties; Japanese profiles
sharply drop while they do not in EC profiles.

(B) Japanese male white collar workers share common profiles
with EC white collar workers.

(C) Consequently, wage diffentials between the male white collar
worker and the male blue collar worker are small in Japanese
large firms when compared with EC countries; because both the
blue collar and the white collar workers have seniority wages
in Japanese large firms, while EC blue collar wages increase
little after the mid-twenties even though white collar workers
are paid seniority wages.

This EC survey also supplies valuable data on the length of service
for the first time for EC countries: the distribution of workers by
length of service, by occupation and by sex.   Compared with the
Japanese counterparts, this distinctly says that the Japanese male
blue collar worker in large firms tends to stay in a firm to the
same, or even lesser extent than the male white collar worker in EC
countries, in terms of percentage distribution of workers with long
service.[8]  If we say Japanese blue collar workers in large firms
enjoy life-time commitments, then we have to say the EC male white
collar workers also hold life-time, or even super life-time, commitments.

This statistical evidence in age-wage profiles and long service
supports a hypothesis that the Japanese blue collar workers in large
firms are "white-collarized" by having skills of wide range.   A
Japanese feature, if any, is that Japan has relatively more workers
with skill of wide range.

G. A General Hypothesis: Career Type

Here, we come to present a general hypothesis which will attempt to
explain both the similarity and dissimilarity in industrial relations
systems as well as economic achievements as far as human capital is
concerned.   The key concept in the hypothesis is career type.   It
implies the character of workers skill through their careers.

The most important variable in human capital is skill.   In the long
history of economics, only one dichotomy has been used for classifying skill: skilled and unskilled.   This dichotomy says nothing about
the possibility of changes in skill over time.   It is quite reasonable and natural that workers can elevate their skill through experience.   Adding this possibility of skill change to the traditional
dichotomy, we can then obtain four career types.

(A) Craftsman type : the grade of skill is high and no change
in skill occurs over time.   Most of skilled trades in building
are practical examples, so that this is called the craftsman
type.

(B) Laborer type: the grade of skill is low and there is no
change in skill over time.   Unskilled laborers are examples.

(C) Internal promotion type: skill increases as experience increases over a long period, that is, a career with late and

high ceilings. As discussed above, this type of career develops
with promotion within a firm, so that it is referred to as an
internal promotion type. This is the very type which promotes
skill of wide range. A tentative and operational definition
would include those whose ceiling is higher than those in their
early twenties by 50% and more in terms of age-wage profiles.

(D) Less internalized type: skill increases to a lesser extent
for a shorter period than with the internal promotion type. A
lower and earlier ceiling is the feature.

These four career types produce different industrial relations
systems. Taking examples of types A and C, and focusing on union
activities, we can describe the hypothesis. Type A has general
skill, and incurrs no loss in moving to other firms. Consequently,
union organizations extend beyond a plant or a enterprise. Type A
has a high grade of skill, which remains constant over time. This
implies that the demarcation between a particular trade and others
is distinct and rigid. Therefore, union organizations cover solely
the relevant trades. That is craft unionism. Contrarily, type C
has a partially specific skill, so that allocation and pricing are
mostly conducted within a firm or a plant. As the principle of
union organizations is to cover the span of a labor market, it is
reasonable that type C prefers workplace unionism.

With a set of assumptions, we would be able to explain both similarity and dissimilarity in industrial relations systems. The
assumptions are as follows:

(A) These four major types commonly exist in any industrialized
society. This yields similarity in industrial relations
systems between countries.

(B) The weight of the four types differs from one country to
another. It is true that technology as well as other environmental variables strongly effect job content, so that little
variance results, if technology is common. It is also true,
however, that there is freedom in the manner of relating jobs
into a career. Because of this, variety in the weight of the
four types by country occurs. A contemporary Japanese feature
is that type C has more weight than in the U.S. and EC countries.
This would be one of the most important grounds of remarkable
economic achievements in recent decades.

H. Workers in Small Firms

Skill formation systems described so far are confined to workers in
large firms. We now need to examine the systems in the majority of
the Japanese work force: the workers in small firms. The first step
in approaching the question of skill is to observe wages which supposedly reflect skills. And this is crucial, because dual structure
or a great gap in wages by size of firm is often said to be the very
foundation of Japanese economy.

The EC Survey on wage structure, 1972, mentioned above, has supplied
reliable figures on wage differentials by size of firm for the first
time for EC countries, though not supplemented by age or by length
of service. Japan has provided more detailed statistics annually
since 1954. A comparison of these two statistics reveals that;

firstly, no country has little wage differentials by size of firm, and secondly that the Japanese gap is not peculiarly large but almost equivalent to that of France, which is located nearly in the middle of the diffusion among EC countries.[9]

Concentrating on Japan, more detailed information is obtained; age-wage profiles can be observed by size of firm. There is little variance in profiles by size of firm till the age of mid-thirties and with less than 10 years of service; both have positive curve. The main difference appears after that age; wages for the male blue collar worker in small firms do not increase, while those for large firms still continue to rise with less growth rate. It is crucial, then, to ask why wages for small firms stop to grow after the mid-thirties and ten years of service.

More insight into skill formation systems can be obtained by observing the careers of workers. Case studies[10] have revealed that workers in small firms consist of various group.

    (A) Firstly, there is the core group, whose careers are as wide as those of the regular workers in large firms, and clearly of internal promotion type. The main difference between large firms and small firms is that this group consists of almost all male workers in large firms, while in small firms, this can consist of only a small minority, say 5% to 20%.

    (B) Secondly, the majority belongs to the semi-skilled, whose careers are narrower than those of the core group, and mostly confined to a part of the positions in a workshop. Hence, wage profiles hardly increase after ten years of experience.

    (C) Thirdly, the remaining consists of laborers who are least skilled.

In other words, the internal promotion type exists also in small firms, though to a far lesser extent. It is not yet clear whether or not this type can grow in small firms. If a higher grade of skill with an understanding of the mechanics of production is required, then, this type might develop. This leads to a question of whether or not the internal promotion type would grow or decline through remarkable changes in technology such as micro-electronics.

I. Micro-Electronics and Internal Promotion Type

Albeit no reliable data being available, it is not unappropriate to develop speculation derived from the white-collarization hypothesis on the impact of micro-electronics to the internal promotion type.

Japan is known to have highly developed micro-electronics and robots on the level of the U.S, though it has not yet been made clear what type of work has increased or declined through technological changes. It is safe to guess, however, that maintenance or monitoring works along with software jobs would definitely increase, whereas routine work would tend to be replaced by machines. Maintenance work requires a workers understanding of the mechanics of machineries and production. Naturally this is better acquired through the internal promotion type career. So far as software work is of white collar type, then it is also fit to be arranged to a career through which workers can acquire necessary skill. All these processes would enlarge the

extent of the internal promotion type, though this never implies
that this type could occupy the majority of the work force.


NOTES

[1]U.S. [18].

[2]They are complied in Fair Employment Practice Cases.

[3]Fair Employment Practice Cases, U.S.  vs U.S. Steel Corp. Vol.7, p.325.

[4]op.cit., p.325.

[5]Rōdōshō, Koyō Dōkō Chōsa (Survey of Employment and Mobility).

[6]Koike [8] pp.64-65.

[7]Koike [5] pp.35-39 and Koike [8] chap. II deals with this issue by far more in
detail.

[8]Koike [8] chap. III.

[9]Koike [8].

[10]Koike [9].


REFERENCES


[1] The Bureau of National Affairs Inc., Fair Employment Practice Cases,
Washington: The Bureau of National Affairs Inc.

[2] Dore, Ronald P., British Factory-Japanese Factory, Berkeley and Los Angels:
University of California Press, 1973.

[3] Koike, Kazuo, Shokuba no Rōdōkumiai to Sanka-Rōshi Kankei no Nichibei Hikaku
(A Comparative Study of Industrial Relations on the Shop Floor between the U.S. and
Japan), Tōkyo:Tōyō Keizai, 1977.

[4] ---, "Japan Industrial Relations: Characteristics and Problems," Japanese
Economic Studies, Fall 1979, 42-90.  This is an English translation of the final
chapter of Koike[1977].

[5] ---, "Employment in Japan, A Superdeveloped Country," Japan Echo, summer 1979,
vol.6, no.2, 34-47.

[6] ---, "Inter-Industry Wage Spillover in Japan-An Insight into 'Shuntō',''
Keizai Kagaku, December (1980a), vol.28, no.2 30-73.

[7] ---, "A Japan-Europe Comparison of Female Labor-Force Participation and Male-
Female Wage Differentials," Japanese Economic Studies, winter (1980b), vol.6, no.2,
3-27.

[8] ---, Nihon no Jukuren (Japanese Workers Skill), Tōkyō: Yūhikaku, (1981a).

[9] ---, "Fringe Benefits in Contemporary Japan-In a Comparative Light with EC Countries," Keizai Kagaku, September (1981b), vol.29, no.2, 1-25.

[10] ---, "Workers in Large Firms," in T.Shirai ed., Comtemporary Industrial Relations in Japan, Madison, Wis.:Wisconsin University Press, (forthcoming a).

[11] ---, "Workers in Small Firms and Women in Industry," In T.Shirai ed., op.cit., (forthcoming b).

[12] Rōdōshō (Ministry of Labor), Chingin Kōzō Kihon Tōkei Chōsa (Basic Survey of Wage Structure), yearly since 1954, Tōkyō.

[13] ---,Koyō Dōkō Chōsa(Survey of Employment and Mobility), yearly since 1964, Tokyo.

[14] Shiba, Shōji, Cross National Comparison of Labor Management, Institute of Development Economies, 1973.

[15] Shimada, Haruo, Earnings Structure and Human Investment-A Comparison Between the United States and Japan, Tōkyō:Kōgakusha, 1981.

[16] Shirai, Taishiro, ed., Contemporary Industrial Relations in Japan, Madison, Wis: Wisconsin University Press (forthcoming).

[17] U.S. Department of Labor, Collective Bargaining in the Basic Steel Industry, Washington:U.S. Department of Labor, 1961.

[18] ---, Bureau of Labor Statistics, Major Collective Agreements, Bulletin, no.1425, 1-14, Washington: U.S. Geovernment Printing Office, 1969.

THE ECONOMIC ANALYSIS OF THE JAPANESE FIRM
M. Aoki (editor)
© Elsevier Science Publishers B.V. (North-Holland), 1984

# LABOR MOBILITY AND JOB TENURE

TOSHIAKI TACHIBANAKI

It has been widely believed that the Japanese labor market has two characteristics: (1) use of the seniority rule in wage determination and promotion, and (2) lifetime employment at a particular firm.[1] This paper attempts to investigate the second characteristic with the purpose of determining whether the lifetime employment paradigm is, in fact, supported on the basis of both the desires of workers and the actual data. At the same time, labor mobility, which is related to lifetime employment, is studied using various data sources, including aggregate data and panel data, and statistical estimation techniques, with emphasis on the relationship between job tenure and mobility. Due attention is paid, for comparative purposes to the American labor market, which supposedly forms a contrast with the Japanese labor market. Section 1 discusses the relationship between lifetime employment and job tenure, and Section 2 is concerned with the relationship between job tenure and mobility. The final section provides a summary and comments.

## 1. LIFETIME EMPLOYMENT AND JOB TENURE

Job tenure (or duration of jobs) is defined by the duration of employment at a particular firm (or organization). Lifetime employment, which is believed to be distinctive feature of the Japanese labor market, signifies that a worker continues to work at the same firm from the time he starts working until his retirement. There are several alternative definitions of lifetime employment. For example, Hall (1982) regards the stable employment of middle-aged and old employees who have remained with the same firm for over twenty years after experiencing frequent job changes during their younger years as lifetime employment for the American society. This paper adopts the traditional definition of lifetime employment-namely, employment at the same firm from the time one starts working until mandatory retirement (about age 55 - 60).

If all the workers in a society were included in the lifetime employment system, the society would exhibit no labor mobility. If the proportion of workers who are included in the lifetime employment system were low, the rate of labor mobility would, in general, be high. Thus, the degree of lifetime employment is related to the degree of labor mobility to a considerable extent. Various statistical sources give the percentage figures of workers who have never changed employers. Those sources are examined with care.

A.  Desires of Employees

Table 1 presents the attitude of employees towards their present
job.  This table has nothing to do with actual turnover but merely
shows the desires of employees.  The table shows percentage
figures corresponding to four categories:  the worker desires to
(1) stay at his present job (i.e. firm), (2) find an additional
(second) job, (3) change his present job, and (4) leave his present
job (i.e. leave the labor market).  The most important feature of
this table is the fact that it is cross-classified by age and
tenure.  The following observations can be made from Table 1.
Firstly, there is no significant difference between men and women
with respect to their attitude towards their present job in
general, except for the slightly higher rate of leaving the labor
market for women than for men, which is the reason for the slightly
lower rate of staying at their present job for women than for men.
Secondly, the rate of staying at their present job is overwhelm-
ingly higher than the rate of changing jobs:  on average, 85.1%
versus 8.3% for males, and 81.0% versus 10.3% for females.  The
great majority of Japanese employees wish to keep their present
job, if possible.  Thirdly, the older the worker, the higher the
rate of staying (or equivalently, the lower the rate of changing).
The youngest group (15-24 years old) shows a considerably higher
rate of changing jobs (about 13%-14%), and their desire to change
does not vary across job tenure classes.  Lastly, the longer the
worker's job tenure, the higher the rate of staying (or
equivalently, the lower the rate of changing).  This rule does not
apply to the youngest group, as noted previously.  The last point
will be examined rigorously in a later section, which is concerned
with the duration dependence.  It is impressive to note that
employees with tenures of more than twenty years hardly ever
express a desire to change jobs.  Such employees are likely to form
the core of the lifetime employment system.  How many employees (or
what percentage of employees) are actually included in the system?
This is another question which will be discussed later.

B.  The Reality Concerning Lifetime Employment

The purpose of this subsection is to examine whether the desires of
employees which have been presented in the previous subsection are
satisfied in the actual labor market.  Incidentally, an effort is
made to estimate what percentage of employees are actually included
in the lifetime employment system.  We employ two published
sources for this purpose, namely the (i) Wage Structure Survey,
published by the Ministry of Labor, and the (ii) Employment Status
Survey, published by the Statistics Bureau, Prime Minister's Office.
Those two sources are expected to complement one other:  the Wage
Structure Survey includes employees in the non-agricultural sector
who are employed by firms with more than ten employees.  Since a
large number of employees are employed by firms with less than ten
employees, the sample in the Wage Structure Survey cannot be said
to represent all employees.  Although the Employment Status Survey
represents almost the entire labor force, the presentation of
cross-classifications (for example, by age and tenure) is inferior
to that of the Wage Structure Survey.

Wage Structure Survey
This data source provides the number of employees by age class and
job tenure class for a large number of industries excluding the

Table III-1A.  Employees' Attitudes Toward their Present Job

(Males) (%)

| Job Tenure (years) / Desire | | Total | -3 | 3-6 | 7-9 | 10-19 | 20-29 | 30- |
|---|---|---|---|---|---|---|---|---|
| Age 15-24 (years) | A | 79.4 | 77.3 | 80.9 | 80.9 | 75.0 | | |
| | B | 6.7 | 6.8 | 6.5 | 8.8 | 12.5 | | |
| | C | 13.3 | 15.1 | 12.3 | 9.6 | 12.5 | | |
| | D | 0.6 | 1.0 | 0.3 | 0.7 | 0.0 | | |
| 25-34 | A | 81.5 | 72.7 | 78.4 | 82.9 | 85.7 | 88.9 | |
| | B | 7.8 | 8.6 | 8.3 | 7.9 | 7.0 | 11.1 | |
| | C | 10.2 | 17.9 | 12.7 | 8.8 | 6.9 | 0.0 | |
| | D | 0.5 | 0.8 | 0.6 | 0.4 | 0.3 | 0.0 | |
| 35-44 | A | 86.1 | 72.5 | 78.1 | 83.1 | 87.9 | 90.6 | 91.7 |
| | B | 6.0 | 8.8 | 8.3 | 6.8 | 5.7 | 4.4 | 0.0 |
| | C | 7.6 | 18.0 | 13.2 | 9.8 | 6.1 | 4.7 | 0.8 |
| | D | 0.3 | 0.7 | 0.5 | 0.2 | 0.2 | 0.2 | 0.0 |
| 45-54 | A | 90.3 | 78.9 | 82.1 | 86.6 | 89.3 | 93.1 | 94.6 |
| | B | 3.3 | 5.3 | 5.2 | 4.8 | 3.6 | 2.8 | 1.9 |
| | C | 5.9 | 15.4 | 11.8 | 8.3 | 6.6 | 3.7 | 2.9 |
| | D | 0.5 | 0.4 | 0.7 | 0.3 | 0.4 | 0.4 | 0.6 |
| 55-59 | A | 89.2 | 80.5 | 86.6 | 86.4 | 88.5 | 92.3 | 92.5 |
| | B | 2.4 | 3.3 | 2.8 | 3.7 | 2.7 | 2.1 | 1.8 |
| | C | 6.4 | 13.0 | 8.8 | 7.4 | 6.5 | 3.4 | 4.2 |
| | D | 1.9 | 2.4 | 1.8 | 2.5 | 2.3 | 2.1 | 1.6 |
| Total | A | 85.1 | 75.8 | 79.7 | 83.6 | 87.4 | 91.8 | 93.3 |
| | B | 5.6 | 7.1 | 7.1 | 6.9 | 5.6 | 3.4 | 1.7 |
| | C | 8.3 | 16.0 | 12.0 | 8.8 | 6.4 | 4.1 | 3.0 |
| | D | 0.9 | 1.2 | 0.9 | 0.7 | 0.6 | 0.7 | 1.9 |

A:  Desires to stay at the present job (firm)
B:  Desires to find an additional (second) job
C:  Desires to change jobs (firms)
D:  Desires to leave the labor market

Data Source:  Employment Status Survey, Prime Minister's Office, 1979.

Table III-1B.  Employees' Attitudes Toward their Present Job

(Females) (%)

| Job Tenure (years) / Desire | | Total | -3 | 3-6 | 7-9 | 10-19 | 20-29 | 30- |
|---|---|---|---|---|---|---|---|---|
| Age 15-24 (years) | A | 75.0 | 75.8 | 74.4 | 72.2 | 75.0 | | |
| | B | 5.4 | 5.5 | 5.5 | 4.2 | 0.0 | | |
| | C | 14.5 | 14.6 | 14.5 | 12.5 | 25.0 | | |
| | D | 5.1 | 4.0 | 5.6 | 9.7 | 0.0 | | |
| 25-34 | A | 79.0 | 69.8 | 77.3 | 84.2 | 86.8 | | |
| | B | 4.7 | 5.9 | 5.8 | 3.4 | 3.3 | | |
| | C | 11.0 | 18.3 | 12.1 | 7.2 | 5.4 | | |
| | D | 5.2 | 6.3 | 4.8 | 5.5 | 4.5 | | |
| 35-44 | A | 81.6 | 72.8 | 79.1 | 83.7 | 87.6 | 91.9 | 100.0 |
| | B | 3.9 | 4.9 | 4.3 | 3.9 | 3.4 | 2.5 | 0.0 |
| | C | 11.2 | 18.7 | 13.4 | 9.2 | 5.9 | 3.5 | 0.0 |
| | D | 3.3 | 3.7 | 3.2 | 3.6 | 3.2 | 2.5 | 0.0 |
| 45-54 | A | 85.7 | 76.3 | 81.1 | 86.9 | 88.7 | 92.2 | 93.4 |
| | B | 2.1 | 3.1 | 2.6 | 1.5 | 2.2 | 1.6 | 1.2 |
| | C | 7.6 | 14.9 | 10.8 | 7.2 | 5.5 | 2.9 | 1.2 |
| | D | 4.5 | 5.7 | 5.8 | 4.5 | 3.4 | 3.9 | 4.2 |
| 55-59 | A | 86.6 | 85.2 | 82.2 | 85.3 | 87.8 | 91.8 | 90.5 |
| | B | 1.5 | 1.6 | 3.2 | 1.3 | 0.5 | 2.3 | 1.6 |
| | C | 6.0 | 11.5 | 8.3 | 6.7 | 5.6 | 2.3 | 3.2 |
| | D | 6.0 | 4.9 | 7.0 | 6.7 | 6.1 | 3.5 | 4.8 |
| Total | A | 81.0 | 74.1 | 77.8 | 84.1 | 87.6 | 91.4 | 91.9 |
| | B | 3.8 | 5.0 | 4.5 | 3.1 | 2.5 | 1.8 | 0.9 |
| | C | 10.3 | 16.2 | 12.5 | 7.7 | 5.4 | 2.8 | 1.6 |
| | D | 4.9 | 4.8 | 5.2 | 5.2 | 4.5 | 4.0 | 5.6 |

A:  Desires to stay at the present job (firm)
B:  Desires to find an additional (second) job
C:  Desires to change jobs (firms)
D:  Desires to leave the labor market

Data Source:  Employment Status Survey, Prime Minister's Office, 1979.

public sector on an annual basis. Twelve age classes (i.e., 17 years old or less, 18-19, 20-24, 25-29, 30-34, 35-39, 40-44, 45-49, 50-54, 55-59, 60-64, 65 and over), and nine job tenure classes (i.e., 0 years, 1, 2, 3-4, 5-9, 10-14, 15-19, 20-29, 30 or more), are used. By considering the ratio of the number of employees who have never changed employers to the total number of employees for a certain age class, it is possible to obtain a rough indication of the prevalence of worker immobility. Table 2 presents such figures. There are several technical shortcomings to the calculations in Table 2. Firstly, this methodology is unable to identify employees who have very long job tenures in their later careers but who changed employers in their earlier careers (for example, a 50-year-old worker who changed employers once at the age of 20 after working one year but who has continued to be employed by another firm since then). This shortcoming would be serious if we were concerned with the calculation of average job tenure for each job. It is not so serious, however, for our particular purpose, partly because under the lifetime employment system in Japan, an employee typically continues to work at a particular firm starting immediately after graduarion from school and partly because job shopping during a worker's younger years, observed often in the U.S. and emphasized by Hall (1982), is much less common in Japan. Thus, we ignore the problem when calculating the prevalence of worker immobility. Secondly, we had to assume that both the age class distribution and the job tenure class distribution of workers were uniform within each age and tenure class in order to simplify the computations. To be more precise, it is desirable to abandon this assumption, as is done for the computation of the hazard functions (Subsection A of Section II). We can make the following observations from Table 2:

Firstly, contrary to the desires of employees given in Table 1, the data indicate that the rate of worker immobility is rather low. Looking only at employees over the age of 45, for whom a job tenure of over 20 years is possible, it is found that the prevalence of worker immobility is extremely low, approximately 10.5% for males, and 1.6% for females. Since the mandatory retirement age is about 55-60 years old, focusing on the 45-49 and 50-54 age classes provides us with a rough estimate of the real degree of lifetime employment. Incidentally, the results obtained from individual panel data yield a very similar figure for the job immobility rate-9.7% for males. It is valid, consequently, to propose that "lifetime employment" in Japan applies only to a very minor group. It is necessary to understand that the vast majority of employees change their employers willingly or unwillingly during their careers. How many times do they change their employers? We will examine this issue later.

Secondly, Table 2 shows an interesting result concerning the characteristics of the very minor group covered by "lifetime employment": male workers have higher rates of job immobility than female workers, as Table 2A shows. The higher the worker's educational attainment, the more likely he is to be covered by the lifetime employment system, as both Table 2B and Table 2C indicate. It is interesting to point out that university graduates show much higher rates than senior and junior high school graduates. As for the effect of occupation, non-manual workers show higher rates (about 10% higher) than manual workers, as Table 2C indicates. Finally, the larger the firm size, the higher the rate of job

*T. Tachibanaki*

Table III-2.   The Ratio of the Number of Workers Who Have Never
Changed Employers to the Total Number of Workers by Age Class,
Sex, Firm Size, Occupation and Education (1980)


Table III-2A.   Age and Sex

|         | 30-34 | 35-39 | 40-44 | 45-49 | 50-54 |
|---------|-------|-------|-------|-------|-------|
| Males   | 0.331 | 0.186 | 0.149 | 0.110 | 0.098 |
| Females | 0.217 | 0.063 | 0.029 | 0.020 | 0.013 |


Table III-2B.   Education, Age and Firm Size

(Male)

| Education / Age / Firm Size | Junior High School | | | Senior High School | | | College and University | | |
|---|---|---|---|---|---|---|---|---|---|
| | 40-44 | 45-49 | 50-54 | 40-44 | 45-49 | 50-54 | 40-44 | 45-49 | 50-54 |
| Large  | 0.177 | 0.088 | 0.201 | 0.292 | 0.279 | 0.251 | 0.521 | 0.391 | 0.341 |
| Medium | 0.122 | 0.090 | 0.028 | 0.174 | 0.110 | 0.078 | 0.481 | 0.266 | 0.228 |
| Small  | 0.085 | 0.076 | 0.028 | 0.106 | 0.066 | 0.039 | 0.291 | 0.128 | 0.126 |


Table III-2C.   Education, Age and Occupation

(Male)

| Education / Age / Occupation | Junior High School | | | Senior High School | | | College and University | | |
|---|---|---|---|---|---|---|---|---|---|
| | 40-44 | 45-49 | 50-54 | 40-44 | 45-49 | 50-54 | 40-44 | 45-49 | 50-54 |
| Manual Workers     | 0.134 | 0.043 | 0.092 | 0.149 | 0.145 | 0.070 | × | × | × |
| Non-Manual Workers | 0.247 | 0.114 | 0.207 | 0.264 | 0.254 | 0.182 | 0.568 | 0.334 | 0.289 |

Source:   These tables were calculated from the aggregate data, presented in the
Wage Structure Survey: 1980, published by the Ministry of Labor.

immobility, as Table 2B shows.

In sum, workers who never change their employers during their careers are likely to be highly educated non-manual workers working for larger firms. These workers are apparently receiving the benefit of seniority rules for wages and promotions to a greater extent than other workers, so it is natural for them to have stronger incentives for staying at their present firm. The crucial point, however, is that the share of these workers (i.e. non-manual, highly educated, large firms' employees) in the Japanese labor force is very small. This subsection ends with the following conclusion: It is quite misleading to suppose that the majority of Japanese employees never changes employers. Lifetime employment applies only to a very minor group of workers.

Employment Status Survey (Japan) and Special Labor Force Report (U.S.) This subsection attempts to provide a comparison of job tenure between Japan and the U.S. Koike (1978) was the first to tackle this issue. International comparisons are difficult to carry out because the data sources of the two countries must be comparable. In addition to this condition, the methodology used must be the same for the two countries. Maehara (1981), who was influenced by the works of Akerlof and Main (1982), provided a very careful study of the duration of jobs in the U.S. and Japan which minimized the inherent shortcomings of comparative studies. This subsection discusses the characteristics of job tenure in Japan in comparison with the U.S. case by taking account of the results obtained by the present author and by Maehara's study. The main statistical source is the Employment Status Survey for Japan and the Special Labor Force Report for the U.S. The two sources are the most comparable among the existing sources.

Table 3, which has been extracted from one of Maehara's detailed and useful tables, presents the average completed length of currently held jobs ($S_{EW}$) and the average length of all spells of jobs ($S_{TW}$) for both Japan and the U.S. Since the distinction between $S_{EW}$ and $S_{TW}$ is explained in detail by Kaits (1970), Salant (1977), Akerlof and Main (1982), and Maehara (1981), no detailed explanations of $S_{EW}$ and $S_{TW}$ are provided. It is worthwhile, nevertheless, to note that $S_{EW}$ tends to emphasize relatively longer jobs, while $S_{TW}$ tends to emphasize relatively shorter jobs. This is due to the fact that $S_{TW}$ weights all spells equally, while $S_{EW}$ weights spells by their length. According to Table 3, Japan shows longer average durations than the U.S. in terms of both $S_{EW}$ and $S_{TW}$. This result confirms the casual observation that American employees change jobs more frequently than Japanese employees. Since the ratio of $S_{EW}$ to $S_{TW}$ is higher in the U.S. than in Japan, the average length of currently held jobs in the U.S. is not as short relative to the average length of all jobs as it is in Japan even though the average length of all jobs is much shorter in the U.S. than in Japan.

*T. Tachibanaki*

Table III-3.  The Average Completed Length of Currently Held Jobs
  ($S_{EW}$) and the Average Length of All Spells of Jobs ($S_{TW}$),
  Japan vs. the U.S.

(in years)

|  | Japan (1974) | | | U.S. (1968-73) | | |
|---|---|---|---|---|---|---|
|  | $S_{EW}^1$ | $S_{TW}^2$ | $S_{EW}/S_{TW}$ | $S_{EW}^3$ | $S_{TW}^3$ | $S_{EW}/S_{TW}$ |
| males | 22.6 | 8.1 | 2.8 | whites  18.3<br>non-whites  14.4 | 3.9<br>2.8 | 4.7<br>5.1 |
| females | 13.0 | 3.8 | 3.4 | whites  11.6<br>non-whites  10.3 | 2.6<br>2.2 | 4.5<br>4.7 |

1. Non-agricultural sector (employees)
2. Non-agricultural sector (employees) excluding construction and
   government
3. All industries

Sources:  Maehara (1981) and Akerlof and Main (1982).


Tables 4 and 5 are given in order to make clear the causes of the
considerable difference in job tenure between Japan and the U.S.
These tables clearly indicate that for all age groups the frequency
of spells of less than one year duration is much higher in the U.S.
than in Japan.   Thus, the main cause of the difference in average
job tenure between the two countries lies in the frequency of very
short job spells, particularly among the younger age groups.   It is
important to note that there are many employees in the U.S. who
have more than 20 years of tenure, as stressed by Hall (1982), even
though their share in the labor force is smaller.

C.  Panel Data

This section attempts to analyze individual panel data on job
history and to discuss the empirical results with emphasis on
comparing the previous aggregate results with the results obtained
from individual panel data.

First, I briefly explain the data source.   The National Institute
of Employment and Vocational Research conducted an invaluable
Survey on Enterprise Mobility.   The Survey asked a large number of
questions on job status such as (i) the duration of jobs (including
the calendar year of both the starting date and the ending date),
(ii) industry, (iii) firm size, (iv) occupation (very detailed 3-
digit level classification), (v) hierarchical status in the
organization, etc., for all jobs which had been held by respondents
during their entire career up to the survey period.   The survey
also includes other useful information on each individual such as
the level of education, earnings and so on.   It is possible to

Table III-4.  Average Job Tenure by Age (All industries, in years)

| Age \ Sex | Japan (1977) Males | Females | U.S.A. (1978) Males | Females |
|---|---|---|---|---|
| 16-19 | 2.12 | 2.12 | 0.96 | 0.83 |
| 20-24 | 4.17 | 3.62 | 1.83 | 1.65 |
| 25-29 | 7.12 | 5.88 | 3.13 | 2.82 |
| 30-39 | 12.37 | 9.10 | 5.95 | 4.11 |
| 40-54 | 19.52 | 15.32 | 11.93 | 7.34 |
| 55-64 | 19.38 | 19.27 | 16.74 | 11.18 |
| 65- | 21.28 | 22.14 | 18.33 | 12.36 |

Table III-5.  Distribution of Job Tenure by Age (All industries,
          males, in percent, 1973 data for Japan
          and 1974 data for the U.S.)

| Tenure | Age 25-29 Japan | U.S. | Age 40-49 Japan | U.S. | Age 50-64 Japan | U.S. |
|---|---|---|---|---|---|---|
| years |  |  |  |  |  |  |
| 0-1 | 7.9 | 30.0 | 3.3 | 11.6 | 3.6 | 7.1 |
| 1-3 | 8.8 | 13.4 | 3.3 | 6.2 | 3.5 | 4.5 |
| 3-5 | 9.7 | 10.4 | 2.9 | 5.8 | 2.8 | 4.3 |
| 5-10 | 8.5 | 4.0 | 2.2 | 3.7 | 2.1 | 3.0 |
| 10-20 | 1.2 | 0.3 | 2.8 | 2.9 | 1.6 | 2.2 |
| 20- | 0 | 0 | 3.0 | 1.2 | 3.8 | 1.6 |

Source:  Maehara (1981).

distinguish between workers experiencing no job changes and workers
experiencing several changes.   More concretely, it is feasible to
classify workers according to the frequency of job changes.   This
part investigates statistically whether workers can be meaningfully
categorized as either workers experiencing no job changes (lifetime
employees) or as "all other."   In other words, we would like to
know who the workers experiencing no job changes are and to examine
what kind of personal characteristics they have.

The Survey includes farmers and self-employed workers, whose
definition of lifetime employment is considerably different from
that of employees.   Thus, we restrict our attention to regular
employees.   The other important sample selections criteria are as
follows:   (1) only male employees are considered, simply because
female exployees often change their labor force status during their
career, which obscures the implications of lifetime employment.
(2) We excluded older workers who have already reached the age of
55 (i.e., the mandatory retirement age in many companies) because
workers are likely to be forced to change employers at that age.
We also excluded young employees (i.e., under the age of 34), who
are too young to be considered lifetime employees.   In addition to
this age requirement, we consider only employees who have had at
least twenty years of work history.   This is due to our judgement
that the duration of lifetime employment should be at least twenty
years.   See Hall (1982) about this condition.   We are left with a
total of 937 observations after sample selection which are fairly
homogeneous in many respects.

The main statistical tool for the classification of employees
according to the frequency of job changes is linear discriminant
analysis.   Our aim is mainly to test statistically whether a
variable is statistically significant enough to classify the sample.
The usual aims of discriminant analysis, namely the estimation of
discriminant functions and the prediction of cases, are not our
concern.   Needless to say, the classification is made according to
the number of job (firm) changes.   For simplicity, we call workers
with no changes the no changers and workers with any changes the
changers.

The explanatory variables are as follows:   (1) years of schooling,
(2) graduation or withdrawal from school, (3) firm size, (4) current
income level, (5) occupation, and (6) marital status.   The method
for quantification is described in Appendix I.   I now describe the
reasons for introducing these variables.   It should be recalled that
our previous analysis of aggregate data on job tenure (Table 2)
suggested that the following three variables were the crucial
factors for determining the likelihood of job immobility (lifetime
employment):   educational attainment, firm size, and occupation
(manual versus non-manual).   Current income level is introduced for
the purpose of examining whether the monetary reward could be a
factor motivating the worker to change jobs.   It might have been
preferable to take the worker's income level at the time of the job
change, at least for the "changers," but since such data were not
available, we were obliged to use current income as an approximation.   Nevertheless, a comparison of the current income level of
"no changers" and "changers" is still very valuable because the
current income level of "changers" gives us some indication of their
income level after their job change.   As for (5) occupation, we are
interested in inquiring whether occupation, which is quantified by

prestige value, is influential in the decision to change employers.
Since this data source provides a much more detailed classification
of occupation than the previous manual versus non-manual
classification, results based on these data should be more
convincing. We add two variables; (2) graduation or withdrawal from
school and (6) marital status, both 0-1 dummies, which will
hopefully supplement the information on individual characteristics.
One may suppose that an individual who has dropped out from school
is deficient in the desire for achievement and/or is quick to give
up. Thus, it is possible to anticipate that such workers have a
higher probability of changing employers than other workers. As for
marital status, it is not unreasonable to presume that since a
married person is more averse to instability, he is more likely to
keep his present job. In the sample in this study, fortunately or
unfortunately, nearly 100% of the people are married, which is quite
understandable in view of the ages of the workers in the sample.
(6) Marital status was, consequently, eliminated from consideration.

Table 6 presents the means and standard deviations of the
explanatory variables and the number of observations for each class.
The share of the "no changers" is 0.097, while the share of the
"changers" is 0.903. It is worth repeating that the proportion of
changers (about 10%) is roughly consistent with the figures
calculated from aggregate data which were presented earlier. The
breakdown of the "changers" is as follows: once: 230 (27.2%),
twice: 262 (31.0%), and more than twice: 354 (41.8%). The share
of the frequent changers (more than two changes) is impressively
large, and the share of those with only one change is relatively
small. There are several interesting results which can be obtained
by analyzing the means and standard deviations in Table 6.

Firstly, both educational attainment and occupational level
(prestige value) are considerably higher for "no changers" than for
"changers", (10.69 years versus 10.03 years and 47.40 versus 43.43,
respectively). Even among the "changers," the less frequently the
worker changes jobs, the higher are his educational attainment and
occupational level (except for those changing more than twice).
Therefore, it is possible to conclude that the higher the worker's
educational attainment and occupational level, the less likely he is
to change his employer.

Secondly, the impact of firm size is very similar to the impact of
education and occupation. The average firm size of "no changers"
is 4.08 (about 300 employees per firm), while that of "changers" is
3.52 (about 120 employees per firm). "No changers" tend to work for
larger firms than "changers." This is also true when we compare
different categories of "changers." Thus, the expectation that the
larger the firm size, the less likely the worker is to change jobs
(or the greater the likelihood of the worker being a lifetime
employee) is confirmed by the individual panel data.

Thirdly, a somewhat surprising but interesting result appears in the
impact of income. The average income of "no changers" is somewhat
lower than that of "changers" though the variance of income displays
the opposite ranking. Moreover, the highest income is earned by
one-time "changers," followed by two-time "changers" and finally "no
changers." This result suggests that job changes (particularly one-
time changes) give workers a good chance of raising their income
level above that of their previous job. There may be criticism

Table III-6. Means and Standard Deviations of the Variables

| | Educational Attainment | Graduation or Withdrawal from School | Firm Size | Income | Occupation |
|---|---|---|---|---|---|
| **No changers** | | | | | |
| Mean | 10.69 | 0.97 | 4.08 | 6.70 | 47.40 |
| S.D. | 2.68 | 0.18 | 1.31 | 3.21 | 10.46 |
| **Changers** | | | | | |
| Mean | 10.03 | 0.92 | 3.52 | 7.05 | 43.43 |
| S.D. | 2.53 | 0.27 | 1.38 | 3.56 | 8.38 |
| **Changers(once)** | | | | | |
| Mean | 10.44 | 0.94 | 3.60 | 7.54 | 44.03 |
| S.D. | 2.56 | 0.24 | 1.51 | 3.45 | 8.42 |
| **Changers(twice)** | | | | | |
| Mean | 10.11 | 0.93 | 3.49 | 7.08 | 42.41 |
| S.D. | 2.56 | 0.25 | 1.41 | 3.70 | 8.01 |
| **Changers(more than twice)** | | | | | |
| Mean | 9.70 | 0.90 | 3.49 | 6.72 | 43.80 |
| S.D. | 2.46 | 0.30 | 1.28 | 3.50 | 8.58 |

The number of observations is as follows.
No changers: 91
Changers: 846 [once: 230, twice: 262, more: 354]

Data source: Survey on Enterprise Mobility (1973)

Note: See Appendix 1 for variable definitions.

against this speculation: for example, the average age of "no changers" might be lower than that of "changers", but the data show that the average age of "no changers" and "changers" are not significantly different. More importantly, it is crucial to point out that although the higher mean educational and occupational attainment of "no changers" would be expected to produce a higher mean income under normal circumstances, in fact, "no changers" show a lower mean income as compared to "changers." One plausible interpretation of this somewhat surprising outcome is the following: "Changers" may have a stronger preference for monetary rewards than "no changers," while stability of employment may be preferred more strongly by "no changers" than by "changers." In accordance with this preference, "no changers" do not accept or seek new job opportunities which may pay a higher salary than their present job if their employment security at their present job is assured. In simpler terms, workers who do not change jobs are more risk-averse than workers who do. Risk-taking workers (changers) have a better chance of receiving higher wages than risk-averse workers (no changers).[2]

Fourth, the variable which specifies graduation or withdrawal from school supports our expectation that changers should display a higher dropout rate. The individual's attitude towards schooling and work is positively correlated, and one's experience during one's dtudent days (i.e., graduation or withdrawal) is, to a limited extent, a determinant of one's career pattern.

So far we have paid no attention to the statistical test for determining whether the explanatory variables are statistically significant for classifying the sample not only between "no changers" and "changers", but also among different frequencies of "changers." We must assume the usual properties such as normality and equality of all of the underlying covariance matrices. A preliminary test rejects the equality of the covariance matrices when the sample is divided into two parts judging from the estimated determinants. Consequently, we abandon the entire test for this case. Fortunately, a preliminary test among the four categories (i.e., no changers, one-time changers, two-time changers, and more-than-two-time changers) does not lead us to reject the equality of the covariance matrices, judging from the estimated determinants of the matrices. We, of course, eliminate the dummy variables.

The estimation of the discriminant functions, whose usefulness has been justified statistically by the high values of the chi-squared values-namely, 62.79 (15 degrees of freedom) for function 1, 28.58 (8 degrees of freedom) for function 2, and 2.87 (3 degrees of freedom) for function 3-gives the order of the statistical significance of the explanatory variables in the following way, judging from the Wilk's $\Lambda$ (lambda): (1) Occupation (0.976), (2) Education (0.958), (3) Income (0.947), and (4) Firm Size (0.935). The interpretation of the coefficients of the discriminant functions and the Wilk's lambda is as follows: The higher the worker's occupational level, the less likely he is to change jobs. This effect, which is in a way contradictory to the results obtained from the aggregate data, is the strongest among the above four factors. It would be interesting to analyze more carefully whether people with higher status occupations (or more prestigious jobs) have a greater preference for stability of their jobs or whether people with lower status occupations (or less prestigious jobs) are more tolerant of unstable jobs. The data seem to support this view. The

next important variable is education the impact of which is
consistent with the earlier results obtained using aggregate data.
For the third variable, income, the interpretation given to the
means and standard deviations of income is again applicable.
Finally, the firm size variable needs no further comment since it
was discussed previously. In sum, the aggregate published data and
individual panel data yield consistent results with respect to the
effect of education and firm size. The results concerning the
effect of occupation and income which were obtained from individual
data fostered interesting speculation, but further investigation is
required before solid conclusions can be reached.


2.   JOB TENURE AND MOBILITY

This section presents principally two empirical results. The two
studies differ mainly with respect to data sources and estimation
techniques:  the first approach uses aggregate published data and
the survival method as a statistical technique, while the second
uses individual panel data and econometric techniques as an
estimation procedure. The concern, however, is the same for both
approaches-namely, job tenure and mobility.

A.   Survivor Approach with Aggregate Data

This methodology is applicable when cross-section data on wastage
(loss or failure) from the system during a given period are
available. In our case, the loss is defined as the number of
leavers, and the system as the stock of workers employed by present
employers. Thus, only the outflow (or separations) and the stock of
employees within a period of time are required as data to conduct
this approach. The merit of this method is not only its less
demanding data requirements but also its capacity to estimate the
future survival rate, when the parameters of the hazard function are
given. More specifically, it is feasible to anticipate the expected
further duration of employment given the estimated parameters of a
specific hazard function. We explain the model and the estimation
procedure briefly. See, for example, Gross and Clark (1975), or
Mann, Schafer and Singpurwalla (1973) for more about the analysis of
survival.

First, we consider the death density function $f(t)$; which gives the
probability that an entrant leaves during the time interval
$t < x < t + dt$. This is a probability density function or frequency
function, where the random variable is time. Second, the survivor
function, $S(t)$, is defined. This is the probability that an entrant
survives at least until time $t(t > 0)$: $S(t) = 1 - F(t)$, where $F(t)$
is the cumulative distribution function. Third, the hazard function,
$\lambda(t)$, is defined. This is the probability, $\lambda(t)dt$, that an entrant
leaves during the time interval $t < x < t + dt$, no matter how small
$dt$ is, given he has survived up to time t. Then, the conditional
leaving rate at time t is defined by $\lambda(t) = F(t)/S(t)$. This hazard
rate is also called the failure rate, the instantaneous death rate,
or the force of mortality in other fields. If the form of the
density function is available, we can induce the form of the hazard
function because the survivor function is expressed by the
cumulative form of the density function $f(t)$. Finally, the average
remaining duration of employment is given by (1).

$$E(a) = \frac{\int_a^\infty S(t)dt}{S(a)} \quad , \text{ where } a \text{ is the initial duration.} \tag{1}$$

We consider a particular density function for our purpose: the Weibull. The following are the mathematical form of the density function and the induced form of the hazard function.

$$f(t) = \alpha\gamma t^{\gamma-1}\exp(-\alpha t^\gamma) \qquad \text{(density)} \tag{2}$$

$$\lambda(t) = \alpha\gamma t^{\gamma-1} \qquad \text{(hazard)}. \tag{3}$$

where $\alpha > 0$ and $\gamma > 0$.

The reasons for the choice of density function may be summarized as follows. (1) Since the Weibull is a two-parameter function, its estimation is relatively easy. It is difficult to estimate three-parameter functions such as the Beta when we employ non-linear least squares, which is our estimation procedure. (2) The value of the shape parameter $\gamma$ of the function conveys information on duration dependence very clearly, as we shall see shortly, and this is one of the most important concerns of this study. (3) The Weibull contains the simple exponential function as a special case, which gives an important special case of duration dependence (i.e., no duration dependence).

It is easily verified that the following three cases can be distinguished depending on the value of $\gamma$:

(i)     $\gamma > 1$:   the hazard rate is increasing,

(ii)    $\gamma = 1$:   the function reduces to the simple exponential form,

(iii)   $\gamma < 1$:   the hazard rate is decreasing.

Since the hazard rate implies the probability that an individual leaves at time t given he has survived to time t, it implies the leaving rate of a person at time t who has been employed to time t, if we interpret the hazard rate in terms of labor mobility and duration (i.e. job tenure). Positive duration dependence signifies a situation in which the hazard rate is increasing and implies that the longer the individual's job tenure, the more likely he is to leave. Negative duration dependence, signifying a decreasing hazard rate, implies that the longer the individual's job tenure, the less likely he is to leave (i.e. the more likely he is to stay). Whether duration dependence is positive or negative depends upon the estimated value of $\gamma$, the shape parameter of the Weibull.

The data source is the same as the one used previously, i.e., the Wage Structure Survey, which was used to calculate the aggregate rate of job immobility (or the degree of lifetime employment). Although the previous section utilized the raw published data without adjustment in view of the small estimated errors, it is risky to use the raw published data without adjustment this time. The leaving rate during a given period is calculated for each tenure class by taking the ratio of the number of leavers to the number of

total employees in that tenure class. The number of leavers is
obtained by taking the difference between the total number of
employees in the previous year and that in the current year for the
relevant tenure class. If data on the number of employees were
available for each uniformly defined tenure class, say consecutive
one-year tenure classes, the above method would be logical and
justified. The actual data source, however, uses the following nine
job tenure classes of unequal length: (1) less than 1 year, (2) 1,
(3) 2, (4) 3-4, (5) 5-9, (6) 10-14, (7) 15-19, (8) 20-29, (9) 30 or
more years. The alternative method is to assume that the distribution of the number of employees is uniform for each of the nine
tenure classes. Then, it is relatively easy, computationally
speaking, to calculate the number of leavers during a year. It
would, however, be highly erroneous if we took the simple difference
between two consecutive years on the basis of the above method
unless we are able to assume that neither positive nor negative
duration dependence exists.

In view of the several difficulties described above, we adopt a
methodology which is necessarily cumbersome but the most reliable.
First, an attempt is made to estimate the number of employees for
each tenure class, defined by consecutive one-year segments, by
applying the interpolation method. In other words, we try to
enlarge the number of job tenure classes from the original nine
classes to more than thirty classes. Second, the difference between
the number of employees in a particular tenure class in the previous
year and the number of employees in the next highest tenure class in
the current year yields the number of leavers. Third, when the
number of leavers has been computed, the calculation of the leaving
rate for each tenure class is a simple matter. Appendix II presents
the actual methodology of the interpolation.

The next problem is how to estimate the parameters of the hazard
function using the given fabricated data. It is possible to
conceive of several alternative methods that could be used for the
actual estimation: (1) matching the moments, (2) minimum sum of
squared residuals, (3) maximum likelihood method, (4) minimum chi-
squared method. We selected (2) and minimized the sum of squared
residuals between the predicted leaving rate and the actual leaving
rate by applying a non-linear estimation procedure, the Davidon-
Fletcher-Powell method. This method of minimum sum of squared
residuals produces fairly accurate results although the estimation
is somewhat cumbersome due to its non-linearity.

Table 7 gives the parameter estimates and the expected further
durations. The shape parameter, which is smaller than unity,
suggests the existence of negative duration dependence: the longer
the job tenure, the less likely an individual is to leave (i.e., the
more likely he is to stay). It is expected that this negative
duration dependence is a universal phenomenon in any society in the
world. This is confirmed by looking at the distribution of job
tenures in an indirect way, without estimating the shape parameter
or the Weibull function for the other countries. Figure 1 presents,
for example, the Japanese and American distributions of job tenures.

These are obtained from the Wage Structure Survey for Japan and the
Job Tenure Survey for the U.S. Although the American distribution
is not a monotonically decreasing function of job tenure, both
countries show, roughly speaking, a tendency for the leaving rate to

Table III-7A.  Parameter Estimates of the Hazard Function
for Japan, All Industries, Males (1979-80)

|  | Weibull |
|---|---|
| Scale α | 0.328 |
| Shape γ | 0.326 |
| Squared error | 0.021 |
| Chi-squared value | 23.45 |

Table III-7B.  Expected Further Durations for Japan,
All Industries, Males (1979-80)

| Tenure class (years) | 1 | 2 | 3-4 | 5-9 | 10-14 | 15-19 | 20-29 | 30- |
|---|---|---|---|---|---|---|---|---|
| Expected further durations (years) | 14.8 | 15.1 | 16.0 | 15.7 | 14.1 | 10.2 | 6.7 | 0 |

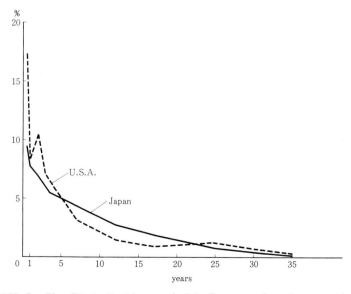

Figure III-1  The Distributions of Job Tenures for Japan and the U.S.

decline as job tenure increases (i.e., negative duration
dependence).

Finally, let us examine the expected further duration curve as
calculated from equation (1). The curve appears to be convex:  it
is relatively low initially-about 15 years. Then, it increases
rather steeply, reaching its maximum level at about 3-4 years.  A
worker who has worked for this length of time at a firm is expected
to work for about another 16 years at the same firm.  Then, the
expected further duration declines gradually.  The total duration,
which is the sum of the expected further duration and initial
tenure, however, becomes longer and longer as initial tenure becomes
longer.

B.   Econometric Approach with Panel Data

This subsection investigates duration dependence and lagged duration
dependence using the same individual panel data used for the
analysis of "no changers" and "changers" in the previous section.
The idea of the analysis is similar to the preceding analysis of the
relationship between job tenure and mobility because it again
employs the hazard rate as a principal tool.  There is an important
difference, however:  the influence of past experience is taken into
account, specifically not only the frequency of changes (i.e.,
spells) but also their duration.  This is feasible only if
individual panel data on job history are available.  This subsection
borrows heavily from Heckman's pioneering work on the structural
analysis of longitudinal data such as Heckman (1978A, 1978B, 1979,
1980A, 1980B), and Heckman and Borjas (1981) and Flinn and Heckman
(1982).

Assuming a simple Markov model of mobility between the two states
(employment and unemployment), and considering the Weibull function
for determining the hazard rate, we obtain equation (1)

$$\lambda_{ij}(t_{ij}) = a_{ij}\gamma_{ij}(t_{ij})^{\gamma_{ij}-1} \tag{1}$$

where $t_{ij}$ is the duration at state i which moves to state j.  $\lambda_{ij}$ is
the hazard rate, $a_{ij}$ is the instantaneous transition probability,
and $\gamma_{ij}$ is a parameter.  Regarding unemployment as a fictitious
point event which makes the transition from one job to another
feasible, and considering the influence of past employment, equation
(1) may be rewritten as follows:

$$\lambda_{ij}\{t_{ij}(\ell)\} = a_{ij}(\ell)\cdot\{t_{ij}(\ell)\}^{\gamma_{ij}(\ell)-1}\cdot\gamma_{ij}(\ell)$$

$$\cdot\exp -\{\sum_{j=1}^{\ell-1}\beta_{ij}(j)\ell nt_{ij}(\ell-j)\} \tag{2}$$

where $\ell$ is the $\ell$-th employment spell, and $t_{ij}(\ell)$ is the duration of
the $\ell$-th employment spell.  $\beta_{ij}(j = 1, \ldots, \ell - 1)$ is the

coefficient for the effect of past spells of employment and their durations.

We consider the most simple parameterization of $a_{ij}(\ell)$, $a_{ij}(\ell) = \exp -\{\rho_{ij}(\ell)Z_{ij}(\ell)\}$, where $\rho_{ij}$ are parameters, and $Z_{ij}$ are exogenous variables. We ignore the unmeasured pure heterogeneity problem. [3] We obtain equation (3), as shown by Flinn and Heckman (1982):

$$\ell n t_{ij}(\ell) = \frac{1}{\gamma_{ij}(\ell)} [B_1 + \rho_{ij}(\ell)Z_{ij}(\ell) + \sum_{j=1}^{\ell-1} \beta_{ij}(j)\ell n t_{ij}(\ell-j)]$$
$$+ W_{ij}(\ell) \tag{3}$$

$B_1$ is equal to $\Gamma'(1) = 0.5772$. The error term, $W_{ij}$, is defined by (4).

$$E(W_{ij}(\ell)) = 0$$

$$E(W_{ij}(\ell))^2 = \frac{B_2}{(\gamma_{ij}(\ell))^2}$$

$$\left. \begin{array}{r} \\ \\ \\ \\ \\ \\ \\ \end{array} \right\} \tag{4}$$

where $B_2 = \frac{d\ell n \Gamma(\theta)}{d\theta}$ (evaluated at $\theta = 1$) $= \frac{\pi^2}{6}$

$$E(W_{ij}(\ell)W_{ij}(\ell')) = 0 \qquad \text{for all } \ell, \ell'$$

There would be two sources of difficulty if we estimated equations (3) and (4) by the usual least squares method. The first is sample selection bias that arises because most panel samples are short in time coverage; some spells may not be completed at the time of the survey. The second is time-varying explanatory variables. This arises when exogenous variables change over time during the panel period and induces simultaneous equations bias. Since our data are longer than most panel data, the first difficulty is partly mitigated. As for the second difficulty, we consider fixed values for $Z_{ij}$, values measured at the start of a spell, namely (1) age at the start of the individual's working life, (2) firm size at the first job, and (3) educational level and ignore values measured after a spell begins.

Past durations, (or lagged durations), which are included as independent variables, are expected to indicate lagged duration dependence in the following two ways: Firstly, if the estimated coefficients of past spells were zero, it would be possible to conclude that the occurrence of past spells does not have any effect on the occurrence of the latest spell. Secondly, if the coefficients were positive (or negative), the duration of the latest spell would be positively (or negatively) affected. In other words, a positive (negative) coefficient on past duration indicates that the longer (or shorter) the past durations, the longer (or shorter) the latest duration. To avoid sample selection bias, the dependent

variable is taken as the $(\ell - 1)$-th spell.  Since the current
employment spell has not been completed, it is natural to consider
only the <u>completed</u> spells.

Initially, we estimated equation (3) by the ordinary least squares
method and included all the explanatory variables mentioned
previously.  The sample is restricted to a homogeneous group of
employees whose ages are between 42 and 51 and whose working
histories amount to at least 20 years.  Appendix III shows the
estimated results.  Since the results were poor in many respects, we
re-estimated equation (3) after excluding age at the first job,
which has a high correlation with education, and also firm size at
the first job from the list of explanatory variables.  It should be
recalled that these two variables are proxies for exogenous
variables which may be time-varying.  Thus, their exclusion is
partially justified even though it causes some deterioration in the
fit.

Table 8 shows the estimated results, which suggest the following
observations.  Firstly, an examination of the coefficients of
education indicate that only regression (ii), $\ell$n(Spell 3) has a
statistically significant coefficient which satisfies the sign
condition.  The other equations do not show any statistical
significance with respect to the effect of education.  Secondly, all
the lagged durations except for $\ell$n(Spell 1) in regression (i) have
negative coefficients, which suggests the following property:  the
longer the lagged durations, the shorter the next duration.  The
negative coefficients of the lagged durations, however, are not
statistically significant.  In other words, the null hypothesis
(i.e., that the coefficient is equal to zero) cannot be rejected in
many cases.  Consequently, the empirical results suggest the
following conclusion:  occurrence dependence, which signifies the
effect of previous occurrences of employment on the probability of
the latest employment, is largely rejected.  This is an important
observation:  the probability of an existing spell of employment is
independent of the number of previous spells.  In simpler terms, it
implies that labor turnover is not strongly influenced by the past
history of labor turnovers.  Thirdly, the coefficient $\gamma$, which is
calculated from the constant term, is smaller than unity.  This
indicates negative duration dependence, which was also indicated by
the aggregate data.  It is important to note that the individual
panel data and aggregate data yielded consistent results with
respect to duration dependence.  However, I have reservations about
generalizing the above observations for the following reason:  the
empirical conclusions are not very decisive in view of the
relatively poor regression results, which in turn, were due largely
to the small size of the sample.  Investigations using larger data
sets and more rigorous estimation procedures would provide more
convincing evidence.

3.  SUMMARY AND COMMENTS

This paper has investigated labor mobility and job tenure in the
Japanese labor market, with the American labor market being
considered occasionally for comparison purposes.  The first concern
was to analyze the relationship between lifetime employment and job
tenure.  Lifetime employment has been believed to be a distinctive

Table III-8.  Parameter Estimates of Duration Equations
Selected Explanatory Variables

| Explanatory Variables \ Dependent Variables | (i) ℓn (Spell 2) | (ii) ℓn (Spell 3) | (iii) ℓn (Spell 4) | (iv) ℓn (Spell 5) |
|---|---|---|---|---|
| Constant | 1.588 | 2.954 | 2.580 | 1.077 |
| Education | 0.010 (0.018) | -0.050 (0.025) | -0.020 (0.030) | 0.010 (0.054) |
| ℓn (Spell 1) | 0.027 (0.064) | -0.145 (0.093) | -0.243 (0.115) | -0.265 (0.220) |
| ℓn (Spell 2) | | -0.195 (0.084) | -0.064 (0.114) | -0.273 (0.199) |
| ℓn (Spell 3) | | | -0.110 (0.107) | -0.083 (0.119) |
| ℓn (Spell 4) | | | | -0.023 (0.163) |
| $R^2$ | 0.001 | 0.068 | 0.061 | 0.065 |
| Standard Error | 0.885 | 0.895 | 0.748 | 1.077 |
| γ | 0.358 | 0.187 | 0.201 | 0.310 |
| Sample Size | 275 | 165 | 97 | 53. |

Notes:  (1)  ℓn (Spell ℓ) indicates the duration of the ℓ-th employment spell.
(2)  Figures in parentheses are estimated standard errors.

feature of the Japanese economy, but we found that the desires of
employees and reality are considerably different with respect to
lifetime employment.  The actual data reveal that only a very minor
group of employees are actually part of the lifetime employment
system.  Also, attention was paid to who is likely to stay longer at
their first job and to be a lifetime employee.  The second concern
was to investigate the relationship between job tenure and mobility.
We used the survival method to estimate duration dependence and
expected further duration.  Regression analysis was also employed to
study duration dependence as well as occurrence dependence.  The
data support negative duration dependence, while conclusive results
were not obtained concerning occurrence dependence.

This paper used, basically, two data sources-aggregate data and
individual panel data to investigate each issue.  Emphasis has been
placed on obtaining consistent results from aggregate and individual
panel data.  Unfortunately, we did not obtain consistent results
concerning the second issue (namely, the relationship between job
tenure and mobility) due largely to the inconclusive results yielded
by the individual panel data, but we obtained more consistent
results concerning the first issue.

APPENDIX 1.

QUANTIFICATION OF THE EXPLANATORY VARIABLES FOR INDIVIDUAL PANEL DATA

The original survey was conducted in 1973. The data include not only job history information since the individual started working but also data on other individual characteristics. This Appendix explains briefly how the explanatory variables were quantified. The empirical analysis was performed after the appropriate sample was chosen. Since the main text of the paper has already discussed the sample used in the analysis, this Appendix explains only the quantification of variables.

(1) Educational Attainment: the number of years of schooling was used.

(2) Graduation or Withdrawal from School: 0-1 dummy, i.e., 1 if the individual graduated from school and 0 if the individual dropped out of school.

(3) Firm Size: firm size is defined according to the number of employees at the firm. 0 if no employees, 1 if 1-4 employees, 2 if 5-29 employees, 3 if 30-299 employees, 4 if 300-999 employees, and 5 if more than 1000 employees. Public employees were treated as belonging to the largest category (i.e., more than 1000 employees).

(4) Income: income was quantified according to the individual's annual earnings. Fifteen income classes of equal size were constructed. The lowest class takes the value 0, while the highest class takes the value 14.

(5) Occupation: occupation was quantified by the prestige value of each occupation. The lowest is 0, and the highest 100. We considered three-digit level occupations (about 300 occupations). The actual prestige values are available in Naoi (1977).

APPENDIX 2.

THE METHODOLOGY FOR ESTIMATING THE LEAVING RATE FOR EACH TENURE CLASS

Section 2 of the main text provides a brief explanation of the method for estimating leaving rates during a given period. This Appendix concentrates on the interpolation method for enlarging the number of job tenure classes. Since the original data source (i.e., the Wage Structure Survey) uses only nine job tenure classes of unequal length, it is necessary to allocate the figures to consecutive one-year tenure classes. Suppose the following exponential equation describes the relationship between tenure class t (defined by number of years) and the number of employees in tenure class t, $N(t)$: $\ln N(t) = at + b$, where a and b are parameters.

Estimating this equation by ordinary least squares for the years 1979 and 1980 yielded the following results:

1979: $\ln N = -0.0789t + 11.62$  $R^2 = 0.984$  D.W. = 2.22
         (0.0038)   (0.058)

1980: $\ln N = -0.0740t + 11.55$  $R^2 = 0.981$  D.W. = 1.39
         (0.0039)   (0.061)

The figures in parentheses are estimated standard errors.  The usual criteria
for regression equations assure the plausibility of this form.  Thus, the
estimated equations above have been used to interpolate the number of employees
in each newly created job tenure class.  The new job tenure classes are all of
uniform length-namely, one year (i.e., 0 years, 1 year, 2 years, 3 years, ...,
29 years, 30 years).  The main text of this paper explains the way in which we
obtained the leaving rate for each tenure class, after the number of employees in
each tenure class had been calculated.


APPENDIX 3.


PARAMETER ESTIMATES OF DURATION EQUATIONS WITH ALL VARIABLES

| Dependent Variables / Explanatory Variables | (i) $\ell$n (Spell 2) | (ii) $\ell$n (Spell 3) | (iii) $\ell$n (Spell 4) | (iv) $\ell$n (Spell 5) |
|---|---|---|---|---|
| Constant | 2.029 | 3.178 | 2.818 | 1.588 |
| Age | −0.043 (0.021) | −0.009 (0.026) | 0.005 (0.032) | 0.046 (0.050) |
| Firm Size | *** | −0.037 (0.052) | *** | 0.036 (0.104) |
| Education | 0.043 (0.025) | −0.042 (0.033) | −0.050 (0.038) | −0.041 (0.063) |
| $\ell$n (Spell 1) | 0.015 (0.072) | −0.098 (0.107) | −0.227 (0.122) | −0.230 (0.226) |
| $\ell$n(Spell 2) | | −0.219 (0.097) | 0.069 (0.121) | −0.268 (0.213) |
| $\ell$n(Spell 3) | | | −0.224 (0.120) | *** |
| $\ell$n(Spell 4) | | | | 0.242 (0.205) |
| $R^2$ | 0.023 | 0.070 | 0.094 | 0.106 |
| S.E. | 0.856 | 0.907 | 0.733 | 1.053 |
| $\gamma$ | 0.28 | 0.18 | 0.20 | 0.36 |
| Sample size | 195 | 123 | 76 | 46 |

The sign (***) indicates that the variable was excluded from the equation
because the preliminary estimates indicated very weak statistical
significance.  $\ell$n (Spell $\ell$) shows the duration of the $\ell$-th employment spell.

NOTES

[1]See Tachibanaki (1975, 1982A, 1982B) about the prevalence of the seniority rule.

[2]Tachibanaki (1981) discusses this subject in a different context by applying the idea of "satisfactions" to Japanese labor tunover.

[3]Unmeasured pure heterogeneity is defined as unobservable variables that differ among individuals and that may differ over time for the same individual.

REFERENCES

[1] Akerlof, G. A., and B. G. M. Main, "An Experience-Weighted Measure of Employment and Unemployment Durations," American Economic Review, December 1981, vol. 71, No. 5, 1003-1011.

[2] Flinn, C. J., and J. J. Heckman, "New Methods for Analyzing Structural Models of Labor Force Dynamics," Journal of Econometrics, vol. 18, No. 1, January 1982, 115-168.

[3] Gross, A. J. and V. A. Clark, Survival Distributions: Reliability Applications in the Biomedical Sciences, New York, John Wiley and Sons, 1975.

[4] Hall, R. E., "The Importance of Lifetime Jobs in the U.S. Economy," American Economic Review, September 1982, vol. 72, No. 4, 716-724.

[5] Heckman, J. J., (1978A), "Simple Statistical Models for Discrete Panel Data Developed and Applied to Test the Hypothesis of True State Dependence Against the Hypothesis of Spurious State Dependence," Annals de l'INSEE, 1978, vol. 30-31.

[6] Heckman, J. J., (1978B), "Longitudinal Studies in Labor Economics: A Critical Review," in Longitudinal Labor Market Analysis, edited by B. Singer and J. Heckman, Academic Press, 1978.

[7] Heckman, J. J., "Sample Selection Bias as a Specification Error," Econometrica, January 1979, vol. 47.

[8] Heckman, J. J., and G. J. Borjas, "Does Unemployment Cause Future Unemployment? Definitions, Questions, and Answers from a Continuous Time Model of Heterogeneity and State Dependence," Economica, August 1981.

[9] Heckman, J. J., (1980A), "Statistical Models for Discrete Panel Data," in Econometric Analysis of Discrete Data, edited by D. McFadden and C. Manski, Cambridge, MIT Press, 1980.

[10] Heckman, J. J., (1980B), "The Structural Analysis of Longitudinal Data," lecture at the World Congress of the Econometric Society, Aix-en-Provence.

[11] Kaitz, H., "Analyzing the Length of Spells of Unemployment," Monthly Labor Review, November, 1970, 11-20.

[12] Koike, K., "Japan's Industrial Relations: Characteristics and Problems," Japanese Economic Studies, Fall 1978, 42-90.

[13] Maehara, Y., The Durations of Jobs in the U. S. A. and Japan, Ph. D. thesis

submitted to the London School of Economics, August 1981.

[14] Mann, N. R., R. E. Shafer and N. D. Singpurwalla, Methods for Statistical Analysis of Reliability and Life Data, New York, John Wiley and Sons, 1974.

[15] Naoi, M., "Classifications of Occupations and Measurement (in Japanese)", in SSM Report (Social Stratification and Mobility), ed. K. Tominaga, 1977.

[16] Salant, S., "Search Theory and Duration Data: A Theory of Sorts," Quarterly Journal of Economics, February 1977, 39-57.

[17] Tachibanaki, T., "Wage Determination in Japanese Manufacturing Industries: Structural Change and Wage Differentials," International Economic Review, vol. 16, October 1975, 562-586.

[18] Tachibanaki, T., "Subjective Satisfaction, and Objective Economic and Social Background in Labor Turnover Behavior," Research Papers in Economics of Factor Markets, Stanford University, No. 5, 1981.

[19] Tachibanaki, T., (1982A), "Further Results on Japanese Wage Differentials: Nenko Wages, Hierarchical Position, Bonuses, and Working Hours," International Economic Review, vol. 23, No. 2, June 1982, 447-461.

[20] Tachibanaki, T., (1982B), "Education, Occupation, Hierarchy and Earnings: A Recursive Logit Approach for Japan," KIER discussion papers, No. 139.

DATA SOURCES

(1) Wage Structure Survey, Ministry of Labor, annual.

(2) Employment Status Survey, Statistics Bureau, Prime Minister's Office, annual.

(3) Survey on Enterprise Mobility, National Institute of Employment and Vocational Research, 1973.

(4) Special Labor Force Report, Job Tenure Survey, U. S. Government Printing Office.

* The author is grateful to Richard Freeman for his penetrating comments as a discussant, and to Masahiko Aoki and Kazuo Koike for their useful advice. Special thanks are addressed to Yasuhiro Maehara, who kindly permitted to cite his excellent unpublished Ph. D. thesis at L. S. E. (1981), and to Robert Hall who drew attention to his thesis. These people are not, needless to say, responsible for possible errors in this paper. Finally, it is gratefully acknowledged that the National Institute of Employment and Vocational Research permitted to use the useful data.

THE ECONOMIC ANALYSIS OF THE JAPANESE FIRM
M. Aoki (editor)
© Elsevier Science Publishers B.V. (North-Holland), 1984

# THE EFFECT OF TRADE UNIONS ON PRODUCTIVITY IN JAPANESE MANUFACTURING INDUSTRIES

KURAMITSU MURAMATSU

Traditional economics has had the common view that trade unions intend to raise wages and improve other working conditions for their members by regulating the supply of labor or interfering with management policies. Behind this view are the two presumptions that labor markets are basically competitive, at least in the long run, and firms are operated constantly by efficient use of technology and management. This framework assumed, there would only be room for trade unions as an impediment to competitiveness in labor markets and to efficiency in management.

In contrast with this traditional view of trade unions, a series of recent papers represented by Brown & Medoff[2], Freeman & Medoff[7] and Clark[3] have offered empirical analyses of the impact of trade unions on productivity or working conditions on the basis of another view focused on the political functioning of trade unions as voice institutions at workplaces. According to this view, trade unions could increase productivity and improve the workers' lot in unionized firms without causing the condition of workers in nonunion firms to deteriorate. This approach and the resultant findings should be noteworthy in the evaluation of the role of trade unions in society, because they give us the point of view that trade unions not only affect the distribution of the pie once made, but also enlarge the potential pie positively.

Trade unions in Japan are well-known to be enterprise-based and concentrated in larger firms. And, the impact of Japanese unions on working conditions and labor markets is commonly viewed to be weak, or rather negligible, and the attitudes of Japanese unions are viewed as cooperative with management, or rather near to being "company unions" (Galenson[8]).

On the other hand, when we see workers' productivity from the aspect of skill formation, promotion-from-within associated with on-the-job-training (OJT) seems to become more important in contemporary workshops (Doeringer & Piore [4] and Koike [13]). In Japan, internal promotion systems seem to prevail more widely and deeply than in the U.S. and European countries, particularly for blue-collar workers. OJT tends to develop firm-specific skills to some extent. In this situation, trade unions could raise the efficiency of skill formation through reducing quits and so on. In Japan, the levels of productivity and wages are likely to be higher in larger firms which are mostly unionized than in the less unionized smaller firms. This apparent phenomenon seems to be inconsistent with the common view that Japanese trade unionism is weak. The functioning of Japanese trade unions should be reexamined from this new viewpoint of unionism and from the aspect of skill formation.

This paper intends to estimate the effects of unions on productivity in Japanese manufacturing industries. The approach and method used are mostly based on that used by Brown & Medoff who estimated the effects in U.S. manufacturing industries. The modified production functions including unionization and labor-quality variables are estimated for two years 1973 and 1978 by using data of two-digit industries by firm size. The positive effect of unionization on productivity was obtained for 1978, holding technological and labor-quality variables constant. This approach using highly aggregated data leaves some ambiguous points when we interpret the findings obtained, but it is worthwile as a first step at least in Japan to examine the effect of unions on labor productivity.


1. THE RELATIONSHIPS BETWEEN UNIONIZATION AND PRODUCTIVITY

The analytical relationships between unions and labor productivity have been discussed in detail in Bok & Dunlop [1] , Brown & Medoff and Freeman & Medoff. Here, we only need to summarize the major possible channels on the effects of unions on productivity.

(1) Restrictive practices by unions
Restrictive practices such as "feather-bedding" or "make-work", are commonly considered to be evidence that union activities affected productivity negatively. These practices, by definition, are assum-ed to have negative effects. But the restrictive practices associat-ed with unions tend to be covered too much by media. Even in non-union firms, restrictive practices by worker groups on workshops might exist, though they are not revealed because they are likely to be concealed. Thus, it might not be so apparent as commonly expected whether the negative effects of restrictive practices in unionized firms are greater than those in nonunionized firms.

(2) Managerial responses to higher wages by unions
According to neoclassical economic analysis of the behavior of the firm, there are two ways for management to respond to higher wages which might be demanded by the monopoly power of unions. The first is to raise the capital-labor ratio, and the second is to hire higher-quality workers, until the value of the marginal product of labor is again equal to the wage. These responses make labor produc-tivity in unionized firms higher than otherwise. But the effects of unions on productivity will not be efficient for the total economy, because they could bring about inequality of productivity between union and nonunion sectors simply by allocating the work force to union sectors less than in the competitive labor market. Thus, these effects should be controlled if we want to investigate the following impact of unions on productivity.

(3) Trade unions as "collective voice"
According to Freeman & Medoff, trade unions are viewed as the politi-cal institution which collectively reveals the average preference of workers about working conditions and environments. They set the work rules, such as seniority and grievance systems by negotiating or consulting with management. Their activities could decrease the com-plaints and frustrations of workers, could mitigate the feelings of rivalry among workers and reduce the potentially arbitrary nature of

management authority. Thus these activities raise the morale and motivation of workers, promote cooperation and teaching among workers, and reduce quits. These effects could possibly contribute to raising worker productivity.

This organizational viewpoint has been almost ignored in traditional economic analysis. Traditional economics has exclusively emphasized the allocational efficiency through turnover, or exit in the labor market (Hirschman[11]and Freeman[6]). And it has assumed that there is no inefficiency within firms, or if inefficient firms existed, they could not survive against competitive pressure in the long run. Furthermore, the quality of labor is assumed to be almost completely homogeneous, and turnover costs for workers and firms are assumed to be negligible in the long run.

On the other hand, when we emphasize the organizational view point, it is to be assumed that there could be some inefficiency in the management of firms ("X-inefficiency" by Leibenstein[14] ), and the quality of labor is not homogeneous with firm-specific skills, so that turnover costs could not be ignored for workers and firms. In the following sections, we try to estimate these organizational effects controlling technological factors and the quality of labor associated with general skills as much as possible with existing data.

## 2. SPECIFICATION FOR ESTIMATION

According to Griliches [9], [10], and Brown & Medoff, we can investigate the effects of trade unions on productivity by estimating the production function modified to include unionization as one of the variables of "quality of labor".

We begin with a modified Cobb-Douglas type of production function,

$$Y = A \, K^a \, ( \, e \, H^c \, M \, )^b \,, \tag{1}$$

where Y = output, K = capital, H = hours worked, M = employees, all on a per-establishment basis. The variable e is the labor efficiency index, the parameter c is the elasticity of efficient labor with respect to hours worked, a and b are each the elasticities of output with respect to capital and labor in terms of efficiency unit.

We estimate the aggregate production function not for each industry, but for all manufacturing by using data of two-digit industries by firm size as samples, mainly because of the limits of sample size. In order to partially allow for the differences of parameter among industries, a is assumed to change linearly according to the capital-labor ratio, and industry dummy variables are used in constant terms.

Dividing both sides of (1) by M and taking natural logarithms gives

$$\ln(Y/M) = \ln A + a(1)\ln \, (K/M) + a(2)(\ln(K/M))^2 + b \, \ln \, e$$
$$+ \, bc \, \ln H - d \, \ln M, \tag{2}$$

where d equals a(1) + b - 1, and represents returns to scale with
respect to capital and employees. This type can also be considered
as one of the first approximations of CES production function (Kmenta
[12]) where a(2) is expected to be positive or negative as the elasticity of substitution is more or less than one.

The next step is to specify the labor efficiency index   e   so that
the factors of general quality of labor and unionization may be
included. Brown & Medoff constructed a quality adjustment factor by
using the coefficients of labor-quality factors such as sex, education and age in wage equations.  They assume wage differentials are
proportional to productivity differentials by factors of labor
quality, based upon the assumption of perfect competition in the
labor market.  As the latter assumption is not tenable in this
framework including unions, we would rather estimate directly these
effects of the labor-quality factors on productivity.

We can use the data on sex, education and age mainly as the variables representing general skills in the quality of labor.  We first
divide employees by sex, and then consider the differences of education and age only for male employees among industries.  Therefore,
the productivity differentials by sex represented by the female
fraction reflect different amounts of education and work experience
between male and female workers, if any, as well as the differences
of innate ability. The average age for male workers, particularly,
for production workers, is assumed to reflect work experience, and
their effects on productivity are assumed to be quadratic.

Assumed that there could be differences in the productivity of union
labor and nonunion labor, the effect of unionization on productivity
is measured by the coefficient of the fraction unionized, according
to Brown & Medoff.  We do not derive rigorously an equation of the
labor efficiency index, but using the appropriate first-order linear
approximations, we specify that by a linear form as

$$ln\ (e) = g(0) - g(1)(FEM) + g(2)(EDU) + g(3)(AGE)$$
$$- g(4)(AGE)^2 + g(5)(UNION), \qquad\qquad (3)$$

where FEM = the fraction of female employees.  EDU = the fraction of
male employees with higher education,  AGE = the average age for
male production workers,  UNION = the fraction unionized.

Replacing  ln (e) in (2) by (3), we can get the equation which can
be estimated given data on  Y/M, K/M, H, M, UNION, and other factors
of labor quality.  From that equation estimated, the effect of
unions on productivity acquired as the coefficient of the fraction
unionized, or

$$ln(Y/M)\ /\ ln(UNION) = bg(5) \qquad\qquad (4)$$

where we can interpret g(5) as the proportional differential in labor
efficiency of union workers, and  bg(5)  as the productivity differential of unionized establishments.  The mostly technological and
general labor-quality factors which could affect productivity being
held constant, this effect of unionization on productivity could be
considered to be due to the net effects of unions through organizational factors, though other interpretations could be possible.

## 3. DATA AND RESULTS

### A. Data

When production functions are estimated on a cross-section basis, regional data are usually used in related studies. But the regional data on the fraction unionized by two-digit industries are not available in Japan. Then, we estimate the production function for total manufacturing sector by using nationally average data of two-digit industries by firm size. The data on output, capital and employees are provided from the Census of Manufacturing by Enterprise (COME: Kōgyō Tōkei Hyō Kigyōhen), which is compiled every year by editing all data on establishments by the name of firm. The published data of this census are classified into at most 9 partitions by firm size for 20 employees and more for each industry. Furthermore, the data are divided by the type of firms which have one establishment or two and more. Then, we get about 260 cells as samples for estimation.

The net value added from COME is used as the output measure. Compared with the productivities among different industries, it is inevitable to use the productivity in terms of value added. Then, we have to assume that the variations in value added reflects mainly the variations in real output rather than that of prices.

We used the book value of physical capital stock from COME as the capital stock measure. It does not precisely reflect the real value of capital stock. Taking account of the different compositions of capital stock by the date of investment, "the recentness variable" (following Griliches) was examined in preliminary regressions, but it was excluded because this effect was negligible.

The number of average employees on an establishment basis, not those on a firm basis, is used from COME as the technological scale measure in production. From the technological viewpoint of production function, the unit of establishment will be more appropriate rather than the unit of firm which might have several plants in separate sites.

The data on hours worked, the fraction unionized and the factors of labor quality are obtained from the various sources published by the Ministry of Labor. But, the partitions by firm size in these data are fewer than in COME. The fewest partitions by firm size in these data are only three in the Basic Survey of Wage Structure (BSWS: Chingin Kōzō Kihon Chōsa), from which the data on average age and the fraction of higher education are taken. Usual analyses are done by aggregating other data into the fewest partitions among available data. But this procedure will decrease the sample size so much that regressions could not be effective. In this paper, we chose not to aggregate the data, but to allocate the same average figure to narrower partitions in a large partition. This method has the merit that the data from COME are effectively utilized, but has the demerit that the errors of measurement of coefficients might be underestimated in the data with fewer partitions such as the variables of age, education and so on.

We can obtain the number of union members of two-digit industries by firm size with 6 partitions from the Labor Union Basic Survey (Rōdo

Kumiai Kihon Chōsa), which is compiled from answers to the quetion-
naire sent to all union offices at the end of June every year by the
Ministry of Labor.  But the number of corresponding employees can
not be obtained from the same survey.  Then we use the number of
employees from COME as the denominator for estimating the fraction
unionized.  These figures tend to be overestimated particularly for
larger firms for the following two reasons.  First, the establishments covered by COME are confined to those in which certain goods
are produced, so that the offices and branches only for sales and
administration are not included in figures reported by union offices.
Second, the data on the number of employees in COME are that at the
end of December every year, which generally tends to be smaller than
that of June. Since there are no ways to modify the raw data, we use
these figure directly.  These errors of measurement are likely to
correlate positively with firm size, then, with the fraction unionized, so that the effects on coefficient estimated tend to be cancell-
ed out to some extent.  The data sources on hours worked and labor-
quality variables are shown in Table IV-1, as well as the other
mentioned.

We chose the two years of 1973 and 1978 as the period of estimation.
Labor productivity tends to change over business cycles, particularly with a decrease just after peak periods because of short-run
adjustment lags between output and employment.  The year of 1973 was
at mostly full operation until the first of the Oil Crisis began.
The year of 1978 was the period of recovery three years after the
severe recession in 1975.  The year of 1979 would be more suitable
than 1978, but the 1978 COME was the newest one available when our
research was done.  During 1975 and 1978, most of the large firms in
almost all indutries faced the "management crisis", and reduced
their employees. And, the labor market was much slacker in 1978 than
in 1973 (for example, the active openings ratio to active applicants
excluding school leavers was 1.76 in 1973, and 0.56 in 1978).  The
environment of industrial relations changed dramatically before and
after the Oil Crisis.  The possible impact of this change on the
union-productivity effect is one of our concerns in this research.

B. Results

Tables IV-2 and -3 present the estimates of production function for
1973 and 1978.  These regressions are estimated by the weighted
least squared method with the number of firms in each cell as weight.
The notations of variables are shown in Table IV-1.  Columns 1 in each
table is the regression including only technological or traditional
variables in production function.  In this column, and also in the
other column, the capital-employee ratio variable has the largest
explanation power judged from the t-value, and the coefficient of
$(\ln(K/M))^2$ is negative and significantly different from zero[1], which
implies that the rigorous Cobb-Douglas type is not appropriate in
this approach.  The coefficient of employees-per-establishment
variable is not significantly different from zero, which implies
that constant returns to scale hold in our sample.  We are not much
concerned with these coefficients, but these results seem not to be
inconsistent with those found in previous related studies.

The central interest in this analysis is the coefficient of the
fraction-unionized variable, which is added in col.2 in each table.
The coefficients of this variable are significantly different from
zero in both years.  At this stage, it suggests unions affect produc-

Table IV-1. Definitions of Variables and Data Sources

| Variables | Definitions | Data Sources |
|---|---|---|
| Yn/M | Net value added per employee (20 employees and more, 9 partitions) | Census of Manufactures by Size of Firm (Kōgyō Tōkei Hyō Kigyōhen: MITI) |
| K/M | Gross book value of capital stock per employee at the end of the year | ---- |
| M/EST | Employee per establishment | ---- |
| M/FRM | Employee per firm | ---- |
| HOUR | Average hours worked (by size of establishment) | Monthly Labor Survey (Maitsuki Kinrō Tōkei Chōsa: MOL) |
| UNION | The fraction of union members (by size of firm, 6 partitions | Labor Union Basic Survey (Rōdō Kumiai Kihon Chōsa: MOL) employees: Census of Manufactures |
| FEM | The fraction of female employees (by size of firm, 5 part.) | Survey of Employment Trends (Koyō Dōkō Chōsa: MOL) |
| EDU | The fraction of higher education attainers (14 schooling years and more) in male employees (by size of firm, 3 part.) | Basic Survey of Wage Structure (Chingin Kōzo Kihon Tōkei Chōsa: MOL) |
| AGE | Average age of male production workers (by size of firm, 3 part.) | ---- |

Table IV-2.   The Estimates of Production Function : Japanese
Manufacturing 1973 dependent variable :  ln Yn/M, case= 260

| Coefficients of | equations | | | | Mean |
|---|---|---|---|---|---|
| | (1) | (2) | (3) | (4) | [SD] |
| ln K/M | 0.613 | 0.572 | 0.541 | 0.509 | 0.356 |
| | (9.65) | (9.02) | (8.38) | (7.78) | [0.42] |
| $(\ln K/M)^2$ | -0.075 | -0.072 | -0.0654 | -0.0648 | 0.304 |
| | (3.21) | (3.16) | (2.85) | (2.86) | [0.57] |
| ln HOUR | -0.0015 | 0.117 | 0.296 | 0.302 | 0.117 |
| | (0.00) | (0.33) | (0.89) | (0.83) | [0.032] |
| ln M/EST | 0.014 | -0.014 | ---- | -0.0084 | 3.87 |
| | (1.22) | (0.99) | | (0.061) | [0.75] |
| ln M/FRM | ---- | ---- | 0.0058 | ---- | 3.95 |
| | | | (0.40) | | [0.89] |
| UNION | ---- | 0.213 | 0.151 | 0.052 | 0.132 |
| | | (3.34) | (1.90) | (0.73) | [0.15] |
| FEM | ---- | ---- | ---- | -0.445 | 0.405 |
| | | | | (3.15) | [0.17] |
| EDU | ---- | ---- | ---- | 0.754 | 0.094 |
| | | | | (2.96) | [0.05] |
| AGE | ---- | ---- | ---- | 0.046 | 36.5 |
| | | | | (1.43) | [3.85] |
| $(AGE)^2$ | ---- | ---- | ---- | -0.00074 | 1350 |
| | | | | (1.59) | [274] |
| Industry dummies | yes | yes | yes | yes | |
| $\bar{R}^2$ | 0.919 | 0.922 | 0.922 | 0.928 | |
| S | 0.0733 | 0.0718 | 0.0719 | 0.0691 | |

Note: The definitions of variables and data sources are shown in Table IV-1.
$\bar{R}^2$: coefficient of determinations modified by degree of freedom
S: standard error, ( ) : t value.
Equations are estimated by weighted least squares method in which the number
of firm is used as weighted factor.

Table IV-3.  The Estimates of Production Function :Japanese Manufacturing 1978 dependent variable : ln Yn/M case= 255

| Coefficients of | (1) | (2) | equations (3) | (4) | Mean [SD] |
|---|---|---|---|---|---|
| ln K/M | 0.646 (6.78) | 0.629 (6.99) | 0.520 (6.01) | 0.575 (6.51) | 1.39 [0.29] |
| $(\ln K/M)^2$ | -0.071 (2.42) | -0.083 (2.99) | -0.061 (2.26) | -0.067 (2.50) | 0.841 [0.85] |
| ln HOUR | -0.020 (0.06) | 0.326 (1.05) | 0.512 (1.70) | 0.683 (2.20) | 0.090 [0.033] |
| ln M/EST | 0.020 (1.46) | -0.030 (1.87) | ---- | -0.030 (1.94) | 3.77 [0.71] |
| ln M/FRM | ---- | ---- | 0.010 (0.64) | ---- | 3.85 [0.84] |
| UNION | ---- | 0.370 (5.45) | 0.256 (3.00) | 0.185 (2.26) | 0.123 [0.15] |
| FEM | ---- | ---- | ---- | 0.313 (1.78) | 0.413 [0.17] |
| EDU | ---- | ---- | ---- | 1.57 (3.67) | 0.116 [0.05] |
| AGE | ---- | ---- | ---- | 0.007 (0.82) | 39.0 [2.48] |
| $(AGE)^2$ | ---- | ---- | ---- | neg. | 1524 [195] |
| Industry dummies | yes | yes | yes | yes | |
| $\bar{R}^2$ | 0.926 | 0.934 | 0.938 | 0.939 | |
| S | 0.0792 | 0.0747 | 0.0723 | 0.0718 | |

Note: see note in Table IV-2.

tivity positively. But it might be viewed to reflect the effect of
firm size on productivity, because the fraction unionized is highly
positively correlated with firm size, and one of the common views in
Japan is that the larger firms apply more modernized and efficient
methods of management than the smaller firms. From col.3 in Table
IV-2 and -3, the coefficient of the firm size variable is not significantly differerent from zero, while the fraction-unionized
variable remains positively significant, though its coefficient is
smaller by about one-third than that in col.2. Therefore, we could
not say that the estimated effect of unions on productivity is not
the mere reflection of firm-size effect on productivity.

Next, column 4 includes the variables of general factors of labor
quality such as the female fraction, the fraction of higher education for male employees and the average age for male production
workers. The variables of the higher education-fraction and the
female fraction are so effective that the coefficient of the
fraction unionized turns out to be insignificantly different from
zero in 1973. In 1978, the coefficient of the fraction unionized
decreased by one-half from 0.370 to 0.185, but still remains significantly different from zero. These results reflect that a higher
quality of labor is likely to be considerably correlated with the
fraction unionized[2] (perhaps more correlated in Japan than that in
the U.S.[3]; cf. Brown & Medoff, p.368). The effect on productivity of
the higher labor quality induced by unions could be reflected by the
difference of the union-coefficient between columns (2) and (4).
The extent of this effect is sizable, and almost the same in both
years (-0.16 in 1973 and -0.18 in 1978). In Japan, workers, in
particular, with higher education tend to want to get jobs and to be
employed in larger firms, which are mostly unionized. It will not
be denied that this tendency might be due to higher wages and more
secure employment mainly brought about by union power.

In 1978, the effect of unionization on productivity even after controlling labor-quality variables is not negligible, which implies
that unionized establishments, other factors being held constant,
are less than 20 percent more productive than those that are not.[4]
This effect is thought to reflect the net effect of union activities
on productivity through organizational factors such as morale,
motivation and specific skill.

One question is why the union-productivity effect is not significant
in 1973, but significant in 1978. We can not give a definite answer
whether it is only a statistical coincidence or due to a substantial
change in the functioning of unions unless further research for
other years is undertaken. But the following hypothesis or interpretation could be given concerning this result from the viewpoint
of unions as a collective voice. The function of trade unions as a
collective voice is mainly to communicate collectively workers'
preferences to management, and reduce complaints among workers.
Whether this function is effective or not depends upon the extent of
potential complaints and the effectiveness of alternatives to re-
solve their complaints such as quitting. When the labor market is
tight, to leave one's job is rather easy because job opportunities
are more abundant, and workers have less complaints during prosperous times than during recession when layoffs and transfers within
firms occur frequently. Thus, union activities such as grievance
relay and negotiations with management would become more active and
effective during recession periods than at boom periods.

In Japan, since the Oil Crisis in 1973, many firms, in particular, the larger firms have experienced a "management crisis", and have made sizable layoffs and transfers among firms as well as within firms. Most trade unions in such firms have actively negotiated with management on the terms of layoffs, transfers and the compensation associated with them. In 1973, on the other hand, the labor market was very tight, and the increasing rate of consumers' prices was 11.7 percent per annuam, so that the unions' main concern was to gain higher real wages (the average rate of wage increase per annuam was about 20 percent in 1973, three times that of 1978), and strike activities were relatively higher than after 1976. These differences of labor markets and economic environments between 1973 and 1978 seem to provide one of the explanations for the different union-productivity effects estimated between the two years.


4. TRADE UNION, QUIT RATE AND PRODUCTIVITY

Our findings of a positive effect of unions on productivity can be interpreted in various ways (Brown & Medoff). The productivity measured by value added might reflect the effects of unions on product prices through cost-push, not on output productivity. There are no effective ways to separate physical productivity from price effect in comparisons of productivity levels between different industries. But the separation between quantity and price is potentially possible in terms of the changing rate of productivity and price. The effect of unions on the rate of productivity change will be another subject for future research. Here, we can only say that the rate of productivity increase has been higher and the rate of price increase rather lower in the sector of larger firms mostly unionized than in smaller firms less unionized in Japan during the past two decades.

The other interpretation is that since the variables of labor quality are not precise and limited, the fraction unionized might be a proxy variable of the unmeasurable quality of labor. More positively, if the mechanism by which productivity is improved by union activities could be isolated, our findings would be more persuasive. The ideas that unions make their workers more productive is mainly thought to be due to the unions' role as the "collective voice". The better unions reflect collectively workers' preferences about working conditions by negotiating and consulting with management, the less workers will have grievances and complaints (but the more workers might reveal complaints through unions), and the higher the morale and motivation for work, and the less workers will quit. Reduction of quits decreases the loss of firm-specific skills and separation. Even if workers dare not quit in spite of having complaints, they will not try to work carefully or to devise earnestly how to work (for example, QC circles). These things will affect worker productivity at workshops.

First, we will examine briefly the relationship between unionization and grievance systems or workers' complaints in a recent survey. Second, we will estimate the effect of quit rate on productivity instead of the fraction unionized.

A. Trade Unions and Workers' Grievances

Grievance systems or rules at workshops are not always connected to
trade unions. There are many nonunion firms which have consulting
committees or grievance systems between management and employee representatives as a management policy. These systems initiated by
management might be thought to be alternatives of mitigating workers'
complaints, or in part of reducing worker desire for unions. But
the countervailing or regulating power of their organizations against
management authority would be weaker in nonunion firms than in
unionized firms. Rather, such systems would work more effectively
in unionized firms than in nonunion firms.

The 1977 Survey on Communicaiton between Management and Workers conducted by the Ministry of Labor is one of the most reliable surveys
available. This survey depended on questionnaires sent to establishments with 100 employees and more selected by random sampling, and
to 20,000 workers within the establishments selected. According to
this survey, Figure IV-1 shows the extent of grievance systems
instituted by unionization and firm size. We can find that the
fraction of workers covered by grievance systems is higher in unionized firms than in nonunion firms in every size of firm, though the
larger firms tend to have them more frequently than smaller firms
whether or not they are unionized.

The survey, also, investigated to what extent the workers made
grievances and complaints about management, and the reasons for not
making them. Unfortunately, the data on these items are published
only by firm size, or by union and nonunion. According to Figure
IV-2 which is classified by unionization, the fraction of workers
who have made complaints during one year is 20 percent whether or
not they are covered by unions. But the fraction of workers who did
not make complaints for the reason that they had no particular
complaints is higher in workers covered by unions than those not
covered. Furthermore, the fraction of workers with potential complaints is likely to be higher in nonunion firms than in unionized
firms.

Figure IV-3 shows the same items by firm size. This figure shows
that the fraction of workers who made complaints decreases as firm
size becomes larger. And, workers in larger firms are likely to
have less complaints than those in smaller firms. These facts could
be explained by the management policies characterized by larger
firms, or the effects of trade unions. But taking into account the
high correlation between firm size and unionization in Japan, we can
not identify these apart from one another only with these limited
data.

In this survey, there was another item which asked workers through
which route they made complaints. The fraction of workers who used
the union route is shown by firm size in the same Figure IV-3. It
is noteworthy that this fraction is higher in smaller firms than in
larger firms mostly unionized, though most workers made complaints
directly through their supervisors in every firm size. These facts
show that the role of unions as voicing mechanisms worked effectively at least in medium or smaller firms, and in the mostly unionized
larger firms, their function is not explicitly revealed, but is not
rejected.

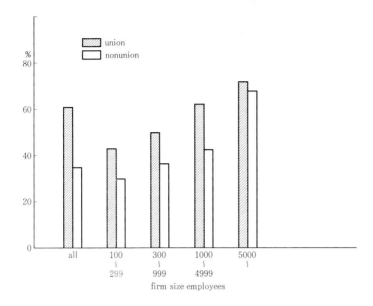

Source: <u>Survey</u> <u>on</u> <u>Communication</u> <u>Between</u> <u>Management</u> <u>and</u> <u>Workers</u>: 1977
(Rōshi Communication Chōsa, MOL) Part. 1, Table 43.

Figure IV-1.   The Extent of Grievance System Covered by Firm
Size and Unionization (the ratio of employees)

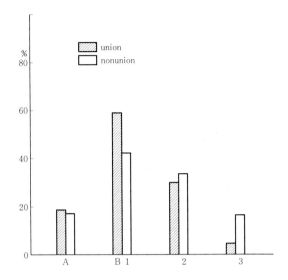

A. the fraction of persons who ever made complaints
   during past one year

B. the fraction of persons by the reasons why they did
   not make complaint:
   1. no particular complaint.
   2. expressing complaint was considered useless.
   3. the absence of formal grievance procedure.

Note: Ibid. Part 2, Table 20, 23.


Figure IV-2.  The Extent of Voice with Grievance and Complaints
             by Unionization (the ratio of employees)

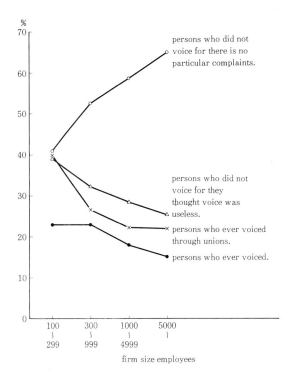

Note: Ibid. Part 2, Table 20, 21, 23.

Figure IV-3.   The Extent and Methods of Grievance
        by Firm Size (the ratio of employees)

B. The Effect of Quit Rate on Productivity

Brown & Medoff used the quit rate as the intervening variable which
connects unions and productivity in their regression analysis.  We,
also, wish to examine this effect in the same way.

The Survey on Employment Trends by MOL investigates the separation
rates by reasons, but it publishes the data only for two-digit
industries by aggregated firm size, or by firm size in the total
manufacturing sector.  The data, we can use, for the two-digit
industries by firm size is only the separation rate including quits,
layoffs and so on.  Then we estimate the quit rates for two-digit
industries by firm size in the following way.  The ratio of the
quits in separations for the ith industry by the jth firm size
(R(i,j)) is estimated by adding the difference of the ratio for the
ith industry (R(i))_and the ratio for the jth firm size (R(j)) from
the average ratio (R̄) for the total manufacturing sector.  Then, the
estimated quit rate (QUIT(i,j)) is obtained by multiplying the
separation rate (SEPA(i,j)) by the estimated ratio (R(i,j)) of
quits in separations; that is,

$$R(i,j) = (R(i) - \bar{R}) + (R(j) - \bar{R}) + \bar{R},$$

$$QUIT(i,j) = R(i,J)SEPA(i,j). \tag{5}$$

The separation rates and the quit ratios can be obtained for male or
female, and for temporarily contracted workers or workers whose
period of contract is not specified (i.e. roughly called "regular
workers").  Female workers tend to leave jobs mainly for the reasons
of marriage or child-bearing, but not usually because of discontent
at their workplaces.  Temporarily contracted workers tend to leave
jobs mainly for management reasons.  For the purpose of this analysis,
it  is desirable to limit the quit rate for male regular workers.

First, we will estimate the effect of trade unions on quit rates
averaged for 1975-1978.  According to Freeman[6], trade unions can
be expected to reduce quits through "monopoly routes" and "voice
routes". Since the effect of unions on wages is sizable and higher
wages are likely to reduce quits significantly, the monopoly-wage
route of impact must be controlled in empirical analyses seeking to
isolate the voice channels to concern.  As the variable of wage
rate, we use the annual hourly wage rate (W/MH) obtained from the
COME 1978, which is classified more finely by firm size than the
BSWS.  But these wages are averaged including female employees.  In
order to adjust the wage rate to that for male employees corresponding to the male quit rate, the fraction of female employees (FEM) is
included in the quit equations for "male" workers.

From the previous studies about quits, the other major determinants
of quits are education, age, the type of job, firm size, and the
type of industry.  In estimating quit equations, we can use the
same variables: UNION, EDU, FEM, AGE and ln M/FRM for 1978.  To
these variables, the fraction of nonproduction employees (NONP) is
added, which is obtained through the same sources as that of EDU and
AGE (see Table IV-1).

The columns 1, 2 and 3 in Table IV-4 are the quit equations of which
dependent variable is logarithm of the annual quit rate averaged
for 1975 to 1978.  Column 1 indicates that the unionized firms had
substantially lower quit rates than in nonunion firms when the
average hourly wage and other personal and job factors are held
constant.  Added industry dummy variables to column 1, column 2
shows that the coefficient of hourly wage rate turns out not to be

Table IV-4. Unions, Quits and Productivity 1978

| dependent variable | Mean [SD] | ln QUIT (case = 94) | | | ln Yn/M (case = 255) | |
|---|---|---|---|---|---|---|
| | | (1) | (2) | (3) | (4) | (5) |
| ln K/M | | | | | 0.549 (6.41) | 0.542 (6.28) |
| $(\ln K/M)^2$ | | | | | -0.066 (2.54) | -0.064 (2.45) |
| ln HOUR | | | | | 0.768 (2.53) | 0.769 (2.53) |
| ln M/EST | | | | | -0.019 (1.46) | -0.015 (0.94) |
| ln M/FRM | 3.87 [0.83] | ---- | ---- | 0.271 (4.30) | ---- | ---- |
| UNION | 0.122 [0.15] | -0.814 (4.60) | -1.16 (4.54) | -1.73 (6.56) | ---- | -0.063 (0.60) |
| FEM | 0.413 [0.17] | 0.029 (0.12) | 0.803 (1.48) | 0.495 (1.02) | -0.261 (1.58) | -0.285 (1.67) |
| EDU | 0.114 [0.05] | 1.92 (2.00) | 2.54 (1.41) | 4.17 (6.37) | 1.28 (3.01) | 1.28 (3.00) |
| AGE | 39.0 [2.46] | -0.052 (4.88) | -0.097 (3.66) | -0.085 (3.56) | -0.162 (0.20) | -0.381 (0.43) |
| NONP | 0.324 [0.094] | -2.14 (3.82) | -3.75 (3.14) | -4.14 (3.88) | ---- | ---- |
| ln QUIT | -2.37 [0.28] | ---- | ---- | ---- | -0.130 (4.33) | -0.063 (3.70) |
| ln W/MH | 0.564 [0.21] | -0.803 (4.60) | -0.248 (0.64) | -1.77 (3.57) | ---- | ---- |
| Industry summies | | no | yes | yes | yes | yes |
| $\bar{R}^2$ | | 0.669 | 0.786 | 0.830 | 0.942 | 0.942 |
| S | | 0.158 | 0.128 | 0.114 | 0.0698 | 0.0699 |

Note: QUIT: the annual average rate of quit for male regular workers from 1975 to 1978. NONP: the fraction of nonproduction employees. W/MH: the annual average hourly wage rate for all employees. The other variables are shown in Table IV-1 and the note in Table IV-2.

significantly different from zero, while the coefficient of the
fraction unionized remains to be stable. Furthermore, in column 3
including the variables of log firm-size, the coefficient of hourly
wage rate again becomes significantly negative, and the effect of
trade unions on quits becomes more significantly negative. Unexpectedly, the effect of firm size on quits is not negative but significantly positive. From these results, we could say that the effect
of trade unions on quits is likely to be relatively stronger than
that of wages and firm size.

Next, we will estimate the effect of quit rate on productivity,
holding other variables but the fraction unionized constant. The
column 4 in Table IV-4 indicates that this effect is significantly
negative. And, in column 5, the coefficient of the fraction-
unionized variables turns out not to be significantly different from
zero. This fact could be interpreted that unionization contributed
to the higher productivity exclusively by reducing quits. This is
contrasted with Brown & Medoff's finding that quit rate reduced the
effect of unions on productivity by only about one-fifth in the U.S.

One of other possible interpretations of the effect of quits on
productivity would be that quits might have been induced in the
industries which happened to be suffered from lower productivity for
various reasons. If this interpretation were true, quit rates would
be expected to be negatively correlated with the net increase of
employment and hiring rates, while positively correlated with layoff
rates. Among the industries by firm size for average rates during
1975 and 1978, however, quit rates were not at all correlated with
the net increase of employment (simple correlation coefficient:
-0.047), highly positively correlated with hiring rates (0.81), and
very little correlated with non-quit separation rates (0.17); quits
are not likely to have the role of labor allocation from the industries with lower productivity to those with higher productivity.
Therefore, lower productivity seems not to be a cause of higher
quits, but a result partly caused by higher quits.


5. CONCLUSIONS

Most of previous literature on the impact of trade unions on economic
variables had concerned with wages or distributive aspects, and they
were solely based on the hypothesis that trade unions have monopolistic  power for the supply of labor including dual monopolies.
Recent research such as Brown & Medoff and Freeman & Medoff has
investigated the effect of trade unions on productivity, separation
rates, and other working conditions from the viewpoint of the trade
unions as the "collective voice". From this point of view, trade
unions could potentially bring about positive productivity and
better working conditions not only into the unionized sector, but
also into the total economy. This approach is noteworthy in that
trade unions could positively enlarge the whole amount of the potential pie distributed, as well as the amount distributed to unionized workers. And, the research based on this view has had impact
by changing or modifying the common view that trade unions always
exist as impediments to efficiency in economies.

This paper tried to investigate the effect of trade unions on produc-

tivity based on this new view of trade unions in Japanese manufacturing industries. The analytical framework is almost entirely based
on Brown & Medoff who analyzed U.S. manufacturing industries. Using
data on two-digit industries and firm size, we estimated the modified production functions including unionization and labor-quality
factors as variables for 1973 and 1978. The main empirical findings
are the following. Controlling for technological differences such
as the capital-labor ratio and establishment size, we noted the
positive effect of unionization on productivity for both years.
But, when labor-quality factors such as sex, education and age were
included, this effect vanished in 1973, while still remained significantly positive in 1978, though this effect was decreased by one-
half. From these findings, we could not reject the kind of monopoly
effect that higher wages by trade unions attract more efficient
workers into the unionized sector, but we could find a positive
union-productivity effect due to other factors such as internal
organizational factors, i.e. morale, motivation and specific skill.
As an intervening variable between unions and productivity, we
examined the quit rate for regular male workers. We could get the
facts for 1978, which were compatible with the hypothesis that
unions would increase productivity by reducing quits.

Our evidence that unionism could increase productivity mainly by reducing quits due to the operation of unions as an institution of
collective voice, has the following implications for the functioning
of labor markets in Japan. It has been well-known that labor markets
in Japan consist of dual sectors usually divided by larger-scale
firms and smaller-scale firms. The former is characterized by
higher wages, higher productivity and stable employment, while the
latter is characterized by reverse phenomena. These characteristics
have tended to be explained mainly by relating to the peculiar
employment system so called "nenko (seniority based) system" or
"life time employment" in larger-scale firms. These view emphasizes
the management policies based on the unique culture in Japan, and
ignored the impact of trade unions which have prevailed in larger
firms. Since Japanese unions are mostly based on enterprise, but
not on craft or industry as western countries, the power of unions
has been presumed to be weak or negligible. But it seems not to be
evident. Rather, the dual structure in Japanese labor markets could
be viewed to correspond to the unionized sector and nonunion sector.
Once we assumed that the impact of unions on wages, productivity and
quits is not negligible in Japan, we could explain many phenomena
consistently by the common logic in western countries. It might be
the most applicable to Japan that "unionism is a major force in the
creation of a relatively permanent enterprise work force", as suggested by Freeman [6, p.671].

NOTES

* The first draft of this paper was presented at Rokko Symposium, Kobe in Japan on
July 26, 1982. I have benefited from discussions and comments from participants
there. Particularly, I am grateful to Richard B. Freemen, Harvard University, for
his detailed valuable comments.

---

[1] The significance criterion of coefficients is t-value larger than 1.97 at both sides of the 5 percent point. In the following, we only state "significant" in this criterion.

[2] The simple correlation between the fraction-unionized and the fraction of higher education is 0.48 and 0.51 each in 1973 and 1978. The correlation with the female fraction is -0.18 and -0.27 each in both years. The former is associated with the fraction-unionized more than the latter.

[3] Brown & Medoff estimated that the effect of unionization on productivity was about 24 percent in the U.S. manufacturing industry, the extent of which is likely to be higher than that in Japan. But the contribution of the labor quality index to productivity is likely to be lower than in this paper, and the correlation with the fraction-unionized, also, seems to be lower than that in Japan. This might be due to the indirect measure of labor quality by wage functions, or this might be due to the substantial differences of organizational forms in trade unions between the U.S. and Japan. Trade unions in the U.S. are organized almost only for blue-collar workers, and unionization for white-collar seems to be still lower, though is increasing recently. On the other hand, in Japan, trade unions are usually organized as a form including both workers within the same company.

[4] The effects on productivity of labor-quality factors such as sex, education and age are different between 1973 and 1978. In particular, the effect of education has sizably increased from 1973 to 1978. Although it might be important to explore the causes of these changes, these changes do not seem to be relevant to the effect of unions on productivity in 1978, because these changes were found in regressions excluding the fraction-unionized variable. It seems to be relevant to the union effect that the overall effect of unions has significantly increased from 1973 to 1978.

REFERENCES

[1] Bok, Derek C., and Dunlop, John T., Labor and the American Community, New York: Simon & Schuster, 1970.

[2] Brown, Charles and Medoff, James L., "Trade Unionism in the Production Process," Journal of Political Economy, June 1978, vol. 86, pp. 355-78.

[3] Clark, Kim B., "Unionization and Productivity: Micro-Econometric Evidence," Quarterly Journal of Economics, December 1980, vol. 95, pp.613-39.

[4] Doeringer, Peter B., and Piore, Michael J., Internal Labor Markets and Manpower Analysis, Lexington, Mass: Heath, 1971.

[5] Freeman, Richard B., "Individual Mobility and Union Voice in the Labor Markets," American Economic Review, May 1976, vol. 66, pp. 361-68.

[6] ---, "The Exit-Voice Tradeoff in the Labor Market: Unionism, Job Tenure, Quits, and Separations," Quarterly Journal of Economics, June 1980, vol. 94, pp. 643-73.

[7] Freeman, Richard B. and Medoff, James L., "The Two Faces of Unionism," Public Interest, winter 1979, pp. 69-93.

[8] Galenson,Walter with the collaboration of Odaka, Kōnosuke, "The Japanese Labor Market," in Patrik, H. and Rosovsky, H.eds., Asia's New Giant: How the Japanese Economy Works, Washington, D.C.:The Brookings Institution, 1976.

[9] Griliches, Zvi, "Production Functions in Manufacturing: Some Preliminary Results," in Brown, Murry ed., The Theory and Empirical Analysis of Production, New York: Nar. Bur. Econ. Res., 1967.

[10] ---, "Production Functions in Manufacturing: Some Additional Results," Southern Economic Journal, October 1968, vol. 35, pp. 151-56.

[11] Hirschman, A.O. Exit, Voice, and Loyalty   Cambridge, Mass.: Harvard Univ. Press, 1970.

[12] Kmenta, J., "On Estimation of the CES Production Function," International Economic Review, June 1967, vol. 8, pp. 180-89.

[13] Koike, Kazuo, Shokuba no Rōdōkumiai to Sanka-Rōshikankei no Nichibeihikaku- (Trade Unions and Participation on Workshops: the Comparisons in Industrial Relations between the U.S. and Japan), Tōkyō: Tōyōkeizai Shinpōsha, 1977.

[14] Leibenstein, Harvey, "Allocative Efficiency v.s. X-Efficiency," American Economic Review, June 1966, vol. 56, pp. 392-415.

THE ECONOMIC ANALYSIS OF THE JAPANESE FIRM
M. Aoki (editor)
© Elsevier Science Publishers B.V. (North-Holland), 1984

*COMMENTS ON II, III AND IV*

# DE-MYSTIFYING THE JAPANESE LABOR MARKETS

RICHARD B. FREEMAN

Japanese workers are lifetime employees of large Japanese firms.

Seniority dominates Japanese personnel practices whereas ability and mobility dominate the U.S. labor market.

Japanese trade unions have little in common with U.S. unions. Japanese unions are company unions and productivity-oriented whereas U.S. unions are industrial unions who reduce productivity.

Japan has a dual labor market structure, with a modern large firm sector and a small firm informal sector, unlike that in the U.S.

These are some of the broad generalities about the Japanese labor market prevalent in the United States. While some aspects of these statements are true, others are false. The three papers on the labor market go a long way to de-mystifying the Japanese labor market and to helping us understand the true differences between the Japanese situation and the American situation.

Tachibanaki asks the questions "how permanent is Japanese employment?" and finds that, yes, Japanese workers have greater job tenure than U.S. workers but that the reason "lies in the distribution of very short jobs particularly among the younger age groups" not so much in the mobility of older workers. 'Lifetime employment', defined as workers staying with the first employer they accept after school is limited to university graduates in large firms. Even here, however, there is an important proviso: large firms in Japan retire workers at 55 whereas those in the U.S. retire workers at 65. Since many older U.S. workers stay with their firm from 55 to 65, the result is that for older workers tenure is quite similar between the two countries. This point can be seen in Tachibanaki's Table III-4, which shows that Japanese male workers age 40-55, 55-64 and 65+ have essentially the same job tenure, whereas U.S. male workers in those age groups experience a striking increase in tenure from 11.8 to 18.3 years. At age 40-54 U.S. male workers have 61% the tenure of Japanese workers; at age 53-64 and 65+ they have 86% the tenure of Japanese workers.

Tachibanaki goes on to show that the effect of tenure on turnover is qualitatively similar between the U.S. and Japan. He finds turnover to drop with tenure both in aggregate and individual panel data. While there is an arbitrariness to the distinction between duration and occurrence dependent which he draws, particularly with this type of data, the rejection of the simple exponential (constant) hazard function is incontestable.

Granting greater increases in tenure among U.S. workers in the
older age group, similar declines in turnover with tenure in
earlier years, the real difference between the two labor markets
which emerges from this paper is in the high turnover/prevalence
of short term jobs in the U.S. compared to Japan.  In the American
context, the job-switching among the young is often explained
in terms of search behavior: looking for the good employee-employer
match.  While Tachibanaki's Table III-1 shows some desire for
job change among young less tenured Japanese workers, and his
Table III-6 shows that changers obtain greater increases in income
than no-changers, he offers no explanation for the striking **difference** between the extent to which young Americans and young Japanese
spend their early work years shopping for work.

What might underlie this difference in behavior?  One possibility
lies in the tenure-earnings profile in the two countries.  The
steeper is the tenure-earnings profiles the greater will be the
return to staying with an employer and the greater the potential
cost of job-shopping.  The observed steeper earnings profiles
in Japan may account for some of the differential in job-search
behavior, though of course, that raises questions about the reasons
for the steeper profiles (see Aoki's introduction for some discussion
of the development of the steep profiles in Japan).  Another possible
explanation relates to the dispersion of wages and personnel
practices.  If firms in the U.S. differ more in their pay and
practices than firms in Japan, U.S. workers will benefit more
from extensive search.  Yet another possibility is that the
education system and labor markets in Japan are more closely tied
together than is the case in the U.S.  Which if any of these
speculations may account for the observed difference should be
the subject of future work. [1]

The contribution of the Tachibanaki paper is to direct attention
at the behavior of young workers and the operation of the youth
labor market as the underlying cause of differences in the tenure
of U.S. and Japanese workers.

Koike's paper deals with the 'seniority dominates labor relations'
generalization.  It shows that, whereas seniority is more important
in wage determination in Japan than in the U.S., seniority is
less important in determination of jobs within a work shop.  In
the 79 workshops of Nippon Steel for which he has data, Koike
finds a large number have egalitarian rotation of jobs, either
regularly (16), irregularly (15) or partially (26).  By contrast
in the U.S. rotation is infrequent and seniority the key factor
in workers obtaining better jobs within a workshop.  Similarly
Koike notes that whereas U.S. workers are laid off in inverse
seniority, in the Japanese plants studied "workers older than
age fifty are the most vulnerable."  While early retirement in
the U.S. partially alters the seniority-layoff pattern for permanent
layoffs, Koike is certainly correct that the junior worker will
lose his job before the senior worker in times of slack demand.

Koike goes on to argue that egalitarian rotation produces a
different carreer pattern and breadth of company specific skills
in Japan than in the U.S. and suggests that this may underlie
some of the differences in worker attitudes toward technological
change and their commitment to the company.  Building on his
first-hand knowledge of the difference between the operation of
U.S. and Japanese workers at the shop floor, Koike concludes by

offerring a general 'human capital' specific skill interpretation
of differences between the labor markets which stresses the greater
importance of internal promotion and training in the Japanese
situtation.   This is a rich and valuable hypothesis which I hope
will be tested by succeeding scholars.

The contribution of a study of what <u>really</u> goes on at shop floors
to our understanding of differences between economies cannot be
overestimated.   Only by studies like Koike's are we likely to
develop new hypotheses, as he does, to explain the true differences
between the operation of internal labor markets.

Few myths have been more enduring or are more erroneous than the
view that U.S. and Japanese unionism are at opposite ends of the
spectrum, with vastly different institutional structures and
effects on firm performance.

To begin with, the generalization that U.S. unions are industrial
unions while Japanese unions are company unions is false.   It
is false because the backbone of American unionism is the <u>local</u>
union organized at a particular work site.   In contrast to European
unionism both U.S. and Japanese union structures are based on
units at the establishment or company level.[2]   U.S. collective
bargaining is not more centralized than Japanese collective
bargaining.   Indeed, to the extent that the Shunto 'Spring
Offensive' produces roughly similar changes in wages in Japan,
it may be that Japanese industrial relations is, in fact, more
centralized, at least on the wage side.[3]

Until the late 1960s and 1970s, any student of U.S.-Japanese labor
markets could point to the strength of public sector unionism
(SOHYO) in Japan and the absence of such unionism in the U.S.
as major differences between the two conuntries.   Indeed, in this
respect, Japan was similar to other OECD countries while the U.S.
stood out as the aberration.   With the growth of public sector
unionism in the U.S.[4] even this longstanding institutional difference
is no longer valid.

Muramatsu's study, which is directly comparable to studies of
the effect of trade unions on productivity in the United States,
yields such similar results to the U.S. studies, as to cast serious
doubt on the belief that Japanese and American unionism has starkly
different impacts on productivity.   Muramatsu finds that productivity
is higher in unionized than in nonunionized parts of Japanese
manufacturing in 1973 and in 1978, with however the 1973 union
productivity effect attributable in large part to the composition
of the work force whereas the larger 1978 union productivity
effect is attributable to differences in quit rates between union
and nonunion workers.   He also finds that, holidng wages fixed,
there is a significant "exit-voice" tradeoff in Japan: As in the
U.S., union workers quit less than nonunion workers paid the same
wages, and he attributes this to grievance systems and work
conditions.   The similarity of results with those for the  U.S.
has to impress the reader.[5]   Muramatus's broad conclusion that
"the dual structure in Japanese labor markets could be viewed
to correspond to the unionized and nonunion sector" in the U.S.
offers a striking reinterpretation of the traditional 'dual labor
market' story about Japan.

The power of Muramatsu's findings about the similarity between

the economic impacts of U.S. and Japanese unionism can perhaps
be seen by presenting his Table 4 (which has <u>no</u> country label)
to a typical U.S. labor economist, as I did recently at an NBER
Conference.  "Oh," said the economist, "You've run the quit and
productivity stuff on the latest (U.S.) census of manufacturing
and got the same results as Brown and Medoff."  Unless one is
told Table 4 refers to Japan, one could easily believe it comes
from regressions for the latest U.S. data.  The econometric
analyses of the union impact on productivity and quits in the
two countries yield findings that similar.

Does this mean that there are no substantive differences between
U.S. and Japanese unionism?

Of course not.  There are several important but often neglected
differences which I hope will receive attention in the future.
First is the striking difference in the unionization of white
collar workers in the two countries.  Whereas in the U.S. white
collar employees are rarely unionized in the private sector and
when they are, generally by different unions than are blue-collar
workers in the same establishment, in Japan, the company union
includes white-collor employees.  It would make a fascinating
study to analyze how these differences in composition of union
membership affect union policies and the outcomes of collective
bargaining.  On the one hand, one might expect smaller white
collar/blue collar wage and work condition differences in the
U.S., as blue collar unions use their strength to benefit only
blue-collar workers.  On the other hand, one might expect greater
mobility from union to management positions in Japan and hence
different attitudes toward internal company policies and
relationships.

A second important difference is in the extent of diversity of
labor management relations in the U.S. as compared to Japan.
American unions and relationships with management vary more
across industry and firms and plants within a firm than I believe
to be the case in Japan.  If, as noted earlier, the Spring Offensive
produces less dispersed wage settlements in Japan than in the
U.S.,  there is also less diversity in wage-setting.  It is
important that studies of U.S.-Japanese unionism deal with the
dispersion of labor relations and outcomes as well as with difference
that appear in averages.

Third are important differences in the <u>attitudes</u> of management
toward unionism and workers.  Aoki's analysis of Japanese mangement
as an arbitrator between the interests of shareholders and workers
differs strikingly from analyses of U.S. management, which show
managers increasingly opposed to unionism.  In the U.S. management
does not view itself as representing the interest of workers as
well as of shareholders.  In part because unionism reduces
profitability in American firms,[6] U.S. management has taken in
many instances a sharp adversarial position to unions.  Managment
views itself as representing shareholders and capital's interests,
not workers' interests.  To see whether different management
philosophies and attitudes in fact affect outcomes, it would be
extremely useful to have a set of comparative company studies
examining how Japanese firms operate in the U.S. environment and
how U.S. firms operate in the Japanese environment.

A theme running implicitly or explicitly through all of the papers on the labor market and the other papers at the Rokko Conference was the extent to which differences between the U.S. and Japanese economies reflects:

a) cultural/historical differences.

b) national adaptations to differing market incentives.

c) innovations in organizational practices which are, in fact, "superior".

The Tachibanaki, Koike, and Muramatsu papers indicate that too much stress has been placed on cultural-historical differences, that similarities in markets, and adaptations to economic incentives are quite important in understanding the differences between the U.S. and Japan, but leave open the possibility that some aspects of Japanese industrial relations may, indeed, prove superior to some aspects of American industrial relations and thus be worthy of adoption in the American context. They also leave open the possibility that some aspects of American industrial relations may prove superior and thus worthy of adoption in the Japanese context.

NOTES

[1] For a study of the youth market in the U.S. See R. Freeman and D. Wise, The Youth Labor Market Problem: Its Nature, Causes and Consequences, (NBER, Chicago 1982).

[2] See Martin Estey, The Unions, Structure, Development and Management (NY: Harcourt, Brace and World 1965).

[3] Grossman, H. and W.S. Haraf, "Shunto, Rational Expectations and Output Growth in Japan," NBER Working Paper No. 1444, draw macroeconomic implications from the Shunto method of synchronized wage settlements.

[4] See R. B. Freeman, "Public Sector Unionism Comes to America," NBER Working Paper, 1984.

[5] Among the modest differences: in Brown & Medoff and in later work in Freeman and Medoff, What Do Unions Do? (Basic Books, NY 1984), differences in quality of workers never account for all of the union productivity effect and only a quarter of the productivity effect in the U.S. is explicable by differences in turnover. At the same time, the U.S. studies show an increased productivity effect in the 1970s, comparable to that found in Muramatsu's work.

[6] R. Freeman, "Unions, Price-Cost Margin, and Returns to Capital," NBER Working Paper, No. 1164, 1983.

Part Two

PERSONAL SAVING AND
CORPORATE FINANCE

THE ECONOMIC ANALYSIS OF THE JAPANESE FIRM
M. Aoki (editor)
© Elsevier Science Publishers B.V. (North-Holland), 1984

# THE BONUS PAYMENT SYSTEM AND JAPANESE PERSONAL SAVINGS

TSUNEO ISHIKAWA
KAZUO UEDA

## 1. INTRODUCTION

In this paper we examine an oft posed conjecture that the institutional form of worker compensation called <u>bonus</u> in Japan is contributing significantly to a high personal savings rate by international standards (with the average of 20.0% during 1958-78). The only close statistical study, so far, addressing this specific question is that of Mizoguchi [20, Chapter 3].[1] By comparing the <u>Family Income</u> <u>and</u> <u>Expenditure</u> <u>Survey</u> (hereafter abbreviated as <u>FIES</u>) data on workers family households for various years Mizoguchi has found that the annual consumption expenditure of the households has a remarkably stable relationship with family head's regular income, the ratio being 1.2-1.3. Furthermore, even when households are decomposed into quintile groups by the size of income, this stability holds for each group except for the lowest quintile. He then argued that households' regular consumption habits are formed on the basis of family head's regular income, and consequently, an increase in the ratio of temporary income (including the incomes of other members of the household and bonus payments as the major parts) to the family head's income is bound to raise the rate of savings (see also Mizoguchi [22, Chapter III]).

In the present paper we will investigate this question from three different angles. First, we will make a detailed probe into the recent (time-series of) <u>FIES</u> cross-section data on worker husehlods which have become much richer since the time of Mizoguchi's study. Our main objective here is to obtain separate estimates for the marginal propensities to consume bonus income, on the one hand, and non-bonus income, on the other. Second, we shall make a time series analysis of a unique survey data <u>(Survey</u> <u>on</u> <u>the</u> <u>Movement</u> <u>of</u> <u>Consumption</u> prepared by the Economic Planning Agency) that contains data on households' expectation on bonus income. Using this data

and estimating the length of the planning horizon of households in
dispensing with the bonus income, we directly estimate the transitoriness, of the bonus income.  This task thus provides us with a
direct test of the permanent income-life cycle savings hypothesis.
Third, we evaluate the effect of the bonus payment system on
savings at the macro level. For this purpose, we have newly constructed aggregate time series data on bonus earnings for the period
1958-78, using the same data source as the data on employee compensation in the National Income Accounts.

The major conclusions that emerge from our study are as follows.
First, the permanent income-life cycle hypothesis does not seem to
apply to Japanese worker households.  They are not rational maximizing
economic agents.  This conclusion follows from our analyses of
both the survey data and the cross-section data.  Our data suggests
that households distinguish bonus earnings from the rest of their
income and regard them as a sort of buffer income, capable of
being dispensed with discretionarily.  Moreover, in the normal
years of stable growth, households seem to follow a conventional
rule of thumb that dictates saving about half of their bonus
income.  This interpretation, which we term the habit-buffer
income hypothesis, is a further elaboration of the viewpoint
implicitly held by Mizoguchi and recently explicitly stated by
Shinohara [26].

Second, in a quantitative dimension, the marginal propensity to
consume bonus income is significantly lower than that of non-bonus
income.  Studies at three different levels all point to the same
conclusion, that the marginal propensity to consume bonus income
is (except for the "turning point" years of 1975-6 as suggested by
the cross-section study) roughly one-half (0.5) whereas consumption
of regular wage income is 0.7.  This roughly twenty percent
difference in the marginal propensity to consume is the source of
quantitative effects of the bonus payment system on Japanese
personal savings.  We should, however, not exaggerate the quantitative
importance of this effect, for simple arithmetic would suggest
that its contribution to the aggregate personal savings rate would
not be more than a few percentage points.  Therefore, the cause of
internationally high personal savings rates yet remain an open
question. Our conclusion thus qualifies the intuitive suggestion
of the importance of the bonus effect so often made by Japanese

economists.[2]

The organization of the paper is as follows.  The following section presents an overview of the movement of the rate of personal savings and its relationship with the relative magnitude of bonus earnings in the aggregate wage income.  The cross-section analysis is presented in Section 3, while the time-series analysis of the survey data is presented in Section 4.  Section 5 gives the analysis of aggregate time-series data, together with the result of simulation concerning the quantitative effect of bonus income. Section 6 summarizes the implications of our analysis and also states various qualifications on our results.  Finally, the Data Appendix provides an account of our estimation procedure for aggregate bonus income series.

## 2.  MOVEMENT OF PERSONAL SAVINGS AND BONUS EARNINGS: AN OVERVEIW

Let us now turn to a brief overview of the movement of the personal savings rate  and its relationship with the share of bonus earnings in the aggregate employment income.  The basic personal savings concept employed here is identical with that of the <u>National Income Accounts</u> (hereafter abbreviated as NIA), namely the difference between personal disposable income and personal consumption, including expenditures on consumer durables.[3]  The period of study is 1958 through 1978, for which we have estimated the aggregate bonus income series.

Figure 1 summarily depicts the now familiar movement of the personal savings (S) over personal disposable income (DY) and the movement of various factors that have previously been suggested to explain the former.  We immediately notice that the personal savings rate series had a definite upward trend until the mid-1970's, starting from 14.8% in 1958, with distinctive rises in 1961 and during the four years 1973-76, reaching the peak of 25.2% in 1974.  Since 1975 it has been declining, and some more recent statistics suggest that by 1980 it had declined to a pre-1973 level.[4]

Out of numerous studies conducted in the past to explain (i) the very high personal savings ratio by international standards, and/or (ii) the trend increase in the rate of personal savings up till the mid-1970's, we have taken up the following four factors for examination.  They are: (a) the so-called "rate of growth"

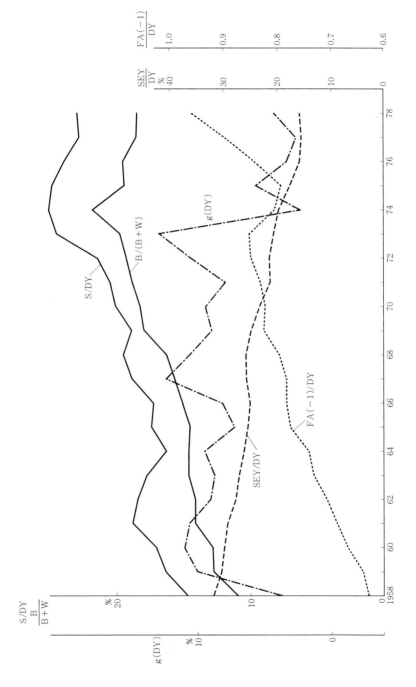

Figure V-1

effect (Ohkawa [24: 171-2]), (b) the importance of the self-
employed sector (Shinohara [25], Komiya [13], Mizoguchi [20]), (c)
the desired financial asset and stock adjustment effect (Mizoguchi
[21, Chapter 3]., [22, Chapter IV]), and (d) the effect of bonus
earnings (Komiya [13], Mizoguchi [20], Shinohara [26]).

Implicit in the rather vague terminology of the "rate of growth"
effect is the notion of habit persistence or of permanent income,
which produces lagged consumption responses to a growth in income.
This factor is represented in Figure 1 by the curve g(DY) which
expresses the annual rate of growth of real personal disposable
income (i.e., g(DY) = (DY-DY(-1))/DY(-1)).  Comparison of this
curve with the curve representing the rate of savings reveals two
particularly noteworthy features.

First, for years before 1974, it appears generally true that
acceleration in the growth of income resulted in a quick rise in
the savings rate, which is an observation consistent with many
theoretical hypotheses on savings, including the permanent income
hypothesis and the habit persistence hypothesis.  Yet when the
movements of the two series are contrasted more closely, we notice
that there exists a lagged response on the part of the savings
rate to the rate of growth of disposable income.  More specifically,
within the period of 1958-74, there are ten turning points in the
g(DY) curve.  However, in six cases out of ten, these points are
followed with a lag of one year by the turning points (in the same
direction) of the savings rate curve.  Thus, the relation between
the rate of growth of personal disposable income and the rate of
personal savings is not that simple.  Moreover, after 1974, there
no longer seems to be any correlation between the two.

Second, and more fundamentally, we must face the fact that any
good theory of Japanese personal savings ought to be able to
explain not only why they are high (query (i) above), but also why
they show a marked long-run increasing trend (query (ii) above) up
until 1974.  The view stressing merely the rate of growth effect
seems to fail on this ground, for even if we again disregard the
years after 1974 and concentrate on the period of rapid growth, no
clear trend in the rate of growth of personal disposable income in
discernible.  High average growth rates during this period may
very well explain high saving rates, yet they fail to explain
their trend increase.  We thus have two points of reservation on

the simple view stressing the rate of growth.

The last point applies even more to the second factor.  As Mizoguchi
[20, 21] has shown on the basis of FIES data self-employed households
(both agricultural and non-agricultural) do save more than worker
households, as expected.  Nevertheless, while it may partly answer
the above query (i), it certainly does not answer our query (ii).
The proportion of self-employed income (SEY) in personal disposable
income exhibits a continual decline from 32.1% in 1958 to 15.9% in
1978 (the scaling for this graph is given in the right-hand margin).

Concerning the third factor, we notice a clear positive trend in
the FA(-1)/DY curve, which expresses the ratio of beginning of the
year net financial assets of the indiviudal sector over the
currenct year personal disposable income, or for short, the net
financial wealth/income ratio.  This ratio fell down significantly
from the trend during 1974-6.  It has been suggested that: (a) in
the face of high growth rates in income a high rate of savings is
required just to maintain the net financial wealth/income ratio
intact (Mizoguchi [22, Chapter 3]), which is a straightforward
implication of the familiar Harrod-Domar formula, and (b) individuals
have a notion of the desired net financial wealth/income ratio and
that the Japanese economy is still undergoing a period of transition,
trying to reach a high target ratio (EPA, Annual Economic Report,
1970, as referred to by Mizoguchi, ibid.).  Clearly, if (b) were
actually the case, it would help in one way to answer our query
(ii).  Moreover, this hypothesis has another apparent appeal, the
off-trend rise in the rate of savings during 1973-76 corresponds
well with the off-trend decline in the net financial wealth/income
ratio during 1974-76, making the interpretation that the former
was caused by the latter conceivable. (Bank of Japan, op.cit.)
While this explanation is certainly suggestive, we must yet see if
it derives from a more basic hypothesis about indiviudals' consumption
behavior, or if it is a mere statistical correspondence.  Important
as it is, a careful analysis of this point is left beyond the
scope of the present paper.[5]

Now we come to the fourth factor, the effect of bonus earnings on
personal savings.  The graph B/(B+W) in Figure 1 depicts the
estimated ratio of bonus earnings B over total employee compensation
(B+W) in the NIA. (W will hereafter be referred to as the regular
wage income.)[6]  As we can see from the figure, the ratio of bonus

income over total earnings, or for short, the "bonus earnings
ratio" shows a steady upward trend until 1974, starting from 10.9%
in 1958, reaching 21.9% in 1974, and then declining to 18.5% in
1978. The average bonus earnings ratio during the entire sample
period turns out to be 16.6%.[7],[8] We immediately observe a high
correlation between the movement of the savings rate (S/DY) and
the bonus earnings ratio (B/(B+W)). Moreover, this high correlation
extends over the period after 1974. The simple correlation coefficient between these two variables is 0.92. This provides prima
facie evidence that the relative magnitude of bonus income in
total earnings might have a significant contribution in answering
our basic queries (i) and (ii). In fact, an aggregate consumption
function we estimate in Section 5 shows a positive and significant
effect of bonus income on savings.

The discerning readers, however, may still question that this
close correspondence might indeed be a spurious one, caused by a
high positive correlation between the bonus earnings ratio and the
rate of corporate profit (or the share of corporate profits in
national income), on the one hand, and a high positive correlation
between the latter and the rate of personal savings on the other.
However, this argument, while theoretically plausible, does not
turn out to be relevant in our case. In the first place, the
correlation coefficient between the share of (after-tax) corporate
profits in national income and the rate of personal savings turns
out to be -.57. In the second place, while the correlation coefficient between the share of the (after-tax) corporate profits
before bonuses are paid out and the bonus earnings ratio is 0.47,
indeed suggesting the presence of a profit sharing element[9], the
correlation coefficient between the (after-tax) corprate profits
(after bonuses are paid out) and the bonus earnings ratio is -.45
(For the source of these calculations, see Table 1.)

What then is the source of the close association between the rate
of personal savings and the bonus earnings ratio? Could we say
that the movement of the latter explains the former? Two familiar
theoretical explanations immediately come to mind. One is based
on the permanent income hypothesis. This hypothesis holds that
the propensity to consume permanent income is higher than that of
transitory income. Then, a rise in the proportion of transitory
income to total income will raise the rate of savings. An interpreta-

Table V-1    Bonus, Corporate Profits and Personal Savings

| Year | (1)<br>B/(B+W) | (2)<br>(P+B)/NY | (3)<br>P/NY | (4)<br>S/DY |
|------|------|------|------|------|
| 1958 | .109 | .114 | .0602 | .148 |
| 1959 | .127 | .123 | .0600 | .165 |
| 1960 | .129 | .153 | .0916 | .173 |
| 1961 | .142 | .155 | .0876 | .189 |
| 1962 | .141 | .146 | .0758 | .185 |
| 1963 | .146 | .140 | .0658 | .178 |
| 1964 | .146 | .145 | .0707 | .163 |
| 1965 | .145 | .130 | .0544 | .175 |
| 1966 | .151 | .145 | .0655 | .173 |
| 1967 | .156 | .159 | .0794 | .189 |
| 1968 | .162 | .174 | .0922 | .196 |
| 1969 | .180 | .182 | .0918 | .190 |
| 1970 | .182 | .190 | .0969 | .202 |
| 1971 | .189 | .183 | .0817 | .206 |
| 1972 | .193 | .175 | .0722 | .215 |
| 1973 | .198 | .154 | .0453 | .247 |
| 1974 | .219 | .124 | -.0046 | .252 |
| 1975 | .194 | .148 | .0332 | .249 |
| 1976 | .196 | .157 | .0407 | .241 |
| 1977 | .186 | .160 | .0465 | .229 |
| 1978 | .185 | .173 | .0628 | .230 |

Notes:  B = after-tax bonus income,    W = after-tax regular wage
                                              income,
        P = after-tax corporate
            profits,                   NY = national income,

        S = personal savings,          DY = disposable income.

        Column (1):  Bonus Earnings Ratio
        Column (2):  Share of After-Tax Corporate Profits
                     before Bonus Payment in National Income
        Column (3):  Share of After-Tax Corporate Profits
                     after Bonus Payment in National Income
        Column (4):  Average Personal Savings Ratio

Source: Calculated from National Income Account Series and Our
Estimates for Bonus Income Series. See also Table A2 in Data
Appendix.

tion of bonus effects on savings can therefore be proposed; it is
just this increase of transitory income that bonus earnings are
creating. The second is the habit persistence hypothesis. It
holds that, in the short-run, individuals' consumption patterns
are geared to historically formed habits, and it takes time to
adjust these habits to an increase in income. Furthermore, the
more temporary the nature of income increases are, the more slowly
(if ever) do they induce revision of consumption habits. Then,
just as in the case of the permanent income hypothesis, a rise in
the proportion of temporary income will raise the rate of savings.[10]

In order for these two hypotheses to be applicable to our context,
bonus incomes must fluctuate relatively more than regular components
of income, so that there are good reasons for them to be regarded
as either transitory or temporary in character. That this is in
fact the case can be shown at two levels; one at the aggregate
level and the other at an industry level. Table 2 below gives the
figures of growth rates for both the bonus and regular wage
income (real, per-capita) series, together with their means and
standard deviations. The standard testing procedure suggests that
the bonus income series exhibits significantly larger fluctuations
than regular wage components. The result is much more pronounced
when we look at the corresponding figures at an industry level.
Table 3 provides the means and standard deviations of the growth
rates of both income series by major industry and by size of
establishments. Also presented are the F-test statistics with
respect to the null hypothesis that both series have identical
variances against the alternative that one has a larger variance
than the other series. As we see from the table, except for the
utility industry for which we observe an opposite tendency (though
barely significant), there is a strong indication that bonus
income series fluctuate much more wildly than the regularly paid
counterparts even at a micro level.

What emerges from our following study, however, is neither the
permanent income hypothesis nor the habit persistence hypothesis
in its pure form. Our explanation is a modification of the latter,
and we name it the _habit buffer income hypothesis_. It holds that,
at least in the short-run, habitual spending rules govern induviduals'
consumption behavior. More specifically, we shall pose the following
to this working hypothesis.

Table V-2   Growth Rates of Aggregate
Regular Wage and Bonus Incomes
(Real and Per Capita)

| Year | Regular Wage | Bonus |
|------|------|------|
| 1959 | 5.9 (%) | 25.9 (%) |
| 1960 | 11.5 | 14.5 |
| 1961 | 10.1 | 20.5 |
| 1962 | 10.6 | 12.1 |
| 1963 | 7.8 | 9.1 |
| 1964 | 8.8 | 12.2 |
| 1965 | 7.1 | 5.2 |
| 1966 | 8.6 | 12.4 |
| 1967 | 9.1 | 15.3 |
| 1968 | 8.4 | 12.6 |
| 1969 | 7.7 | 21.3 |
| 1970 | 10.5 | 15.1 |
| 1971 | 7.8 | 9.8 |
| 1972 | 7.9 | 10.7 |
| 1973 | 8.3 | 13.9 |
| 1974 | 2.3 | 15.8 |
| 1975 | 7.2 | -7.9 |
| 1976 | 1.7 | 2.5 |
| 1977 | 4.8 | -1.3 |
| Mean | 7.7 (%) | 11.7 (%) |
| Std. Dev. | 2.6 | 7.7 |

Source: NIA and our own estimates of bonus income series.
Note: Growth rates for each year are calculated by comparing the
figures of the current year with those of the previous year.
The figures of each year are fiscal year. For institutional reasons
they reflect the sum of "summer" bonuses and "winter" bonuses of
each year more accurately than figures of the calendar year.
Real and per capita figures are obtained after an adjustment with
respect to consumer price index (base=1970) and number in the
population.

Table V-3  Fluctuations in the Growth Rates of Regular Wage and Bonus Earnings: By Industry and by Size of Establishment, 1959-1979; Real and After-Tax, per Regularly Employed Worker

(Establishment Size: 30 or more employees)

| Period | Mining | Construction | Manufacturing | Wholesale & Retail | Finance & Insurance | Transp. & Communic. | Utility | Service |
|---|---|---|---|---|---|---|---|---|
| **Regular Wage** | | | | | | | | |
| 1959-1979 | 4.70 (%) (3.78) | 5.18 (%) (2.43) | 4.86 (%) (3.98) | 4.70 (%) (5.96) | 4.13 (%) (2.87) | 4.43 (%) (2.99) | 4.26 (%) (5.47) | |
| 1959-1974 | 5.15 (3.31) | 5.83 (2.38) | 5.36 (4.11) | 5.51 (6.56) | 4.06 (2.84) | 5.14 (2.87) | 4.13 (4.80) | |
| 1975-1979 | 3.27 (5.19) | 3.18 (1.34) | 3.28 (3.41) | 2.10 (2.24) | 4.37 (3.29) | 2.18 (2.36) | 4.69 (4.69) | 4.45# (%) (4.17) |
| **Bonus Earnings** | | | | | | | | |
| 1959-1979 | 7.40 (11.13) | 7.49 (7.56) | 8.01 (9.08) | 7.35 (8.32) | 6.41 (4.20) | 6.97 (6.95) | 5.80 (4.86) | |
| 1959-1974 | 9.90 (11.09) | 8.30 (8.40) | 11.22 (6.65) | 9.73 (7.86) | 7.22 (4.37) | 9.25 (5.51) | 7.93 (3.13) | |
| 1975-1979 | -0.61 (7.30) | 4.91 (3.14) | -2.27 (8.56) | -0.27 (4.38) | 3.80 (2.32) | -0.33 (6.35) | -0.99 (2.37) | 3.97# (9.42) |
| **Test Statistic** | | | | | | | | |
| 1959-1979 | +8.67** | +9.68** | +5.20** | +1.95 | +2.14* | +5.40** | -1.27 | |
| 1959-1974 | +11.23** | +12.46** | +2.62* | +1.44 | +2.37 | +3.69** | -2.35 | |
| 1975-1979 | +1.98 | +5.49 | +6.30 | +3.82 | -2.01 | +7.24* | -11.20** | +5.10* |

Source: Maigetsu Kinro Tokei (Monthly Labor Statistics) and other sources.
Note: "Year" refers to fiscal year for the same reason as stated in Table 1. For service industry, the figures refer to the period 1972-79. Test Statistic refers to the ratio of variance between the two series. Test of var(g(B))=var(g(W)) against var(g(B)) > var(g(W)) is indicated by the symbol (+) in front of the number, whereas that against var(g(W)) < var(g(B)) is indicated by the symbol (-) in front. Rejection of the null hypothesis at a significance level of 5% is indicated by (*) and that at a significance level of 1% is indicated by (**). Standard deviations are in parentheses. (#: 1972-1979).

(Continued)

Table V-3　Fluctuations in the Growth Rates of Regular Wage and Bonus Earnings: By Industry and by Size of Establishment, 1959-1979; Real and After-Tax, per Regularly Employed Worker

(Establishment Size: 5-29 employees)

| Period | Mining | Construction | Manufacturing | Wholesale & Retail | Finance & Insurance | Transp. & Communic. | Utility | Service |
|---|---|---|---|---|---|---|---|---|
| **Regular Wage** | | | | | | | | |
| 1959-1979 | 6.52 (%) (5.26) | 5.78 (%) (3.54) | 6.05 (%) (3.05) | 5.56 (%) (4.56) | 5.29 (%) (3.47) | 4.91 (%) (3.82) | 4.52 (%) (5.78) | |
| 1959-1974 | 7.40 (3.76) | 6.87 (2.32) | 7.10 (2.65) | 6.67 (4.37) | 5.78 (3.57) | 5.08 (3.13) | 4.29 (6.12) | |
| 1975-1979 | 3.73 (8.54) | 2.30 (4.77) | 2.68 (1.23) | 2.01 (3.37) | 3.71 (2.92) | 4.38 (5.97) | 5.25 (5.03) | 5.41# (%) (5.23) |
| **Bonus Earnings** | | | | | | | | |
| 1959-1979 | 16.40 (25.82) | 9.13 (9.26) | 12.12 (11.22) | 9.39 (11.62) | 7.79 (7.47) | 6.76 (8.18) | 5.48 (6.27) | |
| 1959-1974 | 20.90 (25.80) | 12.36 (7.57) | 15.72 (10.15) | 12.43 (10.92) | 9.44 (7.74) | 9.06 (7.44) | 7.07 (6.24) | |
| 1975-1979 | 20.01 (22.26) | -1.18 (6.26) | 0.59 (4.99) | -0.31 (8.55) | 2.53 (2.97) | -0.58 (6.18) | 3.91 (2.87) | 4.69# (9.79) |
| **Test Statistic** | | | | | | | | |
| 1959-1979 | +24.10** | +6.84** | +13.53*** | +6.49** | +4.63** | +4.59** | +1.18 | |
| 1959-1974 | +47.08** | +10.65** | +14.67*** | +6.24*** | +4.70*** | +5.65** | +1.04 | |
| 1975-1979 | +6.79* | +1.72 | +16.46*** | +6.44* | +1.03 | +1.07 | -3.07 | +3.50 |

Source and Notes: See the previous page.

(i) Households hold a convention that stipulates them to save a certain proportion of their income, which may possibly differ for different income categories.

(ii) Househlods' consumption habits are a historical result of such conventional behaviour.

(iii) Bonus incomes are regarded by households as a very different kind of income from other parts of their income. Namely, they are a sort of buffer income that allows them to dispense with much more freely and discretionarily.

(iv) Under normal circumstances where the conventional mode of behavior defined in (i) satisfies the level dictated by the consumption habit, which in turn, is defined by (ii), bonus earnings are regarded as a convenient source of savings, and thus savings flow out at a higher rate than other parts of income.

That households conceive bonus income to be a convenient source of savings and the households follow a convention of assigning a fixed rate of savings on bonus income have been argued by Shinohara [26], which he termed the lump-sum income hypothesis, albeit on quite an intuitive basis. Our hypothesis can, in fact, be regarded as a further elaboration of his hypothesis, with ours having the qualifications (ii), (iii) and (iv). While in normal years of stable income growth the two hypotheses differ little, they become quite different (and, we argue, Shinohara's becoming unsuccessful) when the economy faces a major downward shock. This point becomes quite relevant when we try to interpret the experience of the major downturn period of 1974-76 (see the next section).

The similarity and dissimilarity between our hypothesis and the original Duesenberry-Modigliani-Brown habit persistence hypothesis can now be stated as follows. The similarity, of course, lies in that we accept already formed consumption habits to persist overtime, or put differently, we accept past consumption to have lasting influence on the present consumption. While accumulated savings would facilitate a source of buffer in the habit persistence world, we are, in effect, adding the current bonus income as an additional source of buffer to the list. On the other hand, we differ from the pure habit persistence world in not regarding savings as a totally passive residual, but rather allowing households to have some degree of "telescopic faculty" (albeit not in such

sophisticated form as in the permanent income hypothesis) and
allow this to participate in the formation of habit itself.

On the other hand, the crucial distinction between the permanent
income hypothesis and our hypothesis (and the habit persistence
hypothesis) lies in the former's emphasis on the households'
forecasting capacity and optimal intertemporal choice behavior.
One of our purposes in this paper is to test the validity of such
a presumption directly.


3.   CROSS SECTION ESTIMATES OF THE EFFECTS OF BONUS

One obvious way of evaluating the effect of bonus payments on
household savings is through the use of cross section data.
Detailed statistical data on composition of income and consumption
expenditure of workers households are available in Japan every
year since 1963 (for population sample covering the whole nation)
in the form of the Family Income and Expenditure Survey (FIES).
Of particular interest for our purposes are the data on households
that are simultaneously classified by levels of different income
categories.   Two such classification tables are compiled in the
FIES Annual Reports, one by level of household annual income, and
another, by level of household head's regular wage income.
Availability of the former table dates back to 1963, while that of
the latter only dates back to 1969.   In this section we will try
to extract as much information as possible from time series (over
the period of 1969-80) of these two bodies of data.[11]

The major limitations of our data are that they are only one-way
classification tables, and no cross classification or joint frequency
tables (not to mention individual household data) are available.
It is well known that simple cross section regresssons relying
solely on data from one-way tables are bound to give misleading
estimates (Haitovsky [8], Maddala [18: 268-274]).   In order to
overcome this limitation we must devise some method to extract
information on the joint distribution of two types of income.   The
basis of the method we propose to employ is the well-known empirical
fact that income distribution, when roughly the top and the bottom
10% are taken out, follows closely the lognormal distribution
(Aitchison and Brown [1], Lydall [17]).   This empirical law also
holds for our two series of data.

For illustrative purposes we have depicted in Figure 2 the plots
of cumulative income distribution on a lognormal probability paper
for three representative years (1970, 1975 and 1980). The plots
are done for both household head's regular wage income (expressed
by $\Delta$) and for total household income (expressed by $0$). The total
household income of each year follows the lognormal law quite
closely even toward the very bottom of the distribution. On the
other hand, the household head's regular wage income follows the
lognormal law in the range above the bottom 6-8 percentile of the
distribution. We notice that there is a mass of households with
none or very little household head regular wage income. In any
case, this finding suggests that we may regard the distribution of
these two types of income as approximately bivariate lognormal.

Model

In view of the nature of the income data discussed above we shall
now suppose that the household's regular income (W) and the household's total income (Y) of each year can be approximated by a
bivariate lognormal distribution such that:

$$(\text{Log } W, \ \log Y) \sim N(\mu, \ \Sigma) \tag{1}$$

where

$$\mu = (\mu_w, \ \mu_y), \qquad \Sigma = \begin{pmatrix} \sigma_{ww} & \sigma_{wy} \\ \sigma_{wy} & \sigma_{yy} \end{pmatrix}_{12}$$

Then by a well-known theorem on the normal distribution, the
conditional distribution of log Y (hereafter expressed by a
lower-case letter y) given log W (hereafter expressed by w) is
normal with

$$y \mid w \sim N(\mu_y + \frac{\sigma_{wy}}{\sigma_{ww}}(w - \mu_w), \ \sigma_{ww} - \frac{\sigma_{wy}^2}{\sigma_{yy}}) \tag{2}$$

while that of w given y is

$$w \mid y \sim N(\mu_w + \frac{\sigma_{wy}}{\sigma_{yy}}(y - \mu_y), \ \sigma_{yy} - \frac{\sigma_{wy}^2}{\sigma_{ww}}) \tag{3}$$

We observe that the expressions for the conditional means $E(y \mid w)$
and $E(w \mid y)$ in (2) and (3), correspond exactly to the manner in
which our one-way classification data are presented. Thus the
parameters of the lognormal distribution (1) are readily estimable

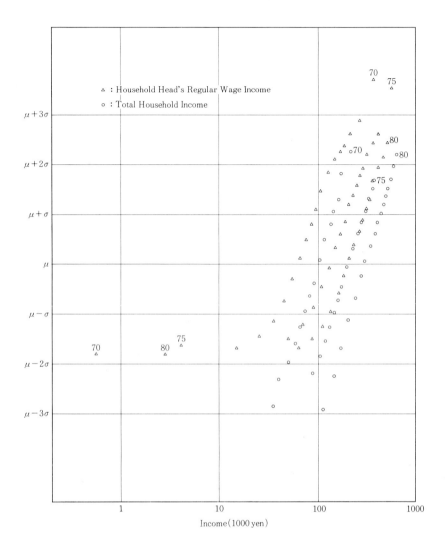

Figure  V-2

(up to a multiplicative constant); we discuss the method shortly.

We next assume that the consumption of a household unit is a function, common to all households, of household regular income (W) and the bonus income, to be denoted by B=Y-W. More specifically, we assume the following log-linear function

$$c = \alpha w + \beta x + \gamma \qquad (4)$$

where $c = \log C$, $x = \log\{1 + (B/W)\}$, and $\gamma = \log \overline{C}$.[13] Equivalently, it can be expressed by

$$c = \overline{C} W^{\alpha}\{1 + (B/W)\}^{\beta} = \overline{C} W^{\alpha-\beta}Y^{\beta} \qquad (4')$$

The meaning of this functional form can be summarized as follows: (i) the elasticity of consumption with respect to income with the proportion of bonus income remaining constant is $\alpha$; (ii) the (partial) elasticity of consumption with respect to income, $n_B (\equiv \frac{B}{C} \frac{\partial C}{\partial B})$ is (after simple algera) $\beta \cdot (B/Y)$ whereas that with respect regular income, $n_w (\equiv \frac{W}{C} \frac{\partial C}{\partial W})$ is $\alpha - \beta(B/Y)$; (iii) The average propensity to consume expressed by $C/Y = \overline{C} W^{\alpha-1}\{1+(B/Y)\}^{\beta-1}$ declines with the rise in the bonus income ratio (B/W) (Y being held constant) if $\alpha > \beta$. Thus the magnitude of $\beta$ is of central importance in the evaluation of the putative bonus effect on savings.

By noting the identitiy $x = y - w$, we can transform the equation (4) into

$$c = (\alpha - \beta)w + \beta y + \gamma \qquad (5).$$

However, since (w, y) is bivariately normally distributed, c (= log C) also becomes normally distributed, and the conditional distributions of c given w and c given y can also be deduced from the conditional distribution of y given w and w given y, respectively. In consequence, we have the following expressions for the conditional mean of consumption:

$$E(c|w) = (\alpha - \beta + \beta \cdot \frac{\sigma_{wy}}{\sigma_{ww}}) w + \beta(\mu_y - \frac{\sigma_{wy}}{\sigma_{ww}}\mu_w) + \gamma \qquad (6)$$

$$E(c|y) = (\beta + (\alpha - \beta) \cdot \frac{\sigma_{wy}}{\sigma_{yy}})y + (\alpha - \beta)(\mu_w - \frac{\sigma_{wy}}{\sigma_{yy}}) + \gamma \qquad (7)$$

With this form we are now able to confront the data available and
estimate the parameters of the consumption function.  An important
feature of our model is that yearly fluctuations of the distribution
of (W, Y) are corrected in the estimation process by substituting
the estimated values of the distribution parameters (done for
each year) into equations (4) and (5) as yearly shifting factors.

Data and Method of Estimation
The above discussion reduces to the following four estimating
equations.

$$y_1^{it} = \frac{\sigma_{wy}^{t}}{\sigma_{ww}^{t}} w_1^{it} + (\mu_y^{t} - \frac{\sigma_{wy}^{t}}{\sigma_{ww}^{t}}\mu_w^{t}) + u_1^{it} \tag{8}$$

$$w_2^{jt} = \frac{\sigma_{wy}^{r}}{\sigma_{yy}^{t}} y_2^{jt} + (\mu_w^{t} - \frac{\sigma_{wy}^{t}}{\sigma_{yy}^{t}}\mu_y^{t}) + u_2^{jt} \tag{9}$$

$$c_1^{jt} = \alpha^{t} z_{11}^{it} + \beta^{t} z_{12}^{it} + \gamma^{t} + v_1^{it} \tag{10}$$

$$c_2^{jt} = \alpha^{t} z_{21}^{jt} + \beta^{t} z_{22}^{jt} + \gamma^{t} + v_2^{jt} \tag{11}$$

where

$$z_{11}^{it} = w_1^{it},$$

$$z_{12}^{it} = (\mu_y^{t} - \frac{\sigma_{wy}^{t}}{\sigma_{ww}^{t}}\mu_w^{t}) + (\frac{\sigma_{wy}^{t}}{\sigma_{ww}^{t}} - 1)w_1^{it}$$

and

$$z_{21}^{it} = \frac{\sigma_{wy}^{t}}{\sigma_{yy}^{t}} y_2^{it} + (\mu_w^{t} - \frac{\sigma_{wy}^{t}}{\sigma_{ww}^{t}}\mu_y^{t})$$

$$z_{22}^{jt} = y_2^{jt} - z_{21}^{jt}$$

$(i=1,2, \ldots, i_t)$, $(j=1,2, \ldots, j_t)$, $t = 1969, \ldots, 1980$.

All variables that appear in the above equations are in natural
logarithms.  The variables with subscript 1 and superscript i
refer to observations provided by the table classified by W,
while those with subscript 2 and superscript j refer to observations

provided by the table classified by Y. The coefficients $\alpha, \beta$ and $\gamma$ of the consumption function carry a superscript t in order to allow for a possibility that household behavior might change from year to year. In view of the above discussion we have discarded certain observations which correspond to the bottom 6-8 percentile group in regular income and the very top 1 percentile group in both income categories. The chosen numbers of observations $i_t$ and $j_t$ for each year range from 12 to 15, and the total sum of $i_t$'s and $j_t$'s over the 1969-80 period is 339.[14] The final term in each equation is a random disturbance term that is assumed to be independently and identically distributed over different classification ranges (i,j) and time periods (t). In addition, we assume that the distribution of $v_1^{it}$ and $v_2^{jt}$ are identical.[15]

The procedure of estimation is as follows. First, we estimate the coefficients of equations (8) and (9), i.e., $(\sigma_{wv}^{t}/\sigma_{ww}^{t})$, $(\sigma_{wy}^{t}/\sigma_{yy}^{t})$, $(\mu_y^{t} - (\sigma_{wy}^{t}/\sigma_{ww}^{t})\mu_w^{t})$ and $(\mu_w^{t} - (\sigma_{wy}^{t}/\sigma_{yy}^{t})\mu_y^{t})$ for each year (t=1969, ..., 1980) by applying the ordinary least squares method to each equation. Second, we substitute the yearly point estimates of these coefficients into equations (10) and (11) (thus correcting for yearly changes in income distribution), and then obtain estimates for the coefficients $\alpha$, $\beta$ and $\gamma$ of these equations. Since equations (10) and (11) have exactly the same form (i.e., linear in parameters $\alpha$, $\beta$, and $\gamma$), and since, by assumption, disturbance terms $v_1^{it}$ and $v_2^{it}$ have identical forms of distribution, we can pool the two equations together, and estimate $\alpha$, $\beta$, $\gamma$'s by using ordinary least squares with the number of observations being $i_t + j_t$. All income variables used in the estimation process are real (deflated by consumer price index 1975=1.00) and adjusted for taxes and social security contributions.[16,17]

## Estimation Results

The results of estimating the parameters of the consumption function are given by Table 4 and 5.[18] Each table gives the estimates based on regressions carried out separately for each year. The difference between the two tables lies in that Table 4 refers to the case where the dependent variable, consumption, includes all durables, while Table 5 refers to the case where the dependent variable is non-durables consumption.

The features of the yearly estimates of the coefficients can be

Table V-4   Estimated Parameters of the Consumption Function, by Year, Consumption Expenditure Including Durables

| Year | $\hat{\gamma}=\log \overline{C}$ | $\hat{\alpha}$ | $\hat{\beta}$ | $(\alpha \hat{=} \beta)$ | s.e. /mean | SSR | # of observ. |
|------|------|------|------|------|------|------|------|
| 1969 | 1.632 (.293) | .853 (.025) | .536 (.211) | .317 (.217) | .0635 11.93 | .105 | 29 |
| 1970 | 1.958 (.190) | .824 (.016) | .554 (.097) | .270* (.102) | .0411 11.90 | .044 | 29 |
| 1971 | 2.060 (.150) | .812 (.013) | .778 (.105) | .034 (.108) | .0290 11.91 | .020 | 27 |
| 1972 | 2.523 (.236) | .775 (.021) | .638 (.136) | .138 (.145) | .0407 11.91 | .038 | 26 |
| 1973 | 1.946 (.223) | .829 (.019) | .471 (.129) | .358* (.137) | .0357 12.04 | .029 | 26 |
| 1974 | 1.361 (.571) | .853 (.051) | 1.420 (.291) | -.567 (.325) | .0776 11.91 | .138 | 26 |
| 1975 | .770 (.462) | .891 (.041) | 1.931 (.264) | -1.040** (.286) | .0821 11.98 | .182 | 30 |
| 1976 | 2.315 (.257) | .778 (.023) | 1.375 (.148) | -.597** (.174) | .0429 12.03 | .050 | 30 |
| 1977 | 2.553 (.286) | .775 (.025) | .597 (.147) | .178 (.162) | .0418 12.02 | .046 | 29 |
| 1978 | 2.556 (.219) | .773 (.020) | .610 (.118) | .163 (.132) | .0275 12.01 | .019 | 28 |
| 1979 | 1.496 (.305) | .871 (.027) | .193 (.165) | .678** (.186) | .0366 12.03 | .036 | 30 |
| 1980 | 1.942 (.239) | .829 (.021) | .481 (.136) | .348* (.146) | .0328 12.16 | .028 | 29 |

Note: Standard errors in parentheses. * indicates significance at 5% level, whereas ** indicates significance at 1% level (in Column 5).

Table V-5   Estimated Parameters of the Consumption Function, by Year, Consumption Expenditure Excluding Durables

| Year | $\hat{\gamma}=\log C$ | $\hat{\alpha}$ | $\hat{\beta}$ | $(\alpha \overset{\wedge}{-} \beta)$ | s.e. /mean | SSR | # of observ. |
|------|------|------|------|------|------|------|------|
| 1969 | 1.759 (.234) | .834 (.020) | .540 (.169) | .294 (.174) | .0507 11.84 | .067 | 29 |
| 1970 | 2.073 (.208) | .808 (.018) | .492 (.106) | .316** (.111) | .0449 11.81 | .053 | 29 |
| 1971 | 2.150 (.183) | .798 (.016) | .712 (.129) | .086 (.133) | .0355 11.81 | .030 | 27 |
| 1972 | 2.514 (.245) | .768 (.022) | .675 (.141) | .093 (.151) | .0422 11.82 | .041 | 26 |
| 1973 | 1.753 (.267) | .838 (.023) | .447 (.155) | .391* (.164) | .0428 11.95 | .042 | 26 |
| 1974 | 1.790 (.508) | .813 (.046) | 1.292 (.259) | -.479 (.289) | .0690 11.83 | .110 | 26 |
| 1975 | 1.258 (.428) | .846 (.038) | 1.867 (.245) | -1.021** (.265) | .0760 11.90 | .156 | 30 |
| 1976 | 2.544 (.288) | .754 (.025) | 1.284 (.166) | -.530** (.180) | .0480 11.95 | .062 | 30 |
| 1977 | 2.883 (.302) | .740 (.027) | .620 (.155) | .120 (.171) | .0442 11.94 | .051 | 29 |
| 1978 | 2.774 (.331) | .750 (.030) | .584 (.177) | .166 (.200) | .0415 11.93 | .043 | 28 |
| 1979 | 1.680 (.333) | .848 (.030) | .237 (.180) | .611** (.203) | .0399 11.95 | .043 | 30 |
| 1980 | 1.926 (.342) | .825 (.029) | .466 (.194) | .359 (.208) | .0468 12.08 | .057 | 29 |

Note: Standard errors in parentheses. * indicates significance at 5% level, whereas ** indicates significance at 1% level (in Column 5).

summarized as follows. First, the estimates of coefficient α are
relatively stable over years, all of them lying in between .77 and
.89 in the case of consumption including durables and between .74
and .85 in the case of non-durables.

Second, quite in contrast, the estimates of the coefficient β are
rather volatile over years. While the normal range of β (for
both consumption categories) seems to be .5- .6. there are
distinctive subset of years for which the actual estimates deviated
substantially from the seeming norm. 1974-76 is one such subset
of years, while 1979 is another. Curiously enough, these two sets
of years correspond to the years corresponding to the period of
(and the period immediately ensuing) the so-called first and
second oil crises. The direction of deviation in these two
periods are, however, just the opposite. While the estimate of β
for 1979 is quite low, the corresponding estimates go sky high
during the 1974-76 period.

Third, except for years 1974-76, the estimate of α is greater
than that of β, indicating the existence of an independent effect
of bonus payments on savings, as expected. However, as the last
column of Tables 4 and 5 show, the standard error of the estimate
of the differential (α-β) is also high, and only in four cases
out of nine (for which we find positive difference) do we find
(α-β) to be significantly different from 0.

Similarity of estimated coefficients over the period excluding
1974-76 suggests a possibility of pooling observations across
years. In fact, using the F-test on linear restrictions among
parameters, (taking the critical significance level to be 5%) we
have come to the following conclusion:

  (i) In the case of expenditures including durables, all non-
  1974-76 years can be pooled toghther; 1974-76 are distinctly
  different years from the rest, and cannot be pooled among
  themselves.

  (ii) In the case of non-durables expenditures, pooling of
  all non-1974-76 years is rejected; however, pooling of
  observations for 1969-73 and 1977-78, on the one hand, and
  pooling of those for 1979-80, on the other, are justified.
  Again, 1974-76 proved to be distinctly different from the
  rest, and cannot be pooled even among themselves.[19]

Statement (ii) confirms our casual grouping of estimation results into three subsets (except that 1980 is also to be considered in the same subset as the year 1979). We designate the first as normal years, the second, post-first oil-shock recession years (1974-76) and the third post-second oil shock years (1979-80). However, according to statement (i), the distinctiveness of the post-second oil shock years does not present itself clearly in the case of consumption including durables. In any case, the result of estimation under alternative way of pooling are presented in Table 6, together with the F-statistics. And, in view of the maxim not to pool observations too easily, we shall in the following discuss our result on the basis of pooling in a manner suggested in statement (ii) (namely, to pool the seven years 1969-73, 77-78 and the two years 1979-80 separately), which passes the test for both categories of consumption used in the regression. We shall continue to designate the same seven years as the normal years.

The major findings from Table 6 are as follows. First, for the period of normal years and for the post-second oil shock years (1979-80), $\beta$ is estimated to be significantly less than $\alpha$. This is the single most important evidence that households treat bonus income differently from other parts of income and that the bonus payment system exerts a positive effect on the savings of the worker households.

Second, the quantitative magnitude of this effect can perhaps more easily be ascertained by transforming these estimates into estimates of elasticities and marginal propensities to consume out of bonus and non-bonus incomes. This task is done in Table 7. For normal years, the figures in the table are calculated in the following manner. Since we know that the average bounus income ratio (i.e., after-tax bonus/disposable income ratio averaged over the sample) is 23.5% while the average propensity to consume disposable income (again over the sample) is 79.0%, the point estimate of the partial elasticity of consumption with respect to bonus income is $\hat{\eta}_B = (.519)(.235) = (.130)$. while the marginal propensity to consume bonus income (evaluated at the sample mean) is $MPC_B = (C/B)\hat{\eta}_B \equiv \{(C/Y)/(B/Y)\}\hat{\eta}_B = .437$. The corresponding figures for non-bonus income, i.e., W+T+R, are $\hat{\eta}_W = .821 - .130 = .685$, and $MPC_W$ (evaluated at the sample mean) = $\{C/(W+T+R)\}\hat{\eta}_W = (.790/.765)(.685) = .707$. Furthermore, the elasticity of consumption with respect to household disposable income when

Table V-6   Estimated Parameters of the Consumption Function, Pooled Regressions

| Period | Depend. Var. | $\hat{\gamma}=\log \bar{C}$ | $\hat{\alpha}$ | $\hat{\beta}$ | $(\alpha - \beta)$ | s.e. /mean | SSR | # of observ. | F-Statistic |
|---|---|---|---|---|---|---|---|---|---|
| 1969-73 & 1977-80 | C | 2.017 (.077) | .821 (.007) | .519 (.045) | .302** (.048) | .0412 11.99 | .423 | 253 | $F_{226}^{24}$ = 1.50 |
| | NDC | 2.048 (.086) | .812 (.008) | .479 (.050) | .333** (.054) | .0461 11.90 | .530 | 253 | $F_{226}^{24}$ = 2.27** |
| 1969-73 & 1977-78 | C | 2.082 (.086) | .815 (.008) | .552 (.050) | .263** (.053) | .0422 11.96 | .340 | 194 | $F_{173}^{18}$ = 1.25 |
| | NDC | 2.146 (.092) | .803 (.008) | .511 (.054) | .292** (.057) | .0449 11.87 | .386 | 194 | $F_{173}^{18}$ = 1.73 |
| 1979-80 | C | 1.773 (.185) | .845 (.016) | .365 (.102) | .480** (.113) | .0345 12.09 | .067 | 59 | $F_{53}^{3}$ = 0.77 |
| | NDC | 1.819 (.230) | .835 (.020) | .376 (.128) | .459** (.141) | .0431 12.02 | .104 | 59 | $F_{53}^{3}$ = 0.68 |
| 1974-76 | C | 1.412 (.265) | .847 (.023) | 1.558 (.147) | -.771** (.160) | .0759 11.98 | .479 | 86 | $F_{77}^{6}$ = 3.78** |
| | NDC | 1.767 (.253) | .813 (.022) | 1.447 (.140) | -.634** (.152) | .0724 11.90 | .435 | 86 | $F_{77}^{6}$ = 4.19** |

Note: Standard errors in parentheses. In Column 2, C designates expenditure including durables while NDC designates non-durables expenditure. In Columbs 6 and 10, * indicates statistical significance at 5% level, while ** indicates statistical significance at 1% level. In Column 10, statistical significance implies rejection of pooling observations.

Table V-7   Estimated Elasticities and Marginal Propensities to Consume Out of Different Components of Income

| Period | Bonus/ Income | Depend. Var. | Cons./ Income | $\eta_W$ | $\eta_B$ | $MPC_W$ | $MPC_B$ | $MPC_Y\vert_{B/W}$ |
|---|---|---|---|---|---|---|---|---|
| 1969–73 & | .235 | C | .790 | .685 | .130 | .707 | .437 | .644 |
| 1977–78 | | NDC | .734 | .683 | .120 | .655 | .375 | .589 |
| 1974 | .237 | C | .745 | .514 | .339 | .502 | 1.066 | .636 |
| | | NDC | .697 | .507 | .306 | .463 | .960 | .567 |
| 1975 | .220 | C | .749 | .466 | .425 | .448 | 1.447 | .667 |
| | | NDC | .706 | .435 | .411 | .394 | 1.319 | .597 |
| 1976 | .228 | C | .776 | .464 | .314 | .466 | 1.069 | .604 |
| | | NDC | .730 | .461 | .293 | .436 | .938 | .550 |
| 1979–80 | .221 | C | .781 | .764 | .081 | .766 | .286 | .660 |
| | | NDC | .739 | .752 | .083 | .713 | .278 | .617 |

Note: This table is constructed by using the point estimates of parameters in Tables 4–6, and using the mean characteristics of our samples for respective periods. "Income" referred to in Columns 2 and 4 of the table is the household disposable income. As in previous tables, C designates expenditures including durables and NDC designates non-durables expenditures.

the bonus income ratio remains constant, denoted by $\eta_Y\big|_{(B/W)}$, is .821. This implies the marginal propensity to consume (at the sample mean), $MPC_Y$, of (.790)(.823) = .644. Similar calculations are performed for other parts of the table. They show that during the normal years there is about 27% difference in terms of margianl propensity to consume (or 28% difference in the case of non-durables, both evaluated at the sample mean) between bonus and non-bonus incomes.

Third, for normal years the difference in consumption categories affects the estimate of β more than that of α. It suggests that expenditure on durables responds to bonus income much more than other parts of income, which confirms our intuition.

The question yet remaining is what happend in the "deviant" years, especially 1974-76. These are the first years of serious and long-lasting depression that this country experienced since the start of the rapid growth era. Simultaneously, these years mark an important turning point in the long-run behavior of Japanese personal savings. While the households' average savings rate reached its peak in 1974 and maintained its high level during 1975-76, the trend clearly began to decline. (See Figure 1. This feature is also true of FIES data on worker households.) What we observe from Tables 4-7 is, however, a wide deviation of micro from macro behavior, or else, a wide deviation of the marginal from the average behavior. The marginal propensity to consume bonus income (evaluated at the sample mean) is roughly two to three times that of the normal years.[20] It implies, ceteris paribus, that households with relatively high bonus income spent a lot, while those with relatively low bonus income saved a lot. And, as Figure 3 shows, since households with high bonus income are relatively more concentrated in the high disposable income class and vice versa, this tended to lower the savings rate of the upper  disposable income class, while raising that of the lower income class.

At any rate, this extremely high β coefficient or extremely high marginal propensity to consume bonus income seems to be the culprit in the now familiar paradox among Japanese economists that, during 1974 and 1975 (though more pronounced in 1975), the average rate of savings declined as annual income (Y) quintile rose, while the savings rate (in proportion to disposable income)

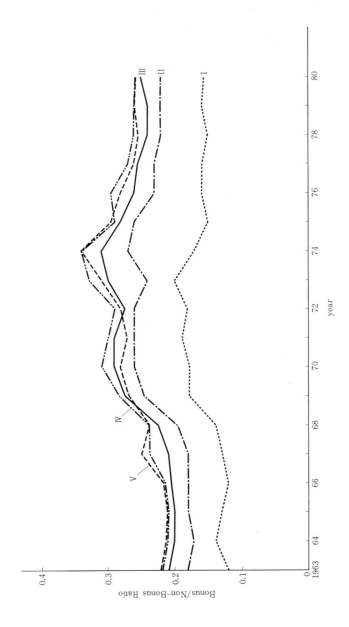

Figure V-3   Bonus/Non-Bonus Ratio of Annual Total Income Quintile-Groups

rose with quintiles of household head regular wage income (W).[21]
In fact, using the estimates for the coefficients of equations
(8) through (11), we can reconstruct the emergence of the paradox.
First, we note that the relationship between consumption and
disposable income as seen from the table classified by Y is
nothing but our equation (11), or its more formal equivalent (7).
On the other hand, the same relationship as seen from the table
classified by W can easily be derived by combining (8) and (10)
(or, equivalently, (6) and the expression for $E(y|w)$ in (3)).
Together, we have:

$$E(c|y) = \{\beta + (\alpha-\beta)S_2\}\cdot y + \{(\alpha-\beta)C_2 + \gamma\} \tag{12}$$

$$E(c\ w) = \{\beta + (\alpha-\beta)/S_2\}\cdot E(y|w) + \{\gamma - (\alpha-\beta)C_1/S_1\} \tag{13}$$

where

$$S_1 = (\sigma_{wy}/\sigma_{ww}), \qquad S_2 = (\sigma_{wy}/\sigma_{yy})$$

$$C_1 = \mu_y - \frac{\sigma_{wy}}{\sigma_{ww}}\mu_w \qquad C_2 = \mu_w - \frac{\sigma_{wy}}{\sigma_{yy}}\mu_y.$$

The fitted equations for each year of the 1974-76 period (using
our yearly estimates of parameters ($S_1$ $S_2$, $C_1$, $C_2$, $\alpha$, $\beta$, $\gamma$))
are given in Table 8. In this table, the estimated slope
coefficient being greater than 1 implies that the average savings
rate declines as income rises. It is then clear that our model
exactly reproduces the features of the savings paradox discussed
above: This feature is more prononunced in 1975, and disappears
in 1976. We also note that equations using non-durables expenditures
shows no paradox for 1974, but do so in 1975.[22,23]

We propose to interpret these abnormal phenomena as the working
of the 'ratchet' effect, or the historically formed consumption
habit asserting itself as in the habit persistence hypothesis,
puls the households' perception of bonus income as buffer income
which admits of discretionary allocation. More specifically, in
terms of our habit-buffer income hypothesis, they are construed
as a temporary deviation from the households' conventional spending
behavior in the face of a severe downward shock (i.e., a rapid
decline in the growth of real income and that use of bonus income
as buffer income maintains the level of expenditure dictated by

Table V-8  Reconstruction of the Savings Paradox

| Year | Table Referred | Expenditures Including Durables | Expenditure Excluding Durables |
|------|----------------|--------------------------------|-------------------------------|
| 1974 | Classified by Y | $c = 1.019\ y - .414$ | $c = .953\ y - .207$ |
|      | Classified by W | $c = .683\ y + 3.715$ | $c = .669\ y + 3.281$ |
| 1975 | Classified by Y | $c = 1.150\ y - 1.969$ | $c = 1.100\ y - 1.431$ |
|      | Classified by W | $c = .631\ y + 4.419$ | $c = .591\ y + 4.840$ |
| 1976 | Classified by Y | $c = .919\ y + .827$ | $c = .879\ y + 1.223$ |
|      | Classified by W | $c = .632\ y + 4.366$ | $c = .624\ y + 4.365$ |

Note: The variables in the equations are in natural logarithm. $(c, y)$ in upper equations of each entry refers to $E(c|y)$ and $y$, while $(c, y)$ in lower equations of each entry refers to $E(c|w)$ and $E(y|w)$. (Cf. equations (12) and (13) in the text.)
Source: Estimated Parameters for equations (8) – (11).

<u>consumption</u> <u>habit</u>.  (The reader is referred back to the conceptual
discussion at the end of Section 2.)  But because of the very
fact that spending of bonus income was largely a protective
measure and that the low savings rate of the upper income class
(with ample source of buffer income) was offset (and presumably
more than offset) by the high savings rate of the lower income
class, the aggregate savings rate did not have to drop sharply;
in fact, it achieved one of the highest levels in the history.
One immediate consequence of this is that we cannot interpret the
close aggregate relationship between the bonus/income ratio and
the personal savings rate observed in Figure 1 as a simple and
direct causal ralationship.  Although the hump in the bonus
income ratio around 1974-76 corresponded very well with the hump
in the personal savings rate of the same period, what went on
inside the <u>micro</u> world of the household was precisely the opposite.

Now we are left with an interpretation of the low estimates for
the years 1979-1980.  We propose to interpret this as a rather
normal response to the exogenous shock of the second oil crisis.
Where this shock differed from the first oil shock is that, by
this time, the economy had already adjusted, and households had
already adapted their consumption habits, to a slow rate of
growth, if not a prolonged stagnation.  Thus the second oil shock
did not have to trigger the buffer mechanism similar to that of
the 1974-76 period to protect the already-formed consumption
habits.  Rather, it acted to depress households' expectations
about the future, and thus to restrain their consumption.  The
households following our habit-buffer income hypothesis would
naturally choose to save a large proportion of their bonus income.

It now seems to be pertinent to comment on the works of earlier
writers.  Mizoguchi argued (based on a study of 1951-60) that
household consumption is very much geared to the household
head's regular wage income (with a remarkably stable ratio of 1.2
to 1.3), and that an increase in bonus payments does not systematically increase consumption, but rather increases savings. Although
this proportionality relationship largely continued to hold
throughout the 1960's, years since 1969 have witnessed a steady
decline in this ratio.  Hence, it is fair to say that the thrust
of Mizoguchi's argument has now lost its power.  We do, however,
share the basic spirit with Mizoguchi's argument (though implicit)

in that bonus income is regarded by households as a different source of income that allows them to decide allocation between consumption and savings discretionarily.

Shinohara's lump-sum income hypothesis, on the other hand, is in accord with our hypothesis for most of our period of study. But Shinohara's view clearly fails to explain the experience of 1974-76. This is the kind of pitfall one sometimes falls into if one looks only at the correlation of aggregate data series.

Incidentally, this pitfall can further be exploited to argue against the rationality of worker households. By concentrating on the observations of the 1970's some Japanese economists have found a negative association between corporate retained earnings and the personal savings at an aggregate level. Then they rather complacently accepted this to be evidence in favor of the 'substitution' or the 'ultra-rationality' hypothesis; that is, households substitute corporate savings for their own savings.[24] The negative correlation observed for the decade of 1970's, however, is very much a consequence of the striking contrast between relatively high personal savings (discussed just above), on the one hand, and the very low corporate profits, on the other, during the period 1974-76. Our present study clearly invalidates these economists' interpretations. In fact, since we know from the Family Savings Survey that the corporate share holding is concentrated in the upper income groups (e.g. in 1980, the top quintile group among worker households held 39.9% of all corporate stock held by the household sector (including self-employed households), and that these groups contain, with higher density, those households who received large bonus income and spent much on consumption during the 1974-76 period, what we actually have at the micro level is a positive, and not a negative, correlation between the corporate savings and personal savings. This is exactly opposite to what we see at the macro level.

## 4.　EVIDENCE FROM SURVEY DATA--A TEST OF THE PERMANENT INCOME HYPOTHESIS INTERPRETATION OF THE BONUS EFFECT ON SAVINGS

So far, we have pointed out that the system of bonus payments seems to exert strong positive effects on personal savings. However, we have not made clear the mechanism by which an increase

in bonus income increases savings.   In this section, we attempt
to shed some light on this point.   More specifically, we would
like to examine the plausibility of a permanent income life cycle
theory interpretation of the bonus effect on savings.   This
theory holds that a transitory increase in income is disbursed
over a long period of time and thus it increases consumption by a
smaller amount than a permanent increase in income.   Hence, if
bonus payments are regarded as a more transitory source of income
than others, an increase in the share of bonuses in total income
leads to an increase in the personal savings rate.

In order to test such a hypothesis we need to know the manner in
which consumers decompose income changes into permanent and
transitory components.   Usually, we make assumptions about the
process whereby consumers generate expectations of future income,
and then test the permanent income hypothesis (hereafter abbreviated
as PIH) jointly with these assumptions.   Recently we have witnessed
an increase in attempts to test the PIH jointly with the hypothesis
of rational expectations.[25]   Some have largely accepted the joint
hypothesis, while others have rejected it.   One difficulty with
such an approach is that a rejection of the joint hypothesis does
not by itself make clear which one of the two hypotheses is
responsible.

In this section we attempt to overcome this difficulty, at least
partially, by using survey data on expectations of future income.
We still have to assume something about the expectation formation
process of consumers. In that sense, results of our analysis
depends on the plausibility of such assumptions.   However, the
assumptions we shall be making are much less stringent than the
ones used in previous works.[26]   Thus, loosely speaking, we can
test the PIH almost independently of assumptions about expectations.
In addition, comparison of income expectations with actual incomes
enables us to test the hypothesis about income expectations.

Our major findings are:

(i) Expectations on bonuses do not satisfy restrictions
imposed by the rational expectation assumption.

(ii) The PIH is rejected; the propensities to consume out of
permanent and transitory bonus incomes are approximately the
same.

(iii) Nonetheless, the propensity to consume out of bonus income is very low--about 46% (irrespective of whether a bonus income is permanent or transitory).

The first two findings cast serious doubt about the permanent income-life cycle theory view that individuals are rational agents, maximizing interpemporal utility functions with expectations of future income reflecting all available information in an optimal manner. According to the first finding, individuals do not use all available information in forming expectations of future bonus payments. The second finding indicates that the distinction between permanent and transitory incomes is not a useful guide in determining current consumption, thus leading to a rejection of the framework in which individuals are forward-looking rational agents.

The third finding shows clearly that the system of bonus payments exerts significant effects on household savings. However, the explanation of the effects must be sought outside the realm of the permanent income-life cycle hypothesis. One possible interpretation of these results is the existence of a conventional spending rule whereby consumers assign a smaller propensity to consume to bonuses than other incomes.

## Specification

As stated above, our analysis focuses on the major theoretical implication of the PIH that the propensity to consume permanent income is higher than that of transitory income. In other words, if households are behaving under PIH, then they must be somehow decomposing the current bonus income (denoted by $B_t$) into a permanent component (denoted by $B_t^P$) and a transitory component (denoted by $B_T^{TR}$). An increase in the transitory component increases household's wealth (upon which consumption is based) less than an increase in the permanent component. Consequently, the propensity to consume out of $B^{TR}$ will be smaller than that out of $B^P$. And to the extent that $B^{TR}$ is larger relative to $B_t^P$, we obtain a strong contribution of bonus payments on personal savings.

The problem then is how households decompose income into two parts. We shall approach this problem by making an assumption that households suppose the permanent bonus income $B_t^P$ to follow a martingale process except for a constant linear time trend[27], and the transitory component $B_t^{TR}$ to be a serially uncorrelated random

noise with mean 0. Then $B_t$ is construed as the sum of these two
stochastic processes. After all, this seems to be a very natural
formalization of the concepts of permanent and transitory
incomes. Nevertheless, to the extent that the above involves a
certain behavioral assumption our study depends on the validity
of this conception.

Households under PIH (and LCH) determine their consumption on the
basis of their perceived wealth, which, in this case, is the
present value of present and expected future bonus income over
the households' time horizon of T periods. This present value,
which we denote by $V_t$, is formally expressed as:

$$V_t = B_t + \frac{E_t(B_{t+1})}{1+r} + \ldots + \frac{E_t(B_{t+T-1})}{(1+r)^{T-1}} \tag{14}$$

where $E_t(\cdot)$ expresses households' expectation as of time t, and
r is the real rate of interest.

We next rewrite (14) using our assumptions about $B_t$. From the
definition of $B^P$ and $B^{TR}$, we have

$$B_{t+s} = B_{t+s}^P + B_{t+s}^{TR} \qquad 1 \leq s \leq T - 1.$$

Then, the assumptions about the stochastic properties of $B^P$ and
$B^{TR}$ imply

$$E_t(B_{t+s}^{TR}) = 0$$

and

$$E_t(B_{t+s}^P) = B_t^P + \beta \cdot s \qquad 1 \leq s \leq T - 1$$

$$\left. \right\} \tag{15}$$

where $\beta$ ($\beta > 0$) expresses the linear growth trend. Using these to
rewrite (14), we obtain

$$V_t = \{\frac{1-(\frac{1}{1+r})^T}{1 - \frac{1}{1+r}}\}B_t^P + B_t^{TR}$$

$$+ \beta\{\frac{1}{r}\sum_{s=1}^{T-1}(\frac{1}{1+r})^{s-1}(1 - (\frac{1}{1+r})^{T-s})\}. \tag{16}$$

Let us now suppose more specifically that consumption of bonus income, denoted by $C_t$, is determined as k $(0 < k \leq 1)$ times the annuitized value of this "perceived bonus wealth" plus a random component (corresponding to transitory comsumption). That is,

$$C_t = k\{B_t^P + g(r, T) B_t^{TR} + \beta f(r, T)\} + u_t \tag{17}$$

where

$$g(r, T) = \frac{1 - \frac{1}{1+r}}{1 - (\frac{1}{1+r})^T} \tag{18}$$

denotes the appropriate annuitization factor,

$$f(r, T) = g(r, T)\left\{\frac{1}{r}\sum_{s=1}^{T-1}(\frac{1}{1+r})^{s-1}(1 - \frac{1}{1+r})^{T-s}\right\},$$

and $u_t$ is a random term with mean zero.

Perhaps a word of explanation is necessary for the notion of 'comsumption of bonus income'. For a _rational_ household, total consumption is a function of total perceived wealth, and, in general, no parts of consumption are earmarked to particular categories of income. However, under the Friedman-type proportional consumption function adopted here (which assumes homotheticity of utility function in the background), households can unambiguously trace consumption of 'bonus wealth', and moreover, it is independent of other parts of their perceived wealth. This is what we have as our $C_t$ here.[28]

In terms of equation (17), the essence of the PIH is that the coefficient $g(r, T)$ is significantly less than unity. In fact, so long as T > 2 (i.e., so long as households are forwardlooking) we can see from (18) that $g(r, T) < 1$ and, as $T \to \infty$, $g(r, T) \to r/(1+r)$.

We now come back to the important question of how individuals divide $B_t$ into $B_t^P$ and $B_t^{TR}$. Note that our foregoing assumptions about the stochastic properites are not, by themselves, sufficient to yield information about how, in fact, households estimate the realized values of $B_t^P$ and $B_t^{TR}$ after the realized value of $B_t$ is observed. Usually, we specify the information set possessed by households at each moment in time and determine the breakdown of

$B_t$ into $B_t^P$ and $B_t^{TR}$. Fortunately, however, our survey questionnaire gives direct data on households' expected bonus income for the next period, or $E_t(B_{t+1})$ to use the above notation. As we now show, we can use this data to infer $B_t^P$ and $B_t^{TR}$. From the martingale property,

$$E_t(B_{t+1}) = \beta + B_t^P \tag{19}$$

and from the identity

$$B_t = B_t^P + B_t^{TR}$$

we have

$$B_t^{TR} = B_t - (E_t(B_{T+1}) - \beta). \tag{20}$$

By substitutiong (19) and (20) into (17), we obtain the final estimating equation:

$$C_t = kE_t(B_{t+1}) + kg(r, T)(B_t - E_t(B_{t+1})) + \bar{C}' + u_t \tag{21}$$

where $\bar{C}'$ is a constant term relating to the trend factor.

We can now confront the model with the data, and test the validity of PIH. We do so by estimating (21) and seeing whether or not $g(r, T)$ is significantly less than 1. If indeed it turns out to be smaller than 1, households' behavior is consistent with PIH. On the other hand, if $g(r, T)$ is equal to 1, then households are in effect determining 'today's consumption on the basis of 'today's income only; hence, PIH is rejected.

Data

The Survey of Movements in Consumption (Shohi Doko-Chosa) has published answers to questionnaires on expected bonus income for each half year (i.e., before the 'summer bonus' or 'winter bonus' time). They ask worker households (the sample size averages roughly 5000 households) ahead of time as to what level of bonus income they expect to receive and what fraction of the income they plan to spend. After bonuses have been paid, they ask what the actual level of bonus income and consumption out of them[29] had been. Such data are available from 1966 to the first half of 1973 and then from 1976 to 1981.[30]

Thus, the time unit of analysis is one half year. We interpret the data as individuals reporting $E_{t-1}(B_t)$ and $E_{t-1}(C_t)$ right before bonus periods and $B_t$ and $C_t$ after bonuses have been paid.[31]

Before we estimate equation (20), let us digress for a moment to examine the properties of the expectations series $E_{t-1}(B_t)$. In particular, let us briefly discuss whether or not the bonus expectations satisfy the rational expectations assumption in view of the widespread use of it in recent literature. As many users of survey data have done[32], we estimate the following equation:

$$B_t = \alpha + \beta E_{t-1}(B_t) + \varepsilon_t \tag{22}$$

If expectations are rational, $\alpha$ should be equal to zero, $\beta$ to one and $\varepsilon_t$ should be serially uncorrelated. The result is the following:

$$B_t = \underset{(.0972)(.0381)}{.321 + .911} E_{t-1}(B_t)$$

$$R^2 = .961, \ D.W. = 1.51.\text{[33]}$$

Thus, all three of the restrictions the rational expectations assumption imposes are rejected. People tend to underestimate bonus payments; errors in expectations are (although mildly) serially correlated. This result indicates at least the danger of using the rational expectations assumption in the analysis of the consumption function.

Of course, in our case we do not have to assume anything strong about expectations, thanks to the availability of the survey data.

Estimation Results

Preliminaly estimations indicated taht there is a serial correlation in the error term of equation (20). Consequently, the error term was assumed to follow a first order autoregressive process and the equation was estimated using nonlinear least squares.[34] The estimation result is shown in Table 9.

Table V-9  Estimated Parameters of
Consumption Function

| $\hat{k}$ | $\hat{g}$ | $\hat{\bar{C}}'$ | $\hat{\rho}$ | s.e. | mean of $C_t$ |
|---|---|---|---|---|---|
| .460 | .941 | .0534 | .626 | .0655 | 1.32 |
| (.0528) | (.0661) | (.0607) | (.206) | | |

* s.e. is the standard error of the regression.
* standard errors are in parenthesis.
* $\hat{\rho}$ is the estimated first order serial correlation coefficient.

First, the table shows that g is not significantly different from
one.  Hence, the PIH is rejected.  In other words, the average
time horizon of worker households is about one half year.  This
means that the distinction between permanent and transitory
income does not play a major role in the behavior of these worker
households.

Second, the propensity to consume bonuses, irrespective of whether
a bonus income is permanent or transitory, is about .46 and is
quite low.  Thus, households do save a lot of their bonus income,
but this effect does not come from the transitoriness of bonus
income, nor the type of household behavior hypothesized by the
life-cycle theory.

One conceivable explanation of our results is, as stated in
earlier sections, that consumers have formed a "habit", accordingly
they save large amount from bonus income than other income;
moreover, at least in the short run (and in normal times), they
do not adjust this habit to changes in the stochastic nature of
bonus payments.  The consumption function estimated here has
become quite similar to the usual Keynesian consumption function
in which the major determinant of current consumption is current
income.  But ours differs from the Keynesian formulation in that
current consumption not only depends on current income, but also
on the breakdown of income into bonus and non-bonus income.[35]  Our
next task would be to explore in depth the historical circumstances
that led to the formation of such a habit and the possibility of

changes in the habit as economic environments surrounding individuals evolve over time. But this is left beyond the scope of the present work.

## 5. THE EFFECT OF BONUS INCOME ON SAVINGS AT THE MACRO LEVEL

In the previous two sections we analyzed households' saving behavior using micro-data and survey data which cover only a fraction of the total households. In this section we turn to macro-data and study the major determinants of aggregate savings of the household sector. This is important because there are many interesting macroeconomic problems directly or indirectly related to the behavior of aggregate savings. Of course, movements of aggregate savings are a reflection of savings behavior at the micro-level. Thus, analysis of worker households might give a reasonable first order approximation of aggregate savings behavior. However, the ratio of non-worker households to total households is still more than 30%; hence, if these households behaved differently from worker households, we would still need an analysis of aggregate savings.[36]

For these reasons we shall estimate a simple aggregative consumption function in this section in order to obtain a rough idea about the determinants of aggregate consumption and the quantitative significance of each. The specification of the consumption function will include most of the variables that were discussed in Section 2. We are especially interested in studying the extent to which the bonus system has increased saving. Thus, in the last part of the section, we shall carry out a simulation which will show clearly the effects of bonuses on saving.

### Specification

Following the discussion in Section 2, we specify an aggregate consumption function as follows:

$$C_t = \alpha_0 + \alpha_1 A_t + \alpha_2 W_t + \alpha_3 B_t + \alpha_4 S_t + u_t. \tag{23}$$

The notations mean $C_t$, aggregate consumption; $A_t$, financial wealth; $W_t$, regularly paid wages; $S_t$, income of the self-employed; $u_t$, error term uncorrelated with included right hand side variables. All variables are deflated by the consumers' price index.

Several aspects of the specification call for an explanation.
First, we have not followed the usual practice of using distributed
lag formulation of income variables.  Such a practice is often
justified by lagged adjustments of expectations or consumption
habits.  However, our analysis in Section 4 indicated that, at
least in the case of bonuses, current income is the major determinant
of current consumption.  Also, specifications that included
lagged consumption terms in equation (24) (in order to introduce,
roughly, the effects of adjustment lags) either did not lead to
major changes in estimates or produced unreasonable results.
Consequently, we decided to use only current income variables in
the equation.

Second, income variables appear separately in the equation.  This
is to allow for differences among propensities to consume from
various income sources.  It would be hard to believe that the
estimate of .460 we obtained for the propensity to consume bonus
income in Section 4 applies to all income sources.

The wealth variable represents income from assets.  As discussed
in Section 2, this variable played an important role in some
previous work in explaining large increases in the savings rate
in the mid 1970's. Our specification attempts to estimate the
significance of such an effect along with other effects.

Data and Estimation Result
The period of study is 1958 to 1978 on a semi-annual basis.  This
choice of time reflects our conclusion in Section 4 that the
average time horizon of households is one half year.  Aggregate
bonus earnings were estimated by multiplying the level of bonuses
per person by the number of regularly employed workers (for
detail, see Appendix).  The beginning period of net household
wealth was constructed by taking the cumulated sum of surpluses
in financial transactions of the individuals' sector (using Flow
of Funds Accounts of Bank of Japan).  This corresponds to the
FA(-1) variable introduced in the previous section. Therefore,
wealth here includes only financial wealth and the latter was
used as a proxy for total wealth.  Other variables come from NIA.

Equation (23) was estimated by OLS with a dummy variable taking
one in the second half of each year added.  The dummy variable
was introduced in order to capture the seasonality in consumption

not explained by included variables. The result of the estimation
is the following:

$$C_t = 15.593 + .1098A_t + .6645W_t + .3759B_t + .6997S_t -7.862D_t \quad (24)$$
$$( \ 2.541) \ (.0225) \quad (.0961) \quad (.1539) \quad (.0890) \quad (2.073)$$

$R^2$ = .9985, s.e. = 2.861, D.W. = 1.474, where standard errors are
in parentheses.[37] All variables are of the right sign and are
significant. In particular, the propensity to consume bonus
income is .376 and lower than the spending propensities from
other incomes.[38] The corresponding number we obtained in Section
4, .460, is slightly higher than this, but within one standard
error of the current estimate. In any case this result supports
the view that the bonus system has had positive effects on the
saving rate.

The propensity to consume the income of the self-employed is
about the same as that of regularly paid wages. This result then
rejects the view that fluctuations in the income of the self-
employed exert significant effects on the savings rate. Equation
(24) also shows that the propensity to consume regular wages is
about .66, which is very close to what we obtained in our cross
section study. This is fairly low by international standards--a
finding which partially explains the high savings rate in Japan
relative to other countries. The propensity to consume net
household wealth seems very large. This, however, is probably
due to the fact that $A_t$ includes only financial assets. The
statistical significance of this variable shows the importance of
the effects of inflation or wealth accumulation on savings. In
sum, the estimation result clearly supports the view that an
increase in bonus earnings relative to regular wages increases
savings.

Simulation

Using the estimation result we may determine quantitatively the
effect of bonuses on savings. For this purpose we ran the following
simulations. We calculated the rate of savings for the sample
period assuming that all bonus income had been paid in the form
of regular wages.

Such a calculation can be done at least in two ways. We may
assume that household wealth is exogenous, or else the effect of
changes in savings (on the path of wealth) may be taken into

account.  Since the wealth variable here includes only financial
wealth, it is not clear how we should calculate its time path
when the time path of consumption changes.  Because of this
difficulty, we report only the result of the first simulation,
although in theory, the second simulation would be more accurate.[39]

Figure 4 shows the simulated path along with the actual savings
rate.[40]  It is immediately clear that bonus payments have exerted
positive effects on the rate of savings.  The difference between
the actual and simulated savings rates were on average, equal to
3.0 percentage points. Consequently, we conclude that the Japanese
personal savings rate would have been (at least) about 17% (on
average) if bonus income had been paid as regular wages.[41]

This numerical figure of at most three percentage points (on
average) seems quite modest.  It certainly does not meet the
expectation so often expressed about the effect of the bonus
payment system.  Moreover, as Figure 4 makes clear, its effect is
not strong enough to wipe out the strong increasing trend in the
rate of savings (up until mid 1970's) even if the bonus payment
system not existed.  In short, it does not explain our query (ii)
raised in Section 2.  In particular, our simulated path shows
that there were large increases in the saving rates of 1973 and
1974, even after the effects of bonus income had been eliminated.
These remarks reinforce our criticism of Shinohara's view made in
Section 3.


6.   CONCLUSION

We are now ready to state our conclusion briefly and also some
qualifications of the present work.  We have confirmed in the
present paper that the bonus payment system has exerted a statistically significant effect on Japanese personal savings (namely, an
approximately twenty percent difference in terms of the marginal
propensity to consume as compared with other parts of income).
However, the quantitative magnitude of its contribution to the
aggregate rate of personal savings is rather small, at most three
percentage points (on average) for the period of 1958-78, when
the aggregate rate of personal savings average 20%.

On the theoretical side, we have seen from our study of the survey
data that this effect on bonuses does not come from the permanent

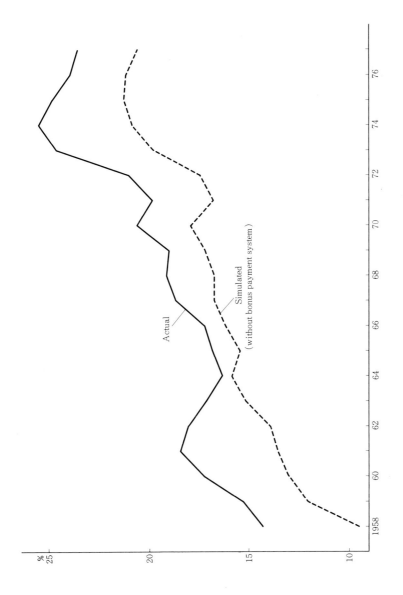

Figure V-4    Actual and Simulated Rate of Savings

income-life cycle hypothesis behavior of individuals.  This
conclusion has been reinforced by our cross-section study which
showed further evidence that households' behavior is incongruent
with the implications of the permanent income-life cycle hypothesis.
As an alternative we have suggested what we termed the habit-
buffer income hypothesis --that, at least in the short-run and
under normal economic conditions, households follow a convention
of spending some fixed proportion of different components of
income.  We do not claim we have proved this hypothesis, yet we
believe it is a workable and plausible inductive hypothesis
waiting to be tested further.

It is important to note that by arguing against the permanent
income-life cycle hypothesis and also suggesting that people
follow conventional spending rules in the short-run we do not
implicate taht they have no concern for future.  As we see clearly
from individuals' answers to various survey questionnaires[42] that
Japanese households do seem to be aware of their savings objectives
(and in this sense their savings are purposive) giving thought to
their expected future needs.  But the point is that households'
foresight capacity of telescopic faculty (à la Irving Fisher) is
fairly limited, and it is also very costly to calculate and
respond to every flow of new information.[43]  Thus households may
set some mild notion of "saving goals" and, on the other hand,
resort to such conventional rule of spending as we discussed in
the present paper. Under normal economic conditions this ensures
satisfying both already formed consumption habits (or the life
space of consumption) and psychological obligations to abide by
their "saving goals".  Here we have left open how people decide
the specific proportion of income they set aside to spend.
Determination of this ratio surely must relate with their long-
run objective.

We have also indicated the role of wealth in governing Japanese
households' savings behavior, albeit in a manner different from
the postulates of the permanent income-life cycle theories.  It
seems that, in the context just stated, the role of wealth should
be studied. These long-run aspects, and the manner in which
household's wealth plays role shall be the next topic of our
study.

DATA APPENDIX

We have estimated the (quarterly) aggregate time series data on
bonus earnings by following as closely as possible the manner in
which the employment income of the national income accounts (NIA)
are estimated.  In making this estimation we have relied heavily
on the Source Materials for Estimating NIA published by the
Economic Planning Agency in 1970 (hereafter abbreviated as SM).
In this appendix, we shall provide a brief account of the estimation
procedure.

The NIA estimate the employment income by (employee compensation)
dividing the economy into the following 13 major industry categories:
A=Agriculture, B=Forestry, C=Fishery, D=Mining, E=Construction,
F=Manufactures, G=Wholesales and Retailing, H=Banking and Insurance,
I=Real Estate, J=Transportation and Communication, K=Electricity,
Gas and other utilities, L=Service, and M=Government.  These
industries are then regrouped as the agricultural sector (consisting
of A, B and C), the nonagricultural and nongovernmental sector
(consisting of D through L) and the government sector (consisting
of M).

Our first major assumption is that bonus earnings within the
agricultural sector is negligible.  While this may not be true
literally, this assumption was necessary because there are no
readily available data on bonuses for the agricultural sector.
We regard this as an acceptable assumption because the proportion
of employed workers in this sector is negligible.  (According to
1975 Census, workers (including managers) in the agricultural
sector are 0.47 million, while those in the non-agricultural
sector are 36.5 million).

As for the non-agricultural sector, NIA employs Monthly Labor
Statistics (hereafter abbreviated as MLS) as the primary source
of material for estimating employment income.  MLS gives monthly
data on both the total wages of regularly employed workers and
the size of regular employment for each industry (D through L.)
These numbers are given according to the size of establishments,
(N.B. not firms) namely those with 5-29 employees and those with
30 or more employees.  It also gives decomposition of total wage
payment figures divided into two components, the portion that is
regularly paid and specially paid.  The latter portion is primarily

constituted by bonus payments. Being unable to decompose further, we have assumed that the specially paid portion of wage payments and bonus earnings are identical. The bonus figure per employee obtained for each establishment size class is then multiplied by the corresponding number of regular employees to give total bonus payments for each industry (D through L (for the establishment size classes 5-29 employees and 30 and more employees)).

The remaining task for this sector is to estimate the total bonus payments for establishments with 1-4 employees. Although MLS does not cover this class on a monthly basis, it conducts a special survey for this class once each year (at the end of July). From this survey, we obtained (for each industry) the figure of the total special payments (which, by our assumption, equals bonus payments) made during the preceding year (i.e., from August of the previous year to July of this year) to regular employees (per worker) and the figure of the number of employees. In estimating the quarterly (and annual) series of regular employees, we have assumed that these yearly payments followed the same monthly pattern as that observed for establishments with 5-29 employees. This assumption is the same as that of the NIA in estimating the quarterly series of total wage payments made to this establishment size class. (cf. SM, pp.18-23)

The above constitutes the basic procedure of estimating bonus earnings in the nonagricultural and nongovernmental sectors. For certain parts, however, we have had to resort to somewhat more ad-hoc procedures. First, NIA treats specially the public school (both national and local) employees (both teachers and administrators) that are already covered by MLS under the title of the serivice (L) industry. Namely, by using the Census of Establishments (conducted every three years) data it estimates the proportion of public school employees within the entire service sector and deducts this portion from the number of employees that MLS gives. It derives the figures from the Fiscal year books of the Ministry of Education (SM, pp.52-3). Although this seemed to be too contrived and perhaps an unnecessary procedure we have followed the same. Since the bonus payments pattern for this group of workers is identical with other government employees, we will describe the procedure of estimating bonus earnings for this group in the next subsection.

Second, there exists a difficulty in that MLS did not have figures
for the service industry prior to 1970. NIA thus resorted to an
ad-hoc method of multiplying wage figures in the Retail and
Wholesale industry (C) by the ratio of wages in the service
industry to the C industry. This ratio is available in the
Survey of Wages and Salaries of Private Employees (Minkan-Kyuyo
Jittai Chosa: Office of Personnels). Our conclusion was that
this method result in a significant underestimation of wages in
the service industry. Hence, we obtained the ratio of wages in
the two industries from a different source. That is, MLS report
annual bonus earnings for the two industries for establishments
with 1-4 employees. From this we obtained the wage ratio in the
two industries and then proceeded the same way as NIA, assuming
that the ratio applies to all establishment size classes.

We also faced some difficulty in estimating the number of regular
workers in the L industry since MLS does not report this prior to
1970. Thus, we first obtained total employment (including partime
workers) from the Survey of Labor Force and then applied to this
the proportion of regular workers total employment available in
the Census of Establishments.

Government Sector

The NIA restricts the coverage of industry M (government) to
those establishments providing general government services.
Annual figures of the total employment earnings of this sector
are available in NIA yearbooks. (They were obtained directly
form government sources). The bonus payments of central government
employees are determined by law (Office of Personnel). For
example, it was stipulated that in fiscal year 1975 public employees
were to receive as bonus payment 2.0 months worth of their regular
salary (the basic part of salary plus certain parts of allowance)
in June, 2.7 months worth in December, and 0.5 months worth in
March. In addition, while each year public employees' salaries
are adjusted by approval of the recommendation made by the Office
of Personnels (usually in December), the adjustment usually goes
back to earlier months and the cumulated amount is paid then.
These payments may very well be regarded as a form of bonuses. By
collecting information on these payments for each fiscal year, we
have divided annual total earnings of government employees into
the regularly paid part and the bonus part. The assumptions we

made are that the bonus ratio and the proportion of salaries on
which the bonus ratio is applied are the same between the national
and local governments.  We have also applied exactly the same
method to public school employees.

After Tax Bonus Payments
The figures obtained above were inclusive of all taxes on bonus
earnings. We then used the average income tax ratio for the
salaries of each year we obtained from the annual financial
reports of national and local governments to derive the aftertax
bonus earnings.  For example, in 1975 this ratio amounted to
3.77% for national government taxes and to 2.45% for local government
taxes.

Consistency with Cross Section Data
The ratio of bonus earnings derived over the entire employment
income in the NIA is contrasted in Table A1, with the corresponding
ratio obtained by the FIES.  FIES figures apply to family households
(excluding single person households) that are drawn from a sample
of cities with population over 50,000.  As the corresponding
Figure A1 shows our estimated series are consistently lower than
the FIES series.  This difference in the two estimates may be
explicable by the fact that FIES households are a more restricted
sample, in the sense that they are older in age and wealthier
than the entire households.  However, it is at once noticable
that the two series are almost parallel.  This shows that our
estimates are at least consistent with the FIES estimates.

Table V-Al   Correspondence of the Bonus Earnings
Ratio between FIES and NIA

| year | FIES | NIA(our estimate) |
|------|------|-------------------|
| 1958 | 14.3 (%) | 10.9 (%) |
| 1959 | 15.4 | 12.7 |
| 1960 | 17.1 | 12.9 |
| 1961 | 17.5 | 14.2 |
| 1962 | 18.0 | 14.1 |
| 1963 | 18.8 | 14.6 |
| 1964 | 18.6 | 14.6 |
| 1965 | 18.7 | 14.5 |
| 1966 | 19.3 | 15.1 |
| 1967 | 19.7 | 15.6 |
| 1968 | 20.2 | 16.2 |
| 1969 | 22.3 | 18.0 |
| 1970 | 23.4 | 18.2 |
| 1971 | 22.8 | 18.9 |
| 1972 | 22.4 | 19.3 |
| 1973 | 23.7 | 19.8 |
| 1974 | 24.5 | 21.9 |
| 1975 | 21.8 | 19.4 |
| 1976 | 21.7 | 19.6 |
| 1977 | 21,1 | 18.6 |
| 1978 | 20.4 | 18.5 |

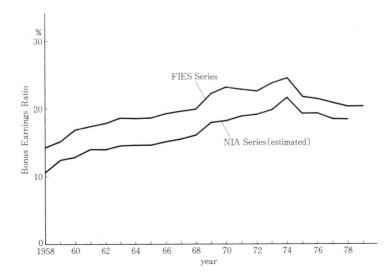

Figure V-Al

*T. Ishikawa and K. Ueda*

Table V-A2  Annual Data

| year | Consumption (C) | Non-Durables Consumption | Household Net Financial Wealth (A) | Regularly Paid Wages (W) | Bonus Earnings (B) |
|------|------|------|------|------|------|
| 1958 | 128.9 | 122.2 | 95.7 | 77.0 | 9.4 |
| 1959 | 138.9 | 130.4 | 107.9 | 82.2 | 12.0 |
| 1960 | 152.8 | 143.5 | 123.6 | 91.8 | 13.6 |
| 1961 | 165.7 | 155.0 | 140.5 | 101.4 | 16.8 |
| 1962 | 181.5 | 169.0 | 158.2 | 114.1 | 18.7 |
| 1963 | 198.9 | 185.2 | 177.5 | 123.9 | 21.2 |
| 1964 | 222.0 | 207.2 | 197.0 | 136.9 | 23.4 |
| 1965 | 234.5 | 218.9 | 219.4 | 148.7 | 25.3 |
| 1966 | 254.1 | 237.0 | 240.4 | 161.4 | 28.6 |
| 1967 | 279.9 | 259.9 | 269.8 | 178.9 | 33.0 |
| 1968 | 306.7 | 282.9 | 303.8 | 196.4 | 38.0 |
| 1969 | 336.2 | 312.9 | 343.5 | 211.9 | 46.5 |
| 1970 | 362.5 | 337.3 | 373.8 | 237.2 | 52.9 |
| 1971 | 389.0 | 360.4 | 407.5 | 263.2 | 61.4 |
| 1972 | 424.9 | 395.5 | 459.6 | 286.2 | 68.3 |
| 1973 | 460.1 | 428.6 | 520.9 | 322.1 | 79.6 |
| 1974 | 467.0 | 434.7 | 503.0 | 325.6 | 91.3 |
| 1975 | 496.0 | 465.7 | 524.1 | 359.1 | 86.3 |
| 1976 | 517.9 | 485.0 | 576.0 | 369.7 | 89.9 |
| 1977 | 540.0 | 510.4 | 628.9 | 389.8 | 89.1 |
| 1978 | 561.8 | 528.4 | 699.5 | 402.2 | 91.4 |

Note:  All data are in terms of billion yen divided by consumer price index: 1970=100.0

Table  V-A3   Expected  and  Actual  Values  of  Bonus  Payments
per  Average  Worker  Household

| year | expected | actual |
|------|----------|--------|
| 1966s | 54.8 | 59.0 |
| 1966w | 73.1 | 77.8 |
| 1967s | 60.5 | 64.5 |
| 1967w | 76.3 | 86.8 |
| 1968s | 67.6 | 74.2 |
| 1968w | 91.1 | 98.5 |
| 1969s | 77.5 | 87.6 |
| 1969w | 114.6 | 115.8 |
| 1970s | 92.3 | 102.8 |
| 1970w | 123.3 | 141.0 |
| 1971s | 116.2 | 133.2 |
| 1971w | 151.3 | 175.6 |
| 1972s | 129.7 | 147.5 |
| 1972w | 179.3 | 201.7 |
| 1973s | 154.5 | 178.4 |
| . . . . . . . . . . . |  |  |
| 1976s | 268.0 | 291.6 |
| 1976w | 395.7 | 352.8 |
| 1977s | 360.1 | 351 |
| 1977w | 428 | 438 |
| 1978s | 376 | 367 |
| 1978w | 444 | 453 |
| 1979s | 387 | 383 |
| 1979w | 448 | 466 |
| 1980s | 417 | 408 |
| 1980w | 481 | 496 |
| 1981s | 420 | 407 |
| 1981w | 485 | 501 |

Source:   Shohi  Doko  Chosa

Note:   figures  are  in  units  of  thousand  yen

NOTES

\* This is an extended and revised version of the paper presented at the Rokko
Econometric Conference held in Kobe, July, 1981. We are indebted to Joaquim de
Andrade, Henry Farber, Robert Feldman, Alberto Giovannini, Nils Gottfries, Mervyin
King, Susumu Koizumi, Masao Kuroda, Stephen Marglin, Franco Modigliani, Jurg
Niehans, Terukazu Suruga, and Martin Weitzman for their helpful suggestions and
criticisms at various stages of our research. We are also indebted to the
National Income Department of the Economic Planning Agency and the Statistics and
Information Department of the Ministry of Labor for their generous support and aid
in our data collection process. Finally, we would like to thank Atsuko Ohashi for
her skillful and perseverant research assistance, and Margaret Leclair for kindly
editing the English of our manuscript.

[1]Most of Mizoguchi's works published earlier in Japanese were assembled and
published in English in [1970]. For example, we find the same material as noted
here in chapter 5 of [1970].

[2]In particular, we differ from Shinohara [1981] in terms of overall evaluation of
the bonus effect.

[3]We did, however, face the problem of discontinuity of data in the NIA after 1977,
as EPA switched to the new System of National Accounts (SNA) series. In order to
obtain estimates of bonus earnings for years after 1977 we have adopted an ad hoc
method of adjusting the SNA series so that it is commensurate with the former NIA
series in case any incongruency occurred between the figures of the two series.

[4]See Bank of Japan, Chosa Geppo (Monthly Bulletin), February, 1981 for a review of
a more recent movement of the personal savings ratio.

[5]We note, however, that our final estimating equation below, i.e., equation (23),
does contain the net financial wealth term, and therefore, any effect that the
relative movement of financial wealth over income might have on consumption should
be caught by this term.

[6]The regular wage component defined in this manner includes wages of temporary and
part-time workers. This is to be contrasted with Mizoguchi's definition that
excludes the parts of household incomes other than family head's regularly paid
wages. In his analysis these are regarded as temporary and thus treated in the
same category as bonus payments. Differences arise when other members of the
family work on a temporary or part-time basis. In our definition, their wages are
included in the regular wage component, whereas in Mizoguchi's they are included
in 'bonus' earnings. We have departed from Mizoguchi because (a) the kind of
decomposition that FIES gives is not readily available at the macro level, and (b)
relatively long duration or tenure of employment of these workers (even though
their status is part-time) makes it difficult to believe that their incomes are
perceived in the same way as bonus incomes. We did, however, impose a substantive
assumption: that part-time and temporary workers do not receive bonus income,
which is, of course, not true as various fragmentary surveys (for instance, see
Rodo Tokei Chosa Geppo (Monthly Labor Statistics and Research Bulletin), Ministry
of Labor, March, 1981) indicate.

[7]To check consistency with FIES data, see the last part of the Data Appendix.

[8]Historically, the bonus payment system started to spread widely over blue-collar
as well as white-collar workers in early 1950's. (The bonus payment system did
exist even before the WWII, but it was limited to white-collar workers employed in
certain large-scale firms.)

[9]We are grateful to Martin Weitzman for pointing out an error contained in an earlier version and suggesting an appropriate manner to evaluate the profit sharing aspect.  A relatively weak correlation found between the bonus earnings ratio and the (before bonus) share of profits share suggests a call for other explanatory factors.  A popular understanding of the bonus payment is that it combines three elements of pay; regular wage paid in the form of lump-sum, incentive pay for extra effort and achievement, and profit sharing.  The degrees to which these three elements are combined seem to vary greatly over industries and firm sizes.  According to Professor Kazuo Koike, bonus payments tend to respond quickly to the current economic performance in small scale firms, while a great deal of inertia governs the adjustment of bonus payments in large scale firms.  Detailed statistical analysis on the determinants of bonus payments in Japan and their movements are certainly due, but to our knowledge, surprisingly little has been done.  To the extent that bonus payments are geared to revenues or profits of firms, they have a very interesting employment-promotion property at the macro level, as recently discussed by Weitzman [1982].  From such a perspective detailed analysis of the system is encouraged.  It is, however, left beyond the scope of our current study.

[10]The classic references for the habit persistence hypothesis are Duesenberry [1949], Modigliani [1949], Brown [1952], Houthakker and Taylor [1970: Chapter 7].  For recent developments of this approach and a detailed probe into U.S. aggregate time series data, see Marglin [1983].

[11]These two tables are, however, not without problems.  Ideally, we would wish these two tables to refer to the data of the same sample households as those classified simultaneously by total annual income and by household head's annual income.  In fact, it is not the case.  Because of a particular rotationary sampling method adopted, and because of the fact that collection of data on annual income is based on households' memory of it over the past twelve month period, while all other data are collected on a current monthly basis and also by use of accounting diaries, the situation is far from ideal.  Indeed, this difference might possibly create a substantial distortion of annual income groups in a period of high nominal income growth, either due to real economic growth or due to inflation.  Nevertheless, we must proceed as if the two tables satisfied the above ideal.  The task of refinement must wait until release of further data by the Statistical Bureau.

[12]By making this formal assumption we are, in effect, ignoring the mathematical constraint that Y must always be greater than W, i.e., $Y > W$.  In other words, we are assuming that a greater portion of the mass of distribution effectively lies above the 45-degree line.  Preferably, and to be more rigorous, we would wish to use a truncated lognormal distribution for estimation; however, in view of the overall quality of our data (Cf. NOTE 11 above), we decided not to pursue this route of refinement.

[13]We would also be interested in knowing if the consumption function itself might be different among income classes.  However, proper handling of this question requires data that are not currently available.

[14]This procedure implies that we ignore the behavior of those who fall within the very bottom of the income classes as classified by household head's regular wage income.  Yet this adjustment is only a partial attempt at eliminating the group of households that fail to conform to the lognormal law.  Ideally we should be able to identify the households we have deleted from our sample and thus to correct the data collected from the table classified by the total household income.  But since this is not possible, we have ignored this adjustment.

[15]Because of the incongruence that exists between the fact that our observations are arithmetic averages within each classification range and the fact the model is

log-linear, we did not follow any weighting procedures in the estimation process. Actually, a simple-minded weighting procedure (using the square root of the number of observations in each classification range), pretending that our observations were geometric averages, produced consistently lower figures for our estimates of β, implying a much stronger effect of bonus income on savings. Thus, at least, we can say we might underestimate, but not overestimate, the effect in question. Another important reservation to the two-step estimation method adopted below is that we have treated the estimates of the distributional parameters as if they were true parameters, which corresponds to our assumption that u's and v's are independent. In fact, however, measurement errors in the estimation of distributional parameters do exist, and they may certainly contaminate the errors in the consumption function, which introduce biases in our estimates of α, β and γ. Ideally we should estimate the four equations (8) through (11) simultaneously, but in this study we resorted to a simpler, albeit yet imperfect, method as a first approximation.

[16]To be more specific, after tax figures were calculated by the following formulas:

$$W = \{ 1 - \frac{\text{household head's regular wage income}}{\text{total employment income}} \text{ (wage earnings tax}$$

$$+ \text{ social security contribution)} \} \{\text{before-tax household head's regular}$$

wage income}

$$Y = \text{total household income} - \text{wage earnings tax} - \text{property and miscellaneous}$$

other taxes

$$= \text{household disposable income.}$$

Strictly speaking, our procedure here is not justifiable, for classification of the tables are based on before-tax quantities and also incurrence of various taxes over different income classes are not proportional. However, since the incurrence of wage earnings tax and social security is in monotonic relationship with wage income (if not proportional), and since miscellaneous other taxes are relatively small in magnitude, we do not expect that the picture has been distorted substantially by our procedure.

[17]One important limitation of our data is that the supposed "bonus" income, B = Y − W does not tell the true bonus income, but rather, it contains other components of income such as "wife and other household members' wage income" and "return from assets and business income" (both of which are not of tax). These two components, when added, constitute roughly 10% of annual disposable income or roughly 30% of what we have termed as "bonus income." (An added complication is that "wife and other household members' wage income" figures include both regular wage and bonus components, for which no decomposition is available.) Since these categories of income are much closer to household head's regular wage income in nature than the true bonus income (except for the proviso just noted), this limitation of data may introduce a serious bias in estimating the elasticity of consumption with respect to bonus income. In order to rectify this bias we have adopted the following procedure. Let our "bonus income", B, be further divided into the true bonus income B', "wife and other household members' wage income", T', and "return from assets and business income", R' (all tax adjusted), so that B = B' + T' + R' holds. Recalling equation (4'), the true model for consumption behavior is now expressed by:

$$C = \bar{C}' \cdot (W + T' + R')^{\alpha'} (1 + \frac{B'}{W + T' + R'})^{\beta'}$$

Where the variable W, i.e., household head's regular wage income, remai. s unchanged. This functional form, however, can easily be rewritten as

$$C = \bar{C}' \cdot W^{\alpha'} (\frac{Y}{W})^{\beta'} (1 + \frac{T' + R'}{W})^{\alpha'-\beta'}$$

or taking the natural logarithm of both sides,

$$C = (\alpha'-\beta')w + \beta'y + (\alpha'-\beta')q + \gamma'$$

where $\gamma' = \log \bar{C}'$ and $q = \log (1 + \frac{T'+R'}{W})$. The new term $(\alpha'-\beta')q$ represents the adjustment factor necessary to correct the bias from inaccurate measurement. The foregoing formulae (6) and (7) should then be modified accordingly, with $(\alpha'-\beta')E(q|w)$ and $(\alpha'-\beta')E(q|y)$ added to the RHS respectively. The final estimation equations are, again, a little modification of the equations (10) and (11):

$$C_1^{it} = \alpha^t(z_{11}^{it} + q_1^{it}) + \beta^t(z_{12}^{it} - q_1^{it}) + \gamma^t + v_1^{it}$$

$$C_2^{jt} = \alpha^t(z_{21}^{jt} + q_2^{jt}) + \beta^t(z_{22}^{jt} - q_2^{jt}) + \gamma^t + v_2^{jt}.$$

[18]The estimates of the coefficients of equations (8) and (9) that were used in the estimation of the parameters of the consumption function presented here are given in the following Table V-F1.

[19]We have also tried pooling the years 1969-73, 77-78 and 80 together. However, the result did not pass the F-test for the case of non-durables.

[20]There is another evidence in support of this finding. Although, for some Mysterious reason, the survey data (Shohi Doko Chosa) which we will examine in the next section do not have bonus related questions for most of the period in question, the data for the winter-bonus period of 1976 is available and it suggests a higher propensity to consume out of bonus than other years. More specifically, the actual average propensity to consume out of the winter bonus of that year was about 55% over all income classes, which was about 10% higher than the corresponding figures for normal years.

[21]See Kosai and Ogino [1980: 192-198] and Akabane [1981: 77-85]. While the former accepts the paradox as a fact and attempts an explanation, the latter dismisses it as a statistical artifact, allegedly caused by the unreliableness of the data coming from the table classified by annual household income. However, the basis of that allegation rested mostly on the fact that the behavior of individual consumption items as given by the table in question fluctuated much. But, in our view, this is not a fair allegation. We all know that narrow items of expenditure data can fluctuate much. What we have shown in our paper is that, even though we corrected for possible fluctuation in the componentwise distribution of income, we still obtain this paradox. Hence, we believe that Akabane's allegation is unfounded and the paradox is real.

Table V-F1   Estimated Lognormal Parameters

(Standard Errors in Parentheses)

| Year | $S_1$ | $S_2$ | $C_1$ | $C_2$ |
|------|-------|-------|-------|-------|
| 1969 | .746 (.024) | .786 (.019) | 3.412 ( .284) | 2.138 ( .228) |
| 1970 | .723 (.027) | .770 (.022) | 3.722 ( .323) | 2.323 ( .259) |
| 1971 | .743 (.013) | .766 (.017) | 3.457 ( .152) | 2.395 ( .209) |
| 1972 | .769 (.020) | .824 (.037) | 3.163 ( .242) | 1.728 ( .445) |
| 1973 | .756 (.022) | .729 (.022) | 3.344 ( .263) | 2.869 ( .276) |
| 1974 | .769 (.017) | .708 (.018) | 3.193 ( .200) | 3.130 ( .217) |
| 1975 | .800 (.158) | .751 (.025) | 2.807 ( .192) | 2.634 ( .303) |
| 1976 | .803 (.021) | .764 (.015) | 2.759 ( .254) | 2.492 ( .178) |
| 1977 | .760 (.019) | .719 (.023) | 3.280 ( .225) | 3.041 ( .277) |
| 1978 | .812 (.013) | .797 (.019) | 2.650 ( .157) | 2.110 ( .223) |
| 1979 | .760 (.019) | .774 (.012) | 3.274 ( .226) | 2.400 ( .151) |
| 1980 | .771 (.025) | .708 (.026) | 3.142 ( .297) | 3.197 ( .317) |

Note:  Estimated Equations: $y_1^{it} = S_1^t \cdot w_1^{it} + C_1^t + u_1^{it}$

$$w_2^{jt} = S_2^t \cdot y_2^{jt} + C_2^t + u_2^{jt}$$

where $S_1^t = (\sigma_{wy}^t/\sigma_{ww}^t)$, $S_2^t = (\sigma_{wy}^t/\sigma_{yy}^t)$,

$$C_1^t = \mu_y^t - (\sigma_{wy}^t/\sigma_{ww}^t) \cdot \mu_w^t$$

$$C_2^t = \mu_w^t - (\sigma_{wy}^t/\sigma_{yy}^t) \cdot \mu_y^t$$

[22]Kosai and Ogino op.cit.'s explanation seems to have relied too much on the role played by the durables consumption. While we agree that it was an important factor, we would still argue that the main explanatory factor lay elsewhere. As described here, the paradox does not disappear in the case of year 1975 even if we subtracted durables consumption.

[23]Obviously the type of behavior just described is not explicable within the strict confines of the permanent income hypothesis. There is an additional reason that works against this hypothesis. The preceding years of sharp inflation have considerably reduced the real value of household financial wealth. However, since the holding of financial wealth is concentrated among households with high annual income (e.g., in 1980, according to the Family Savings Survey, the top income quintile group among worker households held 31.3% of total financial net worth of the household sector (including the self-employed households) as opposed to 8.5% held by the bottom income quintile group (again among worker households), high annual income households were the ones which have been affected most by the inflation. Nevertheless, they tended to consume much, which is against the implication of the permanent income hypothesis. Furthermore, it is clear that one cannot defend the hypothesis by resorting to the shelter of liquidity constraints.

[24]A representative of these studies is Kosai [1981].

[25]This literature includes contributions by Hall [1978], Flavin [1981], Hall & Mishkin [1982], and Hayashi [1982].

[26]If survey data were not available, we would be obliged to assume that the stochastic model proposed below corresponds to the true representation of pay-ments--an assumption much stronger than the one used here. See, for example, Hall & Mishkin [1982] for use of such a procedure.

[27]This is much more general than the Muthian framework (Muth [1960]) where $B_t$ is supposed to be generated as

$$B_t = (B_{t-1} - v_{t-1}) + u_t + v_t$$

with $u_t$ representing a permanent shock and $v_t$ representing a transitory shock.

[28]Under a more general utility function, $C_t$ must be interpreted to mean the amount of consumption that would have to be (marginally) cut back if the 'bonus wealth' were not present. In general, $C_t$ would depend on the magnitudes of other parts of wealth, and the consumption function (17) would have to be modified accordingly. We are indebted to Mr. Nils Gottfries for a helpful discussion on this point.

[29]We interpret the households' answer to this question (as to "consumption out of bonus") to mean the amount of consumption out of annuitized "bonus wealth", a theoretical notion discussed previously. (See also NOTE 28.) In effect, we are assuming that households are much more rational than the persons who actually prepared this question.

[30]Strangely enough, the Survey does not give data for the very period which our cross section studies in the previous section detected irregularities.

[31]Strictly speaking, the time the actual amount of bonus is reported and the time the expectation of the next bonus payment is reported are not the same. During most of the sample period, the former was February and August and the latter was May and November. Clearly, this tends to produce overestimation of the permanent

component and underestimation of the temporary component of bonus changes, possibly resulting in biased estimates of the coefficients. Since it was not obvious how this problem could be avoided, we ignored the problem in the estimation result reported below.

[32]See, for example, B. Friedman [1980].

[33]The D-W statistic reported takes into account the gap in the sample.

[34]The equation was estimated in the following form:

$$C_t = \rho C_{t-1} + k'({}_t B_{t+1} - \rho \cdot {}_{t-1} B_t) + k' \cdot g \cdot (B_t - \rho B_{t-1} - {}_t B_{t+1}$$

$$+ \rho \cdot {}_{t-1} B_t) + c'' + \varepsilon_{t-1}$$

and

$$u_t = \rho u_{t-1} + \varepsilon_{t-1}.$$

[35]In this section we have not estimated an equation which explains consumption out of total income. However, it would be reasonable to assume that the propensity to consume out of regular wages is different from that out of bonus income. We will leave this part to sections 3 and 5.

[36]On the other hand, we are assuming in this section that aggregation biases are fairly small so that the analysis of macro-data give meaningful results.

[37]Equation (24) indicates the existence of a mild serial correlation. When the equation was corrected for serial correlation, the coefficient on bonuses turned out to be unreasonably high--.764. However, when a distributed lag is introduced to the W variable, the estimation result came fairly close to (24) even after correction for serial correlation. This suggests that consumption responds sluggishly to regularly paid wages but not to bonuses. This seems to be broadly consistent with the analysis of the consumption habit carried out so far in this paper. A careful analysis of such a hypothesis is left for future work.

[38]The analysis in section 3 indicated that during the mid 1970's the propensity to consume out of bonus was much higher than in other periods. This possibility was tested here by splitting the sample at the end of the 1960's into two. The estimation result showed that, in fact, there was an increase in the propensity to consume out of bonuses in the latter period. However, the increase was not statistically significant because of large standard errors.

[39]Note that such a simulation tends to overestimate the effects of bonus income on savings.

[40]The figure shows the average of two half year numbers for each year.

[41]The average of the actual savings rate for the sample period of this simulation was about 20%.

[42]Representative examples of survey questionnaires are found in EPA's Survey on the Movement of Consumption used in Section 4 and Bank of Japan's Public Opinion Polls with regard to Savings (Chochiku ni kansuru Seron Chosa) which is conducted annually.

[43]The spirit here is similar to the so-called satisfying approach or Leibenstein's convention approach.(Leibenstein, 1982).

REFERENCES

[1] Aitchison, J. and Brown, J., Log-Normal Distribution, Cambridge:  Cambridge University Press, 1957.

[2] Akabane, T., Hijoshiki no Nihon Keizai-Ron (On Japanese Economy from a Non-Commonsensical Viewpoint), Tokyo:  Nihon Keizai Shimbun, 1981.

[3] Brown, J. M., "Habit Persistence and Lags in Consumer Behavior," Econometrica, Vol. 20, July, 1952.

[4] Duesenberry, J., Income, Saving and the Theory of Consumer Behavior, Cambridge, Mass.:  Harvard University Press, 1949.

[5] Flavin, M., "The Adjustment of Consumption to Changing Expectations about Future Income," J. Polit. E., Vol. 89, October, 1981.

[6] Friedman, B., "Survey Evidence on the 'Rationality' of Interest Rate Expectations," J. Monet. E., Vol. 6, October, 1980.

[7] Friedman, M., A Theory of the Consumption Function, Princeton:  Princeton University Press, 1957.

[8] Haitovsky, Y., Regression Estimation from Grouped Observations, London: Griffin, 1973.

[9] Hall, R., "Stochastic Implications of the Life Cycle-Permanent Income Hypothesis:  Theory and Evidence," J. Polit. E., Vol. 86, December, 1978.

[10] Hall, R. and Mishkin, F., "The Sensitivity of Consumption to Transitory Income:  Estimates from Panel Data on Households," forthcoming in Econometrica, 1982.

[11] Hayashi, F., "The Permanent Income Hypothesis:  Estimation and Testing by Instrumental Variables," J. Polit. E., Vol. 90, October, 1982.

[12] Houthakker, H. S. and Taylor, L., Consumer Demand in the United States, Second and Enlarged Edition, Cambridge, Mass.:  Harvard University Press, 1970.

[13] Komiya, R., "The Supply of Personal Savings," in Sengo Nihon no Keizai Seicho (Economic Growth of Postwar Japan), ed. by Komiya, R., Tokyo:  Iwanami, 1963.

[14] Kosai, Y., "Kojin Chochiku to Sonota Chochiku no Kankei," (The Relationship between Personal Savings and Other Savings) Chochiku Jiho, no. 127, March 1981.

[15] Kosai, Y. and Ogino, Y., Nihon Keizai Tenbo (Japanese Economy in Perspective), Tokyo:  Nihon Hyoron Sha, 1980.

[16] Leibenstein, H., "The Prisoners' Dilemma in the Invisible Hand:  An Analysis of Intrafirm Productivity," A.E.R., Vol. 72, May, 1982.

[17] Lydall, H., The Structure of Earnings, Oxford:  Oxford University Press, 1968.

[18] Maddala, G. S., Econometrics, New York: McGraw-Hill, 1977.

[19] Marglin, S. A., Growth, Distribution and Prices, Cambridge, Mass.:  Harvard University Press, 1983.

[20] Mizoguchi, T., Shohi Kansuu no Tokei-teki Bunseki (A Statistical Analysis of the Consumption Function), Tokyo:  Iwanami, 1964.

[21] _____, Personal Savings and Consumption in Postwar Japan, Tokyo: Kinokuniya, 1970.

[22] _____, Chochiku no Keizai-Gaku (The Economics of Saving), Tokyo: Keiso Shobo, 1973.

[23] Modigliani, F., "Fluctuations in the Saving-Income Ratio:  A Problem in Economic Forecasting," in Studies in Income and Wealth, Vol. 11, New York: National Bureau of Economic Research, 1949.

[24] Ohkawa, K. and Rosovsky, H., Japanese Economic Growth, Stanford:  Stanford University Press, 1973.

[25] Shinohara, M., "The Structure of Savings and the Consumption Function in Postwar Japan," J. Polit. E., Vol. 67, December, 1959.

[26] _____, "Chochiku Ritsu no Nazo" (The Puzzles of Savings Rate), Chochiku Jiho, no. 127, 1981

[27] Weitzman, M. "Some Macroeconomic Implications of Alternative Compensation Systems," Discussion Paper, M.I.T., December, 1982.

THE ECONOMIC ANALYSIS OF THE JAPANESE FIRM
M. Aoki (editor)
© Elsevier Science Publishers B.V. (North-Holland), 1984

# SHAREHOLDERS' NON-UNANIMITY ON INVESTMENT FINANCING: BANKS VS. INDIVIDUAL INVESTORS

MASAHIKO AOKI

The objective of this article is twofold: one is to explore a possible explanation of changes in the observed pattern of investment financing in Japanese firms during the 1960s and 1970s, and the other is to inquire into the nature of the changing role of banks as shareholder-cum-lenders in that process. In order to tackle these problems, I construct a simple general equilibrium model composed of a representative individual investor, a representative bank, and a representative firm. The representative firm, or the non-financial corporate sector, and the representative individual investor are connected directly through the corporate institution, as well as the stock market, and indirectly though the bank. The bank is also a participant in the stock market.[1]

New equity issues have never been a major means of financing investment in Japan until recently.[2]  Theoretically as well, it can be proven that new equity issues are an inferior method of corporate finance from the capital cost point of view when interest payments are tax-deductible at the corporate level (See King [3], pp.91-102). In this article, therefore, possibility of new equity issues is a priori precluded.  Our major concern is the choice between debt financing and internal retention of profits to finance investments of the firm, which we will analyze after allowing for the special features of the Japanese banking sector and of the personal and corporate tax systems.

Even if new equity issues are left aside, however, the stock market is where the values of alternative financial measures are evaluated and the pattern of shareholding emerges. In spite of its importance, the stock market has been largely neglected, or treated only peripherally, in the analysis of the Japanese financial system. According to the standard model, as represented by Suzuki [9], the household is assumed to diversify its portfolio only

between cash and deposits.  The firm is constrained in the determination of its investment level by the availability of bank credit.
City banks play the major role of intermediating between the two
parties.  In performing this function, city banks can increase
their lending capacity through borrowing from the Bank of Japan as
well as through the use of inter-bank markets (such as the call
market and the bill market), in which non-city banks and other
bank-like institutions are primarily lenders.  Elaborate analyses
have been developed regarding banking operations in those inter-
bank markets, but the stock market has never been analyzed seriously
as an integral element of the Japanese financial market. The
standard model is constructed in a rather ad hoc way to explain
banking behavior in credit markets, and the question of why bank
credits became the predominant means of investment financing in
Japan (particularly in the 1960s) in the first place has not been
earnestly addressed.[3]

Professional economists who are trained in Modigliani-Miller
theory might dismiss this question by holding that the tax deductibility of interest payments at the corporate level will make the
cost of debt financing of investments relatively cheap.  They
might further stress that there has been a substantial tax advantage
to individual investors to holding their wealth in the form of
deposits due to the Small Saving Tax-Exempt System introduced in
1963.  However, it is also true that there is a substantial tax
advantage to share-holding as well.  Capital-gains taxation has
been known in Japan only during the brief episode of the Shoup tax
regime (1950-3), introduced pursuant to a recommendation by a
commission headed by Carl S. Shoup and abandoned quickly after the
recovery of Japanese sovereignty.  Further, as explained later,
while deposit and lending rates were more or less regulated under
the Temporary Money Rates Adjustment Act, city banks were able to
manipulate the effective lending rate by requiring debtor firms to
retain a portion of extended credits as compensating balances.
In other words, a substantial portion of interest payments by
firms is, in effect, "taxed" by city banks. Why was borrowing from
banks by firms substantial in spite of such a practice, particularly
in the 1960s?  Some may argue that the rapids growth of the non-
financial corporate sector during that decade made internally
generated funds insufficient to meet investment requirements.
However, as we shall see later (Table VIII-1), the dividend payout

rate was at a much higher level in the 1960s than in the 1970s. The firm could have substituted internal funds for borrowings, at least to some extent, by reducing dividend payouts, if it had desired to do so, but this substitution began to occur only in the 1970s.

The following questions may thus be raised: How is the debt-equity ratio of the non-financial corporate sector determined? Given corporate and personal tax system, can the observed pattern of investment financing be regarded as a result of value-maximizing equilibria? Or is it a consequence of some kind of power balance between primary investors and banks, which might have different interests in portfolio corporations? Is it because the growth of the non-financial corporate sector has declined that the relative importance of debt-financing has been declining? Or is it because the relative power of banks has been eroding? This short essay cannot answer all of these questions in a definitive way but will try to pose these questions in a more transparent way by formulating, and testing statistically, a model which may be useful as a first step toward answering them.

## 1. THE FIANCIAL EQUILIBRIUM MODEL

Let us consider a simple model of an economy composed of a (representative) individual investor, a (representative) bank, and a (representative) firm. The (representative) individual investor is assumed to represent typical primary investors in their tax positions, risk attitudes and wealth. The (representative) firm represents the non-financial corporate sector as a whole. The (representative) bank represents all financial intermediaries engaged in investment financing as well as shareholding. By aggregating the banking sector we ignore the inter-bank markets which have been a major concern of monetary economists. There are two kinds of assets in the model: shares of the firm, which are traded on the stock market, and credits intermediated by the bank. Time is assumed to consist of periods of equal duration, and, when necessary, the values of variables in the model at time period T (= 0, 1, 2, ...) are indicated by the superscript T. When there is no risk of misunderstanding, time superscripts will be omitted.

(a) The individual investor. In order to describe the portfolio selection behavior of the (representative) individual investor, let us introduce the following notation:

  r = the deposit rate.
  V = share price.
  d = dividend per share.
  s = the number of shares of the firm owned by the individual
      investor.
  D = the amount of deposits held by the individual investor.
  W = the initial non-stock wealth of the individual investor.
  $t_r$ = the tax rate on interest income of the individual investor.
  $t_d$ = the tax rate on dividend income of the individual investor.

In view of the Japanese personal tax system, $t_r$ and $t_d$ should be,
ideally speaking, treated as parameters which change step-wise
depending upon the levels of the relevant incomes[4], but they are
assumed to be single-valued parameters for the sake of simplicity.
However, as will be noted later, this simplification does not
affect the performance of the model in any essential way. To allow
for the fact for that deposit rates were fixed until 1970 by the
Council of Money Rate Adjustments, chaired by the President of the
Bank of Japan, and that they have been regulated by the posting of
guidelines by the Bank of Japan thereafter,[5] the deposit rate is
also taken to be a parameter. The value of initial wealth, W, (and
the saving decision by the individual investor implicit in it) is
also given in the model. Other variables are determined endogenously
in the model.

The individual investor selects between shareholdings, s, and
deposits, D, within its budget constraint:

$$D + sV = W + \hat{s}V \tag{1}$$

where $\hat{s}$ is the number of shares held initially. The after-tax
return after one period expected from the current portfolio is
given by

$$R_I = (1 - t_r)r[W + (\hat{s} - s)V] + (1 - t_d)sd + s\Delta V.$$

Note that the return from shareholdings consists of dividends and
capital gains $\Delta V = V^{T+1} - V^T$ and that the latter are not taxable.[6]
Dividends $d^T$ and the next period share price $V^{T+1}$ are stochastic
variables beyond the control of the individual investor, while the
current period price $V^T$ of shares is given to the individual

investor as a parameter determined by the market.

Suppose that the individual investor's risk attitude is represented by a concave von Neumann-Morgenstern utility function, u, defined on the domain of the expected returns $R_I$. Let us denote the after-tax rate of return to the individual investor from shareholdings as

$$\rho_I = (1 - t_d)\frac{d}{V} + \frac{\Delta V}{V} . \tag{2}$$

As we shall see later, $\bar{\rho}_I$, the expected value of $\rho_I$, will depend upon the financial policy chosen by the firm. It is assumed that the variance $\sigma_I^2$ of $\rho_I$ is subjectively believed by the individual investor to be invariant to policy changes.[7] The subjective equilibrium portfolio of the individual investor is attained when the following condition has been satisfied:

$$\left.\begin{array}{l} s = 0, \text{ if } \bar{\rho}_I - (1 - t_r)r < 0; \\[2mm] [(W + (\hat{s} - s)V]E[u'(R_I)(\rho_I - (1 - t_r)r)] = 0, \text{ otherwise.} \end{array}\right\} \tag{3}$$

where $E[u(\cdot)]$ denotes the expected value of u. Approximating the value of u' by a Taylor expansion up to the second order around the expected value of the equilibrium portfolio and substituting it into the second expression yeilds

$$[W + (\hat{s} - s)V]\bar{u}'[\bar{\rho}_I - (1 - t_r)r - A_I\sigma_I^2 sV] = 0$$

where $A_I = -\bar{u}''/\bar{u}'$ is the Arrow-Pratt measure of absolute risk aversion. We assume that the degree of absolute risk aversion is constant. If we define the individual's risk premium for risky shareholding as the difference between the expected value of returns $\bar{\rho}Vs$ and their certainty equivalent, then it is known to equal $(1/2)A_I(sV)^2\sigma_I^2$. (See Pratt [6].) Therefore, if we set the rate of the individual's risk premium for shareholding equal to twice the premium divided by the value of shareholdings

$$\pi_I(sV) = A_I\sigma_I^2 sV, \tag{4}$$

an individual investor's portfolio (s, D) is subjectively in equilibrium if and only if the following condition is satisfied:

$$s = 0 \quad \text{if } \bar{\rho}_I < (1 - t_r)r, \text{ or}$$

$$s = \frac{W}{V} + \hat{s} \quad \text{if } \bar{\rho}_I - \pi_I(W + \hat{s}V) > (1 - t_r)r, \text{ or} \qquad (5)$$

$$\bar{\rho}_I - \pi_I(sV) = (1 - t_r)r.$$

As shown in Table 1, the ex post after-tax annual rate of return
from shareholdings was 17.0% on the average during the period
1962-1977 while the one-year deposit rate was 5.98% on the average
during the same period.  However, there are substantial costs
involved in individual trades of shares, particularly for lower
wealth holders.  Fees charged by stockbrokers for stock trades
are non-negligible and highly regressive.[8]  Therefore, if an
individual investor is substantially risk-averse and his wealth is
not large, the advantage of shareholdings might be more than
offset by the higher rate of risk premium and by the transaction
costs involved in stock trades, and he would hold his entire
wealth in the form of bank deposits.  But if an investor is reasonably risk-taking and his wealth is large enough to make use of
economies of scale in transaction costs, then diversification of

Table VI-1.  The Rate of Return to Shareholding

| Y | (1) d/V | (2) ΔV/V | (3) $t_d$ | (4) (1)×(3) | (5) (2)+(4) |
|---|---|---|---|---|---|
| 1962 | 5.6 | 13.6 | 10 | 5.0 | 18.6 |
| 1963 | 5.2 | -9.0 | 10 | 4.7 | -4.3 |
| 1964 | 5.8 | -0.1 | 5 | 5.6 | 5.4 |
| 1965 | 5.6 | 22.7 | 5 | 5.3 | 28.0 |
| 1966 | 4.9 | 1.2 | 15 | 4.2 | 5.4 |
| 1967 | 5.2 | 11.0 | 15 | 4.4 | 15.4 |
| 1968 | 4.9 | 32.5 | 20 | 4.0 | 36.4 |
| 1969 | 4.1 | 8.2 | 20 | 3.3 | 11.5 |
| 1970 | 4.4 | 15.5 | 20 | 3.5 | 19.0 |
| 1971 | 3.6 | 68.6 | 20 | 2.9 | 71.5 |
| 1972 | 2.4 | 28.0 | 20 | 1.9 | 29.9 |
| 1973 | 2.1 | -13.5 | 25 | 1.6 | -11.9 |
| 1974 | 2.4 | 3.7 | 25 | 1.8 | 5.5 |
| 1975 | 2.4 | 13.9 | 25 | 1.8 | 15.7 |
| 1976 | 2.2 | 9.6 | 30 | 1.5 | 11.1 |
| 1977 | 2.2 | 12.9 | 30 | 1.5 | 14.4 |
| AVE | 3.9 | 13.7 | | 3.3 | 17.0 |
| C.O.V. | 0.36 | 1.35 | | 0.43 | 1.08 |

Note: Estimates of d/V and ΔV/V were provided by the Japan Securities
Research Institute. $t_d$ is the maximum separable tax rate on dividends.

his wealth among deposits and shareholdings would be a non-negligible possibility. Below, we shall assume that the representative individual diversifies so that the third condition (5) above holds. Later I will suggest a way to allow for the existence of risk-averse and/or lower wealth holders who are specialized in deposits and for whom the first condition of (5) holds.

(b) The bank. We deal with a single "bank" and do not make any distinction between city banks, which are normally borrowers in inter-bank markets (such as the call market and bill discount market), and other banks or bank-like institutions, which are normally lenders there. Also, we treat the bank's borrowings from the Bank of Japan only implicitly. Because of these simplifications, we assume away a number of interesting and important aspects of banking behavior. We would like to pick up instead a missing ring in the orthodox analysis of banks' portfolio selection, i.e., the choice between credit holdings and shareholdings. Although the proportion of shareholdings of city banks in their total assets appears to be very small (a little more than 3% in 1981) on their balance sheets, shares are evaluated at their acquisition value, resulting in gross underestimation thereof.[9] If portfolio firms (i.e., firms whose shares banks hold) retain their profits, then this ought to be reflected in their share values. As capital gains are not taxable until realized, the effective tax rate on capital gains of banks is considered to be much lower than the corporate tax rate applicable to profits made by credit holdings. Thus, shareholdings of banks seem to constitute an item in their portfolios which is significant both as an income generating investment and as a tax advantageous reserve.[10] Further, from the viewpoint of portfolio firms, banks are by far the most important and influential shareholders, as we saw in the introductory chapter. This indicates that banks have the potential power to influence the financial policies of their portfolio firms. Issues relating to banks' shareholdings thus seem to constitute an important researchable topic in spite of their relative neglect by monetary economists.

Let us introduce the following notation to describe the portfolio selection behavior of the bank:

$t_c$ = the corporate tax rate on bank's earnings other than capital gains and dividend receipts.

$t_{bd}$ = the corporate tax rate applicable to dividend
     receipts.

$t_g$ = the (effective) tax rate on capital gains.

$r_L$ = the nominal lending rate.

$r_b$ = the interest rate on deposits held by the firm.

$\bar{D}$ = total deposits at the bank.

M = initial cash position of the bank.

n = the number of shares of the firm held by the bank.

L = total loans extended to the firm.

R = reserves.

Among these, $t_c$, $t_{bd}$, and $t_g$ are treated as parameters satisfying
the inequality $t_c > t_g > t_{bd}$.[11] Allowing for the fact that
lending rates were regulated according to the Temporary Money Rate
Adjustment Act until 1971 and by implicit inter-bank agreements
thereafter based on the official discount rate of the Bank of
Japan,[12] both the nominal lending rate of the model, $r_L$, and the
interest rate on deposits held by the firm, $r_b$, are treated as
parameters satisfying the inequality $r_L > r > r_b$. However, as we
shall see presently, this does not imply that the effective lending
rate is beyond the control of the bank.

The budget constraint of the bank is given by

$$L + nV + R = \bar{D} + M + \hat{n}V$$

where $\hat{n}$ denotes the number of shares held initially.[13] The
deposit liabilities $\bar{D}$ of the bank in this model consist of two
parts: the primary deposits D of the (representative) individual
investor and the so-called compensating balances of the firm.
Since the deposit rate is treated as a parameter, the amount of
deposits D chosen by the (representative) individual investor is
not under the direct control of the bank. On the other hand, the
nonfinancial firm to which bank credit is extended is normally
required to set aside a portion of the loan and to hold it as
compensating balances with the bank at a lower deposit rate, $r_b$.
The rate of retention α is actually considered to be determined
through bilateral negotiations between the bank and the firm but
to reflect the general conditions of the financial market. In this
model, it is determined competitively, as specified later. In
actuality, bank deposits also include a portion made by small and
risk-averse individual savers who do not diversify their wealths

into shareholdings and who are not recognized in this model explicitly. I assume that those deposits as well as loans from the Bank of Japan are included in M. M is, together with the reserve requirement R, treated as a parameter. Share price is also determined exogenously in the market and given parametrically to the bank as in the case of the individual investor. Thus, the budget constraint for portfolio selection (n, L) by the bank becomes

$$(1 - \alpha)L + nV = D + n\hat{V} + [M - R]. \tag{6}$$

In selecting its portfolio, the bank is under legal and institutional constraints. A ceiling is set on the shareholdings of banks by the Anti-Monopoly regulation, as described in the introductory chapter. Therefore, we require $n \leq \bar{n}$ for some $\bar{n}$. On the other hand, the bank may be required to hold a minimum number of shares of the firm in order to maintain a stable customer relationship with it and/or to control its financial policy. Therefore, we assume that $\underline{n} \geq n$ for some value of $\underline{n}$. It could happen that $\bar{n} < \underline{n}$, and if that is the case, we assume that only the upper bound constraint is effective.

If the bank increases its lending to the firm by ¥1 but requires ¥$\alpha$ of compensating balances, the net gain to the bank in interest receipts is $r_L - \alpha r_b$, while the opportunity cost of the loan in terms of foregone investment in shares is $1 - \alpha$. The effective lending rate of the bank is then

$$\hat{r} = \frac{r_L - \alpha r_b}{1 - \alpha}. \tag{7}$$

The after-tax end-of-the-period return is given by

$$R_B = (1 - t_c)[(1 - \alpha)\hat{r}L - C] + (1 - t_{bd})nd$$
$$+ (1 - t_g)n\Delta V,$$

where C represents the costs of the bank inclusive of interest payments rD on primary deposits held by the individual investor, on deposits by small savers and on loans from the Bank of Japan. Suppose that the risk attitude of the bank[14] is represented by a concave von Neumann-Morgenstern utility function v of the constant absolute risk aversion type, with the degree of absolute risk aversion being represented by $-v''/v' = A_B$. We assume away the tradability of shares in the bank's profit.

Difine the after-tax rate of return from shareholdings of the bank
by

$$\rho_B = (1 - t_{bd})\frac{d}{V} + (1 - t_g)\frac{\Delta V}{V} . \tag{8}$$

As in the case of the individual investor, the expected value of
$\rho_B$, $\bar{\rho}_B$, depends upon the financial policy of the firm, but it is
assumed that its variance $\sigma_B^2$ is subjectively believed by the bank
to be invariant to policy changes.  Then, as in the case of the
individual investor, we can derive the condition of subjective
equilibrium portfolio (n, L) of the bank as follows:

$$\left.\begin{array}{l} n = \underline{n}, \qquad \text{if } \bar{\rho}_B - (1 - t_c)\hat{r} < 0; \\[2ex] (n - \bar{n})E[v'(R_B)(\bar{\rho}_B - (1 - t_c)\hat{r}] = 0, \quad \text{otherwise.} \end{array}\right\} \tag{9}$$

Equivalently,

$$\left.\begin{array}{ll} n = \underline{n} & \text{if } \quad \bar{\rho}_B < (1 - t_c)\hat{r}, \\[2ex] n = \bar{n} & \text{if } \quad \bar{\rho}_B - \pi_B(\bar{n}V) > (1 - t_c)\hat{r}, \quad \text{or} \\[2ex] \bar{\rho}_B - \pi_B(nV) = (1 - t_c)\hat{r}, \quad \text{otherwise;} \end{array}\right\} \tag{10}$$

where

$$\pi_B(nV) = A_B\sigma_B^2 nV,$$

denotes the rate of the bank's risk premium for shareholding.

Let me comment on some of the limitations of the model, specifically
regarding bank behavior.  First, the risk of default on the repayment
of bank loans is not recognized in this model, and the only risk
that the bank faces is assumed to be the one involved in shareholding.
Secondly, as a corollary of the first simplification, the reserve
requirement, R, is treated as an exogenous policy parameter and
its aspect as a portfolio decision variable of the bank is not
recognized.  Thirdly, by the same token, the role of shareholding
as a reserve is ignored.  This is particularly unsatisfactory in
view of the fact that Japanese banks often write off bad debts
through the tax-free realization of capital gains from shareholdings.

Unsatisfactory as this model of bank behavior may be, however, I
hope that it will serve the purpose of providing us with an understanding of the mechanism of corporate finance in its simple form.

(c) The representative firm. The firm in this model is considered
to represent the non-financial corporate sector. The level of
investment of the firm for the current period T = 0 is given
exogenously. We need only compare the relative advantage of financing
the predetermined level of investment by borrowing from the bank
to that of financing it by the internal retention of (current
period) profits. Suppose that the predetermined level of investment
by the firm is ¥100$I^0$ and that the firm initially plans to finance
$\gamma$% of it by borrowing from the bank. The firm now considers
modifiying its financial policy so as to increase its degree of
reliance on debt financing by one percentage point, which requires
it to borrow $I^0/(1 - \alpha)$ more from the bank including an increase
in its compensating balances. From the cash flow constraint, such
a perturbation of financial policy will cause the firm to increase
dividends in the current period by

$$\frac{\partial d^0}{\partial \gamma} = [1 + (t_c - t_{cd})] I^0 . \tag{11}$$

The borrowing rate net of interest receipts from the compensating
balances is $(r_L - \alpha r_b)$ per ¥1 of debt and is payable in the next
period. Then, the decrease in next period's dividend payout
resulting from the perturbation is given by

$$\frac{\partial d^1}{\partial \gamma} = -[1 + t_c - t_{cd} + (1 - t_{cd})\hat{r}] I^0 \tag{12}$$

where $t_{cd}$ = the corporate tax rate applicable to dividend payouts
and satisfies the condition $t_{cd} < t_c$.[15] It is assumed that the
firm will pursue the same policy after period T = 1 so that

$$\frac{\partial v^2}{\partial \gamma} = 0. \tag{13}$$

How is such a perturbation evaluated by the firm? Suppose that
the firm must choose a financial policy before the opening of the
current stock market. The firm is, in general, expected to choose
a financial policy which is in the "interest of shareholders" who
held stock in the firm at the time of the opening of the stock
market (ex ante shareholders). The problem is that there are two

types of shareholders, i.e., the individual investor and the bank,
and there may not exist perfect unanimity of interest between
them. We shall postpone discussion of how $\gamma$ is chosen and accomodated
until after we introduce the notion of financial equilibrium
relative to a predetermined $I^0$.

(d) <u>Financial equilibrium</u>. Given the tax system, portfolio $(s^T,$
$D^T)$ of the primary investor, portfolio $(n^T, L^T)$ of the bank, share
price $V^T$, effective lending (borrowing) rate $\hat{r}^T$, and the rate of
compensatory retention $\alpha^T$ constitute a <u>financial equilibrium</u> in
period $T(= 0, 1, 2, ...)$ relative to a financial policy of the
firm $\gamma$, an expection regarding next period's share price $V^{T+1}$ and
a deposit rate $r^T$ if:

> (i) For the primary investor and the bank, the portfolios
> are optimal.
> (ii) V equates supply and demand in the stock market:

$$\hat{s}^T + \hat{n}^T = s^T + n^T .\tag{14}$$

> (iii) The firm's borrowings are set equal to the bank's
> lendings through adjustment of the effective lending
> rate.

$$\gamma^T I^T = L^T(1 - \alpha^T)\tag{15}$$

There are four conditions for optimal portfolio selection
[(1)(5)(6)(10)] and three market equilibrium conditions [(7)(14)(15)].
The number of endogenous variables is seven. From (1), (6), (14) and
(15), for an equilibrium to exist for a given $\gamma$, it must hold that

$$\gamma^T I^T = W^T + M^T - R^T.\tag{16}$$

Thus, the rate of debt financing cannot be chosen independently of
the parametric value of M - R. Put differently, a change in the
value of $\gamma$ must be accompanied by a corresponding change in M - R:

$$\frac{\partial [M^T - R^T]}{\partial \gamma^T} = I^T.\tag{17}$$

This condition may be interpreted as stating that increases in the
need for debt financing must be accomodated by corresponding
increases in loans from the Bank of Japan, as well as in exogenous

deposits of small savers, and/or relaxation of the reserve requirement. Below, we assume that M - R adjusts according to (17).

## 2. THE ABSENCE OF SHAREHOLDERS' UNANIMITY

This section proves the following proposition regarding the impact on the firm's financial policymaking of the absence of unanimity between two types of ex ante shareholders: the individual investor and the bank. The proof is rather technical, and those readers who do not care for technical detail might wish to skip it and proceed directly to the next section, which interprets the investment financing behavior of Japanese corporations in light of this proposition.

Proposition. Suppose that the individual investor and the bank diversify their portfolios on a certain region of $\gamma$. Then, the individual investor wants the firm to maximize its share price, whereas the bank wants it to rely upon debt financing to a greater degree than is warranted for share price maximization. Suppose that the firm's financial policy is determined through resolution of this conflict of interest. Then the difference between the after-corporate-tax effective borrowing rate and the rate of returns to individual shareholding, i.e.,

$$\Delta = (1 - t_{cd})\hat{r} - \rho_I , \tag{18}$$

increases monotonically with the relative strength of the bank's influence on the determination of the firm's policy. When this magnitude is sufficiently high, the bank holds the firm's shares only in order to maintain customer relations with the firm.

Suppose that the individual investor diversifies on a certain region of $\gamma$. Then the third equation of (5) always holds. Suppose that the expectation of the representative investor in the current period (T=0) is "rational" in the sense that the expected value of share price is realized in the next period (T=1). Then, by the envelope theorem, the current share price $V^0$ and the expected (and eventually realized) future share price $V^T$ (T = 1) satisfy the following relation:

$$[1 + (1 - t_r)r]\frac{\partial V^T}{\partial \gamma} + \frac{\partial (V^T_\gamma \pi^T_I)}{\partial \gamma}$$

$$= \frac{\partial V^{T+1}}{\partial \gamma} + (1 - t_d)\frac{\partial d^T}{\partial \gamma}, \quad T = 0, 1. \tag{19}$$

where $\pi^T_I = \pi_I(s^T V^T)$. Since the individual investor's utility function is of the constant absolute risk aversion type, it holds for $T = 0, 1$ that

$$\frac{\partial [V^T \pi^T_I]}{\partial \gamma} = \pi^T_I[2 + (V^T\frac{\partial s^T}{\partial \gamma}/s^T\frac{\partial V^T}{\partial \gamma})]\frac{\partial V^T}{\partial \gamma} = \pi^T_I\frac{\partial V^T}{\partial \gamma} \ .$$

Substituting this relation and (11)(12)(13) into (19), we have

$$\underset{T=0,1}{\Pi}[1 + (1 - t_r)r + \pi^T_I]\frac{\partial V^0}{\partial \gamma}$$

$$= (1 - t_d)[-(1 - t_{cd})\hat{r} \tag{20}$$

$$+ (1 + t_c - t_{cd})((1 - t_r)r + \pi^1_I)]I^0.$$

Ignoring the smaller term $(t_c - t_{cd})[(1 - t_r)r + \pi^1_I]$, therefore,

$$\frac{\partial V^0}{\partial \gamma} \gtreqless 0 \quad \text{approximately according as}$$

$$(1 - t_{cd})\hat{r} \lesseqgtr (1 - t_r)r + \pi_I, \tag{21}$$

or considering the third equation of (5),

$$\frac{\partial V^0}{\partial \gamma} \lesseqgtr 0 \text{ according as } \Delta \gtreqless 0.$$

The condition (21) is easy to understand for the case in which the individual investor is risk-neutral so that $\pi_I = 0$. For this case, if the firm increases borrowings by ¥1 per share, it can increase its dividend payment in the current period by ¥$[1 + (t_c - t_{cd})]$ while maintaining a predetermined investment level. If the individual investor maintains the same consumption level as before the change in financial policy, he can increase bank deposits by the amount ¥$(1 - t_d)[1 + (t_c - t_{cd})]$, and his after-tax gain in the next period will be ¥$(1 - t_d)[1 + (t_c - t_{cd})][1 + (1 - t_r)r]$. However, in order to fulfill its increased interest payment obligations, the firm must reduce its dividend payment per share by the amount $¥[1 + (t_c - t_{cd}) + (1 - t_{cd})\hat{r}]$ in the next period, as shown by (12). The after-tax loss per share to the individual investor is, needless to say, this amount times $(1 - t_d)$. Comparing the marginal after-tax benefit and cost, the individual investor is better off by the increase in debt-financing approximately if $(1 - t_{cd})\hat{r} < (1 - t_r)r$ and vice versa, and this ought to be reflected in the share price. If the individual investor is risk-averse, then the risk premium for share price variation in the next period needs to be deducted from the marginal cost of debt financing.

This calculus suggests that share-price maximization coincides with the interest of the individual investor, even if he is risk averse and embedded in a complicated tax system. In order to ascertain this inference, let us differentiate the expected utility of the individual investor $E[u(R_I)]$ with respect to $\gamma$ and denote $E[u'(R_I)]$ by $\bar{u}'$:

$$\frac{\partial E[u(R_I)]}{\partial \gamma} = E[u'(R_I)\frac{\partial R_I}{\partial \gamma}]$$

$$= E[u'(R_I)\{(1 - t_r)r[(\hat{s} - s)\frac{\partial V}{\partial \gamma} - r\frac{\partial s}{\partial \gamma}v]$$

$$+ \frac{\partial s}{\partial \gamma}\Delta V + s\frac{\partial \Delta V}{\partial \gamma} + (1 - t_d)[\frac{\partial d}{\partial \gamma}s + d\frac{\partial s}{\partial \gamma}]\}]$$

$$= \bar{u}'[(1 - t_r)r\hat{s} + s_{\pi I}]\frac{\partial V}{\partial \gamma}, \quad \text{using (3)(19).}$$

Therefore, the individual investor's expected utility is maximized when share price is maximized. Further, going back to (20), it is also found that:

(a) the rate of tax on individual dividend income does not affect the relative advantage of alternative financial policies of the firm from the investor's point of view; and that

(b) the differential tax treatment of firm profits paid out as dividends $(t_{cd} < t_c)$ will make the marginal benefit to the individual investor of debt financing slightly more, thus making this method of financing more attractive to him.

Now let us turn to the bank's side. On the region of $\gamma$ over which the bank diversifies, the current share price $V^0$ and the expected future share price $V^1$ must always satisfy the third condition of (10). Therefore, by the envelope theorem, we have

$$[(1 - t_c)\hat{r}^0 + (1 - t_g) + \pi_B^0]\frac{\partial V^0}{\partial \gamma} + (1 - t_c)V^0\frac{\partial \hat{r}^0}{\partial \gamma}$$

$$= (1 - t_{bd})\frac{\partial d^0}{\partial \gamma} + (1 - t_g)\frac{\partial V^1}{\partial \gamma} . \qquad (22)$$

Substituting from (19) and then (5)(10),

$$(1 - t_c)V^0\frac{\partial \hat{r}^0}{\partial \gamma} = [(1 - t_{bd}) - (1 - t_g)(1 - t_d)]\frac{\partial d^0}{\partial \gamma}$$

$$+ \{(1 - t_g)[(1 - t_r)r + \pi_I^0]$$

$$- (1 - t_c)\hat{r}^0 - \pi_B^0\}\frac{\partial V^0}{\partial \gamma}$$

$$= (t_g + t_d - t_{bd})(\frac{\partial d^0}{\partial \gamma} - \frac{\partial V^0}{\partial \gamma})$$

$$+ [(1 - t_g)\pi_I^0 - \pi_B^0]\frac{\partial V^0}{\partial \gamma} .$$

By assumption, $t_d > 0 > t_{bd} - t_g$ so that, if $\pi_I > \pi_B/(1 - t_g)$,

$$\frac{\partial \hat{r}^0}{\partial \gamma} > 0 \qquad \text{when} \qquad \frac{\partial V^0}{\partial \gamma} \leq 0.$$

Therefore, if the individual investor is at least as risk-taking as the bank in shareholding, then an increase in debt financing (accomodated by an exogenous increase in the cash position of the bank) beyond the value-maximizing point always leads to a rise in the effective lending rate. This property seems to hold even if the bank is more risk-taking than the individual investor because of the discounting factor $(1 - t_g)$. Therefore, one may say that the magnitude, $\Delta = (1 - t_{cd})\hat{r} - \rho_I$, increases monotonically as the firm increases its reliance on debt financing beyond the value-maximizing point.

Finally, let us examine how the bank's expected utility level changes in response to an increase in debt financing of the firm's investment. In so doing, suppose that the bank ignores the possible effect of this change on the amount of deposits made by the individual investor —— in other words, that the bank assumes that $\partial D/\partial \gamma =_B 0$, where $=_B$ denotes the bank's subjective assessment. Differentiating $E[v(R_B)]$ with respect to $\gamma$ and denoting $E[v'(R_B)]$ by $\bar{v}'$ and the marginal cost of increasing cash position, M-R, to meet the increased demand for investment funds by c, we have

$$\frac{\partial E[v(R_B)]}{\partial \gamma} = E[v'(R_B)\frac{\partial R_B}{\partial \gamma}]$$

$$= E[v'(R_B)\{(1 - t_{bd})(\frac{\partial d}{\partial \gamma}n + d\frac{\partial n}{\partial \gamma})$$

$$+ (1 - t_g)(\frac{\partial \Delta V}{\partial \gamma}n + \Delta V\frac{\partial n}{\partial \gamma})$$

$$+ (1 - t_c)(1 - \alpha)((\hat{r} - c)\frac{\partial L}{\partial \gamma} + \frac{\partial \hat{r}}{\partial \gamma}L)\}] \qquad (23)$$

$$=_B(1 - t_c)\bar{v}'\{[\hat{n}\hat{r} + \frac{n\pi_B}{(1 - t_c)}]\frac{\partial V}{\partial \gamma}$$

$$+ (1 - \alpha)[(\frac{nV}{(1-\alpha)} + L))\frac{\partial \hat{r}}{\partial \gamma} + (\hat{r} - c)\frac{\partial L}{\partial \gamma}]\},$$

using (6)(10). The first term within the large brackets represents the capital loss on initial shareholdings and the increased risk cost of new shareholdings when $\partial V/\partial \gamma$ is negative, while the second term represents the gains from the increase in the effective lending rate as well as from the increase in debt financing. Since the second term is positive if $\hat{r} - c \geq 0$, it dominates the first term in the neighborhood of $\partial V/\partial \gamma = 0$, and it holds there that

$$\frac{\partial [Ev(R_B)]}{\partial \gamma} > 0.$$

That is, the bank desires the firm to increase its reliance on debt financing beyond the level warranted by share-price maximization, and there is a clear conflict of interest between the two types of shareholders. The greater the value of $\Delta$, the greater the scope for increasing share price through a reduction in debt financing. Therefore, the magnitude of $\Delta$ can be interpreted as measuring the relative strength of the bank's influence on the determination of the financial policy of the firm, provided that the value of $\gamma$ is not too far from the value maximizing level. Also note that the condition $\hat{r} - c \geq 0$ is sufficient but not necessary to insure that the bank's expected utility will increase due to an increase in debt financing. If the income effect from a rise in the effective lending rate is sufficiently high, then the effect of a marginal increase in the cost of improving the bank's cash position beyond

the effective lending rate (say, by borrowing from the Bank of
Japan) will be more than offset.  Thus, it may be inferred that
the practice of so-called "over-loan" by the Bank of Japan[16] is in
the interest of the banking sector at the expense of the interest
of individual investors.

Finally, let us examine the possibility that the bank does not
diversify except for constrained shareholdings.  Suppose that  n =
$\underline{n}$.  Then, given the firm's financial policy, relations (2)(3) and
(14) determine the equilibrium values of V and D.  Substituting
these values into the first inequality of (10) would leave the
level of $\hat{r}$ indeterminate.  An examination of (23) reveals that
$\partial[E(v)]/\partial\gamma > 0$ when $\partial V/\partial\gamma \leq 0$, even if the bank does not diversify,
so that the first inequality of (10) holds.  Therefore, the stronger
the bargaining power of the bank, the higher the value of $\hat{r}$ and
accordingly the higher the value of $\Delta$.  Conversely, if the value
of $\Delta$ is very high so that

$$\Delta > (1 - t_c)\hat{r} - (1 - t_r)r - \pi_I + (t_{bd} - t_d)\frac{d}{V} + t_g\frac{\Delta V}{V}$$

$$-[\pi_I + \pi_B] ,$$

then

$$\bar{\rho}_B - (1 - t_c)\hat{r} - \pi_B < \bar{\rho}_I - (1 - t_r)r - \pi_I = 0$$

and the bank holds only the minimum number of shares $\underline{n}$ necessary
for maintaining customer relations with the firm.  This completes
our proof of the proposition.


3.   WHY HAS DEBT FINANCING DECLINED?

According to the proposition in the previous section and (21), the
magnitude $\Delta$, equivalent to the difference between the after-
corporate-tax effective borrowing rate and the after-personal-tax
deposit rate plus the rate of individual risk premium, measures
the possibility of increasing the share price through a reduction
in the debt financing of investments. Since the individual investor
is interested in share price maximization while the bank wants the
firm to increase borrowings beyond the share-price maximizing
level, this magnitude may be thought of as an index measuring the
bank's influence over the non-financial corporate firm.  Let us,

for the time being, ignore the rate of individual risk premium $\pi_I$, let $t_r = 0$ by assuming an investor who can make full use of the Small Saving Tax-Exempt System,[17] and consider quarterly time-series data on $(1 - t_{cd})\hat{r}$ and $r$, as depicted in Figure 1. The estimates of the effective lending rate $\hat{r}$ is due to Mr. Wakita of the Bank of Japan[18] and the deposit rate $r$ is the one-year time deposit rate. Evidently, $(1 - t_{cd})\hat{r} - r$ exhibits a declining trend. While the average difference between the two rates was 2.8% between the first quarter of 1962 and the fourth quarter of 1972, it declined to 1.2% between the first quarter of 1973 and the fourth quarter of 1982.

Why has this declining tendency occurred? If banks have no influence over the choice of financial policy of non-financial corporations (in other words, if the firm maximizes its share price and $\Delta = 0$ throughout), then it must hold that the rate of individual risk premium has declined. I have not yet investigated whether, in fact, individual investors became more risk-taking in the 1970s.[19] However, as the time series data on $\Delta V/V$ in Table 1 show, the boom stock market experienced a sudden setback after the first oil shock and many individual shareholders are said to have incurred heavy capital losses in the process. As a result, many individual investors are said to have "fled from shareholding (<u>kabu</u> <u>banare</u>)". The proportion of individual shareholdings, which had been about 40% of total shares outstanding on the Tokyo Stock Exchange at the end of 1970, had declined to 32.7% by the end of 1973. This simple statistic suggests that, if anything, individual investors became more prudent about shareholding.

However, as the model of the previous section indicates, what is relevant to share-price formation is the risk attitudes of individual investors who diversify their financial assets between shareholdings and deposits at the financial equilibrium. Such investors might have become satisfied with lower rates of risk premium because of the increased opportunities for diversification made possible by their accumulation of wealth. Furthermore, throughout the 1970s, the proportion of foreign shareholders tended to increase (from 3.2% at the end of 1970 to 4.6% at the end of 1981). These foreign investors invest in foreign stocks as well, whose returns are not perfectly correlated with those of Japanese stocks, and their investments in Japanese stocks constitute only a small portion of

*M. Aoki*

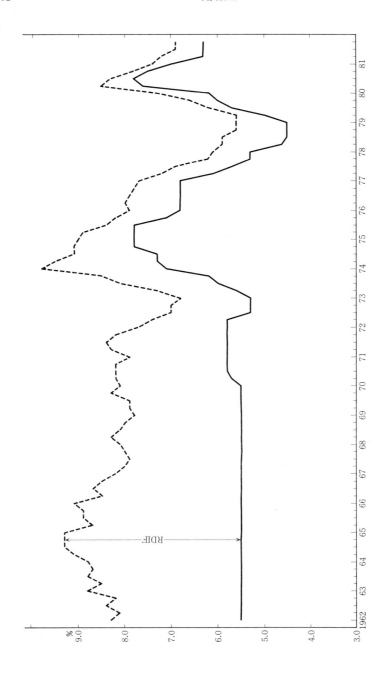

Figure VI-1  The Time Series of the Deposit Rate r ( —— ) and
the After-Corporate Tax Effective Lending Rate $\hat{r}(1-t_{cd})$ (----)

their wealth. Therefore, the risk costs to foreign investors of holding Japanese shares may be relatively smaller.[20] In sum, there are factors which operate on the rate of individual risk premium in the opposite direction, and whether or not the rate has declined on balance must be ascertained through further investigation.

If the declining rate of individual risk premium cannot explain the declining tendency of the difference between $(1 - t_d)\hat{r}$ and $r$, or can explain only a portion of it, then one is led to the conclusion that the power balance between individual investors and banks has been tilting in disfavor of banks during the 1970s — in other words, that the criteria of share-price maximization has become more strongly reflected in the firms' choice of financial structure. And, theoretically, this would decrease the firm's dependence on debt financing for a "given" investment. In actuality, however, the rate of debt financing may be affected by the "level" of investment as well, although this variable was taken to be given in the model. The reason is that, for a given amount of internally generated funds, there may be only limited scope for the adjustment of the dividend payout ratio, and accordingly, even if the power balance between banks and individual shareholders remains unchanged, one might expect an increased level of investment to lead to a higher rate of debt financing.

How did the actual pattern of investment finance vary from the 1960 to the 1970s? To what extent is it related to the changing level of investments in the non-financial corporate sector? To what extent is it caused by a possible change in the relative bargaining power of the banking sector? Or are the two causes not statistically separable?

The data in Table 2 are constructed from the NEEDS Corporate Financial Data and summarize the sources of investible funds of all manufacturing corporations listed on the Tokyo Stock Exchange.[21] The definitions of the variables are:

> DE = annual increase (from the beginning of each calendar year to the end of the next year) in equity capital trough new share issues and the retention of profits.
> DC = annual depreciation charges.
> DR = annual increase in profit-related reserves.[22]
> DW = annual increase in reserves for employees' retirement compensation.

Table VI-2.   Sources of Long-Term Funds
of Listed Manufacturing Corporations

(unit: ¥ million, α: %)

| FY | DE | DC | DR | DW | DBD | DBK | α |
|---|---|---|---|---|---|---|---|
| 1966 | 244892 | 778890 | 92169 | 58915 | 19903 | 118839 | 0.510 |
| 1967 | 468642 | 871138 | 139197 | 86416 | 158996 | 389639 | 0.475 |
| 1968 | 617522 | 997354 | 100153 | 93718 | 162154 | 510061 | 0.469 |
| 1969 | 999318 | 1205007 | 224075 | 118552 | 131321 | 579666 | 0.458 |
| 1970 | 1005238 | 1445948 | 184242 | 126884 | 182147 | 838671 | 0.448 |
| 1971 | 539876 | 1630354 | 96909 | 131773 | 220008 | 392022 | 0.504 |
| 1972 | 931425 | 1722387 | 160541 | 166354 | 52074 | 371974 | 0.474 |
| 1973 | 1275848 | 1913475 | 301952 | 361351 | 141791 | 568134 | 0.444 |
| 1974 | 937403 | 2159673 | 51764 | 415023 | 146218 | 1490147 | 0.395 |
| 1975 | 660550 | 2258196 | -366464 | 231270 | 839492 | 876285 | 0.419 |
| 1976 | 1103003 | 2309061 | -86263 | 247719 | 123519 | 320381 | 0.432 |
| 1977 | 1244916 | 2363237 | -103706 | 234268 | 156479 | -101005 | 0.421 |
| 1978 | 1509766 | 2511757 | -133816 | 180591 | 149568 | -981286 | 0.446 |
| 1979 | 2175797 | 2770689 | -93467 | 227979 | 239396 | -216977 | 0.421 |
| 1980 | 2957438 | 2981806 | -65798 | 211103 | -113841 | 362727 | 0.413 |

Notes: Constructed From NEEDS Corporate Financial Data.   The figures in the table
are for the end of each fiscal year.   The estimates of α used for the calculation
of DBK are by Wakita.   The estimate of α for the end of fiscal year 1965 is 0.539.

Table VI-3.   Regression Data

| FY | Υ | RDIF | NI | V |
|---|---|---|---|---|
| 1966 | 0.090 | 3.22 | 0.0091 | 0.168 |
| 1967 | 0.184 | 2.54 | 0.0401 | 0.172 |
| 1968 | 0.206 | 2.61 | 0.0464 | 0.168 |
| 1969 | 0.178 | 2.47 | 0.0475 | 0.168 |
| 1970 | 0.222 | 2.53 | 0.0487 | 0.179 |
| 1971 | 0.130 | 2.44 | 0.0314 | 0.178 |
| 1972 | 0.109 | 1.76 | 0.0141 | 0.164 |
| 1973 | 0.125 | 1.92 | 0.0241 | 0.181 |
| 1974 | 0.287 | 2.04 | 0.0286 | 0.205 |
| 1975 | 0.195 | 1.04 | 0.0120 | 0.205 |
| 1976 | 0.080 | 1.15 | 0.0088 | 0.189 |
| 1977 | -0.027 | 1.02 | 0.0059 | 0.171 |
| 1978 | -0.200 | 1.14 | 0.0030 | 0.157 |
| 1979 | -0.043 | 0.71 | 0.0048 | 0.157 |
| 1980 | 0.057 | 0.70 | 0.0104 | 0.164 |
| AVE. | 0.106 | 1.82 | 0.0223 | 0.175 |
| S.D. | 0.119 | 0.78 | 0.0163 | 0.014 |

Note:   Constructed from Table 2 as described in the text.

DBD = annual increase in long-term bonds outstanding.

DBK = annual increase in long-term debts from banks net of estimated compensating balances.

  (α = estimate of the rate of retention of compensating balances.)

Profit-related reserves and reserves for employees' retirement compensation are retained within the corporation and are available as long-term funds at the management's discretion (they are classified as long-term debt on balance sheets). Let us define the relative ratio of borrowings from banks to total long-term funds as

$$\gamma = \frac{DBK}{DE + DC + DR + DW + |DBD| + |DBK|} \quad [24]$$

Time-series data on γ thus defined and tabulated in the first column of Table 3 indicate that the dependence of the manufacturing sector on bank debt exhibits a declining tendency in the 1970s except during the adjustment period after the first oil shock (1973-75). The variables shown in the second through fourth columns were chosen because they are possible factors which could explain the changing pattern of investment finance in the manufacturing sector. They are:

RDIF = the estimate of the effective lending rate by Wakita[25] at the beginning of each fiscal year times [1 - the corporate tax rate applicable to dividends] less the one-year time deposit rate at the beginning of each fiscal year.

NI = the level of gross investment in equipment and buildings normalized by sales.

V = the level of inventories at the end of each fiscal year normalized by sales.

Ignoring investors' risk premiums, RDIF may be considered as corresponding to Δ in the last section and hence as measuring the relative degree of a bank's influence over its portfolio firms. V is adopted as a proxy variable which represents the state of product markets as well as the degree of managerial efficiency. A problem is the possible collinearity which may exist between RDIF and NI. Namely, when the level of investment is high, banks may be able to extract a higher interest rate because of the

limited amount of internal funds.  The correlation matrix is
computed as:

|       | $\gamma$ | RDIF  | NI    | V     |
|-------|----------|-------|-------|-------|
| RDIF  | 0.560    | 1.000 |       |       |
| NI    | 0.720    | 0.695 | 1.000 |       |
| V     | 0.630    | 0.029 | 0.136 | 1.000 |

There is, in fact, a considerable degree of correlation between
RDIF and NI.  So one cannot expect to obtain reliable regression
coefficients by regressing $\gamma$ on RDIF, NI and V using the ordinary
least squares method.  In order to cope with the multicollinearity
problem, I employ principal component analysis.[26]  First, the
sample vectors RDIF, NI, and V must be transformed into standardized
sample vectors RDIF*, NI*, and V* by subtracting the average value
from each observation and dividing by the standard deviation of
the variable.  The average value of the standardized variables is
zero and the variance is equal to unity.  The principal components
are the weighted sum of these normalized vectors:

$$x_i = \beta_{i1}\text{RDIF*} + \beta_{i2}\text{NI*} + \beta_{i3}\text{V*} \quad (i = 1,2,3),$$

where the vector of weighting coefficients $\beta_i = (\beta_{i1}, \beta_{i2}, \beta_{i3})$
corresponds to the i-th characteristic vector of the correlation
matrix of RDIF*, NI*, and V*.  Since there are three independent
characteristic vectors in the matrix, the three standardized
sample vectors are transformed into three principal components.
The variance of each principal component is equal to the characteristic root corresponding to the weighting characteristic vector.
Let us order these principal components according to the magnitudes
of the variances (characteristic roots).

The correlation coefficients between the principal components and
the normalized sample vectors are given as:

| principal component | $x_1$ | $x_2$ | $x_3$ |
|---|---|---|---|
| RDIF* | 0.905 | −0.189 | 0.379 |
| NI* | 0.921 | −0.037 | −0.386 |
| V* | 0.212 | 0.975 | 0.058 |
| variance | 1.71 | 0.99 | 0.30 |
| relative contribution to the variance of the sample | 57.1% | 33.0% | 9.9% |
| cumulative contribution to the variance of the sample | 57.1% | 90.1% | 100.0% |

According to this table, 57.1% of the variance of the normalized
sample is explained by the first component $x_1$, which has almost
equal and very high correlations with RDIF* and NI*. The first
component $x_1$ is thus associated with the combined effect of RDIF*
and NI*, i.e., the combined effect of investment demands and
banks' influence. The second component, which accounts for approximately one-third of the sample variance, has a strong positive
correlation with V* and weak negative correlations with NI* and
RDIF*. Therefore, this component may be interpreted as being
related to internal and market inefficiency. The lower the level
of internal and market efficiency, the more inventories accumulate
relative to sales. Further, the rate of investment is affected
negatively albeit weakly. The negative correlation with RDIF*
suggests that increased inventories are normally associated with
decreased pressure from banks to borrow more. The variance of the
third component is relatively small and correlated with RDIF* and
NI* in opposite but equal degrees. This suggests a linear relationship
between RDIF* and VI*, which would be a source of multicollinearity.
In other words, a change in the investment demands of the manufacturing sector is likely to be can called out by an almost equivalent
change in the power of banks, as measured by RDIF.

If we take one, two, and three components successively in descending
order of variance as regressor(s) against the standardized γ with
mean 0 and variance 1, the regression results are as follows:

Regression Results
(t-value)

| | | | |
|---|---|---|---|
| $x_1$ | 0.581<br>(4.38) | 0.581<br>(6.37) | 0.581<br>(6.28) |
| $x_2$ | | 0.492<br>(4.07) | 0.492<br>(4.01) |
| $x_3$ | | | -0.181<br>(-0.79) |
| $R^2$(adj) | 0.578 | 0.801 | 0.795 |
| S.E. | 0.121 | 0.119 | 0.121 |
| D.W. | 1.202 | 1.905 | 1.901 |

As expected, the addition of the third principal component as a regressor reduces adjusted $R^2$, albeit slightly, and the null hypothesis that the coefficient of $x_3$ is zero cannot be rejected even at the 60 percent confidence level.  Therefore, it is more appropriate to remove it from the regression.  We state the resulting regression estimates in original units as follows:

$$Y = 0.047RDIF + 2.85NI + 4.73V - 0.870. \qquad (24)$$

By way of reference, the results of ordinary least squares estimation with the original variables is as follows:

$$Y = 0.028RDIF + 3.78NI + 4.56V - 0.828.$$
$$\quad (1.05) \quad\ (2.89) \ \ (4.32) \ \ (-4.39)$$
$$R^2(adj) = 0.776 \qquad S.E. = 0.058 \qquad D.W = 1.901$$

These results suggest that the regression coefficients of RDIF and NI lack precision.  It seems that multicollinearity causes the effect on $Y$ of changes in the investment level to be overestimated and the effect of banks' influence to be understated.

According to the results of principal component analysis (24), the downtrend of RDIF by 1.15 percentage points on average between 1961-72 and 1973-82 is estimated to have had the effect of reducing $Y$ by 0.054. This is about 34% of 0.160, which is the average value of $Y$ between 1966 and 1972.  From the period 1966-1972 to the period 1973-1980, $Y$ declined on the average by 0.101. The estimated decline in $Y$ due to the decrease in RDIF accounts for about 53.4%

of this downtrend of $\gamma$. The drop in RDIF occurred in parallel
with a decline in NI, and the results of principal component
analysis are obtained by taking into account this correlation.
Accordingly, equation (24) cannot be used to estimate the effect
of a change in RDIF which would take place independently of a
change in NI. However, the above result indicates that the decline
in banks' influence had a statistically significant impact on the
financial behavior of manufacturing corporations.


4.  CONCLUDING REMARKS

The above analytical model and its statistical test are still
simple and elementary. However, before commenting on possible
extensions of the model, let me summarize the important conclusions
drawn so far.

    (1)  It is difficult to explain the dynamics of investment
    financing of the Japanese firm using the orthodox hypothesis
    of share-price maximization. It seems necessary to consider
    the changing power balance between individual investors and
    banks as one of the possible explanatory factors.

    (2)  Banks want firms to rely upon debt financing to a greater
    degree than warranted by share-price maximization. The bank's
    shareholdings may be interpreted as a means of maintaining
    customers' relationships with borrowing firm and realizing
    this preference. The so-called practice of "over-loan" by
    the Bank of Japan has accomodated this preference of banks,
    and increases in deposits by small savers who are risk averse
    and subject to relatively higher transaction cost of sharehold-
    ings facilitated the realization of it.

    (3)  The downtrend of debt financing during the 1970s was
    significantly attributable to the erosion of banks' influence,
    possibly caused by the internationalization, as well as
    strengthening of competitiveness, of financial markets.

    (4)  The decline in the dividends-share price ratio during
    the latter half of the 1970s cannot necessarily be interpreted
    as corporate behavior in conflict with the interests of
    individual investors, as popularly believed. Indeed, it
    might have had a share-price-increasing effect by substituting
    internal funds for debt which was "excessive" from the viewpoint

of individual investors.

These conclusions are based on a number of simplifying assumptions, and I would now like to suggest a few directions in which the present research could be generalized or extended.

First, we have treated only the choice between debt financing and internal financing and have completely ignored the possibility of new equity issues. Theoretical and empirical reasons for doing so were stated in the introduction to this essay. However, there is evidence that new equity issues have become a non-negligible means of corporate financing during the last few years.[27] The incorporation of this possibility into the model is accordingly placed on the urgent research agenda.

Secondly, the possibility of default on the repayment of bank debts by firms was ignored, and the only risk incorporated into the model was that of shareholding. I have already commented on some of the ramifications of this simplifying assumption, but one untouched consequence of it is the rigid treatment of bank reserves as expressed in (16). This might have led to an overemphasis of the role of loans by the Bank of Japan. In order to place the role played by the Bank of Japan and the function of banks' shareholdings in broader perspective, a more satisfactory treatment of risks is requrired.

Thirdly, following the tradition of Modigliani and Miller, the investment level of the firm was treated as being given independently of the conditions in the financial market and the financial state of the firm, and we were concerned only with the choice among alternative means for financing the pre-determined level of investment. In actuality, however, the direction of causality might be in the opposite direction as well. In fact, in many econometric studies, the investment demand function has the availability of bank loans and of internal funds among its explanatory variables. On the other hand, however, a recent study by Moriguchi [5] reports that the significance of the availability variables as predictors of investment demand declined during the 1970s. At any rate, a more satisfactory treatment would involve analyzing a more general theoretical model incorporating investment decisions by the firm as an endogenous variable and testing such a model using time-series data on investments and corporate finance.

NOTES

* Preliminary versions of this paper were presented to, besides the Rokko
Symposium, seminars at Hitotsubashi, Stanford and the Japan Securities Research
Institute. I am grateful to participants of those seminars, particularly
Professor Mervyn King, Susumu Koizumi, Shoichi Royama, Eisuke Sakakibara, Charles
Horioka, for helpful comments. I am also grateful to Mr. Yasuhiro Wakita of the
Bank of Japan for providing me with his unofficial time-series estimates of the
rate of retention of compensating balances at city banks; to Miss Noriko Konya of
the Division of Economics and Econometrics, the Japan Securities Research
Institute, for making available an estimate of the rate of return on shareholdings
(Table 1) and other related information and comments; to Professor Kimio Morimune
and Mr. Jiro Nakamura of the Institute of Economic Research, Kyoto University, for
making their efficient computer programs available; and to Mr. Tatsuya Kikutani,
a graduate student at Kyoto University, for his helpful computational assistance.

[1]As explained in the introductory chapter, Japanese city banks are allowed to
hold up to 10% of the shares of non-financial corporations. At the end of 1981,
19% of the stocks of listed non-financial corporations were held by city and
trust banks.

[2]According to the Funds Flow Table prepared by the Bank of Japan, the proportion
of new equity issues in total corporate finances was 7.2% on average between
1965 and 1970, and 6.4% between 1971 and 1977, but jumped to 9.6% in the period of
1978-1981.

[3]For instance, Sakakibara, Feldman and Harada [1981] enthusiastically argue that
the high growth rate of the Japanese non-financial corporate sector during the
post-war era was made possible by the deepening of debt financing. However, the
question of why other means of financing, such as new equity issues and internal
financing, could not finance the growth is not raised.

[4]Under the Small Saving Tax-Exempt System, interest income from bank deposits and
postal savings not exceeding ¥3 million each are not taxable. Otherwise,
depositors are taxed according to normal income tax rates, which go as high as
75%, [after deductions for which they are eligible have been taken] or they can
opt for separate taxation at a uniform rate (35% at the end of 1982). Shareholders' dividend income can either be taxed at normal income tax rates or at
separate tax rates if dividend income is not too large. Dividend income of less
than ¥100 thousand per stock per year is taxed at 20%, while dividend income of
between ¥100 and 500 thousand is taxed at 35%.

[5]A guideline for the two-year time deposit rate is posted by the Bank of Japan and
other rates are regulated by implicit agreements among city banks, with the price
leadership role being played by the bank which is in charge of the office of the
presidency of the Banking Association.

[6]Capital gains are not taxable if shareholders do not engage in stock transactions
more than fifty times a year and in amounts of more than two hundred thousand
shares.

[7]According to the orthodox corporate financial policy a la Modigliani and Miller,
the variance of returns to investment in corporate stock is assumed as an increasing function of debt-equity ratio reflecting the increasing risk of bankrupcy.
However, in our model, the possibility of bankruptcy is assumed away. It is
possible to treat $\sigma_I$ (and $\sigma_B$ to be defined later) as a function of a corporate
financial policy $\gamma$ to be defined later, but doing so will not alter the essential

result of this paper.

[8]Brokerage fees charged by security companies are regulated by an agreement of the Security Dealers Association. The rate for transactions not exceeding ¥1 million per stock is 2.15%, whereas the rate for transactions of more than ¥100 million is 0.55%.

[9]According to the National Accounts Annual Report of the Economic Planning Agency, the market value of shareholdings by financial institutions at the end of 1982 is estimated at 7.8% of the total asset.

[10]For instance, it may be recalled that of the losses incurred by the Sumitomo Bank due to the bankruptcy of the Ataka Corporation amounting to ¥113.2 billion reported in the financial statement of September 1977, up to ¥26.2 billion was written off by the sale of securities.

[11]The corporate tax rate was set at 42% at the end of 1982. The taxation of dividend income of banks is calculated as follows: the imputed cost of stock acquisition is allowed to be computed as the same proportion of total interest payments as shareholdings at acquisition value are of total assets. This imputed cost is deducted from total dividend receipts and one-fourth of the difference is reckoned as profits subject to the normal corporate tax. The rationalization for this practice is that dividend payouts are taxed at the rate of three-quarters of the normal corporate tax rate (32% at the end of 1982) at the level of dividend-paying corporations. Actually, the effective tax rate on banks' dividend receipts is said to be zero (i.e., the imputed costs exceed dividend receipts) or almost negligible. Capital gains are taxed at the normal corporate tax rate when realized. Therefore, the effective tax rate depends upon the duration of shareholding. Hence, in actuality, $t_g$ is not a parameter independent of n, but it is assumed to be so for simplicity's sake.

[12]Since October 1970, lending rates for short-term loans (one year or less) have been bounded by the minimum "standard" rate and the maximum ceiling rate announced pursuant to the Temporary Money Rates Adjustment Act. The standard rate, which is equivalent to the American prime rate, is fixed at a level 0.25 percentage points higher than the official discount rate. City banks can choose appropriate rates within this band, depending upon the credit worthiness and relative bargaining power of borrowers. There is no formal minimum long-term rate based on the Act, but the preferred rate applicable to loans made to utility companies, which is determined by long-term credit banks after consultation with the Bank of Japan, becomes the de facto minimum standard. Thus, it seems more desirable to treat the nominal rate $r_L$, together with the rate $\alpha$ of retaining compensating balances as defined below, endogenously as Royama [6] does. But within our framework, this embellishment adds little insight into the problem posed.

[13]This equation ignores the possible taxation of capital gains realized by sales of n. Therefore, precisely speaking, this equation is valid only when $n \geqq \hat{n}$.

[14]The risk attitude of the bank may be thought of as an appropriate aggregation of the policy stance of the Bank of Japan, the risk attitude of the management and small depositers, as well as the interests of institutional and individual shareholders.

[15]The corporate tax rate applicable to dividend payouts $t_{cd}$ is approximately three-quarters of the normal corporate tax rate. At the end of 1982, $t_{cd} = 32\%$ and $t_c = 42\%$. This differential treatment is based upon the presumption that shareholders are subject to taxes on dividend receipts. But as we will see later, the effect of this differential treatment is not neutral in its effect on corporate financial policy.

[16]For a description of the practice of "over-loan" by the Bank of Japan, see Suzuki [19].

[17]According to a report by the Ministry of Finance to the Budget Committee, Diet, the proportion of tax-exempted individual deposits in total indiviudal saving accounts at the end of fiscal year 1982 is estimated at 59%. (<u>Nihon Keizai Shinbun</u>, 9 March, 1983.)

[18]See Wakita [10]. His definition of the effective lending rate given in that article differs, however, from ours, as he regards the reserve requirement as a parametrically determined proportion of deposits. Denoting the rate of reserve requirement per unit deposit by $\beta$, the effective lending rate is given as $[r_L - \alpha r_b]/(1 - \alpha + \alpha\beta)$. From the bank's perspective, Wakita's definition may be more appropriate, but an examination of our model reveals that what is relevant in the definition of $\Delta$ is actually the "effective borrowing rate" from the viewpoint of the firm. The estimate of $\hat{r}$ in Figure I is constructed according to our definition from Wakita's estimate of $\alpha$. For a detailed description of the estimation method, see Wakita [10].

[19]One possible way of measuring changes in investors' risk attitude would be to trace the movements of Markovitzs'beta coefficients [4] for manufacturing industries.

[20]Arrow and Lind [1] show that the collective risk cost of an investment tends to become negligible, if the returns from the investment are statistically uncorrelated with other investments and if the investment constitutes only a small portion of investors' total wealth.

[21]The data set below is constructed from aggregated financial data for all manufacturing corporations listed on the Tokyo Securities Exchange (there were 1,102 such corporations at the end of 1981), compiled annually at the end of fiscal years 1965-1981 as <u>Nikkei Electronic Data Bank System</u>, <u>Nikkei Financial Data</u>.

[22]These include Reserves for Doubtful Receivables, Reserves for Price Fluctuations; and Reserves for Losses incurred due to Exchange Rate Fluctuations and were classified as long-term debts until the revision of the Commercial Code in October 1982. Since then, these reserves have been treated as equity reserves.

[23]This variable is estimated by subtracting the amount of long-term debts outstanding (item 63 in the NEEDS) at the end of the previous year times $(1 - \alpha)$ from the corresponding amount at the end of the relevant year times $(1 - \alpha)$. The value of $\alpha$ used for the estimation are given in the last column of the table.

[24]In the neoclassical model, DBD and DBK are treated as being of an essentially homogenous nature. However, in Japan, the transactions costs of bank credit differ substantially from those involved in bond issues because of the practice of compensating balances as well as legal regulations regarding bond issues. We have also tried using a definition of $\gamma$ which includes DBD in the numerator in the statistical analysis, but the results were not good.

[25]See Wakita [10]. Also see note 17 above.

[26]For descriptions of principal component analysis, see, for instance, Chatterjee and Price [2].

[27]See note 2.

REFERENCES

[1] Arrow, K.J. and R.C. Lind, "Uncertainty and the Evaluation of Public Investment," American Economic Review, 60: 364-78, 1970.

[2] Chatterjee, S. and B. Price, Regression Analysis by Example, New York: John
Wiley and Sons, 1977.

[3] King, M., The Corporation and Public Policy, London: Chapman and Hall, 1977.

[4] Markovitz, H., Portfolio Selection: Efficient Diversification of Investments,
New York: John Wiley and Sons, 1959.

[5] Moriguchi, Chikashi, "The Macro Econometric Analysis of the Japanese Economy:
the Experience of the KYQ Project" (in Japanese), in M. Aoki, C. Moriguchi, and T.
Sawa (eds.), Nihon Keizai no Kozo Bunseki (The Analysis of the Structure of the
Japanese Economy), Tokyo: Sobunsha, 1983.

[6] Pratt, John W., "Risk Aversion in the Small and the Large," Econometrica 32:
122-136, 1964.

[7] Royama, Shoichi, Nihon no Kinyu System (The Financial System in Japan), Tokyo
Toyo Keizai Shinpo-sha, 1982.

[8] Sakakibara, E., R. Feldman, and Y. Harada, Japanese Financial System in
Comparative Perspective (mimeographed), Cambridge, Mass.: Center for International
Affairs at Harvard University, 1981.

[9] Suzuki, Y., Money and Banking in Contemporary Japan, translated by J.G.
Greenwood, New Haven: Yale University Press, 1980(1974).

[10] Wakita, Y., "Wagakuni no Kashidashi Shijyo to Keiyaku Torihiki (The Loan
Market and Contractual Transactions in our Country," Kinyu Kenkyu, 2: 47-76, 1983.

Part Three

EXTERNAL RELATIONS

THE ECONOMIC ANALYSIS OF THE JAPANESE FIRM
M. Aoki (editor)
© Elsevier Science Publishers B.V. (North-Holland), 1984

# THE ECONOMIC ROLE OF FINANCIAL CORPORATE GROUPING

IWAO NAKATANI

## 1.  INTRODUCTION

One of the most peculiar aspects of Japanese industrial structure
is that the majority of Japanese firms belong to so-called intermarket business groups - kigyō shūdan or keiretsu affiliations
within which firms are linked through reciprocal shareholding, and
lender-borrower and buyer-seller relations.  These groupgings of
firms do not confine themselves to well-defined commodity markets,
but extend to a variety of complex inter-commodity market relations.
Perhaps more important is the fact that major commercial banks
('city' banks) have been the central organ of the present day groupings of firms.  This type of affiliation among firms and financial
intermediaries is certainly not found so extensively in any other
industrial country.

The central question, then, is whether these groups of firms affect
the behaviour of individual firms in any particular direction.  For
example, are financial and real decisions of the firm influenced by
group formation?  What is the ultimate objective of such an extensive grouping of firms?  In neoclassical economic theory, the firm
maximizes its profits or its market value.  Under this paradigm,
the objective of financial corporate groupings must be to enhance
the profitability, individually or collectively, of the member
firms.  Caves and Uekusa [5] tested the hypothesis of joint·profit
maximization of the member firms, examining whether group-affiliated
firms earned, on the average, higher profits than those companies
which were independent of any keiretsu affiliations.  Their study
shows that while the hypothesis of joint profit maximization applies
to the pre-World War II zaibatsu[1], this is not true of the present-
day corporate groups.  Indeed, profits on total assets for the
period 1961-70 are, if anything, negatively related to group
affiliation.  This finding is confirmed by our study below for the
more recent period 1971-82.

There are several other studies which advance alternative hypotheses
about Japanese firm groups.  Futatsugi [10] emphasises that repro-
cal shareholding among member firms tends to reduce dividend
payments to individual shareholders and increase the proportion of
retained earnings within the corporate sector.  Gotō [12], Odagiri
[23], Teranishi and others [26] attribute the formation of intermarket groups to a desire for cost-minimisation.  It may be that
member firms can make substantial savings on transactions costs by
exchanging information on various aspects of business transactions.
However, this hypothesis is essentially the same as the profit
maximization hypothesis.  Kobayashi [18]  on the other hand,

stresses that control of the demand side of the market is equally important.  According to Kobayashi, grouping increases the monopoly power of individual firms so that they can maintain stable sales networks at a lower cost, and, at the same time, stabilize the price of the product they sell by controlling their markets.  In the neoclassicist conception, again, this hypothesis should raise the profits of member firms, but as Caves and Uekusa have shown, this is not supported by available data.

In this paper, I will put forward a rather novel view of the issue at hand.  Formation of groups does increase the monopoly power of respective members, but the monopoly power is not necessarily used for raising the rate of profits.  Rather, I take the view that the firm in any of the corporate groups maximizes the joint utility of its corporate constituents - employees, financial institutions, stockholders and management.  More specifically, monopoly power is utilized in the pursuit of a desired mode of distribution of output, as well as in stabilizing corporate performance over time.

Of course, this hypothesis cannot be tested directly unless we know the exact shape of the joint utility function of corporate constituents.  Obviously, to specify the joint utility function properly is not an easy task.  To do so would require an explicit modelling of the firm which describes the nature of internal conflicts among corporate members and how they are resolved.  This is beyond the scope of the present paper.  Suppose however, that an equilibrium solution to the problem can be specified in terms of some relevant parameters.  Then, it is certainly of interest to ask if there are any differences in corporate policy, real or financial, among firms which vary with respect to structure of ownership and group affiliation.  At any rate, it seems worthwhile to carry out a comparative study of the behaviour of group-affiliated firms and independent firms and suggest plausible motivations and objectives for a firm participating in group formation.

I shall demonstrate later that the two types of firm - the G (group affiliated) firm, and the I (largely independent of affiliations) firm, are quite distinct in some important aspects of corporate behaviour.  First, the G firm's rate of profit is on the average significantly lower than that of the I firm.  This is consistent with the hypothesis that the firm affiliated with intermarket groups is not a profit maximizer.

Second, as well as having a lower rate of profits, G firms tend to show a somewhat lower growth rate than I firms.  Thus, nor can grouping of firms be explained by a growth maximization hypothesis à la Marris [19].  However, more important is the fact that there is clear evidence that the variability of performance of the group-affiliated firms is smaller than that of the independent firms.  That is, both the rate of profits and growth rate of the G firms are less variable over time than are those of the I firms.

It is of interest to ask why group-affiliated firms show a tendency towards lower profits or growth rates and have smaller variations in these measures.  The tendency may be attributed to the risk attitude of management which seeks to stabilize corporate performance at the cost of lowering the level of performance itself.  Indeed, stability of performance is likely to guarantee the status quo of the managers, unless they perform too poorly when compared

with the average firm. It may also improve the welfare of other
corporate constituents, particularly workers, if they are sufficiently risk-averse.

The assumption that corporate policy reflects the risk attitudes of
management and workers implies 'separation of management from ownership', which in turn requires imperfection in the capital market or
'asymmetric information between management and ownership'. With a
perfect capital market and complete certainty, value maximization
would be the unanimous objective of the firm. In the real world
where management may be separated from ownership, the risk attitudes
of management (and workers) is a relevant factor in corporate behavior. Indeed, the cost of management failure may be much larger for
managers and workers than for shareholders, essentially because the
latter can diversity their portfolio risk, while the former are
ordinarily in a situation where it is more difficult to diversify
their (human) capital. This tendency will be reinforced in the
presence of firm specific skills and when current income derives
mainly from the employment of such skills. Under these circumstances, managers and workers are inevitably more risk-averse
than most shareholders.

It is frequently suggested that member firms of groupings help one
another in times of serious business hardship. When a financial
difficulty arises, for example, the member banks usually render
assistance, financial or sometimes managerial, to the firm in trouble, sometimes at a far greater cost and risk than normal business
reciprocity requires. Likewise, in a buyer-seller relationship,
the buyer will often accept a somewhat higher price if the seller is
in the same group and is facing business difficulties. Of course,
in the reverse case, when the buyer is in difficulty, the seller is
willing to sell at a lower price, or take other measures such as
extending usance on buyer's bills.

This sort of business reciprocity may be taken to imply an implicit
mutual insurance scheme, in which member firms are insurers and
insured at the same time. One of the essential functions of the
capital market is to allocate risks efficiently among different
investors in the economy, but, if the capital market is imperfect
and management is in a position to worry about the business risks in
some way or other, then the grouping of firms can be regarded as an
ingenious solution to the problem of the non-existence of contingent
markets for 'management risks'. In other words, the setting up of a
mutual insurance scheme among group members, and particularly
between the banks and other group members, is an institutional
response by the Japanese firm which aims at coping with apparent
market failure in contingent claims markets of management risks.

It will be further shown in this paper that, while profit rates
are lower, the average income received by the employee of the $\underline{G}$ firm
is significantly higher than that of the $\underline{I}$ firm. This result $\overline{is}$
obtained after adjustments for age structure as well as male-female
ratios of the firm's work force, so that the difference in average
compensation between the $\underline{G}$ firm and the $\underline{I}$ firm cannot be attributed
to difference in worker composition. This finding together with
lower profitability of the $\underline{G}$ firm is worth emphasizing, because it
is indirect evidence that the distribution of the firm's output is
determined in favour of the employee relative to the stockholder.

Perhaps, one of the most interesting results of the paper is that corporate financial policy differs significantly between the G firm and the I firm. Debt-equity ratios of the G firm are significantly higher and the rate of dividend payment per paid-in capital of the G firm is much lower than those of the I firm. While the determina- tion (or even the relevance and irrelevance) of corporation financial policy is still a highly controversial issue in the theory of finance, it is of particular interest to know whether the difference in the composition of shareholders and group affiliation affect the firm's financial policy in a particular direction.

In what follows, these points are discussed in further detail. First, the relationship between formation of financial corporate groups and working of the capital market will be briefly discussed. While a formal model is not developed here, it is important to note that these groupings may be thought of as being deeply related to the so-called 'Japanese-style management'. Section II deals with this question. In Section III, the data are explained. Section IV presents the results of empirical tests to see whether the G firm differs significantly from the I firm. It will be shown there that (1) the level of profits and growth rates of the G firm are gen- erally lower, (2) distribution of output within the firm is biased in the G firm in favour of the employee, (3) the fluctuation of profit as well as growth rates is relatively smaller for the G firm, and (4) financial policy of the G firm differs significantly from that of the I firm. That is, the debt-equity ratio is much higher, and the ratio of dividend over paid-in capital much lower for the G firm. The last section is reserved for a summary and concluding remarks.

## 2.  FINANCIAL CORPORATE GROUPS AND THE CAPITAL MARKET

Under the assumptions of a perfect capital market and certainty, the firm maximizes its profit (or, more formally maximizes the market value of its share price) even if there are differences in pref- erences among shareholders (see, for example, Fama and Miller [7], King [17]). As soon as this set of assumptions is removed, however, the objective of the firm need not (and, perhaps, should not) be described by simple profit maximization. Managers as well as other members of the firm are normally endowed with some discretionary power over corporate decision making processes, particularly when the capital market is imperfect and there is asymmetry in informa- tion between shareholders on the one hand and managers and other corporate constituents on the other.

In this connection, Aoki [1], [2] advances an interesting model in which the firm is viewed as a stockholder-employee co-operative game. It is true that, in monopoly situations, corporate members may wish to engage in a game among themselves, where the aim of the game is to determine important company policies such as the distribution of the firm's output, the growth rate of the firm and corporate finan- cial policy. Of course, the co-operative game approach is possible only when the firm is insulated, at least partially, from the impe- rative of market forces, and then grouping of firms may be regarded as a means of insulating group firms from the pressure of market competition.

Above all, grouping of firms is an effective means whereby imperfection in the capital market is created. Reciprocal shareholding is used to weaken the influence of general shareholders outside the group over policy making processes of group-affiliated firms. The more extensive are reciprocal shareholdings, the more of managerial discretion will reside with management of these firms. Suppose that, because of reciprocal shareholdings, managers are now endowed with discretionary power and in fact act against the interest of general shareholders. Then, naturally, the firm's share price will decline and capital will flow out of the firm. However, the probability of a take-over bid is small because major shareholders are now insiders who would, by implicit agreements, support the present management. The probability of capital shortage is also reduced due to an implicit long-term contract with member banks which guarantees financial support to the firm.[2]

As is well-known, there are two distinct features in the present-day kigyō-shūdan or keiretsu. One is that each group has a major commercial bank (so-called 'city' bank such as Mitsui, Mitsubishi, Sumitomo and Fuji Bank) as the major lender to the member firms within the group. The city bank has been called the 'central organ' of the corporate group today, which implies that it is, in fact, playing the leading role in the financial activities within the group.[3]

Another distinct feature is reciprocal shareholding among member firms. In most cases, reciprocal shareholdings are so extensive that the top shareholder is some corporation or financial institution which belongs to the same keiretsu. Since this relationship is mutual, policies chosen by these firms tend to reflect the interest of the group at large and are often against the interest of general shareholders. This segmentation, or internalization, of the capital market by means of intra-group financing and reciprocal shareholding is certainly effective in insulating group firms from the threat of competition in the capital market. To the extent that this is so, individual members of the group are free to choose their company policies at their discretion. As mentioned before, even if managers do not maximize the market value of the firm but pursue the interest of corporate constituents, they would still be free from a take-over bid because major shareholders are insiders who act in the interest of the present management. Even if the share price is so low that it is impossible to raise enough capital for investment projects in the capital market, the 'city' bank and other financial institutions within the group are willing to help the company in meeting its financial needs.

Are there any merits for city banks and other financial institutions in getting involved in this kind of relationship with borrowers? In a world of uncertainty, financial transactions are normally costly because accurate information required of the borrower is often costly to collect, and it is more efficient to establish stable long-term business relationships with borrowers than to rely exclusively on short-term spot transactions. This line of argument follows the recent development of the implicit long-term contract theory, and the formation of a corporate group can be considered as an ingenious device to establish such a long-term lender-borrower relations.[4]

Further, as we show later, the debt-equity ratio of group-affiliated

firms is considerably higher than that of independent firms.  The
reason for this phenomenon is certainly worth further investigation,
but it seems possible to speculate that a high debt-equity ratio
serves to guarantee stable business opportunities for the city banks
and other financial institutions.[5]  If these statements are correct,
then group banks may find it advantageous to be associated with, and
indeed to remain as an essential member of, a corporate group.


## 3.  DATA AND ASSUMPTIONS

As of 1981, there were 859 non-financial corporations whose shares
were traded in the Tokyo Stock Market (First Section).  In order to
compare corporate performance between G and I firms, I chose 317
manufacturing companies out of the 859 listed firms, and formed the
following eight groups:  Mitsui, Mitsubishi, Sumitomo, Fuji, Dai-
ichi Kangyō (DKB), Sanwa, Subsidiaries and an Independents (or
non-keiretsu) group.  The first four groups have the widest coverage
of industries in their affiliation network, and have historically
shown the strongest ties among member firms.  Other keiretsu groups
such as Dai-ichi Kangyō and Sanwa are important, but are somewhat
smaller in size and weaker in group coherence (see Table VII-1).
Subsidiaries are the group of firms whose management is under direct
control by their parent companies.  We are not analyzing the behaviour of these companies directly, but the empirical study below
shows somewhat similar tendencies to other group members.  There
were 57 companies under this category as of March 1981.


Table VII-1.  Comparison of Six Major Intermarket Groups

(As of March 1981)

|  | No. of Firms | Ratio of Intragroup Borrowing Over Total Debt | Ratio of Reciprocal Shareholdings |
|---|---|---|---|
|  |  | % | % |
| Mitsui | 104 | 17.24 | 18.23 |
| Mitsubishi | 113 | 24.87 | 25.17 |
| Sumitomo | 110 | 23.47 | 26.14 |
| Fuji | 98 | 21.72 | 19.57 |
| Dai-ichi Kangyō | 70 | 15.43 | 15.39 |
| Sanwa | 51 | 19.98 | 11.67 |
| Total | 546 | - | - |

Source:  Keiretsu no Kenkyu, (1983), Keizai Chōsa Kyōkai, Tokyo.


There are other financial combines, such as Tōkai, Daiwa, Taiyō-Kōbe,
Kyōwa, Saitama, Hokkaidō Takushoku, Tokyo, Nihon Kōgyō, Nihon Saiken
Shinyō and Nihon Chōki Shinyō, which are even smaller in size and
too incomplete to be treated as corporate groups.  These financial

combines cover 173 companies, but we regard them as non-keiretsu rather than keiretsu members. A further 83 firms are more or less independent of these groups, but very few of these are 'pure' independents. There are only 54 companies (6.3 per cent) whose affiliations are totally unknown. Others are affiliated with local financial institutions such as Hokuriku Bank and Norin Chukin.

The 317 firms which we have chosen are given in the Appendix. Important qualifications in the selection procedure of these firms are:

i)  Only manufacturing firms were chosen in order to eliminate possible distortions caused by government regulations over certain non-manufacturing industries such as utility, transportation, and banking industries.

ii)  Group affiliation of firms is based on the classification of Keiretsu no Kenkyu [16]. Keiretsu no Kenkyu (Studies on Financial Corporate Groupings) is one of the most-detailed of the annual publications which provide individual company data on reciprocal shareholdings and intra-group borrowings. Group affiliation is determined basically using these data sets, with historical background taken into account. We used annual publications of Keiretsu no Kenkyu for the years 1973, 1977 and 1983 which cover data for 1972, 1976 and 1982 respectively. Only those companies whose affiliations (and non-affiliations) are clearly identified in all of these three years have been included in the data set. For example, if firm A belonged to Mitsui group in 1972, but changed its affliation to some other group in 1976 or 1982, then, such a firm is excluded because it is unclear as to which group this firm should be attached. In other words, only those firms which have been continuously affiliated to a particular group are in our data set.

iii)  In order for a firm to be classified as group-affiliated in a particular year, at least one of the following three conditions must be satisfied:

a)  The member bank should be the biggest lender to the firm for the last three years consecutively and shareholdings within the group must exceed 20 per cent.
b)  The member bank should be lending more than 40 per cent of the firm's total debt for the last three years consecutively.
c)  For historical reasons, the firm is included in a particular group. However, if 30 per cent or more of the equity shares are held by the parent firm, that firm has been classified as being a subsidiary rather than a group-affiliated firm, because it can be no longer regarded as an independent decision-making unit.

iv)  If a firm experienced any kind of merger or separation with other firms, it has been eliminated simply because such events are likely to create discontinuity in the time series data. It is true that mergers or separations are not random occurence, and it is possible that the elimination of these firms produces a certain bias in our result. However, according to preliminary testing, even if they are included in the data, the basic results remain quite similar to those shown in the following section.

All the data used below are taken from the financial statements
(Balance Sheet and Profit and Loss Statements) of individual firms
for the period of 1971 to 1982.  These data are available from Nihon
Keizai Shinbun in the convenient form of Nikkei Financial Data tapes.
The only modification made to the published financial data in these
tapes is that, since the financial settlement term of many Japanese
firms was every six months rather than yearly until recently, these
bi-annual terms were aggregated to annual terms simply by adding up
the bi-annual flow data, component by component.

Table VII-2 shows the ownership structure of the 317 firms selected
following the above procedure.  The figures are the percentage
shares of the various stockholders of the firm — financial institutions, non-financial institutions, individual investors and foreign
residents — group by group, and are averaged over 1974-82.[6]  As is
expected, all of the six groups have lower proportions of individual
shareholdings (30.8 to 36.0 per cent compared with 40.0 per cent for
the non-keiretsu firms).  The share of non-financial corporations
almost offsets the difference between each pair of groups.  Needless
to say, larger shareholdings by non-financial corporations for the
six groups are attributable to reciprocal shareholding among member
firms.  There is no observable difference in the shareholdings by

Table VII-2.  Ownership Structure by Group

(1974-82 Average) (%)

| Group | Shareholdings by | | | | |
|---|---|---|---|---|---|
| | Financial Institutions | Nonfinancial Corporations | Individual Investors | Foreign Residents & others | Total |
| Mitsui | 37.0 | 29.3 | 30.9 | 2.8 | 100.0 |
| Mitsubishi | 39.6 | 22.7 | 34.7 | 3.0 | 100.0 |
| Sumitomo | 34.8 | 32.0 | 30.8 | 2.4 | 100.0 |
| Fuji | 37.1 | 23.4 | 36.0 | 3.5 | 100.0 |
| DKB | 41.2 | 21.9 | 33.5 | 3.4 | 100.0 |
| Sanwa | 40.2 | 22.1 | 35.3 | 2.4 | 100.0 |
| Subsidiaries | 17.1 | 55.1 | 23.6 | 4.2 | 100.0 |
| Non-keiretsu | 37.2 | 19.3 | 40.0 | 3.5 | 100.0 |

financial institutions among these groups except for Subsidiaries.
One reason for this is that the non-keiretsu group includes some
quasi-keiretsu firms affiliated with smaller city banks such as
Tōkai, Daiwa, Taiyō-Kōbe, Kyōwa, Saitama, Hokkaido Takushoku and
Tokyo Bank, long-term credit banks such as Nihon Kōgyō, Nihon Chōki
Shinyō and Nihon Saiken Shinyō Bank, and local financial institutions such as Nōrin Chūkin and Hokuriku Bank.  These quasi-keiretsu
groups are much smaller in size than the other six major groups,
however, and it is impossible to regard them as a complete intermarket business group.

## 4. COMPARATIVE ANALYSIS OF CORPORATE BEHAVIOUR

This section compares the corporate performance of group-affiliated firms and independent firms. Our hypothesis is that, since group-affiliated firms are insulated from market competition (particularly in the capital market) by varying degrees, they need not maximize profits. Instead, they may wish to pay higher wages to employees, and if managers are risk-averse, to stabilize corporate performance over time. Further, it will be shown that there are clear differences in corporation financial policy.

### (a) Profitability[7]

First of all, I will show that the rate of business profits over total assets is significantly lower for $\underline{G}$ firms than for $\underline{I}$ firms. Business profits are defined as operating profits plus receipts of interest and dividends. Since total assets consist of own capital and debt, the rate of return to total assets must include both current profits and interest paid to the financial institutions. If only current profits are counted, the rate of return will appear smaller for those firms whose leverage ratio is higher. Generally speaking, business profit is a better index than current profit because the latter is subject to various artificial additions and deductions which need not reflect the performance of relevant business activities for the period in question.[8]

$$
\left.\begin{aligned}
RBP = {} & 0.0576 + 0.0023\ AW + 0.0045\ TA + 0.0055\ GG \\
& (10.6614)\ (2.7730) \qquad (1.3533) \qquad (13.8928) \\[6pt]
& - 0.0108\ GD(1) - 0.0123\ GD(2) - 0.0122\ GD(3) \\
& \quad (-3.3680) \qquad\quad (-4.0523) \qquad\quad (-3.8328) \\[6pt]
& - 0.0212\ GD(4) - 0.0269\ GD(5) - 0.0120\ GD(6) \\
& \quad (-6.3543) \qquad\quad (-6.4507) \qquad\quad (-2.9257) \\[6pt]
& - 0.0088\ GD(7) + \sum_{i=1}^{16} a(i)ID(i) \\
& \quad (-2.0346)
\end{aligned}\ \right\} \quad (1)
$$

$$
R^2 = 0.3749, \quad F = 19.7626
$$

As equation (1) shows, rate of business profits (RBP) is significantly lower for all the groups including six major keiretsu and subsidiaries compared with non-keiretsu independent firms. In the regression, RBP is explained by average compensation to employees (AW), total assets of each firm (TA), rate of growth of GNP for each year (GG) and Group Dummies.[9] GD(1), GD(2), GD(3), GD(4), GD(5), GD(6) and GD(7) stand for group dummy variables which represent Mitsui, Mitsubishi, Sumitomo, Fuji, Dai-ichi Kangyō (DKB), Sanwa and subsidiary groups respectively. Coefficients for these dummies are relative to non-keiretsu independent firms. For example, the coefficient of GD(1) is -0.0108, which says that, other things being equal, affiliation to Mitsui Group lowers, on the average, rate of business profits by 1.08 per cent compared with non-keiretsu firms. Values in parenthesis are t-values and clearly all the coefficients attached to group dummies which are negative are statistically significant at the 5 per cent level. RBP is positively correlated to average compensation to employees, and assets, as well as the annual growth rate of the national economy. The positive correlation of RBP to the size of the firm (TA) is somewhat surprising,

because it is widely held that the rate of profits declines as the
firm size increases.

Other dummy variables are industry dummies (ID(i)) based on two-
digit classification.  There are 17 industries within the
manufacturing sector and one of 17 ID's is set equal to zero, leaving only 16 ID's in equation (1).  All the coefficients attached to
these industry dummies are again relative to the missing ID, which,
in the present study, is Food Industry.[10]  Since it is not intended
in this paper to analyze differences among industries, actual fig-
uares of these coefficients (a(i)'s) are available but not reported
here.[11]  An F-value of 19.7653 implies that the hypothesis that all
the coefficients are equal to zero is rejected.  We conclude that
group affiliation does not raise profitability of the firm but lowers it significantly.  Apparently, the motivation for the formation
of financial corporate groupings must be found other than in profit
maximizing behaviour.

(b)  Growth Rates
The growth of the firm is measured here as the rate of growth of the
firm's output (value-added), of its sales and of its total assets.
Only the regression result of the growth rate of sales is reported
here,[12] but other estimates based on value-added and total assets
are very similar to it.  In particular, coefficients for the group
dummies are all negative in each of the two estimates.  The rate
of growth in terms of sales values (RGS) is positively correlated to
the annual rate of GNP growth (GG) and negatively correlated, if
anything, to group dummies GD(i) and to total assets of each firm
(TA) (See equation (2)).  Although the statistical significance of
this relationship is not high, the fact that all the coefficients
for GD's except for GD(1) are negative suggests that participation
to corporate groups does not raise the growth rate of the firm,
either.  This result implies that it is also impossible to explain
the motivation for groupings by the hypothesis of growth maximization.

$$
\begin{aligned}
\text{RGS} = &-0.0395 - 0.0012 \text{ TA} + 0.0315 \text{ GG} + 0.0001 \text{ GD}(1) \\
&(-3.3472) \quad (-0.0576) \quad\;\; (28.1194) \quad\;\; (0.0160) \\[6pt]
&- 0.0147 \text{ GD}(2) - 0.0052 \text{ GD}(3) - 0.0117 \text{ GD}(4) \\
&\;\;(-1.6964) \qquad\;\; (-0.5755) \qquad\;\; (-1.2272) \\[6pt]
&- 0.0208 \text{ GD}(5) - 0.0141 \text{ GD}(6) - 0.0081 \text{ GD}(7) \\
&\;\;(-1.7398) \qquad\;\; (-1.1938) \qquad\;\; (-0.6571) \\[6pt]
&+ \sum_{i=1}^{16} a(i)\text{ID}(i) \\[6pt]
&R^2 = 0.4699, \quad F = 35.6335
\end{aligned}
\qquad (2)
$$

(c)  Average Compensation to Employees
Neither profit maximization nor growth maximization were shown to be
appropriate motives for group formation.  Equation (3) shows,
however, group firms pay significantly higher wages to their
employees.

$$
\begin{aligned}
\text{AW} = &\;3.0717 + 2.0663 \text{ RBP} + 0.0091 \text{ KL} + 0.1438 \text{ TA} \\
&(9.1938) \quad (2.9610) \qquad (5.3390) \qquad\;\; (1.6226)
\end{aligned}
$$

$$+ \ 2.006 \ \text{RME} \ + \ 0.4268 \ \text{GD}(1) \ + \ 0.4375 \ \text{GD}(2)$$
$$(5.3362) \qquad (4.0893) \qquad\quad (4.4524)$$

$$+ \ 0.4068 \ \text{GD}(3) \ + \ 0.4657 \ \text{GD}(4) \ + \ 0.1653 \ \text{GD}(5)$$
$$(3.8673) \qquad\quad (4.2642) \qquad\quad (1.2195)$$

$$+ \ 0.3180 \ \text{GD}(6) \ + \ 0.3328 \ \text{GD}(7) \ + \sum_{i=1}^{16} a(i)\text{ID}(i)$$
$$(2.4308) \qquad\quad (2.3842)$$

$$\text{(3)}$$

$$R^2 \ = \ 0.6984, \quad F \ = \ 19.2556$$

AW is, as before, average compensation to employees which is the ratio of the firm's total labour cost (including contributions to fringe benefits and social security) to the number of employees at the end of each accounting period. It is positively correlated to rate of business profit (RBP), which is consistent with our earlier finding that the rate of business profit is positively correlated to the average compensation to employees (see Equation (1) above). The correlation between AW and RBP seems to imply the existence of 'profit sharing' between the worker and the shareholder in Japanese firms.

The average compensation to employees is also positively correlated to capital-labour ratio (KL) and total assets (TA), although the significance level of the latter is low. RME is the ratio of male employees to total employees adjusted also with respect to the age structure of the work force in each firm. More specifically,

$$\text{RME} \ = \ \frac{\text{ME} \times \text{AGM}}{\text{ME} \times \text{AGM} + \text{FE} \times \text{AGF}}$$

where ME, AGM, FE, AGF are, respectively, number of male employees, average age of male employees, number of female employees and average age of female employees.[13] The age-corrected ratio of male employees (RME) thus reflects the age structure as well as the male-female composition of employees. Under a seniority wage system and given that male workers earn more, the coefficient associated with RME is expected to be positive. Equation (3) shows that it is in fact positive.

Coefficients of group dummies are all positive and statistically significant at the 5 per cent level except for GD(5), that is, Dai-ichi Kangyō group (DKB). Note that this result is after necessary adjustments of differences in firm size and composition of employees. Despite of our earlier finding that the rate of profit is lower, the employees of keiretsu firms are receiving higher income than those of non-keiretsu firms. As was pointed out previously, grouping of firms can be regarded as a means to increase their monopoly power. But the monopoly power is used not to raise profits but to pursue a desired mode of income distribution within the firm in favour of the employee.[14]

Top management of large corporations in Japan often define their ultimate goal of corporate policy as being enhancement of the welfare of the firm's employees, which is apparently in sharp contrast with American or European corporate attitudes. In the latter, partic-ularly, in the United States, company objectives are usually

expressed in terms of profitability or shareholders' interest.  It
will suffice here to point out that this difference is related to
the working of capital markets of both countries.  It is segmentation or internalization of the capital market by means of reciprocal
shareholding and intra-group financing that makes the 'Japanese-
style management' (that is, in the present context, a community-
oriented management which points towards the employee's welfare)
feasible in this country.

(d)  Dividend Policy
One of the most interesting findings in the present paper is that
there are clear differences in the corporate financial policy
between Keiretsu and non-keiretsu firms.  More specifically, it
will be noted that dividend policy and debt-equity ratio are
distinctly different.

The question of how corporations determine their dividend payout
rate is still a highly controversial research topic in the theory of
finance.  Here, we examine the inter-group difference in the rate of
dividend over paid-in capital.[15]  As equation (4) shows, the rate of
dividend (RDV) is positively (and rather strongly) correlated to net
profits per share (NPS).  More important in the present context is

$$RDV = 0.1355 + 1.1828 \text{ NPS} - 0.0027 \text{ AW} + 0.0216 \text{ TA}$$
$$(24.2622) \ (34.2926) \qquad (-2.8473) \qquad (5.6014)$$

$$- 0.0100 \text{ GD(1)} - 0.0113 \text{ GD(2)} - 0.0084 \text{ GD(3)}$$
$$(-2.6945) \qquad (-3.1930) \qquad (-2.2967)$$

$$- 0.0156 \text{ GD(4)} - 0.0255 \text{ GD(5)} - 0.0141 \text{ GD(6)}$$
$$(-4.0410) \qquad (-5.2847) \qquad (-2.9659)$$

$$- 0.0127 \text{ GD(7)} + \sum_{i=1}^{16} a(i)ID(i)$$
$$(-2.5649)$$

$$R^2 = 0.6140, \quad F = 73.1786$$

(4)

that the rate of dividend over paid-in capital (RDV) is negatively
correlated with the average wage (AW).  That is, those companies
paying higher wages are paying smaller dividends to the shareholder.
Firm size (TA, total assets) is a positive factor contributing to
dividend payout.  All other things equal, larger firms, as measured
by total assets, tend to pay larger dividends per unit of capital.

As equation (4) shows, all the coefficients for group dummies are
negative and statistically significant at the 5 per cent level.
That is, other things being equal, group affiliation reduces dividend payout.  The reason why the rate of dividend is lower for
these firms is a very interesting topic for future research.  I note
here only some relevant factors.  It is frequently pointed out that
one of the basic difficulties for analyzing why companies pay dividends at all rests on the fact that there are essentially no
individual asset holders for whom capital gains are taxed as heavily
as dividends.  Corporations are somewhat different, however.  They
receive preferential treatment on intercorporate dividends and face
an effective tax rate of very close to zero, while realization of
capital gains is taxed at the regular rate of 42 per cent.[16]  This
fact may be one of the reasons which explains the payment of

dividends by firms whose shareholders are dominated by institutional shareholders.

However, there is a subtle point in this reasoning. If intercorporate shareholdings are financed through borrowings, intercorporate dividends up to the amount of interest payment against such borrowings are treated as profits. Therefore, to the extent that intercorporate shareholdings are financed by borrowings, it is not profitable to receive dividends at all, simply because they are no longer tax-exempt income. Putting it differently, receiving dividends limits the right of the firm in using tax-deductibility of interest payments. Under this circumstance, the firm clearly prefers (unrealized) capital gains to dividends.

If intercorporate reciprocal shareholdings of keiretsu firms are financed largely by borrowings, then we can expect that the rate of dividend is fairly low under the tax rules on dividend just described.

On the other hand, the effective tax rate on personal dividend receipts is relatively low for small investors in low income tax brackets. Taxation on dividends for individual shareholders is subject to choice of overall income taxation (Sogokazei) or separated taxation (Bunrikazei). If the latter is chosen, a flat rate of 35 per cent is used to calculate the tax on dividends. For those investors whose marginal tax rates are lower than 35 per cent, it is profitable to file income returns so that the overall tax rate is applied. In addition, there is a tax credit allowed for dividend income. That is, individuals are allowed to deduct 10 per cent of dividends received out of total tax payments to be made otherwise. For some investors in low income tax brackets, this tax credit is substantial. Given the fact that transaction costs (phyclological as well as pecuniary costs) for selling shares are not negligible for small investors, payment of dividends may be optimal.

Further verification on these points is necessary to determine why group-affiliated firms are paying less dividends than independend firms, but the tax considerations discussed above may be important in the analysis of the observed difference in dividend policy.[17] This will certainly be true in a situation in which management utilizes the knowledge of the shareholders' tax brackets for the determination of dividend policy.

As we saw in Table VII-2 above, institutional shareholding is more dominant in group-affiliated companies and this difference in ownership structure may be the reason why dividend policy differs between keiretsu and non-keiretsu firms.

Another important aspect in analyzing dividend policy of the firm is the role of the dividend as a signal. According to this view, the dividend is used mainly as the signal of the sustainable income of the corporation. If we assume that ownership and management are separated and information is asymmetric between them, the latter may wish to send a signal as a means of communication with the body of shareholders. An increase (decrease) of dividend is intended to show that the future prospects of the firm have improved (worsened), whereas conventional accounting reports are inadequate guides to future prospects of the company.[18] To the extent that management is assured that there will be no take-overs and that ownership

'understands' what management is doing, the need for sending a
sigunal (paying dividends) will be reduced.

In the present context, group-affiliated firms are insulated from
the capital market as a result of intercorporate mutual shareholdings and intra-group financing so that the risk of take-overs
appears to be much smaller than it would be otherwise.  Since member
firms of a group have long-term relationships among themselves, they
know each other better than general shareholders do.  If institutional shareholders within the same group are dominant shareholders
of a firm, then demand from such shareholders for higher dividends
as the signal of the sustainable income of the firm will be small.
In this way, the observed difference in dividend behaviour can be
attributed again to the composition of ownership structure.

One of the most important points in this respect would be 'reciprocity' of shareholding.  Indeed, if, as is the case of group-affiliated
firms, shares are held reciprocally among member firms, a synchronized alteration of dividend policies does not affect the cash flow of
each firm in so far as the reciprocity of shareholding is perfect.
Given the existence of a positive (even if close to zero) rate of
tax on intercorporate dividends, or, as discussed above, of positive
opportunity cost of losing tax deductibility of interest paid against
the borrowing for the acquisition of shares, the smaller amount of
dividends is to the benefit of intercorporate shareholders.  The
larger is the extent of reciprocal shareholdings, then, the smaller
will be the ratio of dividend payout.  This may be another reason
why the rate of dividend is lower for group-affiliated firms.

(e)  Debt-Equity Ratio
Japanese firms are said to have relatively high debt-equity ratios.[19]
International comparison of the financial structure of corporations
involves a variety of complications of accounting practice and tax
rules.  For example, Japanese financial reports are based on book
value so that equity is vastly undervalued.  In fact, the average
price of land has increased 30 to 40 times since 1955, but the values
which appear in financial statements do not reflect such changes in
the price level.  Another point to be made is that there are tax-
exempt special reserves (tokutei hikiatekin) which are substantial in
some cases relative to profits earned.  They are shown as debt rather than equity but since they can be regarded essentially as retained
earnings, they should be included in equity.[20]  Taking these institutional factors into account, Japanese debt-equity ratios could be
much lower and could be fairly close to those in the United States
and European countries.[21]

Apart from these points, however, debt-equity ratios (or equity
ratios) need not be the same over all the Japanese firms.  As
equation (5) shows, the ratio of own capital to total assets (ROC)
is considerably lower for group-affiliated firms (by 4 to 9
percentage points).  Here, 'own capital' includes all the outstanding special reserves such as Reserves for Price Fluctuations,
Reserves for Special Depreciation and Reserves for Overseas Development.  These are regarded essentially as retained earnings even if
they appear as debt in the balance sheet.[22]

$$ROC = 0.3396 - 0.0095 \ TA - 0.0450 \ GD(1) - 0.0417 \ GD(2)$$
$$(32.1074) \ (-0.9904) \quad (-4.8642) \qquad (-4.7415)$$

$$- 0.0419 \text{ GD}(3) - 0.0898 \text{ GD}(4) - 0.0817 \text{ GD}(5)$$
$$(-4.5703) \qquad (-9.3010) \qquad (-6.7538)$$

$$- 0.0570 \text{ GD}(6) - 0.0473 \text{ GD}(7) + \sum_{i=1}^{16} a(i) \text{ID}(i) \qquad (5)$$
$$(-4.7793) \qquad (-3.7821)$$

$$R^2 = 0.4709, \quad F = 37.3306$$

One of the crucial differences between G̲ firms and I̲ firms is the
mechanism by which their investments are financed. The former typically have long-sustained relationships with the group-affiliated
bank, while the latter are not always tied to a particular bank.[23]
Although the average ratio of intra-group financing is only about 20
per cent (see Table VII-1 above), the implicit long-term relation
between the firm and the bank seems to play an important role. That
is, it has the effect of assuring that the probability of default of
such a firm is relatively small. That is, the 'main' bank usually
acts as an insurer of group-affiliated companies and when the latter
are faced with financial and/or managerial difficulties, the former
renders necessary assistance even beyond the level that normal
business reciprocity requires. The group-affiliated non-financial
firms, on the other hand, try to maintain a high and stable outstanding debt against their 'main' bank, even if to do so is incompatible
with short-run profit-maximization. The existence of the implicit
long-term contract between G̲ firms and the 'main' bank is important
in that other banks and financial institutions outside the group can
be more confident in supplying credit to those group companies than
to independent companies, simply because the alleged insurance
scheme of group banks is perceived to reduce the default risks of
those companies significantly.[24] This effect makes the financial
activity of group firms relatively easier than that of independent
firms.

The high debt-equity ratio of the G̲ firm can be regarded as reflecting the preference of the 'main' bank, which is often a major
shareholder of the firm as well. Aoki [3] in this volume shows that
in a general equilibrium framework the bank in this sort of
institutional setting wants the firm to rely upon debt financing beyond the point share-price maximization warrants. The
equilibrium debt-equity ratio in his model is greater than the value
maximizing point of the firm whose shareholders consist of individual investors on the one hand, and banks on the other. When the
bargaining power of the bank is strong relative to individual investors, the debt-equity ratio tends to be higher. Aoki's model is
consistent with our finding that the rate of profits is lower and
debt-equity ratio higher for group-affiliated firms.

An alternative explanation would be that, since the risk of bankruptcy for a given debt-equity ratio is smaller for G̲ firms than I̲
firms, the optimal debt-equity ratio (if it is determinate) will be
accordingly higher. As we have discussed above, financial corporate
grouping can be regarded as an implicit insurance scheme. Indeed,
we will show below that the corporate performance as measured by
rate of profits or growth is more stable over time for G̲ firms. The
less variability of performance of group firms over time may indicate that they are less risky companies.

If the optimal debt-equity ratio can be somehow determined uniquely,
relevant factors to be considered will be such factors as ownership

structure and the existence of bankruptcy costs.  As was discussed
above, since ownership structure differs between G̲ firms and I̲
firms, the optimal debt-equity ratio may differ.

Even if ownership structure were the same so that there is no difference in preference and tax incentives between two types of firms,
however, the difference in perceived probability of bankruptcy
between them would make the optimal debt-equity ratio different,[25]
Obviously, the less risky is the firm, the higher would be the
optimal debt-equity ratio, all other things being equal.  Since
group-affiliated firms are less risky (because of the hypothesis
that there exists an implicit mutual insurance scheme and of the
empirical finding below that the variability of corporate performance over time is smaller), the optimal debt-equity ratio is higher
and equity ratio (ROC) is lower.

(f)  Stability of the Interest Rate
The close relationship of group-affiliated firms with city banks and
other financial institutions can be tested within the framework of
the implicit long-term contract theory.  According to the theory,
under the assumption that the bank is risk-neutral and the firm
(non-financial corporation) is risk-averse, it is to the benefit of
both parties to fix the rate of interest over time.[26]

Equation (6) shows that the variance of the interest rate on
interest bearing liabilities (VRI)[27] is, if anything, negatively
correlated to group affiliation.  The variance of the interest rate
(VRI) is computed for each of 317 firms over the period 1971-82.
It is positively correlated to the average level of the interest
rate over the sample period for each firm (MRI).  The sign of the
coefficient for the average size of the firm measured by total
assets (MTA) is negative but it is not significantly different from
zero.  Although statistical significance is not high, it should be
noted that all the coefficients for group dummies (GD(i)'s) are
negative and the overall effect of group formation upon the fluctuation of interest rate is likely to be such that the lending rate of
interest is made more stable over time for the firm involved in a
keiretsu relationship with the bank.  This is consistent with the
hypothesis that there is an implicit long-term contract between the
bank and the firm in which the rate of interest is stabilized over
time.

$$VRI = -0.00276 + 0.03802\ MRI - 0.00031\ MTA - 0.00035\ GD(1)$$
$$(-5.8905)\quad (11.5249)\qquad (-1.0065)\qquad (-1.2077)$$

$$- 0.00050\ GD(2) - 0.00039\ GD(3) - 0.00047\ GD(4)$$
$$(-1.8396)\qquad (-1.3673)\qquad (-1.5817)$$

$$- 0.00042\ GD(5) - 0.00050\ GD(6) - 0.00036\ GD(7) \qquad (6)$$
$$(-1.1335)\qquad (-1.3559)\qquad (-0.9363)$$

$$+ \sum_{i=1}^{16} a(i)ID(i)$$

$$R^2 = 0.5985, \quad F = 6.3420$$

(g)  Stability of Corporate Performance
In Section I, I pointed out that the financial corporate grouping

may be thought of as an implicit mutual insurance scheme, in which
member firms are insurers and insured at the same time.  Given
imperfection of markets and uncertainty, managers would have reason
to behave as risk-averters.  If this is the case, stabilization of
corporate performance over time becomes an important policy objective of the firm, particularly when other corporate members support
such a policy and the criteria for evaluation of the managers
involve stability of corporate performance over time.

In order to test this hypothesis, first of all, it may be asked
whether variability of the rate of business profits (VBP) over the
sample period 1971-82 differs among the various groups under
consideration.  The variance of the rate of business profits over
total assets (VBP) is computed for each firm over the sample period.
There are then the same number of data of VBP's as the number of
companies (317).  Also, the mean of the rate of business profits
(MBP) and the mean of total assets (MTA) over the period were
computed for each firm.

$$
\begin{aligned}
VBP = {}& 0.0046 - 0.0100 \; MBP - 0.0019 \; MTA - 0.0011 \; GD(1) \\
& (5.7596) \quad (-2.0581) \qquad (-3.0705) \qquad (-1.9478) \\[6pt]
& - 0.0012 \; GD(2) - 0.0013 \; GD(3) - 0.0013 \; GD(4) \\
& \;\;(-2.2859) \qquad\;\; (-2.2490) \qquad\;\; (-3.4621) \\[6pt]
& - 0.0021 \; GD(5) - 0.0009 \; GD(6) - 0.0018 \; GD(7) \\
& \;\;(-1.1484) \qquad\;\; (-2.4372) \qquad\;\; (-2.2693) \\[6pt]
& + \sum_{i=1}^{16} a(i) ID(i) \\[6pt]
& \qquad R^2 = 0.3950, \quad F = 2.1517
\end{aligned}
\qquad (7)
$$

Equation (7) shows that the variance of the rate of business profits
(VBP) is negatively correlated to the average rate of profit (MBP)
and the average firm size (MTA).  Although the negative correlation
of VBP to MTA is an expected result, it is somewhat surprising to
find that the variability of profits is a decreasing function of
average rate of profits.  All the coefficients to group dummies are
again negative, and except for DKB (GD(5)), statistically significant at the 10 per cent level for GD(1) and 5 per cent level for
other dummies.

Equation (8) is the similar test for the growth rate of the firm.
VGS stands for variance of the rate of growth in terms of sales over
the same period.[28]  Statistical significance is not entirely
satisfactory for some of the group dummies, but the signs of the
coefficients attached to group dummies are all negative, which is in
accordance with our hypothesis that group firms prefer a stable
growth path.

$$
\begin{aligned}
VGS = {}& 0.0096 + 0.1156 \; MGS - 0.0145 \; MTA - 0.0067 \; GD(1) \\
& (1.6447) \quad (3.5646) \qquad (-3.2781) \qquad (-1.6791) \\[6pt]
& - 0.0050 \; GD(2) - 0.0057 \; GD(3) - 0.0039 \; GD(4) \\
& \;\;(-1.3106) \qquad\;\; (-1.4502) \qquad\;\; (-0.9438) \\[6pt]
& - 0.0022 \; GD(5) - 0.0096 \; GD(6) - 0.0093 \; GD(7) \\
& \;\;(-0.4235) \qquad\;\; (-1.8722) \qquad\;\; (-1.7175)
\end{aligned}
\qquad (8)
$$

$$+ \sum_{i=1}^{16} a(i)ID(i)$$

$$R^2 = 0.6268, \quad F = 7.5306$$

These results are straightforward, but their implications are far from simple. The fact that corporate performance measured in terms of either profitability or growth is more stable over time in group-affiliated firms might imply, particularly when we recall that the majority of Japanese firms are affiliated with some inter-market groups, that the Japanese economy as a whole tends to be less volatile over time. That is, because of implicit mutual insurance mechanisms which are presumed to exist among group affiliated firms and banks, shocks to a particular firm or industry are not only borne by the firm itself, but are also absorbed by other sectors of the economy. Costs incurred by such shocks which strike a particular firm are borne in varying degrees by the other member firms and banks. Needless to say, the banks play a central role in this process, but there are also other profit-sharing activities, where a relatively prosperous firm will often assist a firm in trouble. For example, if a prosperous firm buys from such a firm, it could agree to pay a price somewhat higher than the market price. If it is a seller, it could ease payment conditions by extending usance on the buyers's bills, or perhaps accept a price somewhat below the market price.

This sort of profit-sharing practice among group members will sta-bilize corporate performance. As a result of these implicit mutual assistance programs, the firm in difficulties is able to recover relatively quickly from even the worst situation. To the extent that this sort of mutual assistance mechanism is effective among group members, there will be fewer bankruptcies and lay-offs at a time of great external shocks. This may be one of the reasons why the unemployment rate has not risen enormously in Japan despite the two recent oil crises.

These points may be most important in interpreting the results of this study. In particular, the question of how the Japanese economy has succeeded in minimizing the external disturbances of the oil crises of 1973 and 1979 in such a short period of time without substantially raising the unemployment rate is still a controversial issue. In the present framework of analysis, groupings of firms serve to mitigate external shocks to those firms which would oth-erwise suffer more seriously, and in a way contribute to the stability of the Japanese economy as a whole. From this perspec-tive, the Japanese economy can be regarded as more resilient to external shocks than other industrial economies, all other things being equal. The relatively high capacity of the Japanese economy for adjustment to changed market conditions may thus be closely related to the industrial organisation in Japan as characterised by group formation.

This fact is also closely related to the efficacy of monetary policy in Japan. After the oil crises, the Bank of Japan adopted tight monetary policy for the purpose of curbing inflation. Similar policies were pursued by many other industrial countries, but as is well known, the outcomes were quite different from that in Japan. In Japan, because of the mutual assistance program discussed above, and the community-oriented operation of group-affiliated firms discussed in the previous sections, the rate of unemployment did not rise significantly. The fact that the Japanese economy can absorb the effects of recession in this way makes it much easier for the Bank of Japan to maintain a strong stance on monetary policy in fighting inflation.


5.  SUMMARY AND CONCLUSIONS

One of the most peculiar aspects of Japanese industrial structure is that the majority of Japanese firms belong to so-called intermarket business groups. The present paper analyzes the motivation of such group formation and its effect upon corporate behaviour using individual firm data for 1971 to 1982. More concretely, I examine whether financial and/or real decisions of the firm are affected by the formatin of corporate groups in any particular direction.

The major findings of the paper can be summarised as follows:

i)  The grouping of firms does not generally either increase the rates of profits or of growth of firms. However, the variation of these rates over time is significantly small for group-affiliated firms relative to independent firms. These facts seem to imply that the formation of groups serves the purpose of stabilizing corporate performance over time at the cost of sacrificing the level of corporate performance. This is made possible through the implicit mutual insurance scheme among member firms and banks. This risk-sharing practice among the group membership is important in understanding the performance of the Japanese economy as a whole, since the majority of Japanese firms are attached to some financial corporate grouping.

ii)  The primary purpose of group formation seems to be the sharing of risks and profits among group members by which stabilization of corporate performance is enhanced, but it is also important to note that group formation makes it possible for individual firms to insulate themselves from the imperatives of market forces, particularly of the capital market. This allows firms to pursue their desired mode of distribution of the output within the firm. Indeed, the average compensation to employees is higher in group-affiliated firms. In other words, these firms pay out income more heavily to wages which are tax-exempt costs. Consequently, profits and corporate income tax are in much smaller proportion for the group-affiliated firm. This is consistent with the hypothesis that group-affiliated firms are not profit maximisers.

iii)  The relationship of group-affiliated firms with banks is very close and coherent. The latter, being the principal lender to the member firms, act also as insurers. When a firm is faced with financial or managerial difficulties, the banks within the group render necessary assistance even at a far greater cost and risk than normal business reciprocity requires. In normal times, however, the non-financial firms try to maintain a high and stable outstanding debt against them. This kind of reciprocity between banks and keiretsu firms is the basis of long-term lender-borrower relations and indeed of financial corporate grouping in Japan. According to the implicit long-term contract theory, if the bank is an insurer (risk-neutral), then it is to the benefit of both the bank and the

firm to fix the interest rate over all possible states of the world.
Our study shows that, the variability of the interest rate over
time is, if anything, negatively correlated to group affiliation,
thus confirming (in somewhat weak sense) that there is a long-term
relationships between group-affiliated firms and banks characterized
by a sticky interest rate.

iv) Because of differences in ownership structure and long-term
relationships with the bank, corporate financial policy between the
group companies and independent companies differs considerably.
The rate of dividend to paid-in capital is significantly lower and
debt-equity ratio is significantly higher for group-affiliated
firms.

v) One of the most important implications of the present analysis
is that the peculiarity of Japanese industrial organization — the
formation of financial corporate groups — may be crucial in
understanding the performance of the Japanese economy as a whole.
In particular, Japanese experience after the oil crises reveals a
relatively high capacity for adjustment to external market disturbances. Our study shows that one of the primary motivations of group
formation is to stabilize corporate performance through various
sorts of risk-sharing arrangements among themselves and with the
banks. There is good reason to believe then that the relatively
high capacity of the Japanese economy to adjust to variable market
conditions is closely related to industrial organization in Japan.
Looking at the problem this way, we may infer that the difference
between Japan and other industrial economies in the effectiveness of
macroeconomic policy may be attributable to a large extent to the
institutional aspects of the industrial structure.

GLOSSARY OF NOTATION

| | |
|---|---|
| AW | Average Compensation to Employees |
| GD(1) | Group Dummy for Mitsui Group |
| GD(2) | Group Dummy for Mitsubishi Group |
| GD(3) | Group Dummy for Sumitomo Group |
| GD(4) | Group Dummy for Fuji Group |
| GD(5) | Group Dummy for DKB Group |
| GD(6) | Group Dummy for Sanwa Group |
| GD(7) | Group Dummy for Subsidiaries |
| GG | Rate of Growth in terms of GNP |
| ID(i) | Industry Dummies for 16 manufacturing industries |
| KL | Ratio of Capital to Labor |
| MBP | Mean of Rate of Business Profits |
| MGS | Mean of Rate of Growth in terms of Sales |
| MRI | Mean of Rate of Interest over Interest Bearing Liabilities |
| MTA | Mean of Total Assets |
| NPS | Net Profits per Share |
| RBP | Rate of Business Profits over Total Assets |
| RDV | Rate of Dividends over Paid-in Capital |
| RGS | Rate of Growth in terms of Sales |
| RME | Ratio of Age-corrected Male Employees |
| ROC | Ratio of Own Capital over Total Assets |
| TA | Total Assets |
| VAW | Variance of Average Compensation to Employees |
| VBP | Variance of Rate of Business Profits |
| VGS | Variance of Growth Rate in Sales |
| VRI | Variance of Rate of Interest over Interest Bearing Liabilities |

APPENDIX

List of Firms in Sample by Group and Industry.

1.  Mitsui Group
    Foods                           Nippon Flour Mills Co., Ltd.
                                    Kyodo Shiryo Co., Ltd.
                                    Taito Co., Ltd.
    Textiles                        Toray Industries, Inc.
                                    Naigai Amimono Co., Ltd.
                                    Atsugi Nylon Industrial Co., Ltd.
    Paper, Pulp                     Honshu Paper Co., Ltd.
                                    Takasaki Paper Mfg. Co., Ltd.
    Chemical                        Central Glass Co., Ltd.
                                    Toagosei Chemical Industry Co., Ltd.
                                    Ibigawa Electric Industry Co., Ltd.
                                    Kanegafuchi Chemical Industry Co.
                                    Mitsui Petrochemical Industries.
                                    Daicel Chemical Industries, Ltd.
                                    Fuji Photo Film Co., Ltd.
    Medicines                       Sankyo Company, Limited
    Glass & Cement                  Onoda Cement Co., Ltd.
    Iron & Steel                    Aichi Steel Works, Ltd.
                                    The Japan Steel Works, Ltd.
    Metal                           The Fujikura Cable Works, Ltd.
                                    Toyo Seikan Kaisha, Ltd.
    Machinery                       Toshiba Tungaloy Co., Ltd.
                                    Toshiba Machine Co., Ltd.
                                    Toyoda Automatic Loom Works, Ltd.
                                    Toyoda Machine Works, Ltd.
                                    Tsubakimoto Chain Co.
                                    Riccar Co., Ltd.
    Electrical                      Toshiba Corporation
                                    Tokyo Electric Co., Ltd.
                                    Takaoka Electric Mfg. Co., Ltd.
                                    Kokusai Electric Co., Ltd.
                                    Sony Corporation
                                    Mitsumi Electric Co., Ltd.
                                    Alps Electric Co., Ltd.
                                    Nippondenso Co., Ltd.
                                    Stanley Electric Co., Ltd.
                                    Yuasa Battery Co., Ltd.
                                    Shibaura Engineering Works Co.
    Ship-Building                   Mitsui Engineering & Shipbuilding
    Automobile                      Toyota Motor Corporation
                                    Hino Motors, Ltd.
                                    Toyota Auto Body Co., Ltd.
                                    Kanto Auto Works, Ltd.
                                    Aisin Seiki Co., Ltd.
    Other Manufacturing             Akimoku Kogyo Co., Ltd.

2.  Mitsubishi Group
    Foods                           Morinaga & Co., Ltd.
                                    Kirin Brewery Co., Ltd.
                                    Sanraku-Ocean Co., Ltd.
                                    Kikkoman Corporation
                                    Ajinomoto Co., Inc.
                                    Chukyo Coca-Cola Bottling Co., Ltd.

| | |
|---|---|
| Textiles | Gunze Ltd. |
| | Toyobo Co., Ltd. |
| | Omikenshi Co., Ltd. |
| Paper, Pulp | Mitsubishi Paper Mills, Ltd. |
| Chemical | Nitto Chemical Industry Co., Ltd. |
| | Nippon Carbide Industries Co., Inc. |
| | Sakai Chemical Industry Co., Ltd. |
| | Osaka Oxygen Industries, Ltd. |
| | Toyo Sanso K.K. |
| | The Nippon Chemical Industrial |
| | Taiyo Sanso Co., Ltd. |
| | Mitsubishi Petrochemical Co., Ltd. |
| | Mitsubishi Plastics Industries |
| | Nippon Kayaku Co., Ltd. |
| | Miyoshi Oil & Fat Co., Ltd. |
| | Dai Nippon Toryo Co., Ltd. |
| Medicines | Nippon Shinyaku Co., Ltd. |
| Petroleum | Mitsubishi Oil Company, Ltd. |
| Glass & Cement | Asahi Glass Company, Ltd. |
| | Nippon Glass Co., Ltd. |
| | Toto Ltd. |
| | NGK Insulators, Ltd. |
| | NGK Spark Plug Co., Ltd. |
| | Ina Seito Company, Limited |
| Iron & Steel | Mitsubishi Steel Mfg. Co., Ltd. |
| Metal | Toho Zinc Co., Ltd. |
| | Mitsubishi Metal Corporation |
| | Tamagawa Metal & Machinery Co., Ltd. |
| | Dainichi-Nippon Cables, Ltd. |
| | Miyaji Iron Works Co., Ltd. |
| | Nihon Kentetsu Co., Ltd. |
| Machinery | Makino Milling Machine Co., Ltd. |
| | Mitsubishi Kakoki Kaisha, Ltd. |
| | Sintokogio, Ltd. |
| | Chiyoda Chemical Engineering |
| Electrical | Mitsubishi Electric Corporation |
| | Omron Tateisi Electronics Co. |
| | Kyosan Electric Mfg. Co., Ltd. |
| | Hochiki Corporation |
| | Japan Storage Battery Co., Ltd. |
| | Jeol Ltd. |
| | Teac Corporation |
| Automobile | Honda Motor Co., Ltd. |
| Other Vehicles | Nippon Yusoki Co., Ltd. |
| Fine Mechanics | Shimadzu Corporation |
| | Nippon Kogaku K.K. |
| Other Manufacturing | Kawai Musical Inst. Mfg. Co., Ltd. |

3. Sumitomo Group

| | |
|---|---|
| Foods | Marudai Food Co., Ltd. |
| | Asahi Breweries, Ltd. |
| | Yoshihara Oil Mill, Ltd. |
| Textiles | Teikoku Sangyo Company, Limited |
| Paper, Pulp | Kanzaki Paper Mfg. Co., Ltd. |
| | Daishowa Paper Mfg. Co., Ltd. |
| | Tomoegawa Paper Co., Ltd. |
| | Settsu Paperboard Mfg. Co., Ltd. |
| | Rengo Co., Ltd. |
| Chemical | Seitetsu Kagaku Co., Ltd. |
| | Daido Oxygen Co., Ltd. |

|                     |                                           |
|---------------------|-------------------------------------------|
|                     | Sumitomo Bakelite Co., Ltd.               |
|                     | Nippon Paint Co., Ltd.                    |
| Medicines           | Takeda Chemical Industries, Ltd.          |
|                     | Yamanouchi Pharmaceutical Co., Ltd.       |
|                     | Daiichi Seiyaku Co., Ltd.                 |
|                     | Dainippon Pharmaceutical Co., Ltd.        |
|                     | Shionogi & Co., Ltd.                      |
| Rubber              | Bridgestone Tire Co., Ltd.                |
| Glass & Cement      | Nippon Sheet Glass Co., Ltd.              |
|                     | Sumitomo Cement Co., Ltd.                 |
|                     | Shinagawa Refractories Co., Ltd.          |
| Iron & Steel        | Nippon Pipe Mfg. Co., Ltd.                |
|                     | Kanto Special Steel Works, Ltd.           |
| Metal               | Sumitomo Light Metal Industries           |
|                     | Sumitomo Electric Industries, Ltd.        |
| Machinery           | Nihon Spindle Mfg. Co., Ltd.              |
|                     | Komatsu Ltd.                              |
|                     | Sumitomo Heavy Industries, Ltd.           |
|                     | Daikin Industries, Ltd.                   |
|                     | Sumitomo Precision Products Co.           |
| Electrical          | Meidensha Electric Mfg. Co., Ltd.         |
|                     | Nippon Electric Industry Co., Ltd.        |
|                     | Matsushita Reiki Co., Ltd.                |
|                     | Matsushita Seiko Co., Ltd.                |
|                     | Osaka Transformer Co., Ltd.               |
|                     | Nissin Electric Co., Ltd.                 |
|                     | Nippon Electric Co., Ltd.                 |
|                     | Toyo Communication Equipment Co.,         |
|                     | Matsushita Electric Industrial            |
|                     | Anritsu Electric Co., Ltd.                |
|                     | Tohoku Metal Industries, Ltd.             |
|                     | Sanyo Electric Co., Ltd.                  |
|                     | Matsushita Communication Ind. Co.         |
|                     | Kyushu Matsushita Electric Co.            |
|                     | Victor Company of Japan, Limited          |
|                     | Hokushin Electric Works, Ltd.             |
|                     | Matsushita Electric Works, Ltd.           |
| Other Manufacturing | Daiken Trade & Industry Co., Ltd.         |

4. Fuji Group

|                     |                                           |
|---------------------|-------------------------------------------|
| Foods               | Nisshin Flour Milling Co., Ltd.           |
|                     | Nippon Formula Feed Mfg. Co., Ltd.        |
|                     | Nakamuraya Co., Ltd.                      |
|                     | Sapporo Breweries, Ltd.                   |
|                     | Nippon Reizo Kabushiki Kaisha             |
| Textiles            | Katakura Industries Co., Ltd.             |
|                     | Nisshin Spinning Co., Ltd.                |
|                     | The Japan Wool Textile Co., Ltd.          |
|                     | Teikoku Sen-i Co., Ltd.                   |
|                     | Toho Rayon Co., Ltd.                      |
| Chemical            | Nippon Sanso K.K.                         |
|                     | The Japan Carlit Co., Ltd.                |
|                     | Dai-ichi Kogyo Seiyaku Co., Ltd.          |
| Medicines           | Tokyo Tanabe Co., Ltd.                    |
| Petroleum           | Toa Nenryo Kogyo K.K.                     |
| Glass & Cement      | Ishizuka Glass Co., Ltd.                  |
|                     | Nihon Cement Co., Ltd.                    |
|                     | Daiichi Cement Co., Ltd.                  |
|                     | Nippon Eternit Pipe Co., Ltd.             |

|                    |                                         |
|--------------------|-----------------------------------------|
|                    | Nippon Hume Pipe Co., Ltd.              |
|                    | Daido Concrete Co., Ltd.                |
|                    | Asahi Asbestos Co., Ltd.                |
| Iron & Steel       | Nippon Kokan K.K.                       |
|                    | Azuma Steel Co., Ltd.                   |
|                    | Yodogawa Steel Works, Ltd.              |
|                    | Nippon Kinzoku Co., Ltd.                |
| Metal              | Showa Aluminum Corpolation              |
|                    | Matsuo Bridge Co., Ltd.                 |
| Machinery          | Enshu Limited                           |
|                    | Tokyo Kikai Seisakusho, Ltd.            |
|                    | Tokyo Juki Industrial Co., Ltd.         |
|                    | Nippon Seiko K.K.                       |
| Electrical         | Origin Electric Co., Ltd.               |
|                    | The Nippon Signal Co., Ltd.             |
|                    | Sharp Corporation                       |
|                    | Yamatake-Honeywell Co., Ltd.            |
| Automobile         | Kayaba Industry Co., Ltd.               |
|                    | Ichikoh Industries, Ltd.                |
| Other Vehicles     | Topy Industries, Limited                |

5. DKB Group

|                      |                                           |
|----------------------|-------------------------------------------|
| Foods                | Meiji Milk Products Co., Ltd.             |
| Chemical             | Nippon Zeon Co., Ltd.                     |
|                      | Asahi Denka Kogyo K.K.                    |
|                      | Toa Paint Co., Ltd.                       |
| Medicines            | Banyu Pharmaceutical Co., Ltd.            |
| Rubber               | The Yokohama Rubber Co., Ltd.             |
| Iron & Steel         | Kawasaki Steel Corporation                |
| Metal                | Furukawa Co., Ltd.                        |
| Machinery            | Niigata Engineering Co., Ltd.             |
|                      | Takuma Co., Ltd.                          |
|                      | Iseki & Co., Ltd.                         |
|                      | Nikkiso Co., Ltd.                         |
|                      | Daifuku Machinery Works, Ltd.             |
| Electrical           | Fuji Electric Co., Ltd.                   |
|                      | Yaskawa Electric Mfg. Co., Ltd.           |
|                      | Shinko Electric Co., Ltd.                 |
|                      | Nippon Columbia Co., Ltd.                 |
| Ship-Building        | Ishikawajima-Harima Heavy Industries      |
| Automobile           | Toyo Radiator Co., Ltd.                   |
| Other Manufacturing  | Nissan Nohrin Kogyo Co., Ltd.             |

6. Sanwa Group

|                   |                                        |
|-------------------|----------------------------------------|
| Foods             | Ezaki Glico Co., Ltd.                  |
| Textiles          | Unitika Ltd.                           |
|                   | Daiwabo Co., Ltd.                      |
|                   | Toa Wool Spinning & Weaving Co.        |
|                   | Teijin, Limited                        |
| Chemical          | Tokuyama Soda Co., Ltd.                |
|                   | Ube Industries, Ltd.                   |
|                   | Toyo Ink Mfg. Co., Ltd.                |
| Medicines         | Tanabe Seiyaku Co., Ltd.               |
| Rubber            | Mitsuboshi Belting Limited             |
| Glass & Cement    | Osaka Cement Co., Ltd.                 |
|                   | Nippon Concrete Industries Co.         |
| Iron & Steel      | Nisshin Steel Co., Ltd.                |
|                   | Nakayama Steel Works, Ltd.             |
| Machinery         | Teijin Seiki Co., Ltd.                 |

|                      | NTN Toyo Bearing Co., Ltd.              |
|----------------------|------------------------------------------|
| Electrical           | Toyo Electric Mfg. Co., Ltd.            |
|                      | Iwatsu Electric Co., Ltd.               |
| Ship-Building        | Hitachi Zosen Corporation                |
| Automobile           | Daihatsu Motor Co., Ltd.                 |
| Other Manufacturing  | Toyo Lenoleum Co., Ltd.                  |
|                      | France Bed Co., Ltd.                     |

7. Subsidiaries

|                      |                                          |
|----------------------|------------------------------------------|
| Textiles             | Ashimori Industry Co., Ltd.              |
| Chemical             | Toyo Chemical Co., Ltd.                  |
|                      | Hitachi Chemical Company, Ltd.           |
| Glass & Cement       | Kurosaki Refractories Co., Ltd.          |
| Iron & Steel         | Toyo Kohan Co., Ltd.                     |
|                      | Daido Steel Sheet Corporation            |
|                      | Nippon Koshuha Steel Co., Ltd.           |
|                      | Hitachi Metals, Ltd.                     |
| Metal                | Hitachi Cable, Ltd.                      |
| Electrical           | Hitachi Koki Co., Ltd.                   |
|                      | The Toko Electric Corporation            |
|                      | Shin-Kobe Electric Machinery Co.         |
| Ship-Building        | Sasebo Heavy Industries Co., Ltd.        |
| Automobile           | Nissan Diesel Motor Co., Ltd.            |
|                      | Nissan Shatai Co., Ltd.                  |
|                      | Aichi Machine Industry Co., Ltd.         |
|                      | Yamaha Motor Co., Ltd.                   |
| Other Vehicles       | Shin Meiwa Industry Co., Ltd.            |
|                      | The Kinki Sharyo Co., Ltd.               |
| Other Manufacturing  | Tosho Printing Co., Ltd.                 |

8. Non-Keiretsu Firms

|                      |                                          |
|----------------------|------------------------------------------|
| Foods                | Fujiya Confectionery Co., Ltd.           |
|                      | Snow Brand Milk Products Co., Ltd.       |
|                      | Godo Shusei Co., Ltd.                    |
|                      | The Calpis Food Industry Co., Ltd.       |
|                      | Hohnen Oil Co., Ltd.                     |
|                      | Nissin Food Products Co., Ltd.           |
| Textiles             | Shikibo Ltd.                             |
|                      | Miyuki Keori Co., Ltd.                   |
| Paper, Pulp          | Chuetsu Pulp Industry Co., Ltd.          |
|                      | Chuo Paperboard Co., Ltd.                |
| Chemical             | Nissan Chemical Industries, Ltd.         |
|                      | Hodogaya Chemical Co., Ltd.              |
|                      | Kao Soap Co., Ltd.                       |
|                      | Shiseido Co., Ltd.                       |
|                      | Japan Synthetic Rubber Co., Ltd.         |
| Medicines            | Kaken Pharmaceutical Co., Ltd.           |
|                      | The Green Cross Corporation              |
|                      | Eisai Co., Ltd.                          |
|                      | Rohto Pharmaceutical Co., Ltd.           |
|                      | Hisamitsu Pharmaceutical Co., Inc.       |
| Petroleum            | Koa Oil Company, Limited                 |
|                      | Daikyo Oil Company, Limited              |
|                      | Fuji Kosan Company, Ltd.                 |
| Glass & Cement       | Danto Co., Ltd.                          |
| Iron & Steel         | Nippon Steel Corporation                 |
|                      | Yamato Kogyo Co., Ltd.                   |
|                      | Tokai Steel Works, Ltd.                  |
|                      | Maruichi Steel Tube Ltd.                 |

|  | Nippon Metal Industry Co., Ltd. |
|--|--|
|  | Nippon Yakin Kogyo Co., Ltd. |
|  | Pacific Metals Co., Ltd. |
|  | Yahagi Iron Co., Ltd. |
| Metal | Dowa Mining Co., Ltd. |
|  | Showa Electric Wire & Cable Co. |
|  | Tatsuta Electric Wire & Cable Co. |
|  | Kawada Industries, Inc. |
| Machinery | Diesel Kiki Co., Ltd. |
|  | Tsugami Corporation |
|  | Ikegai Corporation |
|  | Okuma Machinery Works Ltd. |
|  | Amada Co., Ltd. |
|  | Howa Machinery, Ltd. |
|  | Osaka Kiko Co., Ltd. |
|  | Kioritz Corporation |
|  | Kurita Water Industries Ltd. |
|  | Daido Kogyo Co., Ltd. |
|  | Kato Works Co., Ltd. |
|  | Tadano Ltd. |
|  | Amano Corporation |
|  | Brother Industries, Ltd. |
|  | Nachi-Fujikoshi Corp. |
|  | Nippon Thompson Co., Ltd. |
| Electrical | N C R Japan, Ltd. |
|  | Casio Computer Co., Ltd. |
|  | Hitachi, Ltd. |
|  | Makita Electric Works, Ltd. |
|  | Sanken Electric Co., Ltd. |
|  | Trio Kenwood Corporation |
|  | Pioneer Electronic Corporation |
| Automobile | Tokico Ltd. |
|  | Fuji Heavy Industries Ltd. |
| Other Vehicles | Nippon Sharyo Seizo Kaisha, Ltd. |
|  | Tokyu Car Corporation |
| Fine Mechanics | Aichi Tokei Denki Co., Ltd. |
|  | Kimmon Manufacturing Co., Ltd. |
|  | Ricoh Company, Ltd. |
|  | Minolta Camera Co., Ltd. |
|  | Yashica Co., Ltd. |
|  | Sankyo Seiki Mfg. Co., Ltd. |

NOTES

* An earlier version of this paper was presented at a Rokko Symposium on the Economic Analysis of the Japanese Firm in Comparative Perspective, 26 - 28 July, 1982. The present paper is an extensive revision. (See [20]). The author acknowledges valuable comments from Professors Masahiko Aoki, Mervin King, Eleanor Hadley, Susumu Koizumi, Harvey Leibenstein, and other participants in the Symposium. I would also like to extend my thanks to Professors Peter Drysdale, Michio Hatanaka, Shoichi Royama, Hiroshi Yoshikawa, Kazuo Ueda, Hajime Oniki and other members of the regular Thursday Seminar at Osaka University for their useful comments. Computational assistance by Mr. Noriyuki Ebara was very helpful. I am also grateful to Dr. Peter Drysdale and Ms. C. Boyles for their kindly going over my English in this paper. Needless to say, however, I am solely responsible for

any remaining errors.  This paper was financially supported by Grants-in-Aid for
Scientific Research from the Ministry of Education, Science and Culture No.
58410013.

[1]For a detailed study on the pre-War _zaibatsu_, see Hadley [13].  For the development of post War corporate groups, see Kobayashi [18], Okumura [24].  The
interested reader is also referred to Nakatani [20], [21], [22] for general background readings.

[2]This is one of the reasons why the debt-equity ratio of group-affiliated firms
is substantially higher than that of independent firms, as is shown in Section III.
Equation (5) below shows that the equity ratios of group companies are 4 to 9
percentage points lower than those of independent firms.

[3]For some companies, trust banks and life insurance companies are the most important sources of supply of funds.

[4]The implicit labour contract theory is due to Azariadis.  There are number
of applications of this theory to transactions between banks and non-financial
firms.  See, for example, Fried and Howitt [9], in which non-financial firms are
assumed risk-averse while the bank is risk-neutral.  Under these circumstances,
it is best for both parties to fix the lending rate of interest over all states
of the world.  See Section III below where it is confirmed that the interest rate
is more stable over time for those companies affiliated with corporate groups.
If a firm is not as risk-averse as the bank, however, there may be no such
implicit contract.  Independent companies, then, can be regarded as less
risk-averse than group-affiliated companies.

[5]Another important merit of the bank's association with a corporate group is that
the cost of collecting deposits may be reduced greatly.  For example, suppose
that one of the group-affiliated companies, which have daily business transactions among themselves, borrows from the group-affiliated bank, and that the
borrowed money is used for making payments to other group members.  Since these
group members usually make deposits at the group bank, most of the credit originally forwarded returns eventually to the group's banking sector as deposits.
Other examples are (1) the employee of group companies is required to open personal deposit/savings account with the group bank, to which salaries and wages
are tranferred automatically from the company they work for, and (2) an insurance
company can often sell a collective insurance to companies of the same group.
These examples show that savings can be absorbed relatively easily by group-affiliated banks and other financial intermediaries.

[6]The data before 1974 are not available in accounting reports of the firms.

[7]Glossary of Notation for the regression analysis below is found at the end of
this paper.

[8]'Net Profits' are even worse for evaluating the current period performance of
the firm, since ther are several other artificial additions and deductions between current profits and net profits.  Examples are Special Reserves (_tokutei
hikiatekin_) and once for all capital gains and losses, which can be substantial
relative to current profits.

[9]The inclusion of the rate of growth of GNP (GG) is in order to eliminate the
possible bias of the data produced by macroeconomic business conditions of each
year.  Except for this factor, we assume, as a first approximation, that all the
pooled data (cross-section and time-series) are mutually independent observations.

We follow this assumption throughout the paper.

[10]That is, if a(i) is positive (negative), it means that the i-th industry has an positive (negative) effect on the rate of business profit (RBP) relative to Foods Industry.

[11]These figures are available from the author upon request.

[12]Estimates based on other measures of growth are available from the author upon request.

[13]These data are available in NIKKEI NEEDS COMPANY, a data file supplied by The Nihon Keizai Shinbun Sha. However, they were available only for the latest two years (1981 and 1982), and consequently use of other data in Equation (3) is also ristricted to these two years.

[14]After adjustments of firm size and composition of the work force of each firm, however, it is still possible to speculate that workers with better quality tend to be recruited by group-affiliated firms. If this is true, then the difference in wages may be attributed totally to the difference in quality of workers. However, without detailed data on labour quality, this remains an untestable hypothesis.

[15]The estimation of the payout rate (dividend divided by net profits) using individual firm data involves a technical difficulty. That is, there are a fair number of companies which earned negative profits during the sample period. A majority of those firms pay no dividends at all but some maintain positive dividends out of negative profits. The payout rate in the latter case is clearly infinite, while it is not clear whether zero dividend over negative profits implies payout rates of zero. In order to avoid these complexities, estimation here is based on the dividend ratio over paid-in capital, and this is in turn regressed against net profits per share (NPS).

[16]Taxation in intercorporate dividends in Japan is complex and best understood by a simple example. Suppose that a firm bought x yen worth of stock in some past year, and $\alpha$ of this amount was financed by borrowing at interest rate r and $(1-\alpha)$ by internal funds. In the current year, the company receives dx of dividends, where d is the dividend yield. The amount, $dx-r\alpha x$, is not counted as profits in practice if this amount does not exceed the total dividends paid by this firm. The amount $r\alpha x$ is treated as profits but this is simply to offset the deduction of interest paid against the purchase of the stock from profits of the firm. Therefore, as long as the dividends paid by the firm are greater than the dividends received, there is essentially no tax on intercorporate dividends. This information was supplied to me by Mr. M. Noda, Research Division of The Sumitomo Bank.

[17]An interesting discussion on the effect of the existence of shareholders in diverse tax situations, toghther with the difference in shareholder's risk attitude, is developed in Feldstein and Green [ 8].

[18]See, for example, Stephen Ross [ 25], Roger Gordon and Burton Malkiel [11] and Sudipto Bhattacharya [4] for this line of argument. An interesting discussion is also found in King [17] in which a signal is used as a tool of management strategy.

[19]Recent figures show that, on the average, the equity ratio (equity divided by total assets) of the Japanese firm is 0.19 to 0.20, while it is above 0.50 in the United States.

[20]Recent revision of Commercial Law (shoho) effective as of October, 1982 requires

that all the outstanding special reserves (tokutei hikiatekin) should be shown as
equity rather than debt and there will be non-tax-free special reserves to be
taken away from profits after October, 1982.

[21]Indeed, there are some estimates which show that the adjusted equity ratio of
the Japanese firm is fairly close to that of other advanced countries.  See, for
example, [15].  See also, for a compact discussion on these points, Elston [6].

[22]Unfortunately, however, it is impossible to make adjustments necessitated by
changes in land prices unless we know the details of land ownership of individual
companies including exact location, market price and acquisition date.  If land
owned by group-affiliated firms is more valuable (relative to book values) than
those owned by independent firms, the inflation-adjusted equity ratio of
group-affiliated firms would rise relative to independent firms and may close the
gap entirely in the observed difference in equity ratios (ROC in equation (5)).
Although this remains a mere speculation until we know the details of land ownership of individual firms, it is frequently said that ex-zaibatsu companies
affiliated with Mitsui, Mitsubishi or Sumitomo (and some other firms related to
Sanwa, Dai-ichi Kangyo or Fuji) are in possession of more valuable lands than
those companies outside these groups.  To the extent that this is the accurate
description of reality, equity of keiretsu firms must be more seriously undervalued.  But, in this case, the rate of business profits (RBP) for group companies
will be even smaller than that reported above in Equation (1), since total assets
(denominator of RBP) increases more quickly than independent firms.

[23]Strictly speaking, the non-keiretsu group includes some companies which have
close association with smaller city banks, long-term credit banks or local financial institutions.

[24]This effect will be reinforced if the 'main' bank is sufficiently powerful and
it is believed by other banks that it is firmly committed to act as the ultimate
supporter of the troubled firm.

[25]See for a discussion of bankruptcy costs, Gordon and Malkiel [11].

[26]See Fried and Howitt [9], Ikeo [14] and Wakita [27] for the implicit contract
theory applied to banking sector.

[27]Interest bearing liabilities of the firm include short-term and long-term
borrowing from the bank, corporate bonds, bills discounted and deposits made by
the firm's employees.  The rate of interest over interest bearing liabilities of
the firm is the sum of interest paid by the firm divided by the sum of the liabilities listed above.  Therefore, strictly speaking, the rate of interest here is
not the lending rate of the bank.  Furthermore, in practice, Japanese banks request the borrower firm to leave a certain proportion of borrowings in some form
of bank deposits.  The ratio of compensating balances is determined in reference
to the relative bargaining position of each firm.  It is generally believed that
the average ratio of compensating balances is as high as about 40 percent (see
Wakita [27]), and if this is true, we would have to deal with the effective rate
of interest which takes into account the existence of compensating balances.

[28]Estimates for two other measures of growth, rate of growth of value-added and
of total assets, show very similar results to the one reported here.

REFERENCES

[1] Aoki, M., "A Model of the Firm as a Stockholder-Employee Cooperative Game", American Economic Review, Sept. 1980.

[2] _____, "Equilibrium Growth of the Hierarchical Firm:  Shareholder-employee Cooperative Game Approach", American Economic Review, 1982.

[3] Aoki, M., "Shareholders' Non-unanimity on Investment Financing---Banks vs. Individual Investors", in M. Aoki ed. The Economic Analysis of the Japanese Firm, North-Holland, 1984.

[4] Bhattacharya, S., "Imperfect Information, Dividend Policy, and 'The Bird in the Hand' Fallacy", Bell Journal of Economics, Spring 1979.

[5] Caves, R., and Uekusa, M., Industrial Organization in Japan, Washington D.C., 1976.

[6] Elston, C.D., "The Financing of Japanese Industry", Bank of England Quarterly Bulletin, December 1981.

[7] Fama, E., and Miller, M., The Theory of Finance, Holt, Rinehart and Winston, 1972.

[8] Feldstein, M., and Green, J., "Why Do Companies Pay Dividends ?", American Economic Review, March 1983.

[9] Fried, J., and Howitt, P., "Credit Rationing and Implicit Contract Theory", Journal of Money, Credit and Banking, August 1980.

[10] Futatsugi, Y., Gendai Nihon no Kigyō-shudan (Firm Groups in Modern Japan), Tōyōkeizai, 1976.

[11] Gordon, Roger, and Malkiel, Burton, "Corporation Finance" in Aaron, H.J. and Pechman, J.A. eds. How Taxes Affect Economic Behavior, Brookings, 1981.

[12] Gotō, A., "Kigyo Gurupu no Keizai Bunseki" (An Economic Analysis of Firm Groups), Keizai Kenkyu, April 1978.

[13] Hadley, E., Antitrust in Japan, Princeton, 1970.

[14] Ikeo, K., "Anmoku no Keiyaku to Ginkō Kashidashi Shijō" (The Implicit Contract Theory and Market for Bank Credit), Okayamadaigaku Keizaigaku Zasshi, February, 1981.

[15] Japanese Corporate Finance 1977-80, by International Business Information Service, Inc., Financial Times Limited, 1980.

[16] Keiretsu no Kenkyu (Studies on Financial Corporate Groupings), Keizai Chosa Kyokai, Tokyo (Annual Publication).

[17] King, M., Public Policy and the Corporation, Chapman and Hall, 1977.

[18] Kobayashi, Y., Kigyo-shudan no Bunseki (An Analysis of Corporate Groups), Hokkaido Univ. Press, 1980.

[19] Marris, R., The Economic Theory of Managerial Capitalism, Macmillan, 1964.

[20] Nakatani, I., "The Role of Intermarket Keiretsu Business Groups in Japan", Pacific Economic Papers No.97, Australia-Japan Research Centre, Australian National University, Dec. 1982.

[21] _____, "Risk-sharing Kara Mita Nihon Keizai" (Risk-sharing and the Role of Business Groups in Japan), Osaka Economic Papers, Dec. 1982.

[22] _____, "Nihon Keizai no Himitsu o Toku Kagi" (How Can We Find a Key to the Secrets of Japanese Economic Performance), Ekonomisto, Feb. 15, 1983. (English Summary by ILO, Tokyo Office "Secrets of Japanese Economic Performance", March 1983.)

[23] Odagiri, H., "Kigyo-shudan no Riron" (The Theory of Corporate Groups), Economic Studies Quarterly, Aug. 1975.

[24] Okumura, H., Shin Nihon no Rokudai kigyo-shudan (A New Look at the Six Major Corporate Groups in Japan), Diamond-sha, 1983.

[25] Ross, Stephen, "The Determination of Financial Structures: The Incentive Signalling Approach", Bell Journal of Economics, Spring 1977.

[26] Teranishi, J., Goto, A., and Serizawa, K., "Shikin Shijo to Kigyo Gurupu" (Financial Markets and Corporate Groups), Keizai Hyoron, Nov. 1975.

[27] Wakita, Y., "Wagakuni no Kashidashi Shijo to Keiyaku Torihiki" (The Japanese Credit Market and Contract Theory), Kinyu Kenkyu, Bank of Japan, March 1983.

THE ECONOMIC ANALYSIS OF THE JAPANESE FIRM
M. Aoki (editor)
© Elsevier Science Publishers B.V. (North-Holland), 1984

*MATHEMATICAL APPENDIX*

# RISK-SHARING IN THE CORPORATE GROUP

MASAHIKO AOKI

Let us consider a simple model of corporate group composed of two-vertically related firms. The up-steam firm transforms an externally supplied material (a primary material) into an intermediate product, and the down-stream firm transforms the intermediate product into a final product. Let

$x$ = input of the primary material to the upper-stream firm,
$r$ = supply price of the primary material,
$y$ = input of the intermediate product to the down-stream firm,
$p$ = demand price of the final product of the down-stream firm,

where $p$ and $r$ are stochastic variables uncontrollable by the group of firms. Let F and G be production functions of the up-stream firm and the down-stream firm respectively, each strictly concave and twice differentiable. Suppose that the both firms are risk-averse and that their risk attitudes are represented by concave von Neumann - Morgenstern utility functions u and v respectively, each defined on respective income. Then setting

$q$ = terms of trade of intermediate product,

group-efficiency requires that $x$, $y$ and $q$ are to be chosen contingent upon the state of external markets $\theta$ so as to

$$\text{maximize } E[v(p(\theta)G(y(\theta)) - q(\theta)y(\theta))]$$

subject to

$$E[u(q(\theta)F(x(\theta)) - r(\theta)x(\theta))] = K$$

$$y(\theta) \leq F(x(\theta))$$

for some value K which is considered to represent the relative bargaining power of the up-stream firm vis-a-vis the down-stream firm.

Denoting the probability of the occurence of the state of external markets $\theta$ by $\pi(\theta)$, the necessary and sufficient (Kuhn-Tucker-Arrow-Borch) condition is given by

$$\pi(\theta)v'(s(\theta))[p(\theta)G'(y(\theta)) - q(\theta)] = \mu(\theta)$$

$$\pi(\theta)\lambda u'(t(\theta))[q(\theta)F'(x(\theta)) - r(\theta)] = -\mu(\theta)F'(x(\theta)) \qquad (1)$$

$$v'(s(\theta)) = \lambda u'(t(\theta)), \text{ for all } \theta$$

where $\mu(\theta)$ and $\lambda$ are Lagrange multipliers, and

$$s(\theta) = p(\theta)G(y(\theta)) - q(\theta)y(\theta),$$

$$t(\theta) = q(\theta)F(x(\theta)) - r(\theta)x(\theta),$$

each representing net income of respective firms. From these condition it is easily derived that

$$p(\theta)G'(F(x(\theta))F'(x(\theta)) = r(\theta),$$

$$y(\theta) = F(x(\theta)), \text{ for all } \theta.$$

That is, the amounts of inputs $x(\theta)$ and $y(\theta)$ are to be chosen for each state of the external markets to maximize the aggregate spot incomes,

$$S = p(\theta)G(F(x)) - r(\theta)x.$$

Denote the maximand by $S*(\theta)$. From (1), we have

$$A_v(\theta)s'(\theta) = A_u(\theta)t'(\theta)$$

where $A_v(\theta) = -v''(s(\theta))/v'(s(\theta))$ and $A_u(\theta) = -u''(t(\theta))/u'(t(\theta))$, each representing the measure of absolute risk aversion of respective firms. Since $s'(\theta) + t'(\theta) = S*'(\theta)$, we have

$$s'(\theta) = \frac{A_u(\theta)}{A_u(\theta) + A_v(\theta)} S*'(\theta)$$

$$t'(\theta) = \frac{A_v(\theta)}{A_u(\theta) + A_v(\theta)} S*'(\theta) \qquad (2)$$

This ralation gives the general rule for group-efficient distribution of the maximized joint income. It says that fluctuations of the joint income are to be born between the both firms in a proportion inversely related to respective risk averseness.

This rule is not, in general, observed in the competitive mechanism. For instance, suppose that the production functions of the upper stream firm and the down stream firm are of constant elasticity type so that $F(x) = x^a$ and $G(y) = y^b$ ($0 < a$, $b < 1$). Then the competitive mechanism would determine the relative distribution at

$$s_c(\theta) = \frac{1 - b}{1 - ab} S*(\theta),$$

$$t_c(\theta) = \frac{b(1 - a)}{1 - ab} S*(\theta).$$

This competitive solution will satisfy the above group-efficient distribution rule if $A_v(\theta)s(\theta) \equiv A_v(\theta)t(\theta) \equiv$ a constant. Otherwise, it will do so only by accident. That is, the competitive distribution ("the invisible-hand distribution") is group-efficient, if and only if (1) the production functions of the both firms are of constant elasticity type, and (2) the measures of relative risk aversion of the both firms are constant and identical.

Let us assume that this special case will not hold and accordingly the competitive mechanism is not group-efficient. Instead, for illustrative purpose, let us assume that $A_v(\theta) \equiv A_v$ and $A_u(\theta) \equiv A_u$ for some constants $A_v$ and $A_u (\geq 0)$. Then integrating the condition (2), we have the following group-efficient distribution rule:

$$s*(\theta) = \frac{A_u}{A_u + A_v} S*(\theta) + \beta,$$

$$t*(\theta) = \frac{A_v}{A_u + A_v} S*(\theta) - \beta, \tag{3}$$

where $\beta$ is a parameter to be determined by relative bargaining power of the both firms. To see this, consider a class of distribution rules represented by

$$s_{\alpha,\beta}(\theta) = \alpha S*(\theta) + \beta$$

$$t_{\alpha,\beta}(\theta) = (1 - \alpha)S*(\theta) - \beta$$

for $0 \leq \alpha \leq 1$. The competitive solution $s_c(\theta)$ and $t_c(\theta)$ is a special case of this class for which $\alpha = (1 - b)/(1 - ab)$ and $\beta = 0$. Now by the definition of the measure of absolute risk aversion, we have:

$$E[v(s_{\alpha,\beta}(\theta))] = v(\alpha E[s*(\theta)] + \beta - \frac{1}{2}A_v\alpha^2\sigma_{S*}^2)$$

$$E[u(t_{\alpha,\beta}(\theta))] = u((1 - \alpha)E[s*(\theta)] - \beta - \frac{1}{2}A_u(1 - \alpha)^2\sigma_{S*}^2)$$

where $\sigma_{S*}^2$ is the variance of $S*(\theta)$. Therefore, $E[v(s_{\alpha,\beta}(\theta))] > E[v(s_c(\theta)]$, if and only if

$$\alpha E[S^*(\theta)] + \beta < \frac{1 - b}{1 - ab} E[(S^*(\theta)] + \frac{1}{2}A_v[\alpha^2 - (\frac{1 - b}{1 - ab})^2]\sigma_{S^*}^2$$

$$\equiv G(\alpha).$$

Likewise, $E[u(t_{\alpha,\beta}(\theta)] > E[u(t_c(\theta))]$ if and only if

$$(1 - \alpha)E[S^*(\theta)] - \beta < \frac{b(1 - a)}{1 - ab} E[S^*(\theta)]$$

$$+ \frac{1}{2}A_u[(1 - \alpha)^2 - (\frac{b(1 - a)}{1 - ab})]\sigma_{S^*}^2 \equiv H(\alpha).$$

Consult the diagram. The horizontal axes of the box represent the relative shares of the both firms in uncertain joint income, $\alpha$ and $1 - \alpha$. $\alpha$ is measured from the lower-left corner of the box toward the right, and $1 - \alpha$ is measured from the upper-right corner toward the left. The total width of the box is of course equal to one. The height of the box represents the expected value of the joint income $E[S^*(\theta)]$. The expected income of the down-stream firm $E[s(\theta)] = \alpha E[S^*(\theta)] + \beta$ is measured from the lower-left corner to upward, and the expected income of the up-stream firm $E[t(\theta)] = (1 - \alpha)E[S^*(\theta)] - \beta$ is measured from the upper-right corner to downward. The point C represents the competitive solution. Going through the point C, the graph of the curve $G(\alpha)$ and $H(\alpha)$ as defined above are drawn. If the expected income $E[\alpha S^*(\theta) + \beta]$ is above the graph $G(\alpha)$ for a given $\alpha$, the down-stream firm is better-off under the distribution rule $\alpha S^*(\theta) + \beta$ than the competitive distribution. Likewise, if the expected income $E[(1 - \alpha)S^*(\theta) - \beta]$ is below the graph $H(\alpha)$ for a given $\alpha$, then the up-stream firm is better-off under the distribution rule $(1 - \alpha)S^*(\theta) - \beta$. Therefore the lense-shaped area enclosed by the graph G and H represent possibilities of distribution rules which are Pareto-superior to the competitive solution. The vertical distance between H and G represents the reduction of aggregate risk cost, where aggregate risk cost is measured by the sum of variances of firms' incomes with the respective measures of absolute risk aversion as weights, that is, by the quantity

$$[A_v\alpha^2 + A_u(1 - \alpha)^2]\sigma_{S^*}^2.$$

This measure of aggregate risk cost is minimized at $\alpha$ for which the condition (3) holds. In other words, the intersection of the straight line $\alpha = A_u/(A_u + A_v)$ with the lense shaped area corresponds to the set of group-efficient distribution, i.e., the Edgeworth contract curve. The choice of a point from the Edgeworth contract curve, or the distribution of the saved risk cost, depends upon the relative bargaining powers of the both parties. From the disgram, it is clear that there is one-to-one correspondence between a choice of $\beta$ and the choice of a point from the Edgeworth contract curve.

I shall not go into the discussion of an appropriate measure of relative bargaining powers of members in details, but it is reasonable to assume that each member's bargaining power is affected by its outside opportunity as well as its risk attitude. For instance, Robert Aumann and Mordecai Kurz [1] proposed an interesting concept

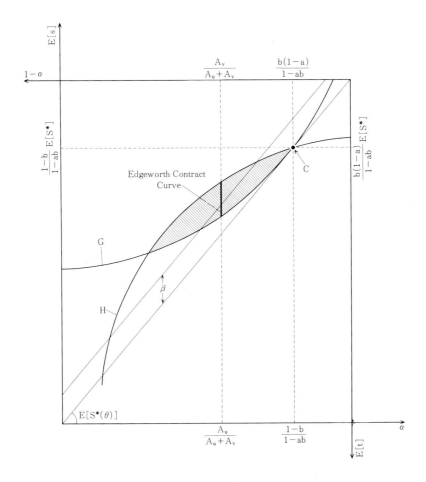

Figure VIIA-1

of <u>pure</u> <u>boldness</u>.  In our analytical framework, the pure boldness
of the up-stream firm can be difined as

$$\frac{E[u']}{A_u(E[u] - E[\bar{u}])} ,$$

where $E[\bar{u}]$ denotes the level of expected utility available outside
the group, once the firm terminates its membership in the group.  A
similar expression holds for the down-stream firm by substituting
v for u.  The aggregate risk cost saved in our model would be distributed to each firm porportional to its pure boldness.  In general,
the slimmer the external opportunity relative to gains available
within the group, the less a firm gets in terms of expected income.

For illustrative purpose, I have employed a simple example in which
efficient intra-group arrangements can be represented by only two
parameters: $\alpha$ to determine the distribution of the variances of net
incomes of member firms, and $\beta$ to determine the distribution of the
expected values of net incomes of member firms.  However, the existence of non-competitive efficient distribution which minimizes the
aggregate risk costs is in general assured, if relative risk aversions
of member-firms are not identical.  In general, if there are n firms
in a group, and if we denote the variance of the i-th firm's income
by $\sigma_i^2$ and its absolute risk aversion at the competitive distribution by $A_i(c)$ (i = 1, ....n), then the efficient distribution of the
joint income of the group ought to minimize <u>ex</u> <u>ante</u> the aggregate
risk cost defined by

$$\sum_{i=1}^{n} A_i(c)\sigma_i^2.$$

Clearly, if any firm, say the i-th firm, is risk neutral so that
$A_i(c) = 0$, then that firm ought to absorb all the risk involved in
the generation of the joint-income by assuring other risk-averse
firms certain fixed incomes regardless of the state of external
markets to evolve.

In the other extreme case in which all firms in a group are alike
in their risk averseness, then the risk involved in the production
of jont incomes should be born equally by all the firms, i.e., it
should be distributed in such a way that the variances of distributed
income become equal <u>ex</u> <u>ante</u> for all the firms.  But it does not imply
that the joint-income itself should be distributed equally among the
firms.  Depending upon relative bargaining power, the expected value
of incomes, or shares in the reduction of aggregate risk costs, for
each firm may differ.

REFERENCES

[1]Aumann, R. and M. Kurz, Power and taxes, <u>Econometrica</u> 45, 1137-1160, 1977.

THE ECONOMIC ANALYSIS OF THE JAPANESE FIRM
M. Aoki (editor)
© Elsevier Science Publishers B.V. (North-Holland), 1984

# THE GOVERNMENT IN A SPIRAL DILEMMA:
# DYNAMIC POLICY INTERVENTIONS VIS-A-VIS AUTO FIRMS. C.1900-C.1960

TAIZO YAKUSHIJI

## 1. INTRODUCTION

The topic of Japan's industrial policies has become conspicuously popular among foreign observers. At times this interest leads to criticism of the Japanese government's overcommitment to industrial affairs. This criticism tends to be particularly intense in regard to auto industry policies. The recent debates over the "local content law" is an example. However, the relationship between the Japanese government and the auto industry is often misunderstood. This relationship has not always been harmonious or antagonistic. For example, the 1981 conflict between the government and the auto industry over export quotas may be puzzling for foreign critics. They may ask, "Can an industry which was believed to have received significant aide from government be antagonistic against its former supporters?" And furthermore, "Why did the government (i.e., MITI) "coercively" set the export quota by 1.68 million units without a sufficient nemawashi (political rooting)?"

In fact, the relationship between the Japanese government and the auto industry changed before and after the early 1970s when auto exports increased sharply. The change occurred as the industry was becoming more and more independent of government interventions, showing a marked difference from the pre-1960s period. During this time, foreign observers, particularly LDCs' or NICs' policy makers, who attempted to implant the Japanese lesson encountered the dilemma: if policies were successfully exercised, it would be highly likely that the promoted industry shrugs government influence, and thus, eventually becomes antagonistic if the government continues to attempt to control the industry's actions (i.e., policy inertia). On the other hand, as a reaction to industry's antagonism, the government's intervention will become more and more coercive. Perhaps, this "boomerang syndrome" is visible in many countries where the governments' interventions were "recursively" or "spirally" practiced.

The purpose of this paper is to elucidate this syndrome (hereafter, called the "spiral dilemma") by examining the sixty-year (c.1900 - c.1960) history of the Japanese government's interventions toward auto firms. The rationale for taking the pre-internationalization period (before the late 1960s) of the Japanese auto firms stems from the assumption that the symptoms of the industry's independent behavior would be readily visible even in the honeymoon period when the industry gradually gained its strength as a result of effective government interventions.

## 2. A CYCLE MODEL: THE SPIRAL PROCESS OF INTERVENTIONS

Talcott Parsons once proposed the so-called AGIL (adaptation, goal-seeking, integration, latency) model to conceptualize the social interactions among polity, economy, society and households.[1] The thesis of this paper explains the interaction between polity and economy. In this regard, the Parsonian model seems to fit our framework. However, his model is primarily conceptual, leaving ample ambiguity for structural specification. With a greater emphasis on behavioral recursion, on the one hand, and a substantiation of the two-sector interactions of the Parsonian model on the other hand, we arrive at the following "cycle" model as shown in Figure VIII-1.

The feature of this cycle model is straightforward. It is the "state-observer" model from the standpoint of policy-makers. That is, this model illustrates the iterative process in which policy-makers observe the firms' reactions to their interventions. Considering the gap between initial expectation and actual output, policy makers can conceive the next intervention. In this respect, the model can be better termed as the "behavioral" or "contextual" model, for interventions are exercised not on the pre-determined or, contextually-free rules like those of economic theory, but on the "real-time" observation of the firms' reactions.

Provided that policy-makers behaved in the manner described above and the interventions were consecutively or spirally employed with respect to the same industry, the cycle model can be interpreted into a matrix form in Figure VIII-2, where our row-wise observations give a picture of development of government intervention over sixty years.[2]

A. The First Policy Intervention: The Law of Support for
   Military Vehicles of 1918 [Figure VIII-3]

There needs to be an initial condition for any operational or descriptive system. The following two incidents are examples of such situations. One is the European precedent for the legal support of motor vehicles for military, which was introduced by a military attaché to the Japanese embassy in Paris. The second was the low import tariff resulting from the Franco-Japanese Preferential Tariff Agreement, which eventually led to an increase of motor vehicle imports into Japan. These two incidents shaped the future trends for military vehicles and civilian vehicles in Japan. The flow of military vehicles led to the enactment of the Law for Support for Military Vehicles in 1918. With this law two large firms, Tokyo Gas & Electric, Ltd. (TGE) and Ishikawajima Motors, Ltd. were established.

Under the recommendation of the Survey Committee for Military Vehicles established in 1912, the Law of Support for Military Vehicles placed a main emphasis on civilian ownership and military commandeering in case of war emergencies. The separation between ownership and commandeering was adopted because the Imperial Army believed that it would be financially difficult to assume all maintenance costs. According to the law, the government gave both purchasing and maintenance subsidies to civilian owners, and for the producers, the law rendered a considerable amount of manufacturing subsidy (less than 2,000 yen per vehicle). It is reported that this considerable manufacturing subsidy lured

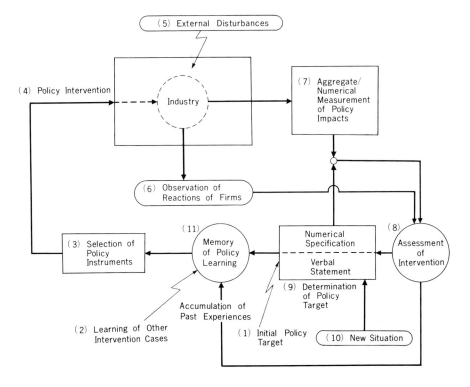

Figure VIII-1   Schematic Model of Policy Intervention

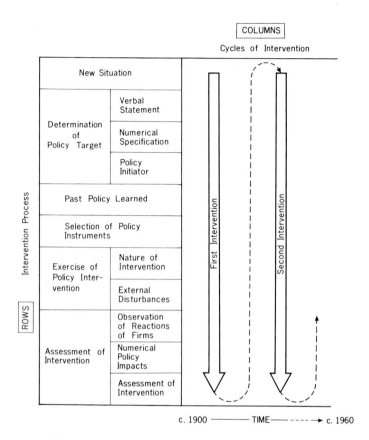

Figure Ⅷ-2   Matrix Framework for Policy Intervention Analysis

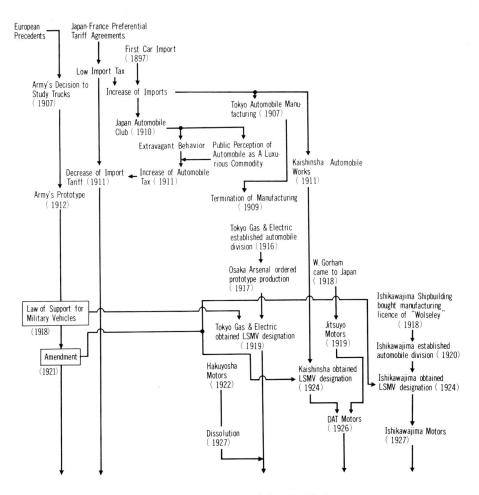

Figure VIII-3    Causal Environment around the First Major Policy Intervention

larger, ambitious firms to take over the role of previous small-
scale firms in an unstable productive capacity.

The flow of civilian vehicles was first characterized by the
establishment of the Japan Automobile Club in 1910. Members were
from the aristocratic class which included members of the Imperial
family and their relatives. Because of these members, passenger
cars at that time, were regarded publicly as an extravagant leisure
item. This notion toward the passenger car lasted until Japan
entered the period of large-scale motor vehicle use and ownership
in the 1960s.

A summary of the 1918 law is best characterized as follows: while
its primary purpose was to secure military vehicles, its indirect
effect was more significant. That is, it established for the first
time the Japanese auto industry. Above all, one should notice that
the government gained confidence in creating the auto industry with
private firms, instead of creating directly-controlled, national
corporations. Furthermore, the mixed policy measures of public
subsidy and detailed technical specifications which were needed for
military standardization determined the scope of government
policies for the future. It is important to notice that the
government attempted not only to support auto manufacturing but
also to create the auto market in the civilian sector. In this
sense, the Law of 1918 can be best characterized not as a "push"
(supply) policy, but rather a "pull" (demand) policy or "indirect"
policy. This is an important but hereafter repeated characteristic
of successive government interventions.

B. The Second Policy Intervention: The Ministry of Commerce's
   Standard Model of 1931 [Figure VIII-4]

The Japanese auto industry created by the Law of Support for
Military Vehicles of 1918 received its second intervention in 1931
when the government authorized the Ministry of Commerce
Standardized Vehicle Model. The direct cause for this intervention
was the Buy-Japanese Campaign stemming from trade deficits at that
time.

Japan enjoyed an unprecedented economic boom in the aftermath of
the First World War, but entered into a period of recession from
1920. A rapid increase in trade deficits which started in 1920,
resulted in the establishment of the Committee for Promotion of
Domestic Products within the Ministry of Commerce (MOC) in June
1926. Three years later, the MOC issued Inquiry #7 to the
Committee regarding the promotion of domestic auto production.
Primarily, the inquiry was concerned with how to deal with national
security and foreign trade implications resulting from a rapid
increase in auto imports.

The primary cause of auto imports came from the Great Kanto
Earthquake in 1923. With the total destruction of its streetcars,
the city of Tokyo purchased 2,000 Ford buses as a temporary
emergency measure. These unexpected sales led General Motors and
Ford Motors to establish their overseas branches. As a direct
consequence, in 1926 and 1927, Japan Ford and Japan GM started a
knock-down assembly production.

Stimulated by the city of Tokyo's successful bus operation, the
Ministry of Railroads (MOR) began to seriously consider installing

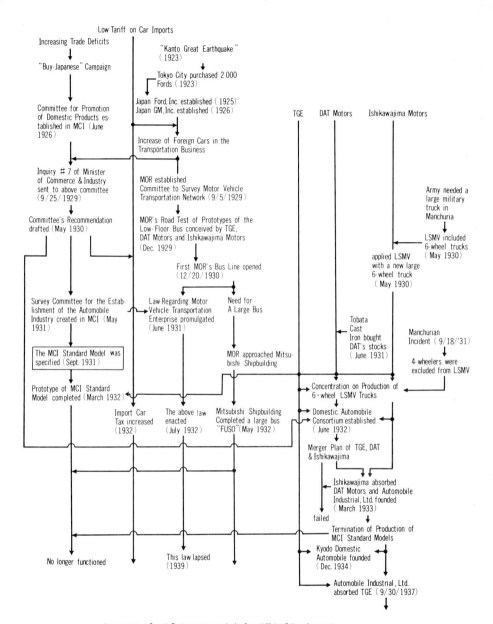

Figure VIII - 4   Causal Environment around the Second Major Policy Intervention

MOR bus routes. In 1929, MOR organized the Committee to Survey
Motor Vehicle Transportation Network and asked Tokyo Gas &
Electric, DAT Motors and Ishikawajima Motors to create a prototype
bus. The salient technical specification of this prototype was a
low floor body which deliberately excluded foreign buses with a
high floor body from the forthcoming MOR bus routes.

In response to Inquiry #7, in 1930, MOC's Committee drafted the
recommendation consisting of a) joint-production target of 5,000
units per year by the major manufacturers of trucks and buses using
the government's technical specifications, b) increasing import
tariff barriers against foreign auto parts and c) promoting the use
of domestic motor vehicles by government officials.

Upon this recommendation, the Survey Committee for the
Establishment of Automobile Industry was founded within the MOC in
1931. While the previous Committee for the Promotion of Domestic
Products was led by MOR, this development implied that the MOC
gained power over the MOR. Three months later, the Committee
announced technical specifications for standardization, and thus, a
new prototype model called "Isuzu" was first introduced in 1932.

The new MOC Standard Model was to weigh between 1 to 1.5 tons and
thus not compatible with existing Ford or Chevrolet cars weighing
less than one ton. The producers to join the production of the
standard-sized cars were given a manufacturing subsidy, and users
of this model were also given tax allowances. The initial
production target was 1,000 units per year. With regard to buses,
the Committee sought to use the standard model solely for bus
transportation.

A closer look at the technical specifications of the standard
model shows that the MOR, which was defeated by the MOC in gaining
overall leadership, then took a lead in technical specifications.
This is evident in that although the MOC insisted that a standard
model be compatible with a Ford or GM model with respect to auto
parts, the MOR supported an incompatible, medium-sized car which
was adopted by the Committee.

The second policy intervention, best characterized in its
emphasis on technical specifications, soon ceased to function.
Three reasons can be given for its malfunction. First, MOR,
because of the cost performance in the operation of bus
transportation, shifted to a larger size bus and thus, asked
Mitsubishi Shipbuilding, Ltd., an entirely new firm, to produce it.
Second, when the Manchurian Incident erupted in 1931, the army
needed large commissariat trucks. In meeting such policy changes,
the application of the military subsidy under the previous 1918 Law
for four-wheel trucks was terminated and new rules were instituted
for only larger six-wheel trucks. Third, the knock-down assembled
small cars by Japan Ford and Japan GM rapidly entered the market.
In particular, these cars were used for taxis and were very popular
as "One-Yen Taxis" for their inexpensive fares.

As described above, the second policy intervention eventually
failed because technical specifications neglected the demand move
in the market. This failure served to shape the scheme of future
interventions.

C. The Third Policy Intervention: The Law Regarding Automobile Manufacturing Enterprise of 1936 [Figure VIII-5]

The rapid and unexpectedly large sales of Ford's and GM's popular cars became a serious problem for the government, since they had a higher utility than that of the army's six-wheel trucks. This was proven by their use in the Manchurian and the Shanghai Incidents. Naturally, the army began research on the popular car and felt it was necessary to promulgate a new law to end the domination of foreign trucks. In addition, economic reasons accelerated the army's move. In 1931 for the second time, Japan banned an export of gold, which in turn resulted in the large devaluation of the yen. The devaluation of the yen increased the prices of foreign trucks and weapon parts on which the army heavily depended.

The army's concern coincided with a nationalist group within MOC led by Nobusuke Kishi, the Director General of MOC's Industrial Bureau. In August 1935, the Cabinet approved the new law, and in June 1936, the Law Regarding Automobile Manufacturing Enterprise was finally promulgated.

However, prior to this, the army, within its Equipment Bureau, established the Committee for Technical Specifications of Domestic Vehicles. Under the contract of this committee, Kawasaki Auto Body, Ltd. made a prototype of this model. Upon satisfactory performance of this prototype, the MOA (the Ministry of Army) and the MOC consulted Tokyo Gas & Electric, Ltd. and Motor Industry, Ltd. (the successor of DAT Motors, Ltd.) regarding the possible production of six to eight-thousand units per year. However, both companies replied negatively because they were heavily dependent on army-subsidized medium-size trucks.

In particular, Automobile Manufacturing, Ltd., inherited the technical knowledge from DAT Motors, Ltd., began to produce a popular size model DATSUN from 1933. Gisuke Ayukawa, president of Automobile Manufacturing, Ltd. believed in private entrepreneurship, and thus, disliked any government intervention. He was negotiating with Japan GM, Ltd. for a possible merger. MOA naturally intervened into this negotiation, when the negotiation met a deadlock. At the same time, Japan Ford, Ltd. collected information of the government's intention to create a new law and started separate negotiations with Asano Cement, Ltd. for purchasing Asano's land for a new plant. Japan Ford sought government approval under the new law for meeting the production capacity proposed by MOA. The government then intervened. This time the government intervened in the Asano-Japan Ford negotiation and felt it extremely urgent to promulgate the new law which would authorize only those firms where managerial decisions are made by Japanese nationals only.

The initial optimistic expectation of the MOC and MOA that the existing auto manufacturers would favorably respond to them was met by a serious opposition. However, the government's plans were rescued by an unexpected event when Toyoda Auto Weaving Machinery, Ltd. submitted to the government a plan to produce 2,000 popular-sized autos per month. The entrance of this entirely new face in auto manufacturing made a considerable impact on the existing firms. As a result, all of the existing firms complied with the MOC and MOA by altering their previous antagonistic attitudes. Thus, all of the problems that existed from the government's

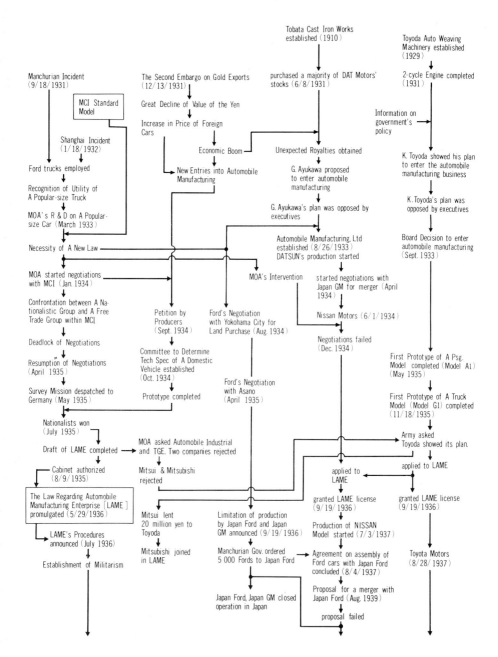

Figure VIII - 5   Causal Environment around the Third Major Policy Intervention

perspective before the new law was passed were finally eliminated.

In essence, the third policy interventions by the Law Regarding the Automobile Manufacturing Enterprise of 1936 was a drastic national intervention in order: a) to expel the powerful foreign subsidiaries, b) to influence the new entry of Toyota Motors, Ltd., and c) to shift the product orientation from a medium-sized to a popular-sized car. Under this law, no one could produce a car without the government's authorization. If authorized, firms were given various favourable treatment such as the exemption of local taxes and the exemption of the profit tax for the first five years, in addition to others. This law provided the government with a strong legal base for the direct control of the auto industry.

D. The Fourth Policy Intervention: War-Time Controls
   [Figure VIII-6]

With the previous three interventions, the Japanese auto industry had been making progress with several outgoing firms as well as new entries. However, a series of war-time legal mandates starting from the Law Regarding Temporal Measures for Exports and Imports in 1937 curbed an upward trend of production and causes its decline.

A crucial incident was when the MOC banned the production of passenger cars in accordance with the "Showa-jyusan-nen Revised Mobilization Plan" instituted in 1938. Later, price controls and supply controls were announced simultaneously. Finally, the establishment of the Association for the National Control of the Automobile Industry in 1941 stopped all manufacturing of motor vehicles in the private sector, and auto firms began to produce aircraft and tanks.

E. The Fifth Policy Intervention: GHQ Controls [Figure VIII-7]

If the auto industry is seen as a big "machine," the previous fourth intervention worked to "switch off" the machine and this fifth intervention by GHQ (the General Headquarters of the Allied Occupation Forces) functioned to "switch it on." Unless the auto industry had been completely dismantled, the post-war auto industry would have begun once again as a continuation of the pre-war period policies, with the initial condition occurring at the time when the MOC ordered the complete embargo of civilian vehicles in 1939. In fact, it is reported that major sections of auto plants did not suffer from serious destruction during air-raids.

In September 1945, the GHQ allowed auto firms to begin manufacturing only trucks in order to compensate for the shortage of transportation. Passenger car production was not fully approved until 1947. After tireless lobbying, JAMA (Japan Automobile Manufacturing Association, the successor of the war-time Association for National Control of Automobile Industry) obtained conditional permission for passenger car production. This conditon specified that Toyota and Nissan could produce passenger cars only within the limits of the existing inventory carried over from the pre-war period. This event marked the re-opening of the post-war development of the Japanese auto industry. Later, the GHQ repealed the conditional permission, and the industry grew quite rapidly, aided by the military procurement during the Korean War.

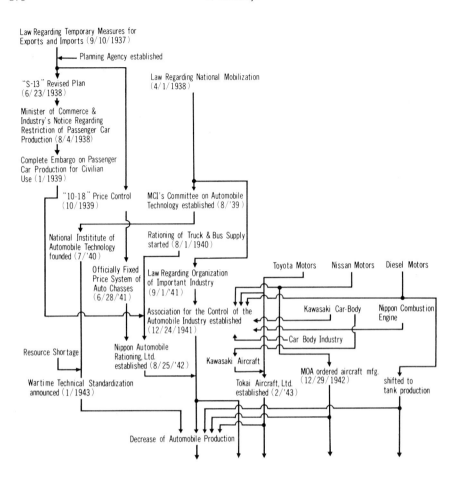

Figure VIII - 6   Causal Environment around the Fourth Major Policy Intervention

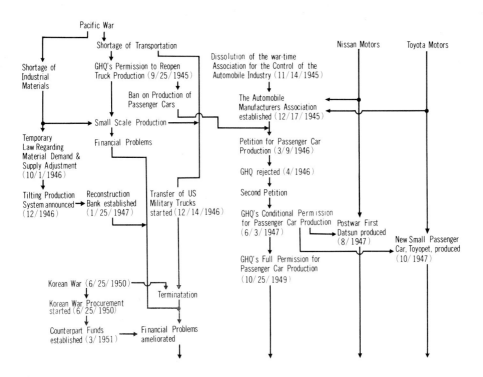

Figure VIII-7  Causal Environment around the Fifth Major Policy Intervention

F. The Sixth Policy Intervention: The Regulation Regarding
   Conveyance of Foreign Vehicles of 1951 [Figure VIII-8]

The auto industry which resumed a steady growth developed an
unexpected problem when passenger cars that were used by the
Occupation Army personnel and their families entered the used car
market for taxi use.

From 1949 to 1950, the Ministry of Transportation (MOT) gave more
or less unconditional licensing to taxi companies. This, in turn,
created a great demand for taxi cabs. Through this unauthorized
channel for foreign currency transaction, American used cars almost
completely dominated the taxi market.

Accordingly, JAMA as a supporter of the domestic industry
strongly opposed this legal loophole. However, triggered by the
problems created by incompetent performance of Japanese-made police
cars, the majority opinion within policy-making circles insisted
that Japan should import foreign vehicles of higher quality rather
than fostering the domestic auto industry. It was MITI (the
successor of the MOC) that considered the issue of the conveyance
of foreign used cars as a serious policy matter.

The problem of conveyance came to an end when the Ministry of
Finance (MOF) stood by MITI's side and regulated the illegal
transactions of American used cars without the MOF's authorization
under the Law of Foreign Exchange. As a joint ministerial mandate
of both MITI and the Ministry of Transportation, the Regulation
Regarding Conveyance of Foreign Vehicles was enacted in 1951.
Subsequently, forty-million dollars were appropriated for
purchasing foreign used cars. This was intended to save the face
of the MOT. As described above, this sixth intervention was a
demand policy in the negative sense, i.e., to choke increasing auto
demands.

The infiltration of foreign cars into the Japanese market was the
primary cause of the third policy intervention. For this sixth
intervention, its causal environment was quite similar to that of
the third intervention. That is, the unsatisfactory performance of
the Japanese cars used for police cars, like the unsatisfactory
performance of domestic trucks used in war zones in the 1930s,
became a serious concern for policy-makers. Furthermore, the sixth
and third interventions resemble each other in that both
interventions applied a direct control over the importation of
foreign vehicles. However, there was a salient difference. It was
the internalization of foreign technology, as discussed below.

G. The Seventh Policy Intervention: MITI's Guideline Regarding
   Foreign Technical & Assembly Contracts for Passenger Car
   Production of 1952 [Figure VIII-9]

The passenger cars made by Japanese firms during the Occupation
Period were the so-called "camouflage" cars that mounted a
passenger car body onto a truck chassis. These uncomfortable cars
obviously could not meet the increasing demands for taxi cabs.
Therefore, the domestic makers began negotiations with their
foreign counterparts for technical cooperation. The first
technical agreement was reached in 1950 between Kaiser-Fraser and
East Japan Heavy Industry, Ltd., which was followed by other
companies. Then, MITI intervened into these contracts for the

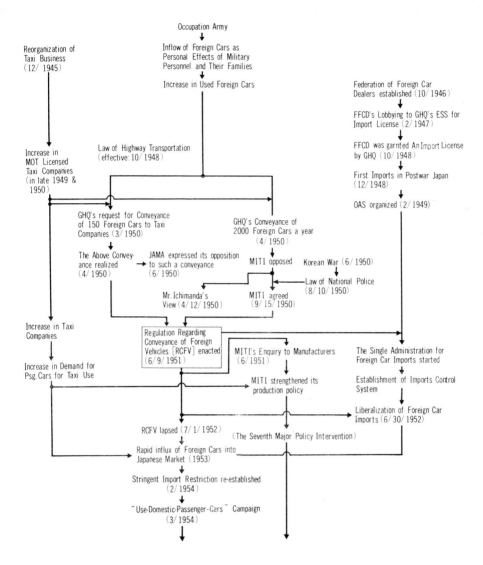

Figure VIII - 8   Causal Environment around the Sixth Major Policy Intervention

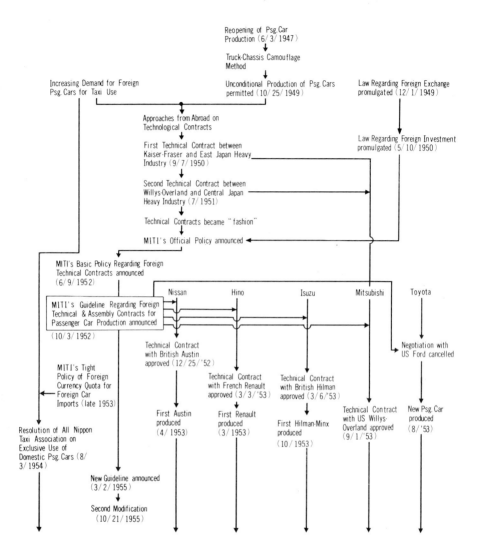

Figure VIII - 9   Causal Environment around the Seventh Major Policy Intervention

protection of domestic companies from powerful foreign makers.
This intervention resembles the army's intervention into Gisuke
Ayukawa's attempt to merge with Japan GM. The rationale for
intervention was the same as before--the protection of the Japanese
market from foreign infiltration.

In October 1952, MITI announced the Guideline Regarding Foreign
Technical & Assembly Contracts for Passenger Car Production which
consisted of three parts: the acquisition of foreign capital, the
introduction of new technology and the assembly of foreign
passenger cars. The essence of this guideline was in MITI's
specifications of eleven auto parts that must be internally
produced by the Japanese contractors when technical cooperation
contracts were terminated. This implies that since major auto
parts were included into these eleven specified items, MITI did not
authorize any technical cooperation with foreign counterparts
unless the contracts clearly indicated that Japanese firms would
gain an exclusive right to produce technically-introduced foreign
parts within a certain period. Thus, MITI's mandate functioned not
to interfere with free contracting, but to help the Japanese
manufacturers stand strongly before foreign introducers. As is
well-known, Hino Motors, Nissan Motors, Isuzu Motors and Mitsubishi
Heavy Industry signed technical cooperation contracts.
Simultaneously in 1953, these companies introduced new models in
which the major parts were foreign-made. However, Toyota could not
reach an agreement with US Ford, and in the same year, it
introduced a domestic model.

H. The Eighth Policy Intervention: MITI's People's Car Plan of
   1955 [Figure VIII-10]

We have already pointed out that the sixth intervention shared
many similarities with the third intervention, but this sixth
intervention differed from its predecessor on the point that the
post-war case did not contain an aspect of the government's direct
intervention. That aspect emerged from an entirely different
context. It was MITI's People's Car Plan that contained a
significant amount of direct, national control over the industry.

In the early 1950s, MITI was preparing for a law that
rationalized the automobile industry recognizing that the
automobile industry would considerably affect national economy.
The nature of this law was that the industry should concentrate on
the production of models with certain types of technical
specification, resembling the war-time controls. For attaining
such narrowly-defined production, the law intended to give a
mandate to producers, unless they spontaneously formed a cartel.

Before MITI's move, the MOT amended the Vehicle Regulations in
1949, and set a new category of vehicle size under an engine size
of 1,500 cc. Accordingly, entirely new small firms entered into
"mini-car" manufacturing. MITI was considering support for mini-
car production by allocating loans of 100 million yen from the
Japan Development Bank and 300 million yen from the Japan Long Term
Credit Bank.

In May 1955, MITI's People's Car Plan was reported by a newspaper
and became a serious political issue in the Diet, because it
appeared as a revival of pre-war, strong government controls. It
first specified in detail the performance of the "People's Car,"

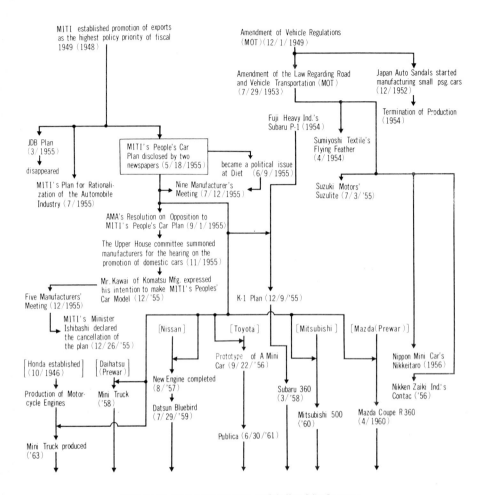

Figure VIII-10   Causal Environment around the Eighth Major Policy Intervention

second, it set a desirable price and third, it suggested that a performance contest be held like that for the MOC's standard model. At last, it assigned only one company the production rights.

All domestic manufacturers fiercely opposed MITI's plan just as they had MOA's popular-size car plan. The industry opposed MITI's plan because it believed that it was technically impossible to meet the performance and prices MITI had established. Only one company gallantly stated that it could make the MITI-specified People's Car. Komatsu Machinery Works, Ltd. announced publicly that Komatsu asked Dr. Porche of Germany to design MITI's People's Car. Auto firms in JAMA were considerably disturbed by Komatsu's move, but finally succeeded in stopping this plan for the People's Car.

A review of post-war interventions suggests a strong resemblance to the pre-war precedents. However, one factor worth noticing is the fact that the industry finally grew strong enough to resist the government's interventions. This is mainly due to the successful assimilation of foreign technology during the 1950s. There is no question that the government assisted the industries in this assimilation. When the strong opposition to the People's Car Plan confronted the government with a dilemma, it can be called the "spiral dilemma," as discussed previously in this paper.[3]


3. NUMERICAL POLICY ANALYSIS

Descriptive information and numerical information are different in nature. Correlatively, a descriptive policy analysis gives a better picture of the dynamic process of policy intervention in a row, while a numerical policy analysis primarily aims either at identifying policy effects or at viewing more macroscopically the policy environment in an attempt to find the rationale for interventions. The purpose of this section is to employ such a numerical analysis as to compensate for insufficiencies in the above, descriptive, causal chains.

A. An Intervention Analysis: Quasi-Experimental Approach[4]

When he first analyzed the effects of policy intervention in the case of the Connecticut Speeding Crackdown, D.T. Campbell assumed the parallel shift of the coordinate axes, as illustrated in Examples A and B of Figure VIII-11.[5]

However, following Campbell's studies, G. Glass [6] and G. Box and G. Tiao [7] advocated structural changes, as shown in Example C. That is, they equivalently proposed the following ARMA (Auto-Regressive and Moving-Average) model:[8]

$$y(t) = \Sigma\ a(i)y(t-i) +\ \Sigma\ b(j)e(t-j) + c.D \qquad (1)$$

where D is a dummy variable to indicate policy-on, and e(t) is the MA process of uncertain disturbances. This model implies that y(t) is the consequence of accumulated uncertainty drives and what we are certain of is only the evidence that a particular policy was on at a particular time. The epistemology associated with this model shows a marked difference from any structural model approach based on theoretical insight.[9] However, because the subject entity

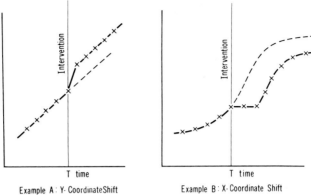

Example A : Y- Coordinate Shift

Example B : X- Coordinate Shift

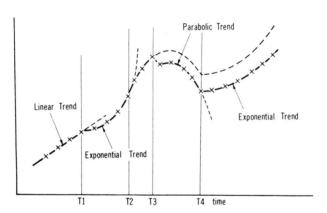

Example C : Structural Change of Dynamic Maturation

Figure VIII - 11    Coordinate-Shift Discontinuity of Maturation Trend vs. Dynamic Change
of Maturation Structure

with which we are concerned is the complicated mix between economic
affairs and political ones, a complete structural model would be
difficult to construct. The model in Equation (1) is too
"probablistic," so that we will adopt the following "time-variant,"
non-linear, regression model of a simpler form:

$$y(t) = a(t)y(t-1) + b(t) \qquad (2)$$

This model can express the three conspicuous patterns observed in
different curves of Figure VIII-12. For example, the production
curve in Figure VIII-12 shows a rapid-stagnation (the first-order
information delay) pattern from 1924 to 1931. This can be
expressed in a form as follows:

$$y(t) = (1-a)y(t-1) + aL \qquad (3)$$

where L is a saturation level and "a" is a time-constant.
Comparing Equations (2) and (3), (1-a) and aL correspond to a(t)
and b(t), respectively.

The exponential pattern in the production curve from 1931 to 1940
can be expressed, letting "g" be a constant growth rate,
as:

$$y(t) = (1+g)y(t-1) \qquad (4)$$

where (1+g) corresponds to a(t) and b(t) in Equation (2) becomes
zero.

Furthermore, the rapid declining pattern from 1940 can be
expressed in a form of the parabolic trend. Since a growth rate of
a parabolic curve "g" in Equation (4) forms a cubic function, a(t)
in Equation (2) correspondingly declines in a parabolic form.

Applying this model logic, the estimations of a(t) and b(t) in
Equation (2) would give information regarding an extent to which a
particular policy intervention made an impact. Our model has some
advantages over the "ignorance model" of Equation (1); for example,
Equation (4) implies an "incremental policy" with a certain fixed
growth rate, while Equation (3) involves a policy dilemma that
policy success soon encounters stagnation.

The results of our estimations of a(t) and b(t) are presented in
(a) and (b) of Figure VIII-13. The data used for estimation was
the total production of four-wheel vehicles in Figure VIII-12,
recognizing that the increase in this kind of vehicles was the
prime policy target throughout an entire period. The method
employed for estimation is the "recursive least-square method"
originally proposed by P. Young.[10] The recursive least-square
method is one simple variation of the Kalman Filter approach.[11]

The basic policy objective might be to let the auto industry show
stable growth. Stable growth is much more important than a
meretricious attainment of a high level of production for a short
term. Stable growth is structurally exponential growth with a
stable growth rate. In terms of Equation (2), this implies a
constant value in a(t) above 1 with b(t) to be zero. How could

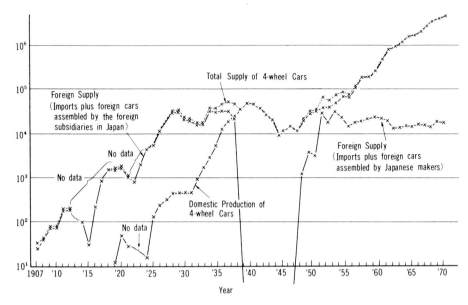

Figure VIII 12   Annual Supply of 4-wheel Vehicles

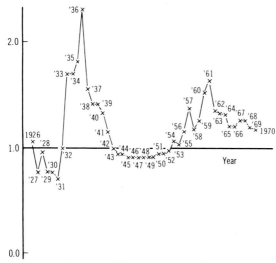

Figure VIII-13 (a)   Estimates of a(t)

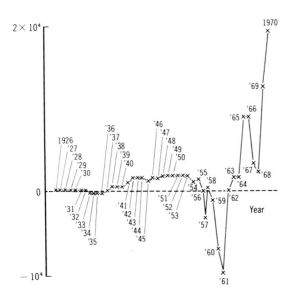

Figure VIII-13 (b)   Estimates of b(t)

this policy objective be attained?

First, Figure VIII-13 [12] shows that, until 1931, a(t) was below 1
and b(t) was slightly above zero (of the order from 100 to 150
units), indicating a typical pattern of rapid stagnation.  If this
pattern were continued, in time, the production would become
stagnated.  Then, we can postulate that the second intervention
occurred with this situation.  The impact of this intervention was
overwhelming.  As a result, a(t) abruptly surpassed the 1-level
border line, satisfying the first requirement of the stable growth,
i.e., an exponential growth.  However, since the policy would have
intended solely to increase the growth ratios, b(t) became negative
as repercussion.  This is because the system "recalled" the
previous system state.  The new state was not healthy, since there
existed an inertia to pull the total production down.  At this
time, the third intervention would have followed.  This
intervention, in contrast, diminished the outrageous growth rate in
an attempt to elevate up b(t) to the positive region.  However, the
third intervention during war-time again destroyed the system where
a(t) continuously declined in a cubic form until 1953.  After the
seventh intervention, the system escaped from the war-time pattern
and a(t) resumed its above-one level.  Later, until 1961, the
system state resembled one of the second intervention, having the
minus b(t) value, and this unstable state lasted until after 1962.
As discussed previously, this period was the one in which the
Japanese auto industry finished the internalization of foreign
technology.  In other words, the production system entered into the
most stable period with a stable a(t) and a positive b(t).

B. The "Exponential" Substitution Policy

In the previous section, we have already found that in both the
pre-war and post-war periods, the identical policy was applied to
expel foreign vehicles.  These were the replacement policies of
foreign vehicles by domestic ones.  Here, we will numerically
analyze the internal logic of this policy.

As shown in Figure VIII-14, domestic production share exceeded
foreign vehicles by 1939 in an exponential pattern.  Also, Figure
VIII-15 shows that the same pattern appeared from 1951 to 1955.
For this reason, we will call the government's replacement policy
the "exponential substitution policy."  There might be numerous
patterns for the substitution curve.  Although a rapid-stagnation
pattern, for example, would achieve a quicker substitution, it must
sacrifice a decline of the total production for some period.  As
discussed in the third policy intervention, the supply of popular-
sized cars was not to be decreased in the army's view.  Thus, we
regard the exponential substitution pattern as the most desirable
and the safest alternative.  In addition, the exponential pattern
indicates a typical, organizational, decision-making policy such as
incrementalism,[13] that is, to gradually expel foreign vehicles with
a constant replacement ratio.

The exponential substitution policy was not an easy alternative
because it involved two imperatives: a) the decrease of the ratio
of foreign vehicles, but b) no decrease in the total production
level.  For the latter imperative, the production curve must, first
of all, increase rapidly.  In other words, the substitution policy
should be coupled with the production policy.  This is most likely
the reason why the third and seventh interventions primarily

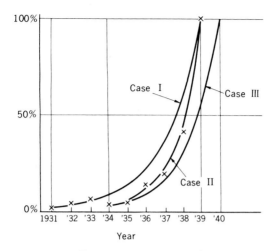

Figure VIII-14    Three Different Projections of The Relative
Share of Domestic Production in Total
Supply of Medium Trucks & Buses

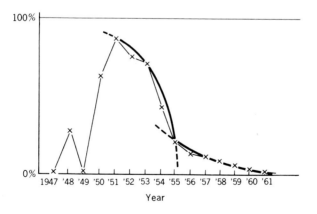

Figure VIII-15    Relative Share of Foreign Imports in Total Annual
Supply of Passenger Cars : Postwar

focused on the production policy.

As indicated in Figure VIII-14, there are three possibilities for
an exponential substitution pattern. Case I and Case II have
different starting years but share the same ending year of 1939,
while Case III assumes 1934 as the starting year and 1940 as a
hypothetical ending year. We roughly estimated the time-constant
parameters for three cases, and applied them into the supply curve
as shown in (a), (b) and (c) of Figure VIII-16. Figure VIII-16
indicates that if the ending year had been set in 1940, the total
production would not have declined, suggesting that the
substitution policy by the MOA and MOC seemed a bit impetuous. In
other words, the expelling policy seemed to be formed without a
good consideration of the production capacity at that time.

In the post-war period, the same policy logic was surprisingly
applied (See Figure VIII-15). But, the post-war situation differed
from the pre-war case in the sense that the target model was a
passenger type for a taxi cab rather than a truck model.
Therefore, it was not necessary for MITI to keep up the total
supply curve during the replacement period.

In fact, as shown in Figure VIII-17, the total passenger car
supply curve became flat for the period until 1955, during which
the production curve of domestic passenger cars grew more or less
exponentially. This coincides with the commencement of different
structural patterns from 1956, as observed in Figure VIII-15.

Evidence strongly corroborates that the government succeeded in
expelling foreign vehicles by using the "exponential substitution
policy" in both the pre-war and post-war periods. In realizing
such a policy, the government should have simultaneously instituted
a production policy in order to compensate for a decline in the
total supply inevitably caused by a rapid substitution policy. For
that reason, assisting the industry in exponential growth might be
a prime policy concern. The third and seventh interventions no
doubt served this purpose.

C. The "Linear" Internalization Policy

The unique pattern in Figure VIII-15 is more vividly observed in
Figure VIII-17, where the import curve "drifted" after 1956 as if
it was freed from suppression. Later, since 1962, the curve
resumed its upward trend. This particular period corresponds to
the time when the auto firms registered their knock-down passenger
cars as domestic vehicles. This coincidence suggests that the
demand for foreign vehicles was replaced by these assembled cars,
and the government suppressed foreign imports until 1962. This
government policy could be called as a "linear internalization"
scheme, since, as shown in Figure VIII-18, the ratio of assembled
cars within the total production of the domestic vehicles declined
"linearly" from 1954, and became zero in 1962. In this sense,
foreign assembled cars were internalized "linearly."

As discussed above in B, the exponential substitution policy
required the growth of domestic models to increase exponentially.
However, it would be quite difficult to attain such a stable growth
in the period of war devastation. At that time, policy makers who
still remembered the pre-war case might have thought that if this
situation continued, the Japanese market would sooner or later be

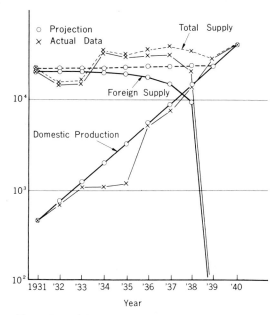

Figure Ⅷ-16 (a)   Projection and Actual Data [Case I]

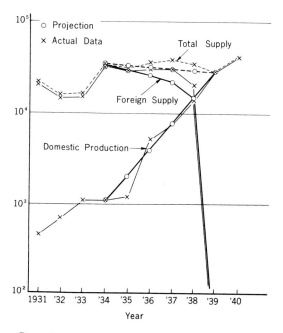

Figure Ⅷ-16 (b)   Projection and Actual Data [Case II]

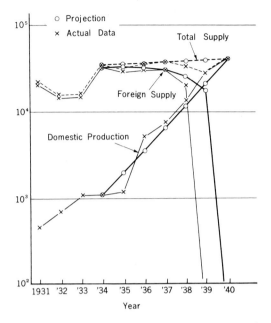

Figure VIII-16(c)   Projection and Actual Data [Case III]

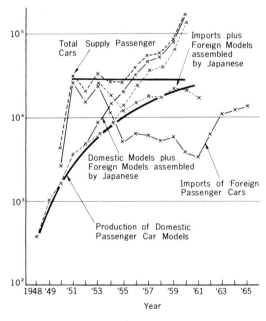

Figure VIII-17   Postwar Supply of Passenger Cars

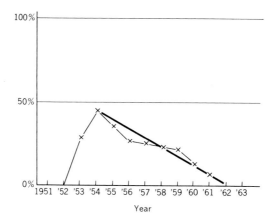

Figure Ⅷ-18   Relative Share of Foreign Small Passenger Cars
Assembled by Japanese Makers in Total Production
of Small Passenger Cars

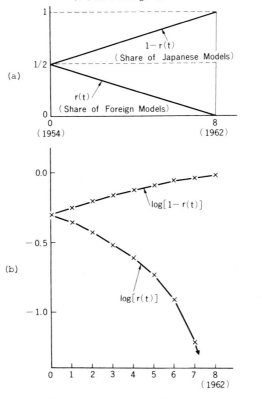

Figure Ⅷ-19  Linear Decline of Relative Share of Foreign
Models Assembled by Japanese in Total Yields
of Passenger Cars

occupied by foreign cars under strong demand pressure from the taxi
market. Policy makers solved this potential problem by realizing
an exponential growth of production that allowed the auto firms to
assemble foreign passenger cars and superimposed them on the poor
production curve of the indigenous models. Concurrently, foreign
imports were limited as in the pre-war period. This is only
conjecture, but similarities between Figures VIII-14 and VIII-15
suggest the relevancy of this postulation.

For corroborating our conjecture, we attempted the following
calculation. First, we drew a line, as shown in (a) of Figure
VIII-19, assuming that the internalization ratio was 50% in 1954
and 0% in 1962. Figure VIII-19 (b) shows the logarithmic pattern
of this line. Denoting A as the sum of assembled cars and
indigenous ones, the logarithmic values of indigenous cars and
assembled ones become, respectively:

$$logB(t) = log(1-r(t)) + logA(t) \tag{5}$$

$$logC(t) = r(t) + logA(t) \tag{6}$$

Since $logA(t)$ is linear, the shapes of $logB(t)$ and $logC(t)$ can be
visually identified from (b) in Figure VIII-19. That is, $logB(t)$
is more or less linear, while $logC(t)$ is of a convex form. Figure
VIII-19 (a) suggests $r(t) = (8-t)/16$, so that the function of
$logA(t)$ is numerically drawn from $A(t)$'s values in 1952 and 1954.
This curve is superimposed in Figure VIII-20, where the actual
curves and the estimated ones resemble each other quite closely.
Thus, we may conclude that the seventh intervention might serve as
a legal base to support the "linear" internalization scheme.

D. Vernon's Model and Its Policy Implications

R. Vernon once argued that technological innovation fit what he
called the "product cycle model." In this model, he stated that
industrial products were diffused through three patterns[14] the
advanced country (such as the US) pattern, the other advanced
country pattern and the less-developed country pattern, as shown in
Figure VIII-21.[15] The purpose of the present analysis is to draw
policy implications from the Vernon model.

A functional pattern of a curve on the logarithmic scale retains
its shape regardless of the level. Then, superimposing the
production pattern on Figure VIII-21 gives (a) and (b) of Figure
VIII-22. We observe that the pre-war and the post-war patterns
correspond to Vernon's less-developed country and advanced country
patterns, respectively. This observation coincides with our
"common-sense" understanding; that is, the pre-war production was
of the less-developed country type, while the post-war pattern was
of the advanced countries type. However, such an observation seems
to be so stereo-typical that no significant policy implication can
be drawn.

Figure VIII-23 illustrates a "patched" curve as if pre- and post-
war production continued unabated by ignoring the period during the
war and the period immediately afterwards. Our artificial patch-
work is based on the fact that the pre-war production facilities
did not receive serious war damages.

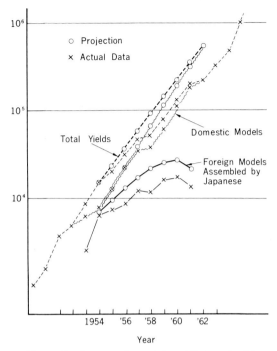

Figure VIII-20   Projection and Actual Data under Linear
Technology Transfer Policy

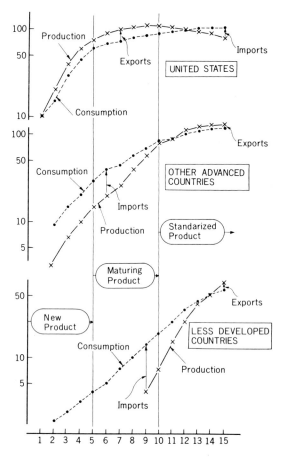

Figure Ⅷ 21  Semi-logarithmic Version of Vernon's Three Patterns

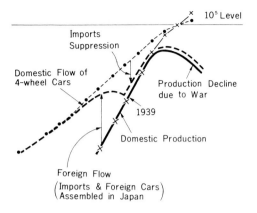

Figure VIII - 22 ( a )    Conceptual Superposition of Prewar Pattern
                         on Less Developed Countries' Case

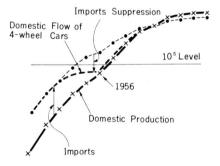

Figure VIII - 22 ( b )    Conceptual Superposition of Postwar
                         Pattern on Other Advanced Countries'
                         Case

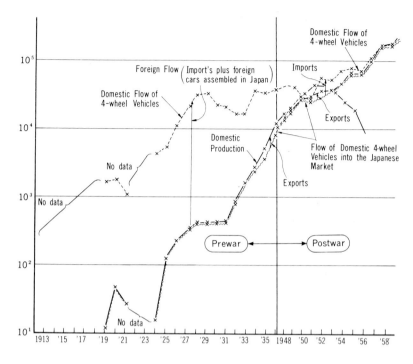

Figure VIII-23  Superposition of Pre and Postwar Data by Shifting Time-scale

Clearly, Figure VIII-23 indicates the less-developed country
pattern. That is, the consumption (substituted by the total supply
curve) forms a log-linear curve, and the production also grew log-
linearly with a high slope constant. A question is raised as to
why the less-developed country pattern was taken. Our conjecture
is that the government had suppressed supply and demand to protect
the domestic industry from foreign dominance. In other words, the
less-developed country pattern was artificially created. This
leads us to re-consider the relevancy of the Vernon model. We
contend that Vernon's less-developed country pattern can be
realized only with policy engineering, but not automatically
realized.

As we observed in the Japanese case, the infant auto industry's
growth soon reached saturation, and this is why policy
interventions were needed to ameliorate a rapid-stagnation pattern.
However, Vernon's argument for the less-developed countries pattern
started with a presumption of a steep log-linear (i.e., exponential
growth) probably because he wanted to stress the transfer of a
product from an advanced country to a less-developed country
through overseas investment. A steep log-linear curve presupposes
a stable implementation of production incrementalism (i.e., the
same growth rate). Can most less-developed countries have such a
stable production system? If a country had such a growth
structure, this country would no longer be "less-developed."

## 4. POLICY ASSESSMENT AND POLICY TRANSFER

Each descriptive or numerial analysis above is a component of the
martix form of our cycle model. The completed matrix is shown in
Table VIII-1. As summarized below, observing each row gives the
dynamic evolution of policy interventions.

Throughout an entire period, the major policy target was to
guarantee Japan's own auto industry, rather than to guarantee auto
supply. In this sense, government interventions were predominantly
on the supply side, except for the first (1918) and the sixth
(1951) interventions which were on the demand side. This is
probably because the Japanese auto industrial policies started with
military purposes. In addition, each policy intervention set its
concrete target in a more or less numerical term. As to policy
initiators, the MOA was followed by the MOC and then by the MITI.

Also, worth noticing is the fact that some of the same measures
were repeatedly applied. This suggests that the government
believed that similar interventions made the same policy impacts by
"learning" the behavior of firms. Furthermore, the successive
firm's behavior were characterized by the strong dependency of the
firms on government help during the first intervention. Later,
with this governmental learning, the auto industry was "reshuffled"
for attaining its targets.

As for policy instruments, the subsidy approach at the early
stage was replaced by more authoritative and hence nationalistic
measures such as the licensing of auto manufacturing enterprise.
The industry which attained stabilizing production with
governmental help, in turn, was gradually escaping from the domain
of intervention and opposed to authoritative government

Table VIII-1   Summary Matrix

| MAJOR INTER-VEVTION | FIRST MAJOR INTERVENTION (THE LAW REGARDING SUPPORT FOR MILITARY VEHICLES:1918) | SECOND MAJOR INTERVENTION (THE MINISTRY OF COMMERCE & INDUSTRY'S STANDARD MODEL:1932) |
|---|---|---|
| NEW SITUATION | | .By accident, Japan Ford and Japan GM were established and started assembly of the Ford and Chevrolet models which occupied more than 90% of the net annual supply of automobiles in Japan. .Due to economic recession, the "Buy-Japanese" campaign began. |
| VERBAL STATEMENT OF TARGET | .Assurance of the supply of military vehicles | .To establish the auto industy .To concentrate on the production of trucks and buses. |
| NUMERICAL TARGET | .Unidentified | .To attain the production scale of 5,000 units per year by 1935. |
| INITIATOR | .Ministry of Army | .The Committee of Promotion of Domestic Product (led by MOR) .The Committee for Establishment Automobile Industry (led by MCI) |
| PAST POLICY LEARNED | .European precedents | .Technical standardization .Manufacturing subsidy |
| NEW POLICY INSTRUMENTS | .Mfg. & Purchase subsidies .Maintenance subsidy .Requisition subsidy .Technical standardization | .Public procurement .Mandatory use of domestic cars by government officials .Tariff rate revision |
| NATURE OF INTERVENTION | .The subsidy measure with technological specification (no procurement) | .The public procurement of the government models |
| EXTERNAL DISTURBANCE | .Not specifically | .The policy shift of MOR to a different model .The Manchurian Incident made MOA shift policy to a larger truck. |
| REACTION OF FIRMS | .The hitherto small inventive firms were cleared. .The three larger firms emerged. .Firms' complainment about complicated government's administration procedures | .Three firms for the military cars were rescued by government procuremenet. .Tobata Cast Iron joined auto production, criticizing government intervention |
| NUMERICAL POLICY IMPACTS | .The hitherto random fluctuating production data ceased. .Since 1924, a smooth growth in a rapid stagnation pattern started. | .The production of trucks and buses departed from the previous stagnation, but soon stagnated again. .The production of small vehicles started growing with the high growth rate. |
| INTERVENTION ASSESSMENT | .The previous concept of a car as a luxurious commodity was upheld to the concept of a practical one. .By this intervention the auto production was incorporated into the recursive system. | .The previous policy orientation to the special military vehicles was broadened to the inter-ministerial national policy. .The nationalistic-minded MCI's policy emerged. .Although the production of trucks & buses resumed the growth, the pattern of a rapid-stagnation was the same. |

Table VIII-1  Summary Matrix (continued)

| MAJOR INTER-VEVTION | THIRD MAJOR INTERVENTION (THE LAW REGARDING AUTO MANU-FACTURING ENTERPRISES:1936) | FOURTH MAJOR INTERVENTION (WAR-TIME CONTROLS: C.1939-1945) |
|---|---|---|
| NEW SITUATION | .The Shanghai Incident (1932), where Ford trucks used. | .The Pacific War broke out. (1941) |
| VERBAL STATEMENT OF TARGET | .For national defence, to establish the domestic supply of all kinds of vehicles. | .To carry out war objectives |
| NUMERICAL TARGET | .6,000-8,000 units/company/year .The planned level unclear | .70,000-80,000 units/year |
| INITIATOR | .MCI backed by MOA | .MOA and The Ministry of Munitions (MCI's successor) |
| PAST POLICY LEARNED | .Maybe the German precedent .Tariff control (as 2nd.) | .Manufacturing license (as 3rd.) .Price control (as 3rd.) |
| NEW POLICY INSTRUMENTS | .Mfg. licensing .Mandatory sales and prices .Financial provisions to complying firms | .Legalized trade consortium .Material rationing .Corporate account control .Product differentiation control |
| NATURE OF INTERVENTION | .The government's direct controls by licensing | .Total national controls for overall areas |
| EXTERNAL DISTURBANCE | .Not specifically | .Material shortage .MOA's order of aircraft mfg. |
| REACTION OF FIRMS | .Toyota suddenly entered. .Nissan finally compelled .The three larger firms .Other firms specialized military large trucks | .Nissan opposed military intervention, but was complied. .The auto trade union was presided by an ex-military official. |
| NUMERICAL POLICY IMPACTS | .An exponential growth started. .Small car procudtion ceased hitherto continuous growth. .The relative share of foreign cars declined parabolically. .The incremental factor lowered. | .All auto productions declined parabolically .The incremental growth mechanism not significantly affected |
| INTERVENTION ASSESSMENT | .Auto industry was again controlled directly by government. .Foreign dominance eliminated .Success for internalization of auto production. .This law invited the entry of Toyota. | .This intervenion caused a parabolic decline of all auto production. .The visible conflict between the industry and government firstly began. .MCI's leadership retreated. |

Table VIII-1   Summary Matrix (continued)

| MAJOR INTER-VEVTION | FIFTH MAJOR INTERVENTION (THE GHQ CONTROL:1945-C.1950) | SIXTH MAJOR INTERVENTION (THE REGULATION REGARDING CON-VEYANCE OF FOREIGN CARS:1951) |
|---|---|---|
| NEW SITUATION | | .The American used cars were disposed and bought by taxi companies. <br> .MOT's unconditional licensing to taxi companies |
| VERBAL STATEMENT OF TARGET | .Conditional production due to the shortage of transports | .To restrict foreign imports to protect the domestic firms |
| NUMERICAL TARGET | .500 units/year of small-psg. cars under 1,500 cc engine size | .Unidentified |
| INITIATOR | .GHQ | .MITI and MOF |
| PAST POLICY LEARNED | .Material rationing (as 4th.) <br> .Technical specification | .Sales control (as 3rd., 4th.) <br> .Buy-Japanese campaign (as 2nd.) |
| NEW POLICY INSTRUMENTS | .Not specifically | .Import restriction by the quota allocation of foreign reserves |
| NATURE OF INTERVENTION | .Mfg. licensing | .Import restriction to protect the domestic firms |
| EXTERNAL DISTURBANCE | .The Korean procurements | .Criticism from international economists <br> .Opposition by taxi companies and MOT |
| REACTION OF FIRMS | .Firms formed political lobbies to the GHQ and government <br> .Firms started the production of a 1,500 cc psg. car. <br> .Nissan produced a truck-based psg. car. | .Firms started seeking foreign contracts. |
| NUMERICAL POLICY IMPACTS | .The postwar upward production curve started. <br> .The new incremental mechanism started. <br> .The new structure contained a damping oscillation. | .Net supply of psg. cars was kept constant. |
| INTERVENTION ASSESSMENT | .This intervention eliminated wartime regulations. <br> .The industry experienced how to attain its goal by colle-ctive bargaining. | .This intervention resembled the third intervention for import control. <br> .But, the use of foreign reserve rationale was a new approach. |

Table VIII-1  Summary Matrix (continued)

| MAJOR INTER-VEVTION | SEVENTH MAJOR INTERVENTION (MITI'S GUIDELINE FOR TECHNICAL CONTRACTS:1952) | EIGHTH MAJOR INTERVENTION (MITI'S PEOPLE'S CAR PLAN:1955) |
|---|---|---|
| NEW SITUATION | .Fashionable technical contracts among auto firms | .General policy mood for industrial rationalization. |
| VERBAL STATEMENT OF TARGET | .To stop unprincipled fashion of technical contracts and protect firms and foreign reserves | .To upgrade the status of a car from a taxi use to a consumer duarable |
| NUMERICAL TARGET | .11 items for permissible tech. contracts | .24,000 units/year |
| INITIATOR | .MITI & MOF | .MITI |
| PAST POLICY LEARNED | .Tech. contracts were MITI's main policy targets. | .Mfg. license (as 3rd,4th,5th) .Financial & tax credits |
| NEW POLICY INSTRUMENTS | .Contract licensing; foreign reserve allocation .Tech. specification for parts | .Selection of a monopoly company |
| NATURE OF INTERVENTION | .The government-backed technical assimilation policy | .The government-authorized manufacturing license for a single firm |
| EXTERNAL DISTURBANCE | .No specific disturbances | .This plan was leaked through a news media, and became a controversial matter. |
| REACTION OF FIRMS | .Nissan, Isuzu, Hino and Mitsubishi applied. .Toyota failed negotiating with Ford, thus decided to stick to its original technology. | .Firms unanimously opposed to this plan. .A new face in auto production acted as a perturbation. .Toyota introduced its own model. |
| NUMERICAL POLICY IMPACTS | .The stagnated production curve resumed an exponential growth since 1954. .The addition of foreign assembled psg. cars to the domestic models yielded an exponential growth. | .The impact on the production curve of mini-cars was large. |
| INTERVENTION ASSESSMENT | .Coupled with the 6th intervention, this helped the psg. production go exponentially upward. | .This intervenion resembles the prewar military intervention, but due to the strong collected bargaining, the industry entered into a new stage of independence. |

intervention.  The failure of MITI's People's Car Plan corroborates
this.  The government intervened into the auto industry to help
attain a stable productive structure.  When such an intervention
succeeded, the industry inevitably started drifting off the course
set by government.  At this stage, the government already had
developed an inertia force and thus, could not change its policy
course.  The adaptive system consisting of both the policy donors
and recipients lost controllability.

A "recursive" government can only continue to control a policy
recipient by extending its assumptions of past circumstances.
Thus, unless the policy objective has been reached, the government
will continue to intervene based on the past and forecasting what
factors will be needed in the future to rectify the situation.  The
government learns by attempting to narrow the gap between
forecasted and actual outcomes.  Thus, the government can
rationalize its intervention only while it can extrapolate and such
a gap is still present.  Hence, when extrapolation has no sense
since the prime policy target is already implemented, the previous
adaptive system soon becomes obsolete.

When the system "matured" in this way, policy makers naturally
expect a new exogenous factor to disturb the stability of the
system.  Rehabilitation of the disturbed system provides a sound
reason for successive policy interventions.  However, since a
policy recipient already possesses its own inertia, only a strong
exogenous intervention can perturbate it.  Appropriate government
interventions may get more and more drastic or coercive in order to
achieve the desired outcome.  Applying the logic of this dynamic
process toward more authoritative policy interventions raises some
implications regarding policy transfer to other countries,
particularly to the less-developed countries.

Our research found that the essence of the Japanese auto
industrial policy throughout both the pre- and post-war periods,
placed great emphasis on the construction of an indigenous industry
in Japan, by preventing the imports of assembled cars, parts and
even domestic assembly of foreign cars.  It may be an imperative
common policy for any industrially developing country to impede the
market infiltration of foreign commodities and thus increase
indigenous industrial products.  If these nations absorb the
Japanese lesson, they may encounter the same constraint as we faced
in this research.  This constraint is the question of how to
extract a "truth" from the "glorified" records of policy events.
It is a typical trait for policy makers to preserve past records
which have been successful and are "worth recording."[16]  Thus, any
developing country which intends to learn from the success of the
Japanese case should take a view based on quasi-experimental
design.  This avoids the usual pitfalls of erroneous and short-
sighted transfer of policy from one particular context to another
context.  This so-called "external validity" question is of
particular importance for policy transfer.

For example, the developing countries might already have a social
and political context where strong authoritative power already
rests on the governments.  If these countries "copied" the past
policies of the Japanese government, it would be quite likely that
these policies will fail.  As described earlier, the system of
government and the auto industry had a recursive controlling
function, and the government gradually became coercive.  If a

strong coercive power is exerted at a premature stage, its recursive control will malfunction and the system will not behave as expected. In other words, the system will explosively oscillate rather than be adaptive. Therefore, it would be advisable that countries which choose to accept foreign strategies for economic development carefully observe the behavior of policy recipients first, and then, calculate the optimal degree of policy strength. In other words, these countries must construct their own policy intervention model as we did in this research by taking into account the contextual difference between the learned countries and the learning countries.[17]

## 5. CONCLUSION

This research has analyzed Japanese auto industrial policies from a historical perspective. The framework employed was T. Parsons' social exchange model and D. Campbell's quasi-experimental design scheme. As a working model, we proposed the "cycle model," with an emphasis on the dynamic process of policy intervention. Based on this model, descriptive and numerical analyses were conducted. The descriptive analysis identified eight major policy interventions exerted by the government from the inception of Japan's auto industry. The analysis also explored the fact that basic policy objectives focused on auto production and the expulsion of foreign dominance in the industry. The numerical analysis, on the other hand, brought the following findings. First, each policy was aimed at helping the industry attain a stable production structure and second, the same policy was used in both the pre-war and the post-war periods to decrease foreign imports. This policy tactically let the ratio of the indigenous production of the total car supply be "1" without a major decline in the total supply. Third, the industry's post-war technology was improved by assembling foreign cars, but evidence suggests that the government intended to "linearly" internalize foreign technology. Fourth, the government intentionally took the less-developed country pattern of Vernon's product-cycle model. Our research contends that this was the best pattern to foster the indigenous auto industry.

These research results were succinctly organized into the matrix form of the cycle model [Table VIII-1]. The following policy implications are readily drawn. First, if intervention is exerted recursively to change a firm's behavior, the government will inevitably become more and more coersive, provided that past interventions were more or less successful. Second, unless a new relation between the industry and the government is created, the policy system under its recursive approach will no longer continue last effectively. Third, there are certain conditions for which the less-developed countries can apply the Japanese lesson. The condition requires that policy makers learn the pattern of firms' behavior. In particular, as long as they adopt the recursive policy intervention scheme, the strong authoritative coercion at the initial stage is not advisable for the following reason. The infant industry will overreact or over-shoot under an authoritative intervention, so that the government will not be able to learn the behavior of firms.

Since this paper focused on the period to c.1960, some comments on the future are necessary. Japan's use and ownership of the

motor vehicle increased dramatically in the late 1960s or early
1970s. Before and during the 1960s, MITI strengthened the parts
industry by the Temporary Measures for Promotion of Machinery
Industry ("Kishinho"). In 1966, Japan became a member of both the
OECD and IMF Article Eight Country. In meeting the membership
requirements, the liberalization of finished vehicles was
officially announced in the same year. However, the import
liberalization of engine and other important parts did not take
place until 1971. In the domestic scene, the Environmental
Protection Agency issued stringent pollution control regulations in
1972, 1974 and 1975, and the energy crisis occurred in 1974 and
1979 and encouraged the development of fuel-efficient and
pollutant-controlled Japanese autos that entered the world market.
The popularity of Japanese passenger cars led to "voluntarily"
restraints as a result of pressures from the US government and the
MITI. This was a period in which the Japanese auto industry
eliminated the jurisdictional scope of governmental interventions
by strengthening and expanding its operation in the international
market. Government policy is, in fact, problem-solving. If a
problem is easily and quickly solved by the private sector, there
is no obvious jurisdictional rationale for the government to
intervene.

NOTES

*This paper is partly from the author's dissertation which was submitted to
the department of political science at the Massachusetts Institute of Technology
in 1977.  He wishes to thank his thesis advisers and readers, Profs. D.A. Hibbs,
Jr., J.H. Hollomon, I.D. Pool, W. Abernathy, J. Utterback and N. Miyatake.
Earlier versions of this paper were presented at the Japanese team meeting of the
Future of Automobile Project and the Rokko Symposium on Japanese Firms in 1982.
He is grateful to Profs. M. Aoki, M. Baba, E. Hadley, E. Sakakibara, S. Sato, K.
Tsunekawa and W. Hayashi for insightful comments and suggestions.  He retains the
ususal responsibilities of authorship.

[1] T. Parsons [1] and [2].

[2] Both descriptive data and numerical data in Sections  2 and 3 were collected
from numerous Japanese sources.  See REFERENCE [3].

[3] The explanation of the failure of the eighth intervention by the lack of MITI's
nemawashi might be erroneous.  For the third intervention, the MOC was said to
encounter a deadlock because the Imperial Army and the Zaibatsu did not support
MOC's idea.  This is the case of the lack of the nemawashi.  As seen before, the
MOC solved this problem by introducing a counter firm, i.e., Toyoda Auto Weaving
Machinery, Ltd.  This strategy seems to have worked well, since the majar opposing
company was G. Ayukawa's Nissan Motors, Ltd.  On the other hand, for the People's
Car Plan, the two leading companies, together with other member companies within
JAMA, strongly opposed MITI's idea.  In this case, MITI's introduction of a
counter firm, Komatsu Manufacturing, Ltd. did not work, even if this strategy was
again taken to remedy the lack of the nemawashi.

[4] The quasi-experimental design advocated by D. Campbell and others is a "spin-
off" from the basic rules of measurement in a laboratory experiment, which are
known among engineers and natural scientists as experimental design.  Experimental
design is particularly concerned with avoiding two fallacies: 1) the erroneous
supposition of a causal relationship between an experimental treatment and effects
on a subject, and 2) the erroneous generalization from a locally-observed
experiment to a general theory.  In their search for comparable rigour in
experimental and educational psychology, Campbell and other psychologists have
adopted the central features of the experimental design.  These reorganized rules
are now widely known among social scientists as the quasi-experimental design.
The term "quasi" denotes the frequent impossibility of repetition of social
science experiments, which makes a true control experiment impossible.  Although
the situation of policy intervention analysis is not exactly identical, there is a
similar need for a rigorous research framework based upon the quasi-experimental
design.

In Campbell's terms, these two fallacies are discussed under the headings of: 1)
threats to internal validity, and 2) threats to external validity.  The former are
fallacies consisting of drawing erroneous conclusions on the efficacy of a policy
interaction in a way analogous to improper reasoning from experimental evidence in
a laboratory.  The latter comprises conclusions improperly extrapolated from a
specific intervention case to a different context, or used in forming a general
theory.

In the context of policy intervention, Campbell raised eight major threats to
internal validity, which are relevant to this research as a post-hoc non-
experimental intervention analysis.  These are: 1) the history threat, 2) the
maturation threat, 3) the instability threat, 4) the instrumentation threat, 5)

the regression artifact threat, 6) the selection threat, 7) the experimental
mortality threat, and 8) the selection-maturation interaction threat.

The history threat means the careless overlooking of causal factors other than
just policy intervention.  The maturation threat consists of a failure to
recognize the time-trend inherent in the data, and thus, concluding incorrectly
that an increase or a decrease has been caused by intervention.  The instability
threat consists of drawing false conclusions regarding the efficacy of
intervention in a situation where measurement errors (or sensor noise) and random
fluctuations of a focused entity (or system noise) are relatively large.  The
instrumentation threat is not the most appropriate description in the context of
this research.  The measurement unit threat would seem to be a closer
apporximation to the true meaning of Campbell's instrumentation threat.  This
consists of drawing false conclusions about the efficacy of intervention as a
result of using improper measuring units.  The regression artifact threat is a
general fallacy in any regression analysis consisting of picking up
unrepresentative extreme data point in a data set and leading to an erroneous
assessment of intervention.  The selection threat means the improper
unrepresentative selection of data to assess policy intervention.  The
experimental mortality threat is evaluating the effect of an experimental
treatment ignoring the fact that a subject itself changes over time or is replaced
by a new one while the treatment is in progress.  The final selection-maturation
interaction threat is a combination of the maturation threat and the selection
threat discussed above.  If a treatment is applied to two different subjects that
have a different maturation pattern, effects may be different since the true
effects, if any exist, are superimposed on such a maturation trend.  Therefore, if
the selection of a subject is biased, it is very difficult to identify the causal
relationship between the treatment and its possible effects.  See Campbell [4].

[5] Campbell [5] and Campbell and Ross [6].

[6] Glass [7].

[7] Box and Tiao [8].

[8] For an ARMA model, see: Box and Jenkins [9] and Nelson [10].

[9] For a good discussion on the difference between the noise-model approach and
the structural-equation approach, see: Hibbs [11].

[10] Young [12].

[11] Young [13].

[12] The initial condition for the recursive least-square estimation took the OLS
estimates.  Hence, the estimates started from 1926.

[13] For the incrementalism, see: Davis [14].

[14] Vernon proposed this model in the context of foreign investment.  However, his
product cycle model receives much attention from students in technology policy.
See Vernon [15].

[15] This figure is reproduced from Vernon's figure on the ordinary scale by
plotting curves on the logarithmic scale.  The picture on the logarithmic scale
would give more accurate information as to structural patterns.

[16] This point is exactly what Campbell emphasized most.

[17] This is equivalent to what Campbell called the "external validity."

REFERENCES

[1] Parsons, T., The Social System, The Free Press, 1951.

[2] Parsons, T., and N. Smelster, Economy and Society, The Free Press of Glencoe, 1956.

[3] References for Japanese Auto Data: Ozaki, Masahisa, Jidosha-nihon-shi (The Japanese History of Automobile), Tokyo: Jikensha, 1955; The Association of the Promotion for the Automobile Industry (APAI), ed., Nihon-jidosha-kogyo-shi-kojyutsu-kiroku-syu (Interview Records of the History of the Japanese Automobile Industry), 1973 (Vol.1), 1975 (Vol.2); Kimura, Toshio, Nihon-jidosha-kogyo-ron- (The Japanese Automobile Industry), Nihonhyoronsha, 1959; Jidosha-nenkan (Almanac of the Japanese Auto Industry), Nikkanjidosha-shinbun; Nissan Motors, ed., Nissan-jidosha-sanjyunen-shi (The 30-Year History of Nissan Motors), 1965; Yoshida, Nobuhide, Gekido-suru-jidosha-sangyo (The Changing Japanese Auto Industry), Tokumashoten, 1967; The Automobile Chamber of Commerce, ed., Jidosha-nenpyo (The Chronology of the Japanese Automobile Industry), 1955; The Automobile Division, MITI, ed., Nihon-no-jidosha-kogyo (The Japanese Auto Industry), 1958; Kodaira, Katsumi, Jidosha (Automobiles), Akishobo, 1968; Yamamoto, Soji, Nihon-no-jidosha-kogyo-wa-donaruka (Where Will the Japanese Auto Industry Go?), Keizaioraisha, 1951; Iwasaki, Matsuyoshi, Jidosha-kogyo-no-kakuritsu (Establishing the Japanese Industry), Itoshoten, 1941; The Automobile Chamber of Commerce, Nihon-jidosha-sangyo-no-hensen-to-syorai-no-arikata (The Future and Past Process of the Japanese Auto Industry), 1948.

[4] Campbell, D.T., "Quasi-Experimental Design," in D. L. Shills, ed., International Encyclopedia of the Social Science, New York: Macmillan and Free Press, 1968, Vol.5, pp.259-263.

[5] Campbell, D.T., "Reforms as Experiments," American Psychologists, Vol.24, 1969, pp.409-429.

[6] Campbell, D.T., and H. Ross, "The Connecticut Crackdown on Speeding: Time Series Data in Quasi-Experimental Analysis," Law and Society Review, 1968, 3(1), pp.33-53.

[7] Glass, G., "An Analysis of Data as a Time Series Quasi-Experiment," Law and Society Review, 1968, 3(1), pp.55-79.

[8] Box, G. and G. Tiao, "Intervention Analysis with Applications to Economic and Environmental Problems," Journal of the American Statistical Association, March, 1975, Vol.70, No.349, pp.70-79.

[9] Box, G and G. Jenkins, Time Series Analysis: Forecasting and Control, Holden-Day, 1970.

[10] Nelson, C., Applied Time Series Analysis, Holden-Day, 1973.

[11] Hibbs, D., On Analyzing the Effects of Policy Interventions: Box-Jenkins vs. Structural Equation Models, A Working Paper, The Center for International Studies, No. c/74-33, MIT, December, 1974.

[12] Young, P., "Discussion on Dr. Bray's Paper," Journal of the Royal Statistical Society, No.3, Series A (General), Vol.134, No.2, 1971, pp.220-222.

[13] Young, P., "Comment on On-Line Identification of Linear Dynamic Systems with Application to Kalman Filtering," IEEE Transactions on Automatic

Control, Correspondence, Vol. AC-16, 1971, pp.369-279.

[14] Davis, O., et.al., "A Theory of the Budgetary Process," American Political Science Review, Vol.LX, No.3, September, 1966, pp.529-547.

[15] Vernon, R., "International Trade in the Product Cycle," Quarterly Journal of Economics, 1968, 80, a, pp.190-207.

THE ECONOMIC ANALYSIS OF THE JAPANESE FIRM
M. Aoki (editor)
© Elsevier Science Publishers B.V. (North-Holland), 1984

*COMMENTS ON V, VI AND VII*

# THE OWNERSHIP AND FINANCING OF CORPORATIONS

MERVYN KING

One of the most valuable aspects of the Rokko Symposium on the economic analysis of the Japanese firm was the extent to which it raised fundamental questions about the nature of long-term contracts within the corporation. Such contracts exist both between the firm and its employees, and among the various suppliers of capital. The analysis of contracts, particularly in cases where the parties have differing information, has become not only an active area of research but also an important ingredient in the modelling of the business cycle. Most of the work to date has focussed on the labour market (see Hart [3] for an excellent exposition of models of asymmetric information). In this paper I shall focus on the role of capital markets and their functioning in Japan, as illustrated by the work of Aoki, Ishikawa and Ueda, and Nakatani.

Before turning to the contributions of these papers, some general remarks about capital markets may be in order. One role of the capital market is to channel savings from individuals and households to enterprises who wish to invest in real assets. Financial inter-mediaries may assist in this process, but the important link is between the individuals who provide the funds, the ultimate source of savings, and the organizations which commit these funds to a real investment project. Of equal importance is the role of the capital market in allocating risks among different agents in the economy. By exchanging claims on future resources, the more risk-averse individuals in the economy are able to hold a higher proportion of their wealth in the form of safe assets than would be the case if such markets did not exist. Through the exchange of securities such as shares and bonds, much of the uncertainty in the economy is shifted to the portfolios of those individuals who are willing to take such risks. In this way a market economy can lead to an efficient sharing of risk.

Although we normally think of capital markets in terms of markets for financial assets such as corporate equity and bonds, individuals do not have preferences defined over the holdings of these assets as such. Instead, their preferences are defined over consumption at various dates in the future, and they are concerned with the possible outcomes of the state of the world. The usual assumption is that preferences are defined over contingent commodities, that is over physical commodities distinguished by the state of the world in which they are delivered as well as the date on which they are consumed. If markets in these contingent commodities exist, then the usual theorems of welfare economics can be used to argue that in a competitive market economy resources will be allocated efficiently. More interesting, is the case in which markets in the basic contingent commodities do not exist, but in which individuals must transact indirectly through financial securities such as shares. In a world of 'incomplete' markets a more restricted concept of efficiency is still attainable if firms behave competitively (Diamond [2]). Because it is clear that there are fewer securities in which to invest than there are states of the world, the analysis of a world of incomplete markets is both interesting and relevant. It turns out that a crucial condition is whether or not these firms, by changing their investment or financial policy, can influence the implicit valuation which individuals in the economy place on consumption in each possible state of the world. In other words, can firms influence the implicit prices of contingent commodities? Provided that firms are in this sense 'small' then no firm can expand the consumption possibility set of its shareholders except by simply increasing their wealth. All stockholders will agree that the firms should maximize its market value thus leading to the increase of their own wealth. Under this basic condition, it is possible to show that not only are all shareholders unanimous, but that they will wish the firm to maximize its market value, and the Modigliani-Miller proposition that financial policy is a matter of indifference will hold in such an economy. In this world, financial policy makes little difference to the firm, and there is no role for managers.

If for some reason the firm is able to influence the implicit prices facing shareholders, then none of the above results hold. In general, shareholders will disagree about the policy which the firm should pursue - both with respect to real and financial policies and there is no presumption that the firm will maximize its market value. (King [4]). Financial policy will no longer be a matter of indifference for the firm and the Modigliani-Miller theorem will not hold. Investment and financial policies will be interdependent, and there is now a possible role for managers in making decisions within the firm given that there is a disagreement among the shareholders. It is evident that one of the important roles played by management is to obtain and utilise for the benefit of the shareholders information which it would be costly or diffi- cult for the shareholders to process themselves. We are therefore back in a world of asymmetric information. Although we do not, as yet, have a satisfactory theory of the firm in these circumstances, a number of propositions are important. First, it is the existence of asymmetric information together with the ability of the firm to influence implicit prices, which creates room for the existence of managers. If this approach is to produce more insights than earlier attempts to construct managerial theories, then the theory must explicitly model the relationship between managers and other groups in the firm, such as shareholders, and it must yield empiri- cal predictions which are at variance with alternative theories. Secondly, there are certain empirical phenomena which it seems difficult to explain within a model based on the assumption that firms are unable to influence implicit prices. The existence of positive levels of dividends, and their time-series stability, together with evidence that firms do care about their own debt- equity ratios, suggest that the view of the world in which firms do have an ability to affect share holders' welfare by altering the implicit prices which they face offers a way of explaining these previously unexplained phenomena. Thirdly, when modelling the relationship between different groups in the firm, it is important to incorporate the firm-specific risks which it is not possible to insure against elsewhere in the economy. These risks affect employees, shareholders, and also managers. It is the existence of such firm-specific risks which is one of the reasons for long-term contracts. It is likely that agents will wish to enter into long-term contracts rather than recontract on the spot market each period. This may provide a way of sharing the residual risk resulting from each firm's operation.

It is against this background that we may examine the contributions by Aoki, Ishikawa & Ueda, and Nakatani. All are in some way concerned with the role of long term contracts in allocating risks among agents in the economy. The paper by Aoki is concerned with a 'managerial corporatist' model of firms in which companies are owned by two major types of shareholders, individual investors on the one hand and banks on the other. Employees are not modelled explicitly in this paper, but some interesting questions on the topic are raised in the paper by Okuno in this volume. The paper by Ishikawa & Ueda does consider one aspect of employees' compensation, namely that part of their income which comes from bonus payments. This means that the wage received by workers is state-contingent. Nakatani is concerned with the role of interlocking shareholdings and argues that their existence may reduce risks. One general point which may be made at the outset concerns that of self-selection. All of these papers are concerned primarily with the larger firms in Japan, and it may well be that the nature of the contracts which link employees, managers and shareholders together in these firms are rather different from the type of contracts one observes in smaller firms. The theoretical implication of this is that the agents who will enter into such contracts will not be a random sample of the population. In the insurance literature this is known as the adverse selection problem, but in this present context the self-selection may mean that higher quality workers and managers are attracted to such firms. For empirical work, the implications of possible sample selection bias are clear and the problems to which they give rise are well known.

One of the central features of Aoki's model is the determination of corporate financial policy in a world where investors differ in both their tax and risk characteristics. He considers a model in which the level of investment is held constant and in which the firm considers how best to finance this fixed investment requirement. The firm's choice is between borrowing and internal equity finance (retentions). It is convenient to ignore the possibility of new share issues, which do not affect the substance of the argument to follow. There are two types of investors, households and banks. Households are assumed to choose between holding shares and investing their savings in banks deposits. Banks may invest in shares and also lend to firms. There is here an immediate asymmetry in that banks may invest in both debt and equity of the corporate sector, whereas households invest only in equity. For a given debt-equity ratio of the firm, Aoki analyses the determinants of portfolio equilibrium for the two types of investor. He then shows that the investors will in general disagree about the direction in which it is optimal to move the debt-equity ratio. In the absence of unanimity, we have no adequate theory for corporate behaviour. Aoki then goes on to propose a way of viewing the firm in terms of a resolution of the interests of the two groups of shareholders. This is clearly an interesting line of development, and one which deserves further investigation. For the moment, however, it is useful to compare this model with an alternative model which has

been analysed by Miller [6] and by Auerbach and King [1]. In this
model, there are investors who differ in their tax brackets with
some investors preferring equity and others preferring debt for tax
reasons.  In general, even when there is uncertainty, no equilibrium
in this model exists unless constraints are imposed to prevent tax
arbitrage.  When such constraints on short sales are imposed, then
there does exist an equilibrium in which the aggregate corporate
sector debt-equity ratio is equal to the ratio of the wealth of
those who prefer debt for tax reasons to the wealth of those who
prefer equity.  In this equilibrium no individual firm cares about
its own debt-equity ratio, and the Modigliani-Miller theorem holds.
Furthermore, all investors are unanimous in agreeing upon share
price maximization as the appropriate objective for the firm, and we
are back to a rather 'traditional' view of corporate finance.  For
this equilibrium to exist, a further set of conditions must hold
which means that despite the existence of constraints, no firm can
affect the implicit valuations of consumption in different states of
the world.  In fact, these conditions are most unlikely to hold in
practice because if short sales constraints are imposed on equity
holdings of individual firms, then the condition for unanimity is
that by holding an appropriate combination of corporate bonds an
individual investor can achieve a portfolio with the same degree of
riskiness as can be obtained by investing in shares.  It seems
unlikely that equity and bonds will be sufficiently close substitutes to make this possible.  Hence unanimity will not in general
hold and we need to model the determinants of corporate behaviour.
Further discussion of this approach may be found in King [5].  A
similar conclusion is reached by Aoki.  There are some similarities
between the two models.  In the model I have just sketched, constraints on short sales are crucial to ensure the existence of
equilibrium.  Aoki does not model such constraints explicitly but
restricts investors to holding only certain securities and hence
imposes implicitly a number of constraints.  One of these is that
households are not allowed to own both corporate debt and equity.
I would conjecture that if in his model households were allowed to
own both assets, then share price maximization would not be optimal
even for households.  But if investors were allowed to own both
types of security, then I suspect that constraints on short sales
would be required in a model with a large number of firms, and this
model would have many similar features to that outlined above.  The
main conclusion will, however, remain the same, namely that except
under very restrictive conditions the wish of investors to diversify
their risks will not coincide with their wish to hold certain kinds
of assets for tax reasons.  The optimal portfolio will involve a
balancing of these risk-spreading and tax saving objectives.  Only
if the optimal portfolio for tax purposes can be separated from that
for diversification objectives will the result of unanimity among
shareholders obtain.  Hence the kind of model which Aoki is trying
to construct is exactly the right sort of model to examine.  The
difficult task here is to examine behaviour in a model where all
agents are acting rationally.  One would like to avoid specifying a
utility function for the 'firm' which is not related explicitly to
the preferences of the agents involved in the firm's activities.

This consideration brings us to the work by Nakatani.  One of his
main arguments is that inter-company shareholdings allow risk-
sharing which the market itself does not provide.  But it is crucial
here to ask the question 'Whose risks are being shared?'.  If we
consider only investors, then they would like to have the maximum

possible scope for diversification which is represented by transactions in the stock and bond markets. The merger of firms, or the growth of inter-company shareholdings, restricts such possibilities. It does not seem intuitively obvious that the growth of such shareholdings benefits stockholders. But it may help to reduce some of the risks faced by managers. Again this requires careful and explicit modelling of the question. Does the existence of the corporate groups in Japan, the ex-zaibatsu, offer economic advantages over and above the traditional ones of economies of scale both in technology and exploitation of market power. Nakatani's paper is concerned with this issue. He proposes that the ex-zaibatsu exist to maximize the joint utility of the firm's constituent components rather than simply joint profit maximization. To develop this idea one needs a more careful definition of 'joint utility' and this leads us in the direction of a bargaining solution. Since the existence of such conglomerates tends to reduce trading opportunities in contingent commodities for agents, we need convincing arguments to accept the proposition that the motive for the development of these groups is risk-sharing. At the level of the firm one might argue that the conglomerates help to avoid the real costs of bankruptcy by reducing the probability that the group as a whole goes bankrupt. But how large are the real costs of bankruptcy? More interesting, perhaps, is the idea put forward by Nakatani that these groups help to insure against 'management risks'. This idea is certainly worth pursuing.

His empirical work examines both the ex-zaibatsu and also 'independent' firms. One problem here is that 84% of the quoted non-financial companies are in conglomerates, and pure independent firms account for only 6% (54 out of 859) listed firms. The sample size is rather small, and there is also the possibility of sample selection bias. This arises because only firms with continuous accounts between 1971 and 1980 are included in samples. Since the births, deaths and mergers of firms are not random occurrences, the existence of both attrition and sample selection bias may affect the estimates. Nevertheless, it is clear that some very important issues can be examined by using this set of data. Finally, the paper by Ishikawa and Ueda examines some extremely interesting data on firms and their payment to workers. The existence of bonus payments means that compensation to employees depends upon the state of the world. This observation is in conflict with the simple implicit contract labour market model which would imply that risk-averse workers would sign contracts with risk-neutral firms involving constant compensation over time. Of course these models involve a number of assumptions, but the most interesting way of relaxing them is to introduce asymmetric information. The fact that management may be able to observe things which workers cannot leads to rather different types of contract. These are analysed in the paper by Hart [3]. One aspect of this theory, however, does not seem to be supported by the results of Ishikawa and Ueda. The kind of information which one would expect managers to be able to observe concerns firm-specific variables. Observation of these is likely to provide information on their future values. Hence one would expect that the size of the bonus payment would not only add to the income of workers, but work also convey to them information about the future prospects of the firm in which they work. To the extent that this is true, then bonus income is not simply a transitory component of income. It also contains information about the workers permanent income. If this is true one would expect to find that the propensity to consume out of bonus income would be larger than that out of transitory income. Yet Ishikawa & Ueda find a rather small propensity to consume out of bonus income. In terms of a life-cycle model, this suggests that current bonus income does not contain very much information about future earnings. This is a most important idea which needs further testing. For one of the problems of models of asymmetric information is that they do not properly explain why firms cannot provide workers with the information required for other contracts to be made under which both parties could be made better off. Clearly, if the payment of bonus income (or profit sharing agreements) provided information then some of the difficulties could be overcome. Hence this empirical evidence about the information content of bonus income is important.

Recent developments in the theory of company behaviour suggest that one of the more promising lines of development is the analysis of long-term contracts. These may exist between employees, share-holders, banks and managers. Some theorists have been using such models to explain the business cycle. But these models have a very important role also in the analysis of individual corporate behav-iour, and empirical studies of these matters are crucial to an understanding of how realistic these models are. With this in mind, the analysis of firms in Japan provides a unique opportunity to test some of the theories. There are many misconceptions about the nature of Japanese firms which the papers in this conference have examined carefully. When the appropriate adjustments are made, it is clear, for example, that the debt-equity ratios of Japanese firms are much closer to those in the US and Europe than is often supposed. If the further adjustments required to Table 1-5 of Aoki's paper were made, it would be interesting to see the differ-ences between debt equity-ratios in Japan and in the US. It will be fascinating, however, to see if there are fundamental aspects of behaviour which are common to the behaviour of firms in Japan and elsewhere, which reflect the nature of the long-term contracts which may underlie the modern corporation. To examine this question would require both explicit theoretical models of how the interests of the different constituent groups of the company are resolved, as well as detailed empirical analysis. The papers in this conference repre-sent a most valuable contribution to this undertaking, and one can only hope that these studies will continue.

REFERENCES

[1] Auerbach, A.J. and King, M.A., "Taxation, Portfolio Choice and Debt-Equity Ratios: A General Equilibrium Model", Quarterly Journal of Economics, (1983), forthcoming.

[2] Diamond, P.A., "The Role of a Stock Market in a General Equilibrium Model with Technological Uncertainty" American Economic Review, 57, (1967), pp.759-76.

[3] Hart, O.D., "Optimal Labour Contracts under Asymmetric Information: An Introduction" Review of Economic Studies, Vol. XLX(1), (1983), forthcoming.

[4] King, M.A., Public Policy and the Corporation, Chapman and Hall, London, (1977).

[5] King, M.A., "Business Taxation, Finance and Investment", in (eds.) Auerbach, A.J. and Feldstein, M.S., <u>Handbook</u> <u>of</u> <u>Public</u> <u>Economics</u>, North-Holland, (1983).

[6] Miller, M., "Debt and Taxes" <u>Journal</u> <u>of</u> <u>Finance</u>, 32, (1977), pp.212-75.

THE ECONOMIC ANALYSIS OF THE JAPANESE FIRM
M. Aoki (editor)
© Elsevier Science Publishers B.V. (North-Holland), 1984

*COMMENTS ON VII AND VIII*

# COUNTERPOINT ON BUSINESS GROUPINGS AND GOVERNMENT-INDUSTRY RELATIONS IN AUTOMOBILES

ELEANOR HADLEY

1.

Professor Nakatani's chapter on "The Economic Role of Financial Grouping", is a fresh approach to a much discussed topic. Eschewing "culturalist" explanations, Nakatani seeks explanation of business groupings in terms of basic economic analysis.

Nakatani poses as the central question whether groupings affect the behavior of individual member firms and finds that groupings do increase the "monopoly power of members" but that this "monopoly power" is not used for raising profits or enhancing the growth rate, but rather for enhancing the "joint utility [I should have preferred 'welfare'] of employees, financial institutions, stockholders and management." Just how "monopoly power" occurs and is enhanced is not explained. Nakatani sees the groupings enabling management to have discretionary power in allocating the returns from production and also stabilizing corporate performance over time. For him the groupings constitute "mutual insurance" schemes.

Professor Nakatani sees the groupings as a factor in Japan's ability to adjust to the shocks following the two oil crises and the efficacy of monetary policy in Japan. "The fact that the economy does not fall into serious recession makes it much easier for the Central Bank to maintain a strong monetary policy against inflation." Thus in seeing the primary purpose of groups in "sharing of risks and profits among group members", Professor Nakatani finds himself concluding that the peculiarity of Japanese industrial organization may be crucial in understanding the performance of the Japanese economy as a whole.

Professor Nakatani has done a most interesting piece of research in this chapter in conceptualizing a hypothesis to be tested and in laying out econometric tests for it. While I have a number of reservations with the way in which the argument is presented, as my comments below indicate, it strikes me that Professor Nakatani may have come upon a significant insight.

Although I will suggest a different micro factor, it is Professor Nakatani who suggests that micro factors may have real bearing on how macro measures play out. With these words of appreciation for Nakatani's research, what are my reservations? They come down to his eschewing history as well as "culturalist" interpretations, and I find I have certain differences of interpretations. It is refreshing to avoid references to Japan's alleged uniqueness; it is not refreshing, however, to have history overlooked.

To the question, how is it that Japan has business groupings centering around commercial banks in a way that other countries do not,
there are such relevant historical factors as:

>    1)   The Occupation did not eliminate groupings, only the family
>    role in them and their top holding companies;
>    2)   In the United States groupings would not be formed around
>    banks because the capital market is the primary source of
>    outside capital, and because banks cannot own shares in
>    industrial companies;
>    3)   Groupings did not occur in Japan because of the separation
>    of ownership and control which followed the Pacific War -- a
>    phenomenon common in all industrial economies today; as indi-
>    cated just above, they carried over from prewar;
>    4)   Commercial banks became key members of groupings (the big
>    older groupings all included a commercial bank, a trust bank and
>    insurance companies) because of the overwhelming need for capi-
>    tal and the underdeveloped state of the capital market;
>    5)   In Japan the capital market has been underdeveloped in con-
>    sequence of a tradition only recently broken under which exist-
>    ing shareholders were offered pro rata subscription rights to
>    new issues at par rather than at market value, making equity an
>    expensive way to raise money; and in consequence of a specula-
>    tive image carried over from prewar.[1]
>    6)   Commercial banks became key to financing because a) Japanese
>    citizens overwhelmingly put their savings in bank deposits, b)
>    by relying on commercial banks for external capital savings
>    could be enhanced through credit creation; and c) it gave the
>    government a handle for steering investments which it would not
>    have had financing been done through the capital market.

The foregoing seems to me a partial answer to the question as to how
Japan has had business groupings centering around commercial banks.

While Nakatani speculates that the higher debt/equity ratio of
companies that are members of business groupings is for the purpose
of "guaranteeing stable and extensive business opportunities for
city banks", one could also speculate that bank/industrial ties make
impartiality difficult and that the higher debt/equity ratio arises
because independents don't have, or in the past have not had, equal
access.  Nakatani suggests an additional interpretation which I find
still less plausible.  Nakatani suggests because workers are paid
higher compensation in group firms, and group firms tend to show a
lower ratio of own capital to total assets, that group firms find
"it is more difficult to raise funds for growth in the capital
market in general and the stock market in particular".  I would put
it just oppositely.  Because member firms have had easier access to
cheaper capital through banks -- interest payments are a deductible
expense -- they chose to borrow.  Now, however, that Japan is
integrating itself into the international financial community, that
growth is slower and that new issues can be offered existing shareholders at market value, equity is being emphasized.

Nakatani finds greater stability of corporate performance among
group firms and suggests this is not a consequence of the mutual
insurance scheme he earlier puts forward but because the managers --
in the face of "imperfections of markets and uncertainty" -- "have
reason to behave as risk averters."  It strikes me as odd to talk
about the leading entrepreneurs of an economy which grew at 10% per

annum in real terms between the early 1950s and the first oil
crisis, as "risk averters". Such headlong growth was full of risk
and the leading firms in the market were part or it.

Nakatani observes that in Japan the impact of monetary policy "tends
to fall on price rather than on quantity." Rather than suggesting
as Nakatani does that this reflects the ability of groupings to
insulate themselves from market forces, there would be many who
would argue that this constitutes prima facie evidence that the
Japanese economy is more competitive.

When economic analysis departs as widely from reality as it does in
assuming the rationality of capital markets, I am not sure how
helpful it is as a tool of interpretation. Nakatani writes, "One of
the essential functions of the capital market is to allocate risks
efficiently among different investors in the economy." The United
States has a broadly developed capital market but what is to be seen
in the United States? According to Robert Reich:[2]

> in 1977 American companies spent $22 billion acquiring one
> another;
> in 1979 American companies spent $43.5 billion acquiring one
> another;
> in 1981 American companies spent $82 billion acquiring one
> another;

Reich writes,[3]

> In 1979, RCA Corporation complained publicly that it lacked the
> $200 million that would be needed to develop a video cassette
> recorder, although recorders are the fastest growing appliance
> of the decade. RCA thereby ceded that video cassette market to
> the Japanese. But RCA had no qualms about spending $1.2
> billion to buy a lackluster finance company that same year. In
> 1979, U.S. Steel decided to scrap its plan for building a new
> steel plant. Instead, it began building a cash reserve to
> acquire some other, more promising company .... [In 1982], U.S.
> Steel ... purchase[d] ... Marathon Oil for $5.9 billion.

The foregoing scarcely sounds like the essence of rationality.

I find myself wondering whether the Keizai Chosa Kyokai's prestigious publication, Keiretsu no Kenkyu on which Nakatani relies for
his data (and on which I myself relied for data in treating Keiretsu
in my Antitrust in Japan) may not have come to overstate membership
in business groupings. For example, Sony and Toyota are listed as
members of the Mitsui Keiretsu, Honda is treated as part of the
Mitsubishi and Matsushita is treated as part of the Sumitomo.[4] When
"Keiretsu-ness" is stretched this far, I would suggest it loses all
meaning.

Sony's Mitsui connection goes back to 1947 when the purged chairman
of the Mitsui Bank Junshiro Mandai became chairman of Sony's board
of directors. On borrowings from banks, it is true that Sony's
largest borrowing comes from the Mitsui Bank which in 1982 accounted
for 36.49% of its total borrowings, and if the Mitsui Trust Bank is
included, 45.63% of its borrowings. But does this automatically
mean the Mitsui Bank is guiding? I think not. One must distinguish
the bank role when borrowers are healthy and when they are in

trouble. In health, I do not believe the bank role is necessarily
large. Furthermore, there are increasing opportunities for borrowing outside of Japan.

Among shareholders the Mitsui role in Sony is quite different.
Moxley and Co. holds 22.89%, Raykay Inc. holds 8.45% and the Mitsui
Bank 4.59% and the Mitsui Trust Bank 2.68%. Sony in my judgement is
an example of an independent company demonstrating the entrepreneurial qualities of its co-founders, Mr. Ibuka and Mr. Morita.

In the case of the Toyota Automobile Co., also listed in the Mitsui
complex, it had zero borrowings in 1982 and hence zero loans from
the Mitsui Bank. Mitsui's ownership position in Toyota is un-
distinguished. In 1982, the Mitsui Bank fractionately held top
position at 4.98% shares compared to the next two largest shareholders, the Tokai Bank at 4.94% and the Sanwa Bank at 4.79%.

While in the case of Honda and the Mitsubishi Keiretsu there is a
seemingly more tangible keiretsu role than in the preceding two
examples, I still question the appropriateness of Honda's inclusion
in the Mitsubishi grouping. With respect to bank credit, Mitsubishi
Bank supplied 12.58% in 1982 while the Mitsubishi Trust Bank
supplied 12.58%. Other major bank sources include the Tokai Bank at
9.81%, the Industrial Bank at 8.09%, the Japan Development Bank at
6.84%. By shareownership, the Mitsubishi Bank is largest at 4.56%,
followed by the other Mitsubishi financial institutions, Mitsubishi
Trust Bank at 4.0%, Tokyo Marine and Fire at 3.91% and the Meiji
Life Insurance at 2.29%. Does this mean that Honda is not an
independent company, the creation of Mr. Honda and Mr. Fujisawa?
I think not.

On the surface, Matsushita Electric looks integrated into the
Sumitomo groupings, but is it? It has zero borrowings in 1982 and
so zero borrowings from the Sumitomo Bank. Among its top shareholders are three Sumitomo institutions -- Sumitomo Bank at 4.86%,
Sumitomo Life Insurance at 4.67% and the Sumitomo Marine and Fire
Insurance at 1.91%. But again to anyone familiar with Matsushita
Electric, one thinks of the extraordinary entrepreneurial talents of
its founder and until recently its head, Konosuke Matsushita. As is
apparent, I do not feel altogether comfortable with all of the data
underlying Nakatani's chapter.

But data -- with or without reservations -- brings me to another
point. I refer to the existence of data postwar. Pre the Pacific
War, the zaibatsu regarded corporate data as their own private
property. Accordingly, corporate directories provided only the
scantiest information on zaibatsu companies. Virtually all key
entries read, "not available". One cannot help feeling the most
immense appreciation for data available today, and notwithstanding
the preceding reservations, to a publisher such as the Keizai Chosa
Kyokai who brings it together so conveniently.

Nakatani's very interesting chapter points up areas for further
research. In what ways does group membership increase the "monopoly
power of its members?" If, as one would expect in a conglomerate
organization, most sales are outside the grouping, how is monopoly
power enhanced? In answering this question it is necessary to bear
in mind that trading companies can no longer bind firms to them
through "sole agency contracts" in the manner of the prewar zaibatsu. Today firms are free to sell on their own altogether or to

use a combination of selling **arrangements** involving direct selling
and the services of one or more trading companies. In this circumstance how do "market insulating" circumstances arise? If there
is merit in the hypothesis that business groupings can insulate
firms from market forces, why haven't business firms abroad been as
eager as Japanese firms to do so -- though in the case of the United
States <u>sans</u> banks.

When and how do banks steer? To what extent is it appropriate to
think of the trust bank, casualty insurance and life insurance of a
grouping as but an extension of the commercial bank in establishing
"keiretsu-ness"? What is different about commercial banks from
long-term credit banks for purposes of foreign business groupings?
The groupings around long-term credit banks are so small that
Nakatani treats them as non-keiretsu or independent companies. With
the lesser dependence on external capital out of lower growth, the
changed character of the capital market and the opportunities for
acquiring funds abroad, is the role of the banks undergoing fundamental change?

To what extent do keiretsu members forego price advantage to help a
member firm in distress? How frequently does this occur? Over what
time period is it likely to happen?

Nakatani argues that the micro factor giving Japan exceptional
flexibility during the 1970s when Japan withstood the oil shocks
more successfully than other industrialized economies is the
groupings. But I wonder. Nakatani says nothing about Japan's
flexible wage system but perhaps it has been wage flexibility made
possible by enterprise unions that is the key factor in stronger
performance. The flexibility of wage arrangements stems from
several circumstances:

  1)  From the fact that union contracts are of one year's
  duration, so it is not necessary to speculate on where company
  growth, inflation and other pertinent factors will be two or
  three years hence;
  2)  That unions are enterprise unions narrows the relevant
  horizon to the firms rather than the industry as a whole,
  increasing solid data and diminishing that which is more
  speculative; (also, of course, giving them a strike fund from
  only their own company.)
  3)  That unions are willing to give credence to management's
  contentions reflects corporate sharing of intimate financial
  information with the union and it also reflects management's
  track record of delivering larger payments to members in good
  times;
  4)  It reflects a <u>de facto</u> re-definition of the corporation
  from "the corporation is the shareholders" to the "corporation
  is the 'people'"; (i.e. staff, blue and white collar.)

These are among the questions and speculations that arise out of
Professor Nakatani's very interesting chapter.


2.

Professor Yakushiji's chapter dealing with the role of government in
Japan's automobile industry for the period, 1900-1960, is written

from a political-science point of view.  The analytic framework is
not, however, designed to capture the "richness" of the relationship.
Professor Yakushiji focuses his attention only on those actions
labelled "automobiles" omitting not only some of these but all of
those measures highly consequential to the industry that are cast in
generic form.  He thinks in terms of discrete measures only,
ignoring ongoing, sustained aspects of the government's role.  He
entitles his chapter, "The Government in a Spiral Dilemma", but his
theme is universal -- that an industry performing below levels of
international competitiveness views government assistance differently than when it attains competitiveness.  The "spiral" aspect of
Yakushiji's framework is simply that the government takes into
consideration the industry's response to its earlier efforts in
formulating subsequent steps (though not all of his interventions
illustrate this.)  This is so much to be expected -- if the government did not do this there would be something wrong -- it is a bit
difficult to understand how it is noteworthy.  It is also difficult
to understand why Yakushiji took as his time period, 1900-1960.  The
period 1910-1970 or better, 1920-1980, would have been considerably
more interesting.

For his story Yakushiji uses eight government interventions.  He
speaks of the industry having two roots, civilian and military.  He
sees the civilian getting support from the low import tariff out of
the Frnco-Japanese Preferential Tariff Agreement (for which he fails
to provide the date) and the military out of the 1918 Law for the
Support of Military Vehicles.  He speaks of an aristocratic Japan
Automobile Club being formed in 1910 on the basis of imported cars.
While Yakushiji explains that under the 1918 law "which established
for the first time the Japanese auto industry" subsidies were given
for production (supply, "push") as well as for purchase (demand,
"pull") he categorizes the legislation as "pull".

Yakushiji sees the second intervention occurring in 1932 in response
to the sharp increase of imports in the 1920s in consequence of the
Great Kanto Earthquake and the substitution of buses for public
transportation.  The encouragement of domestic production was posed
in terms of "national security" and trade deficit.  Interestingly,
the subsidized vehicle was deliberately designed to be non-compatible
with Ford and General Motors, the dominant imports.  Producers were
given both subsidy and tax allowance for manufacture of this
vehicle.

Yakushiji puts his third intervention in June 1936 when the Law for
Automobile Manufacturing Enterprise was enacted owing to foreign
"infiltration" of the Japanese market.  The legislation apparently
was intended both to increase Japanese production of passenger cars
-- Yakushiji writes to shift production from a medium-sized car to a
popular-sized car -- and to exclude foreign producers through the
requirement of a government license for production.  Astoundingly
enough Yakushiji writes in this section that Ayukawa ("Aikawa" today
is the more common form of romanization) of Nissan "believed in
private entrepreneurship and disliked any government intervention!!!
How a scholar could continue to overlook the fact that Aikawa headed
the Army's Manchukuo development company directing the entire
industrial development of Manchukuo -- is a bit difficult to compre-
hend, especially when the point has been called to his attention.

Yakushiji's fourth intervention consists of two actions, the first
in 1937, under the Law Regarding Measures for Export and Import,

dealing with foreign exchange controls and a 1941 act or ordinance
(it is not indicated which), The National Control of the Automobile
Industry, under which Yakushiji cryptically states "all private
effort in manufacturing vehicles ceased and auto firms were incorporated into [firms] producing aircraft and tanks."

The fifth intervention, according to Yakushiji was in two parts,
1945 and 1947 under SCAP. Yakushiji claims it was in 1945 that
MacArthur authorized truck manufacture to compensate for the
shortage of transportation (which seems doubtful to me); that it was
in 1947 that the Headquarters approved Toyota's and Nissan's production of passenger cars but initially "only within the limits of
inventory carried over from prewar" (the form of this stipulation
also seems doubtful to me.) Yakushiji observes that SCAP later
rescinded "the conditional approval".

Yakushiji's sixth intervention occurred in 1951 when the Government
under the Regulation of Foreign Vehicles cut off entry of Occupa-
tion-used cars in order to eliminate such competition from Japan's
fledging passenger-car industry.

The seventh intervention might be termed "domestic content" on
parts. MITI's 1952 guideline specified in the case of 11 auto parts
that the technology licensing agreements must provide upon expi-
ration that Japanese firms would produce the parts.

Yakushiji provides as his eight government intervention MITI's
effort in 1955 to have a model car produced, the "People's Car",
with MITI specifying performance standards and price. That the
industry effectively resisted this, Yakushiji refers to as a "spiral
dilemma".

Not only are Yakushiji's eight interventions odd for what they omit
but it is curious why he decided to conclude on 1960 though he does
in a final paragraph refer to a few post 1960 events. Additionally,
I find certain of his observations difficult to understand. For
example he says that the "import curve drifted upward after 1956 as
if it were freed from suppression." He believes the truth of this
observation is to be seen in Figure 17 which I cannot understand.
But what are the facts of the import trade? Passenger car imports
for the years, 1955-70 are given below together with export figures
for comparison. It will be noted that the "drift" upward was modest
indeed.

Import and Export of Passenger Cars, 1955-70

|      | Import | Export |      | Import | Export |
|------|--------|--------|------|--------|--------|
| 1955 | 5,311  | 0      | 1963 | 9,339  | 31,447 |
| 1956 | 6,684  | 46     | 1964 | 12,185 | 66,965 |
| 1957 | 6,179  | 410    | 1965 | 12,881 | 100,716|
| 1958 | 5,450  | 2,357  | 1966 | 15,244 | 153,090|
| 1959 | 5,994  | 4,884  | 1967 | 14,352 | 223,491|
| 1960 | 3,540  | 7,013  | 1968 | 15,000 | 406,250|
| 1961 | 4,310  | 11,531 | 1969 | 15,748 | 560,431|
| 1962 | 5,646  | 16,011 | 1970 | 19,080 | 725,586|

Note:  Import figures from the Tokyo office of Japan Automobile Manufacturers Association; export figures from Japan Automobile Manufacturers
Association, Motor Vehicle Statistics of Japan, 1982, p. 19.

Yakushiji provides the reader parts of the government role in the
Japanese automobile industry but only parts.  He says nothing about
the governmental contretemps of the early 1950s as to whether it was
feasible for Japan to think of developing an internationally
competitive automobile industry.  MITI argued for the industry;
Ichimada, Governor of the Bank of Japan argued the opposing position.  Ichimada contended, "Since Japan should develop its foreign
trade on the basis of the international division of labor, efforts
to develop the automobile industry will be futile."[5]  He fails to
note Japan Development Bank loans to the industry in the early
1950s which the Boston Consulting Group put at roughly 9 percent of
the total cost of passenger car facilities for the year 1951-55.[6]
He mentions administrative guidance not at all.  He says nothing
about duty rates.  Duty rates in this time period were scarcely
negligible as will be seen below.[7]

|      | Small Cars | Large Cars |
|------|------------|------------|
| 1955 | 40 %       | 35 %       |
| 1965 | 40         | 35         |
| 1967 | 40         | 28         |
| 1968 | 36         | 28         |
| 1969 | 36         | 17.5       |
| 1970 | 20         | 17.5       |
| 1971 | 10         | 10         |
| 1972 | 6.4        | 6.4        |
| 1978 | 0          | 0          |

In addition to the above restrictions against imports the Government
had exchange control.  Up to 1964 (not 1966 as stated textually),
the Government, if it chose, could simply refuses to grant foreign
exchange for the purchase of imported automobiles.  The commodity
tax imposed on the purchase of automobiles was discriminatory
against imports.  The tax was higher on large cars and was applied
on a "cif" basis whereas on domestic cars it was applied ex-factory.[8]

In constructing events affecting the automobile industry it is as if
Yakushiji was of the impression that the regulation, ordinance, law
needed to have the word "automobile" in its title before it was
pertinent.  There was however, a host of general measures that were
of great pertinency to the automobile industry.  There was the 1950
Foreign Investment Law under which the domestic automobile industry
was protected against foreigners producing inside Japan.  There was
the Enterprise Rationalization Law of 1952 under which approved
equipment in approved industries could take a first-year write-off
of 25 percent (first year only).[9]  There were export encouragement
measures.  Rates of depreciation were affected by the proportion of
total production going into exports with extra "brownie points" for
raising the firm's ratio or exceeding the national export growth

rate.[10]   There was the Overseas Market Development Law under which firms could take 1.5% of gross sales (not net profit) for use in market development.   Originally conceived as tax foregiveness, it was changed under GATT complaint to a 5-year tax deferral.[11]

The Government role in the automobile industry did not consist of discrete interventions as Yakushiji would have one believe but instead has been an ongoing partnership.   The roles of the partners changed over time, the techniques employed by the government changed over time, as did its options, but the partnership continues though now in the form of a world-premier industry with the Government calling upon it for export restraint.   I do, however, agree with Yakushiji's summation of Government measures that they were designed to build a domestic industry "rather than to guarantee the auto supply."

NOTES

[1]On new issues, Japanese firms were expected to offer subscription rights to existing shareholders on a pro rate basis at par, typically Y50, whereas the market value might be several times this amount.   The first firm to break out of this tradition was Nihon Musical Instruments (Nihon Gakki) October 1968.   The next firm was Alps Electric (Arupusu Denki) in April 1969.   It was not until the early seventies that it became common to offer subscription rights at market value.

[2]Robert Reich, "The Next American Frontier", *Atlantic* *Monthly*, March 1983, p. 54.

[3]Ibid., pp. 57–58 with the exception of the last sentence which is taken from p. 54.

[4]All corporate data cited in the subsequent paragraphs is taken from the Keizai Chosa Kyokai, *Keiretsu* *no* *Kenkyu*, 1983.

[5]Quoted in Hiroya Ueno and Hiromichi Muto, "The Automobile Industry of Japan", *Japanese* *Economic* *Studies*, Fall, 1974, p. 12.

[6]Eugene Kaplan, Japan:   The *Government-Business* *Relationship*, Government Printing Office 1972, p. 115.

[7]U.S. General Accounting Office, *U.S.-Japan* *Trade*, *Issues* *and* *Problems*, September 1979, pp. 42 and 44.

[8]Ibid., p. 42.

[9]Ibid., pp. 178–79.

[10]Ibid., pp. 179–81.

[11]Ibid., pp. 182–84.

Part Four

# MANAGERIAL EFFICIENCY AND
# THE MOTIVATION SYSTEM

THE ECONOMIC ANALYSIS OF THE JAPANESE FIRM
M. Aoki (editor)
© Elsevier Science Publishers B.V. (North-Holland), 1984

# THE JAPANESE MANAGEMENT SYSTEM:
# AN X-EFFICIENCY-GAME THEORY ANALYSIS

HARVEY LEIBENSTEIN

This paper is constructed like a sandwich: the top and bottom layers are about the systems of management in large Japanese companies and the intermediate layer presents a brief version of an X-efficiency game theory approach to the theory of the firm. We hope to show how the theory can help to explain some basic aspects of actual Japanese experience. Our special focus will be the attempt to understand (1) why large Japanese firms have been generally X-efficient, and (2) why they have been especially efficient with respect to the quality component of output.

In order to describe the management system of large Japanese firms it is necessary to make some rather broad generalizations. Such generalizations are almost always hazardous. Time and space constraints make it impossible to review the literature, and provide the empirical evidence to show that these generalizations are valid. Fortunately, part of this job has already been done by Rodney Clark [8] in his book, The Japanese Company.[1] Clark worked in a Japanese company for a number of years. His book shows a great deal of familiarity with the available literature both in English and in Japanese. Most important he has written an extremely careful and sensitive book from which one learns not only the nature of the generalizations but the extent to which exceptions are possible and likely. Thus, while I would use the artifice of presenting the "stylized facts" about the Japanese firm in order to permit a reasonable degree of logical coherence, I am nevertheless comforted that the stylization has a strong basis in fact.[2]

Of course, important elements are left out such as the subcontractors and the smaller firms. However, in manufacturing, a case can be made that the activities of the larger firms pull the smaller firms along. Among the more significant elements which will be neglected are the distribution sector, the service sectors generally, and the agricultural sector. The best one can do in a short paper is an attempt to understand a bit of the process.

An important aspect of the approach to be taken here is that it represents an attempt to delineate the relative motivational forces involved. From this point of view beliefs about the system, or about the facts, may be just as important, if not more so, than the facts themselves. For example, when we speak about the lifetime employment ideal, the important thing is not whether people work for a given firm for their entire lifetime but whether they believe that this is likely to be the case so that they behave accordingly. Other aspects will be looked at from a similar viewpoint.

## 1. THE JAPANESE MANAGEMENT SYSTEM

The Japanese management system is, in some respects, best understood by contrasting it with characteristics in the West--such as those found in the United States or the United Kingdom. The set of characteristics listed below, written in "telegraphese," is taken from the longer list developed by Clark and arranged in terms of the interests of this paper. However, an ever present problem is to distinguish between items on the list in terms of characteristics essential to the success of the Japanese company, and those that are incidental to it. Of course there are many variations within each style (Japan vs. West) but in general it would seem useful to keep the stylized characteristics in mind in order to see if they lead to any general conclusions.

The brief list below contrasts the two types of systems.

| | Japan | The West |
|---|---|---|
| 1. | Lifetime employment ideal. | No lifetime employment ideal. |
| 2. | Firm recruits people of particular age and education. | People recruited with particular skills (and/or experience) to fill specific jobs. |
| 3. | Company as a community. | Less emphasis on community ideal. |
| 4. | No sharp distinction between managers and workers. | Sharp distinctions. |
| 5. | Strong emphasis on general hierarchical ranks. | Management positions not standardized-related to function. |
| 6. | Age and service length explicitly recognized as a promotion criteria. | Age and length of service only marginally relevant to promotion. |
| 7. | Authority and responsibility diffuse. | Authority and responsibility ostensibly specific. |
| 8. | Managerial authority limited by internal labor mobility. | Managerial authority challenged practically by trade unions. |
| 9. | Enterprise unions. | Trade unions. |
| 10. | On-the-job training for a variety of jobs. | On-the-job training for specific jobs. |
| 11. | Job rotation and boundary flexibility. | Focus on specific job with specific boundaries. |
| 12. | Emphasis on cooperation, harmony, and consensus. | Greater stress on individualistic behavior within bounds of narrow job commitment.[3] |

Both the Japanese characteristics and the Western characteristics may be viewed as possessing motivational components. We will refer to these from time to time as "motivators." A good deal of discussion about the nature of the Japanese management system is either implicitly or explicitly an analysis of how the system works because of its positive or desirable motivating elements. However, even when this type of analysis is done well, it seems to me, it provides only half the picture. Namely, it indicates the way in which each system supplies the motivating elements to which employees respond. However, it rarely indicates the demand side. Surely employees over the world are not identical in their responsiveness to motivating forces. Or if they are, then in some way this assertion has to be argued and supported by evidence.

The idea behind the demand side is that individuals are likely to have certain values, attitudes, and norms for behavior which determine their responsiveness to the motivating forces contained in the working conditions that the firm provides. An example will indicate what we have in mind. Suppose that the two values are monetary reward for work and position in a hierarchy determined by some title. The monetary reward is obviously a cost to the firm. The number of titles the firm gives people may be either costless or cause small inconveniences to the personnel department so that their cost is low. Thus, the firm could choose a wide variety of bundles consisting of money and title graduations as part of their motivational system. Now consider two populations, A and J, so that in A 90% care only about money and 10% care a great deal about hierarchical position, while in J the opposite ratios hold; 10% care only about money, and 90% care about hierarchical positions. Clearly, the system that would work best for A would be one under which the monetary reward is emphasized, while the one that would be best for J is the one under which hierarchical gradation is stressed. Since we assumed that these hierarchical gradations are cheap we would expect that other things equal the cost of labor would be significantly lower in J than in A.

If we assume that the degree to which people care for money as against non-monetary rewards is continuous, then we can visualize trade-offs between the monetary and the non-monetary rewards. Of course there are also trade-offs between degrees of responsiveness and different types of non-monetary characteristics. The general assumption is that those who desire hierarchical recognition will put forth more effort. Conversely, those responsive to monetary rewards will not be concerned especially by hierarchical recognition. We will consider later the nature of the effort. Suffice it to say that for present purposes that we are not concerned with only (a) pace of work as the element that defines effort, but with other characteristics, such as (b) the quality of the effort and (c) the nature of the activities.

The motivational characteristics may be complementary, competing or neutral vis-a-vis each other. Not too much is known about the optimal mix of such characteristics except that it is likely that any motivators are, at some point, subject to a law of diminishing utility, and to a law of diminishing marginal productivity. Thus, beyond some point an increase in certain motivational factors results in diminished satisfaction to some who respond to it. In addition the degree of responsiveness in terms of effort is likely to decrease beyond some point. Of course, these are the traditional neoclassical ideas with respect to monetary rewards. In the absence of other information, we adopt the view that this is also true with

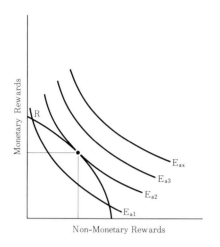

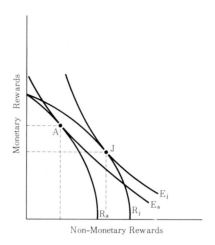

Figure IX-1a                              Figure IX-1b

respect to non-monetary motivating factors.  In figures 1a and 1b we
assume that the curves more or less follow the ideas just enunci-
ated, and hence their shapes reflect diminishing marginal substi-
tutability of one factor for another.

To illustrate the ideas we have in mind we can use a normal indifference curve analysis (as a first step) in order to show how the
level of effort might be determined under some ideal utility
maximizing conditions.  (We relax the maximizing postulate in the
next section.)  On the ordinate (in figures 1a and 1b) we show
money, and on the abscissa we show non-monetary rewards.  The
indifference curves $E_a$ and $E_j$ indicate different levels of effort as
we move from the origin in the northeast direction.  Each indifference curve is an iso effort curve whose slope at any point indicates
the trade-off between the monetary and non-monetary rewards.  The
curves marked $R_a$ and $R_j$ indicate the firms reward trade-offs between
the monetary and the non-monetary aspect.  As usual the point of
tangency between the locus of reward bundles and the iso effort
curves indicates the optimal position that can be reached.  Figure
1b illustrates the situation so that in country J the representative
firm obtains more effort at a lower cost per man than in country A.
One could consider a number of variations of this type of analysis
but space limitations prevent us from going into too much detail.
For present purposes we may view the set of iso effort curves as the
demand side of the motivation problem.

We can now consider some characteristics usually mentioned by
Japanese anthropologists and psychologists (as well as by non
Japanese scholars) as representative of Japanese tradition and

significant in motivating behavior. These characteristics are
frequently associated with such words as amae, on, chu, and giri.[4]
They help to explain such phenomena as the sense of obligation by a
member of the firm to the firm, the extreme importance of intra-
group behavior and peer group interdependence, the high degree of
dutifulness towards the interests of the firm, and dependence on the
firm for a good deal of life's satisfactions.

The concept of amae suggests a desire for dependence on the organization to which one is a member, as well as a mutual dependence
between the organization and the individual.[5] Chie Nakane has
argued that membership within what she refers to as a "frame" rather
than membership in groups that cross vertical lines (e.g., a
professional organization) are the most important to the Japanese.
The "frame" is in a sense all embracing. Examples are: the
household in which one lives, or the organization in which one
works. In the West many forms of membership to which people attach
a great deal of importance depend on narrowly defined economic and
social roles (e.g., membership in a trade union or alumni organization) which cross organizational boundaries. Furthermore, in
Japan dependence on the group motivates service to the interests of
the group, in part, as a consequence of the fear of ostracism.
Ruth Benedict, and other writers, have explained how the nurture and
child discipline systems use threats of desertion or expulsion.
Such nurture practices reinforce the tendency towards group and
organizational loyalty.[6]

The notions behind the words on and chu involve the sense of obligation created by the firm towards its members and the sense of the
need for repayment through performance by the individual member.
They involve "vertical" obligations. The concept of giri involves a
somewhat more diffuse sense of obligation to others, and is likely
to be especially important with respect to peer relationships. It
helps to explain the high degree of dutifulness frequently shown in
the day-to-day working behavior of firm members. While this represents the emotional demands of Japanese employees on the working
organizations which they join, we shall see below, by looking at
some of the characteristics of the management system, that these
demands are frequently met by firm behavior.

The supply and demand aspects are summarized briefly in the table
below.

| Supply | Demand |
|---|---|
| 1. Lifetime employment. | Dependence and desire for belonging. |
| 2. Company as a community | Appreciation of what firm does for individual. |
| 3. General hierarchical ranks. | Sense of duty towards superiors. |
| 4. Job rotation and job boundary flexibility. | Sense of cooperation towards peer group. |
| 5. Emphasis on cooperation, harmony and consensus. | Sense of obligation to repay firm. |

On the supply side we can list some of the other factors which in
general support the points we have emphasized.  Lack of space
prevents us from going into detail but the reader can easily
consider the other factors mentioned in the first table and see that
they fit into an organic picture which meets the demand side that we
have just discussed.  Thus, in terms of the stylized view of both
the supply of motivators and demand for them we can see that the
Japanese management system happens to be exceptionally well suited
to the values, attitudes, and norms of behavior which characterize
Japanese society.

The same approach could be used to show that the bundle of motivating factors which characterizes the Western firm does not
especially meet the demand characteristics of Western employees.
While many Japanese values exist in the West they are of lesser
significance than in Japan.  Thus, desire for peer group approval is
important in the West but the high value placed on individualism
reduces its importance.  In general Western employees hold to some
sort of a fairness ideal in relation to their work.  This is
frequently epitomized by the slogan "a fair day's work for a fair
day's pay."  One might say that the ideal in the West is a short-run
contractual view or contractual ideal of firm association rather
than a long-run belonging ideal.  There is a sense in which the
Western approach represents a series of contracts since there is no
lifetime employment ideal.  Also, employee behavior in the West
involves devotion to a particular skill or job (even a "property
right" in the job) rather than loyalty to the firm in general.

As we go through the various characteristics of the Western firm, we
can see that each of the long-run aspects stressed in the belonging
approach towards the Japanese company is of much lesser importance
in the Western company.  As we will argue in the next section, the
quasi-contractual view is a pseudo contractual approach since a
full-fledged contract cannot be worked out.[7]  Furthermore, the
contractual approach easily leads to concern about deviations from
the presumed contract and hence to the strong possibility of
adversarial relationships between management and employees.
Furthermore, the narrow specification of job boundaries implies that
the interstitial aspects between jobs has to be done by other
employees who may or may not coordinate the various aspects of the
production sequences.[8]  Such additional employees are costly and may
be responsible for some of the relative inefficiencies in Western
firms.

The contractual view also includes the other Western characteristics
with respect to the content of the contract.  Here we are not
concerned so much with the variety and specific nature of employment
contracts, or whether these contracts are implicit or explicit.
Rather, what we have in mind is that there is a contractual attitude
about the nature of work that generally holds, and which is very
different than "the belonging tradition."  Basically, the Western
contractual attitude connects the employee to his or her "job," and
there are strict limits, in the mind of the contractee, concerning
the activities involved in the job.  "That's not my job" is a common
Western expression, and the expression is usually viewed as a
relevant argument--so much so that some Western readers might find
it hard to imagine that things could be otherwise.  This not only
involves a narrow definition of the job itself; but, perhaps more
important, the job is viewed as having fairly clear-cut and specific

boundaries.

The belonging approach involves a sense of generalized commitment to the firm as a whole rather than specific obligation to the job. Thus, the "belonging" commitment is more closely related to the type of attitude frequently found in family enterprises within which specific job characteristics are not clearly defined as such.  Even where they are defined and exist, there is also a strong generalized commitment to firm objectives so that job boundaries are viewed as relatively unimportant, or boundaries that are easily crossed.

Thus, whether or not job definitions exist is really not of the essence.  Whether job boundaries are viewed as being relatively unimportant in carrying out tasks is of the essence.  It is also clear that the belonging approach is much more difficult to define, and very much more difficult to enunciate into a contract than the alternative view.  But, in addition, the belonging view avoids the need for the attempt to set out specific job characteristics, or to be concerned about the effort details of a contract.  Thus, the sort of documentation with respect to job characteristics developed by personnel departments of Western firms either do not or need not exist in the Japanese type firm.

A few statistics on work attitudes between Japanese and American employees may help to illustrate some of the ideas we have attempted to put forward.  In a survey taken in 1976, 49 percent of Japanese workers thought "it is most desirable for my co-workers to work at maximum capacity....helping others when their own tasks are completed."  Only 16 percent of the American workers felt this way. At the same time 75 percent of the American workers felt that their co-workers should "work at whatever level is necessary to perform their own jobs well."  This last clearly reflects a contractual approach by U.S. workers.[9]  Another telling statistic from the same survey is the reply to what workers will do if their company "will experience a prolonged decline in business, and if you can get a job with a more prosperous company."  Only 5 percent of Japanese workers indicated they would leave the company while 36 percent of U.S. workers would leave and 47 percent of young U.S. workers would leave.[10]

The general view taken here is that the outcome depends on reactions to a general system of characteristics and traditions both on the part of the firm and on the part of the individuals.  These are not easily captured by considering the characteristics one at a time. Rather, the complementarity and mutual support of these characteristics are of considerable importance.  Similarly, the complementarity and support of characteristics in the Western type firm, including those which isolate individuals in their work from each other, and isolates jobs from each other, as against those that pressure people to high levels of cooperation, should also be viewed as being closely related.  It is hoped that the various aspects of the general system approach will be clarified as we proceed to elucidate other elements in the argument.


2.  TOWARDS A GAME THEORY-CONVENTION THEORY APPROACH TO EFFORT
    DETERMINATION

The basic idea is that a good deal of X-inefficiency arises as a

H. Leibenstein

consequence of low motivations offered by firms and low effort
levels offered by employees.  The system is determined in part (1)
by the motivational forces within the firm, and (2) in part by the
motivational forces (such as degree of competition) outside the
firm, which in turn penetrate the firm, which in their turn, if
strong enough, causes changes within the firm.  We will argue that
the choice problem is basically different than that indicated by
standard theory in that the outcome depends on the strategic
decisions of various economic agents within the firm.  Thus, we will
try to show that in essence productivity is a theory of games
problem and that in particular the productivity problem is a latent
prisoner's dilemma (PD) problem.  We will also argue that conventions lead to the avoidance of the PD outcome, but usually lead to a
non-optimal solution.  This section is concerned with actual or
latent adversarial behavior, and the relation of such behavior to
productivity.  We will try to show that such behavior is of lesser
significance in the Japanese context than in the Western context.
In addition, we will argue simultaneously that for a number of
reasons such behavior is best analyzed by a theory of games approach
to the problem.  The basic ideas to be developed have already been
published elsewhere (see Leibenstein, AER 1982).  Readers familiar
with these ideas may skip the first half of this section.  However,
the ideas are repeated here for the sake of having the arguments in
one place.  In addition, some concerns not taken up in the AER
article are developed in the second half of this section.  Two such
concerns are (1) whether the fact that production can be viewed as a
repeated game leads to an optimal choice; and (2) whether there is
any advantage in the non-optimizing behavior postulate for the
purposes of the present model.  We shall try to show that non-
optimizing behavior increases the plausibility that conventions will
turn out to be a substitute solution to the prisoner's dilemma
problem.

In order to obtain our results we introduce two assumptions (based
on X-efficiency theory) which differ from the assumptions of
standard micro theory.

Assumption I:  (a)  Relaxation of the Maximizing Postulate:  We
assume that there is a relation between the degree of calculating
behavior and a sense of pressure.  This relation is that of a bell
shaped curve where pressure is the independent variable and degree
of calculating behavior is the dependent variable.  At low pressure
levels people hardly calculate and base their behavior on (1)
habits or (2) conventions.  As pressure increases more effective
calculating procedures are introduced up to the point where "calcu-
latedness" is as complete as possible for the person involved.  This
latter type of behavior approximates utility maximization.  Beyond
some point too much pressure results in disorientation and lower
performance.  Our emphasis will be on (1) the low pressure and (2)
on the optimum pressure segments of the curve.  This assumption is
consistent with and an expression of the Yerkes-Dodson law in
psychology which has been repeatedly confirmed in a large variety of
experiments since 1908.[11]

(b)  We also assume the existence of inert areas so that within
certain values of the independent variable the dependent variable
does not change.  In other words, the independent variable has to go
beyond the inert area bound in order to stimulate a change in the
dependent variables.

Assumption II: Incomplete Contracts: We assume that firm association (employment) contracts are incomplete in the sense that the
payment side is fairly well specified but the effort side, for a
variety of reasons, is either unspecified or specified only in terms
of some rough lower boundary.

The firm can offer its members a wide variety of monetary rewards
and working conditions including career opportunities. Thus every
set of wages and working conditions contain within it some motivating force. Hence, there is a sense in which the firm may be said
to choose among different motivating systems. However, there is no
one-to-one correspondence between the motivating systems and the
amount of effort that employees offer. For each motivating system
there is a range of effort level responses possible.

Assumption II suggests the possibility of effort discretion on the
part of firm members. At the same time, the assumption of non-
maximization under low pressure implies that managers will not
necessarily have the incentive to get the most out of their employees. In any event it is clear that each side can make strategic
decisions. The nature of such decisions are indicated below in
table 1 and figure 2.

In table 1 we show three basic strategic options available to each
side. For employees these are: (1) Maximum commitment: i.e., an
effort level that involves the most he can do for the firm on a
long-run basis. (2) Peer group standard, i.e., an effort level
below the maximum and similar to what other employees put forth.
(3) Selfish max, under which the employee puts forth as much effort

Table IX-1

Management

|  |  | Full Commit $M_1$ | Accept Peer Std. $M_2$ | Min Cost per Man $M_3$ |
|---|---|---|---|---|
| Full Commitment $E_1$ | | 20 / 20 | 25 / 8 | 30 / 3 |
| Peer Std. $E_2$ | | 8 / 25 | 10 / 10 | 15 / 4 |
| Selfish Max $E_3$ | | 3 / 30 | 4 / 15 | 5 / 5 |

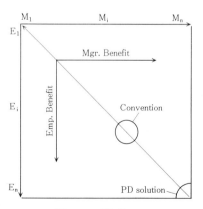

Figure IX-2

as possible for his <u>own</u> purposes rather than firm interests.  The
firm also has three strategies:  (1) It can offer wages and working
conditions ($M_1$) that <u>maximizes</u> <u>that</u> <u>benefit</u> to employees.  (2) The
firm can accept the <u>peer</u> <u>group</u> <u>standard</u> and pay accordingly.  (3) It
can try to minimize the cost per effort unit.  As the payoffs are
written it is clearly a prisoner's dilemma (PD) situation, since
employees will want to choose $E_3$ no matter what management chooses,
and management will want to choose $M_3$ for every choice of the
employees.

Similar ideas are presented in figure 1 for the case of n×n options.
Assume each line is divided into n segments.  The employer has n
motivating options $M_1$....., $M_n$ such that $M_1 > M_2$ .... $> M_n$.
This means that the wages and working conditions contained in $M_1$
cost more than $M_2$ and confer more benefits to employees than $M_2$, and
so on for $M_3$ etc.  Similarly $E_1$ involves more effort than $E_2$, etc.
Note that each value high up on the South-East North-West diagonal
is a Pareto improvement over those lower down.  Also, for any
horizontal movement westward we have shifts in favor of management,
while vertical movements down are moves in favor of the employees.
The direction of values along the diagonal implies that the greater
the <u>adversarial</u> behavior on both sides the lower the effort, or the
effort quality, and the lower the productivity.  It is quite
straightforward that increased adversarial behavior by employees
implies less valuable effort.  But, it should be equally clear that
if managers attempt to minimize cost per effort unit, this increases
resentment among employees, so that the effort level is lower than
otherwise.

It should appear clear that the relative evaluations in the diagram
which imply the nature of the payoff table lead to the prisoner's
dilemma solution.  For <u>every</u> effort option that employees will
choose, the management will want to choose motivational system $M_n$,
and for every motivational system, the employees will want to choose
effort level $E_n$.  The outcome is clearly the prisoner's dilemma
outcome since all cooperative outcomes along the diagonal involve
Pareto improvements over the outcome $E_n M_n$.

We must emphasize that the prisoner's dilemma outcome determined by
the latent two sided adversarial relations between employees and
managers is just one of many prisoner's dilemma situations in the
firm as a system.  At every level in the hierarchy there are other
prisoner's dilemmas expressed by the idea of free rider incentives.[12]  It makes sense for every employee to feel that other
employees should work relatively effectively so that the firm may
prosper and that his job and career be assured.  But since each
employee is only one of many there is no necessity for any one
employee to feel that he himself has to put forth a maximal effort
since his contribution is minute compared to contribution of all
others.  Thus, each employee may feel that he should follow the free
rider incentives and allocate his efforts towards his own rather
than the firm's interests.  In other words, each employee, if he
were a maximizer, would operate on the basis of "the selfish max
strategy".  Exactly the same sort of thing holds for managers at
every level in the managerial hierarchy where the group of managers

remains relatively large. It is worthwhile to keep these ideas in mind when we discuss conventions as solutions to the prisoner's dilemma problem since it will turn out that the conventions that solve the adversarial prisoner's dilemma also solve simultaneously the free rider incentives type of prisoner's dilemma.

The reader might object at this juncture that it is extremely rare that one observes actual (rather than latent) prisoner's dilemma productivity outcomes. Let me quickly agree that this is the case and turn to the argument that conventions become solutions to the latent prisoner's dilemma. We should keep in mind that the reason that the prisoner's dilemma outcome could occur is because there is no simple way in which individuals can turn their choices based on individual rationality into choices of group rationality. This is an aspect of the problem that has been stressed by Anatole Rapoport in his reviews of game theory.[13] Namely one of the contributions of game theory is to raise the question about the meaning and nature of individual rationality in the situation where a given player (e.g., economic agent) does not control all of the variables. This is especially true in prisoner's dilemma type games. Here clearly the prisoner's dilemma outcome where there are many options is Pareto inferior to other "solutions." But these Pareto superior solutions cannot be attained through means of individual rationality. What is required is what might be called a group rationality solution, that is, a cooperative choice made by means which are in some rough sense beyond individual rational choices. An example, but one which is rarely used in real situations, would be for the contending sides to choose a third party to make the choice for them.[14] We will not go into the difficulties involved in such procedures but suffice it to say that it would require that each side somehow (and this is a large order) bind themselves to the choice made by the third party. However, we note that conventions are in important respects similar to such third party choices. They involve "group rationality," even when they are not the optimum solution.

In recent years a formalized theory of conventions has been developed following some basic ideas suggested by Thomas Schelling (see also the writings of D. Lewis, E. Ullman-Margalit, and A. Schotter). Basically the idea is that conventions are solutions to multi-equilibrium coordination problems. For example, if we are not to be involved in an excessively large number of automobile accidents then we have to solve the problem whether all, within a country, should drive on the right or on the left. Since all left and all right coordination solutions are equally good, it is not surprising that some countries have chosen the right and others the left. Perhaps a superior example of a coordination problem requiring a "convention-solution," for our purposes, involves the choice of hours of work. Table 2 shows three possibilities under which the beginning hours determine the rest of the hours. Assume that the number of hours in the day is decided in advance and that lunch is half way through the day. What is clear is that coordinated hours are much superior to uncoordinated hours. Thus any choice on the diagonal is much better than off. However, the utility payoffs on the diagonal need not all be equally good. Figure 3 shows the same thing for the continuous option case. What is obvious is that a coordinated solution must be chosen but that it may or may not be an optimal solution. That is, any point on the curve marked C for the coordinated solution set can be a solution which we will argue below can have certain stability characteristics. Another example would be

Table IX-2

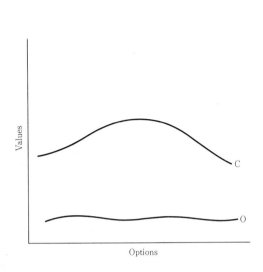

|   | 8 | 9 | 10 |
|---|---|---|---|
| 10 | 10   10 | 2   3 | 3   2 |
| 9 | 3   3 | 11   11 | 2   2 |
| 8 | 3   3 | 3   3 | 10   10 |

Figure IX-3

language.  The coordinated use of a non optimal language is much
superior to no common language at all; i.e., to individually (but
not group) determined connections between sounds and meaning.  We
usually refer to the latter as babbling.

A convention is a behavioral regularity, where there is a multiplicity of such possible regularities, adopted by more than one
individual and under which regular behavior is much superior to non
regular behavior.  Conventions are usually supported by sanctions
applied against those who flout the convention.  Thus, convention
has (1) an informational aspect, i.e., the nature of the regularity,
and (2) a sanctions aspect.  Both of these aspects will be used
below when we consider effort conventions.  Such conventions would
tell people the range within which they should keep their effort,
and for those who flout the convention there would be sanctions at
least in the sense that they would involve the sense of the dis-
approval of others.

We now turn to the question of how effort conventions are determined.  There are two aspects to this:  (1) The creation of the
convention, and (2) adherence to the convention once it exists.
There is no unique way in which a convention gets started.  A
variety of possibilities come to mind:  (a) some people may emulate
others,[15]  or (b) a group may adopt a rule as a reaction to uncoordinated effort, or (c) a small group may receive orders from
above, or (d) a convention may be introduced by those who have
adhered to a similar convention elsewhere.  In some way or other
conventions may get started in a small group as a consequence of
what (for want of a better term) we may call convention creating

activities, but once the convention exists then it is likely to be solidified by adherents who join the group. For later adherents the essential question is whether to follow the convention or not. In most cases if the convention is clearly superior to not following it then clearly additions to the group will help to support the conventions. In addition, new adherents will be influenced by the sanctions applied to temporary deviations, and (usually) in an attempt to show solidarity with the group they will join in applying sanctions to others. It is important to note that the effort level of the convention will depend to a considerable degree on what happened historically, that is on the specific convention creating activity of those who got the convention started.

With the aid of the figures below, and equation (1) to (4) we can illustrate how the effort convention may arise and how it may achieve its equilibrium value. The following relations are assumed to hold.

$$E_i = E_i(O, S) \quad \text{where} \tag{1}$$

$$S = S(E_i, O_{t-1}, \ldots, O_{t-n}), \quad \text{for all } i, \tag{2}$$

$$O_{t-1}, O_{t-2}, \ldots, O_{t-n} \quad \text{are given.} \tag{3}$$

$$E = E(O, S), \quad \text{the average reaction function for all } i. \tag{4}$$

$E_i$ represents the effort supplied by individual $\underline{i}$, O is the observed effort level and S represents the level of sanctions for deviations from some existing standard. The second equation indicates that the sanctions depend on the observed effort level in the past. In equation (4) E is the average effort level for all individuals in the firm. It represents the average reaction of all individuals to the observed effort level. In figure 4a, $E_i$ would be a straight line parallel to the X-axis if the individual did not care about the relation of his behavior to group behavior. We assume that he does care and as a consequence individual $\underline{i}$'s effort level rises, up to a point, as the observed level rises. The effect of sanctions in this case is shown by the entire curve $E_i^*$ being lowered to $E_i'$ because of sanctions applied against the individual for having too high an effort level. In other cases (not shown in the figure) the individual's effort level function may be raised as a consequence of having too low an effort level for almost every level of effort. Thus $E_i$ represents the stable functional relationship which takes into account the effect of sanctions. Figure 4b shows the average reaction function for all individuals. Clearly where the average reaction function crosses the 45° line is the point where the reaction and the observation are the same and hence represents the equilibrium effort level. In other words, it is the level that signifies the particular effort convention that holds sway in this situation.

Should one join a convention which is non optimal? The essential question is whether the convention is better than uncoordinated behavior. If it is that is all that matters. The question of joining or not joining the convention is not really a matter of the

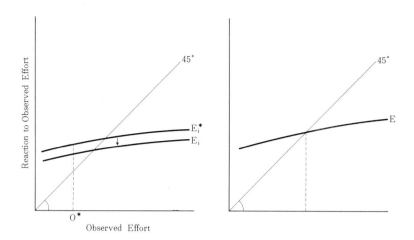

Figure IX-4a                              Figure IX-4b


optimality of the convention.  Whether one should try to change the
convention by getting all adherents to move to a Pareto superior
position is a matter we consider later but is not one that is
relevant at the point of deciding on conventional behavior initially
or on flouting the convention.  The convention is what it is and
that is all that matters at this juncture.

Any stable convention will be imbedded within an inert area.  This
is one of the reasons for introducing the inert area concept among
our assumptions.  For small deviations in the observed effort level
we would expect no reactions from those who behave according to the
convention.  This idea can be shown by a "fat" reaction curve
crossing the 45° line.  If the 45° line is also given a certain
magnitude then the area of the intersection reflects the idea that
within it (i.e., within the inert area) there are no deviations in
behavior.  In other words, it is sufficient for the conventional
effort level to be a rough approximation of the belief about the
observed level rather than an exact equality to exist.  In other
words, the theory does not require that all individuals are precise
measurers of other people's effort levels, and that they are
reactors to small changes.

Perhaps the best way to view conventions is as a non calculating
stimulus-response mechanism.  Once the environment requiring the
convention exists the conventional response occurs.  Furthermore,
everyone behaves as if everyone else will respond to the stimulus in
terms of conventional behavior.  We illustrate how this works in
table 3.  The table contains the two option case indicated in the
payoffs in the lower four squares.  Now suppose the possibility of

Table IX-3

|  | $M_1$ | $M_2$ | $M_3$ |
|---|---|---|---|
| $E_1$ | 2 ⎯ 2 | — | — |
| $E_2$ | — | 3 ⎯ 3 | 4 ⎯ 0 |
| $E_3$ | — | 0 ⎯ 4 | 1 ⎯ 1 |

the convention is indicated by the payoffs under $E_1M_1$. The nature
of the choice is similar to the situation as if each party were
permitted two options each.  Each of them can choose, if he wishes,
the convention plus any other option.  If both parties choose the
convention then this becomes the choice.  The convention rules.
But if one of them does not choose the convention then this nulli-
fies the convention effort choice and each is then left with his
alternative choice.  Since, the alternative leads to the prisoner's
dilemma each might as well choose the convention as his first choice
since that is superior to $E_3M_3$.  But if the convention choice is
nullified then each party is still left with its "best" alternative
option which will be $E_3$ for employees and $M_3$ for the managers.
In the payoff table the convention is superior to the prisoner's
dilemma choice but inferior to $E_2M_2$.  However, the individuals
cannot reach $E_2M_2$ through independent individual rationality.  They
are obviously better off by the convention choice.  The nature of
the choice is also shown in figure 2 by the option marked by a
circle.  Note that the initial developers of the convention, using
some sort of trial and error method, are more likely to have hit on
a non optimal convention than on an optimal one.

Now, will those who adhere to a non optimal convention attempt to
obtain a Pareto improvement?  This will depend on the costs and
incentives for attempting to do so.  If the group is large then the
cost of change for an individual, which involves the cost of
gathering and distributing information and of persuading all other
group members of the desirability of the change, are likely to be

quite large.  In addition there are the costs of facing sanctions at
the hands of those who are strong adherents of the existing convention.   There is also a free rider problem since each person, if he
were completely rational, should feel that he might as well let
others go to the trouble of trying to change the convention.  The
basic point is that the cost of change can be sufficiently great so
that non optimal conventions remain stable.

The major implication of the theory of effort conventions is that
output may be different even if all other aspects of production
circumstances are identical.  Furthermore, the theory helps to
explain the existence of different degrees of X-inefficiency.  That
is, for the same number of employees and the same managers, and
precisely the same equipment and exactly the same knowledge, as
technical knowledge would normally be defined, we can still have
different effort levels and consequently different output levels.
In other words, the production function as usually defined either
does not exist or it does not take effort discretion into account.
A clear cut case which illustrates what we have just said involves
two identical Ford plants, one in Germany and the other in the U.K.,
producing an identical product, with precisely the same knowledge,
but the German plant produced 50% more automobiles with 22% less
labor.  One interpretation is that effort supplies and effort
conventions in the two countries are quite different so that the
lower level effort convention resulted in the much lower output in
the U.K.[16]   There are other cases involving multi-national companies
which operate similar plants in different countries and these lead
to different output levels.[17]

In general two types of historical factors are likely to be responsible for the different effort levels.  On the one hand we have to
consider the in-plant history which influences the effort conventions within the firm.  The other factor deals with effort conventions outside of the firm or plant in question since workers are
likely to bring with them some sense of the appropriate convention
when they move from one plant to another, or as part of the flow of
information between plants.  This is not to say that interplant
influences create equal conventions but simply that the information
flow and employee movements do have an influence.

It is important to note that conventions, once established, need not
stay at that level indefinitely.  The theory of inert areas suggests
that a shock would be required in order to destabilize the convention in question.  In other words, the values of some of the independent variables must go beyond the inert area bounds.  For
example, the type of shock involved in the threat to the survival of
the Chrysler Corporation led to a reconsideration of labor contracts
that could never have occurred in the absence of shocks of this
sort.  Thus new effort conventions could arise as a consequence of
shocks from the economic environment.  Such new conventions may be
Pareto superior to the old ones so that we can imagine some movement
along the diagonal in figure 3 as a consequence of a history of
shocks.

Conventions may be classified in various ways.  The following three
way classification of effort conventions may be useful:  (1)
neutral, i.e., those for which the sanctions are applied with
respect to some deviation in either direction from the average; or
(2) upper bound focus; or (3) lower bound focus.  Those conventions

with an upper bound focus will lead to low effort levels since, in
this case, those adhering to the convention are less concerned about
low effort levels and more concerned that effort put forth by any
individual should not get too high. In conventions with a lower
bound focus the main concern is that everybody should do at least
their part but there is considerably less concern as to whether or
not people do too much. In the Ford plant case cited previously
it can be argued that labor relations in the U.K. are such that
upper bound focus was strongly enforced. In Japan, in some echelons
of management, working conventions may involve a lower bound focus.
In other words those within the group prefer others to do at least a
certain amount of the work but they have no objection if they do
more than the minimum. I am told, for example, that in some government bureaus people will work until midnight frequently because
others keep similar hours. Thus, non optimal conventions may lead
to too much effort while in other cases it may appear to lead to too
little effort.[18]

It is of interest to note that the convention which solves the
adversarial behavior problem between groups also simultaneously
provides a solution for the free rider incentive problems within
groups; i.e., the convention that will usually prevent people from
pursuing what would otherwise be a free rider incentive. But there
is another aspect involved--the postulate that we started with in
this section, namely, the relaxation of utility maximization. We
assumed that when pressure is low non calculating procedures are
employed. It is easier for individuals to choose a convention which
solves the prisoner's dilemma problem if the choice procedure
involves a non calculating stimulus-response mechanism. Thus, our
non maximization assumption allows us to see a little more readily
how we obtain the convention solution to the PD problem. If calculating behavior was always employed then individuals would always
consider whether it pays to follow the convention or to flout it.
We would expect that in many cases flouting the convention would
make sense. Under such circumstances effort conventions would be
rather weak and the prisoner's dilemma outcome would almost always
reappear.

The fact that people under normal low pressure conditions do not
calculate enables them to stick to the convention with ease.
Furthermore, under such circumstances, people are likely to go to
the trouble to employ sanctions against those who do not support the
conventions. Otherwise they would follow the free-rider incentives
and let others do the convention policing work. Hence the existence
of non calculating behavior is supportive of the notion that people
will normally adhere to conventions, and help in their enforcement
through the voluntary application of sanctions.


3.  CONVENTIONS AND MANAGEMENT SYSTEMS

We will argue in this section that there are three classes of
reasons why the large Japanese firm's managerial system has achieved
better results than its Western counterpart. (1) It has solved the
latent adversarial problem by adopting higher level effort standards
than Western companies. (2) The Japanese firm has offered a more
highly motivating mix of non-monetary rewards than Western firms.
And, (3) the broad psychological and cultural characteristics of the

relevant portion of the work force leads to a greater response to
the non-monetary motivators.

The first general point can be illustrated with the aid of figure 5.
In it we show the curve M which is basically the locus of managerial
motivational options.   The curves marked $V(E_1)$ and $V(E_n)$ represent
the iso-effort curves as they respond to the <u>same</u> motivator, $M_i$.
$V(E_1)$ represents the value of effort which reflects the maximum
effort attainable for the relevant mix of monetary and non-monetary
motivators $M_i$.   The curve marked $V(E_n)$ represents the minimum value
of effort achievable for $M_i$.   Thus the range between these two
effort levels will determine the range within which the interaction
between management and employees will determine the actual outcome.
In the figure we show the level J representing an effort convention
which is higher than the level A.   While the reasons for this have
already been suggested in Section 1, we nevertheless restate the
main ideas in general terms.   Basically, the firm provides certain
expectations, possibilities, and almost guarantees which are greatly
appreciated by the employees.   Among these are lifetime employment,
bonuses twice a year, job rotation, movement up an hierarchy, and
finally a basic sense of the firm as a community at each point in
time, and in terms of one's lifetime career.   In response to the
communal spirit, and to the other motivating forces, employees are
likely to show their appreciation and sense of obligation in a
general willingness to operate within a fairly high effort convention.   Thus, a strong likelihood exists for establishing some
initially high effort conventions.

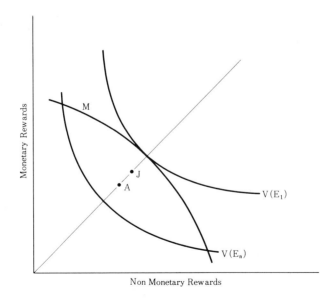

Figure IX-5

The sense of obligation is both towards one's peer group and towards superiors. Towards the peer group each employee is expected to at least "pull his own weight," and hence something like a lower bound effort focus exists. It is precisely the sense of obligation towards peers that minimizes the response to free-rider incentives at the peer group level. Furthermore, the very frequent contact among peers is likely to create sanctions against responding positively to such free-rider incentives. General emphasis on cooperation, harmony and consensus is likely to be a reinforcing element. In addition, a general sense of obligation to the firm is likely to show itself in a sense of duty towards at least some superiors.

Very few of the above elements which determine highly cooperative employee responses exist in the Western firm. On the contrary, the much greater stress on individualism among Western employees, as well as the sense of "property rights" in the job, and the contractual mentality involved, is likely to be associated with potential or clear-cut adversarial behavior. Hence the likelihood of initially lower effort levels. We consider below the relationship of the inert areas to changes in effort conventions, and how they are likely to work themselves out in the Japanese as against the Western cases. Because of our emphasis on the overall system approach to the understanding of competing management systems, it becomes impossible to consider any specific point only once in a given context and let it go at that. Some repetition seems to be necessary in order to see almost identical management characteristics, and employee responses, from more than one perspective.

We consider now in summary fashion some of the major reasons having to do with the characteristics of Japanese management which come to mind, and are responsible for its success. (a) The system of consensus achieved in small groups including the ringi and nemawashi techniques leads to the "creation" initially of fairly high effort conventions. (b) The spirit of harmony which is expected to prevail will mean that these effort conventions, at whatever level, are unlikely to possess an upper bound focus as part of the sanction mechanism. (c) The consensus achieving system, as well as the motivating forces listed below, which creates a close identity between the welfare of the employees and the welfare of the firm, is likely to lead to narrow inert area bounds. Thus fairly small shocks may be sufficient to shift effort conventions in the direction of Pareto improvements.

(d) Most of the large firms are engaged in manufacturing products for international trade in which there is a considerable amount of technical change required (at both the production process and commodity end). This leads to the possibility that such changes will permit, and be accompanied by, changes in the effort level. Furthermore, such changes are generally not resisted under the Japanese management system. The lifetime employment ideal means that there is little fear of job loss. Job rotation and job variety mean that no property rights develop in the job and hence there are no property rights in particular skills for an individual to lose. Furthermore, the emphasis on cooperation and harmony reinforces the lack of resistance to technical changes and the possible accompanying effort changes. In additions age or length of service as a criterion for long run advancement increases the possibility for individuals to identify with the idea that their personal advancement will go hand in hand with improvements in the firm's economic circumstances. In general we have argued that the need for technical change determined by international competition can be seen as an external motivating force which provides small shocks to the system. But the various characteristics of the managerial system allow these shocks to result in improvements in the changed effort conventions.

The nature of the other elements which help to explain the greater success of the Japanese firm are illustrated in figures 6a and 6b. In 6a we show three curves marked O, J, and A representing the optimal managerial motivator locus, the Japanese locus, and the American. Implicit in the figure is that no system is optimal but that the Japanese system comes closer to the optimal locus than the American.

In figure 6b we show three iso-effort curves representing O, J, and A. Once again the idea is that the possibilities of the nurturing and schooling systems are such as to achieve even higher levels of effort than is currently the case. But we argue that the characteristics of the Japanese labor force, as well as the system of selection and recruitment into large Japanese firms, leads to a much higher degree of responsiveness to the non-monetary motivators than is the case for the American labor force. We have tried to show in section 1 why this is likely to be the case. However we did not point to the recruitment aspect, which is in the direction of recruiting those who possess the attributes that work well for the Japanese management system. The way this is achieved is through a double funneling system of the potentially best employees to the

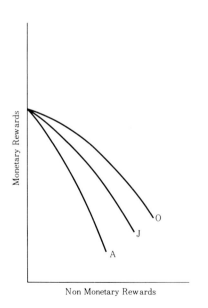

Figure IX-6a

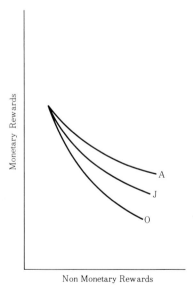

Figure IX-6b

best Universities, and those from the best Universities ending up in
the most successful and prestigious companies. This is in part due
to the ranking consciousness of the Japanese population with respect
to both educational institutions and enterprises. This may mean
that the personnel available for smaller enterprises are somewhat
less gifted than those in the large enterprises. Thus it is possible that part of the reason for the success of large Japanese
enterprises is that they contain a somewhat higher potentially
skillful segment of the population than is to be found in their
American counterparts.

The description of the Japanese managerial system in no way denies
the possibility of latent adversarial behavior. At any one time the
interest of employees, especially of blue collar employees, and the
interests of the higher echelons of management are not identical.
The use of time is still in some fundamental sense different in
terms of the interest of the two groups. The free rider incentives
exist even if they are muted, or almost non existent, by the
conventions and sanctions employed at any specific time. A case in
point is a recent article by a Japanese journalist which explains
the economic difficulties of the J.N.R. (Japanese National Railway).
almost entirely in terms of the adversarial behavior of labor and
management.[19]

Professor Kagano[20] and his colleagues view Japanese management as an
organism whereas the American style management is viewed as being
mechanistic. While in general the analogy seems to be accurate,
nevertheless, one must keep in mind that it is only an analogy. The
organismic aspects may work well as long as other aspects internal
to the firm and the environment also work well. Nevertheless it is
possible for different segments of the "organism" to feel that they
are not treated as well as they might be, and for each segment to
coalesce into an adversarial group vis-a-vis each other. A good
deal of the writing on the Japanese firm hints at the fact that
despite the attempt at maintaining harmonious relations groups do
break up into factions. Probably not enough is understood about the
internal processes at the present time for us to determine whether
the components of the organism will continue to work well as against
the circumstances under which clear-cut adversarial behavior emerges
influences effort supply, and reduces efficiency.

Masahiko Aoki has developed a model which has some resemblance to
the prototype of the Japanese managerial system. Within the model
management plays the role of the referee between the stockholders
and the employees. As Aoki puts it "the management actively tries
to expand the bargain possibility set by formulating more efficien
combinations of resources and specifying Pareto-improving internal
distribution appropriate to those combinations. How is the manage
ment motivated to perform this task? The manager as a personification of the integrative and interest-mediating machinery is
presumed to derive his primary satisfaction from enhanced status anu
legitimacy which will be bestowed on him when he does the jobs
skillfully, efficiently, and professionally." Under this scheme it
could be argued that the potential for adversarial behavior, and
its consequences would be minimized since the referee could make
rational group decisions rather than have the outcome depend on the
individualistic decisions of contending groups. While this might
work as long as management was in fact viewed as a referee by all
sides, and clearly trusted as such, we might argue that for

management to achieve such a position would require the development
of <u>conventions</u> which viewed management in the referee role, and that
these conventions were adhered to by all sides.

Our analysis suggests three general reasons why we should expect the
large Japanese firm to be on the average X-efficient compared to its
Western counterpart. The quantity aspect has been amply discussed.
However an important aspect is the one dealing with <u>quality</u>. Here
it seems clear that the group decision mechanism, and the fact that
jobs are not narrowly specified, helps considerably in the maintenance of high quality standards. If each member of a group feels
responsible to the group, and if the group is held responsible for
the quality aspect of the work, then individuals will have an
incentive to check up and cover for the quality performance of other
members of the group. This is obviously the exact opposite of what
would happen where there is a narrow job definition and each
individual cares only about the performance of his own job (to the
extent that he may care about that) and not at all about how any
other member of the group performs.

The lifetime employment ideal plus promotion by length of service
cannot remain ideal unless the firm operates in such a way so that
the size of the firm and its structure permits a reasonable rate of
advancement for all firm members. This is likely to put pressure
on the firm to grow in various ways so that enough jobs are created
at higher managerial levels as firm members advance through the
ranks. With the normal pyramid shape of the hierarchy the chances
for individual advancement at all levels in the hierarchy increases
with firm growth. This in part may help to explain some of the
elements that led to the high growth rates of Japanese industry
during the two decades from the early '50s to the early '70s. It
may also explain the great concern felt by large firms for the
current slow-down in the world economy and the decreased possibilities for expansion through the expansion of exports.

Some qualifying remarks are in order. We did not consider the
welfare economics aspects. The very long hours put in by some
employees, and the relatively short vacations may be sub-optimal.
It is of interest to note that in the firms that we visited the pace
of work was not in any way especially rapid, unusual, or suggested
exceptional exertion on a physical level. Also, we saw almost no
signs of direct monitoring of any sort. Clearly, it seemed to be
attentiveness rather than pace that makes the difference. To use a
contemporary Western slogan--they were working smart rather than
working hard.

While statistical evidence about cost differences adjusted for wage
differences in the West is hard to come by, the fact of the general
competitiveness of Japanese goods in international markets would
suggest that reaching low cost levels is not an insurmountable
problem. There is some anecdotal evidence which suggests lower
costs apart from lower wage rates for Japanese firms. These are
of the nature of verbal reports by Japanese who have worked in
Japanese and American or European firms of a very similar type.
Other information involves reports of plants purchased by Japanese
firms. Such reports contain interesting comparisons of the output
of the Western plant prior to the Japanese takeover and afterwards.
Such comparisons are almost invariably favorable to the Japanese
management approach. Nevertheless, the reader should note that our

arguments are based on strong impressions rather than overwhelming empirical evidence.[21] Finally, by limiting ourselves to the management system of large firms, we have considered only part of the picture.

NOTES

[1]Ronald Dore, in his book [11] presents a similar list. The recent book by Robert E. Cole [9], which contains quite a bit of survey data, supports the general picture. My conversations with managers in four large Japanese firms also supports the general picture.

[2]An unpublished paper by Naomi Maruo [23] gives the results of a survey of Japanese opinion leaders about the uniqueness of the Japanese Labor-Management Relations. The ten most significant items listed in the order in which they were scored by respondents are: 1) Labor union within a company, 2) Lifetime employment, 3) Trade union consciousness of dependency on the company, 4) Company=family consciousness, 5) Harmony within a group, 6) Active employee education within a company, 7) Informal and daily communication between employers and labor union leaders, 8) Employees' pride in their company, 9) Nemawashi (implicit consensus before formal decision), 10) Strong desire for promotion.

[3]See Clark [8] pp.211 ff. for the full list of characteristics.

[4]For the definition and meanings of these concepts see Doi, Nakane, and Befu.

[5]See especially Doi for a discussion in depth of this idea.

[6]I noted an example of this practice in front of a supermarket in Kyoto. A child about age 3, had apparently taken some candy from the supermarket. The mother got on her bicycle, the child's seat empty, and rode away with the child chasing her on foot, screaming and apprently in a panic. The mother rode the bike just fast enough so that the child could not catch her. The child running as fast as he could, cried and called after her. About 100 meters from the store the mother stopped and spoke to the child, at which point the child started running happily back to the store, where he returned the candy. The mother then permitted the child to get on his customary seat on the bicycle and they left, the child happily reunited with the mother. It is of interest that my Japanese colleagures, when being told this incident, inquired whether this wasn't the way that children were nurtured in the U.S., and were surprised to learn that this is not the case. Since returning to the U.S. (where this paper was revised), I also observed the reverse situation to the one noted in Kyoto. In a park in Cambridge, a mohter dressed in jogging clothes and a three-year old similarly attired were in the park. The mother attempted to get the child to jog along with her. Failing this, she decided to jog ahead and leave the child, hoping the child would pursue her. However, on turning around to see if the child was following, she observed that the child was waving good-bye and seemed entirely unconcerned at the mother's leaving her.

[7]See Section II below on incomplete employment contracts. See also Leibenstein [18] for a fuller treatment of this phenomenon.

[8]This point was made by the production manager of a large Japanese company who had spent three years at a similar company in the U.S.

[9]See Takezawa and Whitehill [40] pp.69, 113, and 129.

[10]Ibid.

[11]See Atkinson and Birch [2], see also Broadbent [6], for a detailed treatment of many aspects of this phenomenon.

[12]See McMillan [24] for a survey of the free rider literature.

[13]Rapoport [35] contains a fairly full treatment of the general problem. See

chapter 3.

[14]Aoki [1] chapter 11.

[15]See the paper by Ishikawa for an interesting treatment of the consequences of the emulation of effort levels.

[16]See New York Times, October 13, 1981, pg. D-1.

[17]The study by C.F. Pratten contains a number of examples of this sort.

[18]See the analysis by Ishikawa for somewhat similar ideas.

[19]See the article by Hideo Matsuoka, Mainichi Daily News, June 29, 1982. The paper by Shimada [38] pp.9-10, makes a similar point.

[20]See Kagono, et. al. [16].

[21]See Nakamura [26] pp.128, and 258-9, and Patrick [33] especially pp.250-4. A recent article in New York Times Magazine (November 14, 1982), pp.79 ff., refers to a study by James H. Harbor which indicates that after taking into account the higher pay of U.S. workers the Japanese still are able to produce cars similar to their most efficient American counterpart (GM) at a cost of something like $1700 less. This probably involves something like a 35-45% lower cost over the American cost figure for the small car.

REFERENCES

[1] Aoki, M., The Cooperative Game Theory of the Firm, Chapter 11, Unpublished.

[2] Atkinson, J.W., and Birch, O., Introduction to Motivation, Van Nostrand, New York, 1978.

[3] Aumann, R.J., "Survey of Repeated Games," Essays in Game Theory, Wissenschafts-verlag, Mannheim, 1981.

[4] Befu, Harumi, Japan: An Authoropological Introduction, Charles E. Tuttle, Tokyo, 1971.

[5] Benedict, Ruth, The Chrysanthemun and the Sword, Houghton, Mifflin, Boston, 1946.

[6] Broadbent, D.E., Decision and Stress, Academic Press, London, 1971.

[7] Chammah, A., and Rapoport, A., Prisoner's Dilemma, University of Michigan Press, Ann Arbor, 1965.

[8] Clark, Rodney, The Japanese Company, Yale University Press, New Haven, 1979.

[9] Cole, Robert, Work, Mobility, and Participation, University of California Press, Berkeley, 1979.

[10] Doi, Takao, The Anatomy of Dependence, Kodansha International Company, Tokyo, 1971.

[11] Dore, Ronald, British Factory - Japanese Factory, University of California

Press, 1973.

[12] Hanami, Tadashi, Labor Relation in Japan Today, Kodansha International
Company, Tokyo, 1981.

[13] Howard, Nigel, Paradoxes of Rationality, M.I.T. Press, Cambridge, no date
(probably 1971).

[14] Ishikawa, Tsuneo, "The Emulation Effect as a Determinant of Work Motivation,"
Published in Japanese, Keizaigaku Ronshu, Vol.47, No.1, April, 1981. English
Version made available by Prof. Ishikawa.

[15] Iwata, Ryushi, Gendai Nippon no Keiei Fudo, (Management Climate in Today's
Japan), Nippon Keizai Shinbunsha, Tokyo, 1978.

[16] Kagono, T., Nonaka, I., Okumura, A., Sakakibara, K., Komatsu, Y., Sakashita,
A., "Mechanistic Vs. Organic Management Systems: A Comparative Study of Adaptive
Patterns of U.S. and Japanese Firms," The Annals of the School of Business
Administration, Kobe University, No.25, 1981.

[17] Koike, K., "Japanese Workers in Large Firms," Keizai Kagaku, Vol.26, Dec.,
1978.

[18] Leibenstein, H., Beyond Economic Man, Harvard University Press, Cambrigde,
1976.

[19] Leibenstein, H., "On Bulls-Eye-Painting Economics," Journal of Post Keynesian
Economics, Vol.4, No.3, 1982.

[20] Leibenstein, H., "The Prisoner's Dilemma in the Invisible Hand: An Analysis
of Intrafirm Productivity," American Economic Review, Vol.71, No.5, May, 1982.

[21] Lewis, D., Convention: A Philosophical Study, Harvard University Press,
Cambridge, 1969.

[22] Marsh, R.M., and Mannari, H., Modernization of the Japanese Factory, Princeton
University Press, Princeton, 1976.

[23] Maruo, Naomi, "The Development of the Welfare State in Japan," Unpublished
paper, 1982.

[24] McMillan, J., "The Free Rider Problem: A Survey," The Economic Record, Vol.55,
(1979), pp.95-107.

[25] Nakagawa, K., Nipponteki Keiei (Japanese Management), Nippon Keiei Shinposha,
Tokyo, 1977.

[26] Nakamura, Takafusa, The Postwar Japanese Economy, University of Tokyo Press,
Tokyo, 1981.

[27] Nakane, Chie, Japanese Society, Penguin Books, London, 1973.

[28] Odagiri, H., "Antineoclassical Management Motivation in a Neoclassical Economy:
A Model of Economic Growth and Japan's Experience," Kyklos, Vol. 35, 1982.

[29] Odaka, Kunio, Towards Industrial Democracy, Management and Workers in Modern
Japan, Harvard University Press, Cambridge, 1975.

[30] Okuno, M., "Wage System as a Work Incentive," Unpublished Paper, March, 1982.

[31] Ozaki, Robert, The Japanese: A Cultural Portrait, C.E. Tuttle, Tokyo, 1978.

[32] Pascale, R.T., and Athos, A.G., The Art of Japanese Management, Senior and Schuster, New York, 1981.

[33] Patrick, H., "The Feature of the Japanese Economy: Output and Labor Productivity," Journal of Japanese Studies, Vol.3, No.2, Summer, 1977.

[34] Pratten, C.F., Labor Productivity Differentials Within International Companies, Cambridge University Press, 1976.

[35] Rapoport, A., N-Person Game Theory, University of Michigan Press, Ann Arbor, 1970.

[36] Schelling, T.S., The Strategy of Conflict, Oxford University Press, Oxford, 1960.

[37] Schotter, A., Economic Theory of Social Institutions, Cambridge University Press, Cambridge, 1981.

[38] Shimada, H., "Perceptions and Reality of Japanese Industrial Relations," M.I.T. Conference, May, 22, 1982. (Unpublished)

[39] Simon, H.A., "Rationality as Process and as Product of Thought," American Economic Review, Vol.68, No.2, May, 1978.

[40] Takazawa, S., and Whitehill, A.M., Work Ways, Japan and America, The Japan Institute of Labor, Tokyo, 1981.

[41] Ullman-Marglit, E., The Emergence of Norms, Oxford University Press, New York, 1977.

[42] Vogel, Ezra F.(ed.), Modern Japaneses Organization and Decision Making, University of California Press, Berkeley, 1975.

[43] Vogel, Ezra F., Japan as Number One, Harper and Row, New York, 1979.

THE ECONOMIC ANALYSIS OF THE JAPANESE FIRM
M. Aoki (editor)
© Elsevier Science Publishers B.V. (North-Holland), 1984

# RESHUFFLING FIRMS FOR TECHNOLOGY?:
# AN AGGREGATE TIME-SERIES ANALYSIS OF B. KLEIN'S "DYNAMIC EFFICIENCY"

TAIZO YAKUSHIJI

## 1. INTRODUCTION: "DYNAMIC EFFICIENCY" VS. "X-EFFICIENCY"

This paper attempts to elucidate the causal links among the external competitive environment, a firm's intramural behavior, and technological yields for all manufacturing industries, the auto industry and the steel industry in Japan for the period from 1956 through 1979.

The present research treats the subject entity, that is, the process to yield new technological outputs, as a system composed of three distinct sets of environment, namely 1) the input environment, 2) the system state environment and 3) the output environment. For this system, our research tests the applicability of Burton Klein's hypothesis that a new external market change (input environment) can be quickly fed-back into managerial decisions in order to plan for organizational changes, manpower allocations, etc. (system state environment) in an attempt to gain market competitiveness by yielding new technological breakthroughs (output environment).

Burton Klein[1] contends that the recent losses in US productivity, which started in the late 1960s, is primarily due to decreases in the market activities. Klein believes that managers are increasingly becoming hesitant at "gambling," namely at risk-taking by introducing new technologically innovative products. According to Klein, such market losses are aggravated by the barriers preventing firms from entering the market, mergers, the institutional difficulties of acquiring capital for R&D and equipment investment. These situations are defined by Klein as the loss of "dynamic efficiency." Here, "dynamic efficiency," means the efficiency of management to feedback market conditions into management policies which eventually lead to the introduction of new products. Obviously, in his argument of dynamic efficiency, Klein focused only on technology developed at the firm level and not on the general conditions of managerial success. In so doing, he stresses that market uncertainty is the only source of technological innovations for firms. According to him, uncertainty forces managers to contemplate technological opportunities no matter how financially difficult. He continued to say that in a competitive market any effort to nullify this uncertainty would lead to business failure. In other words, a stable as well as conservative move by firms would deteriorate their technological basis. One basis for Klein's thesis is his long-time observation of US firms.

Interestingly enough, Klein's view is counter-intuitive. He

places more emphasis on market openness and managerial ability to
quickly respond to market information than on the firms direct
technological efforts such as R&D investment, the size of firm and
the firm's financial status.  Furthermore, what is more important
for firms to be technologically innovative is not cost-benefit
consciousness, but gambling on the future benefits of an initially
costly innovative ("fluid" in W. Abernathy's sense[2]) product into a
well-accepted ("specific" also in W. Abernathy's sense[2]) commodity.
Klein showed many examples to demonstrate that many technologically
innovative products were initially more expensive than the existing
products.  Based on such empirical evidence, Klein even states that
technological leaps come from irrational decisions.  Thus, the role
of managers is of prime importance because they have to screen and
support those irrational ideas which may be beneficial within an
organization which is dominated by rationalism.

Klein's support for a firm's occasional irrational behavior to
promote technological innovation rather than to increase a firm's
cost-benefit efficiency seems to be counter to Leibenstein's so-
called X-efficiency.[3]  The X-efficiency is the efficiency of
producing a given output with fewer inputs.  That is, the
difference between the conceivable output and the actual output
given the same set of inputs.

Although Klein admits that dynamic efficiency is similar to
Leibenstein's X-efficiency, he stipulates several sharp
distinctions as well:

> However, while Leibenstein agrees that competition plays an
> indispensable role in promoting dynamic efficiency, he does
> not discuss what kind of behavior is involved in promoting
> dynamic efficiency, nor how it differs from that involved in
> promoting dynamic efficiency......The key idea in static
> efficiency is to make good use of existing knowledge.  As Adam
> Smith long ago pointed out in his famous discussion of a pin
> mill, the organizational principle in static efficiency is
> specialization; that is, larger tasks are broken down into
> smaller and smaller tasks.  The organizational corollary
> associated with static efficiency is not a firm with high
> degree of openness; on the contrary, the pursuit of static
> efficiency inevitably drives organizations to a lower and
> lower degree of openness......By contrast, dynamic efficiency
> involves undertaking research and development and production
> activities to maximize the likelihood of good luck and
> minimize the consequences of bad luck.[4]

Whether or not the concept of Klein's dynamic efficiency is more
appropriate than that of Leibenstein's X-efficiency in the Japanese
context of the firm-level technology is truly subject to an
empirical test.  Both theories are for theoretical verification as
well as falsification, since both concepts involve quite a lot of
vague aspects.  We will discuss how to employ this empirical test
in the next section.


## 2. NEED FOR PERTURBATION-INFILTRATION APPROACH

There is a methodological difficulty to empirically test B.
Klein's thesis.  This is because we have to measure the impacts of

market uncertainty. However, how can we extract unpredictable and unobservable information from the complex system of mutual interactions? This section addresses itself to this problem. The argument to follow is based on a simple bivariate case.

In contrast to the conventional conjecture of a positive causality from productivity increase to the activation of technological innovation, Abernathy once proposed that the firm's internal efforts to increase productivity (by transferring production processes from the "specific" productive pattern from the "fluid" pattern, or, more simply, by cutting what is generally perceived "wasteful" activities) would deteriorate innovative activities.[5]  This implies that the productivity enhancement paradigm (or, firms' organizational philosophy) contradicts with the paradigm which places a major emphasis on technological innovation.  As already discussed above, this contradiction is somewhat similar to the trade-off between Leibenstein's "X-efficiency" and Klein's "dynamic efficiency."

Given Abernathy's so-called "productivity dilemma" hypothesis, the following negative feedback loop is drawn.  As conventionally thought, the process from innovation to production is assumed to be positive.

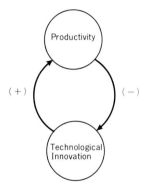

Figure X-1  Feedback between Productivity
and Technological Innovation

The diagram above illustrates that, given an initial level of productivity, the cyclical dynamics through productivity and innovation runs spontaneously.  By spontaneously, we mean that unless management decisions are made to act against the fixed rule (i.e., system structure), the levels of productivity and technological innovation are automatically and successively determined as long as the system runs.  The structure of such a fixed rule is established because the disturbances for both productivity and technological innovation are negligible.[6]

However, more realistically, perturbations are continuously supplied into this system.  Management decisions to change

production equipment or QC circle activities which eventually lead
to a change in productivity are examples of these activities.
Sometimes, perturbations create abrupt achievements of innovation
or failures due to a participation or withdrawl of a very bright
researcher from a particular R&D project.

Given these disturbances, a different[7] diagram of the system is
drawn with the extent to which the two variables, productivity and
innovation, are affected by the disturbances uniquely associated
with these variables (e.g., management decisions to perturbate
productivity or a new entry of able research personnel).  Figure X-
2 exemplifies the impacts (in terms of percentage) of these
disturbances on the two variables:

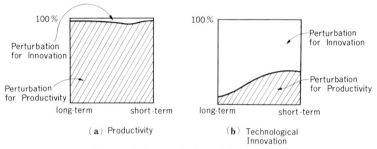

(a) Productivity            (b) Technological
                                Innovation

Figure X-2  Impacts by Perturbations

Figure X-2 (a) indicates that the variation in productivity is
mostly affected by its uniquely associated disturbances, and thus a
feedback from technological innovation is hardly supported.  On the
other hand, Figure X-2 (b) shows that, in the short run, the
variation in technological innovation is significantly affected by
the disturbances for productivity, but in the long run, its
variation is largely accounted for by the disturbances uniquely
associated with the innovative activity itself.  The realized
system chart for Figure X-2 is thus shown in Figure X-3.

In comparing Figure X-3 with Figure X-1, the salient difference
is that the closed feedback in Figure X-1 disappears in Figure X-3.
This implies that a link from innovation to productivity has been
cut off since the noise input for productivity overwhelms the
contribution of technological innovation to productivity.

If productivity is assumed to be a manipulatable variable and
innovation is a non-manipulatable one, the hypothetical result in
Figure X-2 means that management control of productivity is not
functioning well since productivity changes, not because of a
feedback signal from innovation, but because of its own
perturbations (which are, perhaps, a result of the manager's own
discretions).[8]  The above argument can be further elaborated for
the present study.

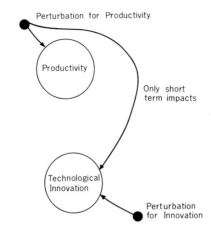

Figure X-3 One-way Influence by Productivity

Market changes contain two kinds of information, certainty and
uncertainty.  The former is the one which is systematically fedback
from some of the firm's internal variables.  The latter is the
exogenous perturbation that is uniquely associated with the market.
In examining Klein's thesis of dynamic efficiency, we are most
concerned with the treatment of uncertainty.  In other words,
rather than discarding "noise" for the normal identification of the
structural parameters, we pay greater attention to perturbation.
For the purpose of clarifying the argument, we are disregarding the
systematically fedback information.  That is, we formulate the
research problem into the following question: To what extent does
market perturbation "infiltrate" into the firm's internal
variables?  Are any of internal variables such as the decision
regarding the allocation of research personnel manipulatable?
Furthermore, if the variation of this variable is significantly
influenced by successively entering market perturbations, we may
postulate that the R&D manpower policy of the firm is made by
responding well to market perturbations.  These firms are in
Klein's terms, "dynamically efficient."  Methodologically, one may
use classical variance analysis for calculating an impact in terms
of the ratio of variances.  The system we are dealing with is
dynamic with multi-feedback loops, so that an ordinary variance
analysis based on a static model cannot meet our purpose.  In this
regard, the best possible approach is TIMSAC (Time-Series Analysis
and Control) developed by H. Akaike.[9]  TIMSAC gives the informaion
exactly as depicted in Figure X-2, by simultaneously identifying
the system structure of multi-feedback loops.  Rather than
variance, H. Akaike adopted the power spectrum density for
measuring the relative impact of one variable on another.  Detailed
discussion of TIMSAC is beyond the scope of this paper.  (See
APPENDIX for a more detailed description of the methodology.)

3. VARIABLES FOR TIME-SERIES ANALYSIS

Unless we employ interviews and directly ask managers for their
specific technological policies, we are eventually confined to an
aggregate level of observation.  As the first approach to this kind
of study, we tentatively chose the following variables: a) market
entropy, b) the ratio of research personnel to total employees, c)
equipment investment, d) firm's operative efficiency, and e) patent
applications.

MARKET ENTROPY: B. Klein believes that "dynamically-efficient"
managers feedback market information.  He does not specify what
kind of market information they perceive, but only that managers
must function in an uncertain market.  Examples of market
uncertainty might include such factors as the ease of new entry,
greater competitiveness of small firms compared to large firms due
to innovative products and changes in consumers demand.

Information-theoretically, uncertainty means the least probable
occurrence, such as high entropy.  A market with a lot of new
entries, high rates of success and failure, close competition in
introducing new products and sales shares contain greater entropy
than a stagnant market.

Figure X-4 shows the entropy changes over 24 years from 1956
through 1979.[10]  As is shown in Figure X-4, the entropy of all
manufacturing industries is the highest, followed by that of the
steel industry and next by that of the auto industry.  In the
1960s, there were many market changes in all manufacturing
industries, but since 1970, share distribution has become more
stabilized.  The highest entropy level of all manufacturing
industries coincides with the fact that this distributional pattern
does not show a skewed curve since there are many smaller firms.

In the steel industry, entropy has been fluctuating, but in the
early 1970s, the product share distribution shifted dramatically.
From the degree of fluctuation, the auto industry is the most
unstable industry because product shares have changed quite
radically.  Figure X-4 indicates that the steel industry is more
equally distributed and stable than the automobile industry.[11]

RESEARCHERS RATIO: Unless we employ microscopic observation for
some selected firms, it would be difficult to collect data for
organizational/personnel changes.  In this analysis, we adopted a
rate by examining the number of R&D personnel divided by total
employees (e.g., the researchers ratio).  In so doing, we assume
that changes in this ratio reflect managerial shifts in the
organization or manpower allocation in an attempt to respond to
market changes, though greater emphasis is on technological
innovation.

According to Figure X-5, the ratios of both the auto and steel
industries have grown.[12]  However, the ratio of all manufacturing
industries shows a logistic pattern which has an inflection point
in the early 1970s.  Since the numbers of both R&D personnel and
total employees are "stock" values, the inflection point indicates
that, during this period, the "flow" of researchers was the
strongest.  In other words, from the point of view of manufacturing
industries, the early 1970s are the most "lively" period when
managers increased R&D personnel.  If the auto and steel industries

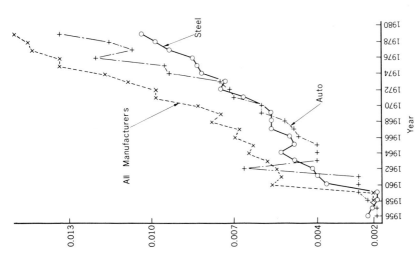

Source : Report on the Survey of R & D, Statistics Bureau,
Prime Minister's Office

Figure X-5   Researchers Ratio

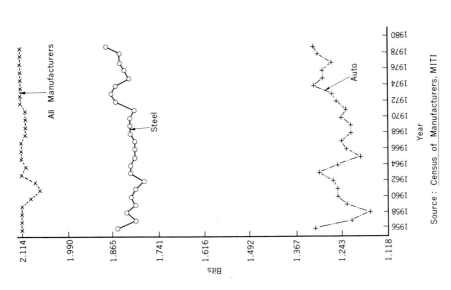

Source : Census of Manufacturers, MITI

Figure X-4   Market Entropy

follow the same logistic curve pattern, then these industries are now in the most "technologically-conscious" period.

EQUIPMENT INVESTMENT: For investment information, we adopted total equipment investment, as shown in Figure X-6.[13]  This figure shows an interesting structural change before and after 1966. Before 1966, all industries, the auto industry and the steel industry show a rapid-stagnation pattern.  Since 1966, the equipment investment of these industries grew quite rapidly, but oscillating in greater magnitude.  In particular, after the "oil shock" of 1973 and 1974, oscillation increased tremendously.

OPERATIVE EFFICIENCY: The most difficult as well as the most controversial task in the present research was the indexing of the firm's operative efficiency.  For example, B. Klein and H. Leibenstein proposed their own indices which contrasted with each other.  Some management economists proposed an index of management efficiency, which is analogous to the technological factor of the Cobb-Douglas production function.[14]  In additiion, one may conceive of labor productivity or the equipment productivity as a suitable index.  Rather than adopting a "ready-made" index, we created our own index for a firm's operative efficiency.[15]

The index that has been adopted is the "L-efficiency," which is the ratio of the productive performance over the cost performance. The productive performance is defined as the ratio of production outputs over inputs.  The cost performance is the ratio of the variable costs over the total costs.  This ratio is 1 plus the ratio of the fixed costs over the variable costs.  L-efficiency is deduced from an intuitive idea, though based on a system theoretic approach (see NOTES 15) in which the firm's operative efficiency would increase if 1) the output/input ratio increases, or 2) the relative weight of the fixed costs decreases.  Using simple mathematical operations, one may find that L-efficiency index represents an output quantity produced by a unit of fixed assets, normalized by the price of inputs.  Roughly, it is an index to indicate how efficiently a unit of production facility produces outputs.  One may have already have noticed that there would be some similarity between L-efficiency and the equipment productivity.  In fact, when we assume that there is no inventory cost (i.e., production equals to total sales), these two indices behave somewhat analogously.[16]

Now, Figures X-7, 8 and 9 respectively show the production ratios, the cost ratios and L-efficiency changes.[17]  Figure X-7 shows the productive ratios for three cases.  Until 1971, the production ratios of all three cases declined and then grew quite rapidly, forming a concave pattern.  Interestingly, the steel industry was affected by the oil-shock immediately, but the auto industy followed two years later having the same receptive pattern.

Figure X-8 shows the ratios of the variable costs over the total costs.  If this ratio is low, a firm's production is more input oriented in terms of cost shares.  On the other hand, if it is high, production is more equipment oriented.  Since the ratio contains the physical dimension of the number of equipment utilized relative to material inputs, or the transfer efficiency from the input costs to the total costs, the lower the ratio, the higher the cost efficiency.

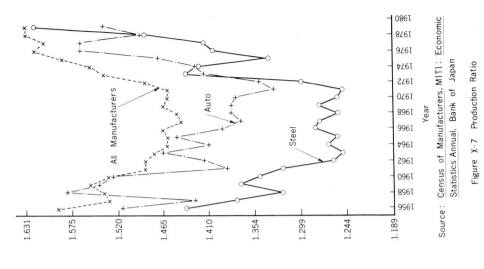

Source: Census of Manufacturers, MITI; Economic
Statistics Annual, Bank of Japan

Figure X-7 Production Ratio

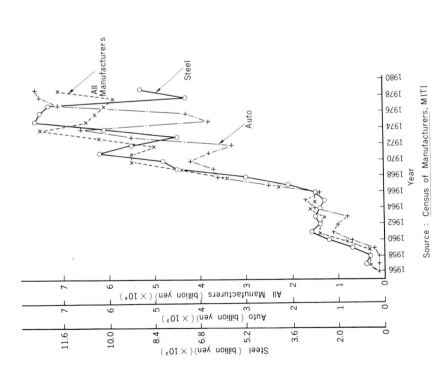

Source: Census of Manufacturers, MITI

Figure X-6 Equipment Investment

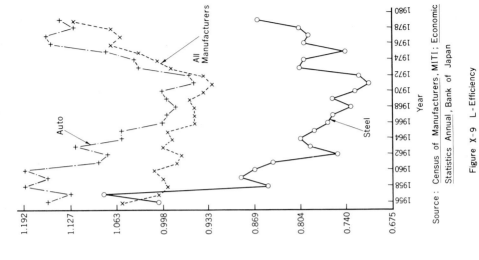

Source : Census of Manufacturers, MITI; Economic
Statistics Annual, Bank of Japan

Figure X-9    L-Efficiency

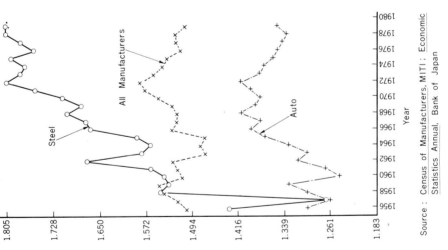

Source : Census of Manufacturers, MITI ; Economic
Statistics Annual, Bank of Japan

Figure X-8    Cost Ratio

Figure X-8 provides the following implications.  The auto industry
has been the most cost-efficient and the steel industry has been
the least cost-efficient, indicating that the steel industry is
more equipment oriented.  Other industries are located in between
these two industries.  All three curves increased up to 1972, and
then declined thereafter.  These declining trends started in 1973
as a result of increases in material prices due to the oil-shock.
Perhaps, the question of whether a price increase automatically
enhances cost efficiency should be asked.  We believe it does.
Since price increases are determined externally and have nothing to
do with a firm's management capability, the lower ratio indicates
that firms could avoid an increase in fixed costs, so that the
cost-efficiency of firms is increased.

Given these production and cost ratios, Figure X-9 shows the
time-series changes of L-efficiency.  As is shown, the auto
industry has the highest L-efficiency, and the steel industry has
the lowest.  All of the curves resemble those for the production
ratios (i.e., forming a concave pattern).  Until 1972 or 1973, the
L-efficiencies of all cases declined, and have since gone up
simultaneously.  The steel industry suffered from a severe decline
immediately after the oil-shock, but resumed a higher level soon.

PATENT APPLICATIONS: As discussed already, this variable was
chosen to indicate the firm's technological performance.  Though
patent applications are not always the best indicator of productive
technology, it nevertheless reflects a firm's technological R&D
level.

Figure X-10 shows a distinct pattern (i.e., a logistic curve) in
which an inflection point is in the mid-1960s.[18]  For example, as
far as the auto industry is concerned, the inflection period is
either 1963 or 1964.  For the steel industry, this period occurs
one or two years later.  Applying the same logic as above, the
firm's innovative activities are the most active during these
inflection periods.

4.  "TIMSAC" RESULTS

The results of the analysis are shown in Figures X-11 through X-
13 and Tables X-1 and X-2.  TIMSAC first estimated the AR
(autoregressive) structure with cross covariances for five
variables.[19]  The lag order of this AR structure was optimally
determined to be 1.[20]  The fitness of the estimated AR parameters
was determined by checking the degree of mutual independence of the
estimation error series (i.e., forecast error called the
"innovation series") for two variables.  If one error series is
highly correlated with the other, the selection of variables is
inappropriate, indicating that there might be some missing
variables that might explain the not-yet-explained part of these
error series.  The lack of serious correlations in Table X-1
indicates that we have successfully identified the model structure.

The estimated AR structure of lag 1 is now shown in Table X-2.[21]
As discussed in Section 2, the structural relationship among five
variables in Table X-2 is established unless there are strong
exogenous perturbations entering this system.  That is, if there is
a perturbation, the variables would not behave as prescribed by

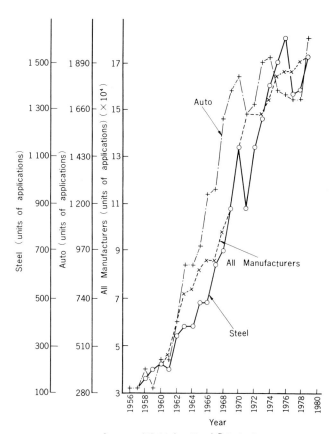

Source : <u>Official Gazette of Patents</u>, Patent Office

Figure X-10　Patent Applications

Table X-1   Normalized Prediction Error Correlations    Case 1: All Manufacturers
2: Auto Industry
3: Steel Industry

| | | Market Entropy | Researchers Ratios | Equipment Investment | L-Efficiency | Patent Applications |
|---|---|---|---|---|---|---|
| Researchers Ratios | (1) | -.068 | 1 | | | |
| | (2) | .404 | 1 | | | |
| | (3) | -.277 | 1 | | | |
| Equipment Investment | (1) | -.169 | -.128 | 1 | | |
| | (2) | .149 | -.063 | 1 | | |
| | (3) | .222 | -.093 | 1 | | |
| L-Efficiency | (1) | .511 | .445 | .089 | 1 | |
| | (2) | .148 | .412 | .124 | 1 | |
| | (3) | -.559 | .287 | .028 | 1 | |
| Patent Applications | (1) | .440 | -.094 | .289 | .383 | 1 |
| | (2) | -.060 | -.232 | .405 | -.279 | 1 |
| | (3) | .001 | -.274 | .442 | .391 | 1 |

Table X-2 First-Order Impulse Response (Estimated Structure of Lag 1)

| | | Market Entropy | Researchers Ratios | Equipment Investment | L-Efficiency | Patent Applications |
|---|---|---|---|---|---|---|
| Market Entropy | (1) | .674 | .0607 | .0170 | -.115 | .0217 |
| | (2) | .112 | .0518 | .485 | -.0230 | -5.08 |
| | (3) | .715 | -.0898 | -.714 | -.0788 | -1.62 |
| Researchers Ratios | (1) | -1.36 | .181 | .0930 | .912 | .183 |
| | (2) | .617 | .201 | 1.89 | .0255 | -33.4 |
| | (3) | -.00277 | .377 | .226 | -.0143 | -6.91 |
| Equipment Investment | (1) | -.0959 | -.278 | .606 | -.00564 | .0150 |
| | (2) | -.0162 | -.0113 | .105 | .0427 | .234 |
| | (3) | .195 | -.0609 | .0595 | .0671 | 8.98 |
| L-Efficiency | (1) | .708 | .180 | -.00799 | .309 | .0350 |
| | (2) | -.0211 | .158 | -.465 | .393 | -10.4 |
| | (3) | -1.24 | .316 | -.350 | -.328 | 23.1 |
| Patent Applications | (1) | 1.11 | .0292 | .521 | -.00467 | -.296 |
| | (2) | -.00716 | .00250 | .0217 | -.00172 | .344 |
| | (3) | .00346 | -.00415 | .0138 | .00468 | .244 |
| R-square | (1) | .518 | .977 | .959 | .623 | .983 |
| | (2) | .371 | .939 | .905 | .696 | .977 |
| | (3) | .875 | .972 | .956 | .725 | .959 |

Table X-2. However, recognizing this limitation, the following two
implications are drawn from Table X-2. First, the diagonal
elements indicate the AR parts. So that, if these values are close
to 1, the respective variable would be more exogenously-created (it
was accumulated with their own past perturbations). Second, if one
of three values in each cell of Table X-2 is exceedingly larger
than the rest, it implies that the impact of this variable would be
relatively large for the corresponding case. However, since the
variation and magnitude in the data sets of the three cases we
examined differed, we need care in drawing the above implications.
Any causal interpretations from Table X-2 are again  subject to the
assumption of no substantial exogenous perturbations.

By transforming the AR structure in Table X-2 into the frequency
response structure, and by transforming its parameter matrix into a
transfer function form,[22] we obtain the input-output structure in
terms of the power spectrum density, where inputs correspond to the
power spectrum densities of perturbations. This input-output
structure indicates to which variables perturbation impacts were
made. That is, we obtained the type of informaion as found in
Figure X-2. Based on the large spectrum frequencies, Figures X-11
through X-13 pick only the short-term (i.e., the high frequency
spectrum) and the long-term (i.e., the low frequency spectrum)
impacts for easy visualization.[23]  In these figures, the bold lines
are for both the short- and long-term impacts; the light lines for
either of the short- or long-term impacts; and the dotted lines for
the weak impacts for both the short- and long impacts. Following
are the implications drawn from these figures.

For all manufacturers, one may extract the following observations
from Figure X-11. The market perturbations made considerable
impacts on the researchers ratio. In other words, R&D manpower
policy was responding well to the market's uncertainty. Thus,
Japanese manufacturing industries have generally been "dynamically
efficient." The market perturbations also affected L-efficiency
and the L-efficiency's perturbations in turn affected the
researchers ratio. According to Table X-2, the impact of market
entropy on the researchers ratio was negative, while the impact on
the L-efficiency was negative. This may indicate that Japanese
industries tried to increase the operative efficiency by relocating
R&D manpower to productive lines. However, the positive linkage
from market entropy to the researchers ratio through L-efficiency
and the negative linkage from the market to the researchers ratio
indicate the possible existence of a conflict in R&D manpower
allocation policy.

Equipment investment policy was responding well to changes in R&D
manpower policy. Discretionary investment policy has affected
changes in patent applications. That is, as long as Japanese
manufacturing industries are macroscopically concerned, the results
corroborate the hypothesis that the "dynamically efficient" firms
respond well to market uncertainty and eventually alter R&D
activities. This is also substantiated by the fact that market
entropy is an exogenous variable (no significant incoming arrows),
and that the patent applications variable is an endogenous one (no
substantial outgoing arrows), and that there are two routes from
market entropy to patent applications. In particular, the short-
term exogenouity and the long-term endogenouity of the patent
applications reflect the reality of innovative activities. That
is, innovation might occur independently and randomly in the short

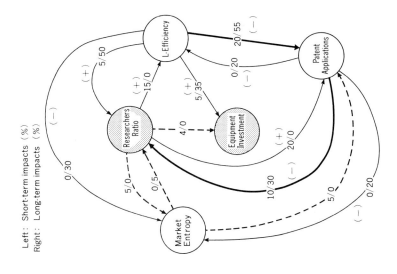

Left: Short-term impacts (%)
Right: Long-term impacts (%)

Figure X-12 Impacts by Perturbations: <u>Auto Industry</u>

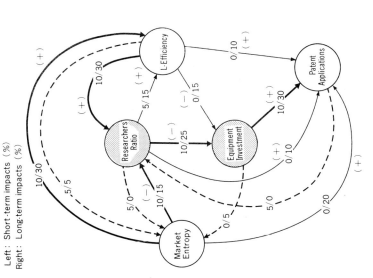

Left: Short-term impacts (%)
Right: Long-term impacts (%)

Figure X-11 Impacts by Perturbations: <u>All Manufacturers</u>

run, but be affected by other known causes in the long run.

For the case of the auto industry, Figure X-12 shows a somewhat
unique picture.  First, the market entropy is rather an endogenous
variable.  This variable is affected by two types of perturbations,
one for the patent applications, and another for L-efficiency but
only in the long run.  The fact that there is no substantial link
between market entropy to one of the firm's four internal variables
indicates that, as far as the auto industry is concerned, Klein's
dynamic efficiency was not established.  It can be said that the
Japanese auto industry has been internally driven in the sense that
firms have successively evolved to influence the market.  Second,
the auto industry's L-efficiency acted as exogenous variable, a
pivotal variable to influence patent applications, the equipment
investment (in the long run), and the researchers ratio (also in
the long run).  Third, R&D manpower policy had a good feedback
response to the perturbations for patent applications.  Fourth, in
general, the auto industry's internal organizations seemed to
establish good feedback interactions.  Fifth, equipment investment
was endogenously determined by L-efficiency in the long run.  That
is, equipment investment policy was sensitive to the change of the
firm's operative efficiency, probably due to process innovation.
Sixth, although the Japanese auto industry did not have "dynamic
efficiency" in Klein's sense, the industry has been very concerned
with operative efficiency.  This operative efficiency has been the
most important.  If our L-efficiency can be comparable to
Leibenstein's X-efficiency, we might say that Japanese auto
industry has been very X-efficiency-consious.  However, despite
Klein's argument that X-efficiency leads to static efficiency with
stalemated R&D activities, Figure X-12 clearly shows that the X-
efficient Japanese auto industry has been also actively changing its
organizational structure to influence R&D activities.  The short-
term impacts of R&D manpower policy on patent applications, and the
strong long-term impacts on R&D manpower policy by L-efficiency and
patent applications indicate that R&D manpower policy has been the
key to these activities.

In contrast, Figure X-13 shows a somehow opposite picture for the
steel industry.  The perturbations for market entropy did affect
firms' internal variable, but it was the equipment investment that
was sensitive to market uncertainty.  Second, as was in the case of
all manufacturers, L-efficiency was affected by market
perturbations.  However, Table X-2 indicates that the causality
between market entropy and L-efficiency was negative, while between
market entropy and equipment investment was positive.  This
suggests that the steel industry responded by increasing equipment
investment due to an unexpectedly large market changes, at the
expense of decreased operative efficiency.  Third, R&D manpower
policy behaved rather exogenously, implying that R&D manpower
policy in the steel industry was randomly made.  Fourth, patent
applications variable acted as an exogenous variable.  This is
striking difference from any of the previous two examples.  In the
Japanese steel industry, R&D activities were conducted especially
without affecting inter-firm interactions.  The uncertainty of R&D
performance always influenced equipment investment, L-efficiency
and even market entropy in the long run.

The diversification of R&D expenditures is another striking
difference between the auto industry and the steel industry (See
Figure X-14).  This figure indicates the very conservative emphasis

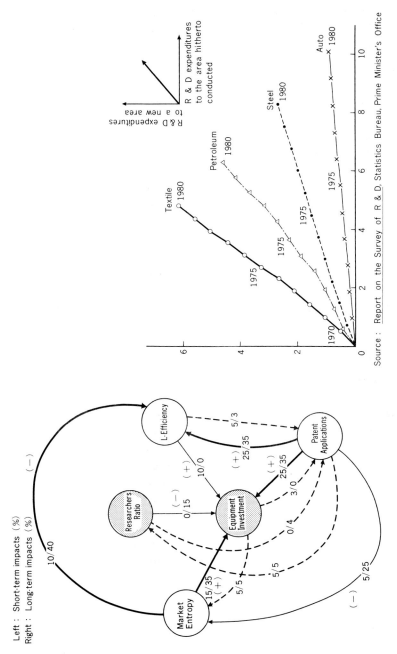

Source : Report on the Survey of R & D, Statistics Bureau, Prime Minister's Office

Figure X-14  Heterogeneous R & D Expenditures  1970-1980

Left :  Short-term impacts (%)
Right :  Long-term impacts (%)

Figure X-13  Impacts by Perturbations : Steel Industry

on operative efficiency by the auto industry.  In contrast, the
steel industry has been constantly diversifying R&D activities.[24]


5. CONCLUSION

One objective of this paper has been to test Klein's provocative
concept of "dynamic efficiency."  A second objective has been to
solve the methodological problems by applying H. Akaike's causal
identification technique (called TIMSAC).  The success or failure
of our approach is subject to the relevancy of our
conceptualization of Klein's market uncertainty into the concept of
perturbations.  This relevancy question is more serious than the
data constraints of the present research.  Such data constraints
are essentially technical problems that can eventually be solved in
future.  Thus, we chose methodological rigour at the expense of
data purity in recognizing that scientific research should avoid
impressionistic non-statistical inference, although practical
applicability can be lost if we are too strict.  Given this basic
epistemological stance, we can now summarize the results below.

Generally, Japanese manufacturing industries have been
dynamically efficient.  Their R&D activities have been influenced
by the firm's dynamic efficiency.  On the other hand, the Japanese
auto industry seems to have been what Harvey Leibenstein calls X-
efficient.  It has been very operative-efficiency-conscious.
However, this X-efficient auto industry has active R&D activities,
perhaps because it has a lot of mutual interactions within internal
organizations (i.e., reshuffling firms).  This finding is a
counter-argument to Klein's thesis, which suggests that an X-
inefficient firm can be technologically innovative.  The validity
of this counter-argument needs further investigation at the
microscopic level of the auto firm.  The Japanese steel industry
has also been dynamically efficient due mainly to equipment
investment policy.  However, the dynamic efficient steel industry
has not effectively perturbated R&D activities.  Hence, the steel
and auto cases are in conspicuous contrast with each other.

APPENDIX

TIMSAC: ITS BASIC IDEA

(A) Granger/Sims/Pierce/Haugh's Approaches to Causality

C. Granger[25] defined causality in such a way that a variable X causes another variable Y if the present value of Y is explained more precisely with the past values of X than without them.

Given this Grangerian causality, two practical approaches were introuduced to statistically test causal relations. The first was the so-called Sims' Test.[26] The second approach is the one proposed by D. Pierce[27] and L. Haugh.[28]

C. Sims' approach is essentially the significance test of the regression parameters of the following dynamic AR model:

$$A(B)x(t) + B(B)y(t) = u(t) \qquad (1)$$

where B in parentheses is the lag operator and $u(t)$ is assumed as white.

By pointing out the practical difficulties of Sims' Test due to the overestimation problems of the parameters $A(B)$ and $B(B)$, D. Pierce and L. Haugh introduced a different approach. They focus on, rather than the above bivariate AR model, the following two distinct univariate time series:

$$F(B)x(t) = u(t) \qquad (2)$$

$$G(B)y(t) = v(t) \qquad (3)$$

where $u(t)$ and $v(t)$ are also independent white noise processes. Given these models, Pierce and Haugh try to find the Grangerian causality by checking the following cross correlation function of the estimated noise processes, namely innovation series:

$$R(x,y:k) = (E(u(t),v(t-k))/(E(u(t))E(v(t)))) \qquad (4)$$

Pierce and Haugh's rationale for taking such a correlation stems from the intuitive notion that since y causes x only if after explaining whatever of $y(t)$ that can be explained on the basis of its own past history, some more should remain to be explained by the past history of x. Therefore, $u(t)$ and $v(t)$ should contain those not-yet-explained remaining parts. If this is true, the above correlation function over the lags k's should be other than zero.

Though Pierce and Haugh's approach is practically better than Sims' Test, it requires laborious work to compute each correlation function over many k's and then to employ many null hypothesis tests for all of R's obtained.

(B) Akaike's Approach (TIMSAC)

H. Akaike introduced, quite independently of the above-mentioned statisticians' work, a different and unique approach based on the orthodox control theory. Akaike's approach consists of two processes. The first process is to formulate a measure of causality under a realistic causal model. In this process, the causality measure is defined in terms of the spectral density of a causing input variable within the spectral density of an effect variable. The second process is to guarantee that this same measure can be calculated from a data-fitting model.

i) The First Process
Consider the multi-variate dynamic linear discrete causal model, of which a simple
bivariate case is:

$$x(t) = A(B)x(t) + B(B)y(t) + u(t) \qquad\qquad (5)$$

$$y(t) = C(B)x(t) + D(B)y(t) + v(t) \qquad\qquad (6)$$

where u(t) and v(t) are "exogenous" input noise processes, and "not" assumed as
white. Thus, they are the actual disturbances that drive the system to generate
values in x(t) and y(t). In other words, without them, the system remains
quiescence. In this regard, u(t) and v(t) can be called the x's "unique" noise
and the y's "unique" noise, respectively.

Once the unique inputs for the respective variables were established, the
spectral density of each variable is easily formulated in the following input-
output Fourier transfer functions:

$$X(f) = W(f)U(f) \qquad\qquad (7)$$

where the column vector $X(f)$ contains the Fourier transforms of x(t) and y(t),
the 2x2 matrix $W(f)$ is the inverse of the matrix $(I-H(f))$ of which $H(f)$ is filled
with the combinations of the parameters in Equations (5) and (6), and the column
vector $U(f)$ contains the Fourier transforms of the exogenous inputs u(t) and v(t).
Given Equations (7), the power spectral density function of $X(f)$ can be obtained
by:

$$P(X:f) = W(f)P(U:f) \qquad\qquad (8)$$

where the column vector $P(X:f)$ contains x's and y's power spectral densities
denoted as p(x:f), p(y:f), and the column vector $P(U:f)$ contains the respective
power spectral densities denoted as p(u:f), p(v:f) for u and v. If we denote the
elements of $W(f)$ as w(1,1:f), w(1,2:f), w(2,1:f), w(2,2:f), the relative power
contributions (RPC) of p(v:f), for example, is:

$$r(x,v:f) = w(1,2:f)p(v:f)/p(x:f), \qquad\qquad (9)$$

and this is exactly the information regarding how much contributions are made by
v(t) to the changes in x(t). Since v(t) is the exogenous cause uniquely
associated with y(t), Equation (9) indicates how much x is caused by y on a
"frequency scale."

ii) The Second Process
In practice, the calculation of r(x,v:f) requires the estimation of the system's
impulse response function (i.e., the system's parameters) as well as the
estimation of the noise inputs. Obviously, these estimations cannot be realized
since the noise processes u and v are not assumed as white. For this reason, we
consider the following data model:

$$X(t) = Z(B)X(t) + E(t) \qquad\qquad (10)$$

where X(t) contains x(t) and y(t), the parameter matrix contains the respective
parameters z(1,1:B), z(1,2:B), z(2,1:B), z(2,2:B), and the column vector E(t) is

filled with the "white" noise processes e(x:t) and e(y:t). Therefore, one can see that Z(B) partially contains the MA (moving-average) structures yielded from the whitening processes for the original input noise processes u, v. In other words, e(x:t), for example, is the whitening part remained in the autoregressive structure of u (which is mathematically proved as z(1,1:B)). Since Z(B) is different from the previously mentioned inverse Fourier transform of H(f), it cannot be substituted into Equation (9). However, if the cross-spectrum for e(x:t) and e(y:t) is zero for all frequencies (in other words, if e(x:t) and e(y:t) are not correlated each other for all lags), we can utilize Z(B) as discussed below.

Now, for a simple mathematical argument, let us express our data model in Equation (10) in the following form:

$$T(B)X(t) = E(t) \tag{11}$$

where T(B) is equivalent to I-Z(B). Multiplying Equation (11) by its transpose from the right side yields:

$$T(B)X(t)X(t)'T(B)' = E(t)E(t)'$$

$$T(B)R(X:k)T(B)' = S \tag{12}$$

where the matrix R(X:k) contains the cross-covariance functions of x and y for the lag k's. If e(x:t) and e(y:t) are uncorrelated each other, S is the diagonal matrix in which the on-diagonal elements are the variances for e(x:t) and e(y:t). Then, taking the Fourier transforms of Equation (12) and reordering the variables give:

$$M(X:f) = T(f) . S . (T(f) )' \tag{13}$$

Note that the spectral density function M(X:f) is the Fourier transform of the cross-covariance function R(X:k) and that S remains the same.

Equation (13) shows the important relation that allows us to calculate causality with data, since M(X:f) in this equation involves the previously mentioned column vector P(X:f) in Equation (8) in diagonal parts. That is, since S is a diagonal matrix with the variances of the white noise processes, m(1,1:f) in the (1,1) element of M(X:f) is the sum of the noise contributions, namely:

$$m(1,1:f) = |t(1,1:f)|^2 s(e(x:t)) + |t(1,2:f)|^2 s(e(y:t)) \tag{14}$$

where t(1,1:f) and t(1,2:f) are the (1,1) and (1,2) elements of T(f), and s(e(x:t)) and s(e(y:t)) are the variances of the white noise processes e(x:t) and e(y:t). This is equal to the denominator of Equation (9).

For the numerator of Equation (9), we simply take the second term of the left side of Equation (14). Hence, the relative power contribution by y to x is calculatable under the data model (10), namely:

$$r(x,y:f) = |t(1,2:f)|^2 s(e(y:t))/ m(1,1:f) \tag{15}$$

Then, we finally have achieved the measure of identifying the bivariate causality.

In comparing the previous Pierce/Haugh approach, Akaike's scheme has the two
salient features.  The first feature is in that Akaike's approach strictly sticks
to the spectral approach based on the orthodox causal model, and not on such a
converted model as that of Pierce and Haugh.  The uniqueness of this approach is
in fact to couple the frequency-domain analysis (i.e., the identification of
causality) with the time-domain analysis (i.e., the estimation of the frequency
transfer function T(f)).  The second feature lies in that though we have discussed
for the simple bivariate case, this approach can be applied for the multi-variate
feedback cases.  This latter feature can not be realized by Pierce and Haugh's
method.  But, for the bivariate case, if the both approaches are equally
efficient, the results by two different approaches must be the same under the same
set of data.


NOTES


* This research was partially supported by a grant from The Twenty-First
Century Foundation.  The author is grateful to Profs. Masahiko Aoki, Fumio Kodama,
Eisuke Sakakibara and Kazuo Ueda for their insightful comments on the earlier
versions of this paper.  He is also grateful to Messrs. Waichiro Hayashi, Shoji
Yoshitake and Minoru Fujihara for valuable assistance in editorial work,
computation and data gathering.


[1] B. Klein [1] and [2].  See: Chapter 3, pp.66-117 in [2].

[2] Abernathy [3].

[3] Leibenstein [4] and [5].

[4] B. Klein [2], p.81.

[5] Abernathy [3].  See, in particular, Chapters 1, 4 and 7.

[6] Technically, these disturbances are called "white noise" whose expected value
is zero.  The structure of such a fixed rule here means the parametrically
identified model, as a result of a variety of econometric methods under the
assumption that the noise inputs are all white.

[7] Mathematically, an AR (auto-regressive) model (e.g., $X = (P)(BX) + U$: B=lag
polynomial, U=noise vector) can be equivalently converted into an input-output
reduced form ($X = QU$: Q=inverse of I-PB).  Since U is a noise vector, Q-matrix
cannot be directly computed.  Instead, one may get the computation like Figure X-
2, by identifying P first, and next by Fourier-transforming it into a frequency-
response function.  As mentioned below, this is the approach taken by H. Akaike
for TIMSAC.

[8] The model we are dealing with is dynamic, so that one-way causation from
productivity to innovation does not mean that innovation is controlled by the
productivity policy.  It is merely influenced by productivity changes without
feeding back the previous level of innovation.

[9] Akaike [6] and [7].

[10] We adopted the following "average" entropy measure as the market uncertainty
at time t:

$$H(t) = - \sum_{i} p(i,t)\log p(i,t)$$

where $p(i,t)$ is a market share by sales for a firm "i" (or a group of firms in a particular category by, for example, firm size in terms of capital or the number of employees). Hence, $H(t)$ is a "scalar" value (bits) to differentiate a different distributional patterns. In so doing, we regard market conditon to be fedback by managers in terms of sales share, under the assumption that technological competition is more intensified by looking at competing firms' sales achievement. This entropy measure has several advantages: a) it incorporates the movement of firms entering into or exiting from a particular market. b) it gives information about both the degrees of concentration and competition even in a highly concentrated market. It is often said that the highly-concentrated Japanese firms are in fierce competition. But, the static measures like Gini's Coefficient or the Herfindahl Index cannot show this fact. However, our entropy measure is not almighty. It certainly has some disadvantages. Among those, the most serious one is in that it is a scalar value so that two different distributional patterns may have an identical entropy. But, this defect can be overcome by the recursive comparison of patterns over time since our main concern is in time changes of a particular pattern, and not in a cross-sectional comparison of one pattern with the other regardless of time. Entropy shown in Figure X-4 was calculated from a distributional pattern where the vertical axis. was for product output shares and the horizontal axis was for firm-group size. We grouped firms into 10 ranks by the size of employees: 4-9, 10-19, 20-29, 30-49, 50-99, 100-199, 200-299, 300-499, 500-999, over 1000 employees. The data source for calculating market entropy is: Census of Manufacturers (Report by Industries), MITI, 1956-1979. Perhaps, a more appropriate categorization would be one which selects companies to compete with each other in a focused particular market. However, practically impossibility precluded us from gathering these "share data" consecutively for 24 years since 1956, so that we adopted aggregare categorization, assuming that each category by the number of employee size would represent a cluster of companies with the same categorization.

[11] The magnitude of variation in Figure X-4 is very small, reflecting the nature of entropy. However, since we are concerned with the power spectrum density (the Fourier transform of the autocovariance function of a series), this small magnitude does not bother our structural estimation.

[12] Researchers are those defined by Statistics Bureau, Prime Minister's Office. Probably, managers would change R&D manpower by mobilizing engineers as temporal workforce, because the definition of researchers are somehow rigorous. Though we needed this supplemental research manpower as a good indicator for dynamic efficiency, we could not obtain those data for consecutively 24 years. Source: Report on the Survey of Research and Development, Statistics Bureau, Prime Minister's Office, 1956-1979.

[13] Source: Census of Manufacturers (Report by Industries), MITI, 1956-1979; Economic Statistics Annual, Statistics Department, The Bank of Japan, 1956-1979.

[14] For example, Hirofumi Itami proposed the management efficiency index M for the Cobb-Douglas functional analogy model:

$$lnY = lnM + (b)lnL + (1-b)lnK$$

where Y, L and K are the value added, the labor productivity and the equipment productivity, respectively. A simple mathematical operation yields:

$$lnM = (b)(\text{fixed assets per employee}) + lnK.$$

Therefore, Itami's management efficiency can be interpreted as being based on
equipment productivity weighted by an equipment-employee ratio which is also
deflated by a factor b.  To compare with our L-efficiency which is discussed
later, Itami's index takes the labor factor into a consideration, while we
regarded it as being absorbed in the equipment factor in recognition that the data
of tangible fixed assets included labor costs.  In fact, we believe that, in the
present era of highly automated production, the simple inclusion of the total
workforce into a production function might be somewhat misleading.  Though we did
not adopt in the present paper because of the similar results with our L-
efficiency, we tried to measure the changes of M by a standard Kalman Filter
technique for time-variant parameter estimation.  See: Itami [8].

[15]Given a block diagram below:

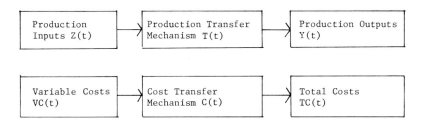

which shows the "transfer function" either from material input quantity to
product output quantity, or from the variable costs to the total costs, the two
different kinds of state variables, i.e., $T(t)$ and $C(t)$, are physical efficiency
(that is, technology in an ordinary sense) and the financial efficiency.  The
larger $T(t)$, the higher technological performance; and the smaller $C(t)$, the
higher financial management efficiency.  It would be a reasonable assumption that
$C(t)$ yields total costs as output, since evidence suffices to corroborate that
firms make every effort to lower the level of the total costs as a major
management achievement.  Note that $C(t)$ involves the information primarily as to
firms' policy regarding how much to incur for the fixed costs such as those for
manufacturing equipment, depreciation reserves, life-time-employed labor force (in
the Japanese context), etc.

Employing a state-space description of the system gives:

(OUTPUT EQUATION)

$$Y(t) = T(t)Z(t) \tag{1}$$

$$TC(t) = C(t)VC(t) \tag{2}$$

(STATE EQUATION)

$$T(t) = f(T(t-1), a) \tag{3}$$

$$C(t) = g(C(t-1), b) \tag{4}$$

where "a" indicates a set of causes to influence changes in the physical (or,
technological) efficiency, and "b" indicates a set of causes to influence the
financial efficiency.  Our primary purpose is to empirically identify the state
equation's functions "f" and "g" in a combined form, i.e., identification of the
combined state function "F" as defined below.

(5)

$$L(t) = T(t)/C(t) = F(T(t-1)/C(t-1), a$$

where L(t) connotes an indicator that takes into account both the physical (or technological) and financial efficiencies of a firm. That is, L(t) increases either when technological capability of a firm is enhanced or when it ameliorates financial constraints to lower the total costs to the variable costs ratio.

Perhaps one would notice that, conceptually, our L(t) is a straightforward interpretation of H. Leibenstein's "X-efficiency." His X-efficiency is, in essence, the transfer efficiency to yield a maximum production output with given firms' cost inbursement, i.e.,

$$Y(t) = h(X(t), TC(t)).$$                                              (6)

X-efficiency (X(t) in the above formulation) is very much static at a fixed point of time, while our L(t) is dynamic. Since X-efficiency appears in the relation between cost measures and physical output ones, it involves both physical technology (or, manufacturing technology in a more concrete sense) and management technology (if one would rather call management know-how a kind of technology); but they are not well differentiated. Our L(t) certainly articulates these two kinds of technology, though it is a simple linear combination of T(t) and C(t).

Some comments on the production function might be necessary, because Equations (1) and (3), in fact, represent a production process. A state-space interpretation of these equations is as follows: 1) the output equation (1) means that it is physical technology T(t) that can be transformed into product outputs, and material inputs Z(t) are regarded as a mere facilitator to activate such transformation. 2) the real inputs are those ( "a" in Equation (3)) that influence a drift of technology over time. On the other hand, the ordinary input-output-minded production functions as exemplified by the following Penrose type:

$$\ln Y(t) = \ln T(t) + p.\ln Z(t) + (other factors)$$                  (7)

are incomplete. The above equation does not show how T(t) would change, and furthermore it does not differentiate between T(t) and p (a diminishing return factor), of which the latter parameter should in fact contain some meanings of technology. For the reasons discussed above, it would be not so absurd if we employ a measure L(t) as a possible candidate for H. Leibenstein's X-Efficiency. However, for protecting his copyrighted term, let us call our L(t) as "Linear Efficiency," which may be assessed by a linear calculation with a given·set of Y(t), Z(t), VC(t) and TC(t).

[16] Our cost ratio is in essence the ratio of the fixed costs over the variable costs, i.e., our original cost ratio minus 1. Adopting this second cost ratio. L-efficiency becomes:

$$\frac{(\text{production output quantity})}{(\text{fixed assets})/(\text{the price of raw materials})}$$

That is, our L-efficiency, though using a slightly different cost ratio, is an indicator for the performance of a unit equipment normalized by the input price. On the other hand, the equipment productivity can be transformed as:

$$\frac{(\text{total sales quantity})(\text{price ratio of a product over raw material}) - 1}{(\text{tangible fixed assets})/(\text{the price of raw material})}$$

Therefore, one may notice, the slightly modified L-efficiency is comparable to the equipment productivity.

[17]The production ratios were calculated by:

total industrial outputs/the whole sale price index
raw material inputs/the consumer price index

Cost ratios were simply the ratios of the fixed costs over the variable costs plus one, where the fixed costs = the costs for sales and general administraive cost + one half of wages + expenses for manufacture + non operating expenses, and the variable costs = expenditures - the fixed costs.  Note that, since BOJ's data of tangible fixed assets include a half of wages, our L-efficiency does include the information of the labor productivity.  In other words, when we say about equipment, it is not always physical machine equipment, but it also contains manpower contributions.  Source: Eonomic Statistics Annual, The Bank of Japan, 1956-1979.

[18]Source: Official Gazette of Patents, Patent Office, 1956-1979.  We could not identify the patent data for the auto industry due to the categorization problem of the patent gazette.  So that, we adopted the data for the general transportation & machinery industry.

[19]In contrast to the ordinary description of a multivariate AR model in the time-domain, control engineers frequently use the algorithm for structural estimation based on the input-output transfer function of the cross-covariances, i.e., the frequency-domain.

[20]The order of lags was determined according to the AIC criterion developed by H. Akaike.  This criterion yields the optimal lag order by taking both the number of parameters to be estimated and the size of time-series data into account.

[21]As the figure of significance, Table X-2 adopted the three-digits level.  For structural estimation, the units of equipment investment and patent applications were 100 trillion yen and 0.1 million units, respectively.

[22]See NOTES 7.

[23]The short-term means the period for two years.  The long-term is, of course, the very long period, i.e., no cycle.

[24]Source: Report on the Survey of R&D, Statistics Bureau, Prime Minister's Office.  The data are available only for the period from 1970 through 1980.  Prof. Fumio Kodama and the author have been conducting the diversification project at Saitama University.

[25]Granger [9].

[26]Sims [10].

[27]Pierce [11].

[28]Haugh [12].

References

[1] Klein, Burton H., Dynamic Economics, Cambridge, Mass.: Harvard University Press, 1977.

[2] Klein, Burton H., "The Slowdown in Productivity Advances: A Dynamic Explanation, Christopher T. Hill and James M. Utterback, eds., Technological Innovation for a Dynamic Economy, New York: Pergamon Press, 1979, Chapter 3, pp.66-117.

[3] Abernathy, William J., The Productivity Dilemma, Baltimore: The Johns Hopkins University Press, 1978.

[4] Leibenstein, Harvey, "Allocative Efficiency vs. X-Efficiency," American Economic Review, June 1966, pp.392-415.

[5] Leibenstein, Harvey, General X-Efficiency Theory & Economic Development, Oxford University Press, 1978.

[6] Akaike, Hirotsugu, "On the statistical estimation of the frequency response function of a system having multiple input," Annals of The Institute of Statistical Mathematics, Vol. 17, 1965, pp. 185-210.

[7] Akaike, Hirotsugu, "On the use of a linear model for the identification of feedback systems, Annals of The Institute for Statistical Mathematics, Vol. 20, 1968, pp.425-439.

[8] Itami , Hirofumi, Nihonteki-keieiron-o-koete (Beyond the Conventional Theory of Japanese Management: A Japan-US Comparison of Management Efficiency, Tokyo: Toyo-Keizai-Shinpo-Sha, 1982, Chapter 2 (pp.14-56) (Japanese).

[9] Granger, C.W.J., "Investigating causal relations by economic models and cross-correlational methods," Econometrica, 37, pp.424-438.

[10] Sims, C.A., "Money, income and causality," American Economic Review, September, 1972.

[11] Pierce, D.A., "Relationships-and the lack thereof-between economic time series, with special reference to money and interest rates," Journal of the American Statistical Association, 72, 1977, pp.11-26.

[12] Haugh, L.D., "Checking the independence of two covariance-stationary time series: a univariate residual cross correlation approach," Journal of the American Statistical Association, 71, 1976, pp.378-385.

THE ECONOMIC ANALYSIS OF THE JAPANESE FIRM
M. Aoki (editor)
© Elsevier Science Publishers B.V. (North-Holland), 1984

# CORPORATE LOYALTY AND BONUS PAYMENTS: AN ANALYSIS OF WORK INCENTIVES IN JAPAN

MASAHIRO OKUNO

It is widely accepted that labor relations in Japan are unique in its institutional characteristics and that they provide some of the critical factors which explain her post-war economic performance. Among the well-known characteristics the most frequently mentioned are: seniority wages, seniority-based internal promotions, life-time employment, enterprise form of unionism, existence of loyalty and affection by employees toward the corporations (i.e., corporate loyalty), the bonus system and mandatory retirement. Although the importance of these characteristics have been recognized for a long time, recently there have been significant changes in the economic analyses of them.

First, some economists (notably Koike [8]) have forcibly argued that some of these alleged features of Japanese labor markets are not necessarily unique when compared internationally. In particular, Koike showed that wages and promotions in both U.S. and West Germany are as much (if not more) seniority based as they are in Japan. He also found that the effective lengths of employment in those two countries are often as long as those in Japan. Second, the volume of research literature that attempts to explain the unique features with economic logic instead of basing them on the cultural and historical pecuriarities of the country is rapidly growing. (See, for example, Okuno [6] for life-time employment, Aoki [1] for seniority-based wages and promotions, Ohashi [15] for mandatory retirement).

The current paper is a contribution to this second line of research on Japanese labor markets. We focus on an aspect that has hitherto been paid little attention in economics literature — that of worker's affective aspects. The existence of corporate loyalty among Japanese workers has been a source of constant amazement to western observers. It is probably one of the most critical factors which convinced many that Japanese labor markets (and her economy as well)

are culturally and fundamentally different from those of the western
counterparts.

In fact, unless we appeal to corporate loyalty, it seems rather difficult to explain some of the behaviors of Japanese workers.  For example: (1) the national average of paid vacation taken by each worker
(in September 1980) is 8.8 days although on the average workers are
entitled to take 14.4 days of paid vacation (i.e., only 61.3% of paid
vacation was actually taken)[1]; (2) among corporations that solicit
suggestions from their employees to increase productivity, employees
make suggestions and recommendations very actively (12.8 suggestions
per employee) although these corporations return only 1/30 of benefits accrued from these suggestions to the employees who made them[2];
(3) a senior worker frequently helps junior workers in the same work
line learn special skills needed for the job.  Yet on-the-job-training is not assigned as a part of the senior worker's job, nor does
he receive any extra reward for his efforts[3].

In this paper, we take the view that Japanese workers have corporate
loyalty because there is an incentive to do so.  More precisely, we
believe that workers employ these behaviors that are normally as-
cribed to corporate loyalty because it is in their own interest to
behave in these manner.  Our logic is rather simple.

A large part (about 26% in 1980)  of Japanese workers' income consists of what is called "bonus" payment.[4]  The Japanese bonus system
differs from that in Western countries.  Bonuses paid in Japanese
companies are paid to entire work force and its amount depends upon
the current performance of the corporation rather than individual
performances.[5]  It is also widely recognized that one of the deciding
factors of wage level in the collective bargaining in Japan is the
corporate performance (profit, growth rate, etc.) of the past year.
Hence, income of corporate employees does (or at least is believed
to, in worker's perception)  depend upon the corporate performance.
In this paper, we shall call such a system (or its perception)
output-related wage system, though it is worker's income and not wage
that depends upon corporate performance (output or value-added).  It
is apparent then  that an output-related wage system will create work
incentive.

Moreover, it is also widely recongnized that employment of an individual employee tends to span a significant number of years.[6]  True
that there is a controversy whether this life-time employment is a

unique feature in Japan or not, and whether such a long-term employment is a consequence of training cost, screening cost, and other
investment in human captial (Oi [16] and Becker [4]), or of risk-
shifting from workers to the firm (Azariades [2], Baily [3]), or of
creating work incentive (Okuno [17]), or of all of these and possibly other factors as well. But it is commonly believed as well that
most of Japanese workers have a perception that their employment is
secure for a considerable number of years unless something unforseen
happens. Given life-time (or long-term) labor contracts and an
output-related wage system, workers would attempt to allocate their
efforts optimally between those to increase firm's production directly and those to increase production indirectly (by improving
other worker's and capital productivity), and between those to improve firm's present performance and future performances. In other
words, workers employed in a firm that provides these institutional
features will attempt to invest optimally in the firm in order to
maximize his life-time benefit from the firm. Viewed this way,
helping other employees learn skills and/or making suggestions for
increasing productivity can be interpreted as investing in firm-specific capitals which take the form of accumulated knowledge of work
skills and stock of technical, organizational and managerial know-
hows.

Interpreting workers' attachment toward their employer by their de
facto investments in the firm in the form of firm-specific capital
has one weak link. Although output-related wage systems can play a
role in creating higher incentive and make the return to those investments positive, such an incentive is usually quite weak. By
working harder, helping other workers, etc., how large an improvement in corporate performance can each worker expect?

Output-related wage system (or sharecropping) creates a proper incentive (in an agency problem) if there is only one agent or if each
individual agent's output is observable. However, in large corporations where the number of employees is high, management-observation
of individual worker's performance becomes virtually non-existent.
As an extreme, suppose for example only the aggregate output is observable. Even if (aggregate) output-related wage system is introduced, unless wages are unreallistically sensitive to the corporate
performance,[7] individual workers normally find it optimal when they
work at a level lower than that which the management (principal) or

workers (agents) as a cooperative group would have chosen. This inefficiency (both from the viewpoint of the firm at large and from
the viewpoint of workers as a group) stems from the fact that, unless wages are extremely responsive to output, workers' gains derived from working less hard outweighs the return from working harder. This problem of strategic behavior (free-rider problem) is the
focus of the second part of this paper.

With an output-related wage system, a worker's strategic behavior
will damage group interest of the body of workers. Therefore, if
individual worker's effort choice is observable by his fellow workers (but not by the management), then fellow workers are apt to
apply pressures on a worker who is found behaving strategically.
Such a social act, such as ostracism (or Mura-hachibu), may eliminate strategic behavior especially when threat from being ostracized
is sufficiently large.

In sections 1 and 2, we shall demonstrate that an output-related
wage system will create a proper intertemporal work incentive when
workers have sufficient knowledge of technology and of the firm's
future plans. Sections 3 and 4 analyze the workers' behavior when
they face the threat of ostracism. We shall demonstrate that, when
ostracism is defined as a social act against players who violate a
social norm, workers will choose a cooperative outcome as non-cooperative Nash equilibrium. All the proofs of the results in Section
4 are gathered in the Appendix. Section 5 concludes the paper.

## 1.  INCENTIVE WAGES AND FIRM SPECIFIC CAPITAL

It is very important to create work incentives among workers when
supervising and monitoring their work performance is relatively expensive. In today's large corporations, organizational structure is
multi-layered and quite complex. Moreover, job requires special id-
iosyncratic skills. Consequently, it is difficult for management to
appraise employee's work performance. These and other factors contribute to create the problem of opportunism. That is, knowing that
management cannot appraise their work performance, workers often do
not work according to management's direction and thereby decrease
the corporation's profit. Provided that it is too costly to super-

vise and monitor, management must rely on mechanisms which would
generate work incentives automatically.

One such mechanism is an output-related wage system discussed in the
principal-agency relationship literature.  Although this wage system
is well-known, we first describe it in a simple framework to clarify
how it works.

Consider a firm which owns some means of production.  To produce
output, this firm must employ a single worker.  Let $\ell \epsilon R_+$ be the
worker's labor (or effort) choice.  The output $y \epsilon R_+$ is a function of
labor choice $\ell$ and production function is written as

$$y = f(\ell).$$

Assume for simplicity's sake that f is concave and monotonically increasing.  We also assume, for simplicity's sake, that the price of
output is always unity.

Potential employees are homogeneous and their utility function is a
function of wage income $w \epsilon R_+$ and labor choice $\ell$, $u(w, \ell)$.  Assume
that u is concave, increasing in w and decreasing in $\ell$.  Let $u_0$ be
the level of utility that potential employees can obtain by choosing
other employment opportunities.  Then assuming that the frim can nei-

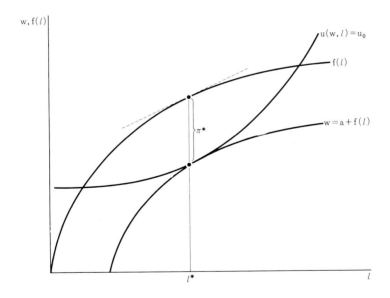

Figure XI-1

ther control nor observe $\ell$, the firm's problem is to choose a wage
function $W: R_+ \to R_+$ to

$$\text{maximize} \quad f(\ell) - W(f(\ell)) \qquad\qquad (1)$$
$$W(.), \ \ell$$

subject to (a) $u(W(f(\ell)), \ell) \geqq u_0$

(b) $\ell \varepsilon \ \arg \max_x u(W(f(x)), x)$.

This problem can be conveniently illustrated in Figure 1. $\ell^*$ is the
amount of $\ell$ that the firm would have chosen had they been able to
control $\ell$ directly (i.e., $\ell^*$ is the firm's first-best labor choice).
At $\ell^*$, the marginal value product of labor, $f'(\ell^*)$ equals the marginal rate of substitution of labor for wage. Therefore, $\pi^*$ is the
maximum possible profit that this firm can obtain under the situation. Even if the firm cannot control $\ell$ (i.e., in the second-best
problem), if the firm offers a wage function $W(f(\ell)) = a + f(\ell)$ (or
any other appropriate non-linear function) with $u(a + f(\ell^*), \ell^*)$
$= u_0$, then the worker will choose $\ell^*$ as his utility maximizing labor
choice. To sum up, the firm (principal) can create proper work incentive and achieve the first-best profit by providing a linear
output-related wage function with a unitary slope.

The role of the output related wage function described above can be
interpreted alternatively as follows. The firm provides the access
to its means of production to the worker in exchange for a fixed fee
$\pi^*$. Once the payment $\pi^*$ is made, the worker is entitled to effectively control the means of production and receive its total revenue.
That is, he can operate the means of production any way he wants and
receive the entire return. Such a procedure will produce the most
efficient allocation.

Although the model we described above is a very simple and static
one, a sequence of output-related wage systems with a guarantee for
life-time employment will provide the same motivation to an employe-
ee. With such wage systems, the worker can allocate his work effort
intertemporally so as to make (the discounted sum of) the firm's returns net of fixed fees. Put differently, he invests in various
forms of capital in the firm whose ownership he purchased by (a sequence of) fixed payments.

We shall formalize this idea in a simple model of a firm-worker relationship. Consider a firm which produces a single output in each
period t. This firm employs labor to produce output. Workers, how-

ever, contribute to the production in two ways. They either work directly to produce output or work to augment the stock of operational and organizational knowledge and the level of his and other workers' work skills. We assume that the stock of operational and organizational knowledge and the level of work skills within the firm in t per employee is represented by an index $A_t$, which we shall refer as the amount of <u>firm-specific capital</u>. For simplicity, we shall assume that the number of employees are constant at N throughout the periods under consideration. Denoting the average of labor hours that each employed worker places directly in production process by $\bar{\ell}_t$, the firm's production function is written as

$$Ny_t = f(A_t, \bar{\ell}_t), \tag{2}$$

where $y_t$ is the amount of output per employee (i.e., the average performance of the employees) in t. We shall assume that

(A.1) <u>f is continuous, increasing and concave in both arguments.</u>

The firm-specific capital will increase when workers spend time on the activity to improve capital. We denote by $\bar{e}_t$ the average of hours spent on this activity by each employed worker. Then

$$A_{t+1} = A_t + g(\bar{e}_t). \tag{3}$$

We shall assume

(A.2) <u>g is continuous, increasing and concave.</u>

For the sake of simplicity, we shall assume that workers are homogeneous (i.e., they have the same characteristics) and live for an infinite number of periods. (i.e., they never die). Moreover, the firm is assumed to offer life-time employment contract which binds both the firm to retain employees for their life span and the employees to remain with the firm. Finally, the number of employees in the firm is assumed to stay constant at N (i.e., the firm recruits no new workers).

$$N_t = N \qquad \text{for all t} \tag{4}$$

Workers are assumed to have the common instantaneous utility function defined over consumption in terms of the firm's output in t, $c_t$, and total hours spent for labor, $\ell_t + e_t$ where $\ell_t$ and $e_t$ are the individual choice of respective work effort. This utility function, $u(c_t, \ell_t + e_t)$, is assumed to satisfy;

(A.3) <u>u is continuous and concave in both arguments, and increasing in</u> $c_t$ <u>and decreasing in</u> $\ell_t + e_t$.

Worker's lifetime utility at time T is the discounted sum of instan-
taneous utilities, $\sum_{t=T}^{\infty} \alpha^{t-T} u(c_t, \ell_t + e_t)$, where $0 < \alpha < 1$. We assume that capital markets are imperfect and workers can neither bor-
row nor lend. Hence they must live solely on wage payments from the
firm in each period.

If the firm can control the optimal choice of each individual worker's efforts, $\ell_t$ and $e_t$, it will be routine to analyze the firm's
maximization problem once its objective function is specified. In
this paper, however, we shall assume that the firm can neither observe (monitor) nor control each individual worker's choice of work
efforts. It can only observe the firm's aggregate performance
($y_t \equiv Y_t/N_t$). Therefore, the firm must provide an appropriate incentive to workers so that they will choose work hours that will
suit the firm's interest. We shall take a wage function, which relates individual worker's wage (in terms of the firm's output) in t
as a function of average performance of the firm's employees in t,
$W_t(y_t)$, as the only vehicle by which the firm can provide work incentive. For the simplicity of the analysis, we shall later confine
our attention to the class of linear wage functions, $W_t(y_t) = a_t +$
$b_t y_t$.

With such a wage function, each individual worker's income depends
upon not only his own work-effort-choice but also other workers'
choices as well. Hence each individual worker is facing a kind of
game situation. In order to analyze worker's behavior, we must carefully describe the rules of this game and choose a proper solution
concept. We shall relegate those game theoretic considerations to
sections 3 and 4. In this and next sections, we shall simply assume
that workers will choose a symmetric cooperative solution as the outcome of this game (hence $\bar{\ell}_t = \ell_t$ and $\bar{e}_t = e_t$).

Assuming that workers are informed of the firm's plan of its wage
functions $\{W_t(.)\}_{t=0}^{\infty} \equiv W(.)$ and that they are aware of the technological possibilities, a representative worker will choose $\{\ell_t, e_t,$
$A_t\}_{t=0}^{\infty} \equiv (\underset{\sim}{\ell}, \underset{\sim}{e}, \underset{\sim}{A})$ to

$$\text{Maximize} \quad \sum_{t=0}^{\infty} \alpha^t u(W_t(f(A_t, \ell_t)), \ell_t + e_t) \tag{5}$$

$$\text{subject to} \quad (5a) \quad A_t + g(e_t) = A_{t+1} \quad \text{for all } t,$$

$$(5b) \quad \ell_t, e_t, A_t \geq 0 \quad \text{for all } t,$$

(5c)    $A_0 = \bar{A}$    is given.

For the firm, we assume that its objective is to maximize the discounted sum of net cash inflows in terms of its output;

$$\sum_{t=0}^{\infty} \beta^t [f(A_t, \ell_t) - w_t]N \qquad\qquad (6)$$

where $\beta (0 < \beta < 1)$ is the discount factor and $w_t$ is the wage (in
terms of output) per worker paid in t.

## 2.   OPTIMAL WAGE FUNCTION

Given the framework of the previous section, the firm's optimal
choice of wage functions, $W(.)$, can be described as a solution of
the following problem:

$$\underset{\underset{\sim}{W}(.), \underset{\sim}{\ell}, \underset{\sim}{e}, \underset{\sim}{A}}{\text{Maximize}} \qquad \sum_{t=0}^{\infty} \beta^t [f(A_t, \ell_t) - W_t(s(A_t, \ell_t))]N$$

subject to (a) $(\underset{\sim}{\ell}, \underset{\sim}{e}, \underset{\sim}{A})$ is a solution of (5) given $\underset{\sim}{W}(.)$,

$$(b) \;\; \sum_{t=0}^{\infty} \alpha^t u(W_t(f(A_t, \ell_t)), \ell_t + e_t) \geq u_0.$$

That is, the firm will choose a sequence of appropriate output-related wage functions that will maximize the discounted sum of net
cash inflows subject to two conditions.  By condition (a), the firm
takes it account that the workers will allocate their labor choice
to maximize their own utilities.  By condition (b), the wage functions are such that behaving optimally the workers will guaranttee
for themselves at least the level of utility they can obtain in other
employment opportunities.

Solving problem (7) is not so simple.[8]  We shall, therefore, take an
alternative route.  Contrary to the assumption implicit in (7), suppose for a while that the firm can directly control a worker's
choice of work efforts.  Then, denoting by $\underset{\sim}{w} = \{w_t\}_{t=0}^{\infty}$ a sequence
of wages that this firm offers to its employees, the firm's problem
becomes:

$$\underset{(\underset{\sim}{\ell}, \underset{\sim}{e}, \underset{\sim}{A}, \underset{\sim}{w})}{\text{maximize}} \qquad \sum_{t=0}^{\infty} \beta^t [f(A_t, \ell_t) - w_t]N \qquad\qquad (8)$$

subject to   (a)  $A_t + g(e_t) = A_{t+1}$    for all t,

(b)   $\ell_t$, $e_t$, $A_t \geq 0$        for all t,

(c)   $A_0 = \bar{A}$      is given,

(d)   $\sum_{t=0}^{\infty} \alpha^t u(w_t, \ell_t + e_t) \geq u_0$.

We shall call this problem the firm's first-best problem.

Assuming that an interior solution exists and the transversality condition is satisfied, necessary conditions for the optimum are

$$\beta^t f_{At} N + \lambda_t - \lambda_{t-1} = 0 \qquad \text{for all } t \geq 1, \qquad (9)$$

$$\beta^t f_{\ell t} N + \mu\alpha^t u_{\ell t} = 0 \qquad \text{for all } t \geq 0, \qquad (10)$$

$$-\beta^t N + \mu\alpha^t u_{wt} = 0 \qquad \text{for all } t \geq 0, \qquad (11)$$

$$\lambda_t g_{et} + \mu\alpha^t u_{\ell t} = 0 \qquad \text{for all } t \geq 0. \qquad (12)$$

where $\lambda_t$ and $\mu$ are auxiliary variables for (a) and (d), and $f_{At}$ = $\partial f(A_t, \ell_t)/\partial A_t$, $f_{\ell t} = \partial f(A_t, \ell_t)/\partial \ell_t$, $u_{\ell t} = \partial u(w_t, \ell_t + e_t)/\partial \ell_t$, $u_{wt} = \partial u(w_t, \ell_t + e_t)/\partial w_t$ and $g_{et} = dg(e_t)/d(e_t)$. Conditions (9) - (12) can be interpreted as follows. From (10) and (11), the marginal rate of substitution of work effort for wages, $-u_{\ell t}/u_{wt}$, must be equated to the marginal productivity of labor, $f_{\ell t}$. From (9), $\lambda_t/\beta^t = \sum_{\tau=t+1}^{\infty} \beta^{\tau-t} f_{A\tau} N$. Economically, $\lambda_t/\beta^t N$ is the value of firm-specific capital at (the end of) t per each worker. (11) and (12) then imply that the MRS in t, $-u_{\ell t}/u_{wt}$, must be also equated to the marginal productivity (evaluated in t) of work efforts, $(\lambda_t/\beta^t N)g_{et}$.

Let $(L^*_{\sim}, e^*_{\sim}, A^*_{\sim}, w^*_{\sim})$ be the first-best solution, namely the solution for (8). Define $W^*_t(y) = a^*_t + y$ for all t where $a^*_t = w^*_t - f(A^*_t, \ell^*_t)$. Then consider the worker's optimization problem (5) with $W_t(.)$ = $W^*_t(.)$. Again assuming that an interior solution exists and that the transversality condition is satisfied, the necessary conditions take the form of:

$$\alpha^t u_{wt} f_{At} + \nu_t - \nu_{t-1} = 0, \qquad (13)$$

$$\alpha^t [u_{wt} f_{\ell t} + u_{\ell t}] = 0, \qquad (14)$$

$$\alpha^t u_{\ell t} + \nu_t g_{et} = 0. \qquad (15)$$

Note first that, by our assumptions, the first-best solution (the solution for (8)) and the solution for (5) with $W(.) = W^*(.)$ are both unique. Moreover, the conditions (9) - (12) and the conditions (13) - (15) are identical. That is, under the proposed wage function, the conditions (13) - (15) are satisfied at $(\underset{\sim}{\ell}^*, \underset{\sim}{e}^*, \underset{\sim}{A}^*)$ if

$$\nu_t = \sum_{\tau=t+1}^{\infty} \alpha^\tau u_{w\tau}(w_\tau^*, \ell_\tau^* + e_\tau^*) f_{A\tau}(A_\tau^*, \ell_\tau^*) = \lambda_t/\mu \quad \text{for all } t.$$

Therefore, under the proposed wage function, this firm can achieve the first-best outcome without directly controlling the workers labor choice.

As we have stressed already, such an incentive mechanism functions properly because under this mechanism the firm is providing workers the opportunity to invest in its firm-specific capital. Consequently, the interests of the management and of the employees coincide. Employees' behavior then becomes as though they are working for the benefit of the firm, for working in a way to improve the firm's (intertemporal) benefit would yield higher payoff for themselves.

Our model lacks reality in many important aspects. In the real-world situations, life-time employment is not a bilateral contract. Employees can and will leave the firm if there is a better employment opportunity somewhere else. Employees are not homogeneous. For example, employees of different generations may have contributed to the firm-specific capital differently and retire at different dates. Hence, employees usually have a conflict of interests. Workers of different generations may therefore receive different wages. Especially senior employees have a certain bargaining power and their wages may not be determined in the way we considered above. [9]

These considerations certainly change the framework and conclusions of the analysis above. However, the fact remains true that the co-existence of output related wage systems and long-term labor contract should create work incentives and provide employees the opportunity to invest in the firm. In the next sections, we shall focus upon another difficulty in interpreting corporate loyalty through workers' attitudes created by output-related wage systems. That is, we shall analyze how strategic behavior among employees may be eliminated by their social act.

## 3.   OUTPUT-RELATED WAGES AND STRATEGIC BEHAVIOR

In this section, we shall demonstrate how an output-related wage
system will create an incentive for strategic behavior.  Throughout
this and the next section, we shall confine our attention upon a
static situation.   Extending our analysis to an intertemporal situation would only yield a more complicated analysis without any substantial difference.

Consider a set of workers $N = \{1, 2, \ldots, n\}$ who have comitted to
work in a firm.   Each worker has a common utility function u:
$R_+^2 \to R$ such that u(w, e) is the level of utility a worker can enjoy
when he earns wage w and works at the effort intensity of e.   We
shall assume

L.1   <u>u is strictly concave, continuous, increasing in c and decreas-</u>
      <u>in e.</u>

L.2   <u>Both w and -e (consumption of a negative amount of e) are normal</u>
      <u>goods</u>

The firm's output, y, is assumed to depend only upon the average ef-
fort level of workers, $\Sigma_{i \in n} e_i/n \equiv \bar{e}$ and we further assume $y = \bar{e}$.
As in the previous sections, we assume that a firm's manager can
identify the total output (and hence the average effort choice), but
it takes a prohibitively large amount of resources to identify the
effort choice of each <u>individual</u> worker.   On the other hand, workers
can find their fellow worker's effort choice without cost.   Therefore, it is crucial for the manager to invent a mechanism which simultaneously provides a proper work incentive to each worker and an
incentive to pursue the group interest.   We shall focus upon one
such mechanism; that is, a wage system which is linearly dependent
upon the total output of the firm (hence dependent upon the average
effort choice of workers).   The reason that we chose this mechanism
singularly should be clear from discussions in the previous sections.
Let this wage system be

$$w_i = a + b\bar{e} \equiv a + \beta e_i + \gamma \hat{e}_i$$

where $w_i$ is the wage paid to individual $i \in N$, $\hat{e}_i \equiv \Sigma_{h \neq i} e_h/(n - 1)$
$= (n\bar{e} - e_i)/(n - 1)$ is the average effort choice of workers other
than i, $a \in R$, b, $\beta$, $\gamma \in R_+$ are constants and, by definition, $\beta = b/n$
and $\gamma = (n - 1)b/n$.   Given this wage system, the utility level which
each worker i can attain is the function of $\hat{e}_i$ and $e_i$.   We shall denote this derived utility by $\phi$.   Namely, the function $\phi: R_+^2 \to R$ is

defined as, for all $(e_i, \hat{e}_i) \in R_+^2$,

$$\phi(e_i, \hat{e}_i) = u(a + \beta e_i + \gamma \hat{e}_i, e_i).$$

By assumptions, $\phi$ is continuous and concave in both arguments, and increasing in $e_i$.

Figure 2 illustrates the choice open to a representative worker $i \in N$. The wage function is depicted as the steeper line which depends upon the average effort, $\bar{e}$. If workers act cooperatively, they will maximize joint utility and choose the cooperative solution $e^C$ as each worker's compulsory effort choice. $e^C$ is characterized as the point of tangency between the wage function and an indifference curve.

Given the average effort of the rest of workers, $\hat{e}_i$, a worker faces an opportunity locus AB(i.e., $w_i = a + \beta e_i + \gamma \hat{e}_i$). His optimal response is to choose $g(\hat{e}_i)$ as his effort and, thereby, makes the point D as his wage-effort combination. By L.2, the locus of optimal response function EF is downward sloping as is depicted in the Figure.

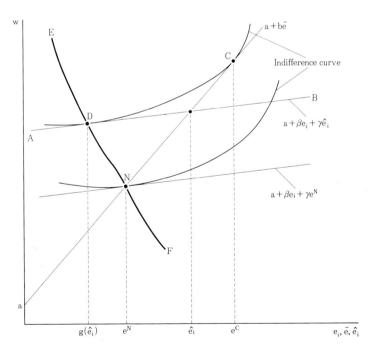

Figure XI-2

The intersection of $a + b\bar{e}$ and EF is the outcome which corresponds to the non-cooperative solution (i.e., a Nash equilibrium). If all the workers have chosen $e^N$ as their effort choice, there is no incentive to divert from this level when each worker considers other workers choices as given. In general, the outcome corresponding to the non-cooperative solution, N, yields a lower utility than that corresponding to the cooperative solution, C.

In the next section, we shall formalize these concepts and introduce the concept of ostracism.

## 4.  OSTRACISM AND COOPERATIVE BEHAVIOR

Let $N = \{1, 2, \ldots, n\}$ be the set of players and for all $i \varepsilon N$ let $S = [0, r]$, a closed interval with a sufficiently large real number r, be his strategy set. We write $\underline{S} \equiv X_{i \varepsilon N} S_i$ where $S_i = S$ for all $i \varepsilon N$. We denote by $\underset{\sim}{s}$ a list of strategies chosen by all players, $(s_i)_{i \varepsilon N}$. Given $\underset{\sim}{s} \varepsilon \underline{S}$, we denote $\Sigma_{i \varepsilon N} s_i / n$ by $\bar{s}$, $(\Sigma_{h \neq i} s_h)/(n - 1)$ by $\hat{s}_i$, i.e., $\bar{s} = s_i/n + (n - 1)\hat{s}_i/n \equiv \bar{s}(s_i, \hat{s}_i)$.

Let $\hat{\phi}: \underline{S} \to R^n$ be the payoff function. Hence $\hat{\phi}_i(\underset{\sim}{s})$ describes the payoff level to $i \varepsilon N$ when the strategy selection is $\underset{\sim}{s}$. We assume that $\hat{\phi}$ has a special property so that any player's payoff depends only upon the choice of his own strategy and the aggregate strategy choice. Therefore, given a strategy selection $\underset{\sim}{s} \varepsilon \underline{S}$, any player's payoff $\hat{\phi}_i(\underset{\sim}{s})$ can be expressed by the value of another payoff function $\phi_i(s_i, \hat{s}_i)$. We shall assume:

G.1   For all i, $j \varepsilon N$ and for all $(s, \hat{s}) \varepsilon S^2$, $\phi_i(s, \hat{s}) = \phi_j(s, \hat{s})$. We shall denote the common payoff function by $\phi$.

G.2   $\phi$ is continuous, strictly concave in both arguments and increasing in s. Moreover, for each $\hat{s} \varepsilon S$ there is $s \varepsilon S$ such that $\phi(s, \hat{s}) > \phi(0, \hat{s})$.

Let $g: S \to S$ be the optimal response function; namely,

$$g(\hat{s}) = \{s \varepsilon S \mid \phi(s, \hat{s}) \geq \phi(s', \hat{s}) \text{ for all } s' \varepsilon S\}.$$

It can be readily proved that g is well-defined, single-valued and continuous. A Nash equilibrium (NE, for short) of the game $(n, \underline{S}, \hat{\phi})$ is a strategy selection $s^* \varepsilon \underline{S}$ such that for all $i \varepsilon N$

$\phi(s_i^*, \hat{s}_i^*) \geq \phi(s, \hat{s}_i^*)$ for all $s \varepsilon S$. Alternatively, $s^* \varepsilon \underset{\sim}{S}$ is NE if for all $i \varepsilon N$ $s_i^* = g(\hat{s}_i^*)$.

We shall assume that:

G.3  $g(\hat{s})$ is decreasing.

The assumption G.3 follow trivially if $\phi$ is constructed from the wage function in the previous section and if L.2 is assumed.

By the usual argument, there always exists a NE $s^* \varepsilon \underset{\sim}{S}$ of the game $(n, \underline{S}, \hat{\phi})$. Moreover, it can be easily proved that there exists a symmetric NE $s^* \varepsilon \underline{S}$ of this game. That is, there exists $s^N \varepsilon S$ such that $s^* \varepsilon \underset{\sim}{S}$ satisfying $s_i^* = s^N$ for all $i \varepsilon N$ is a NE. Henceforth, we shall call $s^N$ the non-cooperative solution. Finally, we shall call $s^C \varepsilon S$ the cooperative solution if $\phi(s^C, s^C) \geq \phi(s, s)$ for all $s \varepsilon S$. (See Figure 3).

We shall now introduce the concept of ostracism. Although the players of the game behave non-cooperatively, as members of an organization (game), they would feel exploited if a player or players of the game do not come up to a standard of the whole group of players. Such a standard or social norm itself arises endogeneously as a consequence of players' behavior. When a player's (or players') strat-

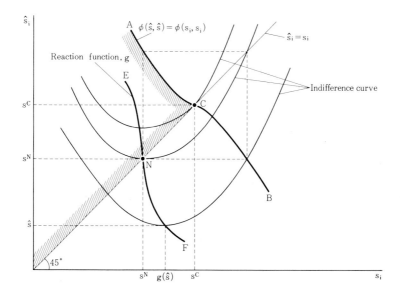

Figure XI-3

egy choice falls short of the social norm, he is (or they are) considered unfair by the rest of players and he is (or they are) ostracized. Being ostracized, a player will be expelled from the organization (the game) and his payoff will be $u_0$ which is guaranteed for anyone who has left the organization.

In the rest of the paper, we shall formulate a game with ostracism in such a manner that ostracism is not a strategy of a player but rather a rule of the game reflected in the payoff function (although social norm itself, which triggers ostracism, is endogeneous). We chose such a formulation not only because ostracism is a social act but because members of an organization take account of the possibility of being ostracized whenever they choose their own strategy. The latter behavior cannot be dealt with by the Nash equilibrium when we define ostracism as a strategy of individual players.

Given a strategy selection $s \epsilon \underset{\sim}{S}$, a player $i \epsilon N$ is called <u>unfair</u> (to the rest of players) if

(Ui)    $s_i < \bar{s}$   and

(Uii)   $\phi(\bar{s}, \bar{s}) > \phi(s_i, s_i).$

We shall denote the set of all $(s, \hat{s})$ so that $(s, \bar{s}(s, \hat{s}))$ satisfiies (Ui) and (Uii) by U. The set U(the shaded area without its boundary) and indifference map of $\phi$ are depicted in the Figure 3.

The idea behind the concept of unfairness is simple. A strategy selection $\underset{\sim}{s}$ will generate a feeling of <u>social norm</u> which is, under our assumption, the average strategy choice, $\bar{s}$. By (i), player i's strategy choice comes short of the social norm and hence harming the rest of players. This is so because, had he chosen the social norm as his own strategy, the rest of players would have benefitted (by <u>G.2</u>) invariably. Moreover, by (ii), it is i's strategy choice, rather than the excessively high social norm, which harms the rest of players.

When a player is considered unfair, he is ostracized. Being ostracized, we assume that he loses the right to receive his wage and his utility will become v(s). In terms of utility function, u, in sections 2 and 3, v(s) may be interpreted as u(o, s). We shall assume that v(s) is continuously differentiable and decreasing in s. If there is a strong possibility of being ostracized, he may leave the game (the firm) voluntarily. For the sake of simplicity, we shall assume that $s_i = 0$ implies the i-th player's strategy that he leaves the firm voluntarily. We shall further assume that the payoff of voluntary quit, $u_0$, is at least equal to $v(0)$, for one should expect $u_0 \geq u(0, 0) = v(0)$.

With this preparation, we can define a new payoff function, $\psi_i$, in the following way. First note $\bar{s}(s, \hat{s}) = s/n + (n - 1)\hat{s}/n$. Let $\psi$ $S^2 \to R$ be

(a) $\quad \psi(0, \hat{s}) = u_0 \qquad$ for all $\hat{s}$,

(b) $\quad \psi(s, \hat{s}) = v(s) \qquad$ if $s > 0$, and $s < \bar{s}(s, \hat{s})$ and

$\qquad\qquad\qquad\qquad\qquad \phi(\bar{s}(s, \hat{s}), s(s, \hat{s})) > \phi(s, s)$ sim-

$\qquad\qquad\qquad\qquad\qquad$ ultaneously hold,

(c) $\quad \psi(s, \hat{s}) = \phi(s, \hat{s}) \quad$ otherwise.

Then define $\psi: \underline{S} \to R^n$ so that for each $i \in N$ $\psi_i(s) = \psi(s_i, \hat{s}_i)$. The optimal response function (correspondence) can be defined as $h(\hat{s}) = \{s \in S | \psi(s, \hat{s}) \geq \psi(s', \hat{s}) \text{ for all } s' \in S\}$.

In order to characterize the optimal response, h, define first $k(\hat{s}) = \min\{s \in S | \phi(s, s) \geq \phi(\hat{s}, s) \text{ or } s \geq \hat{s}\}$. Then obviously the set $U = \{(s, \hat{s}) \in S^2 | (Ui) \text{ and } (Uii) \text{ are satisfied for } (s_i, \bar{s})$ $= (s, \bar{s}(s, \hat{s}))\}$ is expressed as $\{(s, \hat{s}) \in S^2 | s < k(\hat{s})\}$. Then define

$$\hat{h}(\hat{s}) = \begin{cases} g(\hat{s}) & \text{if } \hat{s} < s^N, \\ k(\hat{s}) & \text{if } \hat{s} \geq s^N. \end{cases}$$

It follows immediately that the optimal response function $h(\hat{s})$ takes the form

$$h(\hat{s}) = \begin{cases} 0 & \text{if } \phi(\hat{h}(\hat{s}), \hat{s}) < u_0, \\ \{0, \hat{h}(\hat{s})\} & \text{if } \phi(\hat{h}(\hat{s}), \hat{s}) = u_0, \\ \hat{h}(\hat{s}) & \text{otherwise.} \end{cases}$$

The shape of h when $u_0 < \phi(s^N, s^N)$ is depicted in the Figure 4.

When $u_0$ is sufficiently small, even if a player would prefer to choose a response, $s_i = g(\hat{s}_i)$, which falls short of the social norm, the fear of being ostracized forces him to choose an alternative response $s_i = h(\hat{s}_i) \neq g(\hat{s}_i)$.

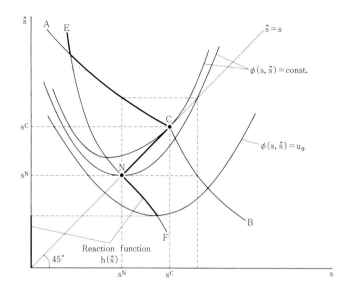

Figure XI-4

A <u>Nash equilibrium</u> of the game $(N, \underline{S}, \hat{\psi})$ (henceforth, by a NE we refer to a NE of $(N, \underline{S}, \hat{\psi})$ rather than a NE of $(N, \underline{S}, \hat{\phi})$ unless othervise indicated) is a strategy selection $s^* \varepsilon \underline{S}$ such that for all $i \varepsilon N$ $\psi(s_i^*, \hat{s}_i^*) \geqq \psi(s, \hat{s}_i^*)$ for any $s \varepsilon S$. <u>A symmetric Nash equilibrium</u> (SNE, for short) of the game $(N, \underline{S}, \hat{\psi})$ is a NE $s^* \varepsilon \underline{S}$ such that for all $i, j \varepsilon N$ $s_i^* = s_j^* = s^*$. We call the common $s^*$ a <u>SNE strategy</u>. Then the following theorem follows immediately.

<u>Theorem 1</u>:  $s^* \varepsilon S$ <u>is a SNE strategy if and only if</u>

(a)  $s^* \varepsilon [s^N, s^C] \cap \{s \varepsilon S \mid \phi(s, s) \geqq u_0\}$,  or

(b)  $s^* = 0$.

As theorem 1 shows there are, in general, a large number of SNEs. In-tuitively speaking, multiplicity of SNEs arises because the fear of being ostracized is not sufficiently strong. Any player can avoid his banishment by choosing a strategy which exactly eliminates the possibility of his ostracism; namely, by choosing a strategy which does not satisfy (Ui) and (Uii) simultaneously. In reality, however, the strategic interaction of members within an organization is very complex — reflecting the imperfect information of game rules and of

other members' strategy choice, uncertainty to which the organization itself faces, difficulty of predicting other players' strategy,
etc. In order to describe the behavior of a player who attempts to
solve the optimal strategy under such a complex situation, we must
explicitly introduce uncertainty and/or incomplete information into
the game. We therefore introduce a concept of (trembling-hand) perfect Nash equilibrium to bring the flavor of uncertainty and/or incomplete information into our model. Let $\xi$ be a random variable
which is distributed uniformly over a closed interval $[-1, 1]$,

Given a real number $\varepsilon > 0$, we define for each $i \varepsilon N$

$$\hat{\psi}_i^\varepsilon(\underset{\sim}{s}) = E\psi(s_i + \varepsilon\xi, \hat{s}_i)$$

where $E$ is the expectation operator. We also define $\psi^\varepsilon(s_i, \hat{s}_i)$
$= E\psi(s_i + \varepsilon\xi, \hat{s}_i)$. Note that $\psi^\varepsilon$ is common to all players. A strat-
egy selection $s^\varepsilon \varepsilon \underset{\sim}{S}$ is a <u>symmetric Nash equilibrium</u> of the game $(N, \underset{\sim}{S},$
$\hat{\psi}^\varepsilon)$ if for all $i$, $j \varepsilon N$ $s_i^\varepsilon = s_j^\varepsilon = s^\varepsilon$ and for each $i \varepsilon N$ $\hat{\psi}_i^\varepsilon(s^\varepsilon, s^\varepsilon)$
$\geqq \hat{\psi}_i^\varepsilon(s, s^\varepsilon)$ for all $s \varepsilon S$. A strategy selection $s^* \varepsilon \underset{\sim}{S}$ is a <u>symmetric</u>
<u>perfect Nash equilibrium</u> (SPNE, for short) if there exists $\{\varepsilon_k\}_{k=1}^\infty$,
$\{s^k\}_{k=1}^\infty$ such that $\lim_{k \to \infty} \varepsilon_k = 0$, $\lim_{k \to \infty} \underset{\sim}{s}^k = \underset{\sim}{s}^*$ and for each $k$ $\underset{\sim}{s}^k$ is a SNE
of the game $(N, \underset{\sim}{S}, \psi^\varepsilon k)$. The following is the main theorem of this
section.

<u>Theorem 2</u>:   <u>There are at most two SPNE strategies</u>:

(a)   $s^C$ <u>is always a SPNE strategy</u>   <u>if</u> $\phi(s^C, s^C) \geqq u_0$,

(b)   $0$ <u>is always a SPNE strategy</u>   <u>if</u> $\phi(g(0), 0) \leqq u_0$.

Although the proof of this theorem is rather involved and is therefore relegated to the appendix, some intuitive explanation may be
called for at this point. As we saw in the theorem 1, if $\phi(s^C, s^C)$
$\geqq u_0$, then any $s \varepsilon [s^N, s^C]$ is a SNE strategy as long as $\phi(s, s) \geqq u_0$.
When a disturbance $\varepsilon\xi$ is introduced to his strategy $s$, a player must
chance his ostracism. If the threat of ostracism is non-zero, he
will attempt to play it safe. In other words, even though $s = h(\hat{s})$
is a SNE strategy of $(N, \underset{\sim}{S}, \psi)$ and therefore $s$ is any player's optimal response in $(N, \underset{\sim}{S}, \psi)$, he will rather choose some $s' = h^\varepsilon(\hat{s})$
$> h(\hat{s})$ as his optimal response in $(N, \underset{\sim}{S}, \hat{\psi}^\varepsilon)$. Consequently, the
optimal response function of $(N, \underset{\sim}{S}, \hat{\psi}^\varepsilon)$ (denoted as $h^\varepsilon(s)$ in Figure
5) is slightly skewed compared to $h(s)$. Therefore, the number of
SNE's in $(N, \underset{\sim}{S}, \hat{\psi}^\varepsilon)$, and hence that of SPNE's, is significantly reduced (see Figure 5). Aside from the trivial SPNE of $s^* = 0$, the
only remaining SPNE $s^* = s^C$ has such desirable properties as symmetri-

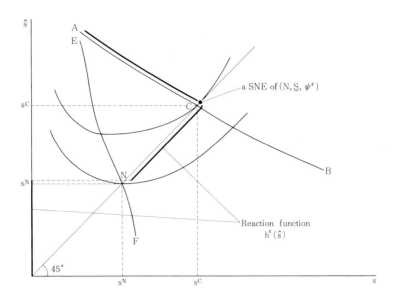

Figure XI-5

city and stability.  We may conclude, therefore, that the ostracism
will create an incentive for a body of players to choose a cooperative outcome, which we assumed in sections 1 and 2.

## 5.   CONCLUSION

In this paper, we showed that corporate loyalty prevalent in Japanese employees can be interpreted as a consequence of incentive
wages and firm-specific capitals.  We also showed that an output-
related wage system will not only create a work incentive but also
induce workers to pursue their group interest when there is a possibility to penalize a worker who is behaving strategically.   In
this paper, we considered ostracism as an vehicle by which the group
of workers penalize that worker.  Although ostracism, which is a
sociological concept, may be considered as without economic foundation by many, the essential mechanism by which ostracism works in
our specification is rather familiar to economics.  That is, the

worker whose performance is the lowest will be expelled from the group and must abide the low utility available outside the organization. This is basically the mechanism of tournament or contest in its reverse form (see Lazear and Rosen [11] and Stiglitz [20]). Put differently, if there is an element of tournament or contest in the (life-time) income determination of individual workers, work incentive existent in an output-related wage system will be enhanced.

One such well-known mechanism in Japanese labor markets is the system of internal promotion. Under this system, vacancies in an organization are filled by lower echelon workers of the same organization by promoting them. Criteria of which workers to promote depend usually upon such factors as who in the lower echelon had the highest evaluation made by supervisors, who has the best reputation among fellow workers, etc. Resulting rank-order competition certainly contributes to a larger work incentive than otherwise.

A critical assumption of this paper is that, in Japan, labor income or wages are respondent to the corporate performance. Some readers may suspect the validity of this assumption, for at least in the U.S., wages are found to be quite sticky. In fact, some economists (e.g., Sachs [18]) keyed the cause of recent stagflation on this observation. We have not found any clear cut evidence that labor income in Japan depends heavily upon the corporate performance. But Gordon [5], for example, found that nominal wage changes in the postwar era are "five to ten times greater in Britain and Japan than in the United States".

These statistical findings may suggest that risks which corporations faced are shared by workers in the U.S. in the form of employment and wage changes (see, e.g., Azariadis [2] and Baily [3]). On the other hand in Japan risks which are shared by workers are absorbed in the form of wage changes but not of employment. Alternatively, it can also be argued that wages are determined in Japan in a manner (such as the one proposed in this paper) which is substantially different from that in the U.S. In any event it should be noted that, for our mechanism to work, what is necessary is the perception of workers that labor income changes as their corporation's performance does.

APPENDIX

Lemma 1: For any $\varepsilon > 0$, $\psi^\varepsilon(s, \hat{s})$ is continuously differentiable in s and $\hat{s}$.

Proof: Straightforward from the absolute continuity of the density function of $\xi$.                                                                        Q.E.D.

Lemma 2: For any $\hat{s}$ and $\varepsilon > 0$, $\psi^\varepsilon(s, \hat{s})$ is decreasing in s for all $s \leq \hat{k}(\hat{s}) - \varepsilon$ and strictly concave in s for all $s \geq \hat{k}(\hat{s}) + \varepsilon$. Moreover, for $s\varepsilon(\hat{k}(\hat{s}) - \varepsilon, \hat{k}(\hat{s}) + \varepsilon)$, when $\varepsilon$ is sufficiently small, $\psi^\varepsilon(s, \hat{s})$ is increasing in s if $v(\hat{k}(\hat{s})) < \phi(\hat{k}(\hat{s}), \hat{s})$ and decreasing in s if $v(\hat{k}(\hat{s})) > \phi(\hat{k}(\hat{s}), \hat{s})$.

Proof: First two properties follow immediately from the facts that v(s) is decreasing in s and $\phi(s, \hat{s})$ is concave in s. To prove properties of $\psi^\varepsilon(s, \hat{s})$ on $s\varepsilon(\hat{k}(\hat{s}) - \varepsilon, \hat{k}(\hat{s}) + \varepsilon)$, define first $x^\varepsilon(s, \hat{s}) = \frac{\hat{k}(\hat{s}) - s}{\varepsilon}$. Then if $s\varepsilon(\hat{k}(\hat{s}) - \varepsilon, \hat{k}(\hat{s} + \varepsilon))$, $\psi^\varepsilon(s, \hat{s}) = \int_{-1}^{x^\varepsilon(s, \hat{s})} v(s + \varepsilon\xi)d\xi + \int_{x^\varepsilon(s, \hat{s})}^{1} \phi(s + \varepsilon\xi, \hat{s})d\xi$.

By differentiation,

$$\frac{\partial\psi^\varepsilon(s, \hat{s})}{\partial s} = \frac{1}{\varepsilon}[\phi(\hat{k}(\hat{s}), \hat{s}) - v(\hat{k}(\hat{s}))] + \int_{-1}^{x^\varepsilon(s, \hat{s})} \frac{dv(s + \varepsilon\xi)}{ds} d\xi$$

$$+ \int_{x^\varepsilon(s, \hat{s})}^{1} \frac{\partial\phi(s + \varepsilon\xi, \hat{s})}{\partial s} d\xi.$$

When $\varepsilon$ is sufficiently small, the first term of the right hand side dominates and the desired property is obtained.                                      Q.E.D.

Lemma 3: For any $\hat{s}$, unless $\phi(\hat{h}(\hat{s}), \hat{s}) = u_0$, the optimal response $h^\varepsilon(\hat{s})$ is single-valued and continuous for sufficiently small $\varepsilon$. Moreover, for sufficiently small $\varepsilon$,

$\quad\quad h^\varepsilon(\hat{s}) = 0 \quad\quad\quad$ if $\quad u_0 \geq \phi(\hat{h}(\hat{s}), \hat{s})$,

$\quad\quad h^\varepsilon(\hat{s}) = \hat{h}(\hat{s}) + \varepsilon \quad$ if $\quad u_0 < \phi(\hat{h}(\hat{s}), \hat{s})$ and $\hat{h}(\hat{s}) = k(\hat{s})$,

and

$\quad\quad h^\varepsilon(\hat{s})\varepsilon(\hat{h}(\hat{s}) - \varepsilon, \hat{h}(\hat{s}) + \varepsilon) \quad$ if $\quad u_0 < \phi(\hat{h}(\hat{s}), \hat{s})$ and $\hat{h}(\hat{s}) = g(\hat{s})$.

Proof: By lemma 2, $\psi^\varepsilon(s, \hat{s})$ has at most two local maxima. Hence single-valuedness and continuity follow immediately. The last property also holds immediately from lemmas 1 and 2.

Proof of Theorem 2:

By lemma 3, for sufficiently small $\varepsilon$, there exists at most two fixed points of $h^\varepsilon(.)$. That is, s = 0 is a fixed point if $u_0 \geq \phi(g(0), 0)$ and $s\varepsilon(s^c, s^c + \varepsilon)$

is a fixed point if $u_0 \leq \phi(s^C, s^C)$. Since $\psi^\varepsilon(s, \hat{s}) \to \psi(s, \hat{s})$ as $\varepsilon \to 0$ and hence $h^\varepsilon(\hat{s}) \to h(\hat{s})$ as $\varepsilon \to 0$, $s = s^C$ is a SPNE strategy if $u_0 \leq \phi(s^C, s^C)$. $\underline{Q.E.D.}$

NOTES

* An earlier version of the present paper was presented at the TCER conference in Zushi, March 1982 under the title of "Wage System as a Work Incentive". The author would like to thank participants of the conference, especially Professors Hajime Oniki, Masahiko Aoki and Ryutaro Komiya for their useful discussions and helpful suggestions. He is also grateful to Professor Kazuyoshi Koshiro for introducing me to many useful references. Financial supports by the 21st Century Culture and Science Foundation and by Research-in-Aid program of the Ministry of Education in Japan are gratefully acknowledged.

[1] The data are for corporations with more than 29 employees (General Survey on Wages and Working Hours System [21]). Also, K. Koshiro has estimated that absentee rate among Japanese workers normally stands around 1 to 2 percent, while in most of Western countries the rate often exceeds 10% (see Koshiro [10] and T. Hanami [6]).

[2] For a brief summary of developments of suggestion system in Japan, see, for example, T. Inagami [7]. Among 427 surveyed corporations in 1980, nearly 600 thousand workers participated in the program and more than 23 million suggestions are made, of which 72% are adopted. Total annual economic benefits (in 278 surveyed corporations) amounts to 225 million yen, out of which only 8 million is paid in the form of compensation for suggestions.

[3] There is no statistical evidence for this phenomenon, although it is widely recognized in Japan. For example, ".... In fact, it is a considerable merit of comtemporary Japan that senior workers ardently teach junior workers. It is in this area where developing countries fail. In those countries, however superior machines there are and however passionate workers are to learn skills, senior workers seldom teach their skills effectively. .... Western countries, where work and wages are directly linked and bonus wages are prevalent, do not do as well as in Japan in this respect" (Koike [9]).

[4] It is the ratio of special payment (of which the bulk is the bonus payments) to annual total cash earnings (Yearbook of Labor Statistics [1980]). The bonus payments are paid biannually in most of the Japanese corporations. In 1980, on the average summer bonus amounts to 1.56 months regular pay and winter bonus 1.85 months regular pay (General Survey on Wages and Working Hours System [21]).

[5] In the survey conducted in 1977, 19.6% of total bonus payments are paid as a fixed payment, 49.1% as a fixed percentage of individual salaries, 8.4% as a payments for job, rank and skills. Only 19.9% are paid according to individual worker's job performance. Among corporations that have explicit agreements with workers about bonus payments 15.1% have profit-sharing clause (General Survey on Wage and Working Hours System [21]).

[6] For example, turnover rate of Japanese workers is estimated as about half of that in the U.S. and about one-quarter of that in Australia (see Koshiro [10] and

and Hanami [6]).

[7]See also Miyazaki [13].

[8]See, e.g., Ross [18], Stiglitz [20] and Mirrlees [12] for various methods to solve similar problems.

[9]For example, Aoki [1].


REFERENCES

[1] Aoki, Masahiko, "Equilibrium Growth of the Hierarchical Firm: Shareholder-Employee Cooperative Game Approach", American Economic Review, December 1982, 72.

[2] Azariadis, Costas, "Implicit Contracts and Underemployment Equilibria", Journal of Political Economy, December 1975, 83, 1183-1202.

[3] Baily, Martin N., "Wages and Employment under Uncertain Demand", Review of Economic Studies, January 1974, 41, 37-50.

[4] Becker, Gary, "Investment in Human Capital: A Theoretical Approach", Journal of Political Economy, October 1962 Supplement, 70.

[5] Gordon, Robert J., "Why U.S. Wage and Employment Behavior Differs from That in Britain and Japan", Economic Journal, 1982, 92, 13-44.

[6] Hanami, Tadashi, "Worker Motivation in Japan (I)", Japan Labor Bulletin, February 1982, 5-8.

[7] Inagami, Takeshi, "QC Circle Activities and the Suggestion System", Japan Labor Bulletin, January 1982, 5-8.

[8] Koike, Kazuo, Shokuba no Rodo Kumiai to Sanka — Roshi Kankei no Nichibei Hikaku [Labor Unions at the Workshop and Their Participation: Japan-United States Comparison of Industrial Relations], 1977, Tokyo Keizai Shimposha, Tokyo, Japan. (English Translation of Chapter 7 appears as "Japan's Industrial Relations: Characteristics and Problems", Japanese Economic Studies, Fall 1978, 7, 42-90.

[9] —————— , Chusho Kigyo no Jukuren [Skill Formation in Small Corporations], Tokyo, Dobunkan, 1981.

[10] Koshiro, Kazutoshi, "Humane Organization of Work in the Plants: Production Techniques and Organization of Work in Japanese Factories", paper Presented at The Sixth Japanese-German Cultural Exchange Seminar, October 1977, mimeographed.

[11] Lazear, Edward P. and Sherwin Rosen, "Rank-Order Tournaments as Optimum Labor Contracts". Journal of Political Economy, October 1981, 89, 841-864.

[12] Mirrlees, James A, "The Optimal Structure of Incentives and Authority within an Organization", Bell Journal of Economics, Spring 1976, 7, 105-131.

[13] Miyazaki, Hajime, "Work Norms and Involuntary Unemployment", Working Paper Series No. 191, Department of Economics, University of California, Davis, 1982.

[14] Nalebuff, Barry and Joseph E. Stiglitz, "Prizes and Incentives: Towards a General Theory of Compensation and Competition", Econometric Research Program

Research Memorandum No. 293, Princeton University, Princeton, January 1982.

[15] Ohashi, Isao, "Kigyonai Rodo Shijo ni okeru Teinen to Naibu Shoshin Sei" [Mandatory Retirement and Internal Promotions in Internal Labor Markets], <u>Nihon Rodo Kyokai Zasshi</u>, October 1981, 12-23.

[16] Oi, Walter, Y., "Labor as a Quasi-Fixed Factor", <u>Journal of Political Economy</u>, December 1962, <u>70</u>, 538-555.

[17] Okuno, Masahiro, "Monitoring Cost, Agency Relationship, and Equilibrium Modes of Labor Contract", mimeographed, Yokohama National University, Yokohama, Japan, 1982.

[18] Ross, Stephen A., "The Economic Theory of Agency: The Principal's Problem", <u>American Economic Review</u>, May 1973, 63, 134-139.

[19] Sachs, Jefferey, "Wages, Profits, and Macroeconomic Adjustment: A comparative Study", <u>Bookings Papers on Economic Activity</u>, 1979, <u>2</u>, 269-319.

[20] Stiglitz, Joseph E., "Incentives and Risk Sharing in Sharecropping", <u>Review of Economic Studies</u>, April 1974, <u>41</u>, 219-256.

[21] Japanese Ministry of Labor, <u>General Survey on Wages and Working Hours System</u>.

[22] ——————— , <u>Yearbook of Labor Statistics</u>.

THE ECONOMIC ANALYSIS OF THE JAPANESE FIRM
M. Aoki (editor)
© Elsevier Science Publishers B.V. (North-Holland), 1984

COMMENTS ON IX AND XI

# SOME REFLECTIONS ON THE JAPANESE MOTIVATION SYSTEM

TUVIA BLUMENTHAL

The question of motivation within the Japanese company, the diligence of the Japanese worker and his devotion to the firm as
manifested by overtime work without pay or skipping vacations has
always intrigued Western economists. Several attempts to explain
this behavior have been made in books on the Japanese economy, from
Abegglen's The Japanese Factory in the 1950s to Vogel's Japan as
No. 1 in the late 1970s. The papers by Okuno and Leibenstein are
both based on a novel approach which regards the intra-company
relations as a game which can be analysed by game-theory methods.
Although both papers have the same departure-point they provide
different solutions to the motivation problem: Okuno, following a
tradition going back to the English philosopher Thomas Hobbes,
argues that Homo Homini Lupus (in Japanese Katakidoshi) and while
each worker seeks only his narrowly defined pecuniary benefit he
is brought into line of making maximum effort by the sword of
ostracism (mura hachibu). Leibenstein, in the best tradition of
another English philosopher, John Locke, argues that social convention is used as a way of saving management and workers from the
low-level equilibrium trap which is the outcome of the prisoner's
dilemma. It is interesting to note that Okuno, the Japanese author,
bases his model on universial principles without any resort to
Japanese idiosyncrasies, while Leibenstein, the non-Japanese,
includes in his model particularistic elements related to Japanese
social structure and psychology.

According to Okuno the Japanese worker belongs to the lowest breed
of "economic animals", his only purpose being to increase his wages
in the form of bonus payments. Since bonus pyments in Japan are
"output based" and given jointly to all workers, the individual
worker lives in constant fear lest his so-called friends will cheat
on him by taking a free-ride on his diligence, and is even more
afraid that if he does not manifest his devotion by staying after
working hours or if he dares use the whole vacation period alloted
to him, they will punish him with the dreaded Tokugawa-era mura
hachibu. This punishment, known to have been exercised only in
extreme cases, meant that the culprit was cut-off from the village
community and his neighbors would not come to his rescue unless his
house caught fire or someone died in his family. The modern version
of mura hachibu, à la Okuno, is that the worker has to leave the
company and his income goes down to $U_O$.

I must confess that this stick-and-carrot explanation of the
Japanese miracle does not appeal to me at all and does not, in my
opinion, capture the essence of labor relations in Japan. The
formidable super-structure of equations seems to be standing on a

very shaky foundation.  Let me first look at the assumptions of the
model.

The utility function includes two variables, wage and labor, where
utility is increasing with wages and decreasing with the amount of
labor.  While it is in accord with the usual formulation of labor
economics, we should inquire whether this utility function ade-
quately reflects the situation in the modern industrial society,
particularly in Japan.  The modern working place, far from the sweat
shop of the early 19th century, has not only an economic but also a
social function.  Thus, for example, the increase in womens' participation in the labor force has at its root non-pecuniary benefits
related to social activities rather than a narrowly defined economic
advantage.  Likewise, I would not be surprised if many a Japanese
worker enjoys his work in an air conditioned office or factory,
where he can chat with his friends and have an occasional "go" or
"shogi" game, more than his one bed-room apartment where he has to
listen to his wife's complaints and help his children with their
homework.  It is interesting to find out whether the term "over
work" does not include a large amount of social activities performed
at the work place rather than work in its proper meaning.

Another shortcoming of the utility function in this model is that it
does not include any non-pecuniary variables such as social status,
security, chance of promotion and satisfaction derived from being a
"sensei" to younger employees.  If a worker is so frightened of
being ostracised by his colleagues he certainly must enjoy their
affection and esteem.  The lifetime committment of the worker to the
firm, taken as granted by this model when describing investment in
firm-specific human capital, is difficult to understand if only
pecuniary rewards are taken into account.  If the only purpose is to
maximize wage income a worker would do better by joining a competitor's firm, taking with him the experience he acquired and receiving
higher wages.  It is interesting to note that while Japan is characterized by fierce (some say "excess") competition in the product
market, there is no such competition in the labor market after the
entrance stage, a phenomenon which is hard to explain without some
non-pecuniary elements.

The raison d'etre of the Japanese bonus system is also not clear in
this model.  If the only purpose of the system is to increase
production, why not use the straightforward Soviet-type bonus system
where payments are made to workers (or teams of workers) according
to their contribution to production?  This seems to be the more
efficient and effective system, saving money for the company and
driving the worker to maximum effort.  The reason that this "first
best" solution is not adopted, according to the paper, is the
perplexing assumption that management cannot observe individual
effort while the worker's peers can do so without cost.  In this
time and age of highly sophisticated productivity measurements this
assumption does not seem plausible, especially since the "first
best" solution is being used in other countries.

Here I would venture the hypothesis that the Japanese way of bonus
payments is itself a part of the motivation system aimed at reducing
friction among workers and increasing the "company spirit".  Rather
than competing against his fellow workers, thriving to get a larger
bonus than others, the worker's ties to the company and to the
company's work force are strengthened and his sense of belonging

enhanced.

Let me turn now to test the model in a different way. Okuno's model is based on the concept of an output-based wage system and is used to explain certain observations about the behavior of Japanese workers e.g. overtime work without pay and skipping of vacations. One way to test the model is to look at other groups of workers whose wage is not output-base and see whether the same observations hold true. If so, it raises grave doubts about the explanatory power of the present model.

One group of workers whose wages are not output-based are government employees, whose bonus payments are determined by collective bargaining, where one important element is the average bonus paid by private companies. If we take Okuno's model seriously, the government employee is a free rider on the effort made by private employees and has no interest whatsoever to put any effort in his work beyond what is demanded of him by the conditions of employment.

While I could not find any statistical information on unpaid overtime or actual vacations of government employees, there is much descriptive evidence to show that the same observations are valid for them as for employees of private companies. Vogel has the following description of elite-track bureaucrats of government ministries:

> "Ordinary employees leave at five or six, but the élite rarely leave work before nine or ten o'clock at night. It is difficult to get ordinary bureaucrats to work on Saturday without special compensation, but elite bureaucrats, who are not officially required to work on weekends, rarely miss a Saturday and rarely leave before two or three o'clock in the afternoon. They are always available for extra duty, and when the work load is especially demanding, they sleep overnight at the ministry on specially provided cots".[1]

Another passage, by a former administrative vice-minister of MITI reads as follows:

> "I cannot say that all the bureaucrats work hard, but certainly some of them are very highly motivated. In my view, they work very hard. It is common for them to work until eight or ten or even twelve o'clock in the evening. They have nabeyaki udon (a pot of noodles) brought to them in the evening, drink a cup of sake, and work with manly determination".[2]

These observations show that high motivation exceeds the boundaries of private companies and that the bonus-cum-ostracism theory leaves much to be desired as a persuasive explanation of Japanese working habits.

In the Leibenstein paper we get a very different picture of the Japanese worker. He has a high degree of dutifulness, likes to be spoiled and is bound by strong ties of loyalty to his company, much as his ancesters, the 47 ronin, were to their feudal lord. This demand side, which represents the workers' attitude, is well met by management in setting the reward system. Non-monetary rewards play a much more important role that in Western societies and the emerging motivation system is a convention which increases the pay-off of both labor and management.

While I am in agreement with the description of Japanese labor relations given in the paper, which emphasizes group spirit and sense of duty, there still arises the question of the direction of causation. Was the motivation system built so as to respond to psychological and traditional characteristics of the Japanese (as argued by Leibenstein), implying a sort of Nihonjinron (a theory that Japanese are different from other human beings), or can the observed qualities be regarded as a result of the motivation system itself (as argued by e.g. Johnson [3]). One way to answer the question is by looking at the history of labor-management relations. Do we find the same pattern in the past, when traditional forces were presumably stronger than today? As shown by Taira [4], the situation has been quite different. Such Japanese institutions as lifetime employment are a product of the interwar period and have become more important during and after World War II. At the beginning of the century labor turnover was high and workers had no qualms in leaving their employer and finding alternative work for higher wages. This points to the conclusion that the motivational system is the cause, rather than the result, of observed behavior of Japanese employees.

To finish on a positive note, each of the two models points to an important aspect of Japanese labor relations. Okuno's model stresses the need for an economic rationale in order to understand the Japanese motivation system, while Leibenstein's model emphasizes the common interest of labor and management in reaching a convention which results in a better outcome for both. These two elements should, I believe, be incorporated in future models of the Japanese company.

REFERENCES

[1] Ezra F. Vogel, Japan as Number 1, Harvard, 1979, p.56.

[2] Yoshihisa Ojimi, "A Government Ministry: the Case of the Ministry of International Trade and Industry" in Ezra F. Vogel (ed.), Modern Japanese Organization and Decision Making, University of California, 1975, p.105.

[3] Chalmers Johnson, MITI and the Japanese Miracle, Stanford University Press, 1982.

[4] Koji Taira, Economic Development and the Labor Market in Japan, Columbia University Press, 1970.

# AUTHOR INDEX

Abegglen, J.   4, 41, 413
Abernathy, W.J.   360, 361, 380, 385
Aitchison, J.   146, 191
Akabane, T.   187, 191
Akaike, H.   363, 376, 380, 384, 385
Akerlof, G.A.   83, 84, 101
Aoki, M.   11, 16, 23, 25, 39, 40, 41,
    128, 230, 241, 257, 311, 351, 355,
    387, 410
Arrow, K.J.   223, 224, 259
Athos, A.G.   357
Atkinson, J.W.   354, 355
Auerbach, A.J.   314, 316
Aumann, R.   262, 264, 355
Azariadis, C.   254, 389, 407, 410

Baily, M.N.   389, 407, 410
Becker, G.   389, 410
Befu, H.   354, 355
Benedict, R.   335, 355
Berle, A.   41
Bhattacharya, S.   255, 257
Birch, O.   354, 355
Blumenthal, T.   38
Bok, D.C.   39, 41, 104, 122
Borjas, G.J.   94, 101
Box, G.   283, 308, 309
Broadbent, D.E.   354, 355
Brown, C.   7, 103, 104, 105, 106,
    112, 113, 118, 120, 121, 122,
    128
Brown, J.M.   145, 146, 185, 191

Campbell, D.T.   283, 307, 308, 309
Caves, R.   24, 41, 227, 228, 257
Chammah, A.   355
Chandler, A.   27
Chatterjee, S.   223, 224
Clark, K.B.   103, 122
Clark, R.   331, 332, 354, 355
Clark, V.A.   90, 101
Cole, R.E.   4, 6, 41, 354, 355

Davis, O.   308, 310
Diamond, P.A.   312, 316
Dodd, E.M.   41
Doeringer, P.B.   103, 122
Doi, T.   354, 355
Dore, R.   4, 39, 40, 41, 74, 354, 355
Dunlop, J.T.   104, 122
Duesenberry, J.   145, 185, 191

Elston, C.D.   256, 257
Estey, M.   129

Fama, E.   230, 257
Feldman, R.   221, 224

Feldstein, M.   255, 257
Flavin, M.   189, 191
Flinn, C.J.   94, 95, 101
Fried, J.   254, 256, 257
Friedman, B.   190, 191
Friedman, M.   191
Freeman, R.B.   7, 38, 103, 104, 105,
    118, 120, 122, 129
Futatsugi, Y.   227, 257

Galenson, W.   103, 122
Glass, G.   283, 309
Gordon, R.   255, 256, 257
Gordon, R.J.   407, 410
Goto, A.   24, 42, 227, 257, 258
Granger, C.W.J.   377, 384, 385
Green, J.   255, 257
Griliches, Z.   105, 107, 123
Gross, A.J.   90, 101
Grossman, H.   129

Hadley, E.   12, 38, 42, 254, 257
Hahn, F.H.   41, 42
Haitovsky, Y.   146, 191
Hall, R.E.   77, 81, 84, 86, 101, 189,
    191
Hamada, K.   42
Hanami, T.   356, 409, 410
Harada, Y.   221, 224
Haraf, W.S.   129
Hart, O.D.   311, 315, 316
Hatade, I.   40, 42
Haugh, L.D.   377, 384, 385
Hayashi, F.   189, 191
Hazama, H.   4, 39, 42
Heckman, J.J.   94, 95, 101
Hibbs, D.   308, 309
Hirschman, A.O.   105, 123
Hirschmeier, J.   40, 42
Hobbes, T.   413
Houthakker, H.S.   185, 191
Howard, N.   356
Howitt, P.   254, 256, 257
Hyodo, T.   4, 42

Ikeo, K.   256, 257
Inagami, T.   409, 410
Ishikawa, T.   7, 311, 355, 356
Itami, H.   381, 382, 385
Iwasaki, M.   309
Iwata, R.   356

Jenkins, G.   308, 309
Johnson, C.   42, 416

Kagano, T.   351, 355, 356
Kaitz, H.   83, 101

Kaplan, E.    39, 42, 327
Kimura, T.    309
King, M.A.    38, 193, 224, 230, 255,
    257, 312, 314, 316, 317
Klein, B.H.    37, 359, 360, 363, 366,
    376, 380, 385
Kmenta, J.    106, 123
Kobayashi, Y.    227, 228, 254, 257
Kodaira, K.    309
Koike, K.    6, 27, 74, 83, 101, 103,
    123, 126, 185, 356, 387, 409, 410
Komatsu, Y.    356
Komiya, R.    32, 39, 41, 42, 137, 191
Kosai, Y.    187, 189, 191
Koshiro, K.    65, 409, 410
Kuhn, H.    259
Kurz, M.    262, 264

Lazear, E.P.    407, 410
Leibenstein, H.    6, 37, 105, 123, 191,
    354, 356, 360, 366, 380, 385, 413
Lewis, D.    341, 356
Lind, R.C.    223, 224
Locke, J.    413
Lydall, H.    146, 191

Maddala, G.S.    146, 192
Maehara, Y.    83, 84, 85, 101
Main, B.G.M.    83, 84, 101
Malkiel, B.    255, 256, 257
Mann, N.R.    90, 102
Mannari, H.    356
Marglin, S.A.    185, 192
Markovitz, H.    223, 224
Marris, R.    228, 257
Marsh, R.M.    356
Maruo, N.    354, 356
Matsuoka, H.    355
McMillan, J.    354, 356
Means, G.    41
Medoff, J.L.    7, 103, 104, 105, 106,
    112, 113, 118, 120, 121, 122,
    128, 129
Miller, M.    230, 257, 314, 317
Mirrlees, J.A.    410
Mishkin, F.    189, 191
Miyazaki, H.    410
Mizoguchi, T.    133, 137, 138, 162,
    184, 192
Modigliani, F.    145, 185, 192
Moriguchi, C.    220, 224
Murakami, T.    42
Murakami, Y.    40
Muramatsu, K.    7, 127
Muth, J.R.    189
Muto, H.    327

Nakagawa, K.    356
Nakamura, T.    355, 356
Nakane, C.    335, 354, 356

Nakatani, I.    14, 24, 25, 254, 258,
    311, 319
Nalebuff, B.    410
Naoi, M.    99, 102
Nelson, C.    308, 309
Noda, M.    255
Nonaka, I.    356

Odagiri, H.    227, 258, 356
Odaka, K.    356
Ogino, Y.    187, 189, 191
Ohashi, I.    387, 411
Ohkawa, K.    137, 192
Oi, W.    389, 411
Ojimi, Y.    416
Okumura, A.    356
Okumura, H.    254, 258
Okun, A.    40, 43
Okuno, M.    7, 38, 313, 356, 387, 389,
    411, 413
Ozaki, M.    309
Ozaki, R.    357

Parsons, T.    266, 309
Pascale, R.T.    357
Patrick, H.    357
Pierce, D.A.    377, 384, 385
Piore, M.J.    103, 122
Pratt, J.W.    197, 224
Pratten, C.F.    355, 357
Price, B.    223, 224

Raiffa, H.    37, 43
Rapoport, A.    341, 354, 357
Reich, R.    321, 327
Rosen, S.    407, 410,
Rosovsky, H.    192
Ross, S.A.    255, 258, 410, 411
Royama, S.    224

Sachd. J.    407, 411
Sakakibara, E.    221, 224
Sakakibara, K.    356
Sakashita, A.    356
Sakisaka, M.    32
Salant, S.    83, 102
Schafer, R.E.    90
Schelling, T.S.    341, 357
Schonfield, A.    32, 43
Schotter, A.    341, 357
Serizawa, K.    258
Shafer, R.E.    102
Shiba, S.    75
Simada, H.    75, 355, 357
Shimokobe, J.    32
Shinohara, M.    134, 137, 145, 163,
    174, 184, 192
Shirai, T.    75
Simon, H.A.    357
Sims, C.A.    377, 384, 385

Singpurwalla, N.D.   90, 102
Smelster, N.   309
Smith, A.   360
Smith, T.   43
Stiglitz, J.E.   407, 410, 411
Suzuki, Y.   193, 224

Tachibanaki, T.   6, 25, 101, 102, 125
Taira, K.   4, 43, 416
Takahashi, K.   63
Takanashi, A.   65
Takezawa, S.   354, 357
Tamaki, A.   40, 42, 43
Taylor, L.   185, 191
Teranishi, J.   227, 258
Tiao, G.   283, 308, 309
Totsuka, H.   63
Tucker, A.W.   259

Ueda, K.   7, 311
Uekusa, M.   24, 41, 227, 228, 257

Ueno, H.   327
Ullman-Margalit, E.   341, 357

Vogel, E.F.   357, 413, 415, 416
Vernon, R.   294, 308, 310

Wakita, Y.   20, 40, 43, 211, 215, 223,
   224, 256, 258
Weibull, W.   91
Weitzman, M.   185, 192
Whitehill, A.M.   354
Wilks, S.   89
Wise, D.   129

Yakushiji, T.   4, 31, 32, 37, 323
Yamamura, K.   40, 43
Yamamoto, S.   309
Young, P.   285, 309
Yoshida, N.   309
Yui, T.   40, 42

# SUBJECT INDEX

Accounts payable    17
Accounts receivable    17
Administrative guidance    326
Adversarial behavior    351
Agency for Medium-and Small-Sized
    Enterprises    26
Agency problem    389
Ageta    26
AGIL model    266
Allocational efficiency    105
Amae    335
Anti-Monopoly Law    10, 11, 12, 39
Anti-Monopoly regulation    201
ARMA (Auto-Regressive and Moving-
    Average) model    283
Asymmetric information    229, 311
Ataka Corporation    222
Auto industry    359ff, 364ff, 265ff,
    323, 374

Balance-sheet    16ff
Bank    193, 199. See also city bank and
        main bank
Bank deposits    15
Bank of Japan    194, 196, 200, 245
Banking Association    221
Bankruptcy    244
    bankruptcy cost    242, 256
Basic Survey of Wage Structure    57,
    107
Behavioral model    266
Belonging tradition    336
Buffer income    134, 145
Business grouping    319. See also
        corporate groups.
    intermarket business grouping    227,
    245
Business reciprocity    229, 241, 245.
    Also see mutual favortism.
Buy-Japanese Campaign    270
Buzumi-ryodate deposits    20. See also
        compensating balance.
Bonus
    effect of bonus on savings    138ff,
    173
    bonus earnings ratio    139
    bonus payment    7ff, 133ff, 315,
    387ff, 409, 413
    bonus payment system 38, 184
    propensity to consume bonus income
    134, 155, 173
    permanent bonus income    164
    transitory bonus income    164ff

Capital-gains taxation    194
Capital-labor ratio    121

Capital market    229, 311
    internalization of
    231, 238
    segmentation of    231, 238
Careers    48, 50ff, 57
    bredth of    48, 56
    depth of    48
    development of    49
    internalized careers    70
    long careers    58, 61
    span of    49, 56
    career type    71
    wide range of    57
Census of Manufacturing by Enterprise
    107, 381
CES production function    106
Chu    335
City bank    8, 227, 231, 242, 256. Also
    see commercial bank.
Collective bargaining    388
Collective insurance 254
Collective voice    104, 112, 113, 120,
    121
Commercial banks    320. Also see city
    bank.
Commercial Code    10, 14
Company unions    103, 125
Compensating balance    20, 23, 194,
    200ff, 256
Consumption function    149
    aggregate consumption function    171
    Keynesian consumption function    170
Consumption habit    133
Contexual model    266
Contingent claims markets    229
Contractual view    336
Convention theory    337ff
Conventions    341ff
Cooperative solution    394, 399
Corporate finance    7
Corporate financial policy    230, 238,
    246
Corporat groups    11ff, 23, 259ff
    ex-Zaibatsu corporate groups    24
    financial corporate groups    230,
    246. See also keiretsu.
Corporate tax    222
Cost-benefit efficiency    360
Council of Money Rate Adjustments
    196
Craft unionism    72
Craftsman type    71
Culturalists    4, 319
    cultualists' view    47
Cycle model    266

Davidson-Fletcher-Powell method    92
Debt-Equity Ratio    16ff, 195ff, 230, 231, 240ff, 246, 254, 320
Debt financing    193ff
Directors    16
Discriminant analysis    86
Dividends
  intercorporate dividends    238ff, 255
  dividends payout rate    238
  dividends policy    238ff
Dual
  dual labor market    127, 125
  dual sectors    121
  dual structure    4, 52, 65, 72, 121
  dual wage structure    3
Duration dependence    91
Duty rates    326
Dynamic efficiency    37, 359ff

Economic Council    32, 33, 42
Economic Planning Agency (EPA)    16-17, 32, 36, 40, 42
Edo Period    25-26
Education    351
  higher education    112
Efficiency    See allocational, dynamic, internal, L-, static, and X-efficiencies.
Egalitarian rotation    See rotation.
Employment Status Survey    78ff, 102
Energy crisis    306. See also oil crisis.
Enterprise Rationalization Law of 1952    326
Enterprise union    6, 27, 323, 332
Enterprise unionism    3, 4, 31, 70, 387
Environmental Protection Agency    306
EPA    See Ecomomic Planning Agency.
Equity ratio    240, 255, 256
Exit    105
Experimental design    307
Export quotas    265

Fair Trade Commission    12
Fairness    336
Family Income and Expenditure Survey    133, 146
Family Savings Survey    189
Feather-bedding    104
Financial intermediaries    8, 31
Firm-specific skill    See skills.
Foreign shareholders    211
Foremen    56, 61, 66
Formal training    62
Free rider incentives    341, 347
Free-rider problem    390
Fukumi-shisan    17

G (Group affiliated) firm    228ff

Game theory    337ff
General Headquarters of the Allied Occupation (GHQ)    275
Giri    335
Goshi    40
Government    31, 323
  government employees    179
  government interventions    265ff
Grievance system    104, 113ff
Groupism    26, 69
Growth maximization hypothesis    228

Habit-buffer income hypothesis    134, 141, 158, 160, 162, 176
Habit persistence hypothesis    137, 141, 185
Hazard function    81, 90
Human capital    127, 389
  human capital theory    6

I (largely independent of affiliation) firm    228ff
IMF Article Eight Country    306
Imperial Army    266
Implicit labour contract theory    254
Implicit long-term contract    231, 241, 242
Implicit mutual insurance scheme    229, 241, 243ff. See also mutual insurance
Incomplete contract    339
Incomplete markets    312
Incremental policy    285
Individual shareholdings    15
Industrial Patriotic Society    31
Industrial policy    3
Industrial democracy    47, 48, 56, 68
Inflation accounting    17
Innovation    360ff, 380
Institutional shareholdings    8ff, 239ff
Integrative bargaining    37
Inter-corporate shareholdings    11ff, 239, 240
Interest rate
  effective interest rate    256
  stability of    242
  standard interest rate    222
  sticky interest rate    246
  variability of    246
Internal efficiency    36
Internal employment structure    27
Internal labor market    5, 70
Internal retention    193ff
Intervention analysis    283
Intra-group borrowing    232ff
Intra-group financing    231, 238, 240, 241
Investment financing    193ff
Irrigation-flood control systems    26

Japan Development Bank    281
Japan Joint Securities Corporation    12
Japanese management system    4, 37, 230, 238
Japanism    4
Job
  job changers    86
  duration of    84
  job ladder    54, 55
  job rotation    332
  job tenure    77ff, 85, 90
Job Tenure Survey    92
Joint profit maximization    227

Kanto Earthquake    270
Keiretsu    11ff, 17, 227, 231ff, 235, 256, 321. Also see corporate groups.
  non-keiretsu    232, 235, 256
Kigyo shudan    227, 231. See also corporate groups
Korean War    275

L-efficiency    366
Labor market    77
  competitive labor market    104
Labor mobility    See mobility.
Labor pool    50ff, 53, 65
Labor Union Act    6
Labor Union Basic Survey    107
Laborer    73
  laborer type    71
Land price    17, 256
Late development effect    39
Law Regarding Foreign Exchange    278
Law Regarding Temporal Measures for Exports and Imports    275
Layoff    49, 70, 112, 126, 244
Less-developed country pattern    299
Leverage ratio    235
Lifetime commitment    70, 71
Lifetime employment    4, 6, 15, 77ff, 81, 121, 125, 331, 332, 387, 393
Liquidity constraints    189
Local content law    265
Long-term contracts    311
Loyalty
  corporate loyalty    387
  to the company    68
  to the group    69
Lump-sum income hypothesis    145, 163

Main bank    241, 256
Management system    335, 347
Manchurian Incident    272, 273
Mandatory retirement    387
Market entropy    364
Markov model    94
Merit-rating    62, 66
Micro-electronics    73
Ministry of Army    273

Ministry of Finance    11, 12, 22, 278
Ministry of International Trade and Industry (MITI)    3, 28, 31, 42, 265, 325, 415
Ministry of Labor    108, 114
Ministry of Railroads    270
Ministry of Transportation    278
MITI    See Ministry of International Trade and Industry.
Mobility    77ff, 90ff
  mobility between workshops    61
  mobility to remote workshops    62
  a wide range of    61
  mobility within a plant    49
  mobility within a workshop    61, 64, 65, 67
Modigliani and Miller Theorem    194, 220, 221, 312, 314
Monetary policy    244, 319
Monopoly power    228, 237
Motivation    413
Motivators    333ff
Mura hachibu    413. See also ostracism.
Mutual favortism    23. Also see business reciprocity.
Mutual insurance    319. See also implicit mutual insurance scheme.

Nash equilibrium    400, 404
  symmetric Nash equilibrium    404
National economic planning    32ff
Nemawashi (political rooting)    265, 307, 349
Neoclassical paradigm    3ff
Nissan Corporation    275
Non-cooperative solution    400
Non-taxable reserves    21

Occupation    320
OECD    306
Off-balance sheet assets    17
Office of Personnel    179
Oil crisis    108, 113, 162, 244. See also oil shock.
Oil-shock    155, 211, 366. See also oil crisis.
On    335
On-the-job-training (OJT)    48, 103, 332, 388
  the cost of    48, 49
Opportunism    390
Ostracism    38, 335, 390, 401ff, 413
Output-related wage system    388, 391
Outside workers    52, 53, 65, 70
Over-loan    210, 219
Overseas Market Development Law    327
Ownership structure    8ff, 234, 239ff

Paid vacation    388
Patent    369

People's car plan   4, 325, 281, 307
Permanent employees   28
Permanent income hypothesis   137, 139, 164ff
Permanent income-life cycle hypothesis   7, 134, 176
Personal saving propensity   7
Personal saving rate   135
Policy engineering   299
Policy inertia   265
Port of entry   52
Presidents' Clubs   12
Principal-agency relationship   391
Principal component analysis   216
Prisoner's dilemma   338ff
Product cycle model   294
Productivity   380
  effect of quit rate on   113, 114ff, 120
  effect of unions on   103, 120, 127, 104, 106
  productivity differentials by labor quality   106
  productivity differentials by sex   106
  productivity dilemma   361
  productivity enhancement paradigm   361
Profit sharing   237, 244, 409. Also see risk-sharing.
Promotion   49, 55, 57ff, 70, 127
  promotion-from-within   72, 103
  internal promotion   103, 387, 407
Public sector unionism   127
Pull (demand) policy   270
Pure boldness   264
Push (supply) policy   270

Quality control circles (QC Circle)   47, 67ff, 113, 362
Quality of labor   105
Quits
  effect of trade unions on   120

R&D expenditures   374
Rank-order competition   407
Rate of growth effect   137
Rational expectation   164ff, 169
Reciprocal shareholdings   227, 231ff, 240. Also see intercorporate shareholdings
Regular workers   65, 66, 118
Researchers   381
Retirement   125. See also mandatory retirement.
Retirement compensation   21ff
Ringi   349
Risk
  risk cost   262
  risk-averse workers   89

risk-taking workers   89
risk-sharing   28, 245, 259, 314. Also see profit-sharing.
Rotation   61, 126
  partial rotation   63, 65
  regular rotation   63

Samurai   40
Saving paradox   158
SCAP   See Supreme Commander for Allied Powers
Search   126
Security Dealers Association   222
Securities Holding Union   12
Seniority   49ff, 55ff, 61, 66, 104, 125, 126
  seniority rule   77ff, 83
  seniority wages   3, 4, 69, 237, 387
Separate taxation   221
Separation rates   66, 118
Shanghai Incident   273
Sharecropping   389. See also profit-sharing and risk-sharing.
Share price maximization   205ff, 219, 241
Shock   346
  shock absorber   52
  shock absorbing   14
Shoko-Chukin Bank   29
Short sales   314
Shoup tax regime   194
Showa-jyusan-nen Revised Mobilization Plan   275
Shunto   127
Skill   47
  firm-specific skill   103, 105, 229
  enterprise specific skill   49, 70
  general skill   105, 106
  skill formation   6, 47ff, 103, 104
  skill of wide range   67ff
Small firms   72ff
Small Saving Tax Exempt System   39, 194, 221
Social norm   402
Special Labor Froce Report   83, 102
Special reserve (Tokutei hikiatekin)   21, 240, 254ff, 256
State-observer model   266
Static efficiency   360
Steel industry   359ff, 364ff, 374
Stock market   8, 193ff
Stockbrokers   198
Stockholder-employee co-operative game   230
Strategic behavior   390
Subcontracting   14, 26ff
Subsidiary   14ff
Subsidiary groupings   11ff
Supply side   299
Supreme Commander for Allied Powers

12, 325
Survey on Employment Trends   118
Survey on Enterprise Mobility   84, 88, 102
Survey on the Movement of Consumption   133, 168
Survival method   90

Take-over bid   231, 240
Temporary Measures for Promotion of Machinery Industry ("Kishinho")   306
Temporary Money Rates Adjustment Act   194, 200, 222
Temporary workers   118, 184
Tenure-earnings profile   126
Three sacred treasures   4, 39, 69
TIMSAC (Time-Series Analysis and Control)   363
Tokyo Securities Exchange   8, 16
Toyota Motors, Ltd.   275
Trade credits   17
Trade union   See union.
Trading companies   322
Transfer   49, 62, 65, 70
  transfer among firms   113
  transfer within firms   112
Turnover costs   105
Turnover rate   409
Turnpike trajectory   33

Ultla-rationality hypothesis   163
Unions   5, 23, 103, 127. See also enterprise unions.

as voice institutions   103
monopoly power of   104
local union   61

Variance analysis   363
Voluntary restraints   306

Wage   236
  wage differentials   73
  wage flexibility   323
  wage function   394
  wage profiles   57
Wage Structure Survey   78, 82, 91, 92, 99, 102
War Economy   31
Water control systems   25
Welfare pension   21
White collar workers   70, 128
White-collarzation   66, 73
Work-place unionism   70
Workers voice   47, 67

X-efficiency   22, 37ff, 331, 360, 383
X-inefficiency   105, 337ff

Zaibatsu   12, 31, 227, 254, 322
  ex-zaibatsu   315
  zaibatsu dissolution   4, 12